International Management

MANAGEMENT, ORGANIZATIONS AND BUSINESS SERIES

Series Editor: John Storey

This wide-ranging series of texts, surveys and readers sets out to define the study of the management of people and organizations. Designed for both postgraduate and undergraduate students of business and management, it draws on the leading authors from the various contributing disciplines, including organizational psychology, sociology and industrial economics. A distinctive characteristic of the series is that these subject specialists make their work available to the general business and management student in a highly accessible way.

Published

Human Resource Management: A Strategic Introduction, Second Edition
Christopher Mabey, Graeme Salaman and John Storey

Changing Patterns of Management Development
Andrew Thomson, Christopher Mabey, John Storey, Colin Gray and Paul Iles

International Management: Cross-Boundary Challenges
Paul N. Gooderham and Odd Nordhaug

Strategy and Capability: Sustaining Organizational Change
Graeme Salaman and David Asch

Learning by Design: Building Sustainable Organizations
A. B. (Rami) Shani and Peter Docherty

Forthcoming

Motivation and Performance
David Guest

International Management
Cross-Boundary Challenges

Paul N. Gooderham and Odd Nordhaug

Blackwell
Publishing

350 Main Street, Malden, MA 02148-5020, USA
108 Cowley Road, Oxford OX4 1JF, UK
550 Swanston Street, Carlton, Victoria 3053, Australia

First published 2003 by Blackwell Publishing Ltd

Library of Congress Cataloging-in-Publication Data

Gooderham, Paul N.
  International management : cross-boundary challenges / by Paul N. Gooderham and Odd Nordhaug.
    p. cm. – (Management, organizations, and business series)
  Includes bibliographical references and index.
  ISBN: 978-0-631-23342-8
  1. International business enterprises–Management. I. Gooderham, Paul N.
  II. Nordhaug, Odd. III. Title. IV. Series.
  HD62.4.G667 2003
  658′.049–dc21

                                  2002156294

A catalogue record for this title is available from the British Library.

For further information on
Blackwell Publishing, visit our website:
http://www.blackwellpublishing.com

Contents

CONTENTS

CONTENTS

▶ The Authors

Paul N. Gooderham is Professor at the Department of Strategy and Management, Norwegian School of Economics and Business Administration and Research Director at the Foundation for Social Science and Business Research in Norway. His research interests are concentrated on international and comparative management, organization theory and the management of small and medium-sized enterprises. He has published numerous articles in international research journals, including *Administrative Science Quarterly, Management International Review* and *Scandinavian Journal of Management*. E-mail: paul.gooderham@nhh.no

Odd Nordhaug is Professor at the Department of Strategy and Management, Norwegian School of Economics and Business Administration. He has published extensively in international research journals, such as *Administrative Science Quarterly, Human Relations, Management International Review, International Studies of Organization and Management, Journal of Portfolio Management, European Journal of Management* and *Scandinavian Journal of Management*. His research interests comprise international and comparative management, organization theory and knowledge management. E-mail: odd.nordhaug@nhh.no

▶ Contributors

Leona Achtenhagen is a Research Fellow at Jönköping International Business School, Sweden.

Jyrki Ali-Yrkkö is Head of the Unit at ETLA, Research Institute of the Finnish Economy, Finland.

Alla Anisimova is a PhD student at the Department of International Economics and Management, Copenhagen Business School.

Julian Birkinshaw is Associate Professor of Strategy and International Management at the London Business School.

Søren Brandi is director of Global Change Management, LEGO Company.

Karen L. Cates is an Assistant Professor of Management and Organization at the Kellogg School of Management, Northwestern University, Illinois, USA.

Jean-Luc Cerdin is an Associate Professor of Human Resource Management at ESSEC, France.

Tim Dickson is executive editor of *European Business Forum*, a quarterly management publication which is the joint initiative of CEMS (the Community of European Management Schools) and PricewaterhouseCoopers (www.ebfonline.com).

Martin Gjelsvik is Research Director at the Rogaland Research Institute in Stavanger, Norway.

Keith Goodall is a Senior Associate at the Judge Institute of Management, University of Cambridge. He also holds a lectureship in Organizational Behaviour at the China Europe International Business School, Shanghai, China.

Kjell Grønhaug is Professor at the Department of Strategy and Management, Norwegian School of Economics and Business Administration.

Snejina Michailova works as an Associate Professor at the Department of International Economics and Management, Copenhagen Business School, Denmark and is European Editor of *Journal of World Business*.

Laura Paija works as a researcher at ETLA, Research Institute of the Finnish Economy, Finland.

Kimia D. Rahimi is a recent graduate of the Kellogg School of Management at Northwestern University, Illinois, USA.

Petri Rouvinen is Research Director at ETLA, Research Institute of the Finnish Economy, Finland.

Winfried Ruigrok is Professor of International Management at the University of St Gallen, Switzerland.

Johannes Rüegg-Stürm is Professor of Organizational Behaviour at the University of St Gallen, Switzerland.

Robbert Nickolaj Stecher is Director of Global Strategic Development, LEGO Company.

John Storey is Professor and Research Director at the Open University Business School, UK.

Siri Ann Terjesen worked as a consultant for Accenture prior to taking a Master of International Business degree at the Norwegian School of Economics and Business Administration (NHH).

Svein Ulset is Associate Professor at the Department of Strategy and Management, Norwegian School of Economics and Business Administration.

Matthias Wagner is Head of Key Account Management Hospitals Fresenius Kabi AG, Germany.

Malcolm Warren is Professor and Fellow, Wolfson College, University of Cambridge and a member of the faculty at the Judge Institute, University of Cambridge.

Pekka Ylä-Anttila is Research Director at ETLA, Research Institute of the Finnish Economy, Finland.

Abbreviations

ABB	ASEA Brown Boveri
ACFTU	All China Federation of Trade Unions
BA	Business Area
BBC	Brown Boveri Cie.
BU	Business Unit
CCT	cross-company teams
CH	Switzerland
COLA	cost of living allowance
CSR	corporate social responsibility
EEO	equal employment opportunity
ETP	executive training programme
GE	General Electric
HQ	headquarters
HNC	host country national
HRM	human resource management
IJV	international joint venture
JV	joint venture
M&A	Merger and Acquisitions
M-form	Multidivisional Form
MNC	multinational corporation
NGO	non-governmental organization
NM-form	Network Multidivisional Form
PMP	Performance Management Programme
PNC	parent country national
P-segment	Power Generation Segment
SESAM	'sales equals cooperation'
SOE	state-owned enterprise
TU	trade union

Acknowledgements

We are both grateful and indebted to the many students who have taken our Master of International Business (MIB) course on International Management at the Norwegian School of Economics and Business Administration (NHH). In addition to those who have come to Bergen to take the MIB degree, others have come to NHH as part of the CEMS exchange programme. Typically students from some 20 different countries have taken the course each time it has been given. The CEMS programme has ensured that there is always a strong contingent from European Union countries while the MIB degree has brought in many other nationalities including North Americans, Chinese, South Americans and Eastern Europeans. The mix of nationalities has been fascinating but also challenging. Our students' enthusiasm for the subject matter and their willingness to provide us with constructive criticism have been immensely valuable in the writing of this book. Therefore the book is dedicated to these students.

We are also indebted to John Storey at the Open University Business School for encouraging us to set about writing this text and for having provided us with sound advice during the process. Blackwell has also at all stages played a significant role in the development of this text. Their anonymous reviewers who commented on our original proposal provided us with many valuable comments.

An earlier version of Chapter 7, co-authored by Svein Ulset at NHH, appeared in *International Business: Adjusting to New Challenges and Opportunities* (2002), edited by F. McDonald, H. Tüselmann and C. Wheeler. We thank Palgrave for granting us permission to use this chapter.

Introduction

The most crucial of the many challenges faced by managers of multinational companies (MNC) is the generation and transfer of knowledge across national settings, organizations and networks. This is not just our view, but it is a view shared by many of our fellow international management scholars. Significantly it is also the view of virtually all of the international managers with whom we have spoken in the past ten years. Among other things, it influences the choice of organizational structure, the choice of human resource management system and the degree and type of expatriation. It is therefore the core of our text on international management.

We have chosen an interactive approach to explore this knowledge challenge. Each of Chapters 1 to 9 consists of three parts:

- a theoretically grounded presentation of a particular aspect of international management;
- a case culled from the real world of international management that is designed to illustrate the theory;
- case assignments that assist the student in relating the theory to the case.

In Chapter 10 we examine four challenges that we regard as being of particular importance for international managers for this decade. By way of supplementary reading we have included a number of readings that address these emerging challenges.

As well as a wide range of MNCs, our text spans a variety of national settings and draws upon contributors based in a diverse range of countries. The result is that the following countries are directly featured: China, Denmark, Finland, France, India, Ireland, Norway, Russia, Sweden, Switzerland, the United Kingdom and the USA. Additionally, the text chapters deal with variations in cultural and institutional conditions in many other countries, including Japan, Germany, Spain and Malaysia.

The book starts with a definition of the multinational corporation, its most important characteristics and challenges. Thereafter a broad picture of the globalization of businesses is drawn, along with a discussion of the triad economies and the issue of national identity. Various strategies for entering the international arena are delineated, and it is emphasized that the book concentrates on equity modes of entry involving fully owned subsidiaries in multinational companies.

The case linked to Chapter 1 goes straight to the heart of the text in that it is first and foremost about cross-national learning in practice. It describes how the chief executive of an insurance company, together with a colleague, ventures out into different countries hunting for novel business opportunities, new avenues to increase learning in the organization at large, and new ways to broaden the scope of the company. It becomes apparent to them that they can achieve this through making foreign acquisitions that grant access to knowledge and capabilities that the parent company does not possess.

The point of departure in Chapter 2 is that a paramount challenge in regard to generating valuable organizational capabilities is that of developing internal structures that are appropriate for the MNCs' strategic needs and that provide control and co-ordination of world-wide operations. Due to continual changes in the environments of MNCs, such strategic needs are rarely stable, no matter whether they involve customers, suppliers, competitors, technologies or governments. Structures are thus constantly evolving and in many instances are becoming more complex and differentiated. Three generic internal structures are defined and discussed, that is, the international, the multi-domestic and the global product division. This classification is based on two analytical dimensions; the degree of local responsiveness that is deemed necessary by the MNC and the degree of global integration it is seeking to achieve. Next, the focus is set on the emergence of a fourth generic internal structure, that of the transnational. However, important as formal structure is, in delineating this new organizational form, a third dimension, worldwide learning, is required. This is because there is a growing recognition of the competitive advantage in ensuring that knowledge flows between increasingly knowledge-intensive subsidiaries. MNCs are responding to this challenge by attempting to develop knowledge exchange networks that are informal systems overlaying the chosen structure, thereby generating new channels of learning across national and organizational settings with the company.

Attached to Chapter 2 is a case study that features the Swedish-Swiss multinational company, ABB. It deals with ABB's attempts to achieve a balance between local responsiveness and global integration through the implementation of a global matrix structure and its reorganization in 1998. Although the case is primarily concerned with ABB's structural features, it also touches on the need to supplement structure with non-structural elements that facilitate open and effective communication.

In Chapter 3 we first discuss the nature of international or cross-national human resource management (HRM) as compared to domestic HRM. This is followed by a presentation of a model for the analysis of cross-national HRM. In this model, the focus is on how environmental forces may influence various aspects of human resource management in foreign subsidiaries of multinational companies. On the basis of this environmental perspective, micro-level and macro-level impacts are discussed that emphasize the need for MNCs and their foreign subsidiaries to develop socio-economic, cultural and institutional sensitivity and awareness in cross-national settings.

Case C, following Chapter 3, describes the joint venture of the French construction materials company Lafarge and the Chinese state-owned company Huabei Mining Company. In particular, it highlights the importance for a venture of this kind in taking into account dissimilar cultural values, epitomized by factors such as differences in work ethics, work discipline, attitudes to reward systems and employees' relationship to different rewards.

MNCs are radically different from purely export-based domestic firms not least because of their foreign subsidiaries. Not only does physical distance pose a challenge for effective communication, even more so, there is the challenge represented by cultural differences. This is the topic of Chapter 4. The concept of national culture is discussed. Research findings from two influential studies of work-related aspects of national cultures are presented and discussed. The aim of this discussion is to underline the importance of having an awareness of the relativity of one's own cultural framework, and thereby the ability to question the notion that there is 'one best way' of managing and organizing regardless of cultural and institutional setting. If foreign subsidiaries are to be integrated for knowledge-sharing purposes, the starting point has to be an understanding of the mindsets of subsidiary management and employees in terms of their work-related values. The management challenge for many MNCs is to be able to adapt their organizations to culturally distinct environments without losing organizational consistency. Finally, recent research results in regard to cultural differences in Europe are presented.

In the following case, Case D, the focus is on the Russian subsidiary of a Danish MNC with subsidiaries in more than one hundred countries. The issue is how cultural differences may cause managerial problems that undermine learning and knowledge transfer and how such problems can be solved.

The aim of Chapter 5 is to compare human resource management (HRM) as it has developed in the USA with HRM as it is currently practised in Europe. In order to facilitate this, a distinction is drawn between calculative and collaborative HRM. On the basis of this distinction, four generic HRM regimes are identified and discussed. Finally, we show how host country HRM regimes influence subsidiaries of MNCs in their choice of HRM system. In certain settings a subsidiary may experience a pronounced tension between host country and parent company expectations.

Case E, attached to Chapter 5, is a description of how a Norwegian bank faced by the deregulation of its industry, and therefore increased competition, attempted to implement an HRM development concept and method derived from the USA.

By showing how the programme had to be adjusted to fit Scandinavian values, the case points to the importance of institutional as well as cultural differences and the need to 'translate' organization and management practices when these are transferred from one institutional setting to another.

In Chapter 6 we focus on aspects of competence management and competence development within MNCs and particularly their subsidiaries. The distinction between the broader term human resources and the more narrow term competencies is discussed, along with the concept of strategic competence management. Thereafter, a classification of employee competencies in MNCs is presented that encompasses meta-competencies, standard technical competencies, organizational multinational company competencies, technical multinational company competencies, organizational subsidiary competencies and technical subsidiary competencies. Finally, a dynamic perspective on the development of competencies in MNCs is introduced.

Accenture is the featured company in Case F, following Chapter 6, and the focus is on knowledge management. The presentation starts with the period when attention was directed at creating an infrastructure that could facilitate knowledge management processes. At a later stage, considerable effort was devoted to the creation of knowledge-sharing activities and thereafter knowledge outfitting. Finally, illustrations of both successful and unsuccessful knowledge management activities are featured.

In Chapter 7 we present a conceptual framework that addresses the issue of knowledge transfer between high knowledge parents and low knowledge subsidiaries, and the challenge in developing the latter. The move from knowledge recipient to centre of innovation is divided into four levels. At the lowest level, level I, a subsidiary is only capable of absorbing explicit knowledge of an elementary type. At the highest level, level IV, a subsidiary is not only capable of absorbing tacit knowledge, but is also capable of independently generating knowledge which may be transferred to the parent or other parts of the MNC. Using extant research, various knowledge transfer mechanisms are identified in the move from level I to IV. These vary in terms of the social interaction they are intended to generate which in turn is contingent on the degree of tacitness to the knowledge that is to be transferred.

Accompanying this chapter is a case study of Kodak in Xiamen in China. The case traces developments at Kodak's Xiamen subsidiary, which was set up as part of a joint venture in 1998 on the back of a Chinese state-owned enterprise. In terms of in-transfer capacity, the state-owned enterprise was at level I. The case describes how Kodak set about changing employee behaviour from the state-owned model to one that would support a high-tech business.

Chapter 8 deals with expatriation, a common feature of most MNCs, particularly those exhibiting either an ethnocentric or geocentric approach to the staffing of their subsidiaries. The aim is to provide an overview of the various functions expatriation plays and to examine factors that are associated with widespread use of expatriates. Furthermore, it deals with the importance of thorough selection and recruitment processes as well as relevant training programmes preparing the personnel selected for expatriation. The challenge for human resource departments is therefore not only to select and train the right candidates for expatriation, but also to elaborate reward and incentives packages that can motivate personnel to overcome the barrier posed by the 'reluctant spouse or partner'. We also examine the repatriation process and the significance of debriefing expatriates when they return to the parent organization of the MNC.

Case H linked to Chapter 8 is that of a leading global luxury brand conglomerate LVMH Moët Hennessy Louis Vuitton. It deals with career development through expatriation and international mobility across the conglomerate's five main world zones, France, Europe, the Americas, Pacific Asia and Japan.

In Chapter 9 it is argued that the recent growth in the number of multinational companies, along with their increased economic and political power, strongly accentuates their ethical and social responsibilities. The aim is to illuminate and discuss the challenges that stem from these responsibilities. The conception of these firms as global corporate citizens is introduced and different stages of ethical development are presented. A focus is put on ethnicity and racial discrimination, corruption, child labour and guest workers, and gender discrimination. Efforts to implement and monitor corporate codes of conduct and ethics are discussed. Other issues that are covered include whistle-blowing and loyalty, ethical absolutism versus relativism, and the relationship between profit seeking and social responsibility.

The related case study concerns the Norwegian MNC Norsk Hydro and the company's so-called Utkal venture. This included the establishment of a bauxite mine, and an aluminium-refining factory in the Rayagada region of Orissa in the eastern part of India. The case is particularly relevant because Norsk Hydro engaged in a rigorous dialogue regarding the ethical challenges involved in acting in a socially responsible manner. The case of the Utkal project juxtaposes this ethical rhetoric with the real and recurring dilemmas confronted since its start in 1993.

The closing chapter contains a discussion of four challenges that MNCs and international managers face in the coming decade. First, we address the issue of whether the increased importance of competencies and networks means a shift of paradigm in the conceptualization of MNC managerial challenges. If so, we will witness the final death throes of the bureaucracy and the rise of the 'flexicracy'. The flexicracy has structural implications and the second managerial challenge that is discussed regards the development of appropriate structures. Flexicratic arrangements also have personnel implications. It is argued that it requires a new type of individual who not only is capable of tolerating change but who is actively seeking it. Hence, the third challenge we review is the challenge MNCs face in respect to attracting and retaining Generation Y employees. Finally, we revisit the ethical dimension of MNCs. The fourth challenge that MNCs must confront is related to meaning. We will argue that the long-term survival of MNCs depends on their ability to create meaning for their employees and that this can only be achieved through acquiring and maintaining their legitimacy and keeping to high ethical standards.

Each of these four challenges is illustrated in more detail through a series of readings, including discussions of the network organization, structural developments, 'Generation Y' and corporate ethics.

chapter

1

The Multinational Corporation

▶ Purpose

The purpose of this chapter is to define the multinational corporation (MNC) and outline its major characteristics and challenges. Various strategies for entering the international arena are delineated. The focus of this book will be on equity modes of entry involving fully owned subsidiaries. First, we paint a broad picture of the globalization of business, the significance of the triad economies and the issue of national identity.

▶ The Globalization of Business

The phenomenon of MNCs has been ascribed to a combination of two main factors: the uneven geographical distribution of factor endowments and market failure (Dunning, 1988). That is, because of their national origins, some firms have assets that are superior to those in many other countries. Moreover, a substantial proportion of these firms have concluded that they can only successfully exploit these assets by transferring them across national boundaries *within* their own organizations rather than by selling their right of use to foreign-based enterprises. More recently, nationally endowed assets have been supplemented by MNCs acquiring, developing and integrating strategically important assets located in other countries, thereby making their national origins somewhat less significant.

To date, this combination of unequally distributed factor endowments combined with difficulties in using market-based arrangements has yielded more than 60,000 MNCs with over 800,000 affiliates abroad. On a global basis, MNCs generate about half of the world's industrial output and account for about two-thirds of world trade. About one-third of total trade (or half of the MNC trade) is intra-firm. MNCs are particularly strong in motor vehicles, computers

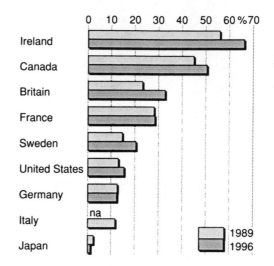

Figure 1.1 Share of foreign affiliates in manufacturing output
Source: OECD © The Economist Newspaper Ltd, London, 8 January, 2000

and soft drinks, having on a global basis 85 per cent, 70 per cent and 65 per cent of these markets, respectively. In some countries they are the dominant manufacturing presence. As figure 1.1 shows, in 1996, affiliates of MNCs accounted for nearly 70 per cent of Ireland's manufacturing output, and over 50 per cent of Canada's. A substantial proportion of manufacturing in Britain, France and Sweden is also accounted for by MNCs. All the indications are that the level of production undertaken by foreign-owned manufacturing will continue to rise. For example, by 1998 for the EU as a whole a quarter of total manufacturing production was controlled by a foreign subsidiary of an MNC compared to 17 per cent in 1990.

The advantages of becoming a global player in manufacturing are more obvious than for service-based firms. In the case of the former, the value chain can be divided across many locations. Parts of the manufacturing process can be located to low-cost countries, while R&D can be located in a region with specialized competencies with its costs spread across many markets. In the case of service firms, much of the value chain has to be generated locally: that is, there is little in the way of opportunity to centralize activities to low-cost locations. To a greater or larger degree, services have to be tailored for each client unlike, for example, pharmaceuticals, which can be mass-produced. Sharing advanced knowledge is also more problematic. In manufacturing companies it can be made available through patented technologies or unique products. In service companies it has to be transferred from country to country through learning processes. Nevertheless with the liberalization of recent years, the share of services in foreign direct investments (FDI) has risen significantly particularly within telecommunications, utilities, investment banking, business consulting, accountancy and legal services.

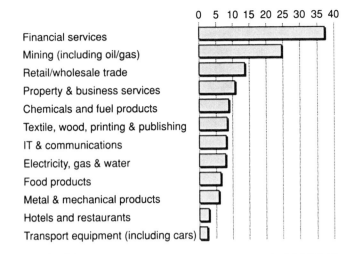

Figure 1.2 Stock of foreign direct investment in Britain, end of 1997, £bn
Source: ONS © The Economist Newspaper Ltd, London, 22 January, 2000

Accenture, the management consultancy, for example, has a staff of 75,000 in 47 countries and the accountancy PricewaterhouseCooper (PwC) has 160,000 in 150 countries. The emergence of new services, such as software, back-office services, call-centres and data entry, has also contributed to the relative growth of services in FDI. At the broad sectoral level, the share of services in FDI now accounts for about half of inward FDI stock in the world.[1] Although Britain is by no means representative of developed economies in terms of spread of foreign direct investment, figure 1.2 nevertheless provides a useful indicator of the diversity of sectors within which MNCs operate.

Despite setbacks such as the Asia crisis of the late 1990s, the long-term flow of foreign direct investment (FDI) is one of inexorable increase. The annual average FDI growth rate between 1986 and 2000 was 30 per cent or more for 65 countries including Denmark, Finland, China, Germany and Finland. Another 29 countries, including Austria, the Netherlands and Russia, had FDI growth rates of 20–29 per cent. For 1999 and 2000 over three-quarters of global FDI inflows went to the developed world partly because of intense cross-border mergers and acquisitions activity. The major recipients at the end of the 1990s were the USA and the European Union (EU), with Germany, the United Kingdom and the Benelux countries figuring particularly strongly. Among developing countries China (including Hong Kong) was by far the most important recipient: nearly 400 of the Fortune 500 firms have invested in China to date.[2]

Within these recipient countries subsidiaries tend to cluster geographically in and around areas with well-developed infrastructures including suppliers, skills and innovative capabilities. In the USA, California, New York, Texas, Illinois and New Jersey are the main magnets; in Japan it is Tokyo, and in China it is the coastal regions.

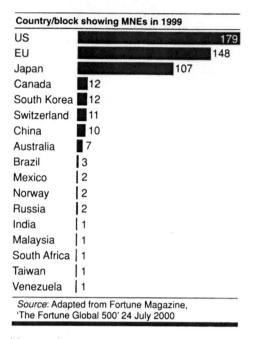

Figure 1.3 The world's 500 largest MNCs
Source: Rugman, 2001

▶ Regional Boundaries

The 'triad' economies, the EU, the USA and Japan, have long accounted for the bulk of global FDI. As figure 1.3 indicates, most MNCs are therefore from the triad. Rugman's (2001) analysis indicates that of the world's largest 500 MNCs, a total of 434 are from the triad. This total has increased from 414 in 1990 indicating the permanency of the triad hegemony. Together, the 434 triad MNCs currently account for 90 per cent of the world's stock of FDI meaning that developed countries are the primary destinations for FDI. The 434 triad MNCs carry out half of all world trade, often in the form of intra-company sales between subsidiaries. However, it should be borne in mind that most of them first and foremost operate in a strong triad home base. In other words, much of the production, marketing and other business activities are organized by regional boundaries rather than being truly global so that the bulk of FDI is concentrated within regions and neighbouring regions. For North America there are strong FDI links with Latin America and the Caribbean, Japan with Asia, whereas for the EU links are strong within Western Europe with some recent strengthening with Central and Eastern Europe. Furthermore, MNCs generally have large portfolios of purely domestic assets. Even the largest MNCs have on average nearly half of their total assets in domestic assets whereas for many smaller MNCs the proportion is substantially larger. Rugman (2001: 10) may be overstating his case somewhat when he concludes that:

> There is no evidence for globalisation, that is, of a system of free trade with fully integrated world markets. Instead the evidence on the performance and activities of multinational enterprises demonstrates that international business is triad-based and triad-related . . . European, North American and Asian manufacturing and service companies compete viciously for market share, lobbying their governments for shelter and subsidies.

However, Rugman's perspective is a useful antidote to naïve notions of the geographical scope of most MNCs, particularly smaller MNCs.

▶ National Identity

Despite the increase in globalization most MNCs have home bases that give them resolutely national identities. General Electric and Microsoft are clearly American just as Honda and Toyota are Japanese. Only one in five of the boards of ostensibly global US companies include a non-US national. Sixty per cent of Honda's sales are outside Japan, but only 10 per cent of its shares are held by non-Japanese. Toyota has 41 manufacturing subsidiaries in 24 countries but no foreign managers among its vice-presidents in Tokyo. Mergers and acquisitions have little impact. Daimler-Chrysler, hailed in 1998 as a merger of equals, soon became a German company with German executives taking control of the US operation while many of Chrysler's most senior executives either left or were forced out. Even within Europe with its single market and single currency, pan-European companies, free of national demarcations, remain elusive. One typical variant is that pan-European ventures end up being dominated by one national-ity. Thus Alstom, the transport and power engineering group, started out as a British-French joint venture but is now dominated by French executives, with the UK managers playing a junior role. The other typical variant is that management structures are specifically designed to take into account constituent national sens-itivities. For example, the European Aeronautic Defence and Space Company (EADS) formed in 2000 through a merger of Aerospatiale Matra of France and Daimler-Chrysler Aerospace of Germany with Casa of Spain as a junior partner, has two chairmen (one German and one French), two chief executives (ditto) and two headquarters (Munich and Paris).

There are exceptions such as Royal Dutch/Shell and Unilever, two long-standing Anglo-Dutch groups with bi-national identities. But there are few com-panies with genuinely multinational identities. The most obvious exceptions tend to be located within professional services. The Boston Consulting Group has now more partners outside the USA and also generates two-thirds of its revenues outside the USA. However, these are nationally owned partnerships that confer a degree of local independence. Outside professional services multinational identities are more elusive. However, because an increasing number of MNCs have more employees outside their home base country, creating some inclusive corporate identity is increasingly important in order to enhance knowledge flow from subsidiary to corporate headquarters. ABB, the Swedish-Swiss engineering conglomerate, from its launch in 1988, has always insisted that it has no national axe to grind. It has a tiny corporate headquarters of only 100 employees in Zurich, an executive board comprising a variety of nationalities, and English as its working language. Swedish Percy Barnevik, ABB's first chief executive, famously insisted on fellow Swedes writing to him in English. And yet it took 14 years from its inception and a substantial crisis before a non-Swede, Jürgen Dormann, became its chief executive.

▶ The Focus

MNCs have a number of advantages over local companies. Their size provides them with the opportunity to achieve vast economies of scale in manufacturing and product development. Their global presence also exposes them to new ideas and opportunities regardless of where they occur. Moreover, their location in many countries can be used as a bargaining chip in obtaining favourable conditions from governments anxious to preserve inward investment and jobs. However, with all the advantages size confers, there are also the potential liabilities of slowness and bureaucracy. MNCs are not necessarily successful. Indeed, the Templeton Global Performance Index (2000, 2001) reveals that in 1998 while the foreign activities of the world's largest MNCs accounted on average for 36 per cent of their assets and 39 per cent of revenues, they only generated 27 per cent of their profits. Over 60 per cent of these companies achieved lower profitability abroad than at home. The report concludes that many MNCs are not particularly good at managing their foreign activities, particularly in regard to digesting acquisitions, and that strong core competencies do not guarantee international commercial success. Furthermore, the gap between the best- and worst-performing companies is growing.

Over 40 years ago Hymer raised the question of why MNCs existed at all given that they are 'playing away from home' both in national and cultural terms. Domestic companies have 'the general advantage of better information about their country: its economy, its language, its laws and its politics' (1960/1976: 34). Certainly the liability of foreignness is particularly severe in the initial entry phase. An MNC will often have to compete head on with domestic companies that have a number of natural advantages. First, domestic companies have a customer base they have cultivated and which is familiar with their brands. This loyalty to a local player has to be overcome in such a way that it does not evoke a nationalistic reaction. In the early 1990s, Norwegian ice cream manufacturers responded to Unilever's entry into the Norwegian market by playing the nationalistic card. In an aggressive advertising campaign that featured Norwegian national symbols, great emphasis was put on the intrinsic superiority of Norwegian ingredients. The public turned its back on Unilever's products and it withdrew from the Norwegian market.

Second, local firms will also have developed supply chain relations that may involve long-term contractual relationships that effectively preclude newcomers. This has been a formidable barrier for companies entering the Japanese market.

A third entry barrier is that national regulators will tend to discriminate against foreign subsidiaries. Except when they are so locally embedded that they are perceived as domestic, foreign firms will be significantly more investigated, audited, and prosecuted than their domestic counterparts (Vernon, 1998). Even in the United States, officially committed to applying the same 'national treatment' to the offspring of foreign companies that they give to their own companies, it has been empirically documented that 'foreign subsidiaries face more labour lawsuit judgements than their domestic counterparts' (Mezias, 2002: 239). As such foreign MNCs such as Honda, Unilever and Novartis, have recognized the need to form a body that monitors and responds to discrimination. The Organization for International Investment (Offi) has found it must remain alert. According to Nancy McLernon, Offi's deputy director, '[Discrimination] can come from any direction, any time.' For example, in 1998:

> someone at the US Interior Department had a bright idea – to conserve the increasingly tight supply of irrigation water in 16 states in the west of the country by forbidding its use to foreign companies . . . Bear Creek, a fruit and flower company belonging to Japan's Yamanouchi, lost its water rights for its roses. It was 10 months before Offi was able to get the Treasury and State Departments to convince the Interior Department to turn the taps back on. (*The Financial Times*, 5 May 2000)

Finally, a fourth entry barrier is the lack of institutional and cultural insight. When Wal-Mart moved into Germany it had little feel for German shoppers, who care more about price than having their bags packed, or German staff, who hid in the toilets to escape the morning Wal-Mart cheer. Added to that were two of factors mentioned above, the inflexibility of local suppliers and the entrenched position of local discounters such as Aldi, but also the strength of trade unions. In the wake of losses of $300m a year, John Menzer, head of Wal-Mart International, admitted, 'We screwed up in Germany.'

To overcome these disadvantages an MNC must possess some unique strategic capability whether it is advanced technological expertise, marketing competencies or scale economies. In addition, an MNC also has to have some form of organizational capability that enables it to leverage more from its assets via subsidiaries than it could through other entry strategies (see below). This capability and the costs associated with developing it must not be taken for granted. Increasingly, one of the most important aspects to this organizational capability involves the management of the knowledge base of the MNC. This comprises not only the transfer of knowledge between the various parts of the MNC, but also the creation of new forms of knowledge by combining knowledge located transnationally both within and beyond the MNC.

The focus of this book is on the managerial and learning challenges that MNCs have to confront in order to create the necessary organizational capabilities. Not only are these challenges substantial, they are also constantly evolving. Even Coca-Cola, one of the most profitable foreign operations in the Templeton Global Performance Index for 1998, acknowledges this. In an open-hearted essay published in the *The Financial Times* (2000), Coca-Cola's CEO Douglas Daft revealed that:

> Sometimes you have to stumble before you realise you have wandered off the right path. That is what happened to our company in 1999. After 15 years of consistent success, we endured a year of dramatic setbacks. Those events provided us with a clear wake-up call that told us we had to rethink our approach for the new century.

In essence the challenge for MNCs is to retain their size, which gives them economies of scale and scope, and their global reach which enables them to exploit new opportunities and ideas wherever they may occur. They also need to maintain their multiple country locations that not only grant them flexibility in deciding where they will source products, but which also enable them to bargain with local governments. However, it is these strengths that also represent their liabilities in that large, globally distributed companies can easily become bureaucratic and therefore non-entrepreneurial and insensitive to the many different environments in which they operate (Birkinshaw, 2000). Indeed, some researchers claim that there is a non-linear inverted U-shaped relationship between international diversification and performance.[3] Beyond a threshold of international expansion, returns diminish due to the limits of the firm and its management. That is, at some point the transaction costs involved in co-ordinating and controlling geographically dispersed units outweigh the benefits of international diversification.

Addressing these liabilities involves developing a corporate culture that stimulates commitment to the company, entrepreneurial attitudes and a non-parochial mindset. This must be supported by appropriate reward and career systems. Added to this is the need for structures that match the strategic thrust of the company by defining the basic lines of reporting and responsibility. However, unlike purely domestic companies, the context within which MNCs operate involves national cultural differences, distance and regulations that vary by national setting and which may be biased against foreign companies.

In short, MNCs must have the capacity to respond to local conditions as well as the ability to benefit from their size through the integration of their activities. How much local responsiveness and how much global integration are needed may vary but to a substantial extent they are the two most important issues MNCs with say 200,000 employees and locations in 30 countries must respond to.

▶ Entry Strategy Alternatives

Once a firm has decided to enter the international arena it must make a choice regarding the appropriate mode for organizing its foreign business activities. There are a number of entry strategies available. These alternatives are not mutually exclusive, indeed, large companies may employ them simultaneously in different contexts. Choice of entry modes can be fruitfully divided into the following:

1 Non-equity modes:
 – exporting,
 – licensing,
 – franchising
 – contract manufacturing and service provision
2 Equity modes:
 – joint ventures
 – fully owned subsidiaries.

These modes vary in terms of the risk they involve. They also differ in terms of their organizational, management and resource demands as well as the amount of control that can be exercised over foreign operations.

Exporting

Exporting is a relatively low-risk entry strategy as it involves little investment and exit is unproblematic. As such, it is an obvious alternative for firms lacking in capital resources. An exporter is, however, entirely dependent on being able to identify efficient and reliable distribution channels. Changing a distributor with whom one is dissatisfied is often contractually difficult. Other critical factors are import tariffs and quotas as well as freight costs.

Licensing

Licensing is another low investment, low-risk alternative that is a particularly useful option in countries where regulations limit market entry or where tariffs and quotas make export a non-viable strategy. It is also a preferred strategy when the target country is culturally distant from the home country or there is little prior experience of the host country. A licensing agreement gives a firm in a host country the right to produce and sell a product for a specified period in return for a fee. The main weakness with licensing is the licensor's lack of control over the licensee. This applies to quality standards that, if disregarded, can be detrimental to the brand's image. It also applies to the monitoring of sales that form the basis for royalty payments. Another risk is that the licensee may appropriate the competence underlying the product, thereby becoming a direct competitor. That is why licensing is primarily suitable for the mature phase of a product's life cycle in which the technology that is transferred to the licensee is older and standardized. In other phases of a product's life cycle direct ownership is a more viable strategy.

Franchising

Franchising is similar to licensing but more comprehensive. For a fee and royalty payments the franchisee receives a complete package comprising the franchiser's trademark, products and services, and a complete set of operating principles thereby creating the illusion of a worldwide company. Holiday Inn and, not least, McDonald's with its 29,000 restaurants in 121 countries are two familiar examples. Both of these franchisers place great emphasis on ensuring that quality does not vary. However, beyond that, management control is so devolved that McDonald's chief executive Jack Greenberg characterized McDonald's as in reality being 'an amalgamation of local businesses run by local entrepreneurs from Indonesia to France.'[4]

Contract manufacturing and service provision

Nike distinguishes between design, product development and marketing, on the one hand, and shoe and clothing manufacturing, on the other. The latter is not integrated in Nike but is contracted out to independent plants in developing economies such as China, Indonesia, Thailand and Vietnam, primarily for reasons of cost. In Indonesia in 2001 its nine contractor factories paid base monthly salaries slightly above the official minimum wage of about $28. The main benefits to Nike are that it has none of the problems of local ownership, nor does it invest its own capital in manufacturing. Nonetheless, various pressure groups have ensured that Nike has become a focus for international scrutiny because of allegations of sexual harassment and physical and verbal abuse of workers at its contract factories. Increasingly it has recognized that it cannot relinquish moral responsibility for conditions at contractor manufacturers. It has even commissioned outside groups such as the Global Alliance for Workers and Communities to examine conditions in its contractor plants as a means of improving conditions.

Mobile phone vendors, including Ericsson, Philips and Motorola, have applied the same model to handset manufacturing. They outsource the production of handsets to Asian companies, such as the Singapore-based Flextronics, on a contractual basis while retaining control of research, design, branding and marketing. The key advantage to mobile phone vendors in not owning their own factories is that they have the flexibility to ramp production up or down in accordance with extreme fluctuations in demand without long-term capital investments or an increase in their labour forces. The disadvantage lies in that they are handing over control of a vital part of their supply chain. Not only is quality control more problematic, there is also a dependency on the contract equipment manufacturer (CEM) possessing or having access to the necessary parts. In 2000, Philips ran into difficulties when it emerged that its CEM was lacking in flash memory chips, thereby jeopardizing production of nearly 20 million handsets. It is these disadvantages that have caused Nokia to resist outsourcing beyond the manufacture of assemblies.

Basically the task of the CEM is to manufacture products according to well-specified designs provided by their clients. Their use is appropriate when technology is less important as a differentiator and value is derived from competing on brand, distribution and style. In the case of mobile handsets, Motorola has concluded that they are no longer complex products but merely commodities. Contracting out involves therefore no loss of critical learning opportunities. In the personal computer industry, the commodity model has been taken a step further. Vendors not only contract out manufacturing but also a large proportion of the work design is allocated to companies that offer original design manufacturing. Distribution may also be outsourced. Contracting taken to this extreme means that the MNC is not a firm in the traditional sense, that is a vertically integrated organization, so much as a network of contractually determined market based obligations that together constitute a complete supply chain. This emerging organizational form makes for a new set of managerial challenges – the management of contracts and relationships across borders. This is a theme we will return to in the final chapter of the book.

Finally, it should be noted that contract arrangements are by no means confined to manufacturing. Nearly half of the 500 largest MNCs regularly use Indian IT service providers on a contractual basis because of their combination of low costs and advanced processing skills. The contracts involve a spread of IT services from low value work, such as systems maintenance, to the more lucrative development of new applications such as Internet-based portals.

International Joint Ventures (IJVs)

The establishment of IJVs have been an increasing trend since the 1970s. By the 1990s IJVs were the mode of choice about 35 per cent of the time by US MNCs and in 40 to 45 per cent of international entries by Japanese multinationals (Beamish *et al.*, 2000). An IJV is an agreement by two or more companies to produce a product or service together. It involves a much higher level of investment and therefore of risk than the previous entry strategies. Generally, an IJV consists of an MNC and a local partner. Equity proportions vary but usually relative ownership approximates to 50–50, although there are many variations including IJVs with more than two partners including relatively passive partners with minority holdings. Control of the five to ten management positions that typically constitute the top management group of an IJV is a central issue in IJV negotiations, particularly in regard to the top position of general manager. This position usually goes to the partner that has the dominant equity position or some other basis of power such as critical technology. The partner that does not win the top position will argue strongly for other slots that guarantee the desired level of representation. Typically members of the management group of IJVs have two agendas: on the one hand they are expected to commit themselves to the success of the IJV, on the other they are 'delegates' of their respective parents. As legal entities, IJVs have boards of directors who set strategic priorities and make decisions regarding the use of profits and investment policy (Hambrick *et al.*, 2001).

Until recently, an IJV was the only means of entry in India because local participation was mandatory. In China, foreign retailers are barred from having full control of mainland operations thus compelling retailers such as Carréfour of France, Wal-Mart of the USA and Tesco of the UK to look for local partners. However, even when local participation is not obligatory, an IJV may be appropriate because a local partner can provide intermediate inputs, such as local market knowledge, access to distribution networks and natural resources, as well as making the MNC an insider in the host country. When Tesco entered the South Korean market in 1999, it chose to do so with Samsung, Koreas's biggest conglomerate and most powerful brand. By choosing to put Samsung's name in the joint-venture title first and by appointing a Samsung executive as chief executive, Tesco went a long way to diffuse potential criticism in a country dominated by small, traditional shops. In addition it was helped by Samsung to develop a hypermarket adapted to Korean tastes including assistants in traditional Korean dress who bow to each arriving customer, and octopus, squid and lobster that are plucked from tanks and chopped up alive, sushi-style.

The benefits of IJVs are that they provide a combination of rapid entry into new markets, risk-sharing and increased economies of scale. The problem they face relates to diverging expectations and objectives. Rarely are the two partners equally matched with the MNC usually the stronger partner in terms of technology and management skills. The result is that the local partner may come to view the MNC as overzealous in protecting its core technology and on imposing its control on the joint venture, while the MNC finds it difficult to trust its local partner. The friction that this generates is a major explanation of why many IJVs result in partner dissatisfaction or outright failure. Indeed, some surveys have suggested such outcomes for about half of MNCs with IJVs (Beamish *et al.*, 2000).

Fully owned subsidiaries

Disregarding local ownership restrictions imposed by host country governments, preferring fully owned subsidiaries to IJVs is largely a product of an assessment by the MNC of the transaction costs involved in obtaining intermediate inputs. Fully owned subsidiaries are preferred when these represent the most efficient solution, a calculation that may well stem from problems in locating a reliable partner. However, it is also to some extent a product of national culture. It has, for example, been shown that all things being equal, the propensity for US firms investing in Japan to choose joint ventures over wholly-owned subsidiaries is substantially higher than for Japanese firms investing in the USA (Makino and Neupert, 2001).

Fully owned subsidiaries can be divided into mergers and acquisitions (M&As), on the one hand, and start-ups, on the other. Although it is often difficult to distinguish between mergers and acquisitions in precise terms, mergers are usually the result of a friendly arrangement between companies of roughly equal size, whereas acquisitions are unequal partnerships, often the product of a hard-fought battle between acquiring and target companies. The scale of M&As as a vehicle for FDI has increased rapidly since the beginning of the 1990s. Most new FDI in 1998 was in the form of M&As. M&As have the advantage of providing rapid entry into a market and therefore economies of scale. Established product lines, distribution channels and insider status are all obtained. They can also be of great value as a means of capturing new expertise. On the other hand the difficulties encountered in integrating the acquisition into the culture and overall strategy of the MNC should not be underestimated, particularly in the case of acquisitions where there may be deep resentment amongst employees in the acquired unit. Frequently, despite due diligence, the acquirer also lacks a proper understanding of what has been acquired. A new identity for the acquired firm has to be developed and as acquired businesses often involve a seat on the parent board, there may be board-level disagreement as to precisely what that identity is. The difficulties are such that as many as 50 per cent of M&As fail.[5] However, as the World Investment Report 1999 comments, MNCs do 'not seem to be deterred by the relatively poor results that have been observed with respect to M&As' (UNCTAD, 1999: xxii).

Start-ups do not involve having to grapple with the problem of integrating cultures and creating a unified purpose. Nevertheless, as an entry strategy it is generally the strategy that carries the highest risk particularly in countries with nationalistic attitudes toward foreign ownership. Start-ups also require the longest time to establish, and require the greatest contribution of know-how.

The choice of start-up versus acquisition tends to be affected by the industry the MNC is operating in. MNCs operating in industries that are driven by unique or superior technical expertise are characterized by a preference for start-ups since they can build their operations in a way that minimizes the costs in transferring their knowledge. An acquisition will often involve dealing with incompatible methods for absorbing and processing knowledge and even a low motivation for new knowledge. For example, Nokia, since it began to focus on mobile phones, has expanded mainly through start-ups, whereas ABB, operating in established technology sectors, has grown mainly through acquisitions. However, there are also cultural factors at work in such a choice. Japanese firms tend to prefer entry through start-ups rather than acquisition, whereas British firms are more comfortable with acquisitive entry. Harzing (2002a) has shown that differences in MNC strategies also have an influence on the choice of entry mode. MNCs that are particularly focused on adapting their products and policies to the local market tend to prefer acquisitions because the acquired subsidiary will at the outset be aligned with host country conditions, while MNCs that regard their subsidiaries as pipelines for standardized, cost-efficient products will prefer start-ups. Finally, there is the impact of prior experience. MNCs that have successfully employed acquisitions will be more likely to choose acquisitions in subsequent entries (Chang and Rosenzweig, 2001).

Collaboration or internalization?

Initial entry mode choices are difficult to change without considerable loss of time and money, making entry mode selection a very important strategic decision for MNCs. In essence, the decision is whether to collaborate in some way with local partners in the host markets or whether to internalize operations. Collaboration allows the firm to extend its competitive advantages into more locations faster and with reduced cost and market uncertainty. This enables it to focus its resources on further developing its core competencies. Another advantage is that a local partner can provide knowledge of the local economy or product-specific knowledge. Despite these benefits there is a high level of managerial dissatisfaction with inter-firm collaboration. In part this is due to the costs associated with training partners and providing technology and management assistance. More important though are the costs involved in writing, enacting, and enforcing contracts with partners. This is a particular problem in dealing with firms in countries with low transparency, that is unclear legal systems and regulations, macro-economic and tax policies, accounting standards and practices, and corruption in the capital markets. PricewaterhouseCoopers have produced an index that weighs the effects of each of these factors for each of 35 countries. The results are displayed in figure 1.4.

However, internalization involves the costs of additional payrolls and overheads, investments in plant, property and equipment and added administrative costs. Because of this, in high-risk countries some form of IJV is often preferable to full ownership (Gatignon and Anderson, 1988). Internalization also means the loss of relevant market knowledge that a local partner might supply. This is particularly valuable when socio-cultural distance is high, explaining why partial ownership is preferred in settings that are regarded as very foreign (Gatignon and Anderson, 1988).

In trying to understand the circumstances under which collaboration is efficient or optimal it has been pointed out that because IJVs involve a partner and therefore considerable risks of free riding and other opportunistic behaviour, IJVs should be avoided whenever there is a significant proprietary content to the intangible

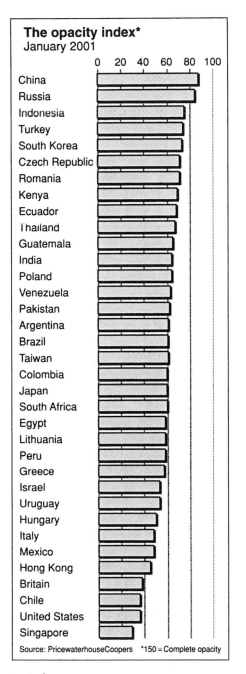

The opacity index*
January 2001

Source: PricewaterhouseCoopers   *150 = Complete opacity

Figure 1.4 The opacity index
Source: © The Economist Newspaper Ltd, London, 3 March, 2001

assets, whether they be technology or brand loyalty. Indeed, empirical research has shown that entry by full ownership is positively related to intangible assets such as R&D intensity and advertising intensity (Anderson and Gatignon, 1986; Gatignon and Anderson, 1988). Another aspect to collaboration concerns the type of knowledge that is to be applied in a host market. Knowledge that is tacit or poorly codified is difficult and costly to transmit across organizational boundaries. In other words, MNCs should avoid collaboration if the international exploitation of tacit knowledge is involved (Shrader, 2001).

In this book we will largely disregard the non-equity modes of entry, export, licensing, franchising and contract manufacturing. Our primary focus is on firms that have fully owned subsidiaries or management responsibility for IJVs. It is these we regard as fully-fledged MNCs.

By MNC we therefore mean a firm which not only has substantial direct investments in foreign countries, but which also actively manages these in an integrated way. In other words, firms that simply export their products fall outside the parameters of this book, as do firms that license their products to foreign firms. Applying these two criteria consequently means that MNCs are a relatively recent development with most of them founded after World War II.

▶ Summary

In this chapter we have defined what we mean by an MNC, i.e. actively managed substantial foreign direct investment made by firms that have a long-term commitment to operating internationally. We have thereby excluded several prevalent forms of internationalization such as licensing and contract manufacturing. MNCs are a historically recent phenomenon whose presence is particularly evident in certain sectors. Despite local resistance, sometimes explicit and sometimes tacit, MNCs have generally proved themselves, as their dramatic growth in numbers and proportions indicate, to be highly robust, at least within the context of their own triads. Nevertheless, their individual positions are always under threat because of their size and geographical dispersion, factors that make communication and control problematic. Success for individual MNCs is far from guaranteed. They are 'playing away from home' and must therefore have the organizational capabilities that enable them to leverage whatever unique strategic capabilities they possess. Increasingly these capabilities are knowledge-based. This book is therefore about the managerial challenges involved in creating and sustaining that necessary organizational capability that in turn enables the MNC to harness its knowledge resources.

The case that follows traces the process of internationalization of Vita, a European financial services company. In terms of entry mode it chose, at different times, both the acquisitions and start-ups route. The case illustrates the necessity of responding to institutional and cultural conditions, in other words, the necessity of some degree of local responsiveness. The issue of national identity is also a feature of the case. Finally, Vita also serves as a precursor for a dominant theme in this book, that of learning and the transfer of knowledge across boundaries.

Notes

1   UNCTAD (2001).
2   UNCTAD (2001).
3   See Geringer, Beamish and daCosta (1989) and Hitt, Hoskisson and Kim (1997).
4   *The Economist*, 3 November 2001.
5   Child, Faulkner and Pitkethly (2001).

case **A**

Vita Insurance: Creation of Cross-National Learning

Martin Gjelsvik and Odd Nordhaug

▶ Introduction

In the following we will present and discuss a case study that highlights a particular mode of cross-organizational learning which is likely to become increasingly commonplace in companies, that is, learning through acquisition of foreign subsidiaries that are very different from each other and from the mother company.

The presentation starts from the following question and related questions: why does a traditional and stable bureaucratic European insurance company open up businesses abroad that are built on entirely new concepts of running insurance companies and, moreover, at a time when its financial returns are high and its image in the home country is outstanding? In other words, why was this course of action chosen in the absence of any visible or evident pressure to internationalize?

First, a background is provided and the headquarter organization, called VITA Insurance, is briefly presented. Thereafter, the process of how and why an entirely domestic insurance company became a multinational is outlined. In this section, the major players are allowed to 'speak for themselves' in their own words as formulated during the interviews. This leads to a presentation of models of scanning, interpretation and learning in the actual empirical context. Observed learning obstacles and needs for transfer mechanisms to facilitate learning throughout the firm are highlighted. Finally, implications are discussed.

▶ Background

During the past few years, a common understanding has emerged that strategic planning has to be replaced with strategy processes in which continuous learning about changes and developments is at the very core. Such learning may take numerous forms, and one important aspect is the degree to which it is based solely on the competences being deployed within the boundaries of the company or on a combination of this and the competences of external firms and individuals. There is little doubt that the latter form has become increasingly widespread over the past few years, illustrated by the soaring number of joint ventures and strategic alliances founded on the pooling of dissimilar, yet complementary, competences.

The basis of this case study is observations made by one of the authors through a managerial assignment, during which he became acquainted with and acquired knowledge not only about the subsidiary VIKING Life, but also about the mother company, VITA Insurance. Being assigned the task of investigating how the company could expand its business into other areas of the financial industry, he had an excellent opportunity to gain first-hand knowledge of the company, both from a strategic as well as an operational point of view. The great difference of operations and strategies between the two companies, as well as the very loose couplings between them, appeared striking and astonishing. The cultures were different, no common products existed, the subsidiaries applied proprietary, local information technology, and the leadership structures were virtually disconnected. The subsidiary in France was operating along the same autonomous principles as the one in Scandinavia. So why establish a multinational company at all? Why not remain solely domestic? No resulting economies of scale and no standardized products across national borders were present. The organizational structures were based on national strategies, and no overarching international scheme was evident. Viewed in the light of common wisdom, it really looked like a mystery and generated a need for further investigation.

The presentation is based on data from the following sources:

- participation in several strategy discussions in VIKING;
- weekly meetings in the management group of VIKING;
- monthly discussions with the Vice President of VITA Insurance who was responsible for international business;
- two meetings with the top management group of VITA Insurance;
- one meeting with the Executive Group consisting of the top management group of VITA Insurance and the CEOs of the foreign subsidiaries;
- comprehensive, separate research interviews with the managing director of VITA Insurance and the Vice President responsible for the international businesses (conducted a year after completion of the employment relationship with VIKING).

▶ VITA Insurance

VITA Insurance was formed in 1939 as a result of the merger of four small VITA Insurance insurers and the branches of five large life insurers in a neighbouring country. During the next 25 years, focus was set more or less exclusively on cost reduction, and recruitment was virtually non-existent. By the early 1960s, survival had been established, but VITA Insurance's competitors were some of the largest mutuals in the neighbouring country who were far stronger financially. It was clear that competing in the traditional way would not be enough. The first step in a new direction came with the launch of equity-linked life insurance in 1964, one of the first such products anywhere in the world. The following years set a pattern of continuing growth as a result of factors such as:

- development of the domestic national economy;
- recruitment of a new generation of managers and specialists;
- increasing demand for life, savings, and especially pension products;
- new financial and investment possibilities;
- growth of a competitive broker market.

Today, the company offers a full range of life and pension products in its home country, as well as non-life insurance, personal finance and loans through an associated building society. Proprietary products are distributed through brokers, its own sales force, banks and building societies.

In 1967 VITA Insurance entered the UK market with products virtually identical to the domestic ones at the time. Since then, the markets have diverged and the UK operation is in effect a stand-alone subsidiary. In 1988 VITA acquired an insurance company in the USA, in 1990 took a majority share in the Scandinavian company VIKING Life, and in 1992 VITA set up a greenfield insurance operation in France.

The national government owned 90 per cent of VITA for many years, although the company was run entirely as a commercial enterprise. In 1991, the government reduced its holding to 34 per cent through a flotation.

In its strategy document, VITA's stated ambition was:

> to be an internationally recognized provider of personal financial services, and to be best in whatever we do. Although this is a deliberately broad statement, it is accompanied by a set of beliefs, characteristics and values which together act as a framework for assessing what we choose to do.

Some of the beliefs about the future are: the future will be quite different to the past and continual change will be the norm. Boundaries between different types of institutions will be less relevant. Our strategies must be market-led, while most of our current competitors are product-led. There will be more scope for transferring knowledge and experience to new markets. Technology will continue to lower cost bases and increase our ability in marketing and service. There will be a greater need to manage risk and resources, both in terms of capital and skills.

In the past few years, VITA has developed by identifying highly selective situations in the US, Scandinavia and France. Each has common characteristics, are market-led, use technology aggressively, are low-cost producers, and have a clearly differentiated competitive position. However, what they do and how they do it, is quite different. This reflects our approach of allowing each to develop their business in a way entirely suited to the circumstances of their market.

In the future, we see VITA becoming a family of different business operations, each a distinctive competitor in its own market, contributing to and drawing on the strengths of the rest of the group and our business partners. Recently we have been making increasing use of partnerships and joint ventures with shareholders, distributors and others – we expect to continue this trend to maximize the mutual benefits from complementary resources.

▶ The First Steps towards Internationalization

In this section, light will be shed on the very process underlying and leading to the internationalization of VITA through acquisitions of foreign companies. Since the purpose is to uncover the rationale underlying the international acquisitions, the formulations of the central actors will be emphasized.

Let us first turn to the issue of why it all started. These are the words of the CEO on what motivated VITA to go international:

> I was the only young person at the time. I was new and wanted some challenge. I didn't think about it at the time, I suppose it was a way of me putting a stamp on the company. I thought it was something I could do. I thought it was necessary. A company of that size where it was a relatively big company in a relatively small country and there was a lot of external factors saying you should diversify. You should spread risk. We had managed to do that on the investment side. We had investments in other countries, so to some extent we had experience outside of Ireland.

First, we note the strong personal motivation that apparently indicates the strong influence CEOs may have on the strategic goals and processes of a firm. Second, we observe what the new institutionalism in organizational theory suggests: Managers tend to imitate successes in other pertinent companies. In the organizational field of VITA (DiMaggio and Powell, 1983), the right thing to do at this time in history was to diversify in order to spread risk. Some proprietory experience was at hand on the investment side. However, there was more to it than that. The CEO explains:

> At the same time, another aspect, one of the reasons why we went international, . . .
> I have been with VITA for ten years now and when I came to the executive office
> I didn't think that we were ready at that stage to set a strategy, it was very difficult,
> so to start the process we had four or five papers written on what were our develop-
> ing opportunities. And the people that wrote the papers came back and said there
> are *no* opportunities. We can do a little more here, we can sell more than we do
> now, we can do some small things, we can do more in the UK.

In other words, the CEO's closest peers had belief structures or frames of reference that hardly stretched beyond the shores of the home country. Bearing in
mind that they had been employed in a stable and state-owned bureaucratic
organization for a long time, their views came as no surprise.

However, the CEO did not give in:

> There was a big debate among 8–9 people who were involved in that afterwards, but
> there *were* major opportunities and if so, were they to get into new businesses at
> home or to get into the same businesses in other countries? And we decided that we
> knew a lot about the business we were in, but not other businesses, so it was better
> to move into the same business in other countries. I don't know if that's right or
> not, but anyway that's what we decided. So we went to other countries and started.
> My concern at that stage was that we had a very big share of a small market and
> I couldn't see how we could double our size. In fact we continued to do very well
> in the home country the following 5–6 years, which gave us opportunities to do
> something else. About that time I knew a man that was running a paper company
> in the home country, one of the biggest in the world, that went international and
> if you were to go international it has to be done by the chief executive officer or
> somebody that has the power. Because when the opportunities come, they may be
> different, and you have to move very quickly, and I was very struck by that.

These experiences told the CEO to initiate and take charge of the process of
international diversification more or less single-handedly. This had important
bearings on what followed. The whole process was actually driven by the CEO
himself and a close colleague, whom the CEO appointed as Vice President responsible for international business. Very satisfactory financial performance facilitated great discretionary muscles. The board did not intervene, in fact, the members
did not care.

▶ The Scanning Process

A scanning process started. In the words of the Vice President:

> The US was the first establishment. It was natural because of the language, the legal
> and financial systems are pretty similar, and we are both members of an international
> network and you find many immigrants from our country there. It is a huge and
> dynamic market. Looking into Europe later, there was no thought-out process. Let's

do it. There's got to be *something* we can do. I was taken out of the organization to do it. It was on nobody's priority list. Nobody had any idea about how to go about it, or any idea about where to go. It was as simple as that. We got the map out.

In order to reduce uncertainty, the start-up was located to the most familiar market. Consequently the USA became the natural goal for expansion. Having initiated the operations in the USA, the process continued in Europe: The Vice President explains:

> Really, we started up with no idea, no preference for where we wanted to look. It was simply information gathering. But quickly you come to some conclusions: the Southern European countries were very immature with very few established market practices. It was difficult to predict where they were going to develop. We concluded that the southern countries were not attractive. In the northern countries we looked for regulations. Germany is such a big country, it's a natural place to look at, but the regulations were used to keep out competition, and it was frightening.

The scanning process was comprehensive and time-consuming. The study of various European countries spanned more than two years. With no plans or procedures at the point of departure, the interpretation process might easily have developed completely out of perspective. Some constraints did exist, however, particularly the fact that there were limits to risk-taking. In the southern European countries, the institutions were not regarded as sufficiently stable. The future market trends could not possibly be predicted. In Germany, it was almost the other way around. Markets and institutions were easily understood, but no trespassing or intrusion was allowed. At the time, foreign financial companies were not welcome in the country.

The fact that the scanning process was a learning process in itself, was confirmed by this statement:

> You're really listening for two things: facts, and people who really understand the business. So it's a two-tiered process. And you repeat the process for each country. You take each market and evaluate the products, the distribution, or if the banks are getting involved in insurance, or whatever. You go back to the people you felt for until you pick up a picture of the market in that country.

Having those pictures in mind, a selection was made:

> We felt that France was a sensible place, because it was big enough to have a range of various managers around and it was well organized. It was highly regulated, but in the process of becoming more liberal.

When the scanning process is non-directional, as in this case, there is no way of telling where one will end up. After some time, certain patterns started to emerge, however, as expressed indirectly by the Vice President:

If you are going to do anything at all in a country, you need to have people who see that opportunity themselves. If that opportunity is something that we started to believe in, things that were really not here today, we started to say: 'This is something for the future, maybe we can look for business today that can lead us in the right direction. Maybe we should look for people with ideas.' There was also a personal preference, I always took a liking in new things, people who are doing things differently.

Having decided on the country and the mode of entry (building a relationship with a local, trustworthy person with ideas), an additional scanning process was carried out:

We first concentrated on the question: whom do we talk to? We talked to everyone from journalists to merchant banks, to banks and dogs in the street, market research people, and insurers as well. The next step was simply to sit down and write down our ideas. Our paper covered what VITA was good at, what we could bring to businesses elsewhere, what it takes to compete, and our conceptions of the French market. We wanted a local person who already had some ideas and believed in our criteria. We gave our paper to 3–4 individual people whom we had met and trusted. Some of them came back and said we've found somebody that has similar ideas. Richard [the CEO] and myself met with him, and I must say that I was convinced that he was the right person. At this time we were nervous of French managers, but we felt there was enough to talk about, and we hired him for three months. After the three months he came up with a business plan and a proposition for the board, and the real big thing here is not France, but the fact that it is non-life. Then people all of a sudden started to get very scared. At that time, VITA as a group also started to talk about financial services, not only life and pensions. This was actually the first time that Richard saw what this really meant.

Ending up with a greenfield non-life company in a foreign country, certainly is a long way to go for a state-owned, bureaucratic insurance company. Non-life (motor and home casualty) insurance differs sharply from the life and pension business the company had so far been involved in. As can be recalled, VITA's expansion route was to find new markets for their existing product portfolio, 'We decided that we knew a lot about the business we were in, but not other businesses, so it was better to move into the same business in other countries.'

All of a sudden the company found itself with a new strategy. Not only did they enter other countries, they started *new lines of business* in a foreign environment. In other words, this provides a clear example of strategy emerging along the route. There was even more innovation to it than that: the distribution system was a novelty, based on small, cheap and standardized street level shops, the technology was developed from scratch, and the risk (for casualties) was calculated on an individual basis. The consequence of the individual risk calculations was that each customer was priced differently. Thus, France became VITA's *laboratory* for testing out new ideas and concepts within a broad context. We have now become familiar with a top management team that at the outset scanned their immediate environments only to find no substantial opportunities. Interpretations were made, but on a very limited scale, namely, the home country. As a consequence of VITA's dominating market share, there were no alternative players that could represent a possible learning arena for the company. There was simply no variation. Concurrently, it was similarly hard to conceive of any demanding new customers in the home country. This might of course also be explained by the arrogant attitude of the majority of the national managers who participated in the strategy process by presenting papers on future directions.

▶ Interpretations

Having experienced the disappointing facts mentioned above, the CEO decided on a strategic reorientation through marketing the present products to new geographical markets. As the CEO and his close associate travelled around the world, they came across people with new ideas and concepts. They physically acted on these events, attending to some of them, ignoring most of them, and talking to a large number of different people to observe what they were doing (Braybrooke, 1964). Interpretation is the process of translating these events, of developing models for understanding, of bringing out meaning, and of assembling conceptual schemes among key managers (Daft and Weick, 1984). In this case, the interpretations resulted in reformulations of the strategy. Actually, the interpretations first resulted in actions: opening a greenfield company in France far beyond the borders of the explicitly stated strategy of the company. Then, and not one second prior to this moment, the CEO realized the actual consequences of the actions taken: 'This was actually the first time that Richard [the CEO] saw what this really meant.' A new conceptual scheme had to be introduced and included in the strategy: 'We go abroad to find idea-generating people and companies.'

As we have seen, top management in VITA started out by analysing their domestic opportunities. The rules and regulations were well understood as they had remained stable for a long period. Customer demands and preferences reflected traditions in the home country. The management had well-established frames of reference and, accordingly, came up with suggestions for incremental changes only. They certainly operated within an analysable context, having gathered information on customers and markets over a long period of time. Emphasis was put on detecting the correct answer already existing in an analysable environment rather than on shaping the answer (Daft and Weick, 1984). Management sought support and data from their own marketing department and external consultants. Marketing surveys, trend analysis, and forecasting methods were the dominant tools applied. Actions and learning were based mainly on interpretations of formal data from a predictable environment.

From his own personal experience, especially from the USA, the CEO sensed the emergence of some radical changes that could alter the basic assumptions underlying the domestic activities. The trend in international financial markets was one of deregulation and, furthermore, the traditional boundaries between banks and insurance companies were becoming blurred. Banks started to develop and sell insurance products within their portfolio, and cases in other countries strongly indicated that banks were able to distribute insurance much cheaper than traditional insurance companies. The latter ones were dependent on very demanding commissioners, whereas the banks had the opportunity to utilize their existing sales force and related slack. From the USA, the CEO picked up information that new technologies were under way. The deregulation process led to bankruptcies and uncovered widespread fraud. Changes in government regulations, which would have tremendous impact on insurance companies, were impossible to predict. In short, the future seemed virtually impossible to analyse. The CEO frankly states: 'I didn't think that we were ready at that stage to set a strategy, it was very difficult.'

Organizations in benevolent environments have weaker incentives to be intrusive (Hedberg, 1981). Only rarely do such organizations use their slack resources for trial and error experimentation or formal search. Based on VITA's international intelligence efforts, carried out by the CEO and his Vice President in persona, a sense of a future hostile environment was intruding. The assumptions about the environment in the process of being altered, the future environment of the company could not be studied and interpreted from a desk in the capital of the home country. The interpretation activities changed from a discovering mode to an enacting mode. The company had to learn to handle future challenges at home, challenges the company was at the time unable to predict. The company needed to prepare for a portfolio of possible futures in which the environment was ambiguous. The method applied was a form of learning by acting to which we shall now turn.

▶ The Learning Process

The interpretation process described above is restricted to a very limited number of persons. It is non-linear, distinctly *ad hoc* and improvisational. Referring to the French experience, the resulting content of the learning process was accidental and highly dependent on the network of individuals that emerged around the two top managers. The actual learning process was quite complex with many feedback loops and iterations.

> things just evolved and evolved. It was mainly me doing it, with Richard backing up. It's really hard to say who thought of what at what time. We went into France with life and pension products, and came out with a non-life product, that's quite a transition.

Having completed the scanning process that generated the decision to open a greenfield non-life business in France, the company had learned how to run the scanning and interpretation activities more efficiently and less *ad hoc*. The Vice President concludes:

> We would do the same process again other places today. The process could be reproduced. The search process [in France] was easy, but it wouldn't have made any sense if we didn't have a clear view of what we wanted. The where- and what-activities changed, the original idea was to find opportunities.

As we have seen, the company did not have any clear view of what it wanted at the outset. However, for the CEO and his Vice President the picture turned clearer as they interpreted the events and acted on this basis. The goals and the respective means did not become clear until after the actions had been carried out.

Scandinavia was the next step. The decision to enter this region was taken very quickly. Again, the Vice President spells it out:

> Why Scandinavia? That was simply because I ran into Kjell and Torger, the managing director and the man in charge of the distribution, plus some specifics about Scandinavia, I mean, Scandinavia was such an uncompetitive market. Something was going to happen sometime in Scandinavia, something that we [in VITA] were good at, something that they [in VIKING] were good at. Plus the fact that they were already working with the banks , which we were looking for, and they seemed to be doing it well. They also had a low-cost mentality and focus, so VIKING was a company which just happened to match. Kjell and Torger had been invited to NEXO, an international association of insurance companies. I just made sure I was seated next to them. Ten days later I went over there to see for myself. I went straight to Richard and said that we should get involved in this. There are some interesting things here that the rest of the group can learn from.

A new learning arena was established. Though unintentionally at the outset, VITA eventually bought all the shares in VIKING. Through VIKING it learned how insurance products could be sold successfully and inexpensively by ordinary bank employees with virtually no background from insurance. Distribution and marketing costs were drastically lower than the figures VITA was accustomed to. The top managers of VITA were also highly impressed by the efficiency of VIKING's information technology solutions. All of a sudden, the trends that the CEO had sensed and maybe envisioned only a short time prior to the acquisition of VIKING, materialized. Through hands-on experiences with prospective acquisitions, the top management had established new frames of reference.

A common thread was found in the subsidiaries (cf. Ansoff, 1965). Some of the actions proved to be more pertinent than others. The CEO relates:

> You may have an overall picture as we have, that you have to run the insurance business more cheaply. You've got to have some structured way of finding them [the customers], and not just throwing things out to the world hoping that somebody would come to you. You've got things like the way the technology enables you to deliver better services.

The world was difficult to analyse, the signals were equivocal and even market surveys could not promise to avoid 'just throwing things out'. In the home country that strategy was costly and could at worst ruin the existing relationship with the company's customers. The company itself needed to take action in order to obtain reliable and pertinent information as a basis for present and future decisions and predictions.

The management was intent on keeping the VITA Group as a portfolio of companies. The traditional hot debates between globalization and local responsiveness had not surfaced. According to the CEO:

> I would be worried by building up a monolithic organization. If I were at the IBM I would have no idea how you could change something like that. It's a particular problem in financial services. In our industry the only examples are some reinsurance companies. It's understandable because in reinsurance customers are big and small in numbers, so the reinsurance companies need to be big and therefore international. The only one purely international retail bank is Citibank. But we are talking about portfolio companies, there is none being near true international companies.

Building a monolithic organization structure was regarded as having a negative effect on learning in a group: the variation of events and actions was greatly restricted, and learning was seriously hampered.

There are also institutional factors that forced financial services companies to act differently in disparate environments. The CEO was asked: 'When you envision the company five years ahead, do you see one company or a portfolio of different companies?' He replied:

> I see a portfolio, I don't see anything like General Motors or Ford where clearly you can sell the same thing in all the countries with just more production. The market of personal financial services is different, there's too many cultural differences, there are too many tax differences. And see what's happened in the home country: tax privileges that insurance companies always have enjoyed were taken away last year.

The Vice President independently expressed an identical view: 'We saw, and still see, that every market is an individual market. For the mass market, and that's where VITA mainly is, you have to provide local services to local people.'

The institutional factors constitute compelling and totally unpredictable forces. It is important to note, however, that the institutional changes may repeat themselves from one country to another. The shift in the domestic tax regime was very similar to the ones experienced in the Scandinavian country a year earlier. Having learned that such abrupt shifts may occur constituted a considerable advantage and even more favourable if one has experienced the direction of the changes.

However, dilemmas had to be solved. The CEO explains:

> There's an interesting conflict in financial services. On the one hand you've got to be big because you have a name and people like security and have trust in big

companies. Look at Life Insurance Company BETA, people have trust in BETA despite the fact that it was almost effectively bust. On the other hand there are advantages with small companies, They can move more quickly and new companies too, because the technology is changing very rapidly and your distribution network is changing very rapidly, then it may be very hard for existing people to change without feeling too big a threat.

Three reasons then emerged for keeping the group as a portfolio of companies and learning arenas: First, the markets were quite different due to cultural and institutional factors. Second, a portfolio of companies was considered to facilitate learning, including more rapid and efficient alignments to changing environments. The clue was to create a broader variation of events and actions. And, finally, this resolved the dilemma of being both big and flexible at the same time.

The ability to unlearn past and present frames of references or belief structures is a crucial prerequisite for new learning (Hedberg, 1981). Especially in the home country, belief structures were fixed. Parts of the management exhibited a strong inertia caused by historical path dependencies. The conception of VITA becoming an international company seemed far-fetched and not very sensible. The CEO regrettably admits: 'People at home weren't so interested in what's going on outside their own companies: We are very big, we are very good, and we are earning money.' This may be interpreted as a typical example of complacent managerial attitudes in a currently successful company operating in benevolent environments, and evidently the CEO under-estimated the learning obstacles: 'It's sometimes hard for me to realize that people haven't worked anywhere else and haven't been outside the home country.' Talking is not enough:

> I have talked often about the idea that if you have common ideas and people thought in the same way, then the rest would follow naturally. You have a problem in that you may have people that stay with their beliefs, they say things but may act differently in practice. That's a real difficulty because people's beliefs are quite strong. I think it's quite stressful, I suspect, when you have this set of beliefs and that's all you have.

It is disappointing that 'the rest [does not] follow naturally'. Evidently, something is missing.

▶ Competence Transfer

According to the CEO, the Executive Group consisted of the top management team of the headquarters in the home country and the managing directors of the foreign subsidiaries. The influence of the group was growing:

> I was very, very struck at the early meetings with the Executive Group. Initially we would meet once a year, now we are meeting three times a year, but because, and

that's interesting in itself, and the group has become more like I want the company to be, they decide on the group's strategy – initially it was just people telling one another what they were doing, and the reason why that has happened is that the best people in the group are no longer from the home country – which would have been true at the outset.

The term negotiated belief structures (Walsh, Henderson and Deighton, 1988) has been used to study how individual schemata are represented and used in group deliberations. It is reasonable to hypothesize that internationally oriented managers offer a broader range of relevant schemata to group discussions, and therefore carry a larger potential of making decisions leading to improved performance than do managers with domestic experience only. This suggestion is derived from the CEO's evaluation of his domestic peers and their fixed and constrained beliefs.

Judging from actions taken in the home country and in the subsidiaries respectively, the CEO recognized that 'the best people in the group are no longer from the home country of VITA'. The Chief Executive Group had turned into an arena where the managers' belief structures were transformed from the individual to the organizational level. Some individual belief structures developed into shared belief structures or common frames of reference. An example was the assumedly great potential of advanced technology in regard to reducing the costs of distribution of insurance products and efficiently utilizing customer data bases to promote products and services.

On the intermediary level of management (heads of departments such as Information Technology, Marketing, Accounting, Internal Auditing), establishment of shared belief structures were sought through so-called skill sharing groups. The CEO gives evidence: 'A year ago he [the Vice President, responsible for the international business] started this concept of skill sharing, where you gather people with knowledge of different markets and systems.'

These were professional groups in which the members could learn from each other's experiences from operations in dissimilar markets and under varying institutional conditions. The most successful group had been the one including Information Technology managers, as pointed out by the CEO:

> This group has worked on the systems side where people talk to one another. We had a big problem in France at the moment, and they got quite some help from the headquarters, equally the headquarters is at the moment looking at the US people, something that they've done. There's a lot of changes on the technology side, experience is just terrifically important.

We may hypothesize that technology in itself, and technology-related knowledge are, in general, relatively easily transferable across individuals, groups and organizational units. As a contrast, the marketing managers did not succeed, which was probably a consequence of the disparity between the different markets and idiosyncratic national institutional barriers.

The board of VITA was a third mediating mechanism. A few years earlier the board members were exclusively home country nationals. Now the board had become somewhat international, although the majority of the members were still recruited from the domestic scene. The CEO explains:

> The board is starting to visit the outside companies. They were here [in the capital of the Scandinavian country] last year, in the US a month ago, and there's an opportunity then to get some impression [of the subsidiaries].

Until recently, the board had played a less than dominant role in multinational activities. However, as the financial leeway tightened, the board intended to monitor the business more actively.

A fourth transfer mechanism was simply imitation or contagion (DiMaggio and Powell, 1983; Rogers, 1962). The CEO had observed, 'It's interesting because when you have been reasonably successful, people will say: yes, they are right, that's the direction business got to go'. In fact this was the mediating mechanism in which the top manager of VITA initially had the most confidence, although until then imitation and contagion processes had been rare. Such processes might work as long as the organizational structure facilitated those processes through skill groups and the Executive Group. The CEO admitted that:

> You need some sort of a group process that says that these things you have to do, and the concept of this group strategy process has to do with that. Instead, people look to the centre a lot more than I thought they would do. People look for direction. I didn't want to give them direction, I didn't want to give them *much* direction, but perhaps they needed to be told that.

Entering into new learning arenas, participants needed to be told what was expected from them. Without a normative pressure and a supportive and visible reward system that could promote competence transfer, the mere intentions and hopes of the CEO would have been insufficient.

▶ Discussion

Models of organizational learning may be useful to further the understanding of the diversified multinational company (DMNC). Doz and Prahalad (1991) argue that organizational learning theories are of great relevance to the DMNC management theories. The conceptualization of the multinational company as a set of learning arenas relates to Ghoshal and Bartlett's (1990) idea of the multinational as a network of exchange relationships among different organizational units.

The observations presented in this case study clearly tell a story of structural indeterminacy, internal differentiation, decision trade-offs between multiple priorities, and the importance of information flows. Furthermore, the pattern of linkages between the subsidiaries was formed more by emergent processes than formal decisions by the top management. By operating the subsidiaries, VITA Insurance allowed for efficient transfer of technologies and knowledge suitable for the repetitive processes in the bureaucratic home organization, as well as differential, innovative change processes in the host countries. Through these innovations, the management of VITA Insurance actually enacted or created an important part of the organization's own environment (Weick, 1979). The elements mentioned above are identical to the criteria for relevance to DMNC management, to which organizational learning theory may prove to be well suited (Doz and Prahalad, 1991).

At a certain point in time, some participants in the organization discovered a discrepancy between what they thought the world ought to be like (given present possibilities and constraints) and what the world actually was like. This discrepancy produced individual behavior which was aggregated into organizational action. Concurrently, the establishment of a set of learning arenas did not automatically lead to a broad organizational learning process. It started with the people who sensed the above-mentioned discrepancy. In this case, the top management had effectively learned through creating new environments for their company. They had gained new insights and knowledge of a broad range of topics that were highly relevant for improving the operations in the headquarter organization. Thus, they had acquired an ability to make adjustments and alignments to changing environments. They even had the capacity to make all the necessary decisions on strategic realignments. Consequently, one might conclude that the development of a new strategy was carried out 'in a single informed brain' (Mintzberg and Waters, 1982: 496). However, the strategic reorientations needed to be implemented. The altered goals, the novel way of learning through experimentation on foreign arenas, the fact that VITA was no longer a purely domestic company, all these elements needed to be included in new belief structures.

In regard to the performance of the learning arenas, the CEO summarized some of the achievements so far:

> Oddly enough, I think the mistake we made wasn't so much that we were imposing direction on the *new* companies, it was that we didn't impose, or *I* didn't impose direction – because I was the only person in charge – on the *existing* companies. We had less time than I thought we had. But if we look today, if we hadn't gone international, we would have been in a much more difficult situation. Strangely enough I'm not sure that the VITA Insurance board would find that so easy, for two reasons: none of them know much about financial services business, they have some ideas, the second is that they are all based in the UK and our home country and it's very difficult to get people to think outside the area which they're familiar with.

The latter part of the quote reminds us of two major conclusions. First, in order to succeed in establishing a multinational company, considerable management discretion is required. The visions of the CEO could not have been carried through with interference from a highly domestically oriented national board. The Vice President frankly stated that:

> at the time we had lots of decisional discretion. The idea of doing motor insurance in France was horrific to the board, motor insurance in the home country is awful. But they never challenged, we produced no dividends, there was no pressure. Today the board is more testing, more risk adverse, and we have to pay dividends. In fact France probably wouldn't get through.

Organizational slack is another precondition for going international. VITA was affluent in terms of cash when the establishment and acquisitions of the foreign companies started. Manpower was plentiful, and one person from the upper echelons, the Vice President, was selected from the established organization to work with international opportunities. No stakeholder was crying for dividends, so the decision-makers could settle for a long-term perspective, in other words, *time* was not a scarce resource. The two major players, the CEO himself and his Vice President, provided sufficient attention to activities that, measured in quantitative terms, were rather marginal. Through long-term financial support, manpower, and management attention, the future potential of the investments could be utilized. Frequent and sustained attention to events in the foreign, enacted environments supported learning activities and improved performance. Furthermore, focus was set on learning on the strategic or top management level and, furthermore, on what some researchers call higher-level learning or double-loop learning (Argyris and Schön, 1978). The context for higher-level learning is typically ambiguous and ill-defined. Overall rules, norms and structures rather than specific activities or behaviours are in focus.

By diversifying into new areas of operation, markets and institutional environments, DMNCs can establish new learning arenas that may serve to facilitate higher-level learning. Thus, a DMNC may create a learning environment, take new actions and thereby generate a large number of events from which the company may gain novel insights by monitoring and interpreting the various performances. Through the testing of new concepts in highly different environments, causal inferences may be drawn and new frames of references elaborated. Firms which establish learning arenas that offer the most efficient facilitation of alignments to new markets and environments, may gain competitive advantages that are very costly and difficult to copy, if at all imitable by competitors.

The present case description supplements the study by Paul Adler (1993) in which he challenges the dominant view that bureaucracies waste human potential for innovation and creativity, suggesting the existence of a learning-oriented form through common goals, participation in defining key policies and standards, including trust and respect. The case of VITA suggests an alternative learning method for mature bureaucracies: design a multinational company and let the subsidiaries play the role of learning arenas and action generators. Establish efficient transfer mechanisms throughout the companies to facilitate learning across organizational levels and geographic areas.

The substance of this case indicates that diversified companies possess the potential to develop better learning skills than do domestic, single-business firms. Multinational companies may create a multifaceted, complex environment in order to improve their learning skills. In the words of the CEO of VITA Insurance:

> You are stuck if you stop learning, then you have a problem. Change becomes very difficult. I certainly got that wrong. I didn't understand, I thought that all you have to do is to talk about it. I never envisaged that people somehow would get stuck.

It is important to emphasize that the process of adaptation and alignment to new competitive and institutional environments requires support from structural elements in the organization. The process does not roll by itself and this insight was a critical part of the learning process that the CEO and his management team went through.

The presentation has offered insights into how well-established, traditional bureaucracies may create new learning through foreign acquisitions that can generate competence transfers which are otherwise impossible to accomplish. VITA invested in innovative, trustworthy, idea-generating people in different countries to gain access to new skills and capabilities. The management considered it too risky to experiment with the bureaucratic mother company. Through foreign investments, management could learn by operating companies with highly different structures, product ranges, technology, and leadership styles. The company actually adopted a model of learning by acting. Through interpretations and experiences from these actions, new technologies could then be transferred and implemented deliberately into the large mother company without running the risk of ruining the efficiency of extant operations. Hence, it was very much like a grafting process (Huber, 1991). The members of the bureaucracy could learn from real examples and experiences rather than through abstract and verbal persuasion. At the time, management had sufficient financial discretionary power to construct relevant novel environments and to utilize this capacity for learning purposes. The result was that the performance of the subsidiaries in important fields gradually became benchmarks for the rest of the organizations.

▶ Conclusion

The conventional interpretation of the rationale underlying diversification within companies and corporations has been that of risk spreading, not carrying all one's eggs in one basket. However, as demonstrated in this presentation, diversification may be motivated by alternative considerations related to competences and learning within the company. In the case of VITA, spread of risk was not an issue at all, since the company was financially very strong and operated within low-risk areas of the insurance industry. What the top managers wanted to achieve through the acquisition of foreign subsidiaries in dissimilar lines of business, was to create a variation within the company that could facilitate transfers of dissimilar competences and experiences to the headquarters organization and across subsidiaries. Hence, the aim was to construct a sort of intra-firm specialization, not in order to secure economies of scale but in order to promote cross-fertilization among organizational units. This was accomplished by utilizing four transfer mechanisms through which new knowledge and adaptation rules could be disseminated throughout an organization:

- the board members;
- the Chief Executive Group;
- skill groups;
- imitation or contagion of visible and presumably viable 'best practice' examples.

The main focus was put on the development of competence bases and learning potentials. This can be called learning-directed diversification, and it is reasonable to expect that numerous such examples will emerge in international business in the near future.

Case Assignments

1 Discuss the situation the CEO of Vita was in and how he handled it.
2 Evaluate the CEO and his colleague's *modus operandi*.
3 Discuss other possible international, learning-oriented strategies that could have been chosen.
4 Is this way of creating cross-national learning recommendable to other firms? If so, what kinds of companies are these?

c h a p t e r

2

Structures and Learning Networks

Purpose

The purpose of this chapter is to review the overarching organizational capabilities required by MNCs in order for them to meet their strategic needs. In the initial part of the chapter our focus is on the challenge involved in developing internal structures that are appropriate for MNCs' strategic needs in the sense that they provide control and co-ordination of worldwide operations. We define three generic internal structures: the international, the multi-domestic and the global product division. These are ordered in terms of two dimensions: the degree of local responsiveness and the degree of global integration the MNC is seeking to achieve. Thereafter we describe the emergence of a fourth generic internal structure, that of the transnational. However, important as formal structure is in delineating this new form, a third dimension, worldwide learning, is required. This is because there is a growing recognition of the competitive advantage in ensuring that knowledge flows between increasingly knowledge intensive subsidiaries. Thus in the latter part of this chapter we discuss how MNCs are responding to this challenge by attempting to develop knowledge exchange networks that are informal systems overlaying the chosen structure. We indicate that because of changes in their environments, whether these involve customers, suppliers, competitors, technologies or governments, MNCs strategic needs are rarely stable. As such, structure is constantly evolving and, in many instances, becoming more complex and more differentiated.

Traditional Motivations

The traditional motivations for firms to internalize their transactions in international markets through the establishment or acquisition of foreign operations, can be divided into three. First, some firms are dependent on having a reliable supply of raw materials that can only be accessed in foreign locations. For example, European tyre companies established rubber plantations in Malaysia and South America while aluminium companies established smelters where cheap energy was available. Internalizing these transactions provide these firms with a supply that may be less vulnerable and therefore, in the long run, cheaper than market solutions.

A second driving force has been the need to expand the market for the company's product by capitalizing on idiosyncratic strategic assets through their application in foreign markets. This has been particularly important for firms with small home markets. A powerful contemporary example of this is developments at Nokia of Finland, a country of 5 million people, during the 1990s. Started in 1865, Nokia is one of Europe's oldest companies. For many years it was a broadly based conglomerate, spanning tyres, cables and television sets, primarily serving the Finnish market. It was not until the 1980s that it made its first concerted attempt to break out of the limitations of its domestic market primarily through electronics-based products, such as televisions. However, it continued to manufacture a wide range of other unrelated products. Indeed, in the late 1980s Nokia was Ireland's leading manufacturer of toilet paper and the world's only supplier of studded winter bicycle-tyres! By 1989 it was obvious that the strategy was a failure and Nokia set about conducting a major rethink. The decision was to maintain a global strategy but to focus the company on one particular comparative advantage. Nokia had been in the Finnish telecommunications business since the early 1960s. While most countries had a national telephone operator that purchased equipment from a national supplier, Finland had always had many telephone companies and equipment manufacturers from all over the world had competed fiercely to supply them, forcing Nokia to constantly develop and improve its products. This advantage was coupled to the nascent technology of mobile phones and the networks that allow them to operate. By 1992 Nokia was selling large chunks of its established businesses in order to focus on this one business. By the end of the decade it had 35 per cent of the global market, with sales of $26.1 billion and pre-tax profits of $5 billion dollars. Finland accounted for a mere 4 per cent of these sales. Over half of Nokia's 45,000 employees consisted of foreigners spread across 26 sites in 11 countries.

From the 1960s onwards, as tariffs declined, firms located in the USA and Europe found themselves at a competitive disadvantage because of their relatively high labour costs. As a result a third driving force for establishing foreign operations emerged, the accessing of low-cost labour. An added incentive to relocate production has been the willingness of some host governments to provide direct or indirect subsidies in the form of low levels of corporate taxation. MNCs are therefore able to spread their production processes across multiple countries, thereby taking advantage of the different factor endowments located in their manufacturing chains. Each link in the manufacturing process is located in a country where the associated costs are the lowest. Production is moved to more favourable locations in accordance with changing wage rates, interest rates and factor prices.

Raymond Vernon's (1966) product cycle theory makes explicit use of the second and third of these drivers. With a particular focus on US firms he portrayed their internationalization as a gradual, incremental three-phase process. A firm located in phase one has all of its production within the USA with some incidental export to developed markets in Europe. When exports reach significant proportions, the firm, almost reactively, moves into phase two in which production facilities are established to serve its major foreign markets. As the product becomes highly standardized and competitors are able to produce similar products and make their presence felt by competing on price, the firm enters a third phase: production is transferred to nations where labour costs are low, and if necessary, doing so repeatedly.

In Vernon's view, then, the primary driver for internationalization was increasingly one of acquiring access to low-cost factors of production, particularly labour which leads to *off-shore production* of specific items which are then exported either for further work or for sale. Any exceptions to this trend would be the product of markets protected by politically created, barriers, such as tariffs. To circumvent these barriers, the common response was to establish factories whose task would be to assemble the home product locally. These *server plants* might make some minor adaptations to suit local needs and engage in some localization of components, in order to overcome political barriers, but product design and development would remain centralized.

In terms of Vernon's product cycle theory we can distinguish two generic multinational strategies. Phase two of the product cycle may be labelled the international strategic phase, whereas phase three is the global phase. Prior to discussing the organizational implications and characteristics of these phases Vernon's perspective must be supplemented by a third generic strategy, the multi-domestic. This strategy has been a particular feature of European firms operating subsidiaries in other European countries. Large national differences in consumer preferences between European countries, logistical barriers and, originally, high tariff barriers all contributed to favouring a strategy involving high national responsiveness. The result was a loose federation of relatively small, decentralized subsidiaries who were generally allowed to significantly adapt products in accordance with local preferences.

▶ Basic Structures

Structure is, or should be, largely a response to strategy, which in turn will reflect the type of business the firm is operating in as well as its internal resources. The basic structures that emerge with regard to international strategy are largely a reflection of the degree of global integration the MNC chooses to exercise over its subsidiaries and the degree to which its subsidiaries are mandated to be flexible and responsive in regard to their local environments. On the basis of our discussion above we can identify three generic variants.

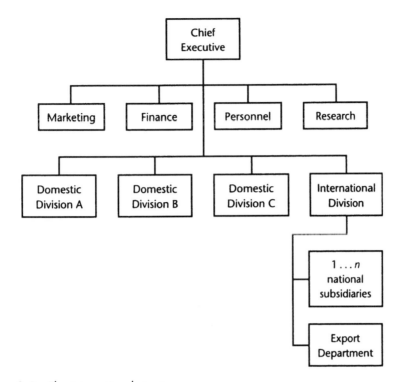

Figure 2.1 The international structure
Source: Leontiades (1985). Reprinted with permission of Rowman & Littlefield Publishing Group

The international

The simplest form of MNC structure involves the establishment of a dedicated international division charged with the responsibility of overseeing and managing the international activities of the firm. These activities are not considered as integral to the company in that it is overwhelmingly focused on its home market. Initially the responsibilities of the international division may involve no more than overseeing the export of the company's products. That is, it is charged with attending to tariff and trade issues and securing and monitoring foreign agents. However, in succeeding phases sales offices are opened and manufacturing capacity established in order to better serve the company's most important markets. Figure 2.1 illustrates this structure in the context of the single product company.

Characteristic of foreign operations is that they have an adjunct or peripheral function. Despite being usually headed by parent company staff, i.e. expatriates, they are not integrated in any of the company's business units. The lack of global strategy means that decisions relating to foreign operations are made in an opportunistic or *ad hoc* manner.

Another trait is that they lack the resources and mandate to adapt, let alone develop, the product to any significant extent. There is a one-way transference of technology and knowledge from the parent company to its foreign subsidiaries resulting in a low degree of local responsiveness. The approach is to exploit home-country innovations in order to achieve incremental sales rather than develop flexible or high-scale operations. In their early days this was how Colgate Palmolive and many other American companies, such as Kraft and Procter & Gamble, operated in Europe. As Vernon suggests, the international organization type is essentially a transitory phase that precedes a more globally integrated form of organization.

The multi-domestic

The main driver behind Nestlé's approach to expansion outside of Switzerland was entirely different to that underlying international expansion. With a small domestic market, expansion could only come from establishing operations abroad. In other words, foreign activities were never viewed as purely incremental and this has influenced the way it has traditionally structured its operations in currently over 80 countries. Today these operations account for 98 per cent of Nestlé's $47 billion turnover. Founded in 1866, by the early 1900s it had operations in Britain, Germany, Spain and the United States. This expansion was accompanied by a profound recognition that as tastes in human foodstuffs vary enormously from country to country, centralization was to be kept to a minimum. From its earliest days Nestlé delegated brand management authority to country managers who independently adjusted the marketing and manufacturing strategies in accordance with local tastes and preferences. In 1994 of its 8,000 brands, only 750 were registered in more than one country. Even research and development was decentralized so that currently some 18 R&D centres are located around the world. As for IT, Nestlé, had 100 IT centres round the world providing separate IT support functions for most of the countries in which it operates. Currently, of its 230,000 employees only 1,600 are employed in Vevey at Nestlé's headquarters. As such, Nestlé has been labelled a multi-domestic company characterized by relatively weak global integration and pronounced local responsiveness. Figure 2.2 indicates the basic structure.

However, developments, such as its 'Globe' (Global Business Excellence) project, since Peter Brabeck took over as chief executive in 1998, indicate a strong desire by Nestlé to try and generate economies of scale through a pronounced consolidation and standardization of its global business processes. This is particularly apparent in its centralization of marketing and IT functions. In terms of the former, Nestlé has been increasingly attempting to focus on its core products resulting in the consolidation of its resources behind key corporate strategic brands such as Nestlé, Nescafé, Friskies and Carnation. The Nestlé brand now accounts for 40 per cent of the total turnover. Additionally there are over

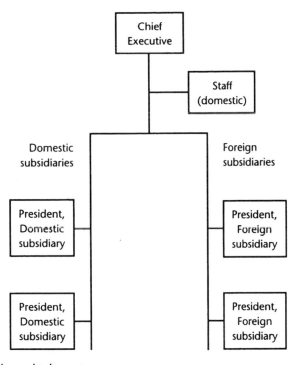

Figure 2.2 The multi-domestic structure
Source: Leontiades (1985). Reprinted with permission of Rowman & Littlefield Publishing Group

40 different strategic world-wide product brands including KitKat, Coffee-mate and Crunch which are now managed from headquarters. Paralleling this Nestlé's 100 IT globally redistributed support centres are being reduced to just five as part of the most fundamental reorganization in the group's 135-year history. For the first time in its history Nestlé's Vevey headquarters has a computer system that enables it to know how many raw materials its subsidiaries buy, in total, from around the world. As a consequence Nestlé is increasingly able to negotiate contracts on behalf of the company as a whole and centralize its production. Between 1998 and 2002 it was able to close or sell about half of its factories. Sylvian Massot, an analyst at Morgan Stanley Dean Witter in London commented that, 'Brabeck has taken a company that is a collection of fiefdoms and turned them into an effective global company.'[1] In other words, Nestlé is moving away from an overtly multi-domestic structure towards what we will refer to as the global product division structure.

In their own ways this has been the case for many other European multi-domestics such as Philips, Shell, Danone and Unilever. It has also been the case for Ford Motor Company, which during the 1990s, in conjunction with a cost-savings plan dubbed the 'Ford 2000' plan, centralized its international and domestic operations.

At the same time, though, Nestlé continues to evince the need to be responsive to different consumer tastes. Peter Brabeck comments: 'The emotional link to the local consumer is extremely important to our business. That is why it remains a fragmented industry and that is why we try to stay as close as possible to local consumers' (*The Financial Times*, 13 March 2000).

Global product division

We have noted that European multi-domestics appear to be converging around a global-product division structure. Additionally, we have pointed to the international as an organization type that precedes a more globally integrated form of organization. By a global product division organization type, we mean that the major line of authority lies with product managers who have a global responsibility for their product line. Japanese MNCs, particularly in the electronics, computer and automobile industries, have invariably adopted the global product division structure from the outset. Highly centralized scale-intensive manufacturing and R&D operations are leveraged through world-wide exports of standardized global products. When foreign subsidiaries are established, there is no intention that they should respond actively to local market demands over and above that which is strictly necessary. In terms of strategy formulation, product development and key manufacturing they have no more than a secondary status, being either *off-shore* or *server* plants.

Sony is a typical global type of MNC. It makes most of its value-added high-tech products, such as chips and personal computers in Japan, where it can monitor quality and where it has location-bound advantages not least in terms of research and development. When products have become highly standardized and are no longer dependent on Sony's location-bound advantages, their production is transferred to other locations either to lower costs or to improve market entry. In relation to Europe, Sony has transferred production of audio-visual products, such as televisions and computer displays to purpose-built greenfield sites that have been managed largely according to Sony's management principles. The standardized capabilities involved are easily transferred through training programmes.

Firms that are pursuing the global-product division strategy have to develop and deploy three distinct organizational capabilities. They must succeed in:

- gaining the input of subsidiaries into centralized activities
- ensuring that all functional tasks are linked to market needs
- integrating diverse functions such as development, production and marketing by managing the transfer of responsibilities among them.

(Bartlett and Ghoshal, 1995: 581)

The main structural features of the global-product division are shown in figure 2.3.

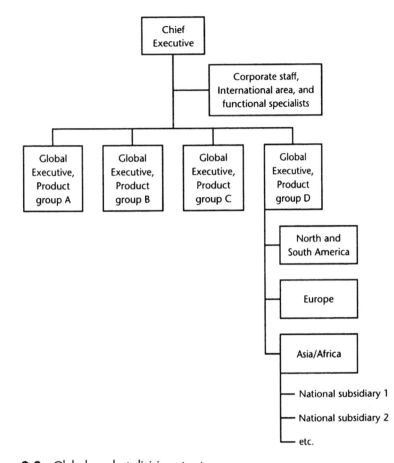

Figure 2.3 Global-product division structure
Source: Leontiades (1985). Reprinted with permission of Rowman & Littlefield Publishing Group

Companies such as Sony epitomize Theodore's Levitt's (1983) thinking. Writing in the early 1980s he envisioned of a world increasingly dominated by MNCs of the global organization type:

> Everywhere everything gets more and more like everything else as the world's preference structure is relentlessly homogenised . . . Ancient differences in national tastes or modes of doing business disappear. The commonality of preference leads inescapably to the standardisation of products, manufacturing and the institutions of trade and commerce. [The global corporation] treats the world as composed of few standardised markets rather than many customised markets. It actively seeks and vigorously works toward global convergence. [It seeks] to force suitably standardised products and practices on the entire globe . . . Companies that do not adapt to the new global realities will become victims of those that do.

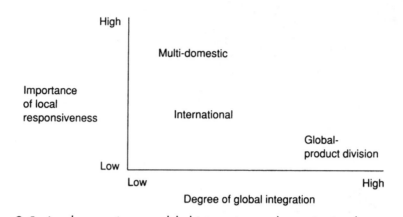

Figure 2.4 Local responsiveness, global integration, and organizational structure

The mentality underlying the global-product division is of course far from exclusively Japanese. Ikea's history is one of having ignored local taste and bucking fragmented furniture markets by producing scale-intensive, globally standardized furniture. Despite serving a range of markets from Russia to North America, purchasing, distribution and design functions remain centrally controlled and served by Swedes. Similarly General Electric functions on the basis of a distinctly uniform corporate mentality although this does not preclude non-Americans. Its ten businesses are global businesses, each with its own president who co-ordinates and integrates activities worldwide.

Framework

The three generic strategy-structure types we have discussed are summarized in figure 2.4.

Figure 2.5 distinguishes different types of subsidiaries according to the degree of knowledge resources they possess. The framework distinguishes the two types of subsidiary common to the global product division type of MNC: off-shores and servers. Additionally it includes a second type of server subsidiary. This is associated with multi-domestics and is different from the global server in that it has the latitude to develop resources that enable it to significantly adapt products for its local markets. Subsidiaries of the more transitory international organization type do not feature, but in principle they will fall into one of figure 2.5's three categories.

The framework includes a second dimension, the learning contribution of the subsidiary to the MNC. For all three subsidiary types this is low, indicating that even multi-domestics have rarely systematically attempted to leverage learning from their various subsidiaries.

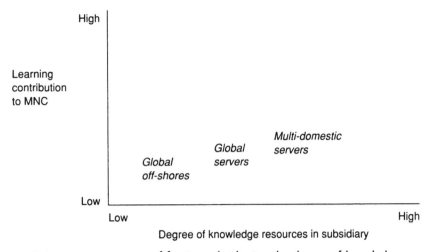

Figure 2.5 A categorization of foreign subsidiaries: the degree of knowledge resources they possess and learning contribution

 Emerging Motivations

In the early 1980s the global strategy was increasingly regarded as mandatory. With increasing competition as a consequence of decreased tariff barriers, product life cycles had shortened dramatically thereby escalating research and development costs. The ability to operate under such a cost burden entailed an expanded scale of production over and above what a firm's domestic market was capable of absorbing. As such, foreign markets had to be sought out just in order to 'enter the game'. A further reason to seek out foreign markets was that without a presence in every market, competitors could achieve dominant positions that granted high profit margins. Dominance and strong profitability in one or more markets could then be surreptitiously used to subsidize loss-making entries into other markets.

At the end of the 1980s, however, it was argued by, for example, Bartlett and Ghoshal (1989), that important as the global integration dimension is, there is also an increasing need to achieve close proximity to local markets or customers to be able to adapt products to local tastes. Customers are no longer prepared to accept a 'one-size-fits-all' product strategy. Furthermore, not only do customers have their idiosyncratic national preferences, host governments increasingly expect both local content and transference of technology. In terms of this perspective global off-shore plants based on cheap labour or global server plants making minor adjustments are no longer the critical modes of internationalization. Instead subsidiaries increasingly involve an ability to adapt and enhance products in line with local market demands. This pressure manifested itself in the thinking of

Corus, the Anglo-Dutch steel and aluminium producer when it in early 2001 set out its plans to double its plant investments for the next five years. Its chairman, Sir Brian Moffat, indicated that most of its new spending would probably be outside the UK and the Netherlands because it needed to invest close to customers. He commented, 'It is difficult to satisfy companies in eastern Europe or China if you have most of your assets in Britain' (*The Financial Times*, 16 March 2001).

MNCs recognized that in acquiring or creating subsidiaries with a developmental capacity these subsidiaries could not only be used to adapt products, but also to enhance them (Kuemmerle, 1997). Coupled to this was the understanding that there were competitive advantages to be derived from integrating product developments stemming from 'enhancers' into the MNC as a whole, which meant that worldwide learning became a motivation for internationalization in itself. Firms increasingly recognized that there were competitive advantages in being able to tap into and integrate critical knowledge resources wherever they may be located. As a result MNCs began to seek out regional centres of excellence in order to tap into world-class specialist knowledge from the local scientific community, including competitors as well as universities, from where it flows back to the company's central R&D site and beyond to other sites in the firm's global network (Kuemmerle, 1997). For example, nearly all of the big European pharmaceutical companies have established an R&D presence in America, particularly in high-technology clusters such as Boston and San Diego. Likewise American pharmaceutical companies, such as Pfizer, have European research facilities. Pfizer's UK research centre has discovered three of its recent blockbuster drugs. The result is that it is the subsidiary that is the centre of excellence within the firm for particular products and technologies (Birkinshaw, 1997). Figure 2.6 illustrates

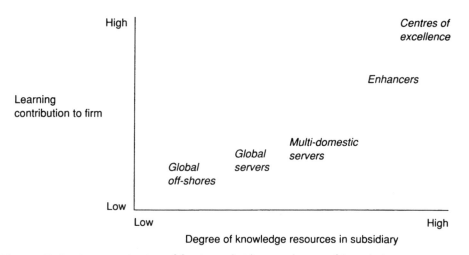

Figure 2.6 A categorization of foreign subsidiaries: degree of knowledge resources and learning contribution to the MNC as a whole

the position of enhancer and augmentor subsidiaries in relation to off-shores and servers.

The notion that what is increasingly driving the internationalization of firms' activities is their need to obtain and create new competencies in order to support and improve overall innovativeness, is viewed by Cantwell (1996) as representing a 'new evolutionary approach' for understanding the strategic intent of MNCs. No longer are MNCs to be exclusively viewed as agents of unidirectional international technology transfer. Instead they should be viewed as being driven by a need to develop technology and knowledge that is met by leveraging their presence in foreign locations to generate internationally co-ordinated learning processes. This is particularly the case in regard to technologically intensive industries such as pharmaceuticals and electronics, where levels of sophistication make labour costs increasingly less of an issue than skills and creativity. So, for example, while Nokia has been driven by the need to expand the market for its product, it has also formalized the learning opportunities internationalization grants it by establishing learning centres outside of Finland, in China, Italy and Singapore.

▶ The Transnational

The requirements for global integration, local responsiveness and world-wide learning meant, according to Bartlett and Ghoshal, that a new MNC organization type, the transnational, was emerging:

> While some products and processes must still be developed centrally for worldwide use and others must be created locally in each environment to meet purely local demands, MNCs must increasingly use their access to multiple centres of technologies and familiarity with diverse customer preferences in different countries to create truly transnational innovations. (Bartlett and Ghoshal, 1995: 127)

Bartlett and Ghoshal took ABB as their core example of this new MNC form. ABB was a heavy engineering firm that was formed in 1988 as the result of a cross-border merger between Asea AB of Sweden and BBC Brown Boveri Ltd. of Switzerland. Its first chief executive officer, Percy Barnevik, expounded a strategic vision that, with its focus on reaping global efficiencies, while being locally responsive and ensuring world-wide learning, constituted an 'almost a perfect description of the transnational' (Bartlett and Ghoshal, 1995: 788). In Barnevik's words:

> We want to be global and local, big and small, radically decentralized with centralized reporting and control . . . You want to be able to optimize a business globally – to specialize in the production of components, to drive economies of scale as far as you can, to rotate managers and technologists around the world to share expertise and solve problems. But you also want to have deep local roots everywhere you operate – building products in the countries where you sell them, recruiting the best local

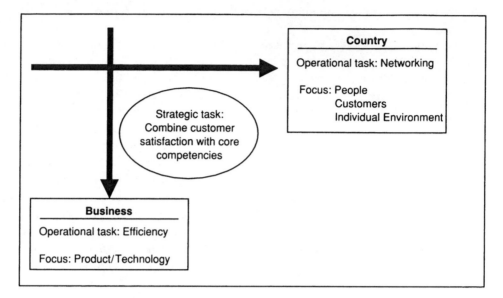

Figure 2.7 The initial balanced global matrix structure at ABB

talent from the universities, working with the local government to increase exports. If you build such an organization, you create a business advantage that's damn difficult to copy. (Taylor, 1991)

But how does one build such an advantage, which not least rests upon the ability to disseminate learning throughout the company? Under Barnevik ABB's primary structural response was the implementation of the balanced global matrix for its 1,300 separate operating companies. Each operating manager was responsible for creating and pursuing entrepreneurial opportunities. Each of these front-line managers reported to a country manager, who was typically responsible for all the operating companies within a specific country, and to a Business Area manager who was responsible for developing world-wide product and technology strategies. Figure 2.7 illustrates the general principle.

In turn each Business Area manager reported to one of 11 executive vice presidents. These vice presidents were the lynchpins of the matrix system in that they not only were responsible for an interrelated set of Business Areas but also several regions. They constituted the Executive Committee that defined overall global strategy and broad performance targets (see figure 2.8). It is significant that of 215,000 employees only 100 people were located at corporate headquarters in Zurich.

A final feature at ABB was its deployment of a centralized reporting system, ABACUS, which collected performance data and compared it with budgets and forecasts. The system also allowed the data to be consolidated or broken down by

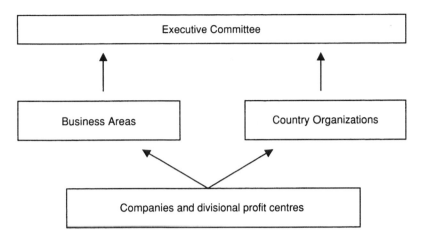

Figure 2.8 The initial overall structure at ABB

business segments and worldwide product lines, countries and companies within countries. In that way the Executive Committee had not only a clear view of the usual measurements such as orders, cash flow and margins, but also emerging trends in performance, both globally and by country.

Bartlett and Ghoshal observed local responsiveness at ABB in its radical de-centralization of assets and responsibilities to local operating units. Managers of the local operating units had a mandate to build their businesses as if they owned them with managers being allowed to inherit results. They also observed global integration in that the mandate of the Business Area manager was designed so as to facilitate horizontal integration between units in respect to knowledge, export markets and production facilities. 'He decides which factories are going to make what products, what export markets each factory will serve, how the factories should pool their expertise and research funds for the benefit of the business worldwide' (Bartlett and Ghoshal, 1995: 853). That is, any local unit may be upgraded by a Business Area manager to take on a central task or requested to contribute its expertise to the realization of a task at another unit. In structural terms the essence of ABB is thus the balancing and integrating of global business managers and geographic management groups. Figure 2.9 summarizes the trans-national in relation to global integration and local responsiveness.

In addition to the objective structural features Bartlett and Ghoshal regarded the development of a structure of shared values at ABB, a 'common organizational psychology', as being of even greater significance. The essence of such a psychology is a shared understanding of and respect for the company's mission and objectives combined with non-parochial, collaborative attitudes. It is, they argue, achieved by selecting and promoting individuals whose personal characteristics predispose them towards non-opportunistic behaviour and by creating an internal

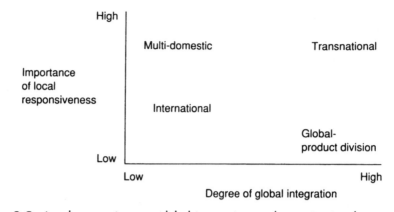

Figure 2.9 Local responsiveness, global integration, and organizational structure

context that encourages people to act in the way they would as a member of a functional family or a disciplined sporting team.

▶ Validation

Employing data from 166 subsidiaries of 37 MNCs headquartered in nine different countries, Harzing (2000) has substantially confirmed the validity of the typology of MNC organizational structures we have presented. Her analysis excludes the transitory international, focusing instead on the issue of the existence of multi-domestics, globals and transnationals. In the first stage of her analysis, Harzing divided her sample into three according to the type of corporate strategy being deployed. Those firms with a focus on global competition and economies of scale were categorized as globals, firms emphasising domestic competition and national responsiveness were classified as multi-domestics, and firms combining these features were labelled transnationals. In the second stage of her analysis Harzing examined the association between the three MNC types and a number of core organizational characteristics. Overall Harzing's findings are in line with our theoretical discussion above. Table 2.1 features Harzing's main findings.

Harzing's research also features an analysis of the main control mechanisms associated with the three MNC types. An expected characteristic of the multi-domestic subsidiaries is that there is little in the way of centralized control over and above an evaluation of their financial results. However, for globals, decision-making is much more than simply output control. Control is highly centralized and at subsidiary level there are surveillance mechanisms in addition to written rules and procedures that have to be adhered to. Transnationals are harder to distinguish from globals than multi-domestics. However, they do appear to be more inclined to use what we referred to above as a 'common organizational psychology' than is the case for multi-domestics or globals.

Table 2.1 Harzing's test of typologies of MNCs

MNC type	Characteristics
Multi-domestic	Decentralized federation Low level of HQ dependence Low level of interdependence High level of product modification, adaptation of marketing
Global	Subsidiaries have a 'pipeline' role High level of HQ dependence High level of interdependence Low level of product modification and adaptation of marketing
Transnational	Network structure, centres of excellence, inter-subsidiary flows Medium level of HQ dependence High level of interdependence High level of product modification and adaptation of marketing

Source: Adapted from Harzing, 2000.

The Evolution of the MNC

For a substantial part of the 1990s it was speculated that MNCs were evolving into transnationals. However, Harzing's research (1999) undermines this thesis since she finds that a significant proportion of transnational firms did not grow out of multi-domestic or global companies. That is, they started out as transnationals. Other research suggests that structure is far from stable and that it is being constantly adjusted in response to strategic shifts (Taggart, 1998). Let us exemplify this by charting changes at Bartlett and Ghoshal's prototypical transnational, ABB.

As ABB moved through the 1990s its structure and the ambition of creating a common organizational psychology were put to the test by the gale of market forces that saw ABB moving out of heavy engineering businesses into IT-related businesses such as process automation. Employee numbers were reduced from 215,000 to 160,000. This change in employee numbers involved much more than a simple reduction in staff. While on the one hand there were 60,000 job losses in Europe, new jobs were created in other regions, not least in the Far East where there was an addition of 40,000 employees. In this turbulent environment the internal rivalries between the various profit-centres, between the business segments and between the business area dimension and the regional dimension were such that fundamental structural adjustments were called for. ABB retained its ABACUS system and its small corporate headquarters. However, its main structural features were subject to radical reorganization. In August 1998 the balanced matrix structure in which an operating manager was equally accountable to regional and Business Area managers was scrapped by Barnevik's successor Göran Lindahl. He replaced it with an industrial divisional structure in which

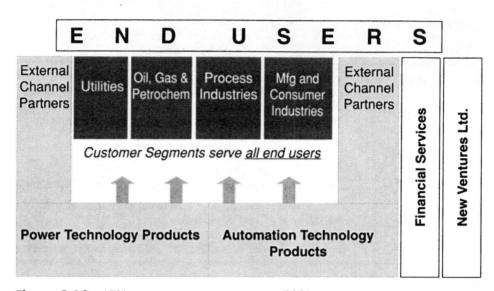

Figure 2.10 ABB's consumer segment structure, 2001–

Business Segment managers and their Business Area managers had the ascendancy and there was no more than a dotted-line relationship to the country manager. In that sense ABB had moved towards a structure similar to that of the global product organization, but without the overt national bias of Sony, Ikea or General Electric. More recently though under its then chief executive, Jörgen Centerman, this corporate structure has been dismantled because there was a perception that customers wanted 'one-stop' shopping. The customer perspective was that ABB was organized in silos along product lines. One key customer had complained that 'If I hear that an organization can do five different things for me, that's great. But not if I have to deal with five different approaches and processes.' ABB replaced its business segments with four customer segments – utilities, oil, gas and petrochemicals, process industries, and manufacturing and consumer industries – that are designed to serve end-users. These segments rest on two product segments that are intended to cover all generic product needs. This consumer segment structure is depicted in figure 2.10.

The Financial Services segment continues to provide services and project support for ABB and for external customers. A new division, New Ventures Ltd., was also created to act as an incubator for new businesses.

By reorganizing itself, ABB wants to be viewed as a flexible supplier, one which is straightforward to do business with. The ambition is to be able to both appear and actually function as an integrated partner providing ABB products and services in a uniform way, instead of as a disparate collection of uncoordinated sales teams. ABB claims that it is the first in its industry fully to organize itself 'around customers rather than technologies'. In effect, ABB has put into place 'global account managers' who are able to serve ABB's largest global customers, such as the Ford motor company, in an integrated way so that these customers deal with one ABB and not a plethora of ABBs. With corporate executive sponsorship the global account managers, using their networks and ABB's databases, select the best solutions available within the geographically distributed business units. Using financial incentives as well as their executive mandate these solutions are combined into customized packages of products and services. Adding complexity to this, however, ABB is also seeking to preserve its ability to be locally responsive because many of its global customers require solutions that are adapted to various locations. This balancing act between global integration and local responsiveness has been a core feature of ABB's mission since its inception. However, of these two, it is global integration that is increasingly in the ascendancy. As one ABB executive remarked, 'Now Zurich is ruling the world [of ABB]'.

In summary, ABB has concluded that a structure with equal stress on two lines of accountability does not work and has opted for a structure that while complex and differentiated, primarily emphasizes global integration. Starting from multi-domestic structures Philips, Nestlé, Shell and Unilever have moved to the global-product division structure. However, to conclude that there is an unambiguous trend towards the global-product division structure would be as misleading as Bartlett and Ghoshal's view that there will be a general movement towards the transnational type of MNC organization. A prototypical global, such as Toyota, is responding more actively to differences in tastes and requirements across its markets. In the USA it has to adapt to a market dominated by light trucks, while also serving the more sedate tastes of its Japanese customers and meeting European aspirations for smaller, sportier cars. But local responsiveness is not just about responding to local taste, it also involves tapping into local managerial and research and development competencies. Coca-Cola, for example, is explicitly attempting to become more locally sensitive by adopting a 'think local, act local' strategy. The essence of this strategy is to promote locally recruited executives to higher posts and to encourage them to develop products tailored to local tastes. In the case of Sony it is planning to break with its tradition of centralized production of high-technology consumer electronics products by shifting production from Japan to Europe.

The reality is that there is no one satisfactory way of organizing a MNC. Moreover, internal structures are becoming increasingly complex and differentiated. As a consequence, 'For most global companies it is a question of choosing the least-bad structure and then figuring out how to mitigate its greatest weaknesses' (Birkinshaw, 2000: 3).

▶ Global Learning and Knowledge Networks

The degree of formal balance that is struck between global integration and local responsiveness is, however, only one aspect to the transnational thesis. There is also the need to develop organizational capabilities that ensure that ideas and information flow across the MNC in order to stimulate cross-national learning. The nature of this flow varies according to the resources located in the subsidiaries. As we have observed in some cases, subsidiaries are centres-of-excellence with global mandates, whereas in others subsidiaries are no more than low-cost, low-skilled, production units or local marketing channels. Involving the latter in a knowledge exchange network is obviously less important than involving the former. In the rest of this chapter we will argue that regardless of the precise balance between global integration and local responsiveness, increasingly MNCs are becoming knowledge network organizations. The knowledge network organization is not an alternative to structures but an informal overlay that makes use of, for example, computer systems and employee transfer policies.

▶ Competence Generation in Foreign Subsidiaries

There is an abundance of evidence suggesting that the competitive advantage of having a portfolio of intellectually proactive sites is increasingly acknowledged. Thus, for example, Asbjørn Birkeland, as managing director of the Norwegian high technology company Nera in the late 1990s, was firmly of the view that 'the old-style colonial mentality' which dictated that product development had to be exclusively concentrated at home had become obsolete. In his view, future global investments will be primarily determined by what they can offer in terms of access to competence and creativity.[2] This is of course by no means an exclusively Norwegian or Scandinavian viewpoint. Toru Takahashi, director of R&D of the Japanese computer printer, copier and camera company Canon, states 'We used to think that we should keep research and development in Japan, but that has changed . . . So now we are looking for a sort of global orchestra, in which say the first and second violin might be in Japan and the cellos in France'.[3] In other words overseas investments will increasingly be knowledge investments as opposed to purely financial investments so that multinationals may be viewed as 'representing alternative international networks of . . . innovative experience' (Cantwell, 1989: 158).

This anecdotal evidence is supported by Cantwell's (1996) analysis of the distribution of R&D on the basis of patents attributable to research in foreign locations (outside the home country of the parent company) for the period 1969–86. Cantwell infers that while R&D has been quite widely dispersed internationally among European MNCs since at least the late 1960s, there has, in more recent years, also been a shift towards the internationalization of US and Japanese MNCs' R&D facilities with technology acquisition as a particularly important motive for the latter.

One should of course avoid positing any simplistic evolutionary logic that states that off-shores and servers will be superseded by enhancers and augmenters. This is not least because firms that contain the latter types of overseas sites will often find it advantageous to include the former. This means that within the

MNC there will be different internal network structures for sharing and combining different kinds of knowledge (Malnight, 2001).

▶ The Network MNC

Increasingly, then, MNCs are seeking to become learning networks in which good ideas are not the monopoly of one site. The conviction is that ideas develop as a product of responding to and interacting with a variety of diverse settings and that great effort should be made in spreading them around. In terms of knowledge there is no pronounced hub or home base. The need to ensure the flow of knowledge means that the challenge is to create considerable integration across sites and even businesses. The question is whether this integration is to be first and foremost created through the implementation of formal structures or through culture. Let us take the example of General Electric (GE), a US conglomerate with ten product groups spanning GE capital, power systems, aircraft engines, plastics and transport. The bulk of its workforce is located outside America and there is a growing layer of non-Americans at management level. The usual objection to a conglomerate, and not least such a geographically dispersed conglomerate, is that managers cannot allocate capital better than the market. However, GE appears to have overcome this by creating a culture of ideas sharing which is given added impetus by tying pay and promotion to 'boundaryless behaviour'. For example, in the late 1990s a new flexible-manufacturing technique invented in New Zealand was transferred to a site in Canada and then to one in America. Equally compelling is the case of GE capital and the inter-business transfer of ideas it now represents. GE capital, under Gary Wendt, used to resist knowledge-sharing pointing to its growth and profits record. However, in 1998, with GE capital no longer the company's fastest-growing group, Wendt left and GE capital became considerably more integrated in terms of ideas sharing with the rest of GE. Within a year GE capital had imported so-called 'wing to wing' techniques from the aircraft engine division to streamline its bureaucracy.

▶ Centres of Excellence in Service MNCs

In the services industry there has traditionally been little interaction between affiliates. Knowledge has been locally generated for local markets with only the corporate logo binding the various affiliates. Alternatively there are service MNCs in which there has been knowledge transfer but it has been centre-driven with foreign affiliates adapting whatever they receive. To overcome the lack of inter-affiliate global learning service, MNCs have attempted to foster informal learning networks by staging seminars, creating international teams and developing knowledge management systems through the application of, for example, Lotus Notes. The drawback with such networks is that they are relationship based. Consultants contact the consultants they happen to know. Moore and Birkinshaw (1998) have observed that most service MNCs have recognized that relying on informal networks is insufficient and that a more formalized approach is needed to ensure knowledge flows throughout the firm. They view the emergence of centres of excellence in service MNCs as the most effective means of obtaining worldwide learning.

Moore and Birkinshaw define centres of excellence as small groups of people who are mandated by top management to make available their leading-edge, strategically valuable knowledge throughout the MNC. They called the most common type of centre of excellence 'focused centres'. These are typically based on a single area of knowledge that has come to be regarded by top management by way of a bottom-up emergent process as representing best practice. They are usually, such as Accenture's multimedia centre of excellence in Windsor, UK, based in a particular physical location. The expectation is that a focused centre's members will travel regularly making their expertise available to other affiliates around the world either as advisors or as members of project teams.

Moore and Birkinshaw's research also indicates though that a significant number of centres of excellence are not fixed in a single geographic location but consist of geographically dispersed individuals who either meet regularly or are connected through their firm's intranet. They termed these 'virtual centres' and observed that they are generally the product of a top-down process by which senior management has come to recognize that certain knowledge areas need to be actively developed within the firm. Unlike focused centres in which the core individuals work together to build a body of tacit knowledge, which they disseminate through interaction with other members of the MNC, virtual centres disseminate codified knowledge by electronic means. The task of the members of the virtual centre is to maintain and renew the system. It is not only the type of knowledge and the means of its dissemination though which differentiate 'focused centres' from 'virtual centres' but also their breadth of impact. Unlike the knowledge developed by 'focused centres', that of the virtual centre can be accessed simultaneously by many, if not all, members of the MNC.

Finally, Moore and Birkinshaw identified a third type of centre of excellence, which they refer to as 'charismatic centres'. These are simply individuals who have achieved the status of authorities in their area of expertise and whose mandate is to transfer this to other professional employees in a master–apprentice style role. These company stars typically travel a great deal acting as expert advisors on projects without getting involved in any of the details. In some cases they may even be outsiders such as academics who are brought in to enable the company to build a capability that has been missing.

Centres of excellence in service MNCs are not permanent. They emerge in response to a strategically defined need and in some cases die a 'natural death' and disappear of their own accord as that need fades away. More generally, though, they need to be closed down by senior management. In many cases the life-cycle of a centre of excellence is no more than five years. In that space of time new areas of knowledge have been identified as needing to developed or disseminated, giving rise to new centres of excellence. For senior managers of service MNCs their role in overseeing the evolution of centres of excellence has become increasingly critical. It involves not only an awareness of client needs, but also an overview of latent sources of expertise in the firm wherever they might be located.

▶ Summary

Developing structures that reflect the need to find a strategically appropriate balance between local responsiveness and global integration is a task that calls for continuous adjustments and fine-tuning. There is no end-state and within one and the same MNC there may be a mix of centralized and decentralized operations making for structural diversity. Regardless of structure there has to be an overlay of relatively informal systems that ensures the flow and combination of knowledge between constituent parts of the MNC. Developing these systems has evolved into an organizational challenge of major significance. An MNC needs to know what it knows, learn what it needs to learn and apply that knowledge as quickly as possible for sustainable competitive advantage. The network MNC is the ideal but it is a mental construct rather than an objective structure. Obviously a variety of paths have to be constructed in order that knowledge may flow, but the degree to which these paths are actually used is dependent on the application of various incentives, the sensitive use of authority and the development of a sense of community across the MNC. Neil Aston, Head of BP's Information Technology Architecture and Strategy, has concluded that: 'Technology is an important enabler, but knowledge management is as much about leadership, culture and behaviour.' It is also about experience – employees must be encouraged to take the time to learn about the available paths for the networks to materialize.

Case B is about ABB's attempts to achieve a balance between local responsiveness and global integration through the implementation of a global matrix structure and its reorganization in 1998. Although the case is primarily concerned with ABB's structural features, it also touches on the need to supplement structure with non-structural elements that facilitate open communication.

Notes

1 Source: *Business Week*, 11 June 2001.
2 Source: Garvik (1997).
3 Source: Dawkins (1996).

ABB: Beyond the Global Matrix: Towards the Network Multidivisional Organization

Winfried Ruigrok, Leona Achtenhagen, Mathias Wagner and Johannes Rüegg-Stürm

▶ Introduction

If there is one European company that over the past ten years has managed to excite management consultants, scholars and business people alike, then it is ABB (ASEA Brown Boveri), the Swiss-Swedish professional engineering group. Repeatedly voted as Europe's most respected company, ABB has become a text-book case of many successes achieved over a short period of time: merging Swedish ASEA and Swiss Brown Boveri into one joint entity, reducing the head office role, implementing a global management development policy, and developing a highly effective international organization (cf. Barham and Heimer, 1998: 175ff.).[1] Bartlett and Ghoshal (1993) combined these elements and used ABB as their most prominent case to claim the rise of an organizational form beyond the multidivisional organization. A few years later, Bartlett and Ghoshal analysed ABB's global matrix structure (in place until 1998) as the appropriate form for companies to deal with the 'global–local dilemma' (1995: 470).

The matrix organization had provided a highly successful model of internationalization for many companies over the 1960s and 1970s, and usually represented a geographical, i.e. international, extension of the multidivisional organization. The main advantages associated with the matrix organization are its parallel reporting systems to geographical and product (and possibly functional) managers, allowing for a coordination of diverging internal company interests; its multiple information channels, enhancing the level of intra-company communication; and its overlapping responsibilities, creating a platform within the company for discussion and decision-making. The matrix provided multinational firms with a model to deal with uncertain and diverging environments, especially in locally responsive industries.

Companies have applied matrix structures successfully in various kinds of activities, such as the development of new products and services (cf. Larson and Gobeli, 1987; McCollum and Sherman, 1993). However, as a model of international organizing, the matrix lost much of its appeal over the 1980s as integrating markets, converging standards and consumer tastes, increasing competition and the shortening of product life cycles forced companies to develop new solutions to manage their products across national borders. Peters and Waterman (1982: 49) even saw the matrix structure as the summit of complicated and ultimately unworkable organizational structures.

ABB's choice for a global matrix structure to manage the newly merged company was therefore far from self-evident. Yet in a widely read article in the *Harvard Business Review*, Bartlett and Ghoshal (1990) suggested that the main problem with 'matrix management' is not so much the need for companies to take into account different product and geographical dimensions, but the fact that 'organizational development has not kept pace [with strategic thinking], and managerial attitudes lag even further behind.' The challenge, they argued, was not to focus on creating the ideal structures, but rather on 'developing the abilities, behavior, and performance of individual managers' (1990: 145). Rugman and Hodgetts (1995: 250) derived three key criteria for a matrix to work well: (1) clarity (how well do people understand what they are doing and why they are doing it); (2) continuity (of the same core objectives and values); and (3) consistency (of managers throughout the organization pursuing the same objectives). ABB, it has been implied by many authors, got this balance right and moved beyond the multidivisional organization (Bartlett and Ghoshal, 1993: 24ff.) to develop a 'dancing giant' (Kets de Vries, 1994; Barham and Heimer, 1998).

So all the more puzzling was the fact that ABB in August 1998 announced that it would reorganize into what would appear to resemble a multidivisional organization. Dissolving its regional management layer, ABB established seven business segments which in turn included a total of 33 business areas. Is this the end of ABB's acclaimed matrix structure, and has ABB become just like any other multidivisional organization? This chapter analyses the overall organizational transformations during the ten years after the ABB merger as well as its 1998 reorganization by asking the following questions: first, has ABB really departed from its global matrix structure, and if so, why?, and, second, has ABB really reorganized towards a conventional multidivisional organization?

In the summer of 1998, we conducted 25 interviews at different levels of the ABB Group. Seven interviews took place at the international head office and at the Financial Services department of the ABB Group, and 18 interviews were carried out at ABB Switzerland (ABB-CH) with managers of the country holding and managing directors of the various front-line companies of ABB Switzerland. ABB-CH is one of ABB's larger country holdings with a very international outlook. The interviews took place just before the August 1998 announcement of ABB's new organizational structure and were aimed at understanding the functioning and weaknesses of the ABB matrix organization. After August 1998, additional communication has taken place with ABB-CH on the interpretations that we have drawn.

This chapter is organized as follows. First, we trace the history of the ABB group and the organizational structure that evolved over the ten years after the merger. Then the external and internal drivers for ABB's organizational change are discussed, and the three stages of ABB's organizational development over the 1988–98 period are presented. Next. the process sequencing of these changes is shown, and the barriers to change at ABB are identified. We then compare the official reasons for ABB's 1998 reorganization with the impressions that we gathered when carrying out our interviews. We identify some management issues yet to be resolved. Finally, we summarize our findings and reflect upon the question as to whether ABB's reorganization indicates a move back to the traditional multidivisional organization.

▶ History, Context, and Organizational Structure of ABB

The history of generating and using electricity started in 1866, when Werner von Siemens invented the principle of the self-exciting generator (dynamo). In 1879, Edison developed the incandescent lamp as a next landmark. Around that time, Charles Brown, who was working at Oerlikon Machinery Corporation (Switzerland), and his colleague Walter Boveri started to think about establishing an electrical equipment factory, following the examples set by General Electric (US), AEG and Siemens (Germany) and a company called ASEA (Sweden).

Brown and Boveri founded their own factory called Brown, Boveri & Cie (BBC) in February 1892 with 100 factory workers and 24 office workers (Steigmeier, 1991: 4). From the very beginning, BBC had a strong export orientation and it gained a foothold in most leading European industrial countries before World War I. After 1945, new business areas, such as electronics and nuclear power, were opened up. In 1987, BBC listed 159 group companies on all five continents and employed about 100,000 people around the world (Catrina, 1991). At that time, BBC also showed low performance rates as a result of high costs, low levels of innovation and a weakness in developing new markets.

Swedish ASEA had been in a similar position in the early 1980s. Percy Barnevik had taken it upon him to reorganize ASEA into 350 profit centres and to decentralize responsibilities. The profit centre managers were allowed to act highly autonomously, as long as they produced profits. Barnevik's attempts had been very successful and ASEA had subsequently begun to expand to the USA.

When ASEA and BBC entered their talks in 1987, both parties recognized the potential mutual benefits. ASEA contributed superior current profit performance, sophisticated management controls and marketing aggressiveness, while BBC brought a strong order book and high technical expertise. ASEA operated in geographic areas and in product spheres that on the whole complemented rather than competed with those of BBC, even though there were some areas, such as Power Transmission, were there was a significant overlap (Catrina, 1991).

On 1 January 1988, both companies transferred their activities to the newly founded ABB ASEA Brown Boveri Ltd. ABB became the world's largest producer of engineering products and services and became a leading supplier of process automation systems, robotics, high-speed locomotives, and environmental and pollution control equipment. The ASEA Holding (former ASEA) and the BBC Holding (former BBC) each possessed 50 per cent of the ABB ASEA Brown Boveri Ltd. (ABB Group) shares. The two parent companies remained independent corporations and maintain their national identities as Swiss and Swedish companies.

ABB now faced the challenge of building one collectivity out of two companies from different countries that had long regarded each other as rivals. Spurred by the expectation that restructuring and post-merger integration efforts would initially hamper performance, Barnevik continued the pattern of reorganizations carried out at ASEA and set out the principles of decentralization of responsibilities and individual accountability.

> The only way to structure a complex, global organization is to make it as simple and local as possible . . . Our managers need well-defined sets of responsibilities, clear accountability, and maximum degree of freedom to execute . . . Our operations are divided into nearly 1,100 companies with an average of 200 people. These companies are divided into 3,500 profit centres with an average of 50 employees . . . We are fervent believers in decentralization. When we structure local operations, we always push to create separate legal entities. Separate companies allow you to create real balance sheets with real responsibility for cash flow and dividends. (Percy Barnevik, in Taylor, 1991: 99)

It took ABB only two months to develop the main features of the new organization (figure B1). Since both ASEA and BBC had had a matrix organization prior to their merger, the matrix structure was a logical choice for the new company as well. The matrix structure enabled ABB to 'think global, act local' – which was more than just a slogan to ABB. Dealing with large public and private customers, ABB had to negotiate at a local level, strike compromises on issues such as local content, while being able to draw components and services from a large and efficient global organization in the background. The ABB matrix was refined in

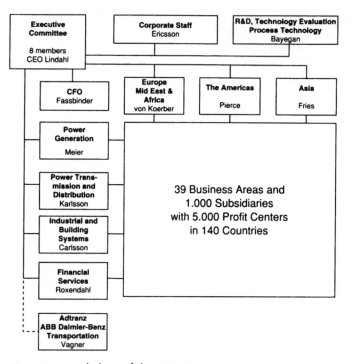

Figure B1 Organizational chart of the ABB Group
Source: ABB Group annual report 1997

1993 and again slightly in 1996, before the new structure was announced in 1998.

ABB Switzerland (ABB CH), where most interviews were conducted, is one of the 140 national holding organizations of the ABB Group. The former BBC head office location was transformed into today's ABB CH and in the overall ABB Group, ABB CH plays an important role. ABB CH is one of the largest national ABB organizations and is well known for its advanced research and development and its highly skilled workforce. ABB CH is highly interconnected with ABB companies around the world, as indicated by its high degree of exports (80 per cent). It owns companies in all business segments as well as in financial services. With its line of products and services, ABB CH covers the entire power distribution spectrum from the generating plant to the wall socket. It also provides products and systems for applications in industry and transportation. At the end of 1997, ABB CH had 25 companies and employed about 12,000 people (ABB Switzerland annual report, 1997).

ABB's major competitors are three other global players: Siemens, Mitsubishi, and General Electric (see table B1). General Electric has been another highly admired company, led by another admired CEO (Jack Welch), which for many years has clearly outperformed ABB and which is expecting a continued profitable

Table B1 ABB compared with its main competitors, 1997

Competitors	ABB	Siemens	GE	Mitsubishi Group
HQ	Zürich-Oerlikon/CH	Munich/Germany	Fairfield/USA	Tokyo, Japan
Number of employees	Group: 215,000	Group: 386,000	Group: 276,000	Group: 322,000
Consolidated revenues	Group: 31,300 mill. $; power related business: about 29,500 mill. US$	Group: 64,750 mill. $; power related business: About 20,500 mill. $	Group: 90,800 mill. $; power related business: about 23,300 mill. $	Group: 166,300 mill. $; power related business: about 28,000 mill. US$
Strategy	Focus on large key plant projects; efforts towards a solution provider; back-end vertical integration strategy; expansion strategy	Innovation strategy at high-end megawatt plants; Product services strategy; International presence by acquisitions	Efforts in globalization (esp. in Asia) by acquisitions; product services strategy; TQM strategy (Six Sigma Quality program); streamlining; portfolio of innovative services and products; strategy aims to be the No 1, 2 or 3 in each business area	Expansion strategy by acquisitions; marketing strategy that focuses on strengthening customer relationships and immediate response to the market; streamlining its investments into areas that have the highest revenue generating potential over the long term.
Area of competition	Plant, components	Plant, components	Plant, components	Plant, components
In-house trends	Towards 'network multidivisional'; focus on product services	Restructuring (10-point program to enhance profitability), cost problems, focus on (financial) services; efforts towards an integrative problem solver (general contractor)	Six Sigma Quality Initiative, leadership program; pushing service activities	Efforts toward an integrative product line; trend towards a solution provider; create new businesses (e.g. product services); further investments in Asia and emerging markets
Organizational structure	Global matrix structure	M-form	(Financial) holding structure	Holding structure
Relative competitiveness	Medium; since 1996 declining revenues, profits and productivity; goal is to regain dominant position in this industry as in the beginning of the 1990s	Low; lagging performance; profit declined to 150 mill. US$ in 1997; strong turnaround efforts	High; steadily increasing revenues and profits; six sigma quality projects achieved 94 mill. US$ in savings	Medium/High; revenues and profit have increased between 1996–1998

Source: Siemens Internet pages 1998; Siemens annual report 1997; General Electric annual report 1997; Mitsubishi Group, 1998; Merrill Lynch report, 1998.

growth over the coming years. Recently, Siemens has started a ten-point pro-gramme in order to achieve a turnaround in its power division. Mitsubishi Group, finally, also has invested a lot in its power related business activities. In addition, Hitachi and Toshiba – previous system providers – offer specialized components and single technologies or services. If one takes into account ABB's emerging activities in financial services (see below), investment banks can also be viewed as competitors. Finally, ABB's activities in the field of services and main-tenance have produced a new type of competition (e.g. privatized plant operating companies).

▶ Drivers for Change at ABB

The basis of both ASEA's restructuring over the early 1980s and BBC's will-ingness to merge with its former arch-rival was a company crisis, leading to slowing growth and performance rates. Performance measurement remained an important tool at ABB and has been guiding change ever since, exposing problems at the business segment and country level. At the same time, as will be shown below, this emphasis on internal accounting at times led to sub-optimal solutions.

Throughout the 1990s, there was a world-wide trend towards deregulation and privatization in power supply markets, with formerly government-controlled utility companies developing into commercially thinking market partners. These 'new' customers now demanded complete turnkey plants with a full range of services, including financial services, operation, and maintenance. This raised the level of complexity of the business, making it more important for suppliers to manage in-house and external deliveries effectively, and posed a huge challenge for each firm to manage its internal knowledge effectively. It also implied that local differentiation (and local bargaining) became less important than a supplier's ability to offer a reliable solution at a reasonable price.

As a consequence, the international power generation and transmission industry has gone through a dramatic consolidation process. In 1990, firms such as Hitachi, Westinghouse, AEG, and Toshiba were still playing a role as independent end producers. Since then, excess capacity has forced Hitachi and Toshiba to leave the business and focus on specialized components; ABB took over Westinghouse's power transmission and distribution divisions in 1990; and in 1996, the rest of the Westinghouse corporation merged with Siemens.

In addition to these external factors, there were a number of internal drivers for change at ABB, often resulting from the inherent weaknesses of the ABB matrix. Despite a range of instruments to enhance internal transparency, for instance, and despite the numerous efforts to explain the ABB structure, many employees (as well as numerous external partners) still felt that they did not understand the matrix. Moreover, the internal negotiations between the small profit centres were occasionally difficult and frequently led to micropolitics.

▶ Content, Scope, and Depth of Organizational Innovations

This section discusses the organizational innovations at ABB over the past ten years in terms of the structural, process and cultural changes. They are analyzed according to their initiation time by giving information about content, scope, and depth of change. The main features are summarized in table B2.

Building the global matrix (1988–93)

Just as he had done at ASEA, Barnevik began decentralizing the operations of most ABB subsidiaries into independent profit centres. The profit centre concept was to enhance internal financial transparency and customer orientation. A key element of the ABB matrix was to make the BA managers and country managers understand their complementary and different roles. The BA managers were to set the strategic framework, coordinate R&D and production, and monitor quality standards and performance. The country managers were to actively supervise the operating business, to foster local contacts and to carry responsibilities for HR activities. Of these two dimensions, the balance was slightly in favour of the country managers, signified by the fact that the country managers of the most important ABB national organizations such as Sweden, Germany, the USA and Switzerland, all had a seat on the executive board.

The first few years after the merger, ABB focused on integrating the world-wide operations, restructuring BAs, outsourcing activities, acquiring companies and selling off other companies or parts of them. In the first five years after the merger, ABB was involved in more than one hundred mergers and acquisitions transactions as well as joint ventures. Various cost-cutting programmes aimed at avoiding duplicate tasks and resources, and reducing administration costs. As had been done with ASEA before, the ABB head office was trimmed down to initially just over one hundred staff. Instead of having centralized corporate laboratories for R&D, ABB created a network of eight R&D centres of excellence, which were closely linked to front-line companies. Finally, a very important ingredient in managing the world-wide activities, ABB developed a simple but very effective and transparent internal financial controlling system, called ABACUS. Its structure followed the matrix idea, by allowing one to analyse financial data in a business-oriented and in a country/regional-oriented way at the same time.

In the early 1990s, ABB CH and various other country organizations were facing one similar problem: the quality of their products, services, and customer orientation was too low, and costs were too high. ABB therefore launched its 'Customer Orientation Programme', initiated at the Group level, but managed by country organizations such as ABB CH. The programme aimed at enhancing

Table B2 History of ABB, 1988–98

Evolution of ABB	Before 1988 Pre-Merger phase		1988–93	1993–97	1998–
	ASEA	BBC			
PHASE DESCRIPTION GENERAL CONDITIONS	• good economic conditions • growing market	• good economic conditions • growing market	Development of global matrix • consolidation in industry • tough competition • chances in emerging markets	Global matrix with regional dimensions • deregulation and privatization of utilities • tough competition	'Network Multidivisional' • market saturation; declining economic conditions
PERFORMANCE/ INCOME* SALES	• superior performance • sales increasing	• weak performance, but strong position in Europe • sales decreasing	• performance affected by post merger integration (income: 1,150 mill. US$) • sales increased up to 28,750 mill. US$	• highest income in 1995 (2,100 mill. US$). Income decreased over time (in 1997: 850 mill. US$) • sales increased up to 31,260 mill. US$	• in 1998 performance still declining • sales decreasing (in 1998)
IN-HOUSE TRENDS	• reorganized by Barnevik early 1980s • rather marketing oriented	• technology oriented • huge units • bureaucracy	• merger was viewed as an opportunity for implementing fundamental change and growth • merger integrating efforts	• growing awareness of insufficient customer and sales orientation • service business identified • region/country oriented	• restructuring efforts towards product/ segment orientation

STRATEGIC CONCEPTS	• internationalization efforts (e.g. US market); • strategic marketing concepts	• technology-oriented strategy • product innovation strategy	• streamlining of corporate activities • enhancing regional presence by acquisitions • reengineering of business processes	• continuing smaller acquisitions • outsourcing • implementation of regions • customer focus concept • focus on Eastern markets	• financial services strategy • solution provider strategy • attempts to achieve critical mass in each business field
CORPORATE STRUCTURE	• global matrix structure • profit center structure (350)	• matrix structure, 6 segments and 8 regions/countries	• matrix organization, 6 business segments • profit center organization • 12 member executive committee	• global matrix organization, 4 business segments • lead country concept • 8 member executive committee	• regional dimension eliminated, business segments dominant line of authority • eight member exec. committee (7 business segments plus CEO)
EMERGENCE OF NETWORK ELEMENTS	• small legal entities • strong decentralization	• focus on technological expertise • first initiatives to horizontal networking among segments	• small legal entities • strong decentralization • international network	• small legal entities • building of cross boundary networks • stronger focus on people and culture	• networking among segments • horizontal communication
HR-MANAGEMENT	• focus on people	• focus on people • high skilled engineers	• decentralization of HR-responsibilities	• strong investments in HR • international personnel transfers	• growing awareness of need to enhance ABB-wide cohesion

Source: ABB Group Internet pages, 1998; BBC annual report, 1987, interviews; * income before taxes.

customer satisfaction, connecting customer needs and innovation processes, and reducing service costs. Around the same time, some other smaller changes took place, such as a reduction of employees due to a European recession, and the establishment of a segment 'environmental systems'. Finally, in 1992 ABB introduced its 'centres of excellence' concept, in which one company per BA was allocated world-wide leadership. ABB was one of the first to introduce such a lead country concept, which aimed at reducing costs by avoiding resource duplications in the ABB national companies, thus simplifying the matrix and providing clear responsibilities. On the downside, however, this approach also gave room to micropolitics and country rivalry.

Redefining the matrix: adding the regional dimension (1993–98)

In 1993, after the establishment of the European Union and the North American Free Trade Agreement, ABB adjusted its organization by adding a regional dimension and by making the regional managers full executive committee members. This reorganization created three regions and five business segments (power distribution and transmission were integrated). In this set-up, ABB attempted to benefit from the fact that country borders became more permeable, allowing for lateral linkages within regional areas. This reorganization did not just reduce the importance of the individual country holdings, but in retrospect also enabled the business segments to attain a more dominant position in the organization.

Thus the ABB matrix from 1993–96 combined five business segments and three regions (which also captured the country dimension). The business segments were split up into 39 Business Areas (BAs), each of them representing a distinct world-wide product market. A BA manager reported (1) to the executive committee member responsible for the business segment's overall strategy and performance; and (2) to the executive committee member responsible for the specific region, who supported and coordinated the operating companies within a world region. This global matrix structure has been ABB's organizational framework for some ten years (cf. table B2).

After redesigning the matrix, ABB undertook another important effort to raise customer orientation. Its Customer Focus programme aimed at improving process orientation, customer relations, and quality management at the same time (Zoller, 1998). Customer Focus became an ongoing programme pursuing continuous analysis and improvement of internal processes on the one hand, and a continuous (re)orientation to the customer on the other. Though initiated by the ABB group, all ABB companies were required to have a Customer Focus manager put in charge of its implementation.

In 1996, the number of business segments was reduced from five to four. By this time, ABB had begun to recognize the scope for further lateral linkages among its segments to improve the project management for turnkey power plants and to increase economies of scale and scope. At ABB CH, various Cross-Company Teams (CCT) were set up to explore such networking linkages. The CCT team members are the managing directors of the various ABB CH front-line companies. This team composition, and the explicit support by the ABB CH top management, indicate the importance ABB CH attaches to these teams. By 1998, eight CCTs at ABB CH were exploring the networking potential in areas such as Marketing, Organization Development, Human Resources, Finance & Controlling, etc., and were evaluating individually or jointly developed concepts or methods. Another example of ABB's attempts to cross business segments is the open spaces concept. In this concept, employees in the same country but from different management levels and segments get together once a month to discuss current organizational issues. Other important tools to enhance networking across segments include joint data base management, international personnel transfers, and numerous kinds of meetings. These efforts, however, are limited to the country level.

Finally, ABB identified that its global matrix structure also required a set of essentially non-structural features, i.e. a corporate culture based on open communication and empowerment. Over 1998, various teams throughout ABB were re-evaluating the overall company mission, its values and the existing policies booklet (Lindahl, 1999: 8).

The emerging problems with matrix management at ABB

Although the 1993 reorganization was intended to simplify the organization, several interview partners indicated that many employees actually had difficulty understanding the overall structure. Frequent problems arose in the fields of business segmentation, in the working of the internal market mechanism, and in the internal decision-making processes.

First, having only four business segments, there was a great heterogeneity within business segments in terms of front-line companies' size, customers, technologies, and business logic. In 1998, ABB recognized that it had somewhat lost the balance between global efficiency and local responsiveness. An internal analysis showed that the horizontal differentiation of the four business segments was highly ineffective. A segment such as 'Industrial and Building Systems' had deteriorated into an 'all-purpose division' whose products were in different phases of the life-cycles, serving entirely different customer segments, therefore offering very little scope for meaningful central coordination. At the basis of this is one of ABB's long-time dilemmas, i.e. of seeking both differentiation and integration. ABB is a company with numerous local, regional and global businesses alongside each other (Barham and Heimer, 1998: 64). The diversity of its products, technologies and markets has made perfect segmentation of businesses very difficult. As it was, the segment managers had difficulties in boosting special growth areas and pushed the restructuring towards a more optimal business segmentation. The country managers did not see the problem in quite the same terms, since their role was to ensure the company's market orientation and customer relations rather than world-wide efficiency in managing segments.

A second problem area emerged in the field of ABB's internal market mechanism – an area in which ABB had also pioneered new organizational solutions. In order to coordinate the vertical and horizontal resource flows among the various profit centres, ABB developed a market-oriented transfer pricing system. ABB's transfer pricing system – undoubtedly one of the most advanced in the world – required a lot of time and energy. Within a single business segment this did not raise any real problems, because at the end of the day the profit centres all contributed to the overall performance of their segment. However, especially the cross-segment margin calculation led to frequent conflicts, because each business segment sought to maximize its own profits. As a result, profit centres from different business segments competed with others in terms of resource allocation and investment decisions, leading to situations in which single profit centre objectives could easily override the overall Group objectives.

With its matrix structure and profit centre philosophy, ABB had deliberately created an organizational paradox: competition and cooperation at the same time. The core dilemma was simple: how to create a spirit of internal competition in order to be competitive, while at the same time provide a cooperative internal environment to exploit the scale and scope advantages offered by the multinational organization? Several interviewees indicated that internal fights and competition at times were more important than fighting external competitors. Thus, the strong autonomy of the small front-line companies, on the one hand, strengthened entrepreneurship and customer orientation, and, on the other, obstructed inter-segment cooperation and corporate strategizing. This even led to a point where some front-line companies understood their role as owner of the business rather than as business opportunity provider for the ABB Group. 'Everybody is seeking to increase his margin. It's not the overall success in the market that counts, but the performance of one's own profit centre. Therefore it's difficult to offer competitive prices to the final customer in the market' (Top manager, ABB Switzerland, summer 1998).

A third fundamental problem was that individual managers found it increasingly difficult to live up to the expectations to the matrix. Particularly in Europe, the dynamism of the first years had waned, the number of staff members had increased and formerly flexible structures had become more rusty. As a result, several managers left the company (often to go to competitors), frustrated with years of pressure from above. Moreover, the regional dimensions in the company had effectively created regional principalities leading to long and complex decision-making processes and contributing to an increasingly political climate within the matrix. Many at ABB felt that the power of these regional barons had become disproportionately large in relation to the reducing importance of the regional dimension, given the changes in the market (see also Bantel and Schär, 1998: 6).

'One of the drawbacks of the matrix structure is that its problems are always a mix of region and segment problems. The company is highly political' (Assistant vice president, summer 1998).

In conclusion, while the matrix organization and the profit centre structure at ABB had long provided a useful organizational framework, ABB increasingly was facing some of the very disadvantages of the matrix organization that Bartlett and Ghoshal had mentioned in their 1990 article: 'conflict and confusion; . . . international logjams . . . ; and overlapping responsibilities produced turf battles and a loss of accountability' (1990: 139).

Beyond the global matrix: the 'network multidivisional organization' (1998–)

As a result of the problems above, ABB in 1998 announced to dissolve its regional layer and eliminate the positions of the business region managers and their staff. About one hundred managers world-wide lost their jobs due to these changes. The country organizations will remain, continuing to represent ABB's 'multi-domestic' presence in markets around the world. However, the business segments have become the dominant dimension within the company. By focusing on segments instead of regions, Göran Lindahl, the new CEO after Percy Barnevik left in 1997, seeks to strengthen ABB's product orientation in particular.

Various press reports have suggested that there was a fierce internal struggle at ABB preceding the reorganization (Bantel and Schär, 1998: 6). In view of the changes that have taken place, such an internal struggle seems quite likely: Eberhard von Koerber, former head of Europe/Africa, saw his position eliminated and subsequently left ABB, and Sune Carlsson saw his industrial and building systems ('all-purpose division') business segment being split up in three business segments (automation; oil, gas and petrochemicals; and products and contracting).

Figure B2 shows the new organization of ABB as of 1998. The first change is that ABB now has seven business segments as the dominant structure. Each executive committee member carries the responsibility for one segment, with the CEO having the overall responsibility. This product-oriented organization aims at promoting growth in areas where ABB has technology advantages and unique capabilities, and to cut myopic internal competition. The newly added financial services business segment is to help ABB provide complete solutions, including financing packages, to newly privatized customers and those in emerging markets. The second change is the removal of the regional layer. As a result, country organizations now report directly to Zurich. Put together, ABB expects to achieve shorter decision-making processes and greater responsiveness to deregulation and privatization.

However, ABB has made a point of communicating continuity in the organization. The Group's head office is to remain small and focused on truly strategic activities. The business segment and business area managers maintain responsibility

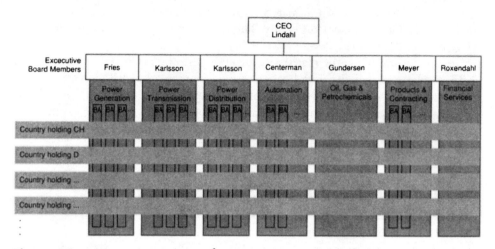

Figure B2 ABB's organization as of 1998
Source: ABB, 1998

for world-wide product strategies ranging from world-wide R&D or investments, world-wide market allocation and sourcing, and for world-wide business results. The country holdings will maintain the relationships with local stakeholders such as customers, governments, labour unions and media, and will remain responsible for local operations, marketing and human resource management within their country. Front-line managers will continue to have direct customer contact and will be responsible for running the daily business. Indeed, the worldwide architecture of small front-line companies, the centres of excellence concept, the internal labour market, the importance of entrepreneurship, the search for cross-segment networking (at the level of country organizations), and the ABACUS information system will remain core elements of ABB's organization. 'The end of the matrix seems to take place as fast as it was introduced in 1988, although the new structure is only about an improvement (instead of an elimination) of the matrix' (Göran Lindahl in *Bilanz*, September 1998: 58).

Thus, the 1998 ABB reorganization does not represent a full departure from the global matrix. Rather, it is an attempt to transform the matrix from a geographical to a product bias, while maintaining the full range of existing internal networking mechanisms. In our view, ABB has not returned to the classical Chandlerian multidivisional organization (Chandler, 1980). Rather, it seems to be transforming to what Richard Whittington and Michael Mayer (1997: 253ff.) have termed the network multidivisional: In their view, the network multidivisional is a flatter version with the emphasis on the lateral rather than the vertical, knowledge rather than scale and scope, and human resources and self-organizing rather than corporate planning and bureaucracy.

ABB has maintained three core features of the multidivisional organization, yet has transformed each of them. First, the overall ABB organization is based on strict managerial hierarchies, and it may be argued that the corporate centre has become more powerful after the 1998 reorganization (*Wirtschaftswoche*, 13 August 1998). However, ABB has supplemented these hierarchies by systematically decentralizing operating and country-specific responsibilities, and by encouraging entrepreneurial behavior. Second, ABB now has a divisional structure, yet at the country level, ABB is deliberately cutting through divisional boundaries by combining operations in country holdings, by having senior management CCTs exploring scale and scope opportunities, and by creating a financial services segment which depends on cooperation with other segments. Third, ABB has an internal capital market in place and closely monitors front-line companies' and business segments' performance, yet it has added an internal labor market as another key resource:

> Our internal labor market really works like a market. Employees can be contracted by other ABB companies once they have been in their jobs for more than eighteen months. The only rule is that the direct superior has to be informed. Jobs are announced in the internal job market on the intranet. Previously, it was considered a bad habit to hunt people internally. The result was that many people left ABB, as they were recruited by external head hunters. This created a change of mentality. (Head of HRM, ABB-CH)

▶ Process Sequencing

In terms of sequencing, ABB used two types of change actions: the first was characterized by a short time frame, top-down initiated and closely managed, but rarely with a cultural impact; the second was characterized by a longer time frame, with various loci of action, managed more loosely with the aim to change modes of behavior. Kanter, Stein and Jick (1992: 492) referred to these two types of change actions as 'bold strokes' and 'long marches'. Bold strokes are strategic decisions, such as M&A or designing the organizational framework, whereas long marches are more operational initiatives, such as transforming quality or customer relationships.

Thus, the past ten years at ABB may be interpreted as a pattern of continuity and change. Figure B3 summarizes the various change programmes at ABB over the 1988–98 period. The combination of this continuity and change can be seen in the fact that many programmes were carried out in parallel, that many programmes stretched beyond individual reorganizations, and that the number of change programmes has increased over time. The 1998 strengthening of the product dimension, moreover, is in line with the fact that from the beginning 'Barnevik [had been] more interested in the products and businesses' than in the country dimension (Barham and Heimer, 1998: 74).

At ABB, there is an explicit view on the sequencing and transition of an organizational form, described by Lindahl (Solenthaler, 1998) and restated by

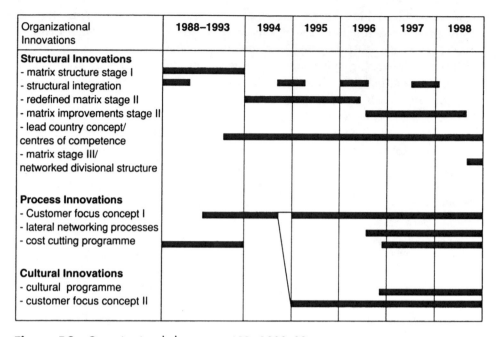

Organizational Innovations	1988–1993	1994	1995	1996	1997	1998

Structural Innovations
- matrix structure stage I
- structural integration
- redefined matrix stage II
- matrix improvements stage II
- lead country concept/ centres of competence
- matrix stage III/ networked divisional structure

Process Innovations
- Customer focus concept I
- lateral networking processes
- cost cutting programme

Cultural Innovations
- cultural programme
- customer focus concept II

Figure B3 Organizational changes at ABB, 1988–98
Source: ABB interviews

one of our interview partners. Given the environmental conditions, organizations develop a form that may enable them to improve performance for a number of years. However, in the view of ABB, organizational life cycles are limited: after some five years, the performance gains of a previously appropriate form have been exploited to the full, and performance begins to decline. At that moment ABB will have to adjust its form to the newly changed environmental conditions. An organizational form can thus be seen as a temporary optimal growth trajectory. Even if the performance benefits of such a new form will not be immediately visible, they will emerge in due course (see figure B4).

▶ Barriers to Change at ABB in the 1990s

To every corporation, change is a real challenge and often creates resistance (Hambrick, Nadler and Tushman, 1998). Frequently, organizational change fails because of implementation problems and internal institutionalization rather than because of inherent conceptual problems of the innovation itself (cf. Kanter, 1983: 301). Even if change at ABB may be interpreted as a combination of continuity and change, there have been some real internal barriers that have affected both the functioning of the matrix and ABB's 1998 reorganization. In

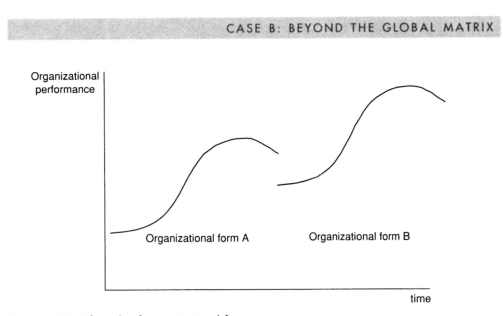

Figure B4 Life cycle of organizational forms
Source: ABB interviewee

the introduction, we referred to Rugman and Hodgetts' three criteria for a matrix to work well (1995: 250). Here we may briefly evaluate these criteria:

- *Clarity* refers to how well do people understand what they are doing and why they are doing it. Based on the views expressed by several interviewees, we have to conclude that ABB had failed to achieve sufficient organizational clarity for the 'matrix in the mind' to develop. Despite Barnevik's energetic attempt to communicate the nature and rationale of ABB's corporate structures and values, too many employees only saw financial clarity, based on the ABACUS system of monitoring profit centres' performance, not organizational clarity.
- *Continuity* refers to the extent to which the company has stuck to the same core objectives (including products) and values. This criterion has been fulfilled partly. ABB has not shifted its product range dramatically, apart from adding a new business segment 'financial services'. The company has also remained committed to its expansion into emerging markets in Central and Eastern Europe and in Asia, even when economic recessions hit these regions. However, in retrospect, adding three regional layers in 1993 (which Barnevik had seen as 'regrettable' but inevitable, see Barham and Heimer, 1998: 286) effectively inserted a seed of disintegration into the organization between the head office and the country organization. The three regional barons and the three segment chiefs had different views of the need to focus on the business dimension, and an equal weight in the executive committee.

- *Consistency* refers to the extent to which managers throughout the organization have been pursuing the same objectives. Perhaps the biggest weakness of the ABB matrix during later years was the internal rivalry and the micropolitics between the various profit centres, among the business segments and between the product and the regional dimension. For instance, the heterogeneity of front-line companies in terms of firm structures, competitive environments and business logic (e.g. semiconductors vs. plant projects) implied that concepts developed by ABB CH did not necessarily fit with each front-line company. Likewise, some interviewees argued that reporting standards had been set along the needs of the machine industry which did not fit their own business equally well Inevitably, the front-line companies' independence often hampered the implementation of such concepts.

An underlying barrier to the development of the matrix may have been that ABB's corporate culture has been based rather one-sidedly on achieving customer focus. Bartlett and Ghoshal (1993: 26) suggested that the *Mission, Values, Policies* booklet provided a strong shared vision and corporate culture. However, we found that by 1998 its influence was rather limited. Various interviewees in fact criticized the lack of a corporate culture functioning as a 'glue' in the overall company, and indicated that it would be difficult to create a strong unifying culture for the whole ABB Group as this would contradict the principle of decentralization and unwavering customer focus.

The 1998 ABB Reorganization: Beyond the Authorized Motives

ABB has presented its 1998 reorganization as a logical and relatively minor organizational transformation, with the prime objective of improving customer focus by separating businesses with local and more global customers and with different product life-cycles. The company has put great effort into communicating continuity rather than change. And for good reasons: despite some occasional incidents in Asia, ABB has long enjoyed a favourable press, which is reflected in the ABB brand reputation, its market capitalization and its ability to recruit talented engineers and managers. 'ABB is very successful in creating an external image of success' (Assistant vice-president).

This section compares the official reasons given for the reorganization with the impressions that we gathered during our interviews at ABB CH. Table B3 summarizes the main points. The ABB case drives home some management truisms and points out the difficulties of building up a network organization:

Table B3 Official reasons and interpretations of ABB's 1998 reorganization

Official reason	Our interpretation
• Simplifying segment business activities	• Three original business segments were too differentiated; too difficult to manage the portfolio
• Creating new synergies	• Countries/regions were creating boundaries; little contacts among profit centers which were within the same segment but located within different countries
• Cost reduction by cutting one hundred management positions	• Eliminating 'regional princes'; more centralized power for the heads of product segments
• Promote growth area and focus along business segments	• Preparation for divestment activities (or even for splitting up the Group); internal competition at international level
• Focus investor attention	• Transparency by publishing data on each of the eight business segments; creates legitimization for further action and integration of Swiss and Swedish shares
• Faster decision-making	• 'Strong men win' as ABB's *de facto* slogan led to slow decision-making based on political power instead of market/product orientation

Source: ABB Group press release, 1998, interviews.

- It is possible to reduce managerial hierarchies and decentralize operational decision-making, but this may easily go at the expense of company-wide coordination.
- Pushing for internal transparency, entrepreneurship and profit responsibility may produce a culture in which 'strong men win' (as ABB's culture is frequently described by employees).
- Establishing a regional management layer (as many large companies have done recently, cf. Lasserre and Schütte, 1995) also implies inserting another power centre.
- Networking between divisions may be obtained within one country but is much more difficult to establish across countries (let alone regions).

▶ Unresolved Management Issues

In order to capture the full potential that the new organization offers, ABB needs to address some yet unresolved management issues. These will be summarized below.

The first challenge is to reduce the internal conflicts and micropolitics which are the unintended consequence of creating an internal market and calculating internal margins. In the view of various interviewees, the internal market has frequently led to myopic competition against other profit centres hindering horizontal networking processes. It remains yet to be seen whether and how the new organization can help tackling that challenge.

The second problem lies in the field of interface management. ABB's lead country concept aims at improving coordination of world-wide processes, yet several interview partners indicated that ABB did not assign clear enough responsibilities to the lead country organizations. ABB has often faced the problem of determining which country organization is to take the lead in which country/ project. As a result, there has been too much duplication of work. Since adding or taking away country organizations' responsibilities in large international plant projects is inherently a critical and political issue, clarity and central leadership are all the more needed here.

The third challenge, mentioned by numerous interview partners, is that of exploiting synergies within and across segments, or, put differently, to make the 'network' element in the network multidivisional work. Many interviewees indicated that with increasing cost and time pressure, exploiting synergy potential represented a great challenge for ABB, though they usually did not have a very clear idea how to achieve that. It is not immediately obvious whether and how such inter-divisional networking between the seven business segments may materialize. One way may be by strengthening ABB's horizontal process focus, which would require a change in incentives and employees' behaviour.

The fourth challenge is to develop an ABB culture beyond financial results, and beyond the front-line company or the country organization. While people are usually very proud to work for ABB, employees talk mostly about the corporate culture of their front-line company or country organization, rather than referring to the ABB Group culture. We found that ABB managers perceive organizational culture as a strong coordination mechanism between head office and units. However, ABB managers do not perceive organizational culture as playing an equally strong role as a coordination mechanism between units or within units. Thus, the influence of the *Mission, Values and Policies* booklet seems to have worn off at last. Developing a horizontally unifying corporate culture is by no means a luxury for a company with such truly worldwide operations.

The fifth challenge resides in developing a new understanding of management's role. The management of front-line companies need to appreciate that, being assigned the responsibility to run a profit centre, they are not the single owner of a specific business, but rather the business opportunity provider for other front-line companies or segments. Only such an understanding may raise internal networking and ultimately improve service to the customer.

The financial implications of ABB's 1998 reorganization could not yet be assessed at the time of writing this case study, though it is obvious that ABB will have to go a long way to match GE's return rates. Finally, it is worth mentioning that many of the above challenges have existed since the merger in 1988. It would appear that problems which are not solved during the first years after a merger continue to haunt the organization afterwards.

▶ Conclusion

ABB has often been referred to by gurus and management scholars alike as a model organization for other companies to follow. This chapter depicted the transformation of the ABB organization over the 1988–98 period, and analysed the nature of its 1998 reorganization to what at first sight would appear to resemble a classical multidivisional organization. The chapter described how ABB transformed itself from a global matrix with a strong country focus (1988–93), through a global matrix with regional focus (1993–98) to what Whittington and Mayer (1997: 253ff.) have termed a network multidivisional (from 1998).

During the first stage of the ABB organization, the key words were turn-around management of individual profit centres, infusing entrepreneurship, creating internal markets and enhancing local responsiveness. The second stage was characterized by the rise of regional trade blocks, fierce international competition, and the increasing importance of emerging markets in Asia and in Central and Eastern Europe, calling for enhanced regional coordination and internal networking. During the third stage, finally, continued tough competition and the need to offer relatively similar products plus a full service package to newly deregulated private sector players further boosted internal networking and strengthened the product versus the country dimension.

We arrived at two major conclusions. First, ABB has not entirely removed its global matrix structure, but rather has transformed it by strengthening its product focus while maintaining the country dimension. Second, ABB has not 'regressed' to a classical multidivisional form but rather has supplemented this form with characteristics beyond its three defining features:

- *managerial hierarchies*: ABB has decentralized operational decision-making to its network of profit centres, whereas strategic decision-making is shared between the business areas and business segments, rather than concentrated entirely at the head office.
- *divisionalization*: ABB is deliberately and increasingly crossing divisional boundaries at the level of the country organizations seeking to reduce costs and create company-wide synergies.
- *internal capital market*: ABB monitors the performance of its profit centres, its business areas and business segments primarily by financial controlling instruments; adding a financial services segment in fact increased the importance of the internal capital market; yet ABB has also added internal labour markets to manage human resources and knowledge as other internal key resources.

The ABB 1998 reorganization seems to have resulted largely from the limitations of the 1993 global matrix organization, i.e. the rivalry between the various profit centres; the internal politics between the business segments, the regions and the head office; the loss of sight of the global business dimension as a result of the introduction of the regions in 1993; and the use of only three business segments until 1998, combining very different businesses in one division. However, we interpreted the 1998 reorganization as a combination of continuity and change, since many structures, responsibilities and processes have essentially remained unchanged as compared to the period before August 1998. This view is in line with more quantitative research which suggests that we 'do not see evidence of a new form supplanting the old, but we do see evidence of new arrangements supplementing the old' (Ruigrok, Pettigrew, Peck and Whittington, 1999).

In our view, ABB continues to be a pioneer of innovative forms or organizing. Its global matrix enabled it to experiment and gain experiences that many other companies have yet to obtain. The openness that ABB employees displayed talking to us and their search for better organizational solutions reflects a strong commitment to the company and its products. And, frankly, we cannot wait to learn about ABB's reorganization in the year 2003, and see the next stage in networking the multidivisional organization.

Acknowledgements

An earlier version of this chapter appeared in Andrew Pettigrew and Evelyn Fenton (eds), *Processes and Practices of New Forms of Organizing*, London/Thousand Oaks, CA: Sage, 2001.

The authors thank Nikolaus von Bock for his research assistance and Norbert Lang at ABB Switzerland for enlightening us on ABB's history. Furthermore, the authors acknowledge the generous support by the HSG *Grundlagenforschungsfonds*.

Note

1   The story even goes that students at one of Europe's leading international business schools got to the point where they left the room as soon as a professor brought up ABB to illustrate effective management practices.

Case Assignments

1   Describe the main elements of ABB's global matrix structure as it evolved between 1988–98.
2   Discuss the advantages of this structure.
3   Describe the problems encountered by ABB in conjunction with its global matrix system.
4   In 1998 ABB recognized that its global matrix structure also required 'a set of essentially non-structural features, i.e. a corporate culture based on open communication and empowerment'. How would you characterize the corporate culture at ABB in 1998?

3

Cross-National HRM

▶ Purpose

In this chapter we will first discuss the nature of international or cross-national human resource management (HRM) as compared to domestic HRM. Thereafter we will present a model for the analysis of cross-national HRM. In this model the focus is on how environmental forces impact on many aspects of HRM in foreign subsidiaries of multinational companies. On the basis of this environmental perspective, micro-level and macro-level influences on the management of human resources in subsidiaries are discussed. Collectively these influences mean there is an acute need for multinational corporations (MNCs) and their foreign subsidiaries to develop socio-economic, cultural and institutional awareness in cross-national settings.

▶ Brief Background

The current expansion in the internationalization of business organizations means that a rapidly increasing number of firms are moving from being purely domestic players to being cross-national players. This development represents a major challenge for these firms' HRM managers. International aspects of human resource management have traditionally been concerned with a narrow range of issues with the principal concern being the expatriation of home country personnel and their compensation. However, particularly during the past decade the range of issues has broadened to encompass cross-national differences in work motivation, job satisfaction, employee commitment, managerial goals and competences, compensation and incentives, supervision and control, employee participation, and management styles.

In a cross-national context it is paramount that managers at corporate headquarters of MNCs recognize that their ways of managing human resources have evolved in relation to the cultural and institutional conditions that are specific to their particular countries of origin. What is more, a particular, idiosyncratic style of management cannot readily be applied to subsidiaries operating in dissimilar cultures and institutional settings. Given this, it is important for these managers to fully accept that their style of management is not necessarily superior, in relation to that of companies in other nations, but simply one way of managing. Indeed, MNCs must not only learn to tolerate their foreign subsidiaries' developing other ways of conducting HRM, they must regard these other ways as potentially enriching for the MNC as a whole.

It is important to bear in mind that in many foreign contexts there is considerable risk attached to mismanaging human resources. This is because MNCs have a higher visibility and a higher exposure to monitoring than their indigenous counterparts. For instance, if a country has a policy requiring that host country personnel are to be preferred for specific positions, the MNC swiftly risks losing its legitimacy if it is viewed as having failed to respond.

▶ Cross-National HRM

Managing human resources embraces a variety of tasks. These may be categorized into five broad, but interrelated HRM areas: (1) the acquisition of human resources; (2) human resource development; (3) compensation; (4) design of work systems; and (5) labour relations.

- *Human resource acquisition* encompasses both the internal and the external selection and recruitment of individuals to jobs. In addition, it includes the hiring of temporary employees and the use of external consultants.
- *Human resource development* includes not only the development of competences among employees but also their maintenance.
- *Compensation* embraces a wide spectrum of employee rewards and incentives. In this chapter we focus on extrinsic or externally controlled rewards, that is, wages and employee stock ownership plans.
- *The design of work systems* refers to the ways in which tasks and responsibilities in the firm are structured and distributed, and the extent to which there are clear borderlines between jobs.
- *Labour relations* span the negotiations with the work force that are necessary in order to put into practice all of the above.

Although these areas are common to both domestic and cross-national HRM, foreign environments often make for a higher degree of complexity because of the cultural, socio-economic, institutional, and political dissimilarities involved. One important consequence of this complexity is that it may make be more difficult to specify tasks and expected performance levels than is the case in purely domestic environments. To succeed, managers with cross-national human resource responsibilities must be equipped with a broader cognitive perspective and more knowledge than their purely domestic counterparts. There is a need for managers who are capable of coping with uncertainty and ambiguity and who are equipped with the ability to develop negotiated solutions to problems that may even lack clear-cut definitions.

The deployment of expatriates

An important cross-national HRM issue that we will discuss in more detail in Chapter 8 involves the composition of subsidiary work forces. Some MNCs have a policy of recruiting parent country personnel to managerial positions in foreign subsidiaries, some recruit host country personnel for such positions, and yet others prefer to hire a substantial proportion of third country managers. Particularly in the first instance, cross-national HRM commits the MNC to a much deeper involvement in the personal lives of employees than is the case for purely domestic operations. Going abroad for a number of years to live and work in a different culture is a major change for most people. Moreover, many expatriates have spouses and children who are also affected by such a move. At a minimum, assistance and advice will have to be given in regard to housing and schooling. For the many dual-career families, the company ought to be proactive in helping the spouse to get a job in the new country or enter a relevant educational programme.

▶ An Environmental HRM Model

Figure 3.1 depicts an analytical model that can be applied as a stepping stone for a discussion of the nature of the cross-national, management of human resources. The model distinguishes between micro- and macro-environmental factors, their direct impact on the management of human resources, and their indirect impact on subsidiary performance. These factors comprise both potential opportunities and constraints.

The macro-environment refers to conditions that are embedded in the surrounding region and/or country in which the subsidiary is located and which are therefore 'givens'. They involve socio-economic, institutional (political/legal), and cultural influences. A range of socio-economic conditions, such as wage levels and the educational infrastructure have consequences for the shaping of a subsidiary's HRM. Institutional conditions include political or legal factors that impact on the types of work arrangements and economic incentives that are feasible, for example, there may be regulations concerning minimum wages and the length of the working week. Employees' rights to exert influence on their work situation may also be regulated by law, as is the case in Scandinavian countries. Cultural conditions embrace factors such as values, symbols, attitudes and patterns of behaviour in a given society. Differences in respect to these dimensions may,

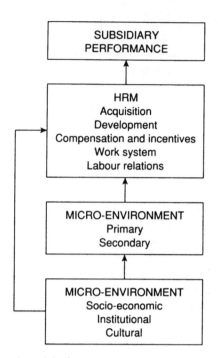

Figure 3.1 An analytical model of HRM

for example, have an impact on the degree of hierarchy employees are prepared to accept.

The subsidiary's micro-environment can be divided into primary and secondary elements. The former includes the subsidiary's relationship to other parts of the multinational company. Secondary environmental elements are made up of closely related external actors, such as customers, competitors, suppliers of resources that are critical for the operation of the subsidiary, and local public institutions and interest organizations.

Finally, it can be seen from the model that HRM is assumed to affect subsidiary performance either in terms of profits, productivity or even creativity. Performance measures are important feedback mechanisms for managers with HRM responsibilities.

▶ Micro-Influences

Our analysis of the influences on HRM policies and practices in foreign subsidiaries starts with those micro-environmental factors that affect the acquisition of human resources, human resource development, compensation and incentive systems, work systems, and labour relations. Table 3.1 provides an overview of the analysis.

Table 3.1 Micro-environmental influences on HRM in subsidiaries of MNCs

HRM functions	Micro-environmental influences	
	Primary	Secondary
HR ACQUISITION: RECRUITMENT AND SELECTION	Internal labour markets	Extended internal labour markets
HR DEVELOPMENT: EMPLOYEE TRAINING	Training policy and programmes in the MNC	Amount of resources spent on training in competing firms
MANAGEMENT DEVELOPMENT	MNC programmes	Availability of managerial competence in the region
COMPENSATION AND INCENTIVES: INDIVIDUAL PERFORMANCE APPRAISAL	Appraisal traditions and principles in the MNC	Attitudes to individual assessment in the local population
WAGES	Remuneration policy in The MNC	Regional wage level in comparable companies
EMPLOYEE STOCK OWNERSHIP PLANS	Attitudes of top management in the MNC	Practices in competing firms
WORK SYSTEM: TEAMWORK	Traditions of and familiarity with teamwork in the MNC	Practices of competing firms
EMPLOYEE AUTONOMY	Job design policy in the MNC	Individualism in local labour market
LABOUR RELATIONS: EMPLOYEE INFLUENCE	Policy and arrangements in the MNC	Degree of influence in competing companies

Acquisition of human resources

One factor that influences the recruitment of new employees is the extent to which an internal labour market exists in the subsidiary and in the MNC as a whole. An internal labour market means that it is company policy that higher-level jobs are normally filled from within the company. A weak variant of this policy is that, in the case of equal qualifications, internal applicants for a vacant job are to be preferred to external applicants. However, the policy may be even stronger, in the sense that higher-level positions are exclusively reserved for company employees.

In addition, though, subsidiaries of MNCs may have to confront so-called extended internal labour markets as part of their secondary micro-environments. These involve expectations that relatives, friends, or acquaintances of employees in the company should be given preferential access to available positions within the firm. Extended internal labour markets are particularly commonplace in cultures where social networks, tribal origin or kinship relations are primary sources of loyalty and identity. In some circumstances it may even be deemed necessary to design a recruitment policy that is in accordance with such traditions even though it lays the company open to charges of nepotism.

Human resource development

The priority assigned to human resource development in a subsidiary is likely to be a result of the particular needs of the MNC and the systems, programmes and traditions that have been established both in the parent organization and in other subsidiaries. The principles and practices in other parts of the MNC therefore constitute important elements in the subsidiary's primary micro-environment.

Within the secondary part of the micro-environment, practices in competing firms may affect the amount of resources spent on human resource development. In regard to attracting and retaining key employees the subsidiary must look beyond the direct compensation and rewards system and take into account opportunities for development. This applies in particular to professional employees who invariably assign a high value to opportunities for personal and professional growth through training, recurrent education and the execution of work tasks. The amount of resources allocated to the development of managers in the subsidiary will often be affected by the access to managerial competence in the region of operation.

Compensation and incentives

The use of performance appraisals in subsidiaries is commonly a function of whether these are part of HRM at corporate headquarters. However, their use is, as we shall see under the discussion of macro-level influences, also affected by the culture of the country of localization. Moreover, their use may also be affected by the degree to which other companies in the host country or region have implemented individual performance appraisal systems.

The compensation and reward practices of other units in the MNC, including the HQ and other subsidiaries, also affect the compensation and design of incentives in each subsidiary. Uniform compensation systems across the various units in MNCs will tend to restrict the local degree of HRM autonomy. On the other hand, particularly when access to qualified personnel is problematic, a subsidiary will have to take into account the rewards system of local firms that compete in the same labour market. Because of this, information about the actual reward systems and wage levels applied in firms operating in the vicinity must be regularly collected and analysed.

Work systems

The way in which work is organized in a subsidiary will be influenced by several factors in the micro-environment. The policies and practices of the MNC and other subsidiaries may be decisive for the design and implementation of teamwork and employee autonomy in each single subsidiary.

An essential element in the secondary microenvironment is the way in which a subsidiary's competitors organize their work systems, including their use of teamwork. In contexts where critical human resources are scarce, substantial use of teamwork may in some instances be a competitive advantage as a means of attracting skilled personnel, since persons with higher education often find teamwork attractive to work in projects and teams. However, this is contingent upon the degree of individualism in the local population. If this is high, the quest for employee autonomy in jobs will also be high (Hodgetts and Luthans, 1991: 166–7).

Labour relations

Following the collaborative precepts in HRM (see Chapter 5), many large Western companies have found it advantageous to involve their employees in discussions concerning strategy formulation and the future development of their companies. When we look at subsidiaries of MNCs, it is clear that the type and amount of influence on decision-making that their employees are granted are likely to be affected by the policy and practices common to host country competing firms.

▶ Macro-Influences

We shall now extend our perspective by focusing on how elements in subsidiaries' macro-environments impact on their HRM systems and practices. Table 3.2 provides an overview of the presentation.

Human resource acquisition

For most subsidiaries of MNCs the local or regional external labour market is one of the most vital socio-economic factors for their operations. However, the size of the local pools of qualified individuals in relation to the jobs that have to be filled

Table 3.2 Macro-environmental influences on HRM in subsidiaries of MNCs

HRM FUNCTIONS	Macro-environmental factors		
	Socio-Economic	Institutional	Cultural
HR ACQUISITION: RECRUITMENT AND SELECTION	External labour markets	Pressure to recruit locals	Women's position in society
USE OF HEADHUNTERS	Availability of services	Legal regulations	Recruitment ethics
HR DEVELOPMENT: EMPLOYEE TRAINING	Access to skilled people in the country	Public educational policy	Values attached to learning
MANAGEMENT DEVELOPMENT	Access to managerial competence	Supply of relevant external programs	Degree of bureaucracy in society
COMPENSATION AND INCENTIVES: INDIVIDUAL PERFORMANCE APPRAISAL	Degree of social inequality	Attitudes of national unions	Degree of egalitarianism
WAGES	Local average wages	Minimum wage policies	Degree of materialism
EMPLOYEE STOCK OWNERSHIP PLANS	Level and distribution of income	Union policies on ESOPs	Ownership traditions
WORK SYSTEM: TEAMWORK	Authority and status relations	National traditions of organizing work	Degree of individualism
LABOUR RELATIONS: EMPLOYEE INFLUENCE	Social stratification	Labour laws and and regulations	Power distance in society

can be highly variable across different countries and regions. Another problem facing subsidiaries is that national educational systems and traditions are often very dissimilar to those of the parent country. This creates difficulties for subsidiaries of MNCs when they set about selecting the right type of personnel for various work tasks, since the credentials may be difficult to 'translate' into the standards of the parent country.

Moreover, the educational background locally deemed necessary for a person to become a manager may vary substantially. In Germany managers often have a technical, engineering background, in France managers usually have a *Grande Ecole* track or a university education, in Spain many managers have studied law or economics, in the USA an MBA is common for managers, whereas in Great Britain managers are recruited from a broad range of educational backgrounds. Recruiting local managers to subsidiaries without the credentials deemed locally necessary may well create difficulties for the subsidiary in its dealings with other local firms and the authorities.

A key question that every subsidiary faces and one that we will return to in Chapter 8, is the issue of whether managers are to be recruited from the local labour market or from other parts of the MNC. The choices MNCs make in this respect partly depend on their need to execute control over their subsidiaries. If this need is important, then they tend to use parent-country managers. However, this decision is also affected by the amount of locally available managerial talent. Scarcity of local labour possessing the skills required may force the subsidiary to hire managers from the home country or from third countries. This may, however, involve problems since knowledge about the specific foreign culture may be crucial in order to operate effectively. Acquiring such knowledge may be both difficult and costly, depending on the cultural distance between the countries in question. Consequently, it may be necessary to recruit and train managers from the local labour market.

Political conditions are yet another factor that may play a key role in recruitment decisions. In some countries or regions it is expected that foreign companies recruit both ordinary employees and managers from the local population. A weaker version of this demand exists when recruitment of managers or specialists from third countries is negatively sanctioned in the local environment, whereas recruitment from the subsidiary's parent country is not. Many foreign companies may, for instance, find it cumbersome to hire personnel in China if they have to go through government agencies.

As noted by Schneider and Barsoux (1997: 134–5), in countries characterized by a high degree of collectivism, various kinds of nepotism follow from the widespread interdependencies among people:

> When an employer takes on a person, a moral commitment is established. There is an implicit understanding that the employer will look after the employee and quite possibly his/her family too. Family ties in turn provide social controls that are often more powerful than the organizational hierarchy.

India is a country characterized by high collectivism and related practices of selective recruitment of personnel As noted by Sparrow and Budhwar (1997), 'social relationships and political connections play a significant role in the selection, promotion and transfer of employees in Indian organizations'. This is largely a function of the caste consciousness in substantial parts of the country's population.

Ethical norms relating to the recruitment of employees are also an important factor to observe. These differ across national borders and constitute an important cultural factor in the macro-environment and are often visible in local legislation. For example, some countries have legislation on equality of employment opportunity in relation to gender, race, and age, whereas in other countries issues of this type are hardly on the agenda at all.

Finally, in some areas, such as the Arab world and parts of Asia, there may be culturally based limitations on the recruitment of female managers. This is often due to religiously sanctioned convictions that women have a subordinate status. Yet in countries like Taiwan and Japan, some companies, including MNCs, have been able to turn such a situation to their own advantage by systematically recruiting women who often have university degrees and who demonstrate above-average work performance (Adler, 1987).

The use of headhunting firms to recruit managers in foreign subsidiaries of MNCs is also subject to socio-economic, institutional and cultural influences. The availability and quality of such services may have an impact along with ethical codes implying that it is unethical to 'steal' employees from other companies.

Human resource development

A subsidiary's opportunity to develop its human resources can be severely restricted by shortcomings in the local education system (see Judy, 2002). For example the experience of subsidiaries of Japanese electronics companies in the 1990s in Brazil was that they were only able to partly disseminate their TQM (total quality management) systems and practices. The reason was the insufficient numeric skills among local employees who were therefore unable to perform the required range of work tasks that the TQM system demands (Humphrey, 1995). Likewise, German MNCs will encounter problems when trying to implement their characteristic functional flexibility in countries where educational standards are significantly lower than in Germany.

Turning to the institutional level, in some instances, support is given by national authorities to facilitate human resource development in firms. Financial support or tax incentives may, for instance, be available for certain types of training and research and development. In France the training regime is characterized not so much by incentives as financial sanctions that are applied to companies that fail to spend a sum on training equivalent to 1.4 per cent of the total wages bill.

Cultural factors that affect human resource development in general and employee training in particular include the local values and status attached to individual acquisition of competencies and development of human resources. These values are closely related to the host population's attitude to knowledge and learning in general.

When it comes to management development, this is partly affected by the actual access to managerial competence in the local or regional labour market. As pointed out earlier in this chapter, this often determines whether a subsidiary chooses to import managers from the home country or a third country, or whether it opts for developing local managerial talent.

A cultural factor that affects development activities in subsidiaries is the local preferred style of learning. As noted by Schneider and Barsoux (1997: 139), German and Swiss managers tend to favour structured learning environments with clear pedagogical objectives, course outline and schedule, and the 'right answer' or superior solution. This is markedly different from the learning style of British managers: 'Most British participants despise too much structure. They like open-ended learning situations with vague objectives, broad assignments and no timetables at all. The suggestion that there could be only one correct answer is taboo with them' (Saner and Yiu, 1994: 962). Hayes and Allinson (1988) have concluded that learning environments and learning activities that promote effective learning in one culture may be quite ineffective in other cultures.

Compensation and incentives

The use of performance appraisal and, with it, performance-related pay is an HRM practice that is considered to be particularly sensitive to socio-economic, institutional and cultural conditions. Such systems appear to be easier to implement in countries characterized by substantial income inequalities among the working population than in countries with a more equal income distribution. Among the most influential institutional factors are the strength and attitudes of local unions. In Scandinavian work life, which is characterized both by relatively small income inequalities and strong unions opposed to individual performance pay, the use of performance appraisal and individualized pay is much less widespread than in most other parts of Western Europe (Gooderham, Nordhaug and Ringdal, 1999). Individual measures of performance are also to some degree determined by the presence of egalitarian values in society. Pinnington and Edwards (2000: 252) have noted:

> Performance related pay is an example of a practice that operates more easily in some cultures than in others: while it is generally accepted in Anglo-Saxon business cultures, it is less widely accepted in France, Germany, or Italy, where there is resistance to the idea 'that individual members of the group should excel in a way that reveals the shortcomings of others.

This is an issue we return to in more detail in Chapter 5.

The designs and levels of wage systems in subsidiaries will also normally be influenced by specific socio-economic conditions in the country of location.

One of the most important of these is the general income level that restricts subsidiaries' degrees of freedom by setting standards that may be difficult to violate. Another is the class structure and degree of socio-economic inequality in the population. If, for instance, a subsidiary located in a country with very low labour costs pays its employees according to the standards in the parent country, it would distort the local social hierarchy and at worst create a widespread hostility towards the MNC.

Government regulations may also have an impact. In China, for example, the authorities have practised a regulation stipulating that foreign companies have to respect rules governing both minimum and maximum wage levels. This has led to higher pay in MNC subsidiaries compared to state-owned companies and collectively owned enterprises: 'In 1995, for example, wages in foreign-invested enterprises were 132 percent of wages in state-owned enterprises and 189 percent of wages in collectively owned enterprises' (Zhu, DeCieri and Dowling, 1998: 72–3; see also Tretiak and Holzman, 1993; Goodall and Warner, 1997).

The motivational role of economic and other material rewards varies across cultures and may thus influence the design of incentive systems. In some countries, such as the United States, there is a strong belief in business life that employee motivation and thereby also organizational performance can be improved by offering co-ownership to employees. On an international basis, however, variations in levels and distributions of income may determine the relevance of such arrangements. Given that employees receive stocks in lieu of wages, such arrangements would be irrelevant to employees in countries with modest levels of earnings.

Finally, differences in general societal values may affect the viability of co-ownership as a means of stimulating motivation and commitment among employees. In countries where there is a strict, inherited social order, the underlying authoritarian values will constitute an obstacle to employee co-ownership since this will be regarded as a threat against existing class or caste boundaries.

Organization of labour and work systems

Decisions regarding the organization of labour and the distribution of work tasks are crucial for organizational performance. The knowledge and skills possessed by employees are important socio-economic premises underlying such decisions. Variations in competencies or the actual mix of skills available in the local labour market may lead to variations in how work systems are designed and implemented across countries. This also applies to legal restrictions regarding safety in the workplace and regulations regarding working hours. One example of the possible impact of the local mix of skills on the use or non-use of teamwork is that German companies in some foreign settings have problems developing efficient teamwork involving functional flexibility, due to insufficient competencies among local employees (Pinnington and Edwards, 2000: 253).

On the institutional level, the national traditions on performing tasks in groups may have an impact. So may also the actual structure and practices that are embedded in the national system of employee relations:

> In German and British plants of the same company, German team members have been found to be more positive about teamwork than their British counterparts. Attitude to teamwork appears to be influenced by the national institutional structure of employee relations, the traditional British adversarial system having negative effects on worker participation and team contribution (Murakami, 1998). On the other hand, direct employee involvement practices are less dependent on the existence of extra-firm supportive structures and, hence, there is more scope for their diffusion. (Pinnington and Edwards, 2000: 253)

A cultural factor that has consequences for the design of work systems is the degree of individualism or collectivism in the national culture of the host-country (Hofstede, 1980a). An interesting illustration of this is the use of job analysis in HRM. This tool is frequently used in firms in the Western world because the strong sense of individual job-ownership among employees means that individuals are regarded as the basic units of organization. In other words, it is meaningful to split work processes into discrete work tasks. However, in Japan, job analysis is non-existent. This is because behaviour is largely group-oriented (Ishida, 1986), so that in Japanese work life it is the group that is the basic building block and not the individual employee. Thus work processes are designed for groups rather than single individuals.

Non-discussables or work taboos provide an additional illustration of how the work system can be influenced by variations in cultural values. In some countries, religious and social norms set limitations on who can carry out certain tasks. For instance, an effect of the Indian caste system is that only casteless persons are allowed to undertake work that religious belief defines as unclean. However, it should be pointed out that Indian law does not sanction this.

At the cultural level, the degree of individualism or collectivism will have at least some impact on how widespread teamwork is. In cultures characterized by high collectivism, it will generally be easier to implement teamwork than in more individualistic cultures since most people are used to solving problems in group contexts. The opposite applies for employee autonomy. In addition, this will be affected by the degree of power distance in society, that is, the degree to which differences in status and power are accepted by the population (Hofstede, 1984; see also Chapter 5 in this book). In cultures with high power distance people are used to being told what to do and in many cases do not want to become empowered or to enjoy a greater degree of individual autonomy (Hodgetts and Luthans, 1991: 167).

Labour relations

The degree of social stratification and inequality in the host country affects the autonomy subsidiaries of MNCs enjoy in respect to implementing employee influence and participation. In cases where there are extensive differences between classes or castes, granting low-status employees substantial influence on decision-making may be highly problematic.

On the institutional level, it may be observed that a country's corporate and labour legislation will affect the degree of employee influence. According to corporate law, in the Scandinavian countries for example, employees are granted the right to select from their own one-third of the board members in firms that employ 50 or more employees.

A cultural factor that is critical to the implementation of employee influence arrangements is that of power distance. The greater the power distance, the more difficult it will normally be to introduce considerable employee influence.

▶ Practical Lessons

The environments subsidiaries of MNCs operate in exert a substantial influence on managerial decisions. This may undermine the efforts of the individual MNC to make decisions it perceives as rational in relation to human resource acquisition, development, compensation, labour relations and in the design of work systems.

In practical terms it is critical for the MNC to be able to identify and assess the significance of the conditions in the various environments in which it operates. The analytical model outlined in this chapter can be applied to environmental factors that influence the future operation of the subsidiary. Particularly before establishing a subsidiary or joint venture in a foreign environment, it is essential that information about environmental factors is compiled and that, on this basis, both possible and probable problems relating to HRM in this specific environment are clarified. Such an analysis may strengthen the MNC's ability to act proactively with regard to human resource issues.

▶ Summary

In this chapter we have highlighted the fundamental differences between domestic and cross-national HRM. On the basis of a micro-/macro-environmental model of HRM we have discussed factors that have a significant impact on HRM in foreign subsidiaries of MNCs. A distinction was drawn between human resource acquisition, human resource development, compensation, work systems and labour relations. The main point of this chapter is that MNCs and their subsidiary managers must take into consideration the socio-economic, institutional and cultural conditions in host countries when designing and implementing HRM practices in the subsidiaries.

Case C contains an account of a joint venture between the French construction materials company, Lafarge, and a state-owned cement works in China. The case deals with a wide range of HRM challenges that stemmed from differences in cultural values and institutionalized ways of working. The case describes how management addressed these challenges.

Acknowledgement

Parts of this chapter build on Grønhaug and Nordhaug (1992).

Lafarge in China: Cross-National HRM

Keith Goodall and Malcolm Warner

▶ Introduction

The 1994 decision of the French construction materials company, Lafarge, to enter into a joint venture with a Chinese state-owned cement works, appeared strategically attractive. Most of the company's assets at this time were in the more mature economies of Western Europe and the USA, while the emerging econo-mies of Asia, Eastern Europe and South America represented less than 4 per cent of annual sales. The company was aiming particularly to expand its operations in Asia. The potential of the region in terms of economic growth and demand for building materials was clear: the demand for cement in China alone was estimated at five hundred million tons a year, one-third of the global total. For the mana-gers in the new joint venture in Beijing, however, this investment decision marked the beginning of a difficult process. They would face, among other problems, rioting redundant workers, sabotaged equipment, demonstrations at Beijing City Hall, adverse media attention, and a major Labour Law court case. Remarkably, the joint venture emerged four years later from these 'interesting times' with an ISO 9000 certificate, reliable high volume production of low-alkali cement, and a highly prestigious award for labour relations from the All China Federation of Trade Unions (ACFTU).

▶ The Chinese Partner

Lafarge's chosen partner for its first joint venture in China was a state-owned enterprise (SOE): the Huaibei Mining Company (HMC), located an hour's drive north of Beijing. HMC had been set up in 1991, partly to provide limestone to Tianjin Alkali Plant. The project was divided into three parts: Huaibei Cement Plant, Huaibei Quarry Company and an administrative unit of about 20 people. Unfortunately, by the time trial production began in 1992, the planned economy was ending, and so therefore was the planned distribution of limestone. In August 1993, the quarry and cement companies merged, but while the quarry worked relatively well, the cement plant, according to one of the managers, 'was never good, producing only 70 to 80 thousand tons of cement each year'. There was hardly any market for the limestone. The project depended entirely upon state loans, and profits were all paid to the bank:

> The good side was that the enterprise settled the employment problem for so many people. At the beginning, the enterprise depended upon state loans. When no more loans were granted, the enterprise soon fell into hardship. The reason why so many people were recruited for this project was because of the designed capacity, but this was never reached during the SOE years. The problems facing us included low utility of facilities, low production, low and unstable product quality. The company faced bankruptcy, and was going nowhere if we did not enter into a JV arrangement.

HMC had some 1300 employees at the plant, 1100 of whom were workers, the remainder were managers and technical staff. Recruitment of workers had been dictated to some extent by the purchase of land on which to build the plant, 'The company had to recruit the peasants whose land was occupied by the plant . . . These peasants had received very little education'.

Additional workers were also recruited through the local Labour Bureau:

> The Bureau advertised the recruitment through posters and the local broadcasting station. Because we needed quite a lot of people, the company just looked at ages, education levels and gender. Workers recruited this way were mostly senior high school graduates. A few had only finished junior high school, and got in because of *guanxi* (personal relationships). Managerial and technical people were recruited through the Personnel Bureau. Some were recommended by acquaintances, and were then transferred through the Personnel Bureau, because there were *hukou* (residence permit) issues involved. Peasant contract workers, township contract workers and regular workers got different treatments on wages and welfare.

The peasant contract workers were, of course, completely inexperienced in industrial work. Some of the workers, according to one Chinese manager, 'could not even write a note clearly enough to make themselves understood. We had supervisors who could not write a working report well, and workers who could not write a receipt when they borrowed things from the store.'

At the beginning of 1989 two hundred people were sent on a two-year training programme. The training included cement production, vehicle maintenance, special equipment, and laboratory testing. These people became 'backbones' (*gugan*), or key workers. Between 1987 and 1993, the annual expenditure on training was RMB 787 ($92.00) per person. There was no more training after production began.

At the start of the HMC project, morale was quite high. But when production began, many problems emerged with the production method and facilities, problems which management failed to settle satisfactorily. The workforce became demoralized, and management at HMC was described as 'quite chaotic', with many managers preferring to listen to reports in their offices 'rather than go to the site in person'. Madam Gao Yueming, the trade union president, distinguished between HMC's formal organization and its management processes:

> In the old enterprise, there was quite a complete set of regulations and management system. But the regulations were not executed very strictly. Under the planned economy and the practice of guaranteed employment, the number of employees was not tightly controlled. There could be more than two people at a single work position.

Messages were also conveyed to staff in the traditional manner:

> Communications were mainly within the management. There were big employee meetings at which the management told the workers about the objectives, development and tasks of the company. But that was not sufficient, because it was one-way communication from the management to the workers.

In these conditions regulations were erratically enforced, and staff were less than motivated:

> Discipline was not taken seriously. There were several people working on one position, so there was not too much to do. People could go to other departments to have a chat when they did not have anything to do. People could tell the manager 'I want to take leave' and go away from the company, sometimes without getting their wages deducted. Being late for work or leaving the company early were seldom punished. You got punished only if you had stayed away from work for more than 15 days.

With too little to do, many workers found alternative activities:

> All kinds of strange things happened. It was common to see workers playing cards or chess during work hours. Outside the plant they made a lot of trouble, drinking, then fighting. You could find beds in offices and workshops, and people could sleep during working hours . . . If the plant stopped, no one cared. Workers could read novels, play mahjong or chat. 'Just be there, and you'll be paid.'

Working conditions were also unsatisfactory:

> The working environment was very bad. There was rubbish, waste materials and
> rusty components everywhere. The dust collector was broken, but the plant did not
> have money to get it fixed. Thick smoke was billowing everywhere, seriously harm-
> ing people's health . . . There were physical examinations, but very infrequent. They
> did only one examination from 1991 to 1994, when the JV started.

In addition to health and safety issues, there was also considerable dissatisfaction
with the reward system. 'Eating from the big pot' (*chi daguofan*) was felt to be
unfair by some of the workers, 'Wage levels were set according to the importance
of positions, but pay differences between positions were quite small. It did not
matter how much work you did – you got almost the same reward.' When asked
to help out with some task, a typical worker's response would be, 'It's not my
job!' Payment at HMC was initially made up of Record Wages (*dang'an gongzi*).
The basic wage level was decided according to regulations stipulated by the
State, and this was supplemented with subsidies (transportation, and meals, for
example), and allowances (quarry allowance, and construction work allowance).
Before production began, the bonus was set at RMB 20 ($2.50) per month for
everybody.

HMC implemented a Position Skill Wage system (*gangwei jineng gongzi zhi*).
This consisted of eight position levels for workers, and 14 levels for managerial
staff. The Skill Wages should have been set according to skill levels, which were
decided by appraisal and exam results. But, because there were too many people,
the company took a different approach: the previous Record Wages plus fixed
subsidies were simply called Skill Wages. After production began, bonuses were
awarded to departments according to the quantity and quality of work. Department managers then 'distributed the money according to the performance of
different groups'. But there was strong pressure to share rewards relatively equally:
pay rises at HMC were felt by many to be a right of all employees:

> So, in SOEs, you have to be 'fair' and stipulate very hard qualifications for pay rises,
> like diplomas received, length of service, etc., in order to avoid trouble. Giving pay
> rises is a government issue rather than a company one. The state is unable to
> increase salaries for everybody. If only one-third of the people can get a rise, you will
> bring about a disaster if you try to identify the qualified ones through an appraisal.
> The only thing you can do is stipulate a clear demarcation which will leave exactly
> one-third of the people with the right to a raise.

Employees who performed very well were honoured as 'Excellent Employees'
(*youxiu yuangong*) or 'Advanced Employees' (*xianjin yuangong*), and were given
certificates of merit. There were few additional material rewards. The management at HMC had in fact promised financial rewards for good performance, 'but
they did not do it. The workers lost confidence in the management.'

The All China Federation of Trade Unions (ACFTU) at HMC played its traditional role:

> The Trade unionrepresented the interests of the employees and was a link between the Party and the masses. In SOEs, the role of the Union was to help the management and the Party branch with the operation of the enterprise, reflect the requests and opinions of the employees to the management, hold entertainments or sports activities, and take care of employees suffering from hardship. Before the joint venture, the Union mainly assisted the management. The Workers' Congress was an organ of power in the SOE, and could approve budgets, decide welfare distribution (including housing distribution plans), and even had the power to dismiss the Factory Director. Workers' representatives decided the issues by voting.

But the real impact of the trade union was, according to another manager who worked there, extremely limited:

> What the Trade union did was to organize small activities like games and sports in order to show the existence of the TU. They were not dealing with welfare, because the plant had no money, and, of course, the TU had no money either and had to do what the Party Committee and the General Manager wanted it to do.

Similarly, the Workers' Congress was seen by a second manager as having had very little substantive role in the enterprise, 'The focus of the Congress was welfare, and the Workers' Representatives presented their suggestions to the management. But no suggestions were really accepted and put into effect.' The HR function at this time was also disconnected from business objectives and served only an administrative, 'policeman' role.

Then, in 1993, just as HMC was struggling to pay the bank interest on its loans and to support its 1300 workers and staff, Lafarge signalled that it was looking for a partner. The negotiations went smoothly, and in August 1994 the new joint venture, Chinefarge, was established on the old HMC site, with Lafarge holding a 51 per cent share. What would the new partners make of one another once their attention turned in earnest to production and profit?

▶ Chinefarge: The New Joint Venture

The choice of the Huaibei Mining Company as a partner fulfilled Lafarge's initial objectives in China very well. As one of the expatriate managers commented: 'Our aims . . . were to get a foothold in the market by buying a small facility in a good location, with a good limestone source, and near a good market, which is what we did. Something where we could have our very first experience of operating a manufacturing plant in China.'

In addition, the cement plant itself had only been recently built, and unlike many others in China, was not hopelessly outdated. But for many Chinese staff the initial stage of the JV was, as a Chinese manager explained, extremely worrying:

> When an SOE looks for a JV partner, normally it is in hardship. Under such circumstances, employees are very demoralized. People are the biggest resource of a company: if the people are not in good shape, the enterprise can never be successful. In this enterprise, the employees did not know what their future would be like, and seriously lacked confidence. 'How will the enterprise change with the new boss? How will the foreigners treat us? What is going to happen to me? Will the company exist for long?' . . . Those who could leave all left the company. Once I met a taxi driver who used to work in this company. I asked him why he left. He said, 'I didn't know what was going to happen. I was not in very good physical condition, and feared I could not endure the intensity of work.' . . . At the beginning, people did not trust the foreign management, and disliked them.

Although some Chinese workers felt the JV would bring 'benefits and bright prospects to the employees' many anxieties were fuelled by the knowledge that Lafarge wanted to reduce the size of the workforce, 'Though we had more than 1300 people, the foreign partner wanted no more than 600 . . . Everybody was anxious about their future and no one was thinking about the work. Production came to a halt. The situation was very miserable.' Chinefarge, in fact, took 650 people out of the 1300 in the plant. Since the joint venture was an important enterprise in Huairou County, the County Government helped arrange the placement of the rest of the workforce. An equivalent plant in Europe would have between fifty and a hundred workers.

The expatriate managers of Chinefarge had their own worries about the efficient day-to-day operation of the plant. In addition, there was a dramatic start to the venture which the Chinefarge managers would rather have avoided:

> On the very first day we found out our joint venture partners had failed to compensate the workers who were being made redundant . . . There were a number of the workers who demonstrated in the Beijing City Hall, and there was sabotage, windows broken and some malicious destruction of property, and there was some very bad media publicity. It was a very unfortunate start.

The new management included an American GM, Brazilian and French Plant Managers, French sales, Maintenance and HR Managers, and a Chinese Deputy General Manager. This latter was the only HMC manager at the senior level, whose main responsibility was to manage the relationship with the Chinese partner and the local government. When they set about trying to reorganize the plant, there were immediate difficulties:

> I think at the very beginning there were a lot of communication problems within the company. First of all, at the senior management level. We had Brazilians, American, French and Chinese all working together. And with no really common language,

we sometimes had to have three different sets of interpreters at a meeting to translate Portuguese, French and English into Chinese and vice versa. So inevitably there
was some communication difficulty, both within the expatriate team and between
the expatriate team and the Chinese middle managers, and more broadly with some
of the other institutions, our Chinese partner and also the Trade Union.

From the perspective of many Chinese staff, the level of trust in the new organization was low:

> The problem was that the relationship between the partners was not harmonious.
> One reason was the workers felt they were watched over. Another thing was vertical
> communications. The employees could only report to their immediate superiors,
> and could not report to higher levels. At that time, the foreigners and the Chinese
> distrusted each other.

Initial attempts to make changes did not, according to one local middle manager,
always go smoothly:

> The Chief Engineer of the old Huaibei Mining Company stayed at first. But he soon
> found it hard to manage the work because so many people had been dismissed. He
> left the company after a short period of time. Initially, the foreign management
> wanted all people in the production department to be able to transfer to another
> position whenever needed. People did not understand this. Maybe it was like this
> abroad, where workers are more versatile, but the Chinese workers were not tech-
> nically capable enough to do that. And, since they were unfamiliar with other posi-
> tions, it might result in accidents. Therefore, after a short while, the management
> fixed the people and the managers for the departments and units in the plant, and
> clarified the division of work responsibilities. Before the JV, it took several people to
> do the work of a single position. But in the JV, one person had to take charge of
> several positions. The eight hours became intensive.

There were also, from the perspective of the foreign partner, problems with basic
work attitudes:

> People weren't used to working hard, or initiating things. Taking responsibility was
> something which was alien to most people because of coming from a state-run
> background. They expected just to be told what to do and when to do it. What
> I saw was a relatively unmotivated group who were not keen to take initiative on the
> basis that if things went wrong, they would lose face.

Attempts to change management processes in the new joint venture met with
resistance. Efforts by the newly restructured HR department to introduce a performance appraisal system in 1995, for example, produced strong reactions:

> The first year that we had a performance-based bonus system, there was a great
> tendency by middle managers to give everybody the same, because that was the

tradition. And we had a succession of appeals and visits by aggrieved employees and even the middle managers themselves when, in the first year, a high proportion of the workforce received no bonus at all, whereas top performers received quite high bonuses to encourage exceptional performance.

As a Chinese manager explained:

> People were very uncomfortable with performance appraisal, because the Chinese like to hear only pleasant words. Some managers thought that only praise was motivating. Before the appraisal process began, some people gave gifts to their bosses and the Personnel Manager, but the managers refused to accept them.

Even in late 1998, there was still resistance to the way in which performance was assessed. Disagreement was expressed most forcefully by the trade union president:

> The JV uses the appraisal system to decide pay rises and bonuses. Employees say that though this system has positive motivating effects, there is one thing about it that deserves consideration. Is it really always like this: 60 to 70 per cent of the people are good workers and 20 to 30 per cent are bad?

At the start of 1996, 15 months after the inauguration of Chinefarge, there were still, according to the recently arrived Chinese plant manager, also serious problems with production:

> Production was very bad, and so was quality. Workers were poorly educated, and the Chinese employees were very depressed . . . The normal work day ended at 5 p.m., and although the plant was paying workers overtime to repair the machines, there was nobody working when I went to the plant at 6.30 p.m. The department manager was reading a newspaper and drinking tea. I was shocked, and said to him, 'The plant is stopped. Our customers are waiting for the cement, and we have to get things moving. But you are drinking tea here! When do you expect the plant to be fixed?' He was embarrassed, but this was actually a very common phenomenon. When the facilities broke down, sometimes no one would stay after 5 p.m., even the Maintenance Manager went home. The workers were dissatisfied. They had thought the JV would bring them a lot of benefits, and had very high expectations. But life in the JV was not as good as they thought. In other words, it did not rain pizzas. They were unhappy about that. What is more, there are differences in the perception of work between the Chinese and the Westerners. The Chinese tended to think that they were working for others, and failed to see they were also working for themselves. While the Western managers thought that you should perform well once the company had hired you . . . The workers would not challenge the management face to face, but they could bring their resentment into their work, sometimes even resulting in sabotage. The windows of the workshops were often broken, and after they were fixed, they were soon broken again. Sometimes workers even vented their spleen on the production facilities. In general, workers did not want to work here, and would leave when they had a chance . . . It really shocked me when six of our best maintenance workers left the plant together.

Workers showed little understanding of how an enterprise functions in a market economy. The recently appointed Chinese HR manager summarized early attitudes:

> The workers tended to think that wages were decided by the boss, who could give them whatever he liked. But where does the money come from? If the company makes money, you can get a rise. But, if not, it would be quite difficult to increase your wages every year. Another thing is the big problem for almost all Chinese enterprises: the departments would not take responsibility for problems and would just push them to other departments. In an industrial environment where all procedures are linked closely with one another, this attitude is especially detrimental. We have to make it clear to the managers that no department is independent and they have to bear in mind cooperation and teamwork.

The management style of Chinese senior managers also appeared to be very controlling, with all important decisions being referred to them by subordinates: not at all the behaviour that Chinefarge needed to develop. There were also concerns about the attitudes of certain middle managers:

> There were two major problems with the middle managers. One was that they did not like to be strict with their subordinates, which was understandable against the historical background. People got to know from the Cultural Revolution that being strict with subordinates could bring you disaster. The other problem was their low management capabilities. The middle managers did not tie themselves with the interests of the enterprise. Therefore, they worked in a perfunctory manner, covering up problems and shirking responsibilities.

If middle managers, who had little real authority of power, tried to be strict with their subordinates, anonymous letters were sent to the senior managers attacking them.

In addition to problems with managerial attitudes, there were also considerable concerns about worker safety in the new organization: over 2,000 hours of lost-time accidents were recorded in 1995. In an attempt to remedy this dangerous situation a Chinese Safety Officer was appointed, but although he was conscientious, the number of accidents remained high.

A shortage of skilled local people meant that Chinefarge was forced to recruit, and pay more for, staff from other locations. This caused a great deal of resentment:

> There are two wage systems. Local people are paid according to local rate, while people from Beijing are paid according to the salary market in downtown Beijing. Though some local people have technical experience, they do not have enough language skills and can only move around in the local Huairou job market. While managers who are capable both technically and linguistically are desirable for joint ventures and can move in the national market. So can university graduates. Here comes the problem: a newly recruited college graduate might receive higher pay than a Workshop Head who is managing 40 people. Some people are unhappy: 'How many days have they been here?'

There was considerable pressure for greater equality of assessment and pay. Given Chinese cultural preferences, should the expatriate managers compromise in some way? Basic living conditions were also better for externally recruited staff:

In the Dormitory Building, the externally recruited people live on the fourth floor, which is well fitted up and equipped with colour TVs and gas cookers. This is for retention purposes, which is understandable. But the second and third floors, where some local employees live, are just the same as before. The company should consider the psychology of the local employees and make some appropriate arrangements for them to reduce their bad feelings. Also, it is not good for the company's image . . . FIEs should consider people more. Big Japanese firms, like Panasonic and Sony, are good at this. They are strict in management, but care very much for the employees. They make the employees feel that 'this is my home'. People are the first priority. If you lose people, you can do nothing successfully.

The Chinese HR manager explained the provision of different accommodation:

Local employees do not regard the dormitory as their homes, and they can go home every weekend. While those recruited from outside do not have this convenience. Some of them can go home only once a year. Therefore we should make their accommodation better so as to give them a feeling of being at home here. We keep explaining this to our people, and I think they should be able to understand.

As well as dissatisfaction among existing employees, Chinefarge also had problems with both recruitment and retention of new staff. The HR manager summarized the situation:

We have met two major problems in recruitment. First, we are located close to the quarry and far away from the city, so we are at a geographical disadvantage. And we want people with high qualifications, who can easily find good jobs in better places. Traditionally speaking, the cement industry is not an attractive business. People who have made achievements in the cement business have mostly left this industry, many going to design institutes. The fact that we value experience makes it even more difficult to find the right people. Second, retention is difficult. Our plentiful training opportunities and respect for personal choices, which are characteristic of Lafarge, are useful. Improving accommodation and living conditions are useful, too. But these are still limited. We have been unable to find the right people to fill certain posts, such as Purchasing Manager and Senior Maintenance Manager. Since a cement plant has all those large and cumbersome machines which people without experience cannot deal with, we can only look for maintenance experts from the cement industry.

There were also fundamental business problems which needed to be addressed. The plant was running at less than 50 per cent capacity. The market for the type of cement produced was highly competitive and making a profit would be tough. An additional problem in trying to make a profit at Chinefarge was the famous

Table C1 Clinker and cement production and turnover, 1993–98

	1993	1994	1995	1996	1997	1998 estimate
Clinker (ton)	84,000	70,000	117,000	187,000	244,000	250–260 thousand
Cement (ton)	None[a]	89,000	120,000	200,000	300,000	320,000
Turnover (RMB)	25,700,000	20,070,000	27,507,645	47,700,798	74,404,330	83.5 million
No. of employees	1,300	1,300	562	525	522	518

Note: [a] 84,000 tons of high quality clinker can be turned into approximately 100,000 tons of cement.

'triangular debt' (*sanjiaozhai*) problem. Salesmen were often being paid commission on sales which were not paid for, since many customers were waiting for payment from their own customers. The General Manager needed to find a way of reforming the system without demotivating the sales team. There was also a large number of customers to deal with, many of whom made relatively small orders. The industry at this time also had somewhat of a bad reputation after cracks were noticed in the bridges on the second and third ring roads in Beijing. This was because high-alkali cement was used – and this was what most companies, including Chinefarge, were tending to produce.

In terms of organizational culture, expatriate managers were actually looking for ways in which Chinese cultural values and preferences might be incorporated into the new JV. There was clearly much to do to improve the new venture. The Chinese plant manager thought the key to the change process lay in developing trust and understanding, 'I thought that the biggest problem for the JV was neither the technology nor the management method. The management method was very good, but the problem was how to let the employees accept our way of management and how to make them trust the company.'

Whether or not trust and understanding were the key to the problem, Chinefarge managers and workers somehow began to work successfully towards a solution. By 1998, four years after start-up, production had nearly quadrupled (see table C1), ISO 9000 had been awarded, and working hours lost due to accidents had been reduced to 5 per cent of their 1994 levels. From a 1995 operating loss of 43 million RMB, the company in 1997 achieved its first gross operating profit. The gross operating profit in 1998 was ten times that of 1997, and the plant was close to break-even. Full net profitability was achieved in 1999. In addition, having experienced severe labour conflict in 1994, Chinefarge was one of only four FIEs in the Beijing area to receive the ACFTU 'dual-love' award (*shuang'ai shuangping*) in 1998. The trade union had considered 50,000 FIEs nationally and made only

88 awards to organizations which both demonstrated high standards of people management, and had workforces which expressed high levels of satisfaction with the company. A great honour for a venture which had begun with rioting workers and sabotaged equipment. How had so much changed in such a short time?

▶ The Change Process

Looking back to the start of the joint venture, one expatriate manager was able, in 1998, to identify a long list of operational difficulties:

> Prior to the JV there were 1,300 employees, half of whom were farmers. A very, very low percentage of graduates, I think 3 or 4 per cent. A very weak skills base. There had been inadequate training. The plant itself couldn't produce cement, or the previous work force had never been able to produce cement effectively. Very poor production, very low productivity. Frequent stoppages and shut downs. Very poor quality. There was no performance management system. Wages were very low, and there was no differentiation of pay. Very poor discipline. Very poor motivation – obviously related to the compensation system. The health, safety and environmental systems were very inadequate and the performance very bad. There were accidents and risks not being addressed. So there were morale problems, discipline problems, performance problems, environmental problems, all of these issues.

How then were these issues dealt with, and the change process managed at Chinefarge?

Health, Safety, and Environment (HSE)

One of the earliest actions in the joint venture was to upgrade the health and safety conditions of the plant:

> The company invested over a million RMB and got things fixed. You can see no smoke now . . . Moreover, the employees have to have physical examinations once every two years . . . In meetings and documents, safety is always the biggest focus of attention.

As a measure of the attention the company paid to safety, lost time accidents were cut from 2,200 in 1995, to 104 in 1998.

Information about progress in achieving safety targets is now displayed for staff on a large board in the factory. A third-party safety audit was commissioned and acted upon, and there is now a safety management structure in place including a safety committee and regular safety meetings.

Table C2 Number of employees, October 1994 and October 1998

	Managerial	Technical	Workers
October 1994	80	105	1,131
October 1998	50[a]	20	450

Note: [a] Including some temporary personnel who were re-employed after retirement.
At the end of October 1994, Huaibei Company had 1,316 employees.
In October 1998, Chinefarge had 514 employees.

Overmanning

Another immediate concern prior to the start-up was how to select the reduced workforce of 650 employees for the new JV:

> They decided which people to keep by giving tests, appraisals and interviews. The new foreign boss interviewed all the managers and asked which people they would like to keep. The JV also asked a Hong Kong consulting firm to give the workers tests on geometry, maths and other basic skills.

By October 1998 there were 520 employees, compared to over 1,300 in 1994. The number of technical and managerial staff was also reduced (table C2), though by European standards the plant was still over-manned.

Work attitudes and practices

The first General Manager, an ex-navy officer, took very tough disciplinary measures in an effort to change attitudes and work practices. Following discussion with the workers, an Employee Handbook was quickly produced, which set rules for everyone to follow. After everyone had agreed its contents, it was distributed:

> Everyone got a copy of the Employee Handbook, which clearly stated all the disciplinary measures. He punished some people who violated company regulations. There was a case in which the worker took a brief nap during working time and was fired instantly. A few people played cards during working time, and were fired at once. Employees felt it was too tough. The management communicated a lot to the workers, saying that the enterprise would be hopeless if it remained that way. Discipline was then relatively good during the day, but was really bad at night. People would notify each other secretly when foreigners came. The management then sent four expatriates on patrol for the whole night. The department managers also took turns to keep watch during the night. Workers felt very uncomfortable and could not accept it. Through discipline, severe punishments and a lot of communication, the situation improved gradually.

Another Chinese manager noted, however, that after this GM had left the company the Chinese staff understood that 'you have to exceed the proper limits when you try to put something right'. Despite the departure of the first GM, the pressure on staff to follow regulations continued to be intense. From the perspective of the trade union, the way in which the regulations were enforced was fair:

> If you do not execute the regulations, it is equal to no regulations at all. The JV executes the regulations very strictly, so at the beginning the employees felt the tough measures were unreasonable . . . When they came to ask for help from the TU, we would not give them protection if the punishment was delivered according to regulations. Of course, if the punishment was unreasonable, we would never agree. The TU protects the legal rights of the employees, and at the same time we support the business objectives of the enterprise.

Constant communication and initial tough discipline began, according to a Chinese manager, to change attitudes, 'After several dismissals, people realized that they had to work conscientiously. Now the employees understand that, if you do not punish the bad ones, you are unfair to the good ones.'

When asked how much the increase of production volume had depended on the improvement of attitudes, and how much on technical progress, the Chinese plant manager had this to say:

> Until 1997, 80 per cent depended on the employees' attitudes and initiatives. At the beginning, it was a problem of willingness to work. Later the problem changed into how to do it better. In 1998, technical progress has played a more important role in improving production. I think 50 per cent will depend on technology in 1999. From 120,000 to 300,000 tons per year, attitude was the main factor. But, if we want to increase from 300,000 to 350,000 tons per year, technology will be the main factor.

The Chinese personnel manager neatly summarized these attitude changes at Chinefarge, 'People's attitudes have changed from 'They told me to do it' to 'I do it', and then to 'I should try hard to do it'. Though the production people are all inherited from the old enterprise, both production and revenues have increased significantly.'

Although there were still disagreements about various aspects of Lafarge's management policies, progress has clearly been made. And, according to another Chinese manager, as a result of increased understanding, the tough initial stance on discipline has been relaxed:

> People were made to realize that tolerating wrong behaviour was harmful to other employees, and that punishing those who did not do well represented the interests of most of the people. After a couple of dismissals, things improved significantly. Now the disciplinary measures are looser than before. Only after thorough consideration would the company dismiss a worker.

The second General Manager, who arrived in mid-1996, was seen as 'amiable and scholarly', 'But the discipline was not loosened at all, because the middle managers had taken charge of it themselves, and the employees had realized that discipline was the foundation of good performance and should be stressed.' he critical decision to nurture middle managers had apparently begun to pay off, and there had been a clear transfer of understanding to this group and beyond.

Middle managers

A key both to the change process and to achieving operational efficiency was seen to lie in the understanding and commitment of the Chinese middle managers:

> Middle managers were very important, because many jobs had to be done through them, and they were key to internal communications. The foreign management made the middle managers realize their status, their responsibilities, and the prospects of the company, and got trust from them. They established the channel for communication between senior managers and workers, and the Chinese workforce began to stabilize.

The Chinese plant manager was also very clear that middle managers were key, 'Management methods and ideas had to be implemented through certain channels. The top management could not talk to everybody individually, and had to rely on middle managers to communicate the ideas. Middle managers are a key link between the top managers and the workers.'

The middle managers were important, but initially their attitudes to change were problematical. The plant manager again:

> I was clear that they were the key to the change process, and that to change them would be the most difficult step. How should we change them? By force? What we could get would only be superficial results. By firing some of them? We would get results very soon, but there would be no essential change and it would result in more lies, deceptions and more disloyalty. The most important thing was to change the minds of middle managers. I analysed why they did not want to take responsibility, and what would happen if they did. If a middle manager was tough with his workers, they would write anonymous letters to attack him, and would oppose him. If the manager chose not to take responsibility, he could make the relations harmonious, but the performance could not be good. I talked with the GM, suggesting that we forget the past and ignore all anonymous letters so as to eliminate the source of fear. And, in their performance appraisal, we should look at both statistical results and worker motivation.

It was also recognized that the middle managers did not have enough authority:

> We empowered them with all the management of their subordinates, including wages, appraisal, work arrangements, reallocation and labour contracts. The top

management respected their decisions. Under this system, the middle managers felt much greater pressure, because they found it hard to shirk responsibilities. If the big boss interfered too much, it would be easy to do that. It was also important to motivate the middle managers by means of praise and criticism from time to time. At the beginning I criticized a lot. Though it was not a good way of handling things, I felt it necessary to make criticism in front of others, because I must tell everyone clearly what was right and what was wrong, and what our objective was. When managing a system, sometimes you need to take some tough measures like criticizing or firing if the system is too chaotic.

Although a lot of work had been done in trying to develop middle managers, their initial reaction to being directly responsible for performance appraisal was, according to the Chinese plant manager, less than enthusiastic:

When I empowered the middle managers to take charge of the appraisal, and the wages and bonuses of their subordinates, every one of them objected. Because they knew that, though they would have power, they would have to do it according to our targets, which required them to pay Grade 1 bonuses to only 10 per cent of their people, and to pay no bonus to 30 per cent. The managers said that previously the plant had paid everyone 1000 RMB ($117) at the end of the year. But now the differences were too great and they could not manage to do it. But we forced the change through, leaving no room for compromise. We forced the middle managers to get tough with their own teams and to clearly distinguish between good and bad. Before doing this, we only discussed briefly. There were obstacles because the Chinese partner and our Trade union did not like the idea. But I insisted because I knew what the results would be like. After two months, the middle managers said: 'It's easy to manage people now. Some people even look for things to do when they are free'.

HR procedures

As well as changing attitudes and understanding, key HR systems urgently needed to be put into place. The vice-president in charge of HR summarized the priorities:

. . . defining the organization properly, operating procedures, a new employee hand-book setting out clear rules and expectations, and individual contracts and a contract renewal process based on individual performance with one, two or three-year renew-als. Clear job descriptions were also written, which were then evaluated using the Hay process. Chinefarge are the only joint venture in China using Hay job evaluation for the whole workforce, not just management but every single worker post. An annual appraisal system was established, backed up by training and good commun-ication. Very focused training based on actual needs and gap analysis techniques. A performance-based reward structure was also introduced. In addition there was more open communication and feedback channels, careful recruitment and localiza-tion plans, a career department and professional planning. These measures were seen as some of the key tools for managing performance and improving motivation.

However, as the HR Vice President went on to note, 'A lot of those systems took two years or more to really communicate and get operating efficiently'.

▶ Performance Appraisal

The JV was set up in October 1994, and performance-related pay, seen as one of the key HR procedures, was introduced by the end of the year. Performance appraisal, linked to the Hay system, was carried out once a year in 1995 and 1996, and twice a year from 1997. The results of the appraisal had a significant impact on the wages, year-end bonus and term of contract. But the implementation of performance appraisal was neither quick, nor trouble-free, as a Chinese manager noted:

> In 1995, the company ranked the employees in the whole company by their appraisal results, and then decided pay rises accordingly. Employees were dissatisfied, saying it was unfair because different appraisers were using different criteria. Therefore, in 1996, the company began to decide pay rises and bonuses according to the ranking within the departments so as to avoid the criteria problem.

There were many other complaints:

> Some people came to the Personnel Department to ask why they did not get a rise. We explained: 'The biggest problem for SOEs is that the income is not linked with performance, which means hard-working people get the same as those who do not work at all. We must change our previous attitudes and decide wages according to contributions and performance.'

Traditional attitudes to relationships, as a Chinese middle manager pointed out, were not compatible with the needs of the performance management system, 'At first, we were not used to it, and did not know what to talk about with the workers. Workers were not used to it, either. Gradually we got experienced. At the beginning, the managers were afraid of hurting their *mianzi* [face] and *guanxi* [relationship].' But the Chinese plant manager faced these barriers to performance appraisal in China head-on:

> Before the middle managers do appraisals on their subordinates, I do appraisals on them. I tell them what is good and what is bad, so that they can use my criteria when appraising their people. I do not consider their *mianzi* [face], and so they would not consider this with their people, either.

Nonetheless, persistence was required in the implementation of the performance appraisal system. For the first two years nobody apparently received a bad appraisal, and training needs were just 'wish-lists unconnected to the needs of the business'. The system still requires constant re-training of staff:

Every time we were about to launch the process, which is normally run on an annual basis, we put all the line managers and supervisors through a certain amount of training again. Why do we have this process, what is the significance of it, and what are the dangers if we don't operate it in the way in which it is supposed to be operated?

Even so, 'We often end up, as we did before, with a lot of strange data which really is meaningless, because people are not being honest about how they rate individuals. That is of no benefit to the individual and is certainly of no benefit to the organization'. The appraisal system has also required continual modification and simplification, 'The principle has been to try and keep it as simple as possible. I think out of the 520 people here, 484 of them actually just have this simple one-page assessment document which is completed on their behalf by their immediate boss.'

By 1998 the appraisal system had become, according to the Chinese HR manager, a very useful, 'hard' management tool, 'Theoretically, there are three purposes: Firstly, it can improve the communications between the superior and the subordinate; secondly, it can help find training needs; thirdly, the results of the appraisal are linked with wages and bonuses.'

Chinese notions of equality of pay were difficult to overcome, but progress began to be made. By the third year 'we had very, very few questions or complaints and a much higher degree of acceptance'. By this time staff, particularly the key group of middle managers had been introduced to the job evaluation system, and been involved in the salary review process. Eventually, the middle managers came to understand the importance of the process:

> Since we had empowered the managers with a lot of work responsibilities, if they could not be fair with their subordinates, they would find it impossible to lead their groups. After thorough consideration, they realized that being fair was the only right thing to do, and that being fair meant being responsible not only for the company but for the employees themselves.

There was gradual acceptance of the new ways of thinking by Chinese staff:

> Previously, in the SOE, peasant contract workers, township contract workers and regular workers got different treatment on wages and welfare. The JV stressed ability and performance, and ignored *guanxi* and seniority, which had been important in the SOE. By doing this, the JV created equal opportunities for everybody. So, after one year, the employees got used to the new way of working.

Although there was pressure on the expatriate HR Vice President to produce a performance appraisal scheme with greater equality, he was not persuaded:

> I think a good counter-argument to the call for greater equality would be to look at the number of individuals who one year received a poor performance and the next

year received an excellent one as a result of seeing the difference in reward being applied between the excellent and the poor performers.

There were also other, practical, reasons for being tough on the appraisals:

We have taken a very gentle approach to our overall staffing levels at the plant. We started off with 650 and we now still have over 500 for what is a medium-sized plant, which in other countries would have between fifty and a hundred workers. After taking into account China's particular circumstances, where you sub-contract much less and you do a lot more work yourselves with your own employees, we still have probably many more workers than we really require on a year-by-year basis. So if the weakest 10 to 15 per cent, say, feel de-motivated by receiving a series of poor performance ratings over a number of years, I think that would constitute a reasonable motivation for them to find employment somewhere else. Alternatively, we counsel them and see whether there might be some others ways of improving their contribution through retraining or reassignment to something more productive.

By 1998, other Chinese staff were beginning to see the advantages of the culture change which had accompanied the introduction of performance appraisal:

Compared with the previous practice of deciding bonuses according to *guanxi*, most people prefer the performance-related payment the new management implemented. Now, when there are problems in production, the employees do not leave before the problem is settled, even if no one asks them to do so. Previously, no matter how big the problem was, people would head for home immediately after five o'clock.

▶ Reward Systems

Not all the skills required for the new venture were available locally, and Chinefarge was forced to recruit in other locations such as Beijing, and therefore to pay premium salaries. For the Chinese staff from the locality such reward differentials were difficult to accept. A senior Chinese manager had this to say:

The wage gap is a phenomenon which I myself dislike very much. We are trying to eliminate it. I expect to get rid of it in a period that is not too long – maybe three years. The gap in wages is a method the company has taken to settle the recruitment problem. But it is unfair. I acknowledge that we have to pay the external people high wages because otherwise they would leave very soon. But the fact that we are paying the inherited staff lower wages only because they would not leave is problematical. The senior management needs to settle this problem. The only way is to raise the wages of inherited staff. Since we are still losing money, we can only make efforts to improve the situation gradually. When we make money, we will be in a better position to deal with it.

The perspective of the expatriate senior HR manager on reward differentials was, however, somewhat different:

> It's not a problem so long as we are prepared to respect the different markets that exist. So in terms of recruitment, if we are recruiting somebody who is coming from a much higher-value market, somebody with scarce skills which are not available in the local area – for instance, a skilled finance professional with experience of operating international accounting principles and working within a foreign joint venture – it is simply impossible to recruit somebody like that locally, so we have to go to the Beijing market and, if we want to keep the individual, we have to pay them a competitive salary for the market in which they are most closely linked . . . If we started to see a big drop in the motivation of our local Huairou workforce, or if we started to see a number of local Huairou managers resigning for salary reasons, we would know that our salaries were incorrect. But actually all our data suggests that we are one of the better payers, one of the better salary providers in the Huairou area and that although there is a gap, and there will be a gap so long as there are different markets, I think the system that we have in place is a reasonable compromise.

▶ Corporate Culture, Recruitment and Retention

Despite problems arising from differential treatment of staff with regard to pay, Lafarge's basic attitudes to people (see Exhibit 1, Principles of Action) were felt by one Chinese manager to be close to Chinese cultural beliefs and so helpful in retention:

> It is the corporate culture of Lafarge to make the employees feel at home when working in the company. This fits the Chinese culture, and is also advocated by Chinefarge. We try to make our employees feel the company is reliable and they do not need to worry. This is very important to the strategic development of the enterprise. If our 'backbone' people want to leave, we will be left in a difficult situation. People who want to leave are all people we don't want to lose. It is a challenge to make them happy and keep them.

The reasons for Lafarge's care for people are partly pragmatic:

> The reason why Lafarge cares so much for people has a lot to do with the industry. The cement industry requires big investments and a long-term commitment. There are no quick returns. Therefore, to be successful in this industry, the company has to have a long-term strategic vision. So we have to give a lot of consideration to the long-term development of people and community relations.

The fact that Lafarge is seen to be committed to China may also be a factor in both recruitment and retention:

I've seen a big improvement in people's consciousness about being part of the Lafarge group, and that in itself is starting to generate loyalty and a desire to be part of this organization in the longer term. And that is particularly being helped by the fact that Lafarge is seen to be developing rapidly and further in China with the signing of further join ventures so it demonstrates to most of the employees that there is a very long-term commitment to China by Lafarge.

Certainly, by 1998 staff turnover was only 4 per cent.

Communication: internal

In the early years of the joint venture, both expatriate and Chinese managers noted a lack of mutual trust. By 1998 Chinese managers had clear opinions about the kinds of activity that had helped to improve relations:

There used to be serious distrust between the Chinese and the foreign partners. At the end of 1995, there were more than 20 expatriates in the JV, and the company held a big Christmas party. All the employees saw a movie, chatted, and danced together. This was very effective in improving the understanding and relationship between the foreign management and the Chinese employees. After that, with working conditions getting better, the misunderstanding and tension were gradually reduced.

Another Chinese manager similarly connected organized social activity with an improvement in morale:

In the last two years, the situation has improved and the company has won a good reputation in Huairou County. At the fourth anniversary of the JV, the company spent 100,000 RMB and organized a 'Family Day' for all the employees. More than 1300 people got together, and enjoyed buffet, entertainment and a tug-of-war for a whole day. The company also holds birthday parties for managers in order to improve the relationship between local and externally recruited managers. Now the company has quite good cohesion.

As well as using social activities, meetings, bulletin boards, suggestion boxes and an 'irregular' employee newspaper, care was taken to involve and inform the workers through traditional channels:

The GM reports to the Workers' Congress on the state of the enterprise, problems and objectives, and solicits suggestions from the employees' representatives. Suggestions are collected and read out at the meeting. They are mostly about issues closely related to the employees' interests, like safety, labour protection, wages and welfare. There are also suggestions about operations, like ways to lower the cost. At the end of every year, the Union makes a summary report to the Congress on the implementation of the suggestions put forward at the last meeting. When the employees have problems, they would more often prefer to tell the trade union representative, who would go to talk with the management about it, and then tell the employees the results or any information they have got.

'Excellent workers' are selected and rewarded publicly:

> Every month, we select an Employee of the Month. Every month, the departments recommend an employee to HR and describe how well he has performed in this month using a hundred words. Then the HR convenes a meeting of all department managers, at which people read the descriptions and vote. The person that gets the most votes is honoured as the Employee of the Month. The second and third persons after him would be praised as excellent workers of the month. They get rewards like bicycles, or pressure cookers, and have their picture taken with the General Manager.

Communication: external

As well as paying considerable attention to internal communications, Chinefarge also manages its relationship with the local community with some care:

> It is one of the Lafarge principles that we should let the community know what we are doing. We make a lot of contributions to education in Huairou. We donated computers to the Huairou Primary School, and sports facilities to another school. On Teachers' Day the GM goes to the schools to give gifts to the teachers and the children.

The expatriate HR Vice President of Lafarge China was also clear about the broader role of communications in reinforcing the relationship between Chinefarge and the parent group:

> From the HR perspective, having very good communication systems with our employees is important in making them feel a part of the Lafarge group within China and globally. So that where people have come from other companies, or from joint venturepartners, they begin to identify first of all with the part of Lafarge that they are working in, the plant or the sales operation, but secondly that they also identify with being part of Lafarge in China. As far as external communications are concerned, it is the whole range of public relations activities, relationship with the media and the government, with recruitment sources such as universities.

▶ Training and Development

The average training spend per person by 1998 was $150, up from $100 the previous year. Chinese managers appeared satisfied with the Lafarge approach to training, 'Lafarge emphasizes systematic training. This is a very good thing to do, and is the key to improving performance.' The importance of Chinese middle managers to the change process, as well as to the effective day-to-day running of the plant, was reflected in the amount and type of training they received. Particularly significant, according to one of these managers, was a period of time spent overseas:

> Ten middle managers, including me, were sent to France. We stayed for a week in a plant and another week in the R&D centre. That was a shocking experience. Chinefarge has come from a total mess to a plant with quite good production, and we all felt we were good. The company also said we had made great progress and that our management was quite advanced in the cement industry in China. But compared with plants abroad, we still have a very long way to go. The overseas tour was very helpful to us.

▶ Expatriates and Localization

As well as local staff issues, consideration had also been given to expatriate staffing. Having begun the joint venture in 1994 with 20 expatriates, by 1998 this number was much reduced. According to the expatriate Vice President in charge of HR:

> When we first operated we had more than ten expatriates at the plant. When I arrived in August 1996, one of my priorities was to look at how to effectively localize those positions. The two choices really are to train up the more junior managers already in place in the plant, or to bring in Chinese managers from outside. And in a sense we did both.

A Chinese manager similarly felt in 1998 that it was time to localize, 'Now the management emphasizes localization. Because the Chinese employees have got used to the management style of the foreign partner, it is time to use Chinese people as substitutes.'

The arrival of an ethnic Chinese General Manager was significant for the Chinese staff:

> Since foreigners were brought up in different environments and cultures, there are bound to be some difficulties for them to adapt to the local situation. So Chinefarge is gradually localising its management. After the American GM and the French GM, we finally have an ethnic Chinese General Manager with China experience. This is very good . . . HR and finance has also been localized. This has facilitated communications. Before, communications were affected by translation. The words of a Chinese person might be misunderstood if you fail to pay attention to the expressions and intonation.

The expatriate Vice President in charge of HR interpreted localization more broadly:

> By localization I mean two things. One is recruitment of high quality Chinese managers to replace expatriates. And secondly, where we have expatriates, to ensure that they have the skills and knowledge to be able to operate effectively in the local environment. And that means Chinese language skills and it means awareness of Chinese business practices and culture. Thirdly, it is early recruitment: at the top end it is experienced professionals and managers, who can come in quickly and be effective in senior management positions, in managing our new joint ventures, and also at the other end, identifying and recruiting high potential young graduates in advance of our new plant needs.

But not all Chinese staff were enthusiastic about localization:

> Generally speaking, my feeling is that it is easier to communicate with foreigners, because they are not so complicated as the Chinese. But the communication is to a large extent limited to work. It is very difficult to communicate feelings with them. Not easy to make friends with them.

▶ The Trade Union

Chinefarge expatriate managers also had to decide how they were to work with the ACFTU:

> There is nothing to be gained by fighting with the union. And there is a lot to be gained by having a very good relationship. There is only one union, the All China Federation of Trade Unions. They are all linked to that and it is a very strong link between the union and the local party so there is a high degree of, let's say, party and government control of unions and their leadership.

From the Chinese perspective there had been significant changes in the role of the trade union since the start of the joint venture:

> Previously the Union had a subordinate status, and had to do what the Party Committee and the General Manager wanted it to do. Now it works independently in the enterprise, having its own opinions on certain issues, and using the TU funds as it sees fit. The TU can stand up for the employees' interests. The TU represents the interests of the employees, and, at the same time, they support the interests of the enterprise, too.

The relationship between the management and the Union was seen as beneficial to the business:

Internally it means that we have the support of the union for difficult decisions that we may have to take with respect to people, managing people, in the future. So if, for instance, we have to fire somebody for whatever reason, we have the understanding with the unions that where we are complying with the law and treating people fairly, that they will support the actions that we take, however tough they might be in individual cases. Externally, it means that our reputation in the local community with the local government with the local party is positive and we build up a climate of good opinion and support for what we wish to do in terms of developing and building our business. So we are very proud of the Dual Love award that we received earlier this year. It's an award which has given us good publicity, not just in the local Beijing area, but also internationally.

By late 1997 the company was able to pay more attention to its customers. The Australian-Chinese GM joined who joined Chinefarge in September of that year began to address the problem of the poor recovery of debt, and also made significant changes to the sales department:

Because of the 'Triangular Debt' (*sanjiaozhai*) problem in China, the company had very high accounts receivable when I came. We changed the compensation scheme for the salespeople. Previously a salesperson got the same pay every month of the year. Now the monthly wages are linked to sales volume and retrieving receivables. A sale is concluded after the money is back. If the sales person chooses a customer who does not pay, his pay will be influenced. This year, our receivables have all been retrieved. Our total figure for receivables has been lowered, too. The change in the sales system met some obstacles. At the beginning, the salespeople feared that, if we were to refuse to sell to customers who do not pay in time, it would be much harder to sell. The salespeople were afraid that their income could be influenced by the new salary structure. So we gave them three months to decide which salary scheme they would like to choose, the old one or the new one. In this period, if the new salary was lower than the old fixed monthly pay, they could get the old pay. At the end of the three months, they all chose the new scheme. Now this system has been implemented for a year. The salespeople are working harder than before, and are more conscientious in choosing customers, because they have bigger responsibilities.

He also addressed the number of small customers that the joint venture was dealing with:

We also did customer segmentation and narrowed our range of customers. Previously the company had many customers and it was quite chaotic. Now we pay special attention to a few key customers. Because of the special features and quality of our cement, they won't use other cement any more. We have ten key customers, who account for 80–90 per cent of our total sales. This enables us to improve our service. We cooperate with our customers to lower their costs. Though our cement is of higher price, our technical service enables them to lower the cost of their concrete by using less cement in the process.

He was now able to focus attention more on the external environment:

Thanks to the efforts of the two previous General Managers, the company's situation had improved significantly when I came. The employees were much better motivated. What I have done is change practices related to the market. First of all, since we did not have competitive advantage in the market we were in, the company changed its target market and began producing low-alkali cement. Our previous product had a very competitive market. In 1997, we changed our product strategy and began producing low-alkali cement, for which there is big demand in the Beijing area. Many of the aggregates would have an alkali-aggregate reaction (AAR) with alkali in the cement, and cause the buildings to crack within ten to fifteen years. One example is that the main bridges of the second and third ring road in Beijing have got cracks on them, because they were built with high-alkali cement. Our strategy was to produce higher-class cement at a higher price, and to differentiate our product into a niche market. We have been enlarging our cement production. The designed capacity was 250 thousand tons per year. But next year we expect to produce 420 thousand tons. If we can do it, we will make a profit even without a second line. The main issues are technology, management, human resource development, and marketing. Secondly, we promoted teamwork, and have introduced a customer focus. We have made people look externally rather than only internally. That is, people have begun to think how the company can survive in this market and how we can keep our competitive advantage.

Lafarge now began to plan their next joint venture in China, and to reflect on what had been the key elements of this successful change process.

Exhibit 1: Lafarge: Principles of action

For the Lafarge Group, strategy implies an ambition, some demands and a sense of responsibility. It is only when these components are brought together, that actions become sustainable and long-term.

Our principles of action have been drawn up and worked on in consultation with all concerned. They epitomize our ambitions, our convictions, our code of conduct and our values.

Our ambition

To be a world leader in construction materials

- Be recognized as an important participant and shape the future of our businesses through our capacity to innovate
- Be a leader in a competitive environment
- Pursue long-term strategies
- Adopt an international approach

Our responsibilities

To anticipate and meet our customers' needs

- Create a perceived difference and be the supplier of choice
- Serve our customers better by knowing them better
- Contribute to the development and progress of the construction industry

To enhance the value of our shareholders' investments and gain their trust

- To provide shareholders with a competitive return on their investment
- To provide them with clear information
- To respect the interests of our partners and minority shareholders

To make our employees the heart of our company

- To base legitimate authority on the ability to contribute to the company's success
- To develop mutual respect and trust
- To provide employees with equitable compensation and a fulfilling professional environment

To gain from our increasing diversity

- To make our cultural diversity an asset
- To delegate responsibility with accountability and control
- To develop an effective cross-operational management approach
- To make use of synergies and share know-how

To respect the common interest

- To participate in the life of the communities where we operate
- To operate responsibly toward the environment
- To be guided by the principles of integrity, openness and respect in our commitments

Acknowledgements

Research for this case was funded and supported by the China Europe International Business School (CEIBS) in Shanghai, and was carried out with the help of CEIBS research assistant Zhang Qiang.

Case Assignments

1   Describe the work ethics that were originally present in Huaibei Mining Company.
2   Discuss positive and negative aspects related to the recruitment of personnel through *guanxi* (personal relations and acquaintances).
3   On the basis of the case, discuss the cultural barriers that had an impact on the introduction and application of individual performance appraisals.
4   Discuss the problems related to the middle managers and how the management tried to solve these.
5   Explain what is meant by the 'triangular debt' problem and discuss how the management coped with this problem.

chapter

4

Cultural Diversity and MNCs

▶ Purpose

The overall purpose of this chapter is to generate an awareness of the relativity of one's own cultural framework and to question the notion that there is 'one best way' of managing and organizing. Our starting point is the concept of national culture. We then review the main findings from two of the most influential studies of work-related aspects of national culture, those of Geert Hofstede and Fons Trompenaars. Finally, we summarize our own recent research findings in regard to cultural differences.

▶ Why Consider Culture?

MNCs are radically different from export-based firms not least because of their foreign subsidiaries. Not only does physical distance pose a challenge for effective communication, even more so there is the challenge represented by cultural differences. In Chapter 2 we indicated that some MNCs have regarded cultural differences as so important that they have preferred to operate as multi-domestics with decision-making, management style and product development highly decentralized. The attitude is that people in the subsidiaries know best and should be allowed to go their own ways. Such was the attitude in the Dutch electronics firm Philips for most of the previous century. The downside of this approach is the fiefdom and 'not-invented-here' mentality, which resulted in Philips' North American subsidiary refusing to adopt the Philips video recorder (V2000) and opting instead for the rival Japanese model. However, many MNCs, including Philips since 1987, require a much greater degree of coordination, particularly in regard to learning. To do so, these firms must develop common practices and common values. If foreign subsidiaries are to be integrated for knowledge-sharing purposes, a starting point is an understanding of the mindsets of subsidiary management and employees in terms of their work-related values. The management challenge for many MNCs is to be able to adapt their organizations to culturally distinct environments without losing organizational consistency.

The Concept of Culture

Culture refers to the systems of meaning – values, beliefs, expectations and goals – shared by members of a particular group of people and that distinguish them from members of other groups. It is a product of 'the collective programming of the mind' (Hofstede, 1991), that is, it is acquired through regular interaction with other members of the group. Cultural differences can be found at many different levels, professional, class and regional, but it is particularly potent at the national level because of generations of socialization into the national community. As individuals, we generally only become aware of our own culture when confronted by another. However, what we usually observe are the artefacts of cultural dissimilarity – the numerous and often pronounced differences in greeting rituals, dress codes, forms of address and taste. The underlying system of values is, however, neither readily observable nor readily comprehensible. The core differences in values between cultures go back to questions of what works for ensuring survival in relation to the natural environment. The Dutch have had to cope with flooding, the Swiss with avalanches, the Russians and the Finns with long cold winters. Trying to understand the origins of various cultural differences is an immense task that lies outside the remit of this book. What is achievable, though, is to equip MNC managers with sufficient insight to be able to determine what values are of particular importance to take into account when designing management systems.

Classifying National Cultures

Dissecting and explaining any foreign culture is potentially a never-ending exercise. As an alternative to in-depth single-country studies scholars have attempted to classify cultures in relation to one another by using a few, relatively broad fundamental dimensions that are particularly relevant to management practice. This method means that cultures can be clustered, thereby pinpointing which cultures are similar enough to make a standardized management approach viable. Two frequently cited contributions are the work of two Dutchmen, Geert Hofstede and Fons Trompenaars.

Hofstede's Four Dimensions

Between 1967 and 1973 Hofstede surveyed 116,000 IBM employees in 40 different nations using a questionnaire containing about 150 questions enquiring about their preferences in terms of management style and work environment

Table 4.1 Small and large power distance

Small Power Distance	Large Power Distance
Those in power should try to be less powerful than they are.	Those in power should try to look as powerful as possible.
People at various power levels feel less threatened and more prepared to trust people.	Other people are a potential threat to one's power and can rarely be trusted.

(see Hofstede, 1980a; 1983, 1984). Among these 150 items were 32, which Hofstede labelled as work-related values. For each of the 40 nations he computed an average score in relation to each of the 32 work-related values. Taking the 32 'average-nation' values he generated a correlation matrix, which was then factor analysed. The initial analysis revealed three factors, the largest of which Hofstede sub-divided thereby creating four value dimensions: *Power Distance, Uncertainty Avoidance, Individualism–Collectivism,* and *Masculinity–Femininity.* Thereafter he compared each of the 40 national cultures in his sample. It should be noted that these dimensions are not intended to describe individuals but are descriptions of national norms.

Power distance

This dimension indicates the extent to which a society expects and accepts a high degree of inequality in institutions and organizations. In a country with a large power distance organizations are characterized by formal hierarchies and by subordinates who are reluctant to challenge their superiors. The boss is very much the boss. In a country with a small power distance subordinates expect to be consulted and the ideal boss is a resourceful democrat rather than a benevolent autocrat. Examples of small and large power distance are given in table 4.1.

Uncertainty avoidance

This refers to the degree to which a society prefers predictability, security and stability. In societies with high scores on this index there is an emotional need for rules, written and unwritten. Thus organizations in these societies will deploy formal rules in order to ensure that work situations are highly structured with clearly defined task roles and responsibilities. Deviant ideas and behaviours are not tolerated. Societies in which uncertainty avoidance is strong are also characterized by higher levels of anxiety that in turns results in a pronounced need to work hard. Table 4.2 shows the difference between weak and strong uncertainty avoidance.

Table 4.2 Weak and strong uncertainty avoidance

Weak Uncertainty Avoidance	Strong Uncertainty Avoidance
There is more willingness to take risks. Uncertain situations are acceptable.	There is great concern with security in life. Career stability is needed.

Table 4.3 Collectivist and individualist attitudes

Collectivist	Individualist
Identity is based in the social system. Order is provided by the organization.	Identity is based in the individual. Autonomy, variety and pleasure are sought in the system.

Table 4.4

Feminine	Masculine
People and the environment are important. Quality of life is what counts. Service provides the drive. One sympathizes with the unfortunate.	Money and things are important. Performance is what counts. Ambition provides the drive. One admires the successful achiever.

Individualism–collectivism

This dimension relates to the extent to which people prefer to take care of themselves and their immediate families rather than being bound to some wider collectivity such as the extended family or clan. In terms of organizational life, in highly individualistic societies there will be a sharp distinction between work and personal life. Task will prevail over relationships. Also, individuals will prefer work settings in which they can make their own decisions. Table 4.3 shows the difference between collectivist and individualist positions.

Masculinity–femininity

Masculine societies value assertiveness, competitiveness and materialism as opposed to the 'feminine' values of relationships and the quality of life. In terms of the workplace organizations in feminine societies will aim for harmonious relations with a strong emphasis on social partnership. In masculine societies organizations will be more task-oriented and motivation more materialistic. Individual assertiveness is acceptable and appreciated. Within nearly all societies men score higher in terms of masculinity. Table 4.4 shows the difference between feminine and masculine attitudes.

Table 4.5 Hofstede's rankings

Country	Power distance		Individualism		Masculinity		Uncertainty avoidance	
	Index	Rank	Index	Rank	Index	Rank	Index	Rank
Argentina	49	35–6	46	22–3	56	20–1	86	10–15
Australia	36	41	90	2	61	16	51	37
Austria	11	53	55	18	79	2	70	24–5
Belgium	65	20	75	8	54	22	94	5–6
Brazil	69	14	38	26–7	49	27	76	21–2
Canada	39	39	80	4–5	52	24	48	41–2
Chile	63	24–5	23	38	28	46	86	10–15
Colombia	67	17	13	49	64	11–12	80	20
Costa Rica	35	42–4	15	46	21	48–9	86	10–15
Denmark	18	51	74	9	16	50	23	51
Equador	78	8–9	8	52	63	13–14	67	28
Finland	33	46	63	17	26	47	59	31–2
France	68	15–16	71	10–11	43	35–6	86	10–15
Germany (F.R.)	35	42–4	67	15	66	9–10	65	29
Great Britain	35	42–4	89	3	66	9–10	35	47–8
Greece	60	27–8	35	30	57	18–19	112	1
Guatemala	95	2–3	6	53	37	43	101	3
Hong Kong	68	15–16	25	37	57	18–19	29	49–50
Indonesia	78	8–9	14	47–8	46	30–1	48	41–2
India	77	10–11	48	21	56	20–1	40	45
Iran	58	19–20	41	24	43	35–6	59	31–2
Ireland	28	49	70	12	68	7–8	35	47–8
Israel	13	52	54	19	47	29	81	19
Italy	50	34	76	7	70	4–5	75	23
Jamaica	45	37	39	25	68	7–8	13	52
Japan	54	33	46	22–3	95	1	92	7
Korea (S)	60	27–8	187	43	39	41	85	16–17
Malaysia	104	1	26	36	50	25–6	36	46
Mexico	81	5–6	30	32	69	6	82	18
Netherlands	38	40	80	4–5	14	51	53	35
Norway	31	47–8	69	13	8	52	50	38
New Zealand	22	50	79	6	58	17	49	39–40
Pakistan	55	32	14	47–8	50	25–6	70	24–5
Panama	95	2–3	11	51	44	34	86	10–15
Peru	64	21–3	16	45	42	37–8	87	9
Philippines	94	4	32	31	64	11–12	44	44
Portugal	63	24–5	27	33–5	31	45	104	2
South Africa	49	36–7	65	16	63	13–14	49	39–40
Salvador	66	18–19	19	42	40	40	94	5–6
Singapore	74	13	20	39–41	48	28	8	53
Spain	57	31	51	20	42	37–8	86	10–15
Sweden	31	47–8	71	10–11	5	52	29	49–50
Switzerland	34	45	68	14	70	4–5	58	33
Taiwan	58	29–30	17	44	45	32–3	69	26
Thailand	64	21–3	20	39–41	34	44	64	30
Turkey	66	18–19	37	28	45	31–3	85	16–17
Uruguay	61	26	36	29	38	42	100	4
United States	40	38	91	1	62	15	46	43
Venezuela	81	5–6	12	50	73	3	76	21–2
Yugoslavia	76	12	27	33–5	21	48–9	88	8
Regions:								
East Africa	64	21–3	27	33–5	41	39	52	36
West Africa	77	10–11	20	39–41	46	30–1	54	34
Arab countries	80	7	38	26–7	53	23	68	27

Source: Hofstede, 1991. Reprinted with permission.

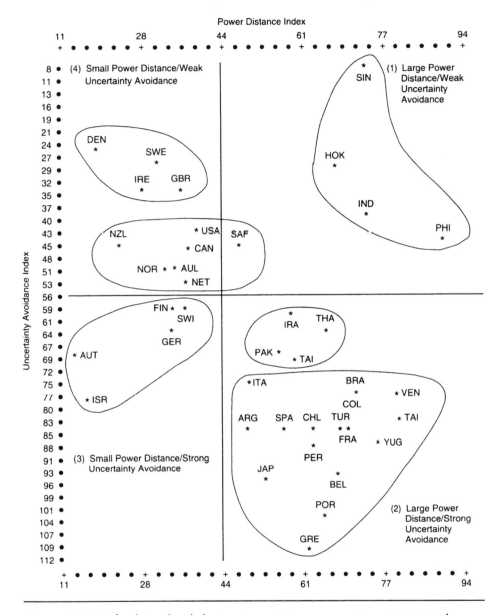

Figure 4.1 Hofstede's cultural clusters: Power Distance versus Uncertainty Avoidance
Source: Hofstede, 1980b. Reprinted with permission

Table 4.5 displays index scores and rankings.

Having ranked countries in terms of four dimensions Hofstede then plotted them along two dimensions at a time. In so doing he identified various country clusters (see figures 4.1, 4.2 and 4.3).

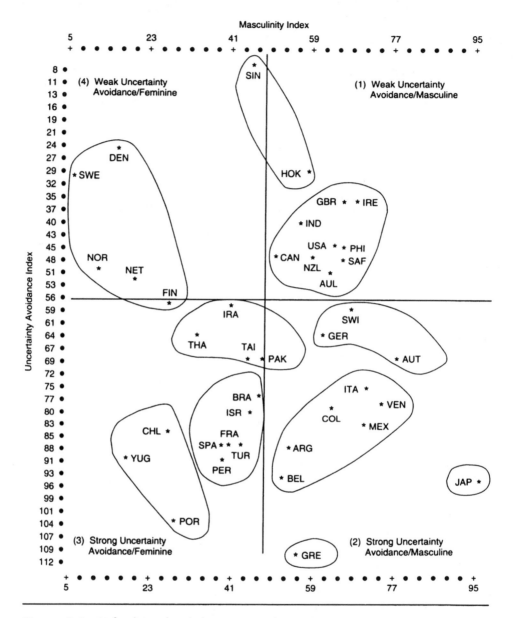

Figure 4.2 Hofstede's cultural clusters: Masculinity-Femininity versus Uncertainty Avoidance
Source: Hofstede, 1980b. Reprinted with permission

Although the boundaries denoting the clusters are somewhat arbitrary, Hofstede argues that they enable us to draw some broad distinctions between the Nordic, Anglo, Latin, and Asian countries. For example, while the Scandinavian and Anglo-Saxon countries are similar in terms of the *Uncertainty Avoidance, Power*

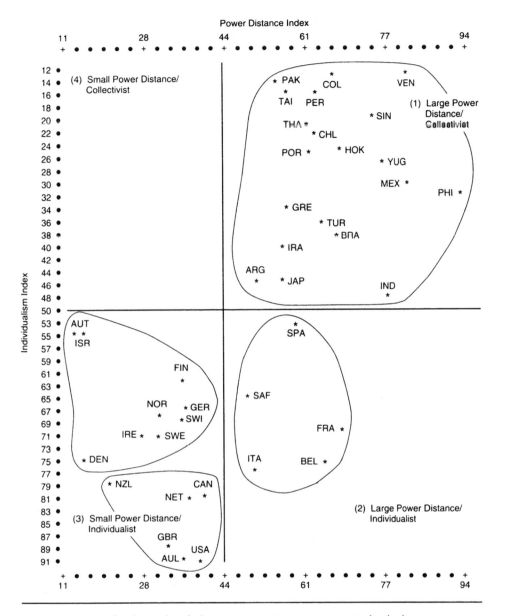

Figure 4.3 Hofstede's cultural clusters: Power Distance versus Individualism
Source: Hofstede, 1980b. Reprinted with permission

Distance, and *Individualism–Collectivism* dimensions, they are markedly different in relation to the *Masculinity–Femininity* dimension. Latin countries coalesce markedly in terms of uncertainty avoidance and power distance, whereas Asian countries such as India and Malaysia are distinguished by their combination of large *Power Distance* and weak *Uncertainty Avoidance*.

▶ Hofstede and US Management Theories

Many MNCs apply organizational designs, systems and procedures in foreign subsidiaries that are derived from, and that are successful in, their own culture. Pay-for-performance, for example, can be successful in the USA or the UK but has often been experienced as difficult to apply in Scandinavia, Germany or large parts of Asia. The assumption behind the transplantation of management practices is that management theories are universal and that what works well in one context will work well in another. Hofstede (1980b) was one of the first to not only question this assumption but to do so on the basis of a theoretical analysis. In particular he focused on American theories of motivation, leadership and organization and their applicability in other cultural contexts. His analysis has important implications for the management of subsidiaries.

David McClelland, Abraham Maslow and Frederick Herzberg developed motivation theories that are, in Hofstede's view, peculiarly American. They all assume a universal achievement motive. For example, Maslow's hierarchy of human needs postulates that when the more basic needs such as physiological needs, security and social needs have been met there is a need for esteem and thereafter for 'self-actualization'. Once our lower needs are satisfied we attempt to satisfy our higher needs.

Hofstede argues that the concept of the achievement motive presupposes (a) a willingness to accept risk (equivalent to weak *Uncertainty Avoidance*) and (b) a concern with performance (equivalent to strong *Masculinity*). This combination is a feature peculiar to the US and other Anglo-Saxon cultures. In the case of Germany or Austria while the *Masculinity* index is strong, *Uncertainty Avoidance* is also relatively strong. Thus the fundamental motivation in these societies is directed towards meeting security needs rather than self-actualization. While Sweden and Norway share the weak *Uncertainty Avoidance* of the USA, on the other hand they have much lower scores on the *Masculinity* index. Thus for these countries while security needs are not fundamentally important, neither is self-actualization. Instead there is an emphasis on the social aspects to the work environment resulting in a de-emphasis on inter-individual competition.

Hofstede's overview of American leadership theories takes in the work of Douglas McGregor (Theory X versus Theory Y), Renis Likert (System 4 management), and Robert R. Blake with Jane S. Mouton (the Managerial Grid). All of these advocate participation in the manager's decisions by subordinates. However, these theories take it for granted that it is the manager's responsibility to initiate the participation. Manager-initiated participative management is, argues Hofstede, a product of the middle position of the USA on the *Power Distance* dimension. In countries with smaller *Power Distances* such as Sweden, Norway and Germany the assumption that it is the manager who unilaterally initiates participation is unacceptable. Industrial democracy is a pronounced feature of work-life in these countries. Interestingly though Scandinavian and German industrial democracy are very different. In Germany, with its strong *Uncertainty Avoidance*, industrial democracy was first established through legislation prior to being put into practice in work life (*Mitbestimmung*). In Norway and Sweden, weak in terms of *Uncertainty Avoidance*, the origins of industrial democracy lie in local experiments. The legislative framework followed an established practice. One implication is that Scandinavian and German managers who move to the USA must learn to manage more autocratically in order to be effective.

Hofstede's analysis of US thinking on the nature of the organization focuses on the 'hire and fire' assumption. In the extremely individualistic US, with only weak mutual loyalty between company and employees, this is tenable. However, warns Hofstede, US organizations may get themselves into considerable trouble in more collectivistic environments if they attempt to operate in this manner.

The core implication of Hofstede's analysis for MNCs is that identical personnel policies may have very different effects in different countries. The dilemma for the MNC is whether to adapt to the local culture or to try and change it. Particularly in the case of acquisitions, the latter may prove to be a difficult route to follow. However, whichever route is taken, it must be based on a thorough familiarization with the other culture.

▶ Criticism of Hofstede

Hofstede's research has been criticized on a number of counts. The first area of criticism concerns the methodology Hofstede employed. Tayeb (1996) objects to the fact that Hofstede's research is entirely based on an attitude-survey question-naire, which he contends is the least appropriate way of studying culture. However, for comparative purposes it is very efficient. Another, and particularly significant, methodological criticism concerns the deliberate choices Hofstede made in defining his four factors particularly in regard to *Individualism–Collectivism*. Bond (2002) reminds us that this dimension was a product of a decision by Hofstede to sub-divide a large factor that emerged through the original three-factor solution. Hofstede labelled the other factor *Power Distance*. Had Hofstede remained true to his original three-factor solution, his findings would have been very different. Bond concludes that it is unlikely that the USA would have been located at an extreme, as it is in terms of the *Individualism–Collectivism* dimension. Without this finding much of Hofstede's critique of the applicability of US management theories falls by the wayside. Bond also questions the validity of this dimension, which comprises six work goals. Personal time, freedom, and challenge were added together to constitute the individualism end of the dimension; use of skills, physical conditions, and training were added together to define the collectivism end of the bi-polar factor. As Bond (2002) remarks: 'The first three work goals bear obvious relations to individualism . . . How the last three work goals described anything resembling collectivism was, however, a mystery to many.'

A second and the most common criticism is that the sample is not representative, because it is drawn from a single company comprising middle-class employees. Hofstede's response has been to argue that IBM employees in different countries constitute suitably matched samples so that the work-value distance between an average IBM employee in Germany and one in the UK is equivalent to that between an average German adult and an average UK adult. The question is though whether IBM, which has a powerful US-derived organization culture, may have socialized its employees so powerfully that their values do not reflect aspects of local national cultures, or, equally that this socialization may have varied from country to country (McSweeney, 2002). Hofstede's (1994: 10) answer is to argue that work organizations are not 'total institutions' and 'that the values of employees cannot be changed by an employer because they were acquired when the employees were children'. This means that the matching of his different samples is based on occupational equivalency. However, even this assumption has been questioned. McSweeney (2002) observes that similar occupations have very different entry requirements and social status from country to country.

A third criticism is that four dimensions are simply inadequate to convey cultural differences. Some years later Hofstede, together with Bond, (1988) identified a fifth dimension, which they refer to as *Long-term versus Short-term Orientation*. Long-term refers to such values as perseverance and thrift, while short-term values include respect for 'saving face', tradition and social obligations in the sense of reciprocation of greetings, favours and gifts. A long-term orientation is mostly found in East Asian countries, in particular in China, Hong Kong, Taiwan, Japan and South Korea. Hofstede attributes the rapid economic growth of these societies to their long-term orientation. However, Hofstede (1994) acknowledges that his research on the implications of differences along this dimension is as yet not sufficient to allow the composition of a table of differences similar to those for the other four dimensions. Moreover, simply adding a fifth dimension does not counter the criticism of over-simplification.

A fourth objection is that Hofstede's four dimensions may not be the most important. It is not improbable that Hofstede would have 'found' different national cultures had he used additional, amended, or alternative questions (McSweeney, 2002).

Finally, his research has been criticized as dated. It is argued that because of globalization that younger people in developed countries are converging around a common set of values. Hofstede (1980b) has been sceptical of this viewpoint arguing that culture changes slowly.

▶ Trompenaars' Cultural Dimensions

Trompenaars' research, published in 1993 and extended in 1997, is similar to that of Hofstede's not least in its use of a series of bipolar dimensions. However, while Hofstede's dimensions were primarily empirically derived, Trompenaars' are theoretically derived largely from the work of sociologist Talcott Parsons. In the 1980s he administered questionnaires to 15,000 managers and administrative staff in a number of companies across twenty-eight countries, expanding this by a further 15,000 during the 1990s. As well as looking at attitudes toward both time and the environment Trompenaars employed five cultural dimensions that relate to the question of inter-personal relationships and work-related values. These are:

- *Universalism versus particularism.* In cultures with high universalism there is an emphasis on formal rules and contracts and to their application regardless of individual circumstances. In high particularism cultures the emphasis is on relationships and trust: rules may be bent to help a friend.
- *Communitarism versus individualism.* In strongly communitarian cultures people regard themselves as belonging to a group, whereas in cultures with strong individualism people regard themselves as individuals.
- *Neutral versus emotional.* A high neutral culture is one in which emotions are not readily expressed in interpersonal communication. In contrast, a high emotional culture is characterized by the free expression of emotions even in a business situation.
- *Specific versus diffuse.* A specific culture is one in which a distinction is made between work and private life. That is individuals tend to compartmentalize their work and private lives. For example, a manager in a specific culture segregates out the task relationship she has with a subordinate and insulates this from other dealings. Almost none of the authority in the work situation diffuses itself into non-work arenas. In diffuse cultures work and private life are closely linked and a great deal of formality is maintained across a wide-range of social situations.
- *Achievement versus ascription.* All societies accord some of their members more status than others, but the principle for doing so varies. An achievement-oriented culture is one in which status is given to people on the basis of how well they have performed their tasks recently, their level of education and experience. In an ascription-oriented culture status is conferred on the basis of durable characteristics such as age, kinship and gender and status differences are thereby more pronounced. Power in such cultures does not require legitimizing in the same way as in achievement-oriented cultures.

According to Trompenaars, these five value orientations greatly influence our ways of doing business and managing as well as our responses in the face of moral dilemmas. One example of the latter that illustrates the *Universalism versus particularism* dimension is the dilemma of how you would respond if you are riding in a car driven by a close friend who is driving at least 25 km per hour over the speed limit in a built-up area and who hits a pedestrian. There are no witnesses. The question is whether you would feel obliged as a sworn witness to testify that your friend was keeping to the speed limit (see table 4.6).

Trompenaars observes that the response to the question varies according to how seriously the pedestrian is injured. For North Americans and most North

Table 4.6 Selected examples of percentage of respondents who would testify against their friend

Russia	44
China	47
India	54
Japan	68
France	73
Spain	75
Germany	87
UK	91
Sweden	92
USA	93

Table 4.7 Selected examples of percentage of respondents opting for individual responsibility

Japan	32
Germany	36
India	36
China	37
Spain	46
UK	48
Denmark	53
USA	54
Russia	69

Europeans the reluctance to not testify on behalf on the friend increases with the seriousness of the accident. However, for Asians and Russians the response is the opposite. In short: in these cultures relationships matter.

In regard to *Communitarism versus individualism*, one of Trompenaars' illustrations is the issue of responsibility in the case of defects being detected that stem from the negligence of a team member. The question is whether the team usually shoulders the responsibility, or whether it is the person who caused the defect who shoulders it. Asians and Germans tend to opt for the communitarian solution, while North Americans, the British and Eastern Europeans such as Russians prefer the individualistic solution (see table 4.7).

Trompenaars exemplifies the *Neutral versus emotional* dimension through the question of the acceptability of exhibiting emotion if you are upset about something at work. Whereas the Spanish, Russians and the French largely find it acceptable to show emotions openly, the Chinese and Japanese do not (see table 4.8).

The *Specific versus diffuse* dimension is illustrated by the question of whether the company is responsible for providing housing for its employees. The proportions that disagree with this are much smaller for China, Russia, Japan and India than for north European countries and North America (see table 4.9).

Table 4.8 Selected examples of percentage of respondents who would not show emotions openly

Spain	19
Russia	24
France	30
Denmark	34
Germany	35
USA	43
UK	45
India	51
China	55
Japan	74

Table 4.9 Selected examples of percentage of respondents who think that the company should not be responsible for providing housing for employees

China	18
Spain	19
Russia	22
Japan	45
India	46
Germany	75
France	81
UK	82
Denmark	84
USA	85

Table 4.10 Selected examples of percentage of respondents who disagree that respect depends on family background

India	57
Russia	74
Germany	74
Japan	79
China	81
Spain	82
France	83
USA	87
UK	89
Denmark	92

The issue of whether the respect a person gets is highly dependent on their family is one of the ways Trompenaars exemplifies the *Achievement versus ascription* dimension. Trompenaars observes that Protestants in particular, such as Scandinavians, North Americans and the British, generally disagree with this. Other cultures tend to be more ascriptive (see table 4.10).

▶ Lessons for MNCs

The lessons that MNCs can draw from Trompenaars findings are many. Here are some examples:

- *Universalism versus particularism.* Companies from universalist cultures negotiating with a potential joint venture partner in China must recognize that relationships matter and take time to develop. They form the basis of the trust that is necessary in order to do business. In a particularist culture, contracts are only a rough guideline or approximation.
- *Communitarism versus individualism.* Companies from individualistic cultures such as the USA will face difficulties in introducing methods of individual incentives such as pay-for-performance and individual assessment in subsidiaries in communitarian cultures such as Germany or Japan.
- *Neutral versus emotional.* Multinational teams consisting of individuals from highly neutral and highly affective cultures need careful management and considerable inter-cultural understanding. Otherwise, the affective persons will view the neutral persons as ice-cold, and the affective persons will be viewed as out of control by the neutrals.
- *Specific versus diffuse.* Managers from specific cultures such as Denmark are much more prone to criticize subordinates directly and openly without regarding their criticism as a personal matter. In the context of a subsidiary in a diffuse culture such as Russia, this may constitute an unacceptable loss of face.
- *Achievement versus ascription.* Sending a young manager to run a subsidiary in an ascriptive culture such as India will involve difficulty. Likewise promoting younger people within the subsidiary on the basis of their performance.

▶ Hofstede and Trompenaars Compared

Making comparisons between Hofstede's research and that of Trompenaars is problematical because they are for the most part exploring very different cultural dimensions. As such their research efforts should be regarded as supplementing one another rather than duplicating one another. However, their research is analogous in regard to one dimension: Trompenaars' *Communitarianism versus individualism* dimension is similar to Hofstede's *Individualism–Collectivism* dimension. An examination reveals broad consistency in the respective classifications of countries. For example, Japan and India are both relatively weak in terms of individualism according to both Hofstede and Trompenaars, while Denmark, the UK and the USA are relatively individualistic. However, many countries appear to be more individualistic according to Trompenaars than Hofstede's research indicates. This is particularly the case for countries such as Mexico, Greece and

Spain. Differences of this kind cannot be entirely explained away by pointing to the differences in the items employed by Hofstede and Trompenaars. Hodgetts and Luthans (2000) have suggested that what is possible is that the differences may be due to the different time frames of the two studies, indicating that cultural change has taken place. In turn this implies that Hofstede's findings are becoming out of date. For example Mexico's integration into the global economy may be generating a move away from communitarian values. In other words, 'Cultures do not stand still; they evolve over time, albeit slowly. What was a reasonable characterization in the 1960s and 1970s may not be so today' (Hill, 2000: 100).

It is also interesting to note that Trompenaars' findings indicate that former communist countries such as Russia, Hungary and the Czech Republic are relatively individualistic despite their communist past.

Trompenaars has also extended his research by examining corporate cultures by nationality. In order to do so he introduced yet another dimension: *equality versus hierarchy*. The hierarchical corporate culture is one that is power-oriented in which the leader has considerable authority and knows best. This dimension is akin to Hofstede's *Power Distance* dimension. Furthermore, there are a number of similarities in their findings: the Scandinavian countries, North America and the UK have relatively egalitarian cultures according to Trompenaars, and are low in terms of *Power Distance* according to Hofstede. France and Spain figure as hierarchical according to Trompenaars and relatively high in terms of Power distance in Hofstede's research. There are, however, pronounced disagreements not least in regard to Germany. Trompenaars' findings suggest that German corporate culture is decidedly hierarchical, whereas Hofstede identifies Germany as relatively low in terms of *Power Distance*.

▶ The Eurobusiness Student Survey

In the late autumn of 2000 we conducted research into work-related values using a sampling methodology akin to Hofstede's (Gooderham and Nordhaug, 2002). Instead of sampling IBM employees, we sampled students at leading European business schools belonging to the CEMS network (the Community of European Business Schools). The 1,335 respondents to the questionnaire were drawn from 11 business schools in as many countries: Austria, Denmark, Great Britain, Finland, France, Germany, Holland, Italy, Norway, Spain and Sweden. Only nationals of these countries were included. Nearly 40 per cent of the sample comprised females and their ages ranged from 19 to 26.

The questionnaire contained 14 items that reflect the examples of the work-related cultural elements comprising Hofstede's dimensions listed above. The items were derived from two main types of question. The first of these was:

How important do you think the following competences are for a person to be a good manager? (scale: 1–5),

Table 4.11 Mean scores on the 14 items derived from Hofstede and grouped according to Hofstede's four dimensions of culture (Gooderham and Nordhaug, 2002)

	All	Men	Women
Power Distance			
Ability to command/control others	3.90	3.90	3.90
Power related political skills	3.79	3.75	3.86
Masculinity v. Femininity			
High annual earnings/salary	3.99	4.05	3.91[a]
Pay based on individual performance	3.67	3.74	3.59[a]
Opportunities for fast promotion	3.65	3.76	3.48[a]
Position has a high status	3.34	3.44	3.18[a]
Individualism v. Collectivism			
Opportunities for personal development	4.37	4.28	4.50[a]
A lot of freedom in the job	3.99	3.97	4.01
A lot of variety in work tasks	4.20	4.13	4.30[a]
Interesting work	4.72	4.65	4.84[a]
Uncertainty Avoidance			
Good job security	3.68	3.51	3.96[a]
The employer has a good reputation	3.74	3.72	3.78
Good personnel policy	3.92	3.75	4.17[a]
Systematic career planning	3.28	3.19	3.41[a]

Note: [a] Men and women are significantly different at the 1 per cent level.

The ability to command/control others
Power related political skills.

The other twelve items were derived from the question:

What importance do you attach to the following factors when choosing your first post-graduation job? (scale: 1–5).

The mean responses to the 14 items, grouped according to each of the four Hofstede dimensions, are listed in table 4.11.

Additive indexes were then formed for each of the four dimensions. Each of these were tested for internal consistency using the Cronbach Alpha test and found to be satisfactory. While the *Power Distance* index ranges between a minimum of 2 and 10, the other indexes range from 4 to 20. The results are displayed in table 4.12.

In assessing whether there are substantial differences between the various countries we took the country closest to the mean for each of the four dimensions as their basis for comparison. Thereafter we examined for statistically significant differences between the 'mean country' and the other countries at the one per cent level.

Table 4.12   Hofstede's four dimensions by country (Gooderham and Nordhaug, 2002)

	Power	Masculinity	Uncertainty Avoidance	Individualism
Austria	8.76[a]	15.39	15.07	18.03
Denmark	6.91[a]	13.90	14.00	16.82
Finland	6.81[a]	13.89	**14.68**	17.36
France	8.24	15.05	12.53[a]	17.24
Germany	8.98[a]	15.43	15.02	17.84
Great Britain	7.71	15.64	15.38	**17.29**
Italy	**7.66**	15.93[a]	14.44	16.37
Netherlands	7.64	14.03	15.01	17.83
Norway	6.67[a]	13.44[a]	14.50	16.83
Spain	9.00[a]	**14.74**	15.04	17.48
Sweden	7.03	15.15	14.85	17.56
Mean	7.69	14.65	14.62	17.28

Notes: [a] Significantly different at the 1%-level from the country closest to the mean for the whole sample.
Bold type indicates the country closest to the mean.

Table 4.13   Hofstede's four dimensions by country (Hofstede, 1980b)

	Power	Masculinity	Uncertainty Avoidance	Individualism
Austria	11*	79*	70*	55*
Denmark	18*	16*	23*	74
Finland	33	26*	**59**	63
France	68*	43	86*	71
Germany	35	66*	65	67
Great Britain	35	66*	35*	89*
Italy	50*	70*	75*	76
Netherlands	**38**	14*	53	80*
Norway	31	8*	50	69
Spain	57*	42	86*	51*
Sweden	31	5*	29*	71
Mean	37	40	57	70
Lowest/highest	11/94	5/95	8/112	13/91

Notes: * Markedly different from the country closest to the mean for the whole sample.
Bold type indicates the country closest to the mean for all eleven countries.

The next stage was to go back to Hofstede's own findings for these 11 countries, the results of which are displayed in table 4.13. Table 4.13 also contains the lowest and highest scores recorded by Hofstede for all the 49 countries in his sample.

For each of the four dimensions we have indicated the country that is closest to the 11-country sample mean (bold types) and we refer to this as the 'mean country'. In addition we have asterisked those countries that are clearly different from the mean country. This is a somewhat conservative estimate on our part because Hofstede has indicated that even a five-percentage point difference can have noteworthy consequences.[1] In the case of *Power Distance*, Austria and Denmark have markedly lower scores than the Netherlands, while France, Italy and Spain are all higher. The *Masculinity–Femininity* dimension is the dimension with the most substantial spread: five countries have clearly lower scores than the mean country Spain, and four higher. There are also substantial differences for *Uncertainty Avoidance* in relation to the mean country, Finland, with four countries having distinctly higher scores and three lower. *Individualism* is the index with the fewest clear-cut differences from the mean country. Only four countries are clearly different, two scoring substantially more and two substantially less.

A significant continuity between our research and that of Hofstede's is to be found in regard to the mean countries. Both in the case of *Masculinity–Femininity* and *Uncertainty Avoidance* our mean countries are identical to Hofstede's, that is Spain and Finland, respectively. For *Power Distance* Hofstede's mean country, the Netherlands, is very close to our mean. In the case of *Individualism*, Hofstede's mean country Norway is not significantly different from that of our mean country, Great Britain.

In terms of the *Power Distance* dimension, Norway, Finland and Denmark in our research all score significantly less than the mean country, Italy. These findings are fairly consistent with those of Hofstede. Indeed, with two notable exceptions, that of Austria and Germany, our findings are generally consistent with his results. According to Hofstede, Austria is a very low *Power Distance* country with Germany somewhat lower than the mean. Our findings suggest the opposite. Moreover, our finding for Germany is consistent with that of Trompenaars.

In our research Spain is the mean country in terms of the *Masculinity* dimension. In terms of whether the countries score higher or lower in relation to Spain, the findings are, with the exception of Sweden, broadly similar to those of Hofstede. However, there is a notable difference: only Norway and Italy differ significantly from Spain. Thus the substantial differences between Spain, on the one hand, and, according to Hofstede, the highly masculine countries of Great Britain, Germany and Austria are greatly diminished. The same applies to Hofstede's feminine countries, Denmark, Finland and, not least, Sweden. As such, our image of Europe is very much more *convergent* in terms of this dimension than is that of Hofstede.

The notion of a largely convergent Europe is given more impetus when one looks at the findings for the *Uncertainty Avoidance* and *Individualism* dimensions. France differs significantly from the mean country Finland in terms of *Uncertainty Avoidance*. Beyond that, though there are no significant differences. Clearly this is a very different Europe to that which Hofstede mapped.

Our findings for *Uncertainty Avoidance* differ from those of Hofstede in other ways. Most notably, France has moved from being relatively high in terms of this

Table 4.14 An ANOVA analysis of the respective significance of gender and country in relation to Hofstede's four dimensions

Dimension	Gender	Country
Power Distance	–	significant
Masculinity–Femininity	significant	significant
Uncertainty Avoidance	significant	–
Individualism–Collectivism	significant	–

Note: Significance at the 1 per cent level.

index to low whereas Great Britain and Sweden appear to have moved in the opposite direction.

Finally, in terms of *Individualism* it is interesting to note that Great Britain's relatively high position in Hofstede's findings is reduced to the European average.

Gender or country?

Table 4.7 indicated that there were a number of significant differences between men and women in relation to most of the components of the four indexes. The question is then whether Europe is more divided in terms of gender rather than in terms of country. We addressed this question by performing an ANOVA-analysis of differences for gender and country. Their findings are summarized in table 4.14.

Table 4.14 indicates that country is a significant differentiator for *Power Distance* and the degree of *Masculinity*. However, gender is also a significant differentiator in terms of the latter dimension. Moreover, whereas gender-based differences are significant for *Uncertainty Avoidance* and *Individualism–Collectivism*, country-based differences are not.

In other words, in today's Europe, on the whole, gender is a more powerful tool for predicting work-related cultural differences than nationality. Only more empirical work can determine whether this trend applies to other advanced economies.

Conclusion

In terms of nationality our findings indicate a significant convergence of values across Europe. It might be argued that when they enter the workplace the values of our sample of young people might change. To this we would reply, as Hofstede has done, that the values acquired prior to entering the workplace are relatively stable. In other words, the cohort we have mapped is substantially different to that of Hofstede's.

Globalization is a multi-faceted concept. It involves not only increased trade and an increased scope for multinational companies but also the dissemination of ideas and values. In the case of Europe, there is the added impetus of the European Union. It is interesting to note that our findings indicate that Norway, which has refused to join the Union, diverges from the mean on two of the four dimensions. Clearly it would be interesting to extend our work to other advanced economies outside the European Union to determine whether the European project of increased institutional harmonization can be shown to be a significant determinant of cultural convergence.

Our findings have particular relevance for the design of management systems. Hofstede (1980b, 1999) has consistently contended that management systems are nationally idiosyncratic and that attempts to apply management systems across borders are courting failure. However, our findings imply that there is increasing scope for pan-European management systems.

Finally, one should also note the relative importance of gender. In terms of two of the dimensions our findings suggest that Italian women have more in common with their Swedish counterparts than with their male co-nationals. It is not unreasonable to speculate that with the increasing importance of European Union political institutions some of the future political movements in Europe could reflect this divide.

The case of Russia

In the autumn of 2001 our student Vladimir Poliakov extended the Eurobusiness Survey to Russia, drawing his sample from the St Petersburg School of Mangement (Poliakov, 2002). We reproduce his main findings in table 4.15. Because of the nature of the case that follows we have, for convenience, repeated the scores for Denmark featured in table 4.12. It should be noted that there are significant differences between Russia and Denmark in terms of all of the dimensions with the exception of *Individualism*.

▶ Summary

It was not the ambition of this chapter to try to understand the origins of various national cultures. Nor have we attempted to provide in-depth analyses of particular national cultures. However, this does not mean that we regard either of these tasks as futile exercises. Instead, we have explored two approaches to comparing many national cultures simultaneously in order to provide a starting point for a discussion of the cultural challenge faced by MNCs. As we will see in the accompanying case, which features the Russian subsidiary of a Danish MNC, there will always be individual variations within one and the same national culture. Likewise, we have indicated that gender is also an important source of the work values

Table 4.15 Hofstede's four dimensions for Russia and Denmark

	Power	Masculinity	Uncertainty Avoidance	Individualism
Russia	8.26	16.67	15.26	17.28
Denmark	6.91	13.90	14.00	16.82

of employees. However, as the case will demonstrate cultural sensitivity is nevertheless of critical importance in the design of management systems if alienation from the MNC is to be avoided and the integration necessary for knowledge exchange is to be achieved. In including our own research we have done so in order to support the argument that cultures are not static, but evolve and change. Hence there will always be a need for the MNC to regularly revise and update its understanding of those cultures within which it operates.

Note

1 See G. Hofstede, 'Motivation, leadership and organization: Do American theories apply abroad?', *Organizational Dynamics* (Summer), 1980b, 44–63.

Russian Voices from a Danish Company

Snejina Michailova and Alla Anisimova

▶ Introduction

This case starts by discussing inclusion and exclusion as key characteristics of local middle managers and specialists working in a foreign-owned company. It then analyses the way these characteristics distinguish two groups of Russians working for a Danish company in Russia – the 'insiders' and 'outsiders' – including how they interpret and react to foreign managers' decision-making and planning. The Russians' ideas and practice of decision-making and planning were very different from those adopted by the Danes. The case concludes by suggesting guidelines on how to reduce cross-cultural conflicts.

Managing across cultures is a major challenge of Western business in Russia, perhaps more than in most countries. Even in organizations established by Westerners, the influence of 74 years of socialist experience on the local culture is usually a serious obstacle to effective communication and co-ordination within the organization. We analyse the challenges from the perspective of Russian middle managers and specialists with the aim of improving Western managers' understanding of the nature of cross-cultural conflicts. Based on a case of a Danish company investing in Russia, we address two questions:

- How do Russians perceive themselves and the foreign organization they work in and how does that influence their behaviour?
- What are the main issues in the Danish approach towards managing that Russians perceive as particularly different from their own and how does this affect the interaction between Russians and Danes?

Our focus is on two issues that so far have not been thoroughly explored either in mainstream international human resources research or in intercultural and cross-cultural management research. First, whereas published research focuses either on the expatriates' perspective (e.g. Fontaine, 1989) or on the interaction between the host and foreign cultures (e.g. Markoczy, 1993), this case is primarily focused on topics related to local workers in foreign-owned organizations: by taking as the point of departure the locals' perspectives and interpretations. Second, whereas research which focuses on host cultures and local workers usually concentrates on local top managers or the most influential executives, our focus is on perceptions and behaviour adopted by local middle managers and specialists in foreign-owned companies. ('Specialist' is a term arising from the Russian classification of professions and refers to a person with a higher education and with a specialization in a particular area of work.)

The key word is 'perception'. Perceptions are of key relevance because:

- They relate to the cognitive process of selecting organizing and interpreting the multitude of stimuli that are perceived.
- They constitute the basis for people's behaviour.

The way individuals interpret messages, view things and provide meaning is varied. The individual's perceptual world is their personal image, map or picture of their social, physical and organizational environment (Buchanan and Huczynski, 1997). Personal characteristics and psychological factors have a strong impact on individual perceptions. At the same time, perceptions are influenced by sociocultural factors (Bowditch and Buono, 1997) and by the culture of the group they belong to, defined as a set of shared meanings and values developed through social actions and/or socialization practices (Nicholson, 1998). Consequently, different individuals react differently to the same stimuli and in the same situations. The notion of perception helps to explain these reactions. Its essence in process terms is the selection of stimuli and their organization into meaningful patterns. The perceived reality, not reality itself, is the basis of their actions and behaviour. 'The world as it is perceived is the world that is behaviorally important' (Robbins, 1998: 90). People's behaviour as a function of their perceived world, as opposed to their objective world, is especially significant in a cross-cultural organizational setting. Developing cohesive patterns, impressions and images of other people through the processes of categorization and stereotyping is mainly based on perceptions.

▶ The Company and the Study

This case study concerns Dancom (not its real name), a large Danish company which is a world leader in some of its areas of business. The organization encompasses significant cultural divergences in its day-to-day interactions since it has subsidiaries in more than a hundred countries and employs more than 20,000 people worldwide. Dancom started its activities in Russia as a sales office in 1993. Currently it is represented by a sales office, a production unit and two branch offices in four different Russian cities.

Our research is a part of a larger study of Dancom's organizational culture, which took place in 1998 (references to Dancom henceforth refer to Dancom's operation in Russia). Data were collected in the sales office and the production unit in one of the company's Russian locations, which employs around a hundred people. The 20 participants in this study were selected from 102 for the way that they represent different national backgrounds (Danes and Russians), and different age, gender, and department affiliations. They also personify different hierarchical positions and have had different length of employment and experience of promotion in Dancom.

Among the 20 participants, ten are managers (three top managers and seven middle managers) and ten are specialists in IT, marketing, technical support, sales, engineering, logistics, administration, finance or (see Appendix for full methodological details). Thirteen of the respondents are male and seven are female. Nine participants were under 30, and five participants were over 40. Five respondents had worked for Dancom for less than one year, and another five for five years.

Three of the managers are Danes – the general manager, the marketing director, and the technical support director. The fourth Dane in the company is the finance specialist. All middle managers, two top managers and all but one of the specialists are Russian. Besides its sales activities, Dancom also has a production unit. It had been involved in Russia for five years – an important criterion for us in selecting the Danish company for our research. One or two years would not really have been long enough for organizational participants to have developed strong impressions and perceptions of the organization and their foreign colleagues. On the other hand, 10–15 years might have made organizational participants accustomed to many of the issues that they found 'strange', 'alien' or 'just very different' in the beginning. A third criterion in our selection was the presence of Danes in the Russian company. Had the Danes been involved in a more marginal or distant way, our respondents, and consequently we as researchers, would not have been able to crystallize the phenomena and processes that are the subject of this study.

The fact that it is a single case limits the representativeness of our study although qualitative sampling improves the quality of data and relegates representatives to secondary importance. We conduct 'analytic generalizations', not 'statistical' ones (Yin, 1994) – in epistemological terms we opt for 'logical inference' rather than 'statistical inference' (Smith, 1991). It is important for us to understand the phenomena themselves. How do Russians perceive themselves and the foreign-owned company they work for and what do they interpret as very different between the Danish and Russian ways of managing? However, the research questions we are concerned with highlight problems common to many foreign-owned companies in Russia (and have relevance for foreign direct investors in many other countries).

▶ Characteristics of 'Insiders' and 'Outsiders'

Inclusion, as defined by Russians working at Dancom, refers mainly to the individual's perception of belonging to the organization and the ability to communicate and share information with people at different levels of the company. The degree of inclusion varies. The collected data suggest that Dancom's middle managers and specialists form two main groups, which we call 'hosting insiders' and 'hosting outsiders'. The term 'hosting' refers to the fact that both groups consist of locals. The division between being inside and outside the organization is suggested by the respondents: they all are members of the organization, however, some of them feel like outsiders – as though they are not really being included in the company's life. These two groups are characterized by a number of specific features (see table D1).

Table D1 Main characteristics of hosting insiders and hosting outsiders

Hosting insiders	Hosting outsiders
Perceive the atmosphere in the company as friendly	Perceive the atmosphere in the company as peaceful but indifferent
Identify themselves strongly with the organization	Do not identify themselves strongly with the organization
Are dissatisfied and even upset with formalization of communication and procedures and lack of informal relations with superiors	Respect formalization of communication and procedures and accept and even appreciate the lack of informal relations with superiors
Have close relations with foreign colleagues	Have no close relations with foreign colleagues
Do not make a clear distinction between Russians and Danes in Dancom	Distinguish strongly between Russians and Danes in Dancom
Distinguish clearly between local Danes and Danes in headquarters	Do not distinguish strongly between Danes in the local office and in headquarters
Are self-motivated and work long hours	Are motivated by money and do not work longer than the official office hours
Have relations with each other apart from work	Do not have relations with other members apart from work
Stay longer and feel very comfortable at company's internal social evens	Leave company's internal social events earlier

Characterize the communication with headquarters in Denmark as formal, inefficient and slow. Tend to interpret that as lack of respect towards Russians.

The hosting insiders

Hosting insiders find the general atmosphere in the organization friendly. They are satisfied with and proud of working for Dancom, identify themselves closely with the organization, refer to it as 'their company', and use metaphors such as 'community', 'friendly village', and 'Dancom nation' when describing the company. Most of them refer to the internal climate as peaceful, calm, and friendly. They perceive the organization's successes and failures as their personal successes and failures, and some refer to Dancom as the most important part of their lives. As two of the Russian middle managers put it: 'I actually don't have any life beyond the work at Dancom'; 'I could not even dream of working for Dancom, it is such a famous name, a leader in the field.'

Hosting insiders are dissatisfied and even upset with the formalization of the communication flow and procedures in the company. They appreciate highly informal relations with their superiors and feel that this increases the level of unity within Dancom in general and their efficiency in particular: 'I could enter my Danish superior's office any time and discuss a problem directly. I did not have to write official request or other papers to solve the problem' (Sales manager). One of the Russian sales engineers describes the early days in the company like this: 'There was a time at the very beginning when we worked in the apartment of my Danish boss, there was no office space yet. It was the best time, we were all so close to each other!' These two quotations confirm previous findings that close relationships and friendship are highly valued in the Russian context. As they also indicate, Russians do not have great respect for other people's private space. Their tendency to be rather intrusive can be associated, among other factors, with the living conditions in *mir* (the communal villages) and in overcrowded communal apartments (Kets de Vries, 1998). The *mir* mentality largely explains the Russian employees' respect for solidarity and loyalty to one another. Russians subordinate their individual interests and priorities to those of the group. Their need for affiliation and belonging is strong and confrontations within the group is treated as a disaster. Obolonsky (1995: 18) has elaborated on this issue in more definitive terms by talking about the 'antipersonnel attitude' at the cost of the group life. He summarizes its essence as 'reject[ing] even a relative independence of the person'.

This aggressive anti-individualism has at least two basic features: a levelling psychology (pseudo-egalitarianism) and a compulsive pseudo-collectivism. They are based on a 'dramatically anti-personal stereotype of "all as one", implying situations where, irrespective of the will of the individual, he is involved in a sectarian joint activity where his personal opinion means practically nothing. The person is sacrificed, victimized in a vulgarized idea of unity and conformism.' The data also suggest that informal relations with superiors are closely associated in Russian minds with organizational validation and recognition and seem to be important for Russian employees' self-perception of their role in the organization.

Close and informal relations with superiors are often seen by Russians as an additional reward from the organization: 'If my boss likes me, if I feel that he respects me, that he is interested in my opinion – then I will work better . . . I mean, I feel satisfaction and pride. It is maybe no less important than the money' (Sales manager).

The hosting insiders' reflections can also be interpreted in the light of the fact that the Russian working climate in general is relationship-oriented (Zaytseva, 1998) and that the relationship orientation is still the key method among Russian managers. A plausible consideration for this finding could be attributed to the fact that formalization is associated with an increasing number of rules, regulations, and procedures and that Russian employees are known as people who dislike procedures (Zaytseva, 1998).

Closer links with foreign colleagues result in the fact that hosting insiders have less tendency than outsiders to judge their colleagues' behavioural standards by their nationality. They claim that they do not distinguish between the Russians and Danes in the company, but make a clear distinction between 'Danes working in Russia' and 'Danes in the headquarters'. 'Local Danes' are perceived as part of the common 'Dancom nation' in the Russian office, whereas Danes in headquarters are perceived as foreigners. Hosting insiders are self-motivated in their work and usually work long hours at the office. They have developed informal relations with each other and with their Danish superiors outside work and tend to stay longer together at the internal company social events.

The hosting outsiders

Hosting outsiders, in contrast, interpret harmony as a surface and superficial phenomenon and mention 'hidden streams, controversies and conflicts'. Some of them explicitly relate the existing harmony to the presence of Danes in the company: 'Who knows how it would be if the Danes were not here . . . Maybe we would have many open conflicts. But it is not good to behave rudely in front of the foreigners' (IT specialist).

Those newcomers who belong to the outsiders' group feel 'lost and lonely' in spite of the 'taking around the office' ritual introduced by the administration and aimed at facilitating the socialization process. They refer to the attitude of other employees as 'polite but indifferent': 'If you need help and ask for it, you will probably get it, but do not expect that somebody will come up to you and ask whether you need help' (specialist in the Technical Support department).

Hosting outsiders are formal in the way they behave. They find the absence of more informal working relationships with their superiors acceptable and even welcome. They claim that a certain level of formalization is necessary in a big company: 'There are many hidden streams, conflicts between departments and people. Structuralization and formalization can solve these problems. Mechanisms, duties, structures must be formalized' (specialist in the IT department).

Hosting outsiders perceive the atmosphere at Dancom as peaceful but indifferent. Some of them claim that they work only for money and do not really identify themselves with the organization: 'The needs and goals of the company and my own goals are two different worlds' (specialist in the marketing department). Hosting outsiders are members whose initial expectations are not met. They tell of experiencing dissatisfaction, frustration and irritation:

> I feel disappointed from a professional point of view. Everyday routine does not leave enough time for self-education. (production specialist)

> I was rather disappointed from a professional point of view when I started working for Dancom. Danes do not apply advanced IT technologies in Russia. In other social divisions and in the headquarters they use them, they pay attention to this, they also have resources. Here they don't. (specialist in the IT department)

The negative attitude toward formalization of relations and procedures could also be interpreted in the light of Russians' wrong expectations towards Western companies. Consider the following: 'We, the Soviet people, had an idea that we had bureaucracy and they – freedom. And now I think that Russia was backward in terms of bureaucracy, it is much more bureaucratic here [i.e. in this Western-owned company]' (Russian sales engineer). Naturally, these respondents tend to compare Dancom with Russian firms and organizations where they previously worked: 'In the bank where I worked before, self-education during working hours was possible, there were no problems' (project specialist).

Some of the hosting outsiders feel restricted in their personal creativity and professional development, and point to the standardization and uniformity of equipment and technologies as the main reason for that: 'In the Russian company where I was working previously, I had complete freedom in my programming activities. This is not the case in Dancom – almost everything is standardized here.'

Dancom employs a selected group of highly educated Russian professionals. When their self-development expectations are not fulfilled, this turns out to be a source of great disappointment. The employees' professional development found that it is not directly linked with the company goals and needs and might not be among the priorities of the company. Since there is a strong connection between expectations and perceptions, a possible explanation for the hosting outsiders' dissatisfaction is the fact that Dancom's managers are not clear and explicit about what the employees might expect in terms of work perspectives and professional development. Hosting outsiders do not have close relationships with their foreign colleagues. They do not distinguish between Danes in Russia and Danes in headquarters. However, they make a clear distinction between Russian and Danes in Dancom. Hosting outsiders do not work longer than the official office hours. Their relationships in the company are strictly based on work. If they attend social gatherings, they usually stay only for a short time.

Another aspect of the inclusion/exclusion or insider/outsider issue is related to language skills. Russians who are not able to speak English constitute the majority of the hosting outsiders group. They often feel excluded from or limited in their access to information and interpretations of organizational events and from the informal oral communication flows. Since part of the formal written communication (memos, letters, orders, etc.) is bilingual (English–Russian), those Russians whose English skills are less than adequate have difficulties, mainly in oral communication with Danish colleagues but also with written information which is not available in Russian. Non-English-speaking Russians do not perceive themselves as part of the whole, as members of a worldwide multinational organization.

▶ Who Are the Insiders and the Outsiders?

The hosting insiders' population is composed mostly but not exclusively by the so-called 'founders' or old-timers – employees who joined Dancom immediately or soon after its establishment in Russia. However, some of the hosting insiders joined the company just recently. In our sample, five insiders had worked in the company for more than four years, three for more than two years, and two (specialists in the IT department) for about a year. There were only two outsiders among those who had worked for Dancom more four years, three among those who had worked there more than two years and five employees for less time. It is worth mentioning that all three Russian top managers are insiders, whereas, among middle managers, two Russians and two Danes belong to the outsiders' group. As far as specialists are concerned, six of them are hosting outsiders and four are hosting insiders. The relations between departmental affiliation and insider/outsider distinctions are shown in table D2.

Table D2 Departmental affiliation of hosting insiders and outsiders

Department	Insider	Outsider
Engineering	1	1
Sales	2	3
Technical Support		2
IT	1	1
Marketing	1	1
Finance and Accounting	2	1
Administration	2	
Logistics	1	
Production		1

▶ United against Headquarters in Denmark

One thing which both hosting insiders and outsiders are agreed on is their attitude to head office in Denmark. For both groups, issues related to the communication with headquarters are especially sensitive. Both groups characterize it as formal, inefficient, and slow: 'Our sales engineers cannot get a response from the headquarters for months. Everything is discussed, documented, but no actions are taken' (sales manager). 'You send a fax to the headquarters but there is either no response or a very formal meaningless reply' (specialist in the Technical Support department). Headquarters are referred to as 'a huge, clumsy monster', 'inflexible structure', and 'slow conservative machine':

> The headquarters are slow and inefficient – they spend a lot of time in order to introduce a new product. As a result some segments of the market are taken by competitors – usually small companies that are more flexible and are able fill the gap and to adjust quickly their products to the specific requirements. (production specialist)

Some Russian employees perceive the formalization and the inefficiency of the communications flows between Dancom and the headquarters in Denmark in the following way: 'It seems that Russia is not the main priority for those who are sitting in Denmark and are responsible for the Russian market' (IT manager). 'There is lack of respect and attention toward Russian colleagues. The headquarters' attitude toward the Russian subsidiary is that of consumption, it is not a true partnership' (specialist in the Technical Support department).

Russians interpret the lack of response from headquarters as a lack of respect for their work and the subsidiary. However, the reason why headquarters do not respond to all requests might be that it is trying not to interfere in the responsibilities of the local managers and employees. The centralization/decentralization debate in terms of relationships between the headquarters and subsidiaries has particular overtones when considered by the Russians: some of our respondents claim that a top-down approach in this relationship is appropriate.

They perceive that lack of communication as a part of the integration of the Russian subsidiary into the 'Dancom world' and as contributing to organizational stability in the subsidiary. Another possible explanation for the slowness of communication is a certain caution at headquarters toward Russia dictated by the instability and unpredictability of the Russian market and the overall Russian political situation. Decisions concerning Russian companies require more discussion and more careful analysis at headquarters than is the case for more stable countries:

> I think they are just afraid to invest in Russia too much, they are never sure what will be here tomorrow. That is why they are very careful. I think they try to behave in such way that if it is necessary they can quit here immediately and leave. (Executive Director's secretary)

Sometimes this 'careful policy' leads to economically unprofitable decisions for Dancom. A story told by one of the specialists in the administration illustrates this:

> In the beginning when the question was raised to about the company's building all the Russians suggested we buy [a building] because the prices for real estate were rather low at that time and it would be cheaper in the long run to buy the building than to rent it. But the Danes said 'No'. And since then the rent has been rising all the time, so if we calculated now how much rent we have paid during five years – it would already be more than if we had bought the building five years ago.

▶ Decision-making

Organizations are networks of decisions, decision-makers, and decision-making (Cyert and March, 1992) and all organizational behaviour springs from decisions. Nutt (1997) has pointed out that inadequate decision-making techniques cost Russian billions of dollars each year in wasted time and money and that 'even a small improvement in the way that decisions are made could have a dramatic effect on Dancom on an everyday basis and to increase the organizational performance' (p. 52).

Decision-making is an issue which Russian middle managers and specialists, both insiders and outsiders, perceive as 'confusing'. There is a striking difference between their way of making decisions and the way Danes do it. According to the Russian respondents, Danes take decisions on the basis of teamwork. They claim that Danish managers repeatedly stress the importance of group discussions, co-ordination of actions and the need to reach consensus when making decisions. They are ready to discuss problems openly and to give and receive feedback. All this confuses the Russian who describe themselves as individualists at work and as preferring the individual mode of decision-making. They do not consider discussions important and try to avoid them especially when they concern problems: 'Russians have strong resistance if somebody tries to step into their business area' (Danish manager).

Russians perceive the collective mode of decision-making, which implies discussions aimed toward consensus, as slow, non-flexible and inefficient:

> Danes discuss the same issue several times and still think they have to discuss more, it takes so much time. (head of the sales department)

> Everything in Russia changes so fast, there is no time for long discussions and slow decision-making. One has to be fast and very flexible. (head of the marketing department)

Russian middle managers and specialists claim that they are oriented toward final results rather than discussions of how to achieve these results. Russians describe their own decision-making methods in Dancom as short-term and result-oriented. They admit that they do not reflect on the status of the events in the working process. For them: 'the job is either done or not done' (specialist in the sales department).

This makes it difficult for Danish superiors to control their subordinates' work and even makes them think that the job is not being done at all:

> The Danish managers worry and want to be sure that everything is being done and is under control. They constantly write check-lists and memos for every single event. It seems to them that nothing is under control. And then they are surprised that the job is done and start asking, how did you manage to do all this? (specialist in the marketing department)

Russian middle managers and specialists find discussions with colleagues, joint setting of priorities, developing frameworks as a team, and informing each other about ongoing issues and process as a 'waste of time'. This is rather different from what they perceive as their own strengths: quick reaction to changing and unexpected situations and ability to act on the basis of fragmented information. Those are features shaped under conditions of instability, scarcity and lack of clarity of information. In a similar study we conducted in another foreign-owned company in Russia, local middle managers perceived the collective decision-making adopted by their Western colleagues as an effort to diffuse responsibility and to hide the absence of knowledge and professionalism.

These perceptions can be discussed within the framework of Eisenhardt's (1989, 1990) findings regarding the behaviour of top management teams in companies dealing with 'high-velocity' environments. She found out that slow decision-makers focused on analysing different alternatives in depth whereas fast ones compared the various alternatives by a quick analysis of the information available. Additionally, planning and information oriented towards the future were typical and significant for slow managers, whereas fast decision-makers relied mainly on current environment and circumstances and current operations. Our respondents' statements are in line with these findings: Russians in Dancom do not discuss details in depth and are focused on the current situation. However, there are three aspects where the case invites interpretations that differ from or are not discussed in Eisenhardt's analysis and conclusions. The first relates to 'sharing information' which, according to her study, is a characteristic of the fast decision-makers. The second aspect modifies the 'current orientation' with little or no time lag by combining it with a strong appreciation of traditions and orientation towards the past. The third is intuition as an element on the decision-making process.

The way Russians in Dancom make decisions is not based on sharing information which leads to two opposite consequences. Either a rather limited access to information or being overloaded with information. According to our observations both in Dancom and other organizations in Russia, Russian participants treat information as a source of power, status and authority rather than as a basis for taking decisions. To use Mintzberg's (1973) vocabulary, they are mainly occupied with playing the 'monitoring' informational role in the sense of seeking and receiving information. At the same time, they try to avoid the 'disseminating' informational role in terms of diffusing, transmitting and sharing information. This then leads to engaging in the role of 'resource allocator' and 'disturbance handler' at the cost of 'negotiating' and 'acting as an entrepreneur'.

The Russian middle managers and specialists continuously refer to their previous experiences and traditional features of the Russian way of handling issues and situations. Whereas efficiency, predictability, professionalism and modernity are seen as the key forces for rationality in the West, belief in fate and destiny dictates an underlying belief system in the Russian environment. While a professionally-oriented modern Western society provides little space for traditions and they are regarded as slowing down the pace of progress, Russians value them very highly. They perceive the future orientation and focus on action and achievement in the Western context as rather different from admiring history and traditions. Russian middle managers and specialists in Dancom tend to make decisions and act on the basis of intuition which often is not understood by their Danish superiors, although they appreciate it when it brings positive results. According to the Russians, Danes value only logical arguments and convincing proofs:

> Sometimes I feel that something has to be done but I can not explain why, I just know so. Then it becomes a problem, because if the Danish manager is not convinced, he will not agree and consequently will not make a decision. What is convincing for a Dane? Logical argumentation but not the specific Russian experience in the specific Russian conditions. (IT manager)

According to the Russian respondents, Danes do not really acknowledge and respect their expertise and experience when they take decisions. This is most often mentioned in relation to recognition of their 'local Russian knowledge' as opposed to 'the Western/Scandinavian/Danish way of doing things' exercised by the Danes. Russians in Dancom characterize the local Russian environment as highly unstable and unpredictable: 'The Danish approach might be good for stable markets where everything is known and can be planned ten years ahead, but it is rather different in Russia – yesterday there was no market and today it is developing so quickly' (head of the sales department).

Russians feel that the Danes should have more trust in the suggestions from Russian middle managers and specialists and in their interpretations of particular situations. A different behaviour is perceived as disrespect and negligence. Russian participants tell of experiencing frustration, feeling personally offended and being held back: 'The Danes don't listen to you., they do what they think is better, then they realize it does not work here, but time and money have already been wasted' (specialist in the accounting department).

> Distrust and arrogance toward Russian services motivated my Danish superior to order computer equipment from Denmark and to use the services of Danish computer firms in spite of my suggestions to use Russian IT firms, which were able to provide the required services under similar conditions. Dancom lost money and quality simply because the Danish manager did not trust anything Russian. (IT manager)

These quotations and our observations suggest that the Russian middle managers and specialists have a strong need to be asked for advice in the process of taking decisions at a more operational level, concerning how a certain task can be implemented after the strategic decision has been already taken. When Western managers fail to do that, Russian employees react negatively and interpret their behaviour as clear disrespect. At the same time, our study indicates that Russian employees feel confused when asked to actively take part in the early stages if the decision-making process. They respect one-man authority and expect their superiors to decide strategically upon setting the overall framework and goal in terms of what has to be achieved.

At the beginning of the decision-making process, Russian employees treat early involvement, showing initiative and coming up with suggestions differently according to whether they are dealing with Russian or with Western managers. In the first case, they interpret such behaviour as interfering in the superior's job, lack of respect towards him or questioning his abilities. One of the sources of that type of behaviour is found in the rule of accepting the leader without any questioning (Bronfenbrenner, 1970). Another explanation might be the employees' traditional alienation from the results of their own work. Work was for decades psychologically regarded as a kind of unprofitable conscription enforced from above (Obolonsky, 1995: 19–21). The ethic of the 'work horse' is well integrated in that approach – individuals do not interfere in things which are 'none of their business'. This is an ethic of one's inferiority and one's boss's superiority: 'Whatever I do nothing happens.' 'They can twist me to a ram horn.' These are justified by a marked loyalty to whatever happens according to the others from 'above', which camouflages a pragmatic, selfish calculation, a practical desire to insure oneself against all sorts of risk: or a cynical disposition to make moral relativism a life-time principle.

If Danish (or Western) managers try to involve Russian employees early in the decision-making process, the Russian perceive the managers as being characterized either by confusion, unnecessary softness and lack of ability (that forces them to consult subordinates) or by complete unfamiliarity with the specificity of the Russian context. This is expressed in statements, such as 'Westerners don't know what to do, that's why they ask us.'

▶ Planning

Russians and Danes in Dancom also define planning differently. Danes interpret planning as a long-term activity. They use active planning as a management tool along with executing and adjusting at different stages of their work as managers. In the minds of the Danish participants planning is an instrumental value, a tool for evaluation of work progress:

> Planning is simply a question of setting goals to have something to focus on. And if do not reach a goal, it is not a defeat, it is not a personal defeat, it might turn out that there is a natural explanation for that and then you just have to adjust your goals for the next period of time. (Danish manager)

However, they confess that 'in Russia it does not work that way'. Danes characterize Russian employees as not interested in planning, especially in long-term planning: 'Russians do not find it very important to settle a plan for the whole year. They think, "OK we know what to do for this month and the next month, and that is enough"' (Danish manager). This is in line with how Russians perceive themselves. They consider long-term planning to be useless. As one of the Russian middle managers tried to explain to the Danish superior: 'It is impossible to plan everything in Russia. There may be some issue where you can plan maximum a year ahead – issues related to big stable customers – but otherwise everything changes so quickly.'

According to the Russian understanding as expressed by our respondents, planning is a strong commitment: 'When you make commitment you also have to be responsible for it. If you don't reach your goal you have to explain why you didn't. Not reaching a goal is a defeat' (sales engineer).

Planning understood as an ultimate value might be seen as a heritage of the socialist system where a planned economy on a societal level reinforced the planned execution by all means, including manipulations and massive collective overtime work (Anisimova, 1999). We suggest that it might also be rooted in centuries-old history, in the times of the village communes. The members of the communes 'openly and uninhibitedly exercised their right to articulate their interests and opinions before decisions were made. However, once a decision had been reached, they were obliged to abide by it' (Vlachoutsicos, 1998: 13). The specific feature, however, is that the decision was taken by one single person who did not necessarily respect the opinions and voices of the others.

The data suggest that insiders and outsiders clearly differ in their attitudes toward Danish work methods in general and certain aspects of decision-making and planning process in particular. Insiders tend to evaluate Danish work methods more positively than outsiders. Among the ten Russian insiders we interviewed, five evaluate them positively, four more or less positively, and only one negatively. However, four outsiders evaluated Danish work methods negatively and three more or less positively. This difference seems to be linked to their perceptions of foreign partners and ways of relating to them. Insiders who have closer and more informal links with foreign colleagues tend to accept their way of doing things, whereas outsiders who perceive Danes as aliens find their work methods alien as well. It is not, then, surprising that self-motivated insiders more positively evaluate the Danish decision-making based on delegation of responsibility than do the hosting outsiders.

There are major differences in the meanings Russians and Danes use in a number of words and phrases in the communication and interaction process. People's understandings are not uniform and notions and terms are not used in a vacuum. They involve different associations in different cultural environments. In that sense, notions themselves might be viewed as cultural artifacts and language as a means of communication in a particular culture rather than a universal means of communication. In a context where different cultures interact, the meaning of the notions is used as a matter of continuous negotiation and change and language is a guide for classifying reality into perceptional units that make a difference for people in the culture. The variety of meanings as such is not problematic. The problem is the failure to clarify and negotiate the meanings. This causes a great deal of uncertainty in the interaction process with a serious impact on organizational everyday life in Dancom.

▶ Conclusion

Our analysis leads to some practical lessons and guidelines for Western investors/managers/expatriates involved in companies with Western participation in Russia.

First, be aware of the variety among the locals in terms of hosting insiders and hosting outsiders. Map the organization; identify who personifies the insiders' and outsiders' 'camps' and what their roles are in the organization.

The degree to which the local organizational members are 'included' in the organization varies. They all are members of the organization, i.e. insiders. But many of them feel like outsiders, perceive themselves as outsiders and are perceived by the others as outsiders. Whereas hosting insiders identify themselves strongly with the organization and are highly motivated in their work, the hosting outsiders look at it only as a place for earning money. While hosting insiders develop good operational relationships with their foreign colleagues, hosting outsiders have difficulties in coping with 'the other' and stick to the rather negative stereotypes and images of foreigners they have developed. In the Dancom case, there is no strong positive correlation between the duration of employment and being an insider/outsider – there are a number of people who joined Dancom when the company was established but still are outsiders and some of the newcomers very much feel insiders.

Second, if possible, select and appoint local members with English language capabilities. Invest effort in learning the Russian language as a sign of respect for your Russian colleagues and their culture. The Dancom case suggests that Russians who understand and speak English have a better chance of being actively involved in the communication and interaction with the foreign managers and specialists and, more generally, of being part of the insiders' subculture. This contributes to their feeling of being 'in' the organization. When foreign managers feel they are 'outsiders', this is largely because they are excluded from the informal life and communication of the Russian company, especially in the cases when Russians do not speak English. Learning Russian is the most efficient bridge to the Russians. Sometimes, the effort alone, without really achieving good results, is a big step towards gaining the trust and respect of the Russian members.

Third, pay a lot of attention to how headquarters handles the communication flow with the Russian company. Russian organizational members are very sensitive towards the intensity of communication flow with the headquarters. A delay or a lack of response from the central units is easily interpreted as a lack of respect towards the Russian subsidiary and even towards the Russian nation rather than as a sign of increasing freedom in solving problems independently. Both hosting insiders and hosting outsiders share this view.

Fourth, when taking decisions, do not be afraid to apply top-down oriented techniques. Be careful in adopting participative approaches inviting initiative and responsibility at the bottom of the organization – they are neither understood, nor welcomed. Top-down management approaches are highly respected by Russian organizational members. At the same time, they perceive long discussions in groups and teams and efforts to reach a consensus in the decision-making process as 'useless', as 'a waste of time', and, even worse, as 'an effort to cover one's lack of knowledge and professionalism by hiding behind the group'. One-man authority, the so-called *edinonachalie*, is interpreted as functioning well and bringing results. Therefore, it makes sense, especially in the initial phase of the development of the Russian company with Western participation, to gain the respect of the local members demonstrating an ability to act as a 'strong leader' able to give directions, define tasks clearly and follow up their execution.

Finally, when introducing strategic plans, formulate short-term oriented tasks with achievable and observable results and assign Russians to work on them. Keep in mind that planning for Russians is a strong commitment, an end that has to be achieved by all means – it is not an instrument for adjusting and evaluating. Russian middle managers and specialists do not respect long-term plans with uncertain outcomes. Many of them have exercised planning in the socialist past and their idea of planning is strongly influenced by those previous experiences. Although the whole planning idea became largely discredited after 1991 and for many people 'plan' became a dirty word, when in use, it is still associated with an ultimate goal.

Consequently, not executing the plan as formulated initially is seen as a defeat. Close monitoring of changes in the organization and its environment and changing the plan accordingly are not understood/applied as an idea or an approach by

Russian managers and specialists. Having pointed out the above features, we do not suggest Western managers adopt the approach 'when in Rome do as the Romans do'. However, we advocate a careful contextualization of the concepts and techniques applied.

Appendix

Methodological details

The departmental affiliations of the participants are shown in table D3.

The research was based on 20 semi-structured interviews with participants (four with the Danes and sixteen with Russians), direct and participant observation, informal conversations, and analysis of documents. Interview questions were centred on the issues of perceptions of Dancom, perception of the foreign partner, interaction, communication, planning and decision-making. Observational data consisted of notes taken during and after interviews and informal discussions. We focus on the perspective of the Russian managers and employees, on their way of perceiving, understanding and interpreting organizational life in Dancom. When we quote Danish managers, we use their statements as a point of reference, not as a basis for comparison. The selected quotations carry out a double function – representation and evocation. When the purpose of quoting was to illustrate our finding we chose those quotations which seemed to be the most typical for the item under discussion and represented idea, notion or concept repeatedly mentioned by different organizational members. When our aim was to stress the diversity and represent the variety of opinions and attitudes, we tried to select polar expressions. One of the categories that emerges from the data in relation to perception of organization by its members is inclusion in the organization. Interview data and observations revealed items which were later grouped around the following notions: belonging to the organization, attitudes to foreign colleagues,

Table D3 The department affiliation of participants

Department	Managerial position	Specialist
IT	1 middle manager	1 specialist
Technical Support	1 middle manager	1 specialist
Marketing	1 middle manager	1 specialist
Finance and Accounting	1 top manager	2 specialists
Sales	1 top manager	3 specialists
	1 middle manager	
Administration	1 middle manager	1 specialist
Engineering	1 top manager	1 specialist
Logistics	1 middle manager	

ability to communicate and share information, and type of motivation. The difference in relation to those items allowed us to distinguish two groups of employees which we have clustered around the inclusion/exclusion debate.

Acknowledgements

The authors are grateful to the respondents in Dancom and the people who made possible fieldwork in the company and to Kenneth Husted and Klaus Meyer, both from CBS and to the anonymous referees. Snejina Michailova gratefully acknowledges the support in the framework of the action research project SODIAC (Sculpturing Organizational Dynamics in a Context: Lessons from Danish Companies Operating in the Russian Market).

Case Assignments

1 Within the context of the case, what are the main issues in the Danish approach towards managing that Russians perceive as particularly different from their own?
2 How do these differences affect the interaction between Russians and Danes?
3 What differentiates 'outsiders' from 'insiders'? How does one become an 'insider'?
4 Discuss the relevance and effectiveness of the managerial measures that were taken in Dancom's Russian subsidiary. And: are there other steps that could have been taken?

chapter

5

Transfer of US HRM to Europe

▶ Purpose

The purpose of this chapter is to address the challenge MNCs face when they attempt to leverage their human resource management (HRM) systems across subsidiaries located in various institutional contexts. The reason we do this is that for an MNC being able to utilize its HRM capabilities worldwide is an important source of competitive advantage. By HRM capabilities we mean the MNC's recipes for motivating its employees to perform in accordance with the overall strategy. However, it is also vital for MNCs to achieve and maintain legitimacy in all environments. To achieve this they must take into account local practices in order to become isomorphic with the local institutional context. 'Hereby lies the tension between the need for global integration, on the one hand, and local adaptation, on the other hand' (Kostova and Roth, 2002: 215). In order to understand this tension we focus on the case of subsidiaries of US MNCs in Europe. Our first step is to delineate the concept of HRM. In so doing, we distinguish between calculative and collaborative HRM. Thereafter, we distinguish the US institutional context from the European. Third, we distinguish, on the basis of the calculative and collaborative dimensions, four generic HRM regimes. Finally, we show how European HRM regimes influence subsidiaries of US MNCs to adapt their HRM practices.

▶ The US Approach to HRM

The question – how should people be managed? – is one of the most fundamental questions to be posed within the field of business management. After all, effective employee management is a major, if not the major, determinant of organizational success. Management theorists have long argued that if one could develop management systems that could be proved to be effective, these could be implemented universally. In other words there is a belief that there is 'a right way' of managing people that can be implemented by management consultants throughout the world. Currently the most significant of these ways may be broadly referred to as HRM.

Although there are different variants of HRM, each variant has as its core premise the necessity of actively aligning the motivations and interests of employees with the strategic aims and interests of the organization. The belief is that there is no inherent reason why this unification of employee–organization interest cannot be achieved, thereby removing 'them' and 'us' attitudes and generating the commitment needed to be able to adapt, change and compete. We will now describe the genesis of HRM followed by a delineation of its major features. In doing so we will emphasize its US origin and development and argue that it therefore has to be understood in terms of its US antecedents.

▶ The Genesis of HRM

Scientific management

In the early part of the last century Taylor (1911) came to the conclusion that US industry was woefully inefficient because of the absence of any systematic approach to management. He observed the lack of a clear structure of command resulting in the confusion in the assignment of tasks combined with a general lack of skills in the workforce. He prescribed a system, *scientific management*, which was designed to enhance the efficient use of manpower. The task of management was to divide the work process into discrete tasks and, on the basis of time and motion studies, to analyse each task in terms of its specialized skill and time requirements. Employees were to be assigned tasks and given the training required for the effective and efficient performance of those tasks and provided with a physical environment designed to maximize performance. Teamwork, or any form of co-worker consultation, was regarded by Taylor as unnecessary and even undesirable. Problems encountered by employees in the course of performing their tasks were to be immediately reported to supervisors who functioned as 'trouble shooters'. Supervisors were also charged with the task of accurately measuring individual task performance. Task performance over and above a prescribed level would trigger individual bonus payments.

It is difficult to gauge precisely the impact of scientific management but it would appear that derivatives of it continued to exert a powerful influence over the mind sets of US managers well into the 1980s: until the rise of HRM.

Arguably HRM can trace its genesis to three reactions to scientific management. The first of these surfaced as early as the late 1920s forming the basis of what is popularly referred to as the *human relations* perspective. The second was *human capital theory* and the third was centred round the text *In Search of*

Excellence by two McKinsey consultants, Peters and Waterman (1982). We briefly present each in turn.

Human relations

During the late 1920s and early 1930s Elton Mayo, a Harvard professor and a keen disciple of scientific management, was engaged by the Western Electric Company of the USA to investigate the causes of chronic low productivity at its Hawthorne works. Mayo assumed that the root problem lay in the physical context and that it needed fine-tuning. He divided the workers into two groups, an experimental and a control group. After explaining his general intentions to the experimental group in an amiable and respectful manner, he began systematically to improve their lighting, noting its effect on productivity. The resultant improvement in productivity, combined with the corresponding lack of change in the control group, appeared to confirm the validity of scientific management. However, Mayo's decision to provide further verification by, after informing the experimental group, decreasing the strength of the lighting caused him to question the scientific management paradigm. This was because instead of the productivity of the experimental group declining, as had been confidently expected, it continued to increase.

Mayo concluded that despite the intentions of the management at the Hawthorne plant, employees had in fact formed informal groups that exerted a powerful independent force on individuals' performance. They had done so, he surmised, because individuals have needs over and above the purely material, i.e. they have social needs, or a need to belong. Not only had scientific management failed to take these needs into account, it had attempted to suppress them. Moreover, it had also failed to recognize that groups that are consulted and informed can generate a commitment that can be harnessed to the aims of the firm.

It is reasonable to say, however, that US managers largely ignored Mayo's conclusions. They continued to be wedded to the tenets of scientific management. During the 1960s the human relations perspective enjoyed a revival, not least in works by Maslow (1954) and McGregor (1960). The former emphasized needs over and above the purely materialistic, arguing that work must be designed in such a way that it provides opportunities for personal involvement and personal growth. McGregor attacked the underlying assumptions of US managers, which he referred to as 'Theory X'. Core assumptions were, according to McGregor, that employees would never seek, let alone exercise, responsibility and were to be treated accordingly. McGregor argued that such assumptions were self-defeating and should be replaced by an assumption ('Theory Y') that employees, given the right conditions, were more than willing to play a responsible role. However, although the ideas of this new wave of human relations theorists enjoyed some measure of academic influence, their impact on either the hearts or minds of US managers was limited.

Human capital theory

During the 1970s economists began to turn their attention to the significance of human resources for productivity. Economic theory had traditionally regarded labour as a cost rather than an asset. *Human capital theory* challenged this view by pointing to the rapid post-war recovery of countries like Japan and Germany. Despite having had much of their physical capital stock destroyed during World War II, these countries recovered much more quickly than had been anticipated by economists. Schultz (1971) argued that this could only be ascribed to the quality of these countries' human capital. Moreover, it became apparent in international comparisons that these two countries were, when one controlled for the effects of traditional assets such as technology and hours worked, out-performing their competitors. It was argued that such differences first and foremost stemmed from the quality of the human capital at these countries disposal. Human capital economists dubbed the source of these differences 'the black box' of economics because of the difficulties involved in assigning values to human capital. Indeed, even today these difficulties have not been successfully overcome although efforts are still being made to do so, not least by the major consultancy firms in conjunction with valuing the assets of enterprises. Given the imprecision of the concept of human capital, it shared the same fate as that of the human relations perspective, namely to be consigned to an academic existence whose impact on managerial thinking was only marginal.

In search of excellence

It was not until the early 1980s that the scientific management approach to management was seriously questioned by US management practitioners. In the light of chronic economic difficulties in the USA, particularly in comparison with the success of Japan, they experienced a severe crisis of confidence. Some ten years after the human capital critique, it became received wisdom that Japanese firms were not only successfully out-competing their US counterparts in terms of price, but more importantly they were also pulling away from them in terms of quality. This crisis of confidence finally opened the door to alternative approaches to management, many of which drew heavily on the ideas contained in the human relations perspective and human capital theory. One of the most influential responses to this threat came from two McKinsey consultants, Peters and Waterman, who attempted to decipher the sources of excellence in those US firms that remained globally competitive. Their findings suggested that in order to achieve quality, the structures of scientific management were considerably less important than the presence of shared values and a shared vision among employees at all levels. It was these properties that created the foundation for a culture of employee commitment to the overarching aims of their firms which

Peters and Waterman concluded was essential if quality demands were to be consistently met.

Human resource management

The issues that crystallized themselves revolved around questions about how managers could succeed in creating inclusivity at all levels and how they could create a link between the ambitions of employees and the strategic aims of the firm. The outcome of this discussion was to propel personnel administration away from its position on the outer fringes of management. Traditionally it had been 'partly a file clerk's job, partly a housekeeping job, partly a social worker's job and partly fire-fighting to head off union trouble' (Drucker, 1989: 269). Now it was to occupy a very much more central position. Personnel administration was re-launched as human resource management.

The theoretical approaches to HRM that emerged as a consequence of the search to provide answers as to how to achieve the strategic deployment of a highly committed and capable workforce have been divided into 'hard' and 'soft' (Storey, 1987; Legge, 1995). Useful as these terms are, they have been taken to imply mutual exclusivity, when it is the case that the practices they encompass are rarely discrete in the workplace. That is, US firms have in practice rarely been wedded exclusively to either 'hard' or 'soft' HRM. With that point in mind, Gooderham, Nordhaug and Ringdal (1999) have introduced the terms 'calculative' and 'collaborative' HRM. Calculative HRM approaches embrace practices whose aim is to facilitate the assessment of each employee's contribution to the firm. Collaborative HRM approaches comprise those practices that aim at creating a culture of partnership between employer and employee.

'Calculative' HRM

In 1984 Fombrun, Tichy and Devanna launched a model, the 'Michigan' model of HRM, which emphasized that organizational effectiveness is dependent on achieving a tight fit between human resource strategy and the overall business strategy of the firm. Only when this has been achieved can HRM systems be developed. Figure 5.1 summarizes their thinking:

Their core recommendation is that the business strategy should be employed to define and determine the types of employee performance required. Once performance has been specified, four systems that ensure its realization must be slotted into place (see figure 5.2).

The first of these is a system for personnel selection; that is a system that ensures the deployment of individuals with the appropriate aptitudes, knowledge and experience. Second, there should be an appraisal system that enables the firm on a regular basis to assess whether performance is satisfactory. Third, there

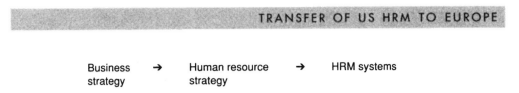

Figure 5.1 Fombrun, Tichy and Devanna's strategic approach to HRM

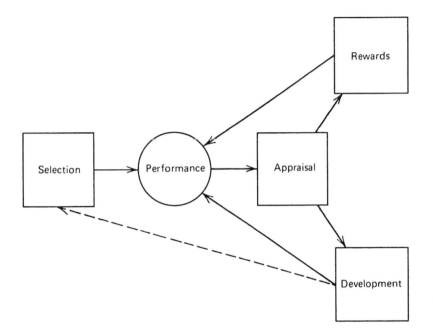

Figure 5.2 The Michigan model of HRM
Source: Fombrun, Tichy and Devanna, 1984. Reprinted with permission of John Wiley & Sons Inc.

should be a system of rewards that differentiates between different levels of performance. Fourth, they recommend that a development system should be available in those instances where the appraisal system indicates performance shortcomings. A final element in the model is indicated by the broken arrow from development to selection: i.e. if development is not forthcoming, then the individual's future at the company will be subject to reappraisal. Although there are no surveys that have established how widespread the use of this system is as a whole in the USA, we do know that the use of rewards differentiation is widespread with as many as 60 per cent of US firms currently using cash-based recognition systems (*The Economist*, 1999a).

On the surface the Michigan model bears a strong resemblance to scientific management. Its four HRM systems – selection, performance criteria, appraisal, rewards and development systems – were all to the forefront in Taylor's thinking. Thus Sparrow and Hiltrop (1994: 7) have characterized the rationale of the Michigan model as being one of managing people like any other resource: 'This means that they have to be obtained cheaply, used sparingly and developed and exploited as fully as possible.' However, beyond the strategic dimension to HRM, the important difference lies in the much greater devolvement of daily responsibility and initiative to the individual employee. Rather than the detailed and precise rules of scientific management, the HRM systems of the Michigan model are aimed at creating a dominant, strategically based, value system within which the employee performs.

One notable refinement to the concept of matching the business strategy to human resource systems in the Michigan model is found in the work of Schuler and Jackson (1987). Borrowing from the work of Porter (1980, 1985) they argued that business strategy could usefully be subdivided into three generic strategies – quality enhancement, innovation and cost leadership. Once it has been established which of these is to be pursued, the structuring of each of the four HRM systems can easily be specified. Thus, for example, pursuing a strategy based on innovation as opposed to one based on cost leadership will mean using group criteria rather than individual criteria in order to encourage the exchange of ideas. Likewise, one would seek to develop a rewards system that offers internal equity rather than market-based pay in order to minimize internal competition and to maximize a sense of group membership.

'Collaborative' HRM

Whereas Schuler and Jackson suggest that HRM systems designed to promote commitment to the group might, contingent upon the nature of the business strategy, be used, the 'Harvard' model developed by Beer *et al.* (1984) argues that they are invariably necessary. In other words Beer regards employee commitment as being of crucial importance for firm success regardless of the type of strategy being pursued. Similarly, Freeman (1984) argued that systematic managerial attention to stakeholder interests, not least those of employees, is critical to firm success because of their capacity to critically affect the achievement of the organization's objectives. 'We need to worry about enterprise level strategy for the simple fact that corporate survival depends in part on there being some "fit" between the values of the corporation and its managers (and) the expectation of stakeholders in the firm' (Freeman, 1984: 107).

In short, employees are not just another resource, they are a critical resource, possibly the most critical resource, so that personnel activities must be guided by an overall management philosophy that seeks to involve them. For Beer *et al.* and Freeman the business strategy should never be considered in isolation but always in relation to the employees.

As a consequence, Beer *et al.* recommend reward systems that aim at tapping into employees' intrinsic motivation coupled to a system of employee relations which delegates authority and responsibility. Typically, to achieve this, considerable effort is expended on creating and recreating mission statements that communicate the business strategy to employees. For example in 1999 Steven A. Ballmer, after nine months as president of Microsoft Corp., concluded that, because of the impact of the Internet, Microsoft needed badly to reinvent itself. One core tool he and Bill Gates employed to generate a change of direction was the introduction of a new mission statement. Out went 'a PC on every desk and in every home' and in came the new rallying cry: 'giving people the power to do anything they want, anywhere they want, and on any device'. For Ballmer the point of this so-called *Vision Version 2* was that Microsoft needed 'to give people a beacon that they could follow when they were having a tough time with prioritization, leadership, where to go, what hills to take'.[1] Coupled to mission statements are employee communication policies and systems for conducting employee briefings at all levels.

Another typical 'soft' HRM initiative has been aimed at creating environments conducive to teamwork. Weinstein and Kochan (1995) point to a clear transition towards the adoption of a variety of Total Quality Management (TQM) practices including employee problem-solving groups, work teams and job rotation. Indeed, by the early 1990s 64 per cent of US manufacturing firms reported that at least half of their core employee were covered by one or more of these workplace innovations, although relatively few were covered by all of these innovations (Osterman, 1994).

It is important to note though that none of these collaborative techniques were rooted in governance systems that involved any increasing role for the employees' trade unions. On the contrary, as HRM established itself in the USA, unions became even more marginalized in an institutional environment characterized by increasing management and shareholder power. Furthermore, the driving force is not intrinsically ethical, but strategic. Collaborative techniques are strictly a means to an end (Berman *et al.*, 1999). They are part of a company's strategy but they in no way drive that strategy. In other words techniques that do not contribute to financial success through increased productivity or improved quality will be discarded.

HRM in US companies

We have remarked that the various HRM practices US firms actually deploy can rarely be exclusively subsumed under either the label of 'calculative' or 'collaborative'. In other words, variable pay is as widespread as is employee communication. This deployment of a mix of calculative and collaborative techniques is particularly apparent at General Electric (GE). GE went from being an old-line American industrial giant in the early 1980s to representing what Noel Tichy, a management professor at the University of Michigan, regards as 'a new, contemporary paradigm for the corporation'.[2] A *Business Week* special report[3] on the leadership style of its chairman, Jack Welch, who succeeded to the post in 1981, states the following:

> Rarely do surprises occur. Welch sets precise performance targets and monitors them throughout the year. And every one of Welch's direct reports – from his three vice-chairmen to each of the operating heads of GE's 12 businesses – also receives a handwritten, two-page evaluation of his performance at the end of every year . . .
>
> As if in lockstep, each business chieftain then emulates the behavior of his boss, and their reports, in turn do the same . . . As Thomas E. Dunham, who runs services in GE Medical Systems, puts it, 'Welch preaches it from the top, and people see it at the bottom.' The result: Welch's leadership style is continually reinforced up and down the organization.
>
> Above all, however, Welch skillfully uses rewards to drive behavior. Those rewards are not inconsequential at GE, in part because of Welch's determination not to hand the kind of $1,000 raise that he got back in 1961. To this day, Welch demands that the rewards a leader disburses to people be highly differentiated – especially because GE is in so many different businesses. 'I can't stand non-differential stuff', he says. 'We live in differentiation.'

In practice, differentiation at GE means that each of its 85,000 professionals and managers is graded in an annual process that divides them into five groups: the top 10 per cent, the next 15 per cent, the middle 50 per cent, the next 15 per cent and the bottom 10 per cent. The top tier will get options; nobody in the fourth tier does, and most of the fifth tier will probably be culled. Each unit must segment its managers in this way each year, so that it cannot get away with claiming that they are all in the first tier.[4]

On the other hand, we also learn that the HRM philosophy at GE encompasses considerably more than a set of calculative HRM practices:

> Welch's profound grasp on General Electric stems from knowing the company and those who work in it like no other . . . More than half (of his time) is devoted to 'people' issues. But most important, he has created something unique at a big company: informality . . .
>
> If the hierarchy that Welch inherited, with its nine layers of management, hasn't been completely nuked, it has been severely damaged. Everyone, from secretaries to chauffers to factory workers, calls him Jack . . .
>
> Making the company 'informal' means violating the chain of command, communicating across layers, paying people as if they worked not for a big company but for a demanding entrepreneur where nearly everyone knows the boss . . .
>
> 'We're pebbles in an ocean, but he knows about us,' says Brian Nailor, a fortysomething marketing manager of industrial products.

Others have observed that:

> One of Jack Welch's early successes was to persuade staff to talk back – a process still used throughout the company, known as 'workout'. Employees are encouraged, in

his words, 'to kick bureaucracy, to hate bureaucracy with a passion'. For a group as hidebound as by rules as GE used to be, that was a revolution.[5]

In sum, Welch believes that because of this mix of practices every member of GE has a very clear understanding of the company's strategy. He once remarked: 'One comment that people give me is that if you go on an airplane ride and you sit next to somebody from any GE division, you will get the same story about where GE is going: that shows the message is pretty clear.'[6]

The essence of US HRM

In essence, US HRM consists of a mix of elements some of which are 'calculative' others of which are 'collaborative'. In particular we have emphasized:

Calculative
- Individual (possibly group) performance appraisals
- Individual (possibly group) rewards systems
- Evaluations of the effectiveness of training and development

Collaborative
- Mission statements that clarify and communicate the vision of the company
- A commitment to employee communication
- Strategy briefings of employees at all levels

▶ Core Assumptions of US HRM

Brewster (1994) has pointed out that a core assumption of US HRM is that the employing organization has a considerable degree of latitude in regard to taking decisions on the management of personnel, including *inter alia*:

- Freedom to operate a contingent pay policy.
- An absence or at least a minimal influence from trade unions.
- An assumption that the organization has sole responsibility for training and development.

In other words, central to the notion of US HRM is the assumption of considerable organizational independence and autonomy. Given the weakness of the trade union movement in the USA, where membership is currently little more than 10 per cent and its activities are predominantly site-based, coupled with the comparatively low levels of state subsidy, support and control, such an assumption is entirely reasonable. The question is though how viable such a critical assumption to US HRM is within the context of Europe.

Closely related to the assumption of firm autonomy is a second core assumption, that the close involvement of HRM and business strategy represents a radically new departure for the management of personnel.

What follows is not intended as a systematic or detailed exposition of the European context, but rather a general introduction to the notion that Europe is different from the USA. In other words we wish to scrutinize the validity of the two core assumptions of HRM as it emerged from the U.S.A. in relation to the assumptions that broadly apply across Europe.

▶ Organizational Autonomy

A culture of individualism

Although the empirical data on national cultural differences is limited, researchers within the field of comparative cultural studies, such as Hofstede (1980a) and Trompenaars (1985) regard the United States as being quite untypical of the world as a whole in terms of its extreme individualism and achievement-orientation. Indeed, it has been argued by Guest (1990) that the US assumption of business freedom and autonomy is peculiarly North American and is related to the North American view of their country as a land of opportunity that rewards success. It is an American's birthright, if not duty, to stand on his own two feet and to have a go at starting up some kind of enterprise.

Certainly, when we examine the proportion of adults who are active in business start-ups, there is a significant gulf dividing the US from Europe. Table 5.1 indicates that while 8.4 per cent of US adults were involved in business start-ups in the winter of 1999, the average figure for European countries, despite generally higher levels of unemployment, was much lower. In Germany and France for example the average was around 2 per cent, whereas for the UK and Italy it was slightly higher.

Table 5.1 Percentage of adults involved in business start-ups, winter 1999

Country	Percentage of adults
Finland	1.7
France	1.8
Denmark	1.9
Germany	2.1
UK	3.4
Italy	3.5
USA	8.4

Source: *The Financial Times*, 1999a.

This culture of individualism or entrepreneurialism is clearly discernible in the thinking underpinning US HRM particularly in regard to its emphasis on performance-based rewards. That is, just as a free market differentiates between successful and unsuccessful individual enterprises, so should firms have the freedom to reward those employees who have made critical contributions to their success. In turn, given the relative lack of a culture of entrepreneurialism in Europe, we equally should not expect any ready acceptance of individual performance-related rewards.

Legislation: the firm and the individual employee

If a culture of individualism is a necessary condition for securing broad acceptance of the differentiation of rewards at the individual level, legislation defines the parameters of actual practice. One German authority, Pieper, pointed out that 'the major difference between HRM in the US and in Western Europe is the degree to which [HRM] is influenced and determined by state regulations. Companies have a narrower scope of choice in regard to personnel management than in the US' (1990: 82). We can distinguish three aspects to this concept of management scope: (1) the degree of employment protection; (2) the legislative requirements on pay and hours of work; and (3) legislation on forms of employment contracts.

In regard to the first of these, Blanchard (1999) has attempted to quantify differences in employment protection, within both Europe and the USA. He argues that employment protection has three main dimensions, the length of the notice period to be given to workers, the amount of severance pay to be paid according to the nature of the separation and the nature and complexity of the legal process involved in laying off workers. Blanchard finds that the USA is significantly different from Europe in general and Italy, Spain and Portugal in particular.

In relation to the legislative requirements on pay and work, there are also marked differences. For example, whereas in Europe legislative developments have ensured that average hours worked have fallen over the last two decades, in the USA, they have increased. Thus in the USA, almost 80 per cent of male workers and 65 per cent of working women, now work more than 40 hours in a typical week.[7] By contrast, in France the working week is by law currently limited to 35 hours with overtime limited to 130 hours a year. This policy of job creation through limiting the amount of work undertaken by individual employees even extends to making unpaid overtime by senior employees a penal offence. Indeed, in June 1999 a director of the defence company Thompson Radars and Countermeasures was fined 100,000 francs after the government's jobs inspectorate had monitored executives, researchers and engineers and uncovered substantial unrecorded overtime. In the USA such a scenario would be inconceivable.

Finally, with respect to legislation on employment contracts, although this varies within Europe, it exists everywhere; legislation governing short-term contract working is non-existent in the USA, where casual employment is more common.

The 'Rhineland' model

The legislation that determines the firm–employee relationship is a product of a wider, normative, conception of what role the state should be play within the economic arena. In his book *Capitalisme contre Capitalisme* (1991), Michel Albert, a former director of the French planning agency, distinguished on the one hand between an Anglo-Saxon capitalism (principally the USA, but also the UK) and on the other a continental, West European type of capitalism which he labelled the 'Rhineland' model. The former is a 'shareholder economy' under which private enterprise is about maximising short-term profits for investors rather than any broader harmony of interests. In contrast, the Rhineland model may be viewed as a regulated market economy with a comprehensive system of social security. Government, employers' organizations and labour unions consult each other about economic goals (in order to) try to achieve a harmony of interests' (Bolkestein, 1999). In short, the Rhineland model is a 'stakeholder economy' in which competition and confrontation are avoided in the belief that it undermines sustainable, stable economic growth. Patrolling this economy is the state, which variously acts as a referee, guarantor, employer and owner.

Table 5.2 provides a first indication of the role of the state in the Rhineland model. Whereas public spending as a percentage of GDP in the EU averages at nearly 50 per cent, it is only 32 per cent in the USA. This difference in attitude between the US and Rhineland economies towards public spending is also manifest in regard to the labour market.

Table 5.2 Public spending as a percentage of nominal GDP, 1997

Country	Percentage of GDP
Sweden	62
Finland	54
France	54
Italy	51
Netherlands	49
EU total	48
Germany	48
Spain	42
UK	40
USA	32

Source: OECD *Economic Outlook*, 1998.

Labour market

As well as being major employers in their own right Rhineland states also subsidize jobs extensively. In France between 1973 and 1997 the number of French workers in subsidized jobs grew from 100,000 to 2.2 million according to the OECD, while the total in unsubsidized jobs shrank from 21.4m to 20.3m. Nearly a quarter of the French labour force now relies on government handouts, whether in the form of unemployment benefit or subsidized jobs. (Pedder, 1999: 11).

On becoming unemployed, Americans initially receive a level of benefit of about two-thirds income, not far below levels in Rhineland Europe. But those benefit levels tail off sharply after six to nine months. In many Rhineland countries, in contrast, benefits are either not time limited or actually increase the longer that people are out of work. In Sweden and Finland the income replacement rate of 89 per cent actually rises to 99 per cent. It has been argued that this virtual absence of a margin between benefits and wages for the low-skilled unemployed represents a serious disincentive to seek new jobs in many European countries. A recent French study reported by Pedder (1999) showed that the unemployed in France take five times as long to find a new job as in the USA *yet those in work are five times less likely to lose their jobs.*

The influence of unions

Another core feature of Rhineland states is the legislative status and influence accorded to unions. Table 5.3 indicates that most European countries are more

Table 5.3 Union density and bargaining coverage

	1994 union density rate	1994 bargaining coverage
Austria	43	98
Belgium	53	90
Denmark	76	90
Finland	81	95
France	9	95
Germany	30	92
Italy	39	82
Netherlands	26	81
Norway	58	74
Portugal	32	50
Spain	22	66
Sweden	91	93
UK	36	47
US	16	18

Source: OECD 1995.

heavily unionized in terms of union membership than the USA. However, in reality, trade union influence cannot be gauged sufficiently by focusing on union density rates. A more important issue is that of trade union recognition, that is whether the employer deals with a trade union in a collective bargaining relationship that sets terms and conditions for all or most of the employees. It is in this respect that Rhineland states diverge to a considerable degree from that of the USA and, to a lesser extent, from the UK. In countries such as Germany, France and the Benelux countries, there is legislation in place requiring employers over a certain size to recognize unions for consultative purposes.

Closely related to the issue of trade union recognition is the Rhineland practice of employee involvement. Typically the law requires the establishment of workers' councils. Legislation in countries such as the Netherlands, Denmark and, most famously, Germany, requires organizations to have two-tier management boards, with employees having the right to be represented on the more senior Supervisory Board. These arrangements give considerable (legally backed) power to the employee representatives and, unlike consultation in the USA, for example, they tend to supplement rather than supplant the union position. In relatively highly unionized countries it is unsurprising that many of the representatives of the workforce are, in practice, trade union officials.

A central theme of HRM is the requirement to generate significant workforce commitment through developing channels of communication. However, in Rhineland countries it is noticeable that the provision of information to the workforce involves the use of the formalized employee representation or trade union channels. And when upward communication is examined, the two most common means in Europe, by a considerable margin, are through immediate line management – and through the trade union or works council channel (Brewster, 1994).

Patterns of ownership

Patterns of ownership also vary from one side of the Atlantic to the other. Public ownership has decreased to some extent in many European countries in recent years; but it is still far more widespread in Rhineland countries than it is in the USA. And private sector ownership often does not mean the same thing in Rhineland countries as it does in the equity-based ownership regimes of the USA and the UK. This is particularly apparent in the case of hostile takeover activity, which is much less widespread in Rhineland countries. Bennett (1997: 100–1) identifies five specific barriers to takeover activity in Rhineland countries:

- In many of the southern European countries particularly, ownership of even major companies remains in the hands of single families rather than in the hands of shareholders. On the other hand, in Germany, a tight network of a small number of substantial banks own a disproportionate number of companies. Their interlocking shareholdings and close involvement in the management of these corporations mean less pressure to produce short-term profits and less exposure to predatory takeovers (Randlesome *et al.*, 1990).

- In a number of Rhineland countries companies hold substantial reserves enabling them to resist unwanted takeovers. Belgian, French and German companies must, by law, create a reserve of at least 10 per cent of their share capital. Italian companies have to retain a 20 per cent reserve; in Denmark the reserve has to be 25 per cent; and in Greece 33.3 per cent.
- In many Rhineland countries there is an extensive use of bearer shares that makes it difficult to identify shareholders willing to sell their equities. Moreover it is lawful in Belgium, France, Spain, Italy, Germany and the Netherlands to conceal the names and addresses of shareholders.
- It is common in Rhineland countries to grant special voting rights to particular groups of shareholders. In Germany, for instance, shares with high par values have more voting rights than shares with low par values. French law permits companies to grant more voting powers to long-standing shareholders than others. France, Germany, Belgium and the Netherlands permit companies to restrict the voting powers of any single shareholder to a low level (e.g., to an upper limit of 5 per cent of all votes). This prevents individuals with large blocks of shares from transferring majority voting powers to takeover predators.
- The compulsory industrial democracy arrangements that large companies in many Rhineland nations are obliged to implement mean that employee representatives have the right to be consulted on takeover attempts, a process that delays such attempts. In Germany and the Netherlands employee representatives have the legal right to delay mergers and acquisitions for several weeks.

The Link between HRM and Business Strategy

One of the most widely discussed distinctions between HRM and old-fashioned personnel management is the closer linking of the former to business strategy. By linking is meant the degree to which the HRM issues are considered as part of the formulation of business strategies. In particular there is an ingrained assumption in the US literature that HRM is the dependent variable and business strategy the independent variable in this relationship. Moreover, North Americans argue that such an integration of business strategy and HRM is inherently advantageous. Our look at GE illustrates this mentality.

However, there is also a strong linkage of human resource issues with business strategy in Europe as well. However, much of this is a product of legislation rather than firm-based decisions. For example, in Germany the Codetermination Act of 1952, as amended in 1976, requires the executive boards of large

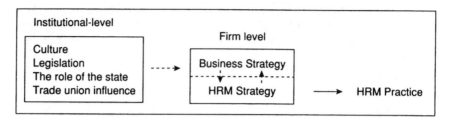

Figure 5.3 A dual level framework of HRM

companies to have a labour director with responsibility for staff and welfare matters. Likewise in the Scandinavian countries any changes to company strategy with employee implications have to be discussed with employee representatives. In Europe, then, it is generally common for personnel specialists to be involved at an early stage in the development of corporate strategy (Brewster, 1994).

▶ A Dual Level Framework

Clearly the practice of HRM cannot be divorced from its institutional context. The US model is a viable alternative or possibility for US firms because of the nature of the context within which they operate. We should not expect to see it replicated in the European context with the exception of the UK, which clearly diverges from mainland Europe. What is needed is an HRM framework that is broad enough to take into account the influence of such environmental factors as culture, legislation, the role of the state and trade union representation. This was the task Chapter 3 addressed. At the same time the framework should accommodate the potential for firm-level activities. It is our contention that HRM theory needs to adopt a multilevel view of the actors in the system if it is to become a theory that can be applied internationally.

The HRM framework we propose in figure 5.3 builds on the framework presented in Chapter 3. It shows, in a simplistic form, that HRM practices are to be understood in part as products of an external institutional environment of national culture, national legislation, state involvement and trade union representation and in part as products of firm level business strategy and HRM strategy. The framework contains three broken arrows that reflect considerable cross-national variation.

- The broken arrow between the institutional-level factors and the firm-level factors indicates that the influence of the former may vary substantially.
- The two broken arrows from business strategy to HRM strategy indicate that the potential for a purely business strategy-driven HRM strategy varies considerably. Unlike in the USA, in the case of Europe there will be an

interaction between the business strategy and HRM strategy as a consequence of institutional-level factors.

The framework indicates therefore that it is conceivable that in extreme contexts institutional-level factors will be a sufficient guide to understanding HRM strategy and that business strategy may be more or less ignored. Equally, in contexts of extreme firm autonomy the importance of environmental-level factors for HRM strategy will be minimal in comparison with business strategy. Our previous discussion suggests that while Rhineland regimes approximate to the former variant, the US regime approximates to the latter.

▶ Four Contexts for HRM in Europe

We have defined and discussed US HRM and located it within its institutional context. We have indicated that in Rhineland Europe organizations are constrained at the national level by culture and legislation, and at the organizational level by trade union involvement and consultative arrangements. It is clear that, with the exception of the UK, European countries are more heavily unionized than the United States and that state involvement is more directly interventionist. Finally, we have indicated that shareholder capitalism, as opposed to stakeholder capitalism, is constrained in Rhineland Europe. We now turn to the question of variations within Europe.

Institutional theorists argue that management practices reflect idiosyncratic principles of local rationality. The character of local rationality has been conceived in a number of ways. One approach has been to distinguish between, on the one hand, countries such as the UK and the Nordic countries in which the state has a limited role in industrial relations. On the other hand, there are the Roman-Germanic countries, such as France, Spain, Germany, Italy, Belgium, Greece and the Netherlands in which the state functions as an actor with a central role in industrial relations. A particular feature of Roman-Germanic countries is their 'comprehensive labour market legislation governing various areas, such as length of the working day (and) rest periods' (Due, Madsen and Jensen, 1991: 90). In other words, unlike either the UK or the Nordic systems, the latitude for firm-level decision making in Roman-Germanic countries in regard to employment issues is relatively small which in turn means that the scope for flexibility initiatives of the collaborative type at the organizational level is constrained.

Hollingsworth and Boyer (1997) represent a second approach in which the focus is on the presence or absence of communitarian infrastructures that manifest themselves in the form of strong social bonds, trust, reciprocity and co-operation among economic actors. They distinguish between social contexts characterized by self-interest and those in which 'obligation and compliance with social rules are the guiding principles shaping human actions' (Hollingsworth and Boyer, 1997: 8).[8] It is their contention that the UK has a pervasive market mentality that

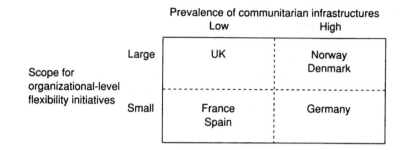

Figure 5.4 Four social contexts for the implementation of HRM in Europe

limits trust and co-operation between workers and managers within firms. In contrast, German and Scandinavian firms are embedded in an environment in which the market mentality is less pronounced with trusting relationships and communitarian obligations. Finally, Hollingworth and Boyer distinguish France as an environment that, while not having a market mentality, is nevertheless deficient in communitarian infrastructures. Instead, the public authorities play a *dirigiste* role in the economy. Hence, there is an environment in which employer–employee conflict is endemic and there is an absence of 'a spirit of generous co-operation' (Maurice, Sellier and Silvestre, 1986: 86). Given its authoritarian legacy from the Franco regime, Spain is another country in which communitarian infrastructures are weakly developed. The presence of communitarian infrastructures constitutes an obstruction for the introduction of calculative mechanisms.

Taken together the two dimensions suggest four broad national contexts for personnel management in Europe. These are indicated in figure 5.4, which we have exemplified with six countries.

▶ HRM in Europe

On the basis of the Cranet data set[9] we shall now look at HRM practices in Europe. Figure 5.4 predicts high levels of calculative HRM practices in contexts with a low prevalence of communitarian infrastructures and widespread use of collaborative HRM practices in contexts characterized by a large scope for organizational-level flexibility initiatives.

Calculative practices

In line with the prediction contained in figure 5.4, tables 5.4, 5.5 and 5.6 indicate a number of substantial differences between on the one hand, Norway, Denmark and Germany and, on the other, Spain, France and the UK. In general calculative practices are more widespread in the latter than the former.

Table 5.4 Use of performance appraisals for various employee categories

Employee category	Norway	Denmark	Germany	Spain	France	UK
Managerial	48.1	44.4	54.1	58.5	83.4	89.4
Professional/technical	37.6	42.8	59.6	75.0	73.8	86.8
Clerical	25.9	40.8	56.0	58.9	56.9	79.3
Manual	23.3	23.0	38.7	48.7	42.3	47.1
N	189	304	364	224	385	859

Table 5.5 Use of performance-related individual reward systems for various employee categories

Employee category	Norway	Denmark	Germany	Spain	France	UK
Managerial	21.2	14.8	19.8	48.7	69.6	64.5
Professional/technical	16.9	12.8	37.1	57.6	54.5	57.2
Clerical	11.6	8.9	35.4	41.4	46.2	48.8
Manual	16.9	24.5	28.8	29.5	35.1	25.8
N	189	304	364	224	385	859

Table 5.6 Formal evaluation of the effectiveness of training in firms

Evaluation	Norway	Denmark	Germany	Spain	France	UK
Immediately after training	44.4	31.9	47.8	83.0	82.3	80.4
Some months after training	24.3	22.0	27.5	53.6	46.0	61.4
N	189	304	364	224	385	859

Collaborative practices

When we examine tables 5.7 and 5.8, which together contain the three core collaborative practices, we find that these practices are significantly more a feature of Norway, Denmark and the UK than of Germany, Spain and France.

Overview

In figure 5.5 we have summarized the results using a scaling procedure while controlling for industry and firm size. Figure 5.5 indicates four distinct European HRM regimes. UK firms have high scores on both types of HRM practices, French and Spanish firms have high scores on calculative practices but only medium scores on

Table 5.7 Proportions of firms with written mission statements and written employee communication policy (%)

	Norway	Denmark	Germany	Spain	France	UK
Written mission statements	96.3	87.3	59.8	57.6	41.0	78.8
N	189	300	361	210	366	845
Written employee communication policies	67.7	48.0	26.6	38.4	33.2	46.3
N	189	304	364	224	385	859

Table 5.8 Proportions of firms which formally brief employees about the strategy of the firm by employee category (%)

Employee category	Norway	Denmark	Germany	Spain	France	UK
Managerial	98.4	94.1	93.4	96.9	94.5	94.4
Professional/technical	76.7	60.2	42.3	70.1	49.9	72.9
Clerical	71.4	50.7	21.7	27.2	32.2	50.4
Manual	66.7	38.5	11.3	20.2	24.9	42.3
N	189	304	364	224	385	859

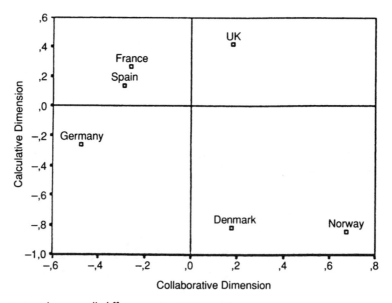

Figure 5.5 The overall differences in HRM practices

collaborative practices. German firms exhibit below average scores on both practices, whereas Danish and Norwegian firms have low scores on calculative practices but high scores on collaborative practices.

▶ When in Rome, Do They Do as the Romans Do?

In their pursuit of being effective global competitors, MNCs will typically seek 'the unimpeded right to coordinate and control all aspects of the company on a worldwide basis' (Bartlett and Ghoshal, 1995: 119). That is, MNCs will attempt to apply the management practices they are most familiar with regardless of the location of their subsidiary. As we pointed out in Chapter 1, national identity is generally strong, so inevitably these are the practices of their countries of origin. However, in order to maintain legitimacy MNCs also have to take into account the demands and expectations of their various host environments. These may necessitate the modification of their management processes. As such, there is a potential for tension between the need for global integration, on the one hand, and local adaptation on the other hand (Kostova and Roth, 2002). That tension will be particularly great when the MNC is trying to establish a subsidiary in an institutional context that is markedly different to its own and when it is not prepared to accept a multi-domestic solution with comprehensive local responsiveness and little in the way of global integration. Increasingly, fewer MNCs can be characterized as multi-domestics as they move to the more integrated and centralized modes associated with US and Japanese MNCs (Edwards and Ferner, 2002).

We have pointed to US firms as being strong in terms of both the calculative and collaborative HRM dimensions. The question is what happens when they establish subsidiaries abroad such as in Europe. Do they do as the Romans do, that is, do they adapt their HRM practices to the local setting, or do they attempt a wholesale implementation of their HRM practices?

The Cranet data set enables us to contrast the use of calculative HRM practices by US MNCs in four different European contexts, the UK, Ireland, Denmark and Norway combined and Germany. We have already noted that the UK is strong in terms of calculative practices while Denmark, Norway and Germany are weak. Ireland is characterized by greenfield sites offering freedom from local institutional constraints. As figure 5.6 indicates, US subsidiaries make more use of calculative practices in all four contexts than their native-owned counterparts. In that sense they clearly are able to exert a distinct country-of-origin influence on local HRM policy. However, there is a marked difference between US subsidiaries in the calculative HRM-friendly environments of the UK and the green-field sites of Ireland to that of Denmark/Norway and Germany. In short, in Denmark/Norway and Germany US MNCs are succumbing to institutional pressures to

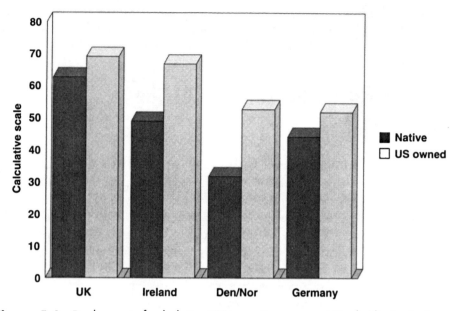

Figure 5.6 Deployment of calculative HRM practices among US subsidiaries in the UK, Ireland, Denmark/Norway (Den/Nor) and Germany and their native counterparts controlled for size, industry and age of establishment

moderate their use of calculative HRM practices. This process of semi-adaptation results in hybrid organizational practices that are partly rooted in practices emanating from headquarters, and partly in local institutional conditions.

These findings do not only apply to MNCs. As the case accompanying this chapter indicates they also have implications for international consultancy firms that attempt to transfer best practice.

▶ Summary

The starting point of this chapter was the potential tension MNCs are exposed to when they attempt to transfer their organizational capabilities to their foreign subsidiaries. Our focus has been on the US approach to HRM and the potential for US MNCs to experience tension in the European context. As we have demonstrated, the UK regime appears to be unique in Europe in that both collaborative and calculative practices are widespread. As such, it clearly resembles the US HRM regime and, like Irish greenfield sites, provides a relatively benign environment for US MNCs in terms of the transfer of HRM practices.

In the following case a Norwegian bank is featured that is located in a context that in terms of HRM is highly collaborative and weakly calculative. The case describes what took place when management attempted to introduce US-style

HRM. Although the case does not involve a subsidiary of a US MNC, it is reasonable to assume that its experiences are similar to cases involving acquisitions of Norwegian firms by US MNCs.

Notes

1 Source: *Business Week* (1999a).
2 Source: *Business Week* (1999b).
3 Source: *Business Week* (1999b: 40–51).
4 Source: *The Economist* (1999b).
5 Source: *The Financial Times* (1999b).
6 Source: *The Financial Times* (1999b).
7 Source: *The Economist* (1999c).
8 See also Maurice, Sellier and Silvestre (1986) and their analysis of work systems in France and Germany.
9 The Cranet set comprises the results of identical surveys of firms in EU and EFTA countries. The overall strategy has been to mail appropriately translated questionnaires to personnel managers in representative national samples of firms with more than one hundred employees. Problems in ensuring that the selection and interpretation of topic areas were not biased by one country's approach, as well as problems related to the translation of concepts and questions, were largely overcome by close collaboration between business schools located in each country (for a detailed description, see Brewster *et al.*, 1996).

case E

SR-Bank: Cultural Translation of a US Concept

Martin Gjelsvik and Odd Nordhaug

▶ Introduction

This case offers a detailed description of an organization being forced to leave the shelter of strict, predictable government regulation and cartel-based non-competition to face and ride through the storms caused by deregulation. This story has repeated itself in many industries throughout Europe. Like other businesses exposed to dramatic changes, the bank had to learn how to compete more or less from scratch. The bank decided to base its turnaround on a redefinition of the former roles of the employees and their managers through a comprehensive organizational development project. A programme was imported from the US and transformed into the Norwegian context. This process challenged the wide cultural differences between the American and Norwegian management traditions, role identities and work organizing.

It is thus a story of how an organization suddenly was confronted with a fundamental turnaround challenge by profound changes in its external environment. The institutional rules of Norwegian banks were turned upside down in the latter part of the 1980s. The deregulation and liberalization of the financial markets swiftly and radically altered the rules of the game in the banking industry. This development coincided with a serious downturn of the economy, causing big losses for the banks. The case presented here deals with a bank and its people that survived what may be called a close-to-death experience, as the bank was on the verge of bankruptcy in 1991. Since then, the bank, with its roots back to 1839, has reinvented itself through a strong belief in linking its overall strategies to a human resource policy of continuously enhancing the knowledge and skills of the employees, close and long-term customer relations and a strong physical presence in the region. The bank has become a learning organization where management consciously facilitates and encourages learning opportunities.

What was then conceived of as a programme or a project is today a continuing process to leverage the knowledge and skills of all employees; and turning those competencies into sales and solid profits. The story centres on the introduction and implementation of an organizational development programme that has been running for 12 consecutive years. The final part of the chapter tells the story of how this programme in itself has been reinvented to serve the needs for the organization and its people.

To better appreciate the story here being told, we first offer a description of the bank's cultural and historical context.

▶ Cultural Context

In this section we briefly describe the historical and cultural context to better understand the Norwegian industrial and labor markets. On reading this section, bear in mind that the context is under transformation with a stronger belief in market solutions and great individual differentiation. During the period after the Second World War, Norway was predominantly ruled by social democratic governments through the Labour Party. The party has advocated social equality as an over-arching value, and until recently, favoured nationalized industries. The other ruling parties, the Conservative Party and the Christian Democratic Party, compared to the dominant European scene, pursued a policy which has not been unaffected by mainstream egalitarian values.

The emphasis on equality, or more precisely the absence of great inequality, has gone hand in hand with a very high unionization, and powerful local and national unions that have played, and still play, an active part in the public arena. In banks and insurance companies, the principle of job security was regarded as sacred until the end of the 1980's. Hence, downsizing and outsourcing were not deemed necessary, and the banks would rather find alternative solutions when change of business strategies and cost-cutting during economic recessions were on the agenda.

Owing to these egalitarian values and the strong unions, wage differentials have stayed relatively small. In addition, employees and unions in many industries have resented individual performance assessments, and compensation has to a substantial degree been determined through collective bargaining.

Traditionally, Norwegian banks were among the most conservative work organizations in the country. This is partly due to their shelter from competition through cartel agreements that determined the interest rates and prices. The cartel arrangements were given the blessing of most politicians and public authorities and were not considered illegitimate by most people at that time. Starting in the 1980s, these rules of the game changed dramatically. These changes offered new business opportunities for the financial industry. New products and new markets were opened. Put differently, the temptation to stretch for opportunities beyond the competencies of the employees and the capabilities of the organization was great. When this temptation became a reality in the late 1980s and the beginning of the 1990s, it is easy to understand why investments in knowledge and skills became a viable competitive strategy.

▶ Norwegian Savings Banks

Norwegian savings banks have their roots in the local communities where they were established from 1840 onwards intended to deal primarily with local financial needs. Many savings banks have thus been important institutions for the local industrial development and the economic well-being of the consumers. Norway's first regional savings bank was established in 1976 when 22 savings banks merged to become Sparebanken Rogaland, which later became SR-Bank.

The former local Egersund Sparebank was formed in 1839 and is the oldest part of the bank. Several other banks have joined gradually since 1976. Today the bank consists of 39 former individual savings banks and is the region's leading bank. In 1996 Sparebanken Rogaland took part in establishing the SpareBank1 Group together with three other regional banks along the West Coast of Norway and an alliance of collaborating savings banks in the eastern part of the country. Sparebank 1 was established to secure a nation-wide and regional alternative institution to the major financial conglomerates with headquarters in the capital of Norway, Oslo.

In 1977 a new Savings Banks Act was implemented in which the savings banks were granted practically identical competitive conditions as the commercial banks. Yet the ownership structure remained very different. Furthermore, the savings banks were not obliged to keep mandatory capital ratios. There was no need for such requirements since losses were virtually non-existent. The lack of mandatory capital ratios turned the banks into vulnerable organizations when the bank crisis struck in the latter part of the 1980s. In addition, the banks had no systems for analysing or measuring the overall credit risk they were exposed to. The financial industry was indeed unprepared for the turmoil the subsequent deregulation and the economic downturn would bring.

The new regime provided the foundation for a strong expansion in the savings banks' operations. The product range was substantially widened, and savings banks became full service banks for business and households. Compared to the rest of Europe, Norwegian savings banks command a unique position in their domestic market. Product development and technological innovations have been a continuous process in the past decades.

▶ SR-Bank's Strategy

We present the bank's business proposal and strategies to explain how the organizational development programme fits with the overall human resource policies and overall strategies. In the annual report from 2000, the bank presents itself as follows:

Business idea

SpareBank1 SR-Bank shall

- be conceived of by the customer as the recommended and preferred partner.
- offer competitive financial products and services that meet the needs of the customer.
- offer its products through modern, easily accessible and local distribution channels, which ensure that the customer receives good quality and service.
- secure the bank's position as the recommended and leading bank by ensuring that its employees are customer-oriented and qualified.
- actively participate in the effort to strengthen growth and development within its market.
- be a profitable and independent bank with local ties, and shall be a regional alternative to the competing financial corporations through the SpareBank 1 alliance.

Operations

SpareBank1 SR-Bank is today organized into five districts with headquarters in Stavanger with 50 offices. The group also consists of the bank's two subsidiaries; a real estate agency chain and a finance company. The bank is part of the Sparebanken1 Group and the Sparebank1 Alliance. The Sparebank1 Group is presently the fourth largest banking ad financing group in Norway and commands NOK 180 billion in total assets. The total assets of SR-Bank were close to NOK 44 billion at the end of 2000.

The SpareBank1 alliance

In 1998 Sparebank1 and Sweden's second largest bank, FöreningsSparbanken AB, decided to enter into a strategic alliance. The alliance is a Scandinavian banking and product alliance where SpareBank1 banks in Norway and FöreningsSparbanken AB in Sweden collaborate through the jointly owned SpareBank 1 Gruppen AS.

The agreement with FöreningsSparbanken strengthens the regional competitiveness and we have access to expertise and capital that enables us to compete with the other major Norwegian and Scandinavian banks in our market.

We note the strong people orientation in the assertion that 'SpareBank1 SR-Bank is first and foremost the people who work there – and the people we work for.' Furthermore, we recognize the strong belief in physical presence and the closeness to the customer. Third, through the alliance and their subsidiaries, the bank has ample and strongly competitive opportunities for product development.

In their primary market the bank commands a 50 per cent market share. In 2000 the bank acquired 8,000 new customers, consolidating its position as the region's leading bank for both private customers and business and industry. The growth in deposits and lending was substantial, 15 per cent and 20 per cent respectively. A 70 per cent increase in commission revenues from the sale of insurance and securities, added to the bank's profits and constitutes tangible proof of the bank as a sales- and customer-oriented organization.

In the annual report of 2000, the managing director stated that 'We believe that the relationship between customer and bank is founded on personal contact, mutual respect and confidence. Therefore, we have never been interested in following a strategy that would replace personal contact with automation.'

Loyal to this strategy, the bank has chosen a relatively expensive distribution strategy. The customers will be able to choose between the bank's network of offices, telephone service and the Internet bank. The strategy entails a very high level of service and access to competent personnel.

▶ Key Financial Figures

Table E1 presents the financial results of Sparebank1 SR-Bank for the past 11 years; in other words from the time of the introduction of the organizational development programme. All figures are percentages of average assets.

Note the disastrous results at the turn of the previous decade, and the gradual improvement from 1992 to 1995, when profits were back to a satisfactory level.

Table E1 Key financial figures

	2000	1999	1995	1992	1991	1989
Net interest income	2.46	2.98	3.52	4.87	3.14	3.78
Other operating income	0.70	0.77	1.13	1.28	1.02	1.24
Total operating income	3.16	3.76	4.65	6.15	4.16	5.02
Total operating costs	1.76	1.83	2.93	3.41	3.56	3.43
Profit before losses and write-downs	1.40	1.93	1.72	2.74	0.60	1.59
Losses and write-downs	−0.18	0.17	0.08	2.12	3.96	1.50
Result of ordinary activities	1.58	1.76	1.65	0.62	−3.36	0.09

Table E2 Key economic indicators

	2000	1999	1995	1992	1991	1989
Growth in loans from private customers	23.1	19.5	8.0	13.0	14.8	13.5
Growth in deposits from private customers	13.9	11.6	0.0	12.2	11.9	11.0
Income per cost NOK	1.72	1.86	1.59	1.80	1.17	1.46
Number of man years	711	677	711			757
Number of branches	50	57	57			60

In the period from 1989 to 1992, losses and write-downs on loans were extraordinary due to the abrupt decline of the economy, with subsequent bankruptcies among the business customers of the bank. Worth noting also is the long-term trend if slender interest margins (net interest income), which has to be partly substituted by off-balance sales (other than loans and bank savings). From the accounting point of view, this trend is a strong motivator for SESAM, enabling the organization to sell other products and services.

Other key figures relevant to the presentation and discussion of the SESAM programme is presented in table E2.

The number of branches and bank offices has been stable throughout the decade. In 2001 the bank planned to establish five new bank offices. The growth in loans and deposits has been substantial and the bank has gained market shares in the period. Productivity has greatly improved, and the growth has occurred in parallel with a reduction of employees. The income/costs ratio is satisfactory compared to the industrial average, but the stretch target is 2.

▶ SESAM – The Antecedents

The decision to keep and develop the branch network was first taken back in 1989, and has been confirmed through the crisis in 1991–93 and the recent technology development with the appearance of Internet banks. The challenge thus became to generate higher revenues, which was more a dream than a reality. Bank employees were not primarily sales people. On the contrary, the most prevalent motive for seeking a job in a bank had traditionally been the desire to obtain a stable income and security.

To include the broad branch network as a part of the bank's strategy was not an obvious decision. In 1989 the issue of the distribution network was the subject of a heated debate. The branch network occupies considerable resources and incurred a major part of the fixed costs. An advanced and well-functioning ATM (automatic teller machines) network together with an electronic payment transfer system significantly reduced the customers' needs to visit the bank in person. Consequently, there were several good reasons for downsizing the branch network. The recommendations from the experts and consultants were also straight-forward: get rid of the brick and mortar!

In the internal discussion, two opposing points of view were presented:

- The bank needs to cut costs. Since the branch network incurs large costs, it must be reduced as much as possible. This is also in line with what our competitors are doing. The basis for this line of reasoning is purely cost-oriented. The contribution of bank employees to revenues was not taken into consideration.
- The branch network, including both the physical and human resources it comprises, represents a unique competitive advantage. No competitor has a similar distribution system. Such an advantage must be developed and exploited, not dismantled.
- Associated with the argument above, a humanistic point of view was present at that time: We are responsible for our employees and their jobs. The challenge is: How can we use these strategic resources more efficiently than in the past?

When the smoke settled, the two latter points of view surfaced as winners. However, the distribution network had to be modernized both physically and by enhancing the employees' communication skills and product knowledge. At this point in time, there was no appreciation of crisis and real need for change. The necessity for change was not recognized either by employees or by a large number of bank managers. The ideals of improving the knowledge and competence of employees as well as providing high quality were easily agreed upon, but the process of transforming these ideas and intentions into practical actions gave rise to considerable differences of opinion. There were disparate views regarding the need for change in recruitment policy, career procedures and reward systems. The new ideas collided head-on with the dominant logic of the old way of doing bank business and customer service.

The former status of lending is very illustrious. In determining the salary of employees working for the retail market (individuals and households), the traditional practice involved linking salary to the amount of loans the employee was authorized to grant. Lending was 'good', it implied more authority and power *vis-à-vis* the customer, it provided status within the organization, and it meant more pay at the end of the month. Lending was associated with more status than deposits, which in turn ensured more status than working with payment transactions. 'Sales' was a four-letter word.

A common description of bank employees engaged in work with private customers was 'order takers'. This kind of reactive work behaviour was adequate as long as there was no reason for a customer to frequent more than one bank; as long as the customer, regardless of the service required, had to physically visit the bank. In the not too distant past, the banks offered the same products at practically identical prices. In addition, switching costs were high. But the bank market had now changed radically. The main questions were now these: How could a sales-oriented culture be developed? How could prevalent attitudes and work behaviour be changed? What kind of knowledge and skills do the employees and managers need? Do we have any tools or systems to aid us in this process?

The internal answers varied. For several years the management had preached 'We must get better at selling' and 'We must become better at understanding customers' needs'. There was no end to what the employees had to get better at. But can anyone be expected to improve without having the relevant tools or instructions indicating how this is to come about?

The notion of 'needs-oriented sales' was introduced to distance the employees from the common perception of an aggressive insurance salesperson; a salesperson more interested in his or her bonuses than in the customer's needs. 'Soft sell' was the buzzword, the starting point was always to meet the customer's actual needs. People were convinced that 'over-selling' would backfire in the form of complaints about poor and sloppy financial advice.

The Human Resource department assumed responsibility for arranging sales courses. These courses were typically one day or weekend courses aimed at teaching employees various sales techniques. However, this approach was unsuccessful. The reasons were plenty. The courses were not specifically directed at sales in banks: the ideals and techniques were copied from traditional retail business. The concepts of 'soft sell' and the focus on long-term customer relations were not at the forefront. Moreover, it had to be acknowledged that courses that were not part of a larger organizational context would easily result in only short-term enthusiasm among the participants, at best. The need for structural changes that could facilitate for learning with lasting effects through organizational capabilities such as improved routines and revised computer programmes became increasingly evident. The instructor's job was completed when the course was completed; he or she had no responsibility for the use or implementation and follow-up of the individual learning that had taken place. And there was no system to indicate what had been learned and if the performance in any substantial way had been improved. The bank had realized that they did not possess the knowledge or skills to design and implement a system to develop radical changes in the organization to change attitudes and business processes.

▶ SESAM: The Initial Steps through Knowledge Import

The manager of the retail market came across a sales training programme that seemed suitable for the task. On a business trip to the USA for quite other purposes, he was introduced to a programme with a good track record in US financial institutions. In a persuasive and entertaining 45 minutes, the designer of the product package convinced the astonished bank manager of its relevance also for a Norwegian savings bank.

On his return to the bank, efforts were made to spread the enthusiasm. Needless to say, this turned out to be rather difficult. Comments such as 'this will be expensive' and 'the US is different from Norway' were indications of profound scepticism. On the other hand, the programme was tailor-made for banks; it could pride itself on an outstanding track record. It had gradually evolved through practical experience and testing. The programme was not 'theory', a well-known taboo in the banking business; it represented condensed practice. Not only was it practice, it was real banking practice!

After a year's tug of war within the organization, a contract was signed. By that time the American developer of the programme had visited the bank twice. His presentations combined with internal alliance building, the marketing manager and manager of human resources were early converts, and persuades top management. A decisive prerequisite was a translation of the programme not only into Norwegian, but into the bank's own culture and intentions as well.

American businesses, not least in the banking industry, are characterized by a higher degree of management by directive than are businesses based on the more participative Scandinavian model. Therefore, bank employees in the USA typically have less autonomous jobs than their Norwegian counterparts. Empowerment has a long tradition in the Norwegian workplace. Employee behaviour was at the time directed more through detailed manuals than through development-oriented, cooperative projects. This is illustrated by the fact that the bank's management was a far more active and visible participant at all stages of the project than was management in the USA. They became actively engaged in the training programmes, used and disseminated the 'new language' and discussed further development of the project in the top management team.

A new position as coordinator for the entire programme was established on a contract basis. The coordinator, an external consultant and the bank manager in charge of the retail market division completed an intensive two-week training session in the USA. It was at this time the programme was 'Norwegianized'. The entire and very comprehensive programme was reviewed and scrutinized in great detail, and the two representatives from the bank were in charge of adapting the programme to allow for local Norwegian conditions. The main challenge for the consultant was to become familiar with the programme and to be up-dated on pedagogical matters.

There was another important reservation regarding the project. Relying largely on detailed manuals and use of consultants in the training sessions, the programme was explicitly built on behaviouristic theory and assumptions, an observation made by management as well as some employees. In this context, conflicts could be eliminated with a reference to SESAM as an authoritative source. This provides considerable opportunity for managerial manipulation of employees. A renowned organizational psychologist was asked to consider the ethical implications of the project. His advice was that the programme was ethically sound given that the employees were informed about the measures taken and the tools to be used.

SESAM: The Explicit Phase

Having been 'Norwegianized', the programme was introduced in 1989. The target group was all employees in the retail market division, including managers at all levels. More than 500 employees were involved. The programme thus constituted a comprehensive organizational development process.

The primary objective was to offer a tool and a learning environment that provided understanding and opportunities to utilize the process of communication between the customer and the bank employees providing services to the customer. The aim was to develop the skills to determine the customer's present and future needs and to suggest the right products and services to fulfil these needs.

The sales and organizational development project was called SESAM, the Norwegian acronym for 'Salg Er SAMarbeid' (sales equals cooperation). The emphasis on the collaborative aspect was related to the customers' tendency to perceive the bank branches as one single bank. The customer wants to be recognized, regardless of whom they approach in the bank. Therefore it became crucial to stress the significance of intra-organizational cooperation, also across departmental boundaries. For example, information about the customer must be exchanged and made available to all customer service and support personnel.

The SESAM project had a long-term perspective. The organization was to be transformed from an 'order-taking station' into a 'proactive sales train'. Notwithstanding, the process was called a project, indicating a temporary perspective. The process consisted of a number of training manuals defining the new roles of employees and managers combined with 2–3 days training sessions. Inspired by Nonaka and Takeuchi (1995) the introductory year may be called the explicit phase. The new roles and the related necessary skills were explicitly formulated in manuals. The training sessions were designed to transform this explicit knowledge into practice. The employees were expected to learn the content in the manuals in two ways, by repeating their contents, and by internalizing the content through learning by doing. The latter process, internalization, embodies explicit knowledge into tacit knowledge (Polanyi, 1966). By introducing the tacit aspect of knowledge, Polanyi pointed to the fact that 'we can know more than we can tell'. Tacit knowledge is difficult to verbalize and deeply rooted in an individual's action and experience as well as in the ideals, values or emotions he or she embraces. When knowledge becomes internalized in employees' and managers' tacit knowledge bases in the form of shared mental models or know-how, it becomes a valuable asset both for the individual and the organization. This internalized knowledge may be deepened and broadened through interaction with colleagues.

Below we offer detailed descriptions of two of the new roles, the one for tellers and the one for the manager of the retail division. Thus we illustrate their complementarities. Each individual employee's role was defined through the so-called 'winning plays'. These plays were used for tellers, customer service representatives (financial advisors) and support personnel. All levels of management were also equipped with winning plays, from the first-line managers ('sales leaders' in the new language) to the managing director. The sales manager of a bank outlet (for instance, the local branch manager) was familiar with his subordinates' wining plays. Conversely, employees also knew their superior's winning play. Thus the different levels could check each other, and measures were generated so that everybody could continuously perfect his or her role performance.

The new role for the teller was defined in this way:

Winning play for tellers
1. Greeting and presentation
   - Greet the customer politely so that he or she feels important and welcome
   - Look up, smile and establish eye contact
   - Even if you are busy with something else, greet the customer by saying something, nodding or waving
   - Ask how you may be of assistance
2. Carry out the customer's wishes
   - Deal with the customer's requests in a competent and polite fashion
   - Use your knowledge to deal with requests, be precise and effective
   - Address the customer by name
   - Draw the customer into conversation – establish contact
3. Uncover needs
   - Discover what PNO's[1] a customer may have, show interest and consideration
   - Comment as you serve the customer
   - Listen for sales opportunities in what the customer says
4. Give recommendations
   - Find out which service best suits the customer and recommend it
   - Explain the solution
   - Use brochures actively
   - Recommend that the customer talk with a member of the customer service personnel
5. Refer the customer to relevant colleagues
   - Use a customer presentation card
   - Write the customer's name, the services you suggested and your name on the card
   - Enclose your business card and any other relevant documents
   - Refer the customer to the right person
   - If possible, escort the customer and introduce him or her

- If you are unable to escort the customer, explain who or she is to see and give the customer the customer presentation card
6. Conclusion
   - Thank the customer politely, using his or her name
   - If possible, shake hands
   - Welcome the customer back and offer your help in the future

The winning play revealed a very important and previously controversial point for the tellers' role. The tellers themselves were not asked to cross-sell, they were asked to refer the customer to a customer service representative if an opportunity for cross-selling arose. However, the tellers have previously responded negatively to any suggestion that they assume a more proactive attitude towards sales. They claimed that sales activity would 'only lead to long line at the counters'. The management had until now been unable to provide any specific suggestions as to how these two seemingly conflicting demands, prompt service and active cross-selling, could be met simultaneously. The paradox had finally been resolved, and the tellers' attitudes towards sales immediately became more positive.

The second example of a wining play was deigned for the general manager of the Retail Market division. Note the hierarchical system of roles and their complementarity.

Winning Play for the Division General Manager
1. Define and communicate the results you expect from each manager
   - Establish 'Winning plays for sales managers' as a standard for sales management and training
   - Set targets together with the managers
   - Obtain acceptance for expected actions and set targets, both for superiors and subordinates, so that the desired behaviour is measurable
2. Be a good example
   - Practise what you preach
   - Be optimistic and enthusiastic
   - Practise the three C's (Competence, Courtesy and Consideration)
3. Empower your employees
   - Share information
   - Arrange monthly follow-up meetings with your managers
   - Give your managers opportunities for individual development
   - Delegate authority and responsibility
   - LISTEN! LISTEN! LISTEN!
4. Build team spirit
   - Set goals and map progress for the region
   - Communicate goals and results
   - Don't forget the humorous side of things
5. Check on your expectations
   - Execute hands-on management by visiting the local banks and branches

- Review the local bank's results monthly with each manager, using the sales reports
- Ask the customers if they are satisfied with the bank

6. Reward and recognize
    - At your monthly meetings, reward and recognize those who have achieved good results
    - Reward and recognize both individual employees and teams
    - Express your approval for a well-done job on a daily basis
    - Catch your employees doing a good job

Performance evaluation

Considerable emphasis was placed on measurable behaviour. Behavioural change was to be observed and reinforced through various forms of rewards: attention, praise and prizes. Reinforcing positive behaviour was a priority. During the first year, managers were instructed not to react negatively towards those employees that did not succeed. Realizing that the project would lead to considerable changes in behaviour, the first year was designated a trial-and-error period. Employees unable to adjust during this period were helped to overcome their problems in their current job position or transferred to another job.

'Catch your employees doing a good job' was the slogan that expressed the positive team spirit the organization sought to nurture. This proved to be a great challenge, especially for managers. Contrary to the American or southern European spirit, Norwegians are introvert and seldom brag about the peers. Even if you believe you are good at something, you are not supposed to show it.

The bank had virtually no experience in sales and performance evaluation. Sales measurement at the individual level, with an accompanying reward system, was a central element in the American version of the programme. This part of the programme was de-emphasized because:

- American business is more individual-oriented
- American motivational theories are frequently based on a conception of the individual as an inherently egoistic and materially oriented being.
- Participation in the project would be motivating in itself. Higher sales would provide the necessary basis to ensure the survival of more of the existing jobs
- Measuring individual sales could result in overly aggressive, short-term sales, leading to deterioration of good customer relations. The bank's goal was to develop stable long-term customer relationships.

Employee sentiments were mixed. Many wanted to demonstrate and visualize their own skills, for example as expressed in sales figures. Others, particularly the more union oriented, were sceptical. They partly expressed concern with the assumed 'weak' performers, and partly argued on the basis of their natural right to stick to the main provisions of the National Bank Agreement, which prohibited individual performance measurements. Evaluations conducted at the group level were accepted, on the condition that nothing could be traced back to the individual employee. The bank's management contested this formal argument, however, since the point in question was included under the main section in the National Bank Agreement dealing with electronically based systems. The management claimed that registration using an electronic medium was forbidden, while manual recordings and measurements were allowed.

Many possible avenues to compromise were attempted. One suggestion was that manual measurements of individual employee performance could be carried out at the workplace and the results then collected by the closest line manager. Union representatives opposed this suggestion, even though the employees in many divisions found this solution desirable. However, the management was not interested in letting the issue evolve into an open conflict. A project that otherwise had been so positively received was not going to be spoiled by a feature not considered vital to the success of the project.

Ultimately, the following agreement was reached: each individual employee would manually record his or her own sales figures every week. These were in turn registered on a form without specifying the respective persons. The sales manager added up the figures and calculated the results of the branch/department. The individual could benchmark himself or herself against the calculated average sales scores.

Each sub-unit's results (or in the new terminology: the results of the single sales office) were then collected centrally and published every month for the entire bank. These figures formed the basis for the selection of a Sales Office of the Month. This recognition consisted of a symbolic sum of money and considerable positive PR in the Bank Newsletter. Similarly, each year the bank rewarded two prizes as Sales Office of the Year and Sales Manager of the Year. Furthermore, the sales offices achieving their sales targets were eligible for membership in the 'Hundred Percent Club', which was restricted to those offices that reached their predetermined sales targets. Thus, virtually all performance measurement took place at the branch office or team level. The only individual reward, 'Sales Manager of the Year', was based on a number of qualitative criteria and was awarded by a committee.

An equally contentious issue was the question of *what* ought to be measured or evaluated. The bank's management ultimately decided the issue, on the advice of the project coordinator and the head of the Retail Market Division. Ten representative products were chosen, partly on the basis of their measurability, partly on the basis of their importance to the bank. The product selection was also designed to grant all bank offices equal opportunities to reach the targets (too much emphasis on deposits, for example, would put the offices that primarily sold loans at a disadvantage).

The development of sales targets and subsequent rewards undoubtedly had an effect on sales. This was not a function of the material goods accruing to the winners of the competitions. The positive recognition, the chance to be the centre of the new rituals, and the internal competition between similar offices were the essential elements. A sales office could, for example, aim to be better than other offices of the same size or others operating in the same market.

During the first year, the level of the fixed sales targets was determined locally, without any particular influence or help from the bank's headquarters. As could be expected, this led to certain instances of tactical budgeting. During the course of the year, however, this became a somewhat awkward and embarrassing matter, as a couple of offices were constantly being named sales office of the month even though their results were mediocre. In the subsequent year, this practice was then changed. Each individual sales office presented its target figures to the regional administration, which coordinated the figures for that region. At the next step, the five regions were coordinated by the bank's headquarters. A number of key figures were set up as guidelines, for example, it was considered reasonable to expect that an equal percentage of a bank's salary account customers used a cash card. In several areas such 'objective' criteria were used.

It had thus taken the bank two years to establish a simple system for performance measurement that most employees and interest groups could accept. A crucial cultural barrier had been overcome, but in such a way that the new system could be integrated into the established culture without directly challenging the culture.

Branches and Departments: The New Learning Communities

The responsibility for training employees at the operational level was assumed by their immediate superior, the sales manager. An external consultant trained the 60 sales managers. He was also in charge of training 20 bank employees to act as on-the-job instructors. These instructors assisted the sales manager in their training of their personnel.

Initially, the on-the-job instructors and sales managers completed a five-day course with the consultant, the coordinator functioning as his assistant. At the operational level, a session spanning 2–3 days, depending on the specific job category, was implemented. It was only at this initial stage that the training took place off-site. At later stages all groups had one-day sessions once every six months. These meetings functioned partly as a forum for mutual exchange and information, partly as a corrective to activities that had been put into effect, and partly as an introduction to new activities.

However, the most important and encompassing learning process took place in the local branches and support departments. The sales managers were responsible for arranging weekly personnel meetings. These meetings were held in the morning before the bank opened the doors for customers. Typically they lasted for half an hour. The meeting followed a fixed pattern in one-month periods. Two meetings were designated for service improvement, one meeting for product knowledge, and one for presentation and discussion of sales targets. The cycle was repeated every month. This responsibility was a new challenge for the sales manager, and the quality and results of the meetings varied greatly. Some attempts were made to avoid the meetings altogether on the grounds of practical excuses, but no deviation from the plan was accepted. Management simply required that these arrangements were part of the sales managers' job, something he or she was committed to through SESAM.

The weekly meetings were regarded an appropriate vehicle to institutionalize the learning process at the organizational level as well as with the individual employee and manager. It was an important tool for the transition from project to organization, from experiment to organizational routine. Learning was to be an organizational capability to leverage the competitive position of the bank.

The weekly meetings were always based on local experiences. Employees were encouraged to present good or bad examples of customer service or responses. These examples served as the basis for a discussion of improvements, changes, needs for new system solutions and advertising material. This institutionalized arena for learning through experience transfer was also important for political and ethical reasons. Local learning based on the team's own experience could serve as an important counterbalance to the more centralized and behaviourist learning model on which the project was originally founded. This local learning, which became increasingly significant, led to a 'democratization' of the organizational development that took place, and successful agendas for weekly agendas for weekly meetings were exchanged among the sales manager.

The weekly meetings represent a telling example of what Nonaka and Take-uchi (1995) have coined the 'socialization' process in the knowledge creation spiral. At the individual level explicit knowledge (the SESAM manuals and the winning plays) was internalized through learning-by-doing in their respective jobs and communications with customers and peers. Explicit knowledge becomes embodied in new skills and attitudes, and gradually part of the individual's automatic routines, and thus made tacit. Since tacit knowledge is context-specific and difficult to formalize, transferring tacit knowledge requires sharing the same experience through joint activities and spending time together. Thus the weekly meetings became an important supplement to the formal training sessions. The combined learning arenas facilitate the blend of internalization and socialization processes that allow for leveraging both from the explicit and tacit knowledge potential.

As we will see in the following chapters, learning from experience has become the dominant knowledge creation method in the bank. Gradually, the explicit and formal manuals have been replaced with broad socialization processes across all levels of the bank.

▶ SESAM 12 Years Later: Best Practice in Practice

Today, 12 years after the introduction, the programme is still healthy and running, an extraordinary achievement in itself. The programme has survived three managing directors. All three have been enthusiastic about the programme. Furthermore, today the programme has expanded to involve the whole organization. The reason is not hard to explain: The bank can pride itself on its stunning results. Within the alliance of regional savings banks, SR-Bank outperforms the others in sales results. These internal benchmarkings are valid indicators of the programme's success as the differences in results occur within a corporation with the same strategy, the same product mix, common plans for implementations and simultaneous product launches. As indicated above, although the basic beliefs and elements are the same, the programme has undergone a transformation. Today all training sessions are based on the employees' own experiences.

In 1989 the programme was introduced to transform bank employees from order taking to proactive selling. Today this is no longer an issue. The employees have all learned how to sell and the managers at all levels know how to motivate their employees to do just that. In fact they are themselves part of the sales force. The programme's content and intentions have become an integral part of the culture of the bank. The sales programme is perceived as a 'cultural development programme'. This is underscored by the fact that whereas the programme initially included the retail bank, today the entire bank is involved. Corporate banking and all service functions are engaged in the programme, not only to improve sales but also to develop a common culture and a common experience-oriented knowledge base. This implies that the programme comprises 700 employees in 50 branches in five districts.

In other words, while the programme is still running at unabated speed, the goals and intentions have changed. Initially, the goal was to learn new roles. The role of the teller was transformed into the role of the proactive financial advisor and seller of products and services. The present objective is to improve the performance of the existing roles, not to create new ones. The challenge is how to pose the most relevant questions to the customer to discover and fulfill present and future needs.

Experience transfer is the main mechanism. The present managing director wants to see 'best practice in practice'.

The transformation of a programme to a culture

When SESAM was introduced in 1989 no one could imagine it still running more than ten years later. Certainly, the intentions were long-term, and everybody expected that instilling a sales culture would be a hard struggle. But what is long-term when it comes to organizational change and development programmes? They often come and go with new bosses and new trends in the market of superfluous consultancy fads.

The first test of the viability of the programme came with the new managing director of the bank in 1991. The main structure of the programme was then in place, including the rather cumbersome negotiations with the union as to performance measurements and the policies towards those employees who did not want to change their roles. The new director was recruited outside and was new to the finance industry. At the time of his entry, the bank was next to bankruptcy (see table E1: Key financial figures).

Contrary to the development in other banks in similar situations, he decided to keep all the bank branches as a strategy to stay close to the customer through human interactions. He attacked the staff functions instead, which he cut by 25 per cent practically overnight. The return on the investments in the ensuing fixed costs associated with the branches and its employees had to be earned by leveraging the sales. He soon became convinced of the potential of the SESAM programme, and dedicated much of his time to being visible at their training sessions and ceremonies. His message was clear and simple: 'We have SESAM, let's use it, and let's install great ambitions for ourselves and our customers.'

The managing director strengthened the importance of performance measurement and was a vigorous advocate for a strong sales culture. With the financial performance of the bank as the immediate backdrop, the message was appealing and easy to grasp. Without increased sales efforts and proven results, bank offices had to shut down and employees laid off. The position as SESAM manager became a two-year assignment job with high status. The right candidate was handpicked from the high ranks of the bank hierarchy. The fact that the position had been occupied by bank managers proves the point. SESAM provides an arena where talented people are allowed to test their ambitions and competencies. It is an extremely visible and transparent position that brings you in contact with most employees and managers in the organization.

Initially the creator of the original American version behind SESAM took part in the implementation of the programme in the bank. He met with the board and the management team to explain the philosophy and intentions of the programme. A Norwegian consultant was also hired to run the training sessions the first couple of years. However, after four years the external consultants were ousted. They had played an important role, but their roles were no longer needed for the new cast. This evidences the new pride and self-confidence the success of the programme fostered. The sales performance was surprisingly successful and sustainable, and the financial results more than indicated that the bank and the employment were no longer in danger.

As described above, the programme formally consisted of written routines of roles and processes. The goal of the training sessions was to transform this explicitly formulated information into practical knowledge and skills for sales managers, financial advisors, tellers and support people. In daily language, 'theory' should be converted to practice. This 'theory' was imported through external consultants and those bank employees who had been acquainted with the programme and its systematic approach in the USA. After three to four years, this theory could no longer inform practice in the bank. 'Theory' had become practice. The winning play is no longer in use as an explicit template, the routine has become an internalized competence.

Learning from theory was replaced by learning from practice. Only good and bad experience from practice could further improve practice. It was time for the bank employees to take charge of the programme and the further development of the organizational culture of their work place and their common learning arenas.

This development coincided with the coming of the next managing director. As a former member of the board of directors, he was well acquainted with SESAM and its performance and its significant impact on the economic results of the bank. His vision was formulated in his view of SESAM as the vehicle for 'implementing best practice in practice'. What is needed in the present stage of the continuing process is learning arenas where the employees can share and reflect upon their own experiences. Two formal arenas serve this important purpose: the weekly local meetings at the branch under the leadership of the sales manager, and the training sessions under the leadership of the SESAM manager.

Learning with pleasure and fun became the guiding principle at the training sessions. The sessions combined fun and play with learning from experience. The good and personally experienced story can carry loads of tacit knowledge across to colleagues. This requires a caring and open atmosphere at the sessions where employees have courage to share failures as well as successes. The sales culture has become more differentiated than the traditional banking culture, where rule following was the hallmark of quality. When following predefined roles and routines is the most important rule of the game, it is difficult to differentiate between the excellent and the average employee. Today, you are encouraged to do your utmost, and you are allowed to show that you are indeed way above the average. The present managing director is also visible at the training sessions, where he insists that the employees tell how good they are.

New roles in a new culture

Sales leaders

The bank manager, who used to be an administrator ensuring that the employees did in fact follow the rules and routines, is today a sales leader. The role of the bank manager includes the role of the sales leader. Contrary to widespread present management rhetoric, middle managers play a major role in the development of the bank and its prevailing culture. All bank managers are also expected to perform as sales leaders. They are not allowed to withdraw to their paperwork in

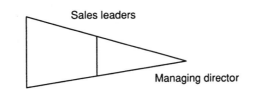

Figure E1 The training arm

secluded offices. They are expected to serve as a good example as a sales leader and a relentless motivator of his or her colleagues. These middle managers are all a vital part of the 'training arm' (see figure E1).

Figure E1 may look like a modest attempt to demolish the traditional pyramid and hierachical order (banking society is often associated with traditional values and half-hearted attempts to change). We have all encountered the advice of consultants to turn the pyramid on its head. Such advice is often embraced but is seldom implemented beyond window dressing. According to the bank, however, their sales organization actually works horizontally. The managing director, the sales leaders and the advisors/sellers support and serve each other throughout the value chain.

Sales managers are evaluated on an annual basis. Two dimensions are important:

1　Sales results over time.
2　Feedback from the employees, by means of an annual internal appraisal and analysis. The analysis includes leadership and organizational qualities such as climate, job satisfaction, openness, and trust. In addition, a score of his or her individual capacity is provided.

In other words, the sales manager's performance is evaluated along quantitative sales statistics and more qualitative dimensions at both the organizational as well as the individual level. If the sales manager does not perform as expected, he or she will be offered other opportunities in the bank.

The managing director

The managing director actively supports the programme. He often takes part in the training sessions, and challenges the employees to propose chores for him do in order to support them in their daily tasks and struggles. He frequently asks 'What can I do to make you perform a better job?' And the employees are responsive: 'We want better systems, we need more people, and we want a more visible leader.' He invites a dialogue with the employees, and he listens to the stories of the employees. In the sessions the employees tell juicy stories to transmit their views of being an employee in the bank and what is on the mind of the customers.

The managing director is part of the process and the employees have learned to expect exactly that. He takes care not to control the process. He puts his head on the block in the same token as the sales managers and employees in their common efforts to improve their sales capabilities and relational processes. This is the logic of the 'training arm' illustrating that the strength of the arm is dependent on everybody playing their respective roles to serve the customers.

The bank has been blessed with down-to-earth and practical managing directors who give credibility to their presence in the SESAM process. Their changing role is a demanding challenge. The role of the coach and visible supporter is very different from the controlling and distanced bookkeeper and the commander of detailed work instructions. Bank employees will easily unmask window dressing and empty rhetoric.

The SESAM learning structure

The programme is managed by a SESAM leader. The position is an appointment for two years and is highly regarded within the bank culture. In recent years bank managers have served as managers and motivators for the programme. The position may serve as a career opportunity, which is evidenced by the fact that former SESAM leaders now command positions as bank managers. Others view the position as a break from a long-held job, witnessed by the present SESAM leader who was recruited from a position as a bank manager. The SESAM leaders may choose to go back to their former job or head for an alternative position.

The SESAM manager coordinates all the activities at the bank level. That includes the management and administration of two central and very comprehensive activities that encompass all managers and employees it the bank: training of sales managers and financial advisors/sellers. The first three activities reach across the bank, fostering experience transfer and knowledge dispersions across branches and departments. The two latter activities are part of the daily routine within the local or regional structure.

1 Training of sales managers
   Twice a year the sales leaders gather for $1^1/2$ days' training sessions. The groups include branch managers, bank managers and department managers in the retail bank. The sessions focus on central themes that differ from session to session depending on perceived challenges at the time of the gathering. Five sessions are orchestrated, one for each region. The $1^1/2$ days' format is consciously chosen as a means to further develop the social relations between the managers from different branches of the region.

2. Training of financial advisors

   All the financial advisors and sellers meet twice a year for a one-day training session. They gather in groups of 25 people across the bank. In sessions led by external consultants, the participants focus on the sales process. With more than 600 financial advisors, tellers and support people, approximately 25 meeting are held annually. The external consultants are aided by the SESAM manager at all meetings.

3. Training of team leaders

   In the larger bank branches, the financial advisors are organized in teams. The team leaders have no personnel responsibility, they are engaged to motivate for sales. These jobs are coined 'performance positions' as they command additional wages. The teams are interdisciplinary as the members hold complementary competencies like financing, savings, insurance, and payment transactions. The team leaders have this year been offered $1^{1}/_{2}$ days' training in how to coach their sales group. These training sessions will continue twice a year in the future.

4. Regional meetings

   The regional bank manager has monthly meetings with his or her local sales leaders (branch managers). The bank is divided into five regions and the regional bank manager is responsible for the activities in his/her region.

5. Local meetings

   The sales managers conduct weekly sales meetings with the local advisors and sellers. The sales manager is typically identical with the branch manager. Presently there are 70 branches with comprehensive responsibilities for the sales. The agenda at these weekly consists of three fixed themes:
   (a) Presentation of the sales results.
   (b) Sales training. Each branch has adopted it own model according to their own needs and opportunities in the market. The market knowledge is local, hence a locally developed model for training.
   (c) Product training.

   The weekly local meetings have become an integral part of the organizational routines. Everybody knows what is expected. The SESAM managers may show up at some of the meetings to be informed and pick up clues to explore in common training sessions. It's worth mentioning that these meeting have been part of the internal rules of the game for ten years. It took some time to have them introduced and actually implemented, today their relevance is no longer disputed.

The SESAM structure

The SESAM manager does not work on his own. He reports to a steering committee that includes the directors of the retail and corporate market, the marketing and the human resource manager. This group makes the formal decisions as to the content of the SESAM programme and training session. Before a proposition is presented to this committee, a broad process has taken place. First, the SESAM manager consults with top management and the marketing and the human resource department. Even more important, resource groups, representing all organizational levels and geographical areas of the bank, respond to where they feel the competitive pressure and the need for more knowledge and training. They are also consulted on the methods to be used at the training sessions, the need for external consultants, etc. The SESAM manager sets off the resource groups and presents the proposed content of the next sessions to the groups before the final decision in the steering committee. This embracing process ensures that the goals and processes of the next training sessions are firmly rooted in the needs and experiences of the employees as well as in the strategies of management.

Performance measurement

Performance measurement has become an integral part of the SESAM programme since its first introduction in the bank. At that time measuring sales ran contrary to the existing bank culture. The initial steps included discussions and negotiations with the union, which expressed scepticism. Management partly shared some of the reluctance, being aware that the programme has its origin in the USA with very different traditions. The negotiations with the union settled on a compromise: Sales at the branch level were accepted, but individual sales should not be reported.

A selection of products is measured. In accordance with the principles of the 'training arm' the branches decide on which products and services after a consultation with the marketing department and the top management group. The range of products is small, because the organization wants to focus on some initiatives. Typically these will coincide with marketing campaigns, seasonal sales or the utilization of new technologies such as Internet banking. The mix of products may change from one quarter to another and products may have differentiated relative weights.

The sales performance is in turn related to economic incentives through an elaborate system. On a monthly basis branches that reach their sales budgets receive NOK 400 per employee. Branches that achieve their quarterly budgets are granted a bonus of NOK 1500 per employee. The budgets and sales goals are stipulated on the basis of a combination of three factors: the bank's overall ambitions, the average of similar branches, and the local conditions and opportunities. Thus a centrally prepared algorithm is used to define differentiated goals for the respective branches.

Note the absence of individual rewards. An internal competition is introduced between the branches by rewarding the five best performing branches with NOK 3000 per employee, the next five branches (numbers 6–10) are granted

NOK 500. In addition to these regular bonuses, economic incentives are used for certain campaigns. All in all the employees in the best sales branches may pocket the equivalent of 3000 Euros annually. Roughly speaking this adds another 10 per cent to their wage.

To avoid complacency the bank has implemented various schemes for benchmarking at three levels:

- internally between the branches of SR-Bank;
- between SR-Bank and the other member banks of the savings bank alliance;
- nationally through Gallup polls.

The effects of the economic aspects of the programme are indisputable. Statistics from the bank alliance document beyond doubt that SR-Bank is the superior sales organization. According to the bank, the SESAM programme claims the honour. (The banks within the alliance market the same products in very similar markets, so internal factors are the most obvious reasons for this good result.) All experience also testifies to the fact that those products and services that are included in the SESAM measurement scheme outperform those that are not included. As explained above, the same product may be part of measurement system for some periods to be excluded in other periods. Again, the bank witnesses that the sales increase in the inclusion intervals.

Above we hinted that performance measurement was a controversial issue at the start-up of the SESAM programme. It still is, but for a different set of reasons. As described above, the economic incentives do make a difference to your wage. The continued scepticism is today rooted in the short-term character of economic incentives. On the other hand, the bank wants long-term customer relations. Consequently, the bank is witnessing the paradox that short-term successes may harm their long-term goals. Reports reveal several examples of too aggressive selling. The sales philosophy tells the employees that their products and services are supposed to be solution-oriented, lasting sales, based on the discovery and mapping of the present and future needs of the customer.

Much to the surprise of management, economic, external incentives are very effective motivational factors. Strong emotional and competitive forces are set in motion. Paradoxically, the training sessions put much effort into discussions of the 'good examples of what we are not supposed to do'. Management is presently trying to balance these unintended consequences by stressing ethics and norms as the most viable basis for customer relations. A balanced scorecard has been introduced to include these features in a broader measurement system.

Looking back to the introduction of SESAM, it was explicitly stated that the model of aggressive insurance salespersons be discarded. Instead the bank introduced the term 'soft selling', underscoring the intention of avoiding obtrusion and pushing sales to reach short-term performance goals. The success of SESAM is in this respect close to becoming the best intentions' enemy.

▶ The Future: Improving Best Practice

The SESAM programme has a 12-years' track record in the bank. Will it go on forever? The answer is most likely yes. It is no longer conceived of as a programme; it is the way the bank carries on with its primary business and customer contact. The bank persistently argues that it has taken six to seven years to implement the present sales culture. The employees have internalized the knowledge and skills that make them successful in the competitive banking environment. It has never been considered to drop the programme. So what are the issues to be resolved in the future? The SESAM manager lists the following:

- The conflict between short-term performance measures and the goal of long-term and profitable customer relationships needs to be resolved. Solutions are not obvious. A potential path is to focus on the drivers of sales, not the actual sales output. Sales referrals, teambuilding and the quality of the financial advice may serve as potential candidates. Needless to say, the discovery and documentation of such drivers are not easy tasks.
- Developing the role of the sales leader. The sales leader is the key performer on the stage of sales actors. They need to internalize their role and the expectations from management, employees and customers. The sales leader has the responsibility to define the right quality of their services and employees to serve their local market effectively. To become a better leader they must command the courage to become more explicit on their feedback to the sales force.
- Goal and development assessment talks with the employees, including the ability and courage to raise difficult issues and resolve controversies.
- Develop the human and social relations in the workplace and within the sales teams. A caring organization is the best basis for open and honest experience transfer and knowledge creation.
- Develop stretch targets. Stretch targets go beyond the budgets and reflect hopes and ambitions of teams and individuals. In people's efforts to reach such targets the bank is tolerant of failures. The main point is to make people more creative and ambitious in what they want, and how they imagine getting there.

Note

1   PNO: Problems, Needs and Opportunities. The rationale is that the customer comes to the bank with a problem that may be transformed into a need, which is a sales opportunity for the bank.

Case Assignments

1 The SESAM programme was modified on the basis of a belief that it was not fully compatible with the culture of Norwegian work-life. Discuss the degree to which the programme could be adapted to a selected bank in your own country and, if needed, outline which adjustments should then be made to make the programme more compatible with the local conditions.

2 Discuss courses of action that can be taken by higher-level managers who want to obtain top management support and commitment to an organizational development programme that these managers consider vital for aligning the organization and its competence base with a radically changed strategy involving a shift from internal to external focus.

3 Discuss whether the bank could have used economic incentives and rewards more actively in order to increase the sales of credits more effectively.

4 Explain which types of incentives in your opinion should have been used as well as how a tailored reward system should have been designed.

5 The bank chose to implement the SESAM programme in order to accomplish realignment of its competence base to the new strategy. However, an important question relates to what the bank alternatively could have done to promote such realignment. Suggest and discuss at least two alternative ways that could have been considered from the wide range of organizational and human resource management measures that can be applied to promote this type of realignment.

chapter

6

Competencies in MNCs

▶ Purpose

The purpose of this chapter is to discuss human competencies among employees in MNCs and their subsidiaries, and how competencies can be generated. After briefly discussing the various forms of intellectual capital in MNCs, we present a six-fold classification of employee competencies in MNCs. The ways in which these critical human resources can be generated are also discussed, together with their significance for multinationals and their subsidiaries. This is followed by a discussion of the generation of competencies in MNCs based on a model elaborated by Nonaka and Takeuchi (1995). Finally, practical implications are discussed.

▶ Background

In Chapter 1 we pointed out that the essence of the competitive advantage possessed by MNCs lies in their potential to combine geographically specific and dispersed resources, such as cheap labour and natural resources with firm-specific resources, such as reputation and idiosyncratic competencies. In Chapter 2 we indicated that, of these, it is the management of idiosyncratic competencies that is now regarded as the key challenge for MNCs. Not only do these have to be generated but they also have to be transferred across spatial and national boundaries.

But what are the constituents of these competencies? We will argue that it is not only important to focus on the core competencies of MNCs but also to bring to light the nature of the various competencies carried by employees, not least because these form the building blocks for the development of core competencies.

Competencies may be analysed as sub-individual units in that they are dispersed across individuals. This approach has several advantages. Among these is the opportunity to aggregate competencies across individuals. This is reflected in the use of concepts such as competence stocks, competence portfolios, competence configurations, team competencies and organizational competence (Winter, 1987; Nordhaug, 1994; Hamel and Heene, 1994). In addition, it is analytically useful to conceive of organizations needing specific types of competencies rather than specific individuals.

▶ Intellectual and Human Capital

There are many factors that account for the growing significance of competencies carried by employees or teams during the last decade. One is the increased globalization of business that forces MNCs to refine and develop their human capital. International operations require a much broader set of competencies than their national counterparts because of their relative complexity and the uncertain environment they face. Another factor is that competition in most industries has significantly increased in part as a consequence of the deregulation of markets. In addition, the significance of possessing unique technologies as a source of sustained competitive advantage has diminished. Previously, firms could develop technologies that conferred competitive advantage for many years. Given the current pace of technological development, this is now only rarely the case. The decline in the importance of technology as a source of competitive strength has compelled firms to look for other factors that confer competitive advantage.

Since sustained technological leverage has become more difficult to obtain and maintain, the focus has turned to companies' various types of intellectual capital. This capital can be divided into the following main elements:

- organizational capital;
- customer capital;
- human capital.

Organizational capital comprises the structure of the MNC and its subsidiaries, their way of organizing work processes, their routines, their competence configurations and their various systems. In regard to competence resources, e-based knowledge management systems provide one illustration of an element of organizational capital. Moreover, various types of property rights, such as patents, licence agreements, production recipes and franchising rights are also a part of the MNC's organizational capital.

The customer capital is made up of the company's customer or client base, its customer relations and the reputation of the MNC and its products. This capital differs from organizational capital in that it is predominantly located outside the organization, that is, it rests in 'the eye of the beholder'. However, it is of course heavily influenced by internal factors such as the MNC's product or service quality, its ethical conduct and historical reputation. In other words the MNC's customer capital is largely a result of its application of competencies over an extended period of time.

Human capital in MNCs consists of competencies in the form of knowledge, skills and abilities among employees, along with individual energy and motivation. In the same way as for organizational capital, since human capital is predominantly controlled from within the MNC, it is a particularly important parameter for the creation of high performance and organizational success.

A central issue relates to the relative importance of competencies compared to traditional sources of competitive advantage: financial capital and technology. Part of our research has focused on how top managers evaluate the importance of a variety of resources for the success of their companies. Our main finding indicated that they regarded access to various intangible resources as critical for sustainable competitive advantage. In particular, they emphasized the significance of employee competencies, the reputation of the company and its products and customer relations. They also indicated that corporate culture, that is an aspect of their organizational capital, was of importance. In contrast, the more traditional sources of competitive advantage, financial capital and technology were assigned significantly less importance primarily because they are relatively easily obtainable (Nordhaug and Gooderham, 1996).

▶ Classification of Competencies

When work-related competencies are to be classified as sub-individual units of analysis, valuable insights are offered by economic human capital theory. It was originally economists such as Becker (1983) and Schultz (1981) who launched the notion of 'human resource specificity' in conjunction with what is known as human capital theory. At the core of human capital theory is a distinction between those competencies that are firm-specific and which have little or no applicability beyond the individual firm, and those which are firm non-specific and which may applied across firms. According to human capital theory, firms will tend to avoid investing in the latter. Furthermore, firms develop internal labour markets in order to encourage employees to invest in firm-specific competencies despite their lock-in effect.

Useful as the distinction between firm-specific and firm non-specific competencies is, it fails to take into account task related differences at the micro-level (Nordhaug, 1994; 1998). In other words there is a need to add a task specificity dimension. We shall define task specificity as the degree to which competencies are linked to the performance of a narrow range of work tasks. Low task specificity is characteristic of competencies that are not particularly relevant to any one particular task. Instead they have a bearing on the successful performance of a wide range of different tasks. They include, for example, analytical skills, problem-solving capacity, social skills, and the ability to work independently. However, when the degree of task-specificity is high, competencies are linked to one

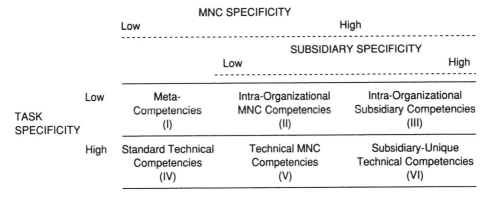

Figure 6.1 Classification of competencies in subsidiaries of MNCs

specific task only and cannot be deployed for the performance of other tasks. For example, 'touch-method' typing can only be applied to the task of operating a standard keyboard. In contrast, social skills may be utilized across a wide spectrum of tasks.

If a competence can be used in one firm only, it is firm-specific and, by definition, has little or no potential value for other firms. In contrast, competencies that are not firm specific can be sold in external labour markets. Firm-specificity is thus fundamentally different from the dimension of task specificity in that it is defined in relation to the external environment of the firm.

Because MNCs have subsidiaries, there is a need to supplement firm or MNC specificity with the notion of *subsidiary specificity*. This is particularly necessary when subsidiaries have strong competencies of their own that are important to the MNC as a whole (see Chapter 2 and the concepts of 'enhancers' and 'augmentors').

In figure 6.1 the dimensions of task specificity, MNC specificity and subsidiary specificity have been combined to form a three-dimensional competence typology comprising six cells. The cells contain different variants of competence idiosyncrasy and thus dissimilar types of competencies within cross-national settings.

The first competence type (I) is both MNC and subsidiary non-specific. It encompasses a broad range of knowledge, skills and aptitudes. Examples are literacy skills, learning capacity, analytical capabilities, creativity, knowledge of foreign languages and cultures, the ability to perceive and process environmental signals and events, the capacity to tolerate and master uncertainty, the ability to communicate and to co-operate with others, general negotiation skills, and ability to adjust to change. We label these forms of competencies *meta-competencies*, because of their relevance for the accomplishment of a variety of different tasks.

The second competence category (II) is characterized by low task specificity, low subsidiary specificity but high MNC specificity. Because this category contains those competencies that denote familiarity with the MNC as an organization, it can be labelled *intra-organizational MNC competence*. Illustrations of intra-organizational MNC competencies include knowledge about the company's history, its strategy and goals, its structure, its market position, its culture and its overall range of products or services. Additionally, it includes knowledge of those persons, networks and alliances that are critical for getting decisions made. A further illustration is familiarity with the different sub-units and their operational conditions which is developed through measures such as job rotation and comprehensive courses for new employees. The aim of this is to provide a broad overview of the MNC and its subsidiaries. The nurturing of managerial generalists within MNCs, that is employees who possess a substantial amount of MNC specific, intra-organizational competencies, is a particular feature of Japanese companies, many of which have extensive job-rotation arrangements.

Type III competencies incorporate competencies that exhibit low task specificity, low MNC specificity and high subsidiary specificity. Consequently, we can call them *intra-organizational subsidiary competencies*. Although they are essentially the same as the types of competencies associated with MNC specific competencies, they are different in that their value is restricted to one and only one subsidiary. Examples include knowledge of the subsidiary's organizational culture (e.g., its symbols, subcultures, history, norms, organizational dialect or code, and ethical standards), its communication channels, informal networks and internal political conditions.

High task specificity, low MNC specificity and low subsidiary specificity are characteristic of type IV competencies, which may be labelled *standard technical competencies*. These embrace a wide range of operatively oriented competencies. Examples include the ability to operate PC keyboards ('typing'), knowledge of generic budgeting and accounting principles and methods, skills in computer programming, knowledge of standard computer software, and craft skills and professional task-oriented skills that can be applied across companies and industries.

Type V comprises those competencies that are task-specific, MNC-specific but subsidiary non-specific. *Technical MNC competencies* can only be used to accomplish a limited number of work tasks and are not portable across companies. They include the skills that are required to operate an individual MNC's IT, budgeting and accounting systems. These have usually been developed to meet the unique needs of the individual MNC and are rarely duplicated in other MNCs.

Type VI, *subsidiary-unique technical competencies*, can only be applied to solve a limited number of tasks within one particular subsidiary. They include the knowledge and skills required to operate the unique elements in an individual subsidiary's technology and routines. Examples are skills related to the use of specialized tools crafted in the subsidiary, knowledge about procedures and recipes developed exclusively within the subsidiary, skills in repairing unique technology and in operating specialized local filing or data systems as well as skills related to the administration and maintenance of organizationally idiosyncratic routines or procedures in general.

The six competence types will now be discussed more thoroughly.

Meta-competencies

The importance of meta-competencies lies in their broad applicability. As such, they form a crucial foundation for work and organizational performance in general. Not only are they critical in regard to most current tasks, but they also constitute a potential for mastering future tasks. That is, meta-competencies constitute a potential for facilitating organizational and strategic change. It is not only managers who need to be equipped with meta-competencies, but they are needed wherever in the organization change is necessary.

Traditionally, the formal educational system has been the main source of meta-competencies. However, there are now many other important sources. One example is that of the training programmes many MNCs have aimed at facilitating the cross-national transfer of their personnel. These comprise a variety of activities whose main aim is the development or refinement of employees' meta-competencies. Indeed, most listings of the competencies needed for management in cross-national settings comprise only meta-competencies. For example, Alkhafaji (1995) lists the following as those abilities that are essential skills for global managers:

- the ability to perform in a team setting;
- the ability to manage change and transition;
- the ability to manage work force diversity;
- the ability to communicate in various cultural settings;
- proficiency in developing global strategic skills and turning ideas into action (implementation);
- the ability to change the way he or she thinks and operates;
- the ability to be creative, learn, and transfer knowledge;
- the expertise to form joint ventures or strategic alliances and to operate with a high degree of personal integrity and honesty.

In addition to this, relational skills that make it possible to develop relationships with host country nationals and to find mentors in the MNC's HQ also frequently figure in this literature. Likewise perceptual skills that relate to being able to understand how host country nationals think and behave as well as the ability to be non-judgemental when confronted with confusing situations are often included.

Intra-organizational MNC competencies

As with meta-competencies, the importance of intra-organizational competencies (IOMCs) has been discussed in the management and leadership literature but also within politically oriented organization theory concerned with power relations (e.g., Kotter, 1982; Pfeffer, 1992). The focus has been on internal networking capabilities, knowledge of and capacity to manage firm-specific symbols, and familiarity with the culture of different parts of the organization. In addition, the significance of knowing how key individuals and coalitions of individuals think and operate is emphasized.

IOMCs are inextricably linked to the organizational culture of the MNC and vice-versa. The corporate culture of an MNC comprises knowledge about past successes and failures that is communicated to and *learned* by new members. This acquired knowledge becomes generalized through successive communication and reinforcement processes. Culturally related IOMCs can be further illustrated by Sackmann's (1991) discussion of cultural knowledge in organizations, noting that cultural cognitions and knowledge become *habits* – that is, habitual thinking translates into habitual actions. She notes that once these habits exist, the carriers of cultural knowledge apply them without prior reflection when faced with a specific situation.

It should be noted that certain meta-competencies are of no value unless they are combined with relevant intra-organizational competencies. For instance, there is a need to blend general leadership skills with knowledge about specific organizational conditions, especially an understanding of internal power structures. In order to act effectively in the organization, the employee needs to be politically adept.

Whereas meta-competencies can be transferred to different contexts, IOMCs have to be acquired anew when individuals move to other companies. A period of several years may be needed to develop the necessary network of contacts. Whitley (1989: 213) notes that the search for general properties of managerial work *per se* has tended to play down the organizational specificity of managerial tasks: 'This specificity means that managerial problems are not easily abstracted from their contexts for solution with general models and procedures. It also suggests that the generalizability of successful practices in one situation to other contexts – across space, time, and cultures – is limited.'

To further illuminate the difference between meta-competencies and IOMCs, we may say that acquiring knowledge of the basic principles of strategic analysis represents an example of the former, whereas the ability to analyse the specific competitive conditions of the MNC *per se* is an example of the latter. Familiarity with the MNC is developed mainly through experience gained while working within it.

Normally, it is employees in managerial and higher-level professional positions who possess most of the IOMCs. However, it is increasingly the case that it is advantageous for the MNC if employees at lower levels also possess basic knowledge about its mission, strategy and policies, its products, competitive situation and competitors. This is particularly the case in service industries where front-line employees have to cope with a variety of dissimilar situations that cannot be encapsulated in work manuals.

IOMCs are mainly acquired through day-to-day interaction with and observation of colleagues. However, companies usually also take steps to enhance IOMCs by implementing job rotation, trainee and mentoring programs, on-the-job coaching, internal executive-development programs, and campaigns aimed at disseminating core values and information about the MNC's goals.

IOMCs need to be generated and maintained. Introduction programmes for new recruits are a common example of the former. The aim is to start the internalization of company norms and values. For example, Accenture has a learning centre outside Chicago where their newly recruited trainee consultants are immediately sent to go though such programmes. Maintenance of IOMCs is the purpose of mentoring for expatriates. The mentor is an experienced person who remains at the MNC corporate headquarters and keeps the expatriate posted on those developments that may be critical for his or her future career development.

Intra-organizational subsidiary competencies

Intra-organizational subsidiary competencies (IOSCs) are normally tacit and are acquired within the subsidiary through interaction with other members of the subsidiary. While they are critical for the operation of the subsidiary, they are of limited value beyond its boundaries. For example, the ability to interact with personnel in one particular subsidiary is of little immediate value in other contexts. As a consequence, if the investment in IOSCs is to yield a satisfactory return, employees must stay in the subsidiary for a substantial period of time.

As we have indicated, most of the training programmes designed for expatriates are intended to enhance their meta-competencies. However, some companies also try to disseminate IOSCs to personnel prior to their expatriation by locating some of their training to the subsidiary. This gives in-coming expatriates an opportunity to get to know managers within the subsidiary and to acquire some knowledge of its products, processes, organization and culture. Other possible arrangements are field trips to the subsidiary in question and internships. Many companies also use former expatriates to brief new expatriates about the specifics of the various subsidiaries.

Standard technical competencies

The leadership literature distinguishes technical competencies such as knowledge about procedures and techniques for performing a specialized activity, and the ability to use tools and operate equipment related to that activity, as a competency category. However, our classification goes further by subdividing technical competencies into three distinct categories:

1 standard technical competencies;
2 technical MNC competencies;
3 subsidiary-unique technical competencies.

Standard technical competencies embrace a wide range of operatively oriented competencies. Examples include knowledge of generic budgeting and accounting principles and methods, skills in computer programming, knowledge of standard computer software, and craft skills and professional task-oriented skills that can be applied across industries.

Important generators of standard technical competencies are the educational system, adult vocational education and training, parts of company in-house training programmes and apprenticeship arrangements. Another source of standard technical competencies is the training provided by suppliers of information and communication technology.

Technical MNC competencies

Technical MNC competencies are those competencies that are specific to the technology of the individual MNC. Some of these are important elements of an MNC's core competencies while others, such as company-specific routines and policies, are of more marginal value. What they have in common is that they have little immediate value beyond the individual MNC.

Typical ways of generating technical MNC competencies are through vocational training specific to the task-related needs and technology of the individual MNC. Common examples are company trainee programmes and apprenticeship arrangements and, not the least, experience gained through concrete, practical work within the MNC. In addition, training aimed at making people knowledgeable about MNC specific routines and procedures may provide an illustration of this.

Together with intra-organizational MNC competencies, technical MNC competencies may create an organizational lock-in of employees if their possession of these competencies is high relative to their meta-competencies and standard technical competencies.

Subsidiary-unique technical competencies

The narrowest type of technical competence in our classification is that of subsidiary-unique technical competencies (SUTCs). Their immediate relevance is exclusive to that of the subsidiary. The main significance of SUTCs lie more in their contributions to generating congruence between personnel and tasks than in their contribution to facilitating change and mobility within the MNC. Idiosyncratic technical competencies are typically generated within the one subsidiary and are developed through channels such as informal learning, job rotation, in-house training and apprenticeship arrangements.

It is therefore SUTCs that have the greatest potential for creating lock-in of employees, since their value is not only confined to one organizational unit, but to a narrow range of work tasks. Employees whose competencies are primarily located within this category cannot be deployed in other subsidiaries without substantial supplementary training. This is often the case for the local employees of subsidiaries located in developing countries because most of the training they receive is narrowly subsidiary specific.

However, in a dynamic perspective it must be emphasized that SUTCs may become MNC specific if they form the basis for technology or product development that is disseminated to other parts of the MNC whether these are other subsidiaries or corporate headquarters. This is the case for enhancer and augmentor subsidiaries.

▶ Discussion

Four important lessons for competence development in MNCs can be derived from the above. First, many jobs can no longer be reduced to a bundle of discrete operational tasks, each demanding easily definable task-specific competencies. Their successful execution involves overarching competencies, for example, those related to communication and co-operation with colleagues as well as to adjustment to working in teams. Second, jobs are enclosed in wider organizational contexts that affect employees, job content and performance standards. These contexts require that employees go beyond technically correct job performance. There is now an increasing need to communicate with colleagues either in one's own department or in other departments or subsidiaries. Knowing whom one should approach to develop a solution to a problem is thus vital. Third, if subsidiaries of MNCs only invest in the development of subsidiary-specific technical competencies, inflexibility may be the outcome. Fourth, it is important that individual employees possess a broad range of competencies. Managers of subsidiaries, for example, need both meta-competencies, such as communication skills and co-operative abilities, and intra-organizational competencies such as knowledge about informal communication channels and power structures together with knowledge about central persons in the company:

The need to blend competencies may be triggered by structural changes in MNCs, for instance, in respect to the emergence of a network organization:

> The substitution of flexible networks for top-down hierarchies means employees need interpersonal skills to get along with customers and co-workers, listening and oral communication skills to ensure effective interaction, negotiation and teamwork skills to be effective members of working groups, leadership skills to move work teams forward, and organizational skills to utilize effectively the work processes, procedures, and culture of the employer institution. More flexible organizational formats in combination with more powerful and flexible technologies also grant individual employees greater autonomy at work. Employees need sufficient self-management, goal setting, and motivational skills to handle this new autonomy. (Carnevale, 1991: 157)

In a similar vein MNCs need to integrate certain classes of complex and sophisticated technological knowledge in their activities. This requires an internal staff of technologists and scientists who are both competent in their fields and concomitantly possess intra-organizational competencies such as knowledge about the firm's strategy, organizational procedures and routines.

The typology we presented in this chapter may be applied as a tool for internal analyses and assessments of the existing pool of competencies in the organization. For example, subsidiaries can apply it as a means for assessing their latent adaptability. Using the typology may expose an over-investment in developing standard technical competencies, technical MNC competencies and subsidiary-unique technical competencies, and an under-investment in meta-competencies, and intra-organizational MNC competencies.

However, there is also a need for a dynamic perspective on competencies in MNCs. We will therefore discuss how various types of competencies can be transformed into new competencies.

▶ Competence Creation

In their renowned book, *The Knowledge-Creating Company*, Nonaka and Takeuchi (1995) outline a dynamic model of competence generation developed on the basis of empirical observations in corporations within manufacturing. The analytical distinction between tacit and explicit knowledge forms the foundation of the model. One key feature of the model is that knowledge is transferred through the interaction of individuals. A second is that knowledge is created as a result of 'the interaction between tacit and explicit knowledge' (1995: 62). On this basis Nonaka and Takeuchi construct a four-cell matrix that encompasses all the possible conversions of existing knowledge into new knowledge. This is shown in figure 6.2.

The first conversion is from tacit knowledge to tacit knowledge and is labelled socialization. Nonaka and Takeuchi's concept of socialization is largely congruent with the sociological concept of socialization in that it includes the internalization of cultural norms and mental models. However, their concept is somewhat broader in that it also comprises technical skills. One illustration of the latter is when

	Tacit knowledge	To	Explicit knowledge
Tacit knowledge	Socialization		Externalization
From			
Explicit knowledge	Internalization		Combination

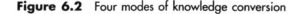

Figure 6.2 Four modes of knowledge conversion

apprentices learn through observing and imitating the master craftsman. Nonaka and Takeuchi emphasize that this method of learning is not confined to traditional crafts and arts, but can also be found in other industries. Nonaka and Takeuchi exemplify socialization with reference to the 'brainstorming camps' Honda regularly employs. These camps use a mix of dialogue and constructive criticism in order to develop new mental models that become part of Honda's tacit knowledge. Another illustration Nonaka and Takeuchi employ centres on Matsushita's development of their home bread-baking machine in the late 1980s. First, Matsushita's engineers selected a number of highly esteemed master bakers. Thereafter they spent considerable periods of time simply observing these master bakers at work in order to get an insight in how they go about kneading the dough. In this way they gained a 'feel' for the mechanics involved in the making of good bread. It was only after they had acquired this tacit knowledge that they set about designing the bread-making machine.

In regard to MNCs, their socialization processes embrace the generation of intra-organizational MNC competencies and intra-organizational subsidiary competencies, and to some degree the generation of technical MNC competencies and subsidiary unique technical competencies. Much of the task non-specific but organizationally specific competencies are transferred through informal interaction and listening to colleagues talking about the MNC's organization, its products and central employees.

The second conversion process in Nonaka and Takeuchi's model proceeds from tacit to explicit knowledge and is called externalization. It occurs as a function of dialogue that results in individuals' tacit knowledge being articulated in such a way that it has explicit meaning for others. This conversion process typically takes place in groups of employees and involves the articulation of tacit knowledge through the use of sense-making metaphors or analogies. Nonaka and Takeuchi illustrate this conversion with reference to Canon's development of its Mini-Copier. The challenge faced by the development team was to design and construct an inexpensive, lightweight disposable metal drum that could be easily replaced by Mini-Copier owners in the event of breakdowns. The team solved their problem during a lengthy beer-drinking session in which their aluminium beer-cans were used as a means of representing the drum.

Nonaka and Takeuchi's illustrations of their four conversion modes are all taken from manufacturing companies. However, externalization of knowledge is a common feature wherever R&D is carried out in teams. For instance, centres of excellence that are based on the spatial co-location of experts will normally be characterized by high degrees of externalization. However, in the case of virtual centres of excellence where the team members are geographically dispersed, live in different time zones and interact at a distance, externalization becomes a considerable challenge. A recent study of 14 Swedish manufacturing industry MNCs (Rognes, 2002) demonstrated that geographically dispersed R&D activities may pave the way for new and more differentiated sources of expertise. But at the same time problems related to communication, lack of direct interaction, lack of social context and different cultural behaviours may seriously hamper the efficiency of dispersed expert networks. Thus there is a latent friction between the new technological means of communication and basic social mechanisms:

> At a strategic level (or macro level) new technologies and the urge to utilize global resources are uppermost, with communication and people issues less central. At the operational level (or micro) level, by contrast, communication, team processes and productivity, and integration challenges, are the major concerns. A key lesson therefore is what seems to work at a strategic level may not be especially feasible in practice. Co-operation over distance is therefore likely to take place when necessary to obtain certain knowledge or technology, but not spontaneously. (Rognes, 2002: 61)

Combination is the third conversion mode and describes the processes whereby existing explicit knowledge is transformed into new explicit knowledge. For example, when middle managers operationalize the corporate vision and strategy or otherwise interpret and translate information coming from higher corporate levels in the MNC, a combination process unfolds. Likewise, much of the work within typically cumulative research is based on combination and syntheses of existing scientific findings in order to make incremental progress or to create entirely new concepts and models that may challenge conventional wisdom. If we return to Rognes' study of Swedish MNCs, it is reasonable to surmise that dispersed R&D functions and virtual, in the sense of not co-located, teams will not have any particular disadvantages as to accomplishing combinatory processes, because explicit knowledge can normally be easily transferred and shared.

The fourth conversion mode is internalization and signifies the transformation of explicit knowledge into tacit knowledge. According to Nonaka and Takeuchi this is closely linked to 'learning by doing', a process in which individuals internalize their experiences.

In MNCs internalization is important particularly in respect to the creation of task specific competencies, that is, technical MNC competencies and subsidiary-unique technical competencies on the level of individual employees. However, Nonaka and Takeuchi also emphasize that internalization may generate collective competencies when shared experiences change into collective, tacit mental models that become part of the organizational culture. One of the examples they use is when CEOs publish books about themselves and their companies that have such a profound impact on their employees that a new mental, shared tacit model emerges.

▶ Summary

In this chapter we have classified competencies carried by employees in MNCs and their subsidiaries. The classification was based on three dimensions: task specificity, MNC specificity and subsidiary specificity. On the basis of these three dimensions a typology of employee competencies in MNCs and their subsidiaries was derived that included meta-competencies, standard technical competencies, organizational MNC competencies, technical MNC competencies, intra-organizational subsidiary competencies and subsidiary-unique technical competencies.

These human resources, together with organizational and reputational capital, constitute opportunities for building unique capabilities that are difficult to imitate and that create competitive advantage. However, in building these capabilities there is always an inherent danger of creating rigidities that may hamper change processes and mobility across subsidiaries in the MNC. This is particularly the case for the development of subsidiary specific knowledge and skills.

Using Nonaka and Takeuchi's model, we also discussed how different competencies are created through conversion processes whereby existing knowledge is transformed into new knowledge. This model has had a strong impact on the development of knowledge or competence management in many companies, as will be seen from the case study that follows this chapter. It deals with knowledge management systems and processes in the world's largest management consulting firm, Accenture. The presentation starts with the period when managers first began to recognize a need for the creation of an infrastructure that could facilitate knowledge management processes. Later, considerable effort was devoted to the creation of knowledge-sharing activities and thereafter knowledge outfitting. Finally, the case contains illustrations of both successful and unsuccessful knowledge-sharing activities.

Knowledge Management in Accenture: 1992–January 2001

Siri Ann Terjesen

Accenture is the world's leading management consulting and technology services company with more than 75,000 employees in 47 countries. (See Appendix A for a comparison with other management consultancies.) The company generated net revenues of US $11.6 billion for the fiscal year ended August 31, 2002. Accenture split from Andersen Worldwide in August 2000. Accenture went public in a $1.6 billion initial public offering in August 2001, and trades as ACN on the New York Stock Exchange. Accenture consultants work in eight service lines: Strategy and Business Architecture, Human Performance, Customer Relationship Management, Finance and Performance Management, Supply Chain Management, Technology Research and Innovation, Solutions Engineering, and Solutions Operations. These capabilities are then matrixed across five operating groups: Communications and High Technology, Government, Financial Services, Products, and Resources. Careers are stepped in a five-tier hierarchy: Partners, Associate Partners, Managers, Consultants and Analysts. Accenture's Knowledge Management (KM) organization mirrors the consulting practice, but has different promotion time frames and fewer top executives. Partner Jill Smart reports directly to Gill Rider, Chief Leadership Officer and Managing Partner, Human Resources on company KM efforts (See Appendix B). Accenture has invested 15 years, countless people hours, and over US $500 million to support the KM strategy's technological and organizational aspects. According to Chairman and CEO Joe Forehand, 'The execution of our business strategy is dependent on how we create, share and protect knowledge. Knowledge sharing is the essence

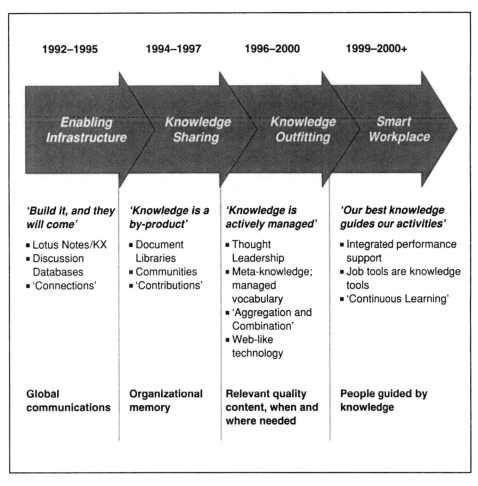

Figure F1 Accenture's KM progress, 1992–2000+

of how we bring innovations to change the way the world works and lives.' The company estimates savings each year, but does not have quantified benefit data. Moreover, the vast KM databases and people networks give Accenture an edge over competitors and a platform for the future. Thomas Davenport, director of an Accenture research center and a frequent author on KM, shared 'Companies have come to realize that there is a benefit to effective and explicit management of knowledge and that the opportunity cost – e.g. the cost of ignorance – is even harder to quantify than its benefits.'[1]

Accenture's KM capabilities have developed over the past 15 years from a predominantly hierarchical, technology first, top down perspective to a bottom-up, people driven process. This is similar to most former Big-5 consulting firms.

Karl Liander, former Head of Nordic KM, illustrates KM progress with a four-step model: Enabling Infrastructure, Knowledge Sharing, Knowledge Outfitting, and Smart Workplace. The following sections review Accenture's chronological progress, including critical organizational and technical milestones. Years overlap as strategies have been pursued concurrently.

Enabling infrastructure: 1992–1995

From the consulting practice beginnings in the 1980s, Accenture employees have shared knowledge through employee conferences, phone calls, faxes, and regular post. Client deliverables, which were devoid of confidential information, were stored in an office repository file, later evolving into subject files and industry binders. Consultants could 'borrow' the files but the materials did not travel further than the local office. These KM methods were effective in the early days but unmanageable as the company grew exponentially in the digital age.

In 1991, the partners decided to pursue a more global, standard and inclusive KM policy, establishing the 'Horizon 2000' task force. A 'Knowledge Management Strategy' was developed to 'leverage the skills, knowledge, and experience of the individual with the cumulative knowledge and reusable experiences of the global community of Accenture, connected electronically and culturally' and a task force created a 'Knowledge Management' organization to 'ensure the leading edge currency of our knowledge capital, and to keep the knowledge exchange demand driven rather than supply driven.'[2]

As then Chief Information Officer Charlie Paulk said, 'We did it as a strategic initiative. At the outset, we looked at some of the benefits in terms of reducing faxing, FedEx, and mailing expenses. But a much more important barometer is 'are we delivering client solutions more quickly?' If one assignment leads to another engagement with a client in part because these investments supported our consultants in doing even better quality work, do I count that and if so, how?'[3]

Accenture's KM technology was based on Lotus Notes® and discussion databases. The first version of the company's internal 'Knowledge Xchange'® (KX) repository of knowledge was released to partners in 1993. Based on the existing Lotus Notes application, KX contents included information about client's, company methodologies and tools, industry best practices, external information, examples of project deliverables, discussion databases, company-wide policies, and employee skills and knowledge. The KX vision was designed 'to be a virtual place where personnel can build and share knowledge internally and with external groups, forming global electronic communities of practice that transcend the barriers of geographical and organizational boundaries.' At that time, a business case was not asked for to support KM. Nor was initial spend analysed in order not to derail what was considered to be a critical strategic imperative.

The KX is organized first by a Directory Database such as the KX Yellow Pages or the KX Front Page; or Reference Databases which are industry or capability libraries. Under each of these, Discussion Databases (e.g. Financial Services Industry Discussion), Homepages (e.g. Consumer and Pharmaceutical Projects) and External Databases (e.g. newsfeeds or Gartner Group reports) are available. There are also Application Databases whose capabilities include call tracking.

Each contribution to a KX database includes the name, career level, home office, e-mail address, and OCTEL voice-mail number for at least one project contact. This enables individuals who locate the document to solicit more information, including specific project details and context, from the primary author(s).

Knowledge sharing: 1994–1997

The second phase of Accenture's KM growth was characterized by knowledge sharing activities. The company utilized both technological and organizational elements to stimulate contribution, use, and improvement of the KX and other KM tools. Knowledge was seen as a by-product of client work that should be shared throughout the organization. According to Paulk:

> The use of [technology] groupware works better in organizations that are into teaming and collaboration. I have relied on the people that I work with to help me for the past 31 years. Groupware shouldn't replace those kinds of interactions. But it can build on and extend the benefits of those interactions, and I think we have seen that it can also have a significant impact when it comes to facilitating creativity.[4]

Technically, the KX was rolled out to most management levels in the company. By 1996, partners, associate partners, managers, and consultants could access ever-growing repositories. (By 2000, all employees would have access.) Continuous improvements provided enhanced catalog and search possibilities, including 'KX Doc Finder' and 'KX Profiler,' off-line systems with search capability and return of e-mail results that enable consultants to devote more time to other tasks. These advancements were developed after feedback about the difficulties of locating and utilizing information. During an interview, one manager shared, 'There's so much out there that you don't even know where to start.'

Organizationally, the KM electronic databases reflected the company's people structure. This encouraged knowledge sharing among professionals interested in similar projects and industry. Geographic offices were segmented into communities, based on industry groups and consulting expertise, e.g. 'Financial Services-Technology.' These networked groups met quarterly and also communicated related new ideas and information through OCTEL voice mail, e-mail, and electronic newsletters. Informal networks also existed, e.g. lunch conversations at home office and cafeterias while on a project site.

These knowledge-sharing initiatives can be interpreted through Nonaka's SECI framework. Accenture's socialization modes included brainstorming sessions, executive retreats, discussion databases, on-the-job training, brown-bag discussions and training at the The Q Center in St Charles, Illinois. St Charles training includes primers on the company's KM resources. Individuals are encouraged to access company repositories when examining problems at projects and creating new deliverables. According to one consultant, 'There is this mentality that 'not invented here' is okay. We learn to cut and paste. All the while preserving client confidential information'. Another example of socialization is the video training library of successful partners sharing best practices and lessons learned, e.g. techniques for assembling and presenting a winning proposal. Externalization is accomplished through brainstorming and problem identification in project team and community meetings; and also library repositories. For example, the Business Integration Methodology and other performance tools attempt to describe learned processes. Combination modes include follow-up meetings, the data warehousing and mining features of the KX. Accenture internalization modes incorporate the development of shared vocabulary, learning-by-doing at the project site, reading newsletters, and use of specific tools such as ARTES time reporting, OCTEL voice-mail, and Look-Up employee address book. On-line tools such as databases for best practices and search tools also characterize internalization.

Accenture increasingly began to sell KM client solutions during this time period. These offerings were based in part of the company's internal lessons learned; and included capabilities processes and infrastructure, ongoing change management programs, shared organizational interface, data warehousing, systems integration, and intranet consulting.

Accenture developed a framework (in research at its Institute for Strategic Change) to help companies understand unique KM challenges and models that best meet these needs. Level of interdependence (e.g. do individuals need to work individually or collaborate?) is paired to work complexity (e.g. do individuals need to use judgment while completing tasks?). According to one Accenture manager, 'there is no "one-size-fits-all" approach.' Accenture generally operates within the collaborative model, the framework for knowledge-based industries.

The **Transaction Model** (low interdependence, low complexity) delivers consistent performance with limited interaction. Routine, automated tasks (e.g. factory assembly lines) require low-level employee skills. Knowledge is learned through formal rules, procedures, and training. KM should be codified KM, e.g. job aids.

The **Integration Model** (high interdependence, low complexity) relies on transferring knowledge around the organization to improve performance. Knowledge is indwelled in processes, tool kits, and rules. Systematic and repeatable tasks

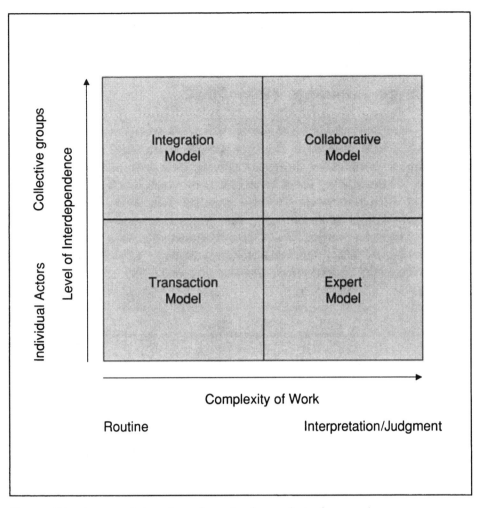

Figure F2 Accenture's interdependence/work complexity framework

must be tightly integrated across different functions, e.g. supply chain management. Organizations can implement a process-oriented strategy emphasizing cooperation and standardized procedures.

The **Expert Model** (low interdependence, high complexity) requires experts or star performers with highly specialized skills and expertise who exercise good judgment and discretion, e.g. a mutual fund manager. KM strategy must enable these top individuals to research and analyze the environment, and share these ideas with colleagues.

The **Collaboration Model** (high interdependence, high complexity) involves experts partnering to create new knowledge through improvisation and learning-by-doing. A team must possess individuals with deep expertise across functions; they become 'fluid' members of flexible teams. Management consulting is a good example.

Knowledge outfitting: 1996–2000

The next phase of Accenture's KM journey was active management and outfitting of relevant, quality content to the right people at the right time and place. Organizational dynamics had changed: migrating from strong-control hierarchies that 'push' information top-down to flexible networks in which individuals 'pull' information from bottom-up. The new paradigm was driven by the growing importance of knowledge-based (rather than physical) assets and service industry growth – comprising roughly 70% of developed countries' GDP and 50% of developing countries' GDP.[5] Karl Liander, Senior Manager of Nordic KM, utilizes the following model to demonstrate the changing dichotomy of work during the third phase:

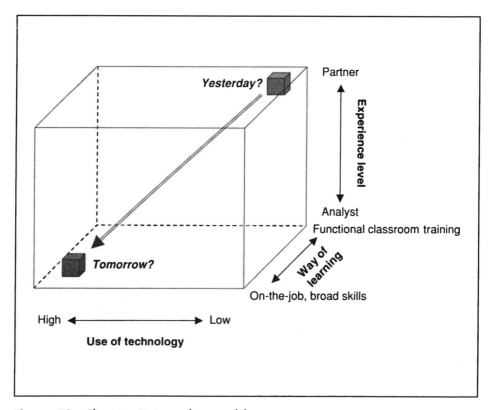

Figure F3 Changing KM paradigm model

The first KM efforts were initiated in a partner-centric knowledge arena. Accenture partners held relationships and knowledge, sharing with subordinates and colleagues on an as-needed basis. The company's work relied on skills that could be learned in a classroom setting and low technology. Partners with years of experience were provided front-line decisions. Consultants and analysts filled back office roles. Increasingly, however, client problems demanded more technology and a broader toolbox of skills. As client-facing roles increasingly included less-experienced consultants, it became imperative to outfit these individuals with the company's OM and a robust set of KM tools.

The company initiated the 'Emerald City' project to focus on six components of the KX vision: KX training, Contribution, Collaboration, Finding, Communities, and Access. The company aggregated and combined knowledge – cutting 16,000 databases to 7,500. In 1998, Pocket Xchange® (PX) was created to enable Accenture consultants with offline access because the KX's 1,000 gigabytes of data were too large to replicate down to a laptop. Other technical refitting of knowledge included business unit e-mail updates and newsletters, tailored Jupiter News, Accenture news wires, and mobile WAP delivery.

Organizationally, Accenture expanded its use of 'Centers of Excellence' (CoE), groups of people geographically or virtually positioned who gather and distribute leading information in a given discipline. In total, the company's 40 solution center CoEs employ 5,000 knowledge works focusing on specific business capabilities. Accenture CoEs include the Chicago-based Accenture Technology Labs, which employs leading academics, consultants, and librarians dedicated to cross-practice technological knowledge. Company technology research CoEs include Silicon Valley and Sophia Antipolis locations.

Accenture's 500 employees working in KM capacities could be considered a virtual and global CoE. Two hundred KM professionals, 'Knowledge Managers,' are deployed across industries, competencies, and geographic locales. Their tasks include knowledge creation, database management, and content management. The company also employs 150 'Knowledge Integrators.' These individuals have deep expertise in a given field and helped to determine and synthesize the most valuable knowledge. They also provide secondary research, help desk support, and external content acquisition and management services. KM employees also began to 'clean the KX' – eliminating data that did not offer value, and highlighting 'best practice' knowledge.

During this period, Accenture received the Most Admired Knowledge Enterprises award, placing 15th in 1998 (later #6 in 1999 & #14 in 2000). Nominated by Fortune 500 CEOs and KX experts, award recipients were ranked against eight key knowledge drivers.

Smart workplace: 1999–2000+

'Smart Workplace' describes today's Accenture where people are guided by knowledge. Integrated performance support and job tools enable continuous learning. The KX now contains over 7,500 databases with over 400,000 documents; and consultants need help mining this vast repository. Accenture created an Internet-based internal company-wide portal in August 2001. Available via a secure Internet connection, employees have instant access to an ever-growing selection of databases.

Industry knowledge maps were created to provide access to best industry specific knowledge. This is a 'one step guide' to the best KX assets including products, services, distribution channels, customer segments, key players, internal operations, and hot topics. Options include Delivering the Solution (tools, practice aids, and frameworks), Market Insight (industry overview, though leadership and point of view, subject matter experts, and sample engagement deliverables), and Selling the Application (sample proposals, credentials, engagement solutions). The Credentials Mart offers 'one stop shopping' of company expertise across all industry and service lines. Credentials are approved for external use and include 220 case studies, key references and resources, analyst reports, stock photography, and information on the Accenture brand.

The latest step in Accenture's KM journey is characterized by the need to align robust organizational and technological strategies to ever-changing external and internal environments. Externally, clients once satisfied with tailored workable solutions based on consultants' research and analysis may now demand primary research and adopt a do-it-yourself approach. Strategic alliances with small and large companies will necessitate increased inter-firm knowledge sharing. KM professionals were asked to take on additional responsibilities. Another key internal change is Accenture's new status as a public company. Consultants recognize that personal compensation hinges on company-wide performance and thus contribute in ways that enable organization-wide success. As shareholders, employees will focus on company revenue maximization, not just optimization of their own situation, e.g. work load.

New policies directed at part-time partner incentives and more flexible work hours will create more virtual teams. These individuals may have less personal contact with colleagues and therefore increasingly rely on technical KM infrastructure. Accenture will also develop an increased focus on retaining top performers otherwise lured to competitors, start-ups, and other opportunities. KM tracking systems could identify rising stars.

▶ Ongoing Challenges

Accenture has faced numerous challenges as it implements a KM strategy, including culture, employee turnover, incentive systems, and usage.

Culture

According to Paulk, Accenture

> always had a (knowledge) sharing culture . . . But we are changing the ways in which we share. To some of our colleagues using a computer is second nature. For others technology can sometimes be a barrier . . . Our firm is increasingly focusing on new ways of training people in the way we want information and knowledge shared. Firms like ours need to make it as easy as possible for busy consultants to contribute their knowledge.[6]

Liander believes that this strong culture aids KM, 'If you feel that you belong to an organization, then you automatically want to contribute to the organization and ensure its survival.'

Although the idea of knowledge sharing is central to organizational culture, the KM organizations and systems are peripheral – and at some times divorced – from the rest of the company. Strong company culture reinforces a sense of community with fellow consultants in the office and on the client engagement who work face-to-face with one another on a daily basis. Meanwhile, consultants' contact with KM employees may be limited to e-mail, OCTEL voice mail, and the occasional office meeting, especially when KM professionals are located all over the globe, from Chicago to Stockholm to Bombay.

Consulting employees have larger compensation packages and faster promotion timelines than their KM counterparts. Liander acknowledges the difference in rewards distribution, 'Supporting clients and generating revenue is seen as more important than storing and sharing knowledge.'

Turnover

Accenture's turnover of 15–20% per annum is par with the industry accustomed to a pace-based workforce model. As one consultant said, 'Accenture is a place where you grow – but not where you grow old. Most of us aren't thinking "I want to be a partner someday." There are a lot of other opportunities out there.'

With roughly one in five or six employees leaving each year, the company risks valuable knowledge walking out the door on a daily basis.

Incentives

Although the knowledge sharing culture is overarching, Accenture has experimented with numerous intrinsically- and extrinsically-focused incentive programs to facilitate KM. Contribution-targeted incentives have ranged from implementing KM-oriented performance evaluation criteria to raffling Palm Pilots to KX contributors. Intrinsic motivations are based on altruism, reciprocity, and feelings of self-worth. Accenture employees want to be helpful, and expect help in return. An individual may also get a sense of worth from establishing him/herself as a source of knowledge for others. He or she will be admired by colleagues and may have the opportunity for challenging projects in the future. An experienced consultant enthused about her role as a 'Knowledge Champion' on an SAP implementation project:

> It was really important to me to be the KC [for the project] ... We were doing [SAP] implementations all around the US and abroad. I was constantly getting e-mails and connecting teams and project information. I spent a lot of time working with senior executives at the company and client ... I was definitely recognized for my work.

Extrinsic motivations are visible to others and focus on compensation such as a career promotion or gifts. Paulk describes Accenture as 'constantly evaluating the way we assess performance.' [7] Accenture employees view KM activities as one of many important inputs to the performance evaluation and promotion process. Most performance criteria could be broadly interpreted to include KM activities. The current performance evaluation, Global Assessment Tool, includes the following criteria (possible KM interpretation given in parentheses): 'Establishes Personal Credibility with Clients and Others' (serves as an expert in a given field and shares knowledge with colleagues and clients), 'Drives to Add Value' (contributes to the KX), 'Builds and Applies Skills and Capabilities' (acquires and applies personal knowledge effectively), 'Community Building' (shares lessons learned with other community members), and 'Maximizes Team's Performance' (uses KX efficiently or trains others on KM tools). KM-oriented performance criteria are now included for every level of the organization. The South Africa practice is particularly keen on supporting knowledge management. In fact, nearly all of the individuals promoted to consultant in the South Africa practice had served as 'Knowledge Integrators', a role in which they encouraged KX contribution and use.

Accenture's extrinsic rewards have also included freebie presents (e.g. t-shirts and pens) and raffles for larger items (e.g. Palm Pilots). These efforts seem to bring short-term results in the form of a flood of documents – only some of which will be useful to others.

Users

Accenture has unique sets of 'top KM contributors' and 'top KM retrievers.' Each user group is driven by a unique set of personal motivations, project tasks, and other goals.

The trend of top contributors tends to be young, relatively experienced, technically savvy and analytically minded individuals who have been with the firm for at least three years. They recognize the value of contributing and make it a critical part of their projects. One manager shared, 'My project managers are usually good about quickly reviewing my sanitized deliverables and then I stick them on the KX . . . usually just the best stuff.' These high contributors know 'what's out there' on the KX and can often suggest the best database repository or key search words for their own and others' documents. Contributors also enjoy the recognition. According to one experienced consultant, 'I like being the "go to" guy. People know who I am.' A top contributor is usually well connected to his/her specific competency group and office, and will continually grow these critical networks. Eventually, contributors become more involved with project management and sales and spend less time with the KX. It is possible to search some KX databases by 'Contributor' view and find individuals who have submitted dozens or even hundreds of documents.

Americans contribute more that 80% of the KX documents. European countries follow as the next largest contributors. Asian counterparts contribute the smallest number of documents. The difference in contribution may be due in part to cultural differences among nations. The different levels also reflect Accenture's client-driven nature – most but not all of Accenture's clients request English documentation. Accenture's heaviest contributors are generally native English speakers who contribute English documentation. Of the documentation in languages other than English, most can be found on country or project-specific databases. The remaining non-English documentation can be found on the KX, and includes a brief abstract in English. The idea of such a short summary is that readers could then contact the project leaders directly to gain more insight. In some cases, a machine translation was used to create the abstract or the entire document. One KM manager reflected on how this mechanization resulted in some very awkward English renditions. Accenture's relative contribution levels are generally on par with other management consulting firms.

On the retrieval side, top users tend to be inexperienced consultants who are new to the company and tasked with KX searches. Due to their relative lack of experience, they may not be able to locate valuable information effectively and efficiently. These individuals don't know what they are looking for and may waste a lot of their personal and project time. One experienced analyst reflected, 'I remember the first time I used the KX. My project manager asked me to search for projects which had created similar deliverables. I didn't even know where to start.' New users may also locate, download, and peruse documents, which are not relevant to their tasks. Liander estimates that only five per cent of retrieved documents are actually of use. Theoretically, these individuals should develop searching skills over time.

Another primary group of data miners are individuals in the business development stage of a project. They are concerned with materials that will help to prepare project proposals. According to one manager, 'I always use the KX to get the latest and greatest credentials. It's also good to see who did what [task] and where [client].'

▶ Case Studies

Successes
Implementation success: From a Manager, KM Enterprise Business Solutions

A Manager in the KM Enterprise Business Solutions (EBS) met with her team members to review the local progress of the Enterprise Business Solutions' (EBS) Global Knowledge Network (GKN). The manager joined Accenture as an analyst eight years ago after receiving her Master's degree from the Stockholm School of Economics.

EBS was one of Accenture's most successful lines of business, incorporating integrated solutions for SAP, PeopleSoft, Oracle, Baan, and ERP. Her GKN team was responsible for creating and storing knowledge that could be transferred and used in pre-sales and delivery environments. The company would benefit from leveraging of intangible assets, gathering and dissemination of experience and know-how, and increasing competitive advantage. It was also anticipated that clients would reap benefits from improved productivity and reduced costs.

The EBS GKN project spanned 13 countries and had a high profile within the company. The manager recalls, 'We were the pioneers. The future was in globally integrated KM . . . Our successes and failures would be watched closely.' Each geographic region had ten to twelve team members. Knowledge Integrators (KIs) were full-time KM professionals responsible for the process of knowledge sharing and outfitting across the global EBS practice. Deployed by geography, software, competency, and market unit, KIs were tasked with training and communicating KM to consultants, developing knowledge-sharing tools and processes, and supporting KM efforts. Database managers created home pages, discussion forums, searchable databases, and other electronic tools.

The manager and her team were responsible for the Nordic region's (Denmark, Finland, Norway, and Sweden) contributions. As KIs, they had spent much of the last six months introducing the company to the project and the mutual benefits to employees, clients, and the firm. The manager recalled the dozens of office and client site meetings with colleagues in Copenhagen, Helsinki, Oslo, and Stockholm, 'I was always impressed by the strong levels of 'buy in' from analyst to partner. People really believe in it [EBS GKN].'

Analysts and consultants were particularly 'charged up' to be able to contribute and have their participation reflected in performance appraisals. These relative newcomers to the company saw the project as a unique personal development opportunity. Individuals with at least 12 months experience with the company were honored with selection as 'Knowledge Champions' (KCs). In this role, they served as the primary client contact for all knowledge sharing activities. KCs were responsible for adding at least two project deliverables each month and for keeping all of their project information current on the KX. They also monitored and encouraged project members' contribution and use of the KX. KCs were ambitious analysts close to the consultant promotion timeline, and often worked extra hard to guarantee personal rewards. 'The really hard workers were often promoted. It was win-win.'

After reviewing the first six month's results, her team was pleased with the high contribution levels and good productivity among the 250 EBS consultants on 16 projects in the Nordic region. Each project had its own client home page and KC who was trained and supported by Solution Center KCs in the larger offices. So far, EBS KM had gathered over one hundred contributions to the EBS Library and over two hundred questions and responses in the discussion databases. All KCs had been rewarded with excellent feedback as either 'Gold' or 'Green,' the two highest possible ratings.

The team discussed success factors. Certainly, buy-in at all levels of the company had helped. Everyone seemed to believe in the project and want to contribute. The business integration across the four company competencies also ensured that all parts of the company were working together. The team also discussed the future challenges. She emphasized the need to ensure capturing of the 'right knowledge.' She wanted to focus more on client team's knowledge needs and develop 'velocity services' that would target the most valuable needs. Furthermore, the team wanted to ensure that the short-term contributions and successes they had witnessed would actually lead to long-term behavior and results. They resolved to continue to install knowledge sharing culture and action through regular communication and training.

Her team also pondered how KM efforts could help drive future EBS work. EBS was still a very strong area for the company, but not growing as fast as e-Commerce. She wondered, 'Would EBS, and our EBS KM efforts, be valuable to the company in the future?' As Accenture was constantly reorganizing, the team also considered how a future organization would challenge and inevitably change the EBS efforts. For example, if the company shifted from competencies to market units, the EBS KM would have to reorganize to mirror this structure. Also, she thought privately, 'How would future cost-cutting initiatives impact the EBS KM program? Would KCs still devote time to the project without a charge number?' She thought there was a real need to quantify the financial benefits of the EBS KM program.

Sharing success: From an Analyst, Human Performance

An analyst in Accenture's Human Performance practice faced the most daunting task in her 12 months with the company. She had two weeks to draft role and job descriptions for 150 employees at a large telecommunications client. She joined Accenture's Washington D.C. office straight out of her undergraduate Business degree at the University of Richmond. Like all new employees, she was introduced to the Accenture culture through rapid-fire training in her home office and then St Charles, the worldwide training facilitated located in the suburbs an hour outside Chicago.

She learned that she had been staffed on the telecommunications project in an e-mail from her future project manager. The project manager emphasized that she would need to play a leading role as content provider for the job descriptions, and asked her to look over the attached project proposal and contract to stimulate ideas. She was expected at the client project site the next morning. This hasty project start was par for the course at Accenture. Employees were expected to 'roll-on' (and 'roll-off') projects as quickly as business needs demanded. Sometimes this would entail a few hours notice before a Red-Eye flight across the country or, occasionally, across the ocean.

After 12 months with the company on telecommunications clients, she was familiar with the industry but had no experience writing job designs. As she recalls, 'I was definitely overwhelmed but I wanted to get up to speed quickly and hit the ground running.' She read the project documentation carefully and then logged onto the KX to search for relevant deliverables from similar projects. She used the KX Doc Finder utility to order archived information she hoped would be pertinent. The KX Doc Finder searches multiple databases and e-mails possible relevant documents. This KM tool saved her the time of a manual search. She justified her KX search, 'Accenture sells this type of work all the time. I don't want to 'reinvent the wheel.' I'd rather spend time getting to know my client and customizing the documents . . . I just hope that someone archived some good frameworks.'

Later that day, she ate lunch with a member of her 'start group.' A 'start group' is a group of employees who began their Accenture careers on the same day. The group (generally five to twenty individuals) often grows close during shared orientation and training experiences. She shared the exciting news of her new project and asked her start group member for ideas on how to gather more information. The member of her start group recommended the KX, and then paused as he remembered that one of his friends from recent St Charles training at the Centre for Professional Education had spoken of a similar engagement – albeit 3,000 miles away in London. The Center for Professional Education brings employees together from all over the world for three day to two week classes. Evenings are often spent socializing at the on campus sports center or the town country line dancing bar 'Cadillac Ranch.' Accenture encourages both work and play time to build trust and long-standing working relationships among employees from all over the world. It was during one of these evenings that she and her London friend had discussed their experiences in the telecommunications industry. The member of her start group suggested that she contact the London-based consultant for general insights on how to approach the work and, if possible, more specific guidance on deliverables.

After lunch, she sent her London counterpart an Octel voice mail and then perused the 50 documents highlighted by Doc Finder and retrieved the most promising. She shared, 'With the KX, you never know what you might get. Sometimes you can't even imagine how something got out there. It just doesn't fit what you want. Luckily, I found some stuff that I hope will give me some ideas.'

The next day, she spent her first morning at the new project – meeting her clients and colleagues, and settling into a cubicle by the window. The project manager scheduled a meeting the following morning for which she would propose a work timeline and action plan for the next critical two weeks. She checked her OCTELs and agreed to call her London counterpart earlier that afternoon. The firm's OCTEL voice-mail system enables employees worldwide to leave and retrieve messages from one another and clients. This system facilitates round-the-clock communication and saved on a long distance phone call.

On the call, the London-based consultant identified with her situation, recalling a similarly challenging project with short deadlines at a leading British telecommunications client. He asked her to explain the client environment and project demands, and then offered some universal guidelines in terms of a reasonable timeline, necessary client inputs and feedback, and lessons learned. He also promised to send her some of his own relevant documents which had not yet been archived to the KX. She thanked him for the input, and he offered to look over her work and answer any additional questions.

She compared her notes from the phone call with some of the relevant KX documents, and designed a workable project timeline. She established deadlines and milestones for each of the project phases, and allowed for feedback sessions with key stakeholders. She also prepared a rough draft of an interview checklist and potential job description templates. Her new project manager was impressed with her efficiency, and approved the schedule and ideas with few modifications.

As she proceeded with the project, she checked in occasionally with her London counterpart and a few others who had contributed valuable KX documents. The client and project manager were pleased with her work. At the conclusion of the project, she sanitized her documents and added them to the knowledge repository. She thought her efforts might help her bid for an early promotion to consultant level, 'I made sure my GAT [Global Assessment Tool performance evaluation] mentioned those KX dumps.' She also wondered how many people would read and use her documents in the future. Perhaps someone would even contact her for further explanation and help.

Partial success: From a Consultant, Technology

A Consultant in Accenture's technology practice leaned back in his chair after typing in the last lines of PeopleSoft code. He had just finished the 'build' phase of a People Soft implementation project at a large financial services client in New York. The next step would be product test and retest, followed by refinement.

He had written most of the code from his prior project experience and information gathering. In his three years with the company, he had compiled sanitized code from different stages of several implementation projects. He had also retained some key programming from his undergraduate degree in Computer Science at the University of California.

He also occasionally searched the KX for code and copied the useful pieces onto his c:/drive files. He enthused, 'Sometimes you find real "gems." You can use them to fix "kluges."' Kluges are code written by programmers that is indecipherable to anyone but the original author. Kluges can wreak havoc on technology projects and can create 'real nightmares' for future programmers. Other times, he found outdated, unworkable code. He never alerted the KX database administrators to problems of inaccurate postings, 'I don't want to get all high and mighty and try to shut other people down. Who knows? Maybe some of that code is worthwhile to someone.' Instead, he learned to recall the names of contributors to seek out, 'I just try to remember who sends in the good solutions and use their information.'

He had built a good repertoire of code and other technology solutions on his laptop's c:/drive. He also backed up a copy on a shared drive. It would be time-consuming and perhaps impossible to locate another copy on the KX, 'I can't afford to lose this stuff even though I don't use all – or even most – of it.' He intended to someday contribute some of the most useful code for the KX, but it was to be a time intensive process and he felt that he didn't have the time beyond his 70-hour week.

He reflected on the most challenging aspect of the project. He had to write a piece of code that would link the PeopleSoft program to the client's software. Although the client's software wasn't very common, he was sure that someone else in the company had seen the problem before. He thought that he could come up with a solution after hours or days of writing and testing the code, but he didn't have the time. The build phase was supposed to wrap up in three days' time, 'I didn't want to hold up the entire project.'

He scanned through dozens of KX technology-oriented databases, but couldn't locate any relevant documents. He posted a question on three relevant discussion databases and awaited replies. Discussion databases on Lotus Notes enable individuals from all over the company to communicate questions and answers to tasks. Although he occasionally checked the discussion databases, he wasn't confident that most of his Technology colleagues around the world were using them. Still there were no replies.

Finally, he sent an e-mail to five programmers whom he knew and trusted from prior projects. Three were unable to offer any solutions. One former colleague sent back code for a related program, but it didn't quite work. The last reply referred him to a project manager in Zurich who then put him in touch with the programmers at a Danish financial client. He e-mailed the programmers and soon received the code as a Lotus Notes e-mail attachment. At first he didn't understand how the solution would work, and contacted the programmers. They traded Octel voice mails and eventually arranged a conference call to discuss the code and its context. As he recalled, 'The Danish guy's information was customized so I had to fine-tune and tweak it a bit.' In the end, the code worked, but he was annoyed to realize that he had spent much of the last two days trying to get information that should have been more readily available.

This was a mild success because he didn't share his lessons learned and workable code with others in the company. The KM tools were not as effective as he had hoped. He did not initiate any action to improve KM documents, processes, and tools.

Technical failure: From a Partner, Strategy

A Partner in Accenture's Strategy practice was preparing to leave the company. One week from now he would begin his first day of work at a smaller strategy firm close to his family home in Connecticut. He stopped into the office's technical support center to pick up a copy of a CD burned from his laptop hard-drive. The support crew asked if there was anything else that he or others might want from the laptop before they deleted the c:/drive and prepared it for another employee. He replied 'no' – after all, no one else would know how to begin to look – let alone use those old client deliverables. He was certain that at least one other copy existed on the laptop of one of the other project managers.

As he walked through the lobby, he reflected on his five years with Accenture. Following an Ivy League MBA and an eight-year career at a leading strategy firm, he joined Accenture at age 35. He had worked directly with client top management and good junior consultants on challenging projects – traveling the world over for meetings, projects and training. Although his peer group of associate partners and partners had been fiercely competitive at times, he reveled in their intellectually stimulating contributions and hoped to stay in touch with many of them.

Holding the CD in his hand, he reflected on how five years of work could be contained on one little disk. He had spent many a long plane ride and late night hunched over his laptop – drafting client contracts, reviewing client deliverables, and answering e-mails. Well, he recalled, it was better than when he first started consulting so many years ago. Without Power Point, he and other junior consultants would spend hours cutting and pasting words and diagrams onto overhead slides for client presentations. Now, everything was electronic and he had a copy of it to pass on to his successor for posterity's sake.

He had always been protective of his work. At Accenture, he never personally archived deliverables or other knowledge onto the KX. In part, he didn't think that the material would be valuable to 99.99% of the firm. He was also unaccustomed to this technical method of knowledge sharing. His first firm had adapted a more bottom-up approach – calling colleagues personally rather than searching databases electronically.

At Accenture, he continued this practice of directly contacting APs and partners for their insights and old deliverables. He felt comfortable sharing the material when he could provide a context. He liked knowing who in the company knew about his projects and what aspects they knew about. Sharing knowledge personally gave him the confidence he could trust others to use the material wisely. In return, his peers would call on him for ideas. Sometimes, if the project was large enough, knowledge sharing might lead to a role in the selling or management of one aspect of the client engagement. These opportunities augmented his firm résumé and, more importantly, his growing list of client and firm contacts.

He never searched the KX but would occasionally ask his project team members to search for relevant documents. These members would also search independently.

He had consistently received good feedback on his performance. He worked well and shared knowledge with others, though not through the technological mechanisms provided by the company. His subordinate project team members weren't particularly strong KX contributors. This was in part due to the lack of a rule or discipline to send documentation to the KX at the conclusion of project phases. He never encouraged KX documentation. If another project member took the initiative, he was not quick to approve the sanitized documents. This could result in weeks or months of delayed posting to the KX. Also, the younger employees followed their partner's lead and aimed to establish and use personal contacts. None of his work was ever archived to the KX.

Exploitive task failure: From an Associate Partner and her Proposal Team

At the end of a tough day, the Accenture project team regrouped in the hotel's restaurant to discuss the day's events and next steps. The Associate Partner (who was also the lead project manager) and her team members were disappointed with the sale of just one piece of the client need for a full SAP implementation. They had poured most of the last three weeks into a strong proposal that would integrate Strategy, Process, Technology, and Organization and Human Performance work.

Collectively, the lead project manager and her four team members had 20 years of experience with SAP implementations. This project was especially large and potentially lucrative as it might have led to additional sell-on work. The lead partner for the client had especially encouraged the team to solicit advice from colleagues running similar projects around the globe. The partner had even sent a 'broadcast OCTEL' to other SAP implementation executives asking for specific insights on this client proposal and referring follow-ups to the lead project manager. She and her team spent much of their time gathering electronic and personal input from others.

The team recalled how they spent weeks reviewing gigabyte after gigabyte of old project proposals, including budgets and timelines. Some documents located on the KX were really outdated. More time-consuming were the countless hours spent organizing and holding conference calls and meetings with executives from all over the world. As she recalled, 'Accenture certainly has a knowledge-sharing culture! Everyone wanted to be helpful and offered a lot of input and documentation.'

The lead project manager reflected, 'I had lot riding on this project.' She had worked in industry for five years before graduating from a top-20 MBA program and joining Accenture's Chicago office. In her six years at the company, she had built a reputation as a strong contributor, but not as a 'rain maker' who regularly sells large projects directly to clients. If the client bought this entire project, she thought that she was sure to be recommended for partner in two or three years' time. The promotion to partner was heavily influenced by revenue contributions to the company's bottom line.

She thought she had spoken to everyone, 'We talked to people who had sold work to the same client several years ago. We talked to project managers running SAP implementations in a half-dozen other countries ... No stone was left unturned.' These calls were difficult to schedule and she thought that a lot of their insights weren't really applicable outside a particular client or country. Sometimes her team provided internal billing charge numbers for these executives' time and this became an expensive aspect of the business development budget. As the process wore on, the team couldn't help but ask themselves if they were wasting their time.

In the end, the team put together a lengthy proposal that incorporated most of the internal feedback. Some of the extensive information gathering was indeed effective. The team saved time by utilizing aspects of the proposal that described Accenture's extensive experience with SAP implementations. But in other cases, there were long descriptions of seemingly peripheral detail. In retrospect, the lead project manager thought that the client was confused by the multiple perspectives and alarmed by the extensiveness of the proposal. This could have led to the client's decision to purchase only one piece of work. The lead project manager hoped that the client had found the material to be personally customized, but she wasn't quite sure.

As the team finished dinner, the lead project manager thought back to the beginning of the project, 'We knew what we had to do.' In fact, together the team had enough experience to prepare a solid proposal. She felt disappointed by the wasted time and effort, and the inability to win the job, '. . . but we just didn't do it. We got distracted – way too distracted.' As a result, the team only sold one portion of the work proposed. The lead project manager would have to wait for another 'rain-making' opportunity.

Notes

1   Ostro, N. 1999. The Corporate Brain. *Chief Executive*, May.
2   Davenport, T., & Hansen, M. 1996. Knowledge Management at Andersen Consulting. Harvard Business School Case, 9-499-032.
3   Reimus, B. 1997. Knowledge Sharing within Management Consulting Firms. Kennedy Information.

4   Reimus, B. 1997. Knowledge Sharing within Management Consulting Firms. Kennedy Information.
5   World Trade Organization. www.wto.org
6   Reimus, B. 1997. Knowledge Sharing within Management Consulting Firms. Kennedy Information.
7   Reimus, B. 1997. Knowledge Sharing within Management Consulting Firms. Kennedy Information.

Case Assignments

1   Describe how Accenture in the second phase of the company's knowledge management development endeavoured to stimulate increase knowledge sharing.
2   Discuss the implications of Accenture's 'Interdependence/Work Complexity Framework' for knowledge management in different types of companies.
3   Explain what is meant by 'Smart Workplace'.
4   Accenture has developed a performance evaluation tool called 'Global Assessment Tool'. How is this composed? Are there, in your opinion, any essential missing elements in this?
5   Discuss the following statement from the Accenture case:
    'Americans contribute more that 80% of the KX documents. European countries follow as the next largest contributors. Asian counterparts contribute the smallest number of documents. The difference in contribution may be due to cultural differences among nations.'

Appendix A Largest management consulting firms (1998)

Firm	Consulting revenues worldwide 1997 ($M)	US consulting revenues 1997 ($M)
1. Accenture (Andersen Consulting)	5,726	2,863
2. CSC*	3,000	2,000
3. Ernst & Young	2,680	1,798
4. Coopers & Lybrand	2,400	1,270
5. Deloitte Consulting	2,300	1,500
6. McKinsey & Co.	2,200	900
7. KPMG Peat Marwick	2,011	1,066
8. Cap Gemini	1,648	198
9. Price Waterhouse	1,400	806
10. Mercer Consulting Group	1,338	823
11. Towers Perrin	1,120	817
12. A.T. Kearney	1,100	550
13. Booz-Allen & Hamilton	1,075	800
14. Arthur Andersen	953	483
15. Sema Group	888	N/A

Source: *Consultants News*, Kennedy Information.
Note: * Revenues for this group are derived from a number of business units, including CSC Index, CSC Consulting, and European operations (among others). The number for this group is a rough estimate.

Appendix B   Accenture Organization prior to January 2001

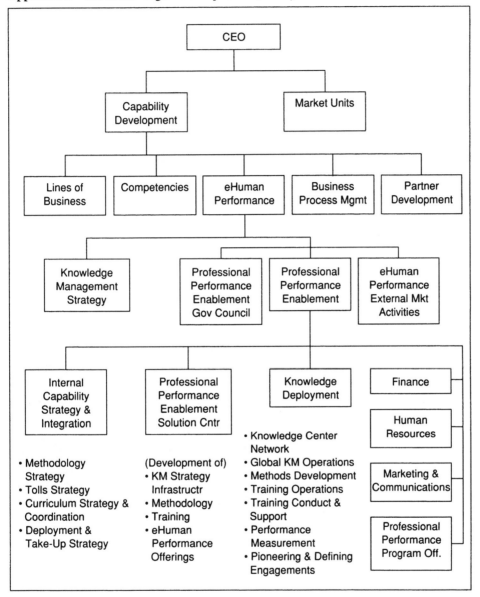

chapter **7**

Knowledge Transfer between HQ and Subsidiaries

▶ Purpose

The purpose of this chapter is to provide a conceptual framework that facilitates the study of knowledge transfer between high knowledge parents and low knowledge subsidiaries. In particular our concern is with knowledge transfer by MNCs to foreign subsidiaries in developing countries. The upgrading of a subsidiary from being a knowledge recipient to that of a centre of innovation is divided into four levels. At the lowermost level, a level I subsidiary can only absorb explicit knowledge of an elementary type. At the uppermost level, a level IV subsidiary is not only capable of absorbing tacit knowledge, but is also capable of independently generating knowledge which may be transferred to the parent or other parts of the firm. Using extant research, various knowledge transfer mechanisms are identified in the move from level I to IV. These vary in terms of the social interaction they are intended to generate which in turn is contingent on the degree of tacitness to the knowledge that is to be transferred.

▶ Background

The success of an MNC is ultimately dependent on its ability to replicate its domestic advantage in foreign locations. This domestic advantage may be due to the possession of unique brands and managerial skills. However, its main source usually resides in unique technologies that rest on the possession of distinctive knowledge-based assets. Indeed 'the primary reason why MNCs exist is because of their ability to transfer and exploit knowledge more effectively and efficiently than through external market mechanisms' (Gupta and Govindarajan, 2000). In short, the more distinctive knowledge content assets possessed by a firm, whether these are related to production, marketing or other activities, the greater the potential for international expansion. To a greater or lesser extent distinctive knowledge-based assets have to be transferred to, adapted to and then implemented in foreign locations.[1]

Traditionally the scope of the transfer task has been limited. Beyond gaining access to raw materials or markets, foreign direct investment has been confined to utilizing low cost unskilled or semi-skilled labour on the basis of established technologies involving limited training. However, since at least the mid-1980s increasingly firms are investing abroad in order to buy into foreign knowledge assets in order to protect or extend their core competencies (Cantwell and Piscitello, 1997; Kogut, 1990; Kogut and Chang, 1991; Teece, 1992). This would appear to be particularly the case for technologically intensive industries, like pharmaceuticals and electronics (Kuemmerle, 1997). Knowledge transfer capabilities are a critical prerequisite for developing these investments into integrated centres of innovation.

The costs involved in codifying and transferring complex knowledge can vary greatly. Teece (1977) estimated that the cost of technology transfer ranged from 2 per cent to 59 per cent of total costs of the 27 projects he analysed. The transfer process is affected by the out-transfer capacity of the transferor, the in-transfer capacity of the recipient in addition to factors such as the cultural distance and the local environment of the recipient (Leonard-Barton, 1995; Martin and Salomon, 1999). Additionally, the degree of tacitness involved in the knowledge to be transferred is a significant factor. Tacit knowledge involves 'causal ambiguity' (Lippman and Rumelt, 1982; Reed and DeFillippi, 1990), that is, there is a basic difficulty in comprehending the precise nature of the causal connections between actions and results that is critical when one is attempting to replicate a capability in a new setting.

Clearly, with such potential costs, attention should be paid to developing and selecting the most appropriate mechanisms for knowledge transfer.[2] In this chapter our aim is to provide a theoretical conceptual framework that addresses this issue with a particular focus on knowledge transfer between high knowledge parents and low knowledge subsidiaries in developing countries. In the case of developing countries it can take decades to develop a knowledge recipient into a centre of innovation. However, rising educational standards and government-induced aspirations increasingly make at least some technology and knowledge transfer mandatory.

We will argue that knowledge transfer mechanisms vary in terms of the degree of social interaction they are intended to generate. We will further argue that the degree of social interaction being aimed at is contingent on the type of knowledge transfer the MNC is seeking to achieve. As a prelude to this discussion we first briefly explore the concept of knowledge.

▶ Knowledge: Explicit-Tacit

As pointed out in Chapter 6, knowledge may be divided into information or know-what and tacit knowledge or know-how (Polanyi, 1962; Kogut and Zander, 1992). Information is defined as easily codifiable, explicit knowledge that can be transmitted 'without loss of integrity once the syntactical rules required for deciphering it are known. Information includes facts, axiomatic propositions, and symbols' (Kogut and Zander, 1992: 386). In the case of global service companies such as McDonald's or Hilton Hotels, tasks have been standardized and are therefore relatively easily transferable to franchisees through well-defined mechanisms such as procedure manuals, routines and franchisee-friendly technology. In addition to its transferability, information can also be relatively easily stored in electronic document systems and reused across a variety of situations as long as these situations are standardized. For example, the consulting arm of Ernst & Young has developed a firm-wide infrastructure for standardizing and centrally storing material deriving from its engagements around the globe. The raw material generated by engagement teams will usually include work-plans, interim and final reports, analytical models, and PowerPoint presentations. Teams have to decide what parts of their material is valuable enough to retain, scrub it for client confidentiality, write an abstract, fill out a 'wrapper' that identifies critical parameters (e.g., industry, business process, engagement director) and then send it electronically to the Center for Business Knowledge. In this way information on previous engagements is readily available for application by other engagement teams regardless of geographical location. The use of databases for the storage of information is not confined to management consultants. In industries where development is strongly routinized, or in industries that have particular routine test procedures, such as pharmaceuticals, food, agro-chemical products, and mechanical engineering, extensive use is made of electronic databases (De Meyer, 1995b).

In companies where activities are less standardized or more complex, databases are generally not used. Partly this may be because 'the available commercial databases are not yet powerful enough to present unstructured information in a standardized and efficient form' (De Meyer, 1995b: 186). More importantly, though, it is because of the nature of tacit knowledge. For Nonaka (1994) tacit knowledge is deeply embedded in action within idiosyncratic contexts. It involves knowledge that is complex, difficult to codify and therefore 'sticky' (von Hippel, 1994; Szulanski, 1996). Thus while information consists of factual statements, know-how comprises recipes, many of which are difficult to articulate in precise terms because they involve experiential insights which may only be transferable by the exchange of employees (Bresman, Birkinshaw and Nobel, 1999). Trying to turn inherently tacit knowledge into explicit knowledge can lead to serious problems if inappropriate transfer mechanisms are used;

Xerox, for example, once attempted to embed the know-how of its service and repair technicians into an expert system that was installed in the copiers. They hoped that technicians responding to a call could be guided by the system and complete repairs from a distance. But it turned out that technicians could not solve problems using the system by itself. When the copier designers looked into the matter more closely, they discovered that technicians learned from one another by sharing stories about how they had fixed the machines. The expert system could not replicate the nuance and detail that were exchanged in face-to-face conversations. (Hansen, Nohria and Tierney, 1999: 115)

Whereas explicit knowledge can be extracted from the person who developed it, made independent of that person, and reused for other purposes, tacit knowledge can generally only be transferred through some form of social interaction (Nonaka and Takeuchi, 1995). However, if we discount the cost involved in transferring it to foreign sites, it is tacit knowledge that results in sustainable advantages not least because it is difficult for competitors to imitate (Kogut and Zander, 1993). However, the protection this source of causal ambiguity offers against competitors also impinges on the firm's ability to transfer its proprietary assets and skills across its own organization (Szulanski, 1996). Thus the greater the tacitness of the knowledge, the more expensive it is to transfer across national borders (Teece, 1981). For example:

A Hewlett Packard team recently developed a very successful electronic oscilloscope with a Windows operating system and interface. Executives wanted to be sure that other divisions understood and applied the interface. To keep the costs of knowledge transfer low, they considered trying to codify the acquired know-how. They realized, however, that the knowledge they wanted to capture was too rich and subtle to incorporate in a written report. And they understood that writing answers to the many questions that would come from HP's divisions would take an extraordinary amount of time. So they took the person-to-person approach and sent engineers from product development teams to meetings at divisions around the world and to a companywide conference.

The executives' decision didn't come cheap: by one estimate, the company spent $1 million dollars on communication costs alone on this process. But the investment paid off as the interface gained widespread acceptance throughout the company. (Hansen, Nohria and Tierney, 1999: 112)

The degree to which tacit knowledge is, or can be, exchanged depends on the out-transfer capacity of the parent and the in-transfer capacity of the subsidiary.

▶ Out-Transfer Capacity

Out-transfer capacity can be subdivided into the transferor's ability to transfer explicit knowledge and its ability to transfer idiosyncratic, tacit, knowledge. The former involves the ability to codify and disseminate necessary information through operating manuals, routines, procedures and physical systems that enable the user to know what to do. Just as some manufacturers of consumer products are more able than others to design clearly articulated operating manuals and user-friendly end products, so some firms are more efficient than others at communicating explicit knowledge to their subsidiaries.

In regard to tacit knowledge, there are a number of factors that make out-transfer of it relatively problematic. One factor is that the generation of tacit knowledge is often the product of organizational routines (Nelson and Winter, 1982). These routines have evolved as a consequence of individuals interacting with one another, face-to-face, over an extensive period of time. As a result there will be a strong sense of collective identity. Strong-tied, multilateral social relationships are not readily duplicated. Pathways between the out-transferor and the recipient have to be deliberately created to facilitate the social ties that make tacit knowledge flows possible (Dyer and Nobeoka, 2000). One increasingly common type of pathway consists of intranet systems that enable employees to pinpoint relevant experts within the firm together with e-mails, the phone and video-conferencing systems. However, many MNCs, such as Ericsson, consider over-reliance on Web-based systems for competence networking as jeopardizing the loss of continuity and responsiveness in knowledge building and competence sharing (Hellström, Kemlin and Malmquist, 2000). While not abandoning Web-based tools, Ericsson, like Bain, Boston Consulting Group and McKinsey, also makes extensive use of face-to-face dialogue not only on a one-on-one basis but also by transferring people between offices for brainstorming sessions.

A further constraint on the out-transfer of tacit knowledge is that individuals or groups of individuals have to be motivated to share their valuable knowledge despite the fact that their income and status within the firm are closely linked to their know-how. This problem is particularly acute when there is no prospect of receiving an immediate payback in equally valuable knowledge, or when there is a fear that proprietary knowledge may be leaked to competitors (Porter, 1985). For intra-firm knowledge transfer to take place a motivation system must be designed that provides the source with sufficient incentive to engage in transfer (Porter, 1985). At ABB one of the most important functions of business area managers is to ensure that knowledge is spread from best-practice sites to other subsidiaries. Coupled to this function are reward systems that have been designed to reward knowledge sharing. However, in addition, somehow the sense of a shared identity that gives rise to the tacit elements has to be expanded to include employees in distant subsidiaries.

Last, but by no means least, is the issue of the initial strategic aim of the out-transferor. As we have previously pointed out in this book, MNCs are often initially motivated to establish foreign subsidiaries in order to benefit from inexpensive labour or to achieve market access. In knowledge terms, not only is the subsidiary totally dependent on the parent company, but also the parent company has a restricted view on what knowledge is to be transferred. The aim is often limited to the transference of technical know-what information, rather than the transference of tacit know-how knowledge.

Maintaining subsidiaries in a knowledge-dependency relation would appear to be the case in regard to Japanese MNCs. Research by Reger (1997), in which he examined the degree of internationalization of R&D in 18 major Japanese and Western European multinational enterprises indicates that, regardless of location, R&D activities are overwhelmingly concentrated in Japan. For example the share of foreign R&D in 1993 at Hitachi was 2 per cent, Mishibushi, 4 per cent, Sony 6 per cent and Matsushita 12 per cent. In contrast corresponding figures for Siemens were 28 per cent, Hoescht 42 per cent, Philips 55 per cent and Roche 60 per cent. In other words Japanese innovation processes are predominantly 'centre-for-global'.

▶ In-Transfer Capacity

Going beyond a knowledge dependency relationship is a theme that Leonard-Barton (1995) has focused on in the context of the in-transfer capacity of subsidiaries located in developing countries. Research by Szulanski (1996) on intra-firm knowledge transfer identified this factor, which he labels absorptive capacity (Cohen and Levinthal, 1990), as a particularly salient factor. Likewise, Lyles and Salk (1996) have demonstrated the importance of absorptive capacity as a determinant of knowledge acquisition from foreign parents within the context of international joint ventures.

Leonard-Barton (1995) distinguishes four levels of in-transfer capacity at the subsidiary level:

- the capacity to operate assembly or turnkey equipment (I);
- the capacity to adapt and localize components (II);
- the capacity to redesign products (III);
- the capacity to independently design products (IV).

While moving from the one level to the next is dependent on the transferor's out-transfer capacity, it is also heavily influenced by the subsidiary's ability to develop its in-transfer capacity. In developing countries, because of levels of education and relevant experience, most subsidiaries will only possess a *level I* in-transfer capacity. Level I operations are characterized by the construction of a complete working plant (a turnkey factory) or an assembly plant. Usually the equipment involves older technology that has been tried, tested and successfully debugged so that it is 'fool-proof'. Beyond the advantage of ease of use, older equipment means that proprietary knowledge is not revealed.

At level I there is little or no capacity for the receipt of tacit knowledge. Knowledge transfer is limited to explicit knowledge that either is embodied in the equipment, software or other physical systems, is recorded in manuals or is communicable through instructions and demonstrations. The only skill required by the recipients is the ability to use the equipment and to perform routine maintenance.

However, even vertical, formal transfer of explicit knowledge may be subject to severe constraints. One major constraint involves finding a match between the functioning of the equipment and the existing infrastructure in developing countries. For example:

> Firms wanting to set up in Nigeria are faced with a problem known locally as 'BYOI' (Bring Your Own Infrastructure). Cadbury Nigeria, for instance, in the absence of reliable power or water supplies, generates eight megawatts of its own electricity and drills 2,500 feet down to obtain the 70,000 gallons of water an hour it needs for its Lagos food-processing plant. Since the water spurts out at 80°C, it has to be cooled before it can be used. According to Bunmi Oni, the firm's managing director, BYOI adds at least 25% to operating costs. (*The Economist*, 2000a)

Another challenge in a level I transfer is to ensure that there is a clear understanding among employees as to what is required of them not only in terms of level of output but also in quality.

Moving from level I to *level II* means that the recipient has developed the ability to adapt the product to local tastes and is able to produce it using a substantial portion of local components. For the recipient to be able to fine-tune the technology and make use of opportunities for the procurement of locally produced components, the explicit knowledge transferred must be upgraded to include the basic engineering principles underlying the successful operation of the transferred technology. In turn, this is dependent on the efficacy of the explicit knowledge transfer mechanisms between parent and in-transferor.

A basic problem for a move to level II is to obtain local managers of a sufficient quality:

> More than half the firms questioned in a recent survey of MNCs in China by the Economist Intelligence Unit [a sister company of *The Economist*] admitted they were disappointed by their performance in China. Many complained about difficulties with their joint-venture partners, but nearly all said the most pressing problem was obtaining good local managers. As a result, many factories are still heavily dependent on expensive expatriate managers. This hurts them. (*The Economist*, 1997)

One particular shortcoming of local Chinese managers is that few have any experience in working with suppliers outside their own vertical chain. Thus one critical input of explicit knowledge involves the training of local managers in logistics and in working with a network of suppliers.

Adapting the product to take into account local conditions depends on being able to go beyond the mechanistic order-taking approach at level I. It means developing a workforce that is capable of assuming responsibility, co-operating with other employees and contributing to the development of local knowledge building. The discipline and the quality consciousness involved in this move may preclude substantial numbers of employees who lack the necessary potential to be able to contribute to a move to level II. Indeed, their presence may be a hindrance for such a move. However, large-scale dismissals may be politically unacceptable thereby blocking a move from level I. Institutional factors of this kind are as much a part of the local infrastructure as the reliability of the local power and water supply.

Finally, it should be noted that these explicit-knowledge transfer mechanisms must not only embrace the subsidiary but also the entire network of local suppliers. A common experience in China has been that local sourcing of components has been problematic because of the amount of training suppliers have needed in order to meet necessary quality standards. This has acted as yet another constraint on a move from level I to level II.

At *level III* the in-transfer capacity embraces the ability to redesign the whole product in order to arrive at a superior product. As such, the recipient is able to do more than adapt components. This capability comprises both a strong theoretical grounding and a great deal of practical experience. Building on the more advanced Japanese infrastructure it took Fuji Xerox less than ten years to reach this level (Leonard-Barton, 1995), whereas Hewlett-Packard's Singapore facility took 20 years (Thill and Leonard-Barton, 1993). Although recipients at this level are still dependent on the transferor for the scientific knowledge underlying the product, there is a move from know-what to know-how, or from the transference of explicit to tacit knowledge.

One factor determining the move from level II to III is the degree of initiative at all levels in the recipient. This may have to be developed in a purposive manner by implementing mechanisms that permit informal social interaction and thereby the communication of values and norms. At Hewlett-Packard the successful transference of tacit knowledge was contingent on the development of substantial opportunities for interaction, involving actual physical co-location, between recipient engineers and managers and their transferor counterparts.

Leonard-Barton (1995: 241) records that:

> When Larry Brown, a manager in the Hewlett-Packard peripherals division with over ten years' experience in research and manufacturing, first took on the task of setting up research in the Singapore facility, he had to learn how to formulate questions so as to leave his authority-conscious engineers options on how to respond: 'If I suggested answers to my engineers, to them this became the only possible solution'.

To some extent this innate unwillingness to disagree openly with a figure of authority is a facet of a particular national culture, but it also a facet of any subsidiary that has developed a dependency relationship with its parent company. Ultimately though the move from level II to level III will be a product of the type of interaction between parent and subsidiary over and above the mechanical transference of technical know-how. Nonaka and Takeuchi (1995) use the notions of socialization and internalization for such interaction. The former refers to the acquisition of culturally embedded knowledge through exposure to the foreign parent, while the latter refers to the conversion of explicit knowledge into routines as a product of experience.

Iveco, the truck-making subsidiary of Fiat, was particularly focused on parent–subsidiary interaction mechanisms when it introduced its management-training programme to its Chinese subsidiary. In the late 1980s, it selected nearly 400 Chinese engineers and workers, trained them in Italian and transferred them to Italian factories. Mr Donati, the chief representative in China of Iveco, explains:

> 'The Chinese wanted the technology. I said 'No, we will give you know-how.' In 1986 Mr Donati arranged for 32 Italians to come to Nanjang to teach 370 local mechanics and other staff basic Italian. Then they were all transferred to Iveco's various factories in Italy to gain on-site technical expertise in how the trucks and vans were assembled, as well as a sense of the corporate and national culture. For Iveco, more than most international automotive groups, such a substantial language programme was a necessity. 'At that time we had a problem in how to communicate,' explains Mr Donati. 'The Chinese didn't speak English and, in fact, the Italians too didn't speak much English either.'
>
> There were loftier reasons for doing more than merely handing over the technical specifications on paper. 'If you wanted to plant a tree in China, then you had to create the ground for it that we had in Italy,' he explains. (*The Financial Times*, 1999a)

What characterizes a level IV in-transfer capacity is that the original recipient is able to absorb the knowledge that enables him/her to design products independently of the original out-sourcer. A move from level III to level IV is dependent on a substantial bi-directional knowledge flow that in turn implies an acceptance of the recipient as a potential equal. Roles and relationships have to be redefined if synergies are to be created. Pathways for knowledge exchange have to be established, coupled to incentives that encourage the sharing of knowledge. In the case of Fuji Xerox, it took about eight years to develop an in-transfer capacity that enabled it to produce its first copier based on its own design concept (Leonard-Barton, 1995).

Possessing level IV subsidiaries, either through subsidiary development or acquisition, means that the MNC's sources of innovation are geographically dispersed. The hierarchical relationship between headquarters and the subsidiary is replaced by a network of equals, in which the foreign subsidiary is a member of a set of interdependent knowledge generating sub-units. Bartlett and Ghoshal (1983) have called this organizational form the transnational, whereas Hedlund (1994) refers to it as the heterarchy. Specialized knowledge about the product or product line resides in the subsidiary, with the subsidiary managing the research and development activities on a global basis. Because of this, 'The challenge is not to divide a given task in a way ensuring maximally efficient performance. Rather, it is to position the company so that *new* tasks can be initiated, often on the basis of a combination of separate knowledge pieces from different organizational units' (Hedlund, 1994: 87). Some studies have suggested that while this dispersion undoubtedly poses challenges, it may come to facilitate the technological development of the firm, 'since the MNC can tap into alternative streams of innovation in different centers, and establish favorable cross-border interactions between them' (Cantwell and Piscitello, 1997: 166).

The question we shall now address explicitly is the role and development of knowledge exchange mechanisms involved in the upgrading of the in-transfer capacity of subsidiaries from level II, through level III to level IV.

▶ Beyond Formal Vertical Mechanisms

Challenging as knowledge transfer is at levels I and II, while taking the local infrastructure into account, to a large extent headquarters can exert unilateral control over the process. This means that although the absence of proximity makes it difficult to supervise directly the behaviour of foreign subsidiary managers, it can nevertheless monitor them through rules, programmes and procedures as well as through expatriates (O'Donnell, 2000). In other words, it can largely determine the flow of knowledge from headquarters to subsidiary as well as its application through formal, vertical mechanisms. A decision to move beyond level II entails a substantial increase in subsidiary autonomy. To some extent at level III, but much more so at level IV, the intention is that through a synergistic transfer of tacit knowledge subsidiaries should have knowledge assets equivalent but different to that of headquarters such that they can take on global responsibility for a set of value activities. In order to achieve this move, the relative importance of the use headquarters makes of supervision and monitoring mechanisms, that is formal, vertical mechanisms, should decrease as increased effort is invested in generating the co-operative behaviour and trust needed for bi-directional knowledge transfer (O'Donnell, 2000). A perceived lack of trust may lead to opportunistic behaviour on the part of the subsidiary, in the sense that knowledge is surreptitiously withheld from other parts of the network (De Meyer, 1995; Ghoshal and Moran, 1996).

In order to create the conditions for tacit knowledge exchange that enables a move from level I/II to level III, vertical knowledge transfer mechanisms of an increasingly interpersonal character are necessary.

Informal vertical mechanisms

Both Reger's (1997) research and De Meyer's (1995) interviews with managers in 14 large MNCs with international R&D operations, indicate that the majority expend a considerable amount of effort in developing mechanisms that facilitate social interaction. The function of these mechanisms is thus to create what Kogut and Zander (1992) have termed a 'social community', that is, a set of shared values and beliefs across subsidiaries, or what Gupta and Govindarajan (2000: 479) refer to as 'interpersonal familiarity, personal affinity, and convergence in cognitive map between the interacting parties'. O'Donnell (2000) lists a variety of informal vertical mechanisms that are used to facilitate the interaction needed to increase subsidiaries' identification with the organization as a whole. Among these are the assignment of subsidiary managers to corporate headquarters and headquarter-based training programmes, both of which the Iveco example above featured. In addition comes the use of parent company personnel as mentors for managers of foreign subsidiaries.

As subsidiaries move from level III to IV, the intention is that the firm should move away from operating on the basis of hierarchy to that of heterarchy, that is the balance of power, at least in knowledge terms, within the corporation is undergoing radical change. This implies a development of knowledge exchange mechanisms that permit and enable either partner to initiate knowledge exchange. Although many of these lateral mechanisms are formal, their aim is to facilitate informal corporate socialization processes by extending opportunities for more open and richer communication.

Lateral mechanisms

Strategic committees generally consisting of the head of central research and heads of development from the subsidiaries are widely used formal lateral mechanisms, as are planning departments which have the purpose of developing and coordinating R&D and technology portfolios (Reger, 1997). Both of these mechanisms represent efforts at providing relatively durable structures for lateral knowledge exchange. Frequently, lateral mechanisms are temporary in character. They include temporary inter-unit committees that are set up to allow managers from different international locations to engage in joint decision-making on a project by project basis. They also span temporary task forces for the co-ordination and facilitation of international collaboration between subsidiaries on a specific project, expatriate assignments between subsidiaries, and training programmes that involve participants from multiple international locations.

Another lateral mechanism is executive development programmes that bring together participants from both headquarters and subsidiaries. In some cases, these develop into being corporate universities. For example, in 1999 ABB founded its own academy not because it was disappointed with the output of the world's business schools but because an arena for lateral as well as vertical interaction was deemed necessary. As Arne Olsson, head of management resources, explained, ABB initiated its academy because it was felt that [business schools] cannot deliver information on where we are going, what the issues, problems and challenges are. People told us they want to get straight messages directly from the top, to build networks with peers, to get a better understanding of ABB's culture and values, and to get specific tools, ideas, and project management techniques to help them manage better. This is a large and very decentralised company. It may sound like a paradox but the more decentralised you are, the more you need some kind of mechanism to build that organisational glue. To manage a company of this size cannot only be done by instructions and memos. You have to have that glue of people contact and trust. (*The Financial Times*, 2000c)

Yet another lateral mechanism in evidence is the use of central staff members as liaison personnel. De Meyer's (1995) interviews indicate widespread use. Their specific job is to co-ordinate the efforts of international functional areas. Frequently they have to travel around constantly to follow up on the evolution of the technology. Part of their mandate is to actively trigger the contacts between different individuals and groups across the company. A second task is to get involved in coaching, guiding and monitoring the research and development activities. A third task is to bring to the attention of the corporate head office potentially significant developments within the network. De Meyer (1995) records that the success of such a person is dependent on, at a minimum, a combination of technological credibility, social skills and integrating skills. Another factor is knowing and being familiar with the decision-makers at corporate headquarters.

▶ Cultural Distance

Thus far we have not considered the impact of cultural distance on knowledge transfer. As we have previously noted, Hofstede (1980a: 43) defines culture as the 'collective mental programming of the people in an environment' with the nation constituting one particularly salient environment. His research indicates that some nations are closer in some cases irrespective of geographical distance. For example, the UK has a culture that is significantly more similar to that of the USA than that of France. Even when linguistic difficulties have been reduced, by employing a common business language, cultural differences impinge on the ability of people to successfully interact and to interpret the subtleties of meaning involved in tacit knowledge transfer. For instance, Nonaka (1994: 22) detects that 'Japanese firms encourage the use of judgment and knowledge formed through interaction with customers – and by personal bodily experience rather than by "objective", scientific conceptualization.' This represents a fundamentally different epistemological tradition from that of the West and contributes to causal ambiguity. It is reasonable to suppose that the degree of cultural distance is a particularly salient factor in the initial stages at level I and II. Beyond these initial stages, given that the appropriate knowledge transfer mechanisms are in place, it would seem that the impact of cultural distance is of less significance. Research by Simonin (1999) on the transfer of marketing know-how in international strategic alliances indicates that there is a significant mitigation of cultural distance as the degree of collaborative experience increases. This result was consistent with Meschi's (1997: 218) findings that 'all cultural differences in an international joint venture, regardless of their nature or intensity, will ultimately recede over time.' It may be supposed that the same would apply to integrated MNCs. Certainly research by Bresman, Birkinshaw and Nobel (1999) on post-acquisition knowledge transfer within Swedish MNCs indicates communication processes improving with time to a point when cultural differences have virtually no significance. In other words, effective informal vertical and lateral mechanisms mitigate the effects of cultural distance.

▶ The Model

The model in figure 7.1 summarizes the factors that determine the move from level I to level IV knowledge in-transfer capacity. The initial capacity of the parent for the out-transference of explicit knowledge together with the subsidiary's in-transfer capacity is the model's starting point. The cultural distance between the parties, as well as the quality of the local infrastructure, will impact on these capacities. The efficacy of the formal exchange mechanisms that are established will determine the move to level II, signified by an extensive capacity for the in-transfer of explicit knowledge. Both the cultural distance and the quality of the local infrastructure will impact on the efficacy of formal exchange mechanisms. A move to level III, that is a limited capacity in the subsidiary for the in-transference of tacit knowledge, is conditioned by the ability of the parent to establish effective informal vertical exchange mechanisms that promote social interaction. Their implementation depends on the parent's strategic aim for the subsidiary. Likewise, a move to level IV, that is a substantial capacity for the in-transference of tacit knowledge, will be determined by the implementation and efficacy of social exchange mechanisms of a more lateral type. Again, their implementation will be a consequence of the strategic intent of the parent, that is, whether it regards the development of a heterarchical organization as advantageous. Once a subsidiary is positioned at level IV it is no longer a subsidiary in the conventional sense, but rather corporate technology and/or production centre that transfers technology and/or intermediate products to other production or assembly facilities.

Although the model has been given a linear form, in practice the sequencing of the appearance of the various exchange mechanisms may be less orderly. This is not least the case for the informal vertical exchange mechanisms. For example, level I subsidiaries managed, or co-managed, by Western-educated locals may readily develop such mechanisms without any impetus from the parent

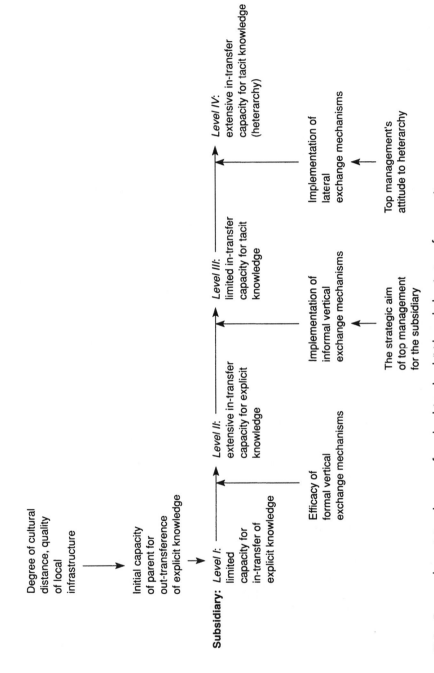

Figure 7.1 Factors determining the move from from level I to level IV knowledge in-transfer capacity

company. However, it is less certain whether on this basis such mechanisms can comprehensively embrace the subsidiary as Michailova and Anisimova's case study of the Russian subsidiary of a Danish company reveals (Case D in this book).

▶ Summary

The knowledge-exchange mechanisms we have listed in this chapter are well documented. Further research will undoubtedly uncover additional examples and may be able to rank them in regard to their knowledge transfer efficacy. The tendency, however, has invariably been to present knowledge transfer mechanisms with only scant regard to the context in which they evolve. The purpose of this chapter has been to provide this context. We have argued that it is largely determined by the interaction between the parent company's out-transfer capacity and the subsidiary's in-transfer capacity which is dependent on the ability and willingness of the parent to develop appropriate knowledge exchange mechanisms.

This is particularly the case in regard to the development of lateral exchange mechanisms, not least because they depend on the parent company being prepared to redefine its relationship with its subsidiaries. Hence, we emphasize that the role of top management in defining the self-identity of the company is critical for moving beyond the use of vertical knowledge transfer mechanisms.

Although the framing of this chapter has been within the context of the development of subsidiaries with low knowledge content to high knowledge content, the model we have proposed also has applicability to high knowledge content mergers and acquisitions. Successful knowledge exchange depends on the development of a combination of informal vertical mechanisms and lateral exchange mechanisms. Without regard to these mechanisms, the synergies that are so often claimed as the *raison d'être* for mergers and acquisitions will simply not materialize.

The case that follows, Kodak in China, features developments at Kodak's Xiamen subsidiary, which was set up as part of a joint venture in 1998 on the back of a Chinese state-owned enterprise. In terms of in-transfer capacity the state-owned enterprise was at level I. The case describes how Kodak set about changing employee behaviour from the state-owned model to one which would support a high-tech business. The case features many of the knowledge-exchange mechanisms this chapter has described.

Acknowledgements

An earlier version of this chapter, co-authored with Svein Ulset, was published in F. McDonald, H. Tüselmann and C. Wheeler, *International Business: Adjusting to New Challenges and Opportunities*. London: Palgrave, 2002.

Notes

1 We prefer to employ the term 'transfer' rather than 'diffusion' in order to signal that the movement of knowledge within the organization is a distinct experience rather than a gradual process of dissemination (Szulanski, 1996).

2 Simonin recently claimed that 'very little research has focused on the process of knowledge transfer and on the barriers to successful learning' (1999: 465). A more correct view would be that very little systematic empirical investigation has been conducted over and above case studies and analyses involving small-scale samples.

case **G**

Kodak in China: Transferring 'Know-How' to the Xiamen Plant

Keith Goodall and Malcolm Warner

Had it not been for the Kodak investment, the whole enterprise would have collapsed long ago.

▶ Kodak in China

Eastman Kodak opened their first China office in Shanghai in 1927, following many decades of successful business relations. In 1996, China was the 17th largest market in the world for Kodak products and services. Only five years later China is their second largest market for roll film. The company's chairman and CEO, Daniel Carp, recently noted that the future of the Eastman Kodak company is 'closely linked to China's development', and the importance of China to the company is reflected in the breadth and scale of its recent investments there.

The vehicle for this investment is the Kodak China Company limited (KCCL), a foreign invested share-holding company registered in Shanghai. It was established in 1998 with a total investment of around US$800 million, and makes Kodak the only imaging company authorized by the government to produce sensitized goods in China.[1] As a cross-region company there are two branches, in Xiamen (manufacturing colour films and papers) and Shantou (medical x-ray films), with headquarters in Shanghai. The company manufactures, sells, and exports imaging products and provides related services.

Kodak's investments in China have progressed at a very fast pace. In 1994, for example, Kodak launched 'Kodak Express', providing independently owned and operated stores with technology, and marketing and training support. Then, in March 1998, Kodak announced a US$1.2 billion investment to manufacture, distribute and market sensitizing products and photochemicals in China. The agreement with the Chinese government allowed Kodak to 'acquire most of China's state-owned enterprises in the photographic industry'. Kodak currently has 23 liaison offices in China, as well as substantial investments there in the production of film, paper, cameras and film processing equipment. In June 2001 Kodak further expanded its China operations, announcing a deal with China's oldest camera maker, Seagull Camera, to manufacture digital cameras in the Pudong district of Shanghai. First-phase investment in this project is expected to be around US$4 million. A US$20 million plant to produce Single Use Cameras, Kodak's first such plant in Asia, also went into production in June 2001. Although Kodak has not said how much profit it makes in China, between 1998 and 2000 it claims to have paid over US$200 million in taxes to the Chinese government. The company has also donated RMB 1.2 million (US$144,500) to the Sichuan provincial government to help fund the training of professional staff needed in the west of China.

According to the Kodak CEO, the quality of products produced in China meets the company's world standards, with Kodak's first six-sigma camera production being achieved in their Shanghai factory. The company has also recently achieved ISO 9001-2000 for film and equipment made in China, and now exports both film and photographic paper from China to Japan.

▶ The Xiamen Plant

The initial contract to transfer technology to Fuda was signed with Kodak in July 1984. Fuda was anxious to be able to sensitize colour products, such as Kodacolor and Ektacolor, but did not want to wait for the two or three years it would have taken to supply the technology and train staff. Kodak therefore agreed to sell sensitized film to Fuda in wide rolls, and to train Fuda staff to do the finishing. The colour product was then marketed under their joint names. This early cooperation between the two companies was basically a turnkey project, finally completed in 1989. The KCCL Xiamen plant was set up in the old Fuda factory in March 1998, mainly producing colour films and colour papers. Fuda, according to one manager:

> . . . had every problem that SOEs usually have. Some people were not suitable for their positions, and there was not enough supervision. While it was easy to control the manufacturing process, there were many problems in supervising other employees, such as sales and purchasing staff . . . The first few General Managers were used to a traditional SOE management style. They were quite confident and aimed to

make Fuda . . . a Chinese Kodak. This was in keeping with the fashion of the early reform era, when people seemed to be expecting to modernize the country in a day or two.

There were also problems with productivity and quality, though, as we shall see there were also positive things to be said about the achievements at Fuda.

After renovation work on buildings and equipment, the new company went into production at the end of August 1998. Kodak had succeeded in transferring technological 'know how' in a very short period of time. Given the state of the Chinese photographic industry, how did Kodak achieve such results so quickly? Part of the answer can be found in the company's approach to setting up its Xiamen factory.

▶ Partner Relations

Kodak had a clear idea of the changes that needed to be made in order to transfer their technology successfully. It was important, therefore, that they had control of the new venture. From the start, there was a clear separation of management responsibilities between the new joint venture and the old state-owned enterprise: 'The management [of KCCL Xiamen] has nothing to do with the Fuda company. Fuda has a presence on the board of directors, but they do not have any management authority. The remaining problems concerning the SOE are handled by Fuda Company.' However, both Chinese and expatriate managers at KCCL Xiamen were clear about the importance of managing the relationship. There is clearly little point in transferring technology and then discovering that the company cannot function properly in what is still a mixed economy:

> We hope to maintain a good relationship with Fuda. With our operation expanding, we will recruit more employees, and possibly we'll hire more Fuda people. Fuda has been here for a long time, and can give us a lot of help. We also maintain very good relations with the municipal government. In the Greater Asia Region we have a senior manager who is very experienced in dealing with the Chinese government.

▶ Majority Shareholding

The new venture was organized to give Kodak a great deal of decision-making power. However, in order to successfully transfer technology it is also necessary to listen to those with local knowledge. One Chinese manager was very clear about the potential dangers of Kodak's majority share holding for day-to-day management at KCCL:

> Fuda is one of the shareholders of this enterprise. We, both Chinese and expatriates, are employees working for this joint venture. It is very wrong to think that, if an

employee is a secondee from the majority shareholder, the employees who originally worked for the minority shareholders should listen to him, whatever he says. We are all employees of this enterprise, and should say whatever we think is beneficial to the company. Sometimes even some local managers say that something should be done this way because the expatriates said so. If we have to regard the expatriates as always right, the Kodak management has a problem. Kodak invested more money than other investors, but the money belongs to Kodak's shareholders, not Kodak employees. Both expatriates and local employees seem to have, more or less, got this wrong. If everyone understands this, the cohesion and initiatives of the workforce would be enhanced significantly.

Certainly, not all the Chinese managers and workers were comfortable with the prospect of the joint venture, and Kodak were likely to experience some resistance to their new technology and its associated management practices;

> My previous company also formed a JV. Through my experience with joint ventures, I find that, on one hand, foreign investment can bring technology, funds, better compensation and better prospects for the development of the enterprise. But, on the other hand, working in JVs is very competitive, and the number of workers is often significantly reduced. Different people have different concerns about working in the JV. Workers feel that the workload is heavy and the discipline is tight. Managers know that communicating in English would be a problem for them, and they are very unhappy about it. The managers think they are capable, and are just deficient in one or two things. Older people think they will not have bright prospects in the JV, and worry about losing their jobs.

There was also a worry that language skills would be more highly valued than technical expertise. As one Chinese manager put it, 'Here, even the English-speaking high-school kids will have better career prospects than the non-English-speaking professionals'. Kodak clearly needed to make sure that those Fuda staff with relatively poor English but high levels of technical expertise were not demotivated or lost to the organization.

▶ JV Preparation

Kodak understood that it was the recruitment, induction and training of staff that would present the biggest hurdle to technology transfer. They therefore wanted to move quickly, and preparations were made for the new venture even before the contract was signed. HR staff were involved at an early stage:

> Before the JV contract was signed, we had already hired some people in Xiamen and Shantou. In 1995, we set up a Xiamen office with about ten people who were mostly translators and secretaries. In Shantou we had only two or three people because we have a bigger office in Guangzhou. On the one hand, the offices explained Kodak practices to the senior State-Owned Enterprise managers;

on the other hand, they also tried to understand how the State-Owned Enterprise worked.

These attempts to move fast and understand the State-Owned Enterprise (SOE) were not without their problems however:

> The SOE management were very reluctant to reveal certain of their practices and data to us. For example, they did not want us to know their compensation data. They said that such 'secret information' could not be disclosed before the JV negotiation was complete. They did not give us the data until the last minute.

▶ Selection

Staff selection was obviously critical to bringing to the new enterprise the skills, aptitudes, and attitudes demanded by the new technology. Again this began at a remarkably early stage of the process:

> When we knew that the negotiation would be ultimately successful, we began planning the staff selection process according to whatever information we could get about the workforce of the Chinese partner. That was about six months before the completion of the negotiation. In order to avoid interference from back-door dealings (*zou houmen*) and *guanxi*, which is prevalent in the mainland, I made it very clear to the Chinese partner that an interview should be guaranteed for every employee. We decided to bring in HR personnel from other Kodak operations who had no connections with Fuda people to interview the employees. We hoped they could trust the credibility of Kodak.

A manager offered this overview of the staffing campaign, a process 'driven by HR and the key managers':

> All the HR people in the Greater China Region gathered in Xiamen, so we had about 15 to 20 people, including Hong Kong and Taiwan staff. We first arranged interviews with the employees whom the Chinese partner thought could work as managers or supervisors. The idea was to hire them first and then let them help in recruiting other people. During the screening interview, the candidate was interviewed by one mandarin-speaking HR person, who would give grades to the candidate according to the Kodak HR practice. Those who got good grades would get a second interview, during which the candidate talked with one expatriate manager and one HR person. In order to get more perspectives, the HR interviewer for the second interview was different from the one who did the screening interview with the same candidate. If a candidate who had been highly thought of by the Chinese partner got a bad assessment during the interview, we would give him another opportunity and let another HR person and another expatriate manager interview him. We tried to be as fair as possible. Some people even got four interviews. If a person was interviewed for a position that was not suitable for him, but we felt that

he was a useful person, we would ask him if he was interested in another position that he might be suitable for. On the one hand, we did not want to lose any useful people; on the other hand, we were willing to give people opportunities which had been denied in the SOE.

Fuda cooperated closely in setting up the selection process:

Fuda gave us a namelist of 2,500 people. Every Fuda employee received a package which included a letter from Fuda informing employees of the decision to transfer the enterprise into a JV, and a letter from Kodak talking about staff selection, Kodak values, and the principles of selection. Then Fuda convened a meeting of all employees, which was actually attended by about 2000 people. Officials from the Xiamen Municipality and executives from Kodak talked at the meeting about the procedures of the selection process. 1500 people came to the first round of interviews. After the screening interviews, the candidates went through a written test of logic and numeracy, and more than four hundred of them chose to take an English test which was not mandatory. Then we first selected some people to fill the key positions of managers and supervisors. We told them about Kodak policies and values, and then let them recommend other people to the JV. We told them, 'You will be responsible for this department. Whom would you like to work for you?' Then the second round of interviews were conducted with those who did well in the tests and those who got recommended. These interviews were done by one HR person and a line manager, who was in most cases an expatriate. Altogether we recruited 735 people from Fuda. It was a very smooth process.

Already, Kodak were involving their Chinese managers in critical decisions which would affect the success of the technology transfer: Chinese managers needed to be confident that they had the best available staff to work with on the new technology. One of the American managers explained, however, how the 'smooth process' described above had to be adapted to Chinese conditions, especially when the interviewees did not speak English:

We had some translators involved . . . and we learned pretty fast that it is difficult to translate technical terms if you are not involved. One of the methodologies that we used was to make drawings. . . . We started to do process drawings for the people that we were interviewing. And this worked a lot better. We learned that on the first day that this was good . . . The process that we used is normally two managers and a translator going to interview with the first round managers and engineers that we hired. And the process went well because if you were not doing the interview, you were just watching the interview. And you could try to understand the body language of the people that are on the other side of the table. And if they were uncomfortable, if they did not understand what we are asking, in a lot of cases we stepped back and started all over again to make sure we had the right communication taking place.

The average age of the selected staff was 35. But age and gender were never used as selection criteria. 'We even took a person who reached retirement age one year after the JV started.' Again, Kodak were very quick to provide new staff with a rich context for understanding their technical tasks:

> After the interviews, those selected were given job offers, and labour contracts were signed with the company. Then the selected employees were convened for a series of training programmes on the Kodak company, Kodak values, development plans, working with Westerners (WWW), working with Chinese (WWC), and technology. Everyone was given an Employee Handbook which was intended to let the employees understand the Kodak culture, values, and regulations concerning personal leave, awards and punishments, etc. This Handbook, based on similar documents Kodak uses in its plants elsewhere, was modified according to the local situation.

Additional work was immediately done with regard to safety:

> One of the areas into which we put a lot of energy just after the hiring process was safety. Our feeling was that people were not prepared to follow the safety standards that we wanted them to follow. And again, we tried to put things back on track again with a lot of training and talk about safety. We had a pay back, because we haven't yet had any lost-time accidents.

A Chinese manager commented on attitudes to safety at Kodak:

> We had some accidents in Fuda. I should say Kodak has higher safety requirements than Fuda . . . The understanding of safety management is quite different from before. In Kodak, people try hard to eliminate potential dangers, rather than just to adapt to them. For instance, if a door knob was badly designed and could hurt somebody's hand, Fuda would attach a note to the door to remind people to handle it with care, while Kodak would simply take it away.

In the selection process Fuda Company was compensated well enough to come up with clear procedures for dealing with the two-thirds of Fuda staff who were *not* chosen:

> They were offered early retirement or jobs elsewhere. Of course some of these people were unhappy, but the generous compensation made it easy for them to readjust. Some of them got tens of thousands of RMB, and they could do what they wanted. Conflict was reduced to a minimum, and by doing this the company both reduced risks in the operation and ensured social stability.

Another potential problem was that in the selection process Kodak might transfer unwanted elements of SOE culture to the new venture, with obvious consequences for the success of the technology transfer. A number of older, senior managers were not offered jobs precisely for this reason:

> They grew up within a state-owned enterprise and they had certain responsibilities to central government and to the local government organizations and they were

responding to quotas, and directives, and the party. So they had a different set of responsibilities in addition to running a quality-conscious, cost-competitive operation. They had just grown up with a different set of values which were required at that time to be successful in China . . . But it if you take managers with that type of background, and try to remould them to function in a more flexible organization with less structure and more involvement of lower levels of the operation, it just wasn't going to work out.

However, even Kodak's careful planning could not cope with all eventualities, 'We did not have too much difficulty in the selection process in Xiamen. But in Shantou, some SOE employees did not understand Mandarin. We only had one HR person who could speak Shantou dialect, so he was the only one who could deal with those people.'

There were also early decisions to be made about key positions in the enterprise, and again Fuda wanted a say in these:

> Fuda wanted to impose a Trade Union on the JV. They wanted us to accept the TU president of Fuda as a Chinese representative in the JV, with the status of a Deputy GM but without taking any other work. Fuda also thought the Chinese partner should send a representative to the JV, but Kodak held that this enterprise is not like the usual type of joint ventures, and that the Chinese partner did not have the right to allocate representatives here. Therefore, Kodak refused to accept that, and we do not have a Trade Union branch here. Kodak did not obstruct the establishment of a TU organization, but just followed the policy concerning our new type of enterprise.

The Chinese Trade Union has a reputation for supporting management rather than workers, and can be a positive force for solving misunderstandings and disputes. Kodak's decision here might therefore be to do with their experiences in the USA.

Even though the expatriate managers were very positive about the quality of the employees who were eventually taken from Fuda, many of whom were college graduates, a Chinese manager noted that SOE culture did have an impact on staff behaviour:

> their way of thinking is often outdated. For example, the managers are reluctant to criticize their subordinates directly. In the Performance Assessment, apparently everybody has been performing well, and everybody should get a pay rise. After a lot of training, people are gradually accepting the Western idea which stresses performance and does not pay too much attention to personal relationships and face.

The new technology demanded certain attitudes and behaviours from Chinese operators and managers, which, despite Kodak's early and extensive investment in training, were difficult to fully achieve. An American manager noted some of these behavioural issues:

There are occasions where operators see things but don't bring them to people's attention as we would like them to do. That happens frequently but it doesn't happen all the time. And so sometimes we find ourselves into a quality problem where it could have been identified and prevented much earlier. So we need to continue to work on making sure people understand their responsibilities and help contribute to improving the operation by having open communication and not putting anybody in a threatening position. And I think that is a change for people. I think we've come a long way and need to continue to work on it. I think historically they were told to do a job and they'd just go off and do it and not give too much thought to going beyond a very defined set of guidelines. I think we are trying to broaden that as much as we can and that works with some people but not with all. And it is only with time that I think we will get more and more successful at getting a lot of people involved in owning the job and taking action.

Active participation from Chinese staff was also regarded as a problem by another expatriate manager:

One thing that I don't think we have broken yet is people participation in terms of comments when you are making a presentation to them. They don't ask questions. And I think this is interesting because there is no reaction. You cannot feel or see in terms of body language or questions how they are feeling about what you are trying to say. I think this is one thing that we didn't break yet. You have 50 people that we are giving a presentation to and there are no questions . . . I don't know if it's culture, I don't know if it is to try to save face.

Another manager emphasized the need for initiative:

I think people here wait for someone to tell them what they need to do. I think people need to change in that area. They need to have the initiative to do things by themselves. I think this would be the point that we're going to say yes, people have really changed.

The same manager went on to stress the importance of the Xiamen plant becoming Chinese, of local staff taking ownership:

This is truly their operation, they are part of the Kodak family . . . this plant will be one of the three major plants world-wide in the manufacturing of coloured film and paper and we will be on a par with the Europe operation, and with the US operation, yet we will be an Asian operation . . . The American participation or expat participation is only over a relatively short period of time and we need a lot of people to help get us started. We will be stepping back very rapidly and turning the operation over to the local management team. And as we place people into local management positions and give them managerial training and exposure to other Kodak operations worldwide, I think they will sense that this is really going to happen. It's not a typical joint venture. It's not an American company coming in to dictate our future and run this operation. It is going to be a Chinese company but with the Kodak name on it.

This ambition to produce a Chinese Kodak had, however, demanded a huge amount of attention to the conditions under which ingrained SOE behaviours could be changed. Kodak managers, both expatriate and Chinese, had a great deal to say about the management of such an ambitious change process.

Organizational Changes

Kodak had to move behaviours from the SOE model to one which would support a high-tech business. Both training and the behaviour of foreign managers as role models were seen as crucial to the change process:

> Intensive training was very important in the change process. The employees received training for months before starting to work. And the expatriate managers set a good example with their own behaviour, which had a huge impact on the Chinese workforce. The expats are seldom arbitrary, and you can discuss with them even if your level is very low. There is almost no hierarchy in Kodak. People call each other by their first names.
>
> At the beginning, the training was mainly about company policies and corporate culture. Later, technical training gradually increased. Cultural transformation can't be done solely by training. The key is to do things according to the new culture, and let the employees see for sure that it is really working in the new way.

Management Style: Loose vs Tight?

An American manager gave an overview of their attempts to involve and inform Chinese staff:

> We have an open-door policy. And every four months we have a 'snap-shot', which is a meeting of all Kodak employees presided over by the GM. The employees are informed of what is going on in the company, and what plans Kodak has for the Greater Asia Region and the Greater China Region. And survey results on issues of general concern are publicized. Employees are also given the opportunity to raise any questions they have for the management, which the General Manager and the HR manager then answer in detail. But not many people raise questions in public. So most the questions are raised in writing beforehand. Most are about welfare and benefits.

A Chinese manager contrasted attitudes to the management of technical trouble-shooting at Fuda and Kodak:

> In Fuda, when the facilities broke down and were hard to fix, the management would convene a repair meeting, at which technicians would propose ways to fix it. The management would agree to the small changes made to the machines if they worked, while in Kodak it is impossible to do it that way. All modifications to the

equipment must be approved through certain procedures before they are made. In Fuda, if some film was dropped on the floor, operators would pick it up and clean it. In Kodak, it will definitely be thrown away.

Chinese managers commented further on the Kodak style of management, 'I admire the expatriates for their performance and their professionalism. If some people set an example with their behaviour, others will be inspired and influenced by them. This is one of the biggest differences between Kodak and Fuda.'

One Chinese manager suggested that the Kodak management style was 'even looser than the SOE':

> Kodak give a second chance even to those who would be dismissed by an SOE. Once a worker touched facilities which were not in his working area, and hurt his hand. Though this was a violation of safety regulations, his department did not punish him. Two months later, this person again violated the regulations by driving a forklift without a license, and hurt another worker. He was punished this time, but was not fired. The company gave him a final warning, and appointed him as a safety coordinator, talking to new employees on safety regulations and checking other employees' safety performance. Sometimes people feel it is too loose. Our system is very human, and is very respectful to people. The company seldom fires people. Sometimes, when dismissal is necessary, we ask the person to resign, and do not publicize the resignation in order to save face for him.

An American manager defended the 'looseness' of Kodak management:

> The key to the success of the operation is these people at the operations level. They know the job better than anybody else. They are spending eight hours a day, five days a week working on the job and they know what is required to produce good products, to produce products more efficiently, cost effectively, reduce waste. So you really need to have an operation that allows people to operate in that environment. So they know it best, and you want them to feel free, to take ownership and show initiative.

▶ Discipline

There were clear differences between Chinese and expatriate managers with regard to the degree of overt control and discipline needed to manage the work force in this new technological environment. One Chinese manager had this to say, for example:

> Without discipline, an enterprise cannot have stable performance over a long period. Now we have two problems. First, there are not very clearly defined disciplinary procedures. We have values, we have the Employee Handbook, but we have not stipulated under what circumstances the employee can be punished or fired. We require the employees to be honest, but have not stipulated what we will do if they

are not. If these are not clearly stipulated, problems may arise if there is an arbitration case. Second, discipline has been kept quite well because the employees have been conscientious. Though our workers behave very well, there should still be some enforcement and deterrent. Some people say, 'Isn't it working quite well?' Actually we have been relying on the deterrent formed by what people think of foreign-invested enterprises. If nothing happens to those who break the rules, after a while we will lose the deterrent. We do not wish to punish employees, but there must be some deterrent.

Again, with regard to safety, another Chinese manager stressed the importance of punishment, 'I told the expatriates that many Chinese never looked at the red lights when walking or bicycling, a habit which makes it difficult to enforce safety regulations. We need time to overcome this, and we may need some severe punishments along with training and motivation.'

Other Chinese managers were less worried about discipline in Xiamen, especially when compared to the old Fuda plant:

We do not think discipline is a problem here. We are no longer concerned about attendance. People know that employment is not guaranteed in a foreign-invested enterprise, and they follow the rules. In Kodak, the supervision is not very tight, and a lot of power is delegated to the supervisors and group leaders. The expatriate management want people to manage themselves. Of course, if you cannot manage yourself properly, they will come and do it. But those with self-respect would take care of their own behaviour. The company offers a good working environment and good compensation. The employees follow regulations not because they are forced to do so, but because they value their opportunities to work here. In Kodak people are motivated rather than compelled. The supervisors and group leaders often talk with the workers, and record their performance. There are also punishments. If the supervisor does not praise or punish his subordinates for a long time, the workers may become slack. But that is caused by the bad management of the supervisor, rather than anything wrong in the Kodak system.

Management processes at Kodak were again compared to those at Fuda:

Management should be established on the basis of systems. The problem with Fuda was that it did not have well-designed systems, and that it did not have a supervisory mechanism. Kodak is very efficient. Maybe that is partly due to cultural differences. Westerners are straightforward and result-oriented. Since they emphasize results, the managers have bigger pressures on their shoulders. While the Chinese attach more importance to the process rather than the outcome.

Another comparison with Fuda emphasized the importance of certain kinds of rules and procedures in the Kodak manufacturing system:

When I was in Fuda, the superiors sometimes would assign some exacting work which could be harmful to the workers' health and safety. Though I knew those were not responsible orders, I had to execute them. Also, because of the loopholes in the system, many people broke the regulations. 'Since everybody does it, I guess I can do it too.' But now, in Kodak, everything must be done according to the rules.

The biggest difference between the Chinese and the expatriates lies in the way they work. The expatriates handle every problem according to the procedures, while the Chinese managers think that they have over complicated some otherwise simple undertakings. The expatriates do have their reasons – there could be hidden safety problems. Following the procedures may cost more time, but by doing this we can avoid many safety and quality problems.

▶ Trust and Teams

Team-building between the various parties was seen by a senior expatriate manager as key to success in transferring technology successfully:

> Building trust between the KCCL expatriate management team and the local management team, and then between that combined management team and the rest of the workforce. I don't treat that lightly. I think that's key to any operation. Again, these people are the ones that understand the operation best and they will contribute and help build the operation if they can trust and understand and communicate and deal with their management. If they are repressed, suppressed, over-managed, directed too finely into the job when it's being done, that's where they will operate and things won't change, you won't have continuous improvement. You really need an open environment where people can communicate, can trust their management. And that is something we will continue to strive for.

Beyond connecting the teams on site, there was a wider issue of the Chinese relationship with the wider organization, 'From my perspective, building the skills of supervisors, the B supervisors and building the skills of the deputy managers to be managers, and then building their skills so that they can interact with the global Kodak world, those are the key objectives that we need to focus on.'

Kodak managers consciously demonstrated trust in their fellow managers from the start of the new venture:

> We started working on building the trust base from day one. We selected the 27 managers, the key personnel who were going to select the next 300, and we trusted them to do that process. And we continue to do that through what we call snap-shot sessions and the open-door policy and those types of open trust is something that you need to continue to reinforce and build day after day after day.

Time was also invested in discussing Kodak values (respect for the dignity of the individual, integrity, trust, credibility, continuous improvement and personal renewal, recognition and celebration), 'I think that was extremely valuable for us because we really determined that they weren't Kodak values or Eastern values or

Western values, but they were human values. And there was a lot of good discussion and I think that really helped bring the groups together.'

Looking back, and despite the evident skills and rapid progress of the Chinese managers, Kodak felt they had made a mistake with the level of expatriate staffing:

> I think the only thing that we initially planned on and I think we were very naïve was how long and how many expats we would need. I think we planned for too few and for too short a period of time. I say that but things have changed in that with the export activity that originally wasn't anticipated for the first two or three years. The first two or three years it was just going to be domestic production and a very limited number of products we were going to produce. That has exploded tremendously, so that has provided a tremendous challenge to everyone. So we have required more expats and we need them longer because of the complexity that we've brought into the operation.

Nevertheless, US managers were able to identify changes in the management style of the Chinese managers since they came into the Kodak plant:

> I saw a lot of change between 1998 and now. This is the reason that I am saying that I think we are being successful. Because in the beginning we had the same problem with the managers that we have now with the operators. When you are in a meeting with operators, people don't ask questions, and our first level managers didn't ask questions at that point. They didn't expose themselves. Right now, they have already changed. I think they already understand that this is the way that we do business. We need to talk more. We need to change ideas. We may even ask stupid questions once in a while in front of everybody, but this is the one way that you improve communications and learn. And again, I saw that also is starting to happen some time ago in the supervisor level. And I hope this will cascade down to the operational level pretty soon. Again, the hierarchy is the way to show people that this is the way to do it, especially here in China where the hierarchy is very important for people. If they see the deputy manager doing it, the supervisors are going to do the same. If the operators see the supervisors doing it, I think they are going to do the same. But these things do not happen from one day to the other. It takes time.

▶ Training

An emphasis on training is an important part of the Kodak philosophy:

> Kodak spares no effort to make sure that training is well delivered. The company sends employees to ABB and Westin House, and also to Kodak operations elsewhere. It is a traditional Kodak idea that, if you make a mistake, and if that is not deliberately done, the way to solve the problem is to give you more training.

So it is no surprise that Kodak offered a wide range of training from the start of the Xiamen branch, 'We had a programme called Kodak in Focus, which introduced the operation and culture of the corporation. There were also quite a lot of management courses on leadership, compensation and benefits, performance assessment, and many other things.'

What was the basic approach to getting people to change, to make them suitable for a high-tech operation?

> Planning is extremely important in a change process. You must coordinate all aspects of the operation carefully beforehand, from which facilities to buy, how to get high-quality human resources, to finances and technology. In our case, we had planned to begin sensitizing materials production on June 1, 2000. So we selected employees in 1998, and sent many of them to the US and France for technical training, many for over six months. And when they came back from abroad, they began testing the equipment with expatriate technicians. Had it not been for the accurate and careful planning, we could not have come to this stage so smoothly.

There was also cross-training, 'For about a year or a year and a half staff in Sensitizing did finishing work and vice versa. Right now they are all back in Sensitizing because they are in the training phase here.'

Chinese views of Kodak training were positive:

> Kodak is extremely generous when it comes to training. In Kodak, we have an Employee Development Planning Process (EDP). In addition to the training required by his current position, the employee can also apply to take other courses. And so long as they are in keeping with his development needs, the application will be approved. Managers had to go through a lot of training at the beginning. When they had just entered the JV, Kodak invited professional trainers and held a one-month training programme for all the managers and supervisors . . . What we've learned during the two years in Kodak is more than we got in the ten years in Fuda.
>
> The average annual training budget is one thousand RMB per person. Last year it was more than that, because we sent more than a hundred people, mostly technicians, abroad to receive technical training. Overseas training can make people understand better how it works and how people think in the West. Who should be sent abroad is not decided by position levels, but decided based on need. The usage of new equipment must be learned abroad.

What was the effect of the overseas training from the perspective of the American managers?

> I think it broadens them significantly. They come back with more confidence in what we are doing. They have seen another Kodak operation and they can relate to that Kodak operation. People come back feeling confident that this is just like any other place in Kodak and we are doing a good job here. I think they just come back with broader appreciation for the job that is being done here in China.

A Chinese manager contrasted the Kodak approach to training with that in Fuda:

In SOEs, there is also quite a lot of training on things like safety, regulations, technology, etc. The Chinese training and education system tries to tell the trainee what not to do and what they are expected to do. While the training we have in Kodak tells you what objectives you should achieve and encourages the trainee to think for himself what he could do to attain the desired target. Take water control as an example: when you want to prevent a flood, do you just try to block the water from flooding around or do you channel the water so that it can go down smoothly? Previously our training was intended to block unwanted behaviour, while now the training is done to channel people's initiatives into the right direction. Previously, in order to keep a workshop clean, many regulations were formulated, stipulating that the windows must be cleaned five times a day and the floor must be swept three times a day, and that the management must check the sanitation regularly. When the inspector came and saw that it was not clean, workers would say, 'We've cleaned the place as stipulated.' Now, the management has made the employees understand the importance of cleanliness, and what standards we should maintain. Though you have not told him to sweep the floor three times a day, he may do it five times.

There had, then, been changes:

Our employees are apparently different from before. At first many people did not understand why some engineers, managers and supervisors did not get paid when they worked overtime. But gradually they have come to understand the common practice of FIEs. They are very eager to learn, because they know their compensation is not determined by their seniority but by their performance and capabilities.

▶ Cross-Cultural and Linguistic Differences

The Chinese are traditionally hard-working, which is very helpful to our work.

In addition to the points already noted by managers, a variety of opinions were offered about the significance, or otherwise, of cross-cultural and linguistic differences within the plant:

Language barriers are the biggest barriers in working with foreigners. Most Chinese employees cannot communicate well in English. Some expatriates are irritable and are not easy to get along with. And there are some basic cultural conflicts. For example, once a machine broke down, and a group of people were repairing it. Westerners seem to be very flexible with dining time, but the Chinese normally cannot hold on without eating for too long. Dinner time had passed a long time ago, but the expat was still working without mentioning dinner. Chinese employees began to be unhappy. Some could not hold on, and wanted to go to get something to eat. The expat went mad, 'We are going to finish! Why don't you eat after you finish?'

Another Chinese employee had a different perspective, 'I don't think the cultural difference is a big problem to us. We Chinese are quite tolerant, and most expatriates are very polite. Sometimes there can be unpleasant situations, but it's not caused by cultural differences but by different expectations.'

One Chinese manager remained adamant that cultural differences were important:

> The expatriate management must consider the huge differences in laws, mindset and culture. If adjustments are not made according to the local situation, there might not be too much left of the Kodak management after it goes through the cultural filter. Communication is needed to avoid this. For example, Kodak training courses often include situational role play. Local employees are bewildered, 'What's this? What does this say?' The Chinese are not very good at analysing situations like this, and always want to know what the teacher has to say. It's not because they are dumb, but because of different cultural habits. They just think it's not the way teachers are supposed to be like. After the role play, discussion is very important, and it is important for the trainer to give a conclusion.

By contrast, when a senior American manager was asked if Kodak had any problems with cross-cultural difference, replied, 'No, we don't. And where we do have differences, I think we talk about them to a point where we understand them and recognize them and appreciate them, but I don't see them as problems or roadblocks. It is more just understanding and accommodating more than anything else.'

Though he added that early cross-cultural training had helped, 'It really helped open people up so that there was good dialogue, good interchange, and helped people understand some of the potential differences. But I think it helped more in terms of building trust in terms of communication.'

▶ Communication

Linguistic and cultural differences clearly affected the ability of the two sides to communicate about key technological issues. Although the American managers confessed that they had found little time to learn Chinese, fortunately, 'the local people have the interest and the desire and the capability to learn English. The total population of the company right now is up around 1100 people, and over 700 people signed up to take English courses.'

Despite this interest in language development, one Chinese manager was less sanguine about the quality of communication in the company:

> The communication between the Chinese and the Americans is still a problem. We have different cultural backgrounds, and the lack of communication has caused some misunderstandings. It is a challenge for Kodak to localize its operation here, and at the same time to keep its brand-name and practices that have been shaped over a hundred years. Everybody is confident about Kodak's facilities, technological

capabilities and managerial expertise, but it remains a problem how all those things can take root in the Chinese soil. Obviously, communication is the key factor in the change process. But we have met with some obstacles in communication, the first one being the language barrier, and the second being different ways of thinking. Kodak has some very strong convictions about how to run an operation. Their handling of backup materials and components seems pretty wasteful to us, but sometimes they become extremely stingy towards very small sums of money. And often, when we think this should be done this way, the expatriates think it should be done in another way.

He went on to give practical examples of these communication difficulties:

For example, during the construction of the new plant, the Chinese workers cleaned the floor of the workshops with tap water, but the expatriates said it should be cleaned with high-purity water, because the floor cost over a thousand RMB per square metre, and they did not trust the quality of tap water here. They emphasized that dirt could never be taken into the workshop, and could only be cleaned out. However, people were still allowed to walk on the floor in their own shoes. This was beyond the understanding of the Chinese workers.

He gave another example:

Whenever the cables are rearranged, the expatriates throw away the old cables. We think this is rather strange, but we cannot communicate well with them because most people do not speak good English. Sometimes they do take advice from the Chinese technicians about problems with certain procedures and facilities during the installation and testing process. But still the communication is far from easy.

The same manager went on to further analyse what he saw as a key problem:

What we need urgently now are communication and coordination. According to my observation, though our overall performance is quite good at this moment, we are very inefficient in some aspects of the operation, and some things should not take so much trouble to get done. And, since people are from two different cultures, and speak different languages, we have some difficulties in communication. For instance, in Fuda, we knew which department to go to for help when we encountered a production problem. But now in Kodak, sometimes no Chinese employee has been trained to maintain a certain machine. The trouble is, when such a machine breaks down, we can't ask for help from an expatriate engineer directly, and have to go through the reporting process, which takes a lot of time and trouble.

The same manager had interesting things to say about conversations between expatriates and Chinese staff:

In this company, most employees think that the Chinese staff and the American staff had different status. Americans are very polite, and we have a good atmosphere at work. But you can see some subtle differences in status from their attitude and their way of doing things. For example, some expats often speak with a commanding tone, and some Chinese managers always listen to expats, even if those Chinese staff have higher positions than the foreigners, just because they were expats.

Despite these differences the American managers seemed, overall, extremely pleased with the quality of staff they had hired:

> I think what we are benefiting from is that we had a workforce that was employed by Fuda who were very smart, had good technical training and really wanted to demonstrate their capabilities. And it was kind of like they were bottled up and weren't able to really show what they could do. And Kodak was in the fortunate position of being able to take the lid off the bottle and let them really demonstrate what their capabilities are. I think we have been overwhelmed and impressed tremendously with their work ethic, with their ability to learn, with their dedication to the job, with their commitment to getting the job done. Some of these deputy managers, it's incredible, the amount of personal dedication and the hours that they put in, and how smart they are, what their capabilities were. We've been really impressed with all of that.

Another senior American manager agreed that attitudes to openness and ownership had changed significantly over an 18-month period:

> One of the concerns that I had was that open communication was going to be difficult and their taking responsibility and initiative would not come easily. I think all three of those areas have all been very pleasant surprises to me. I think we've got managers who will take initiative, who do feel ownership to the operation, and will communicate openly and will be proactive. That was something we tried to encourage and I don't know if it was because we were successful in the training in establishing an environment where they felt comfortable doing that or if we just selected the right people in the selection process. But it has been a very pleasant surprise to see them take ownership of the day-to-day operation now. Whereas a year and a half ago, we are all very much involved in the day-to-day operation, today the deputy managers are dealing with all of that on a regular basis . . . They have taken the initiative on a variety of different programmes to improve the operation.

He then connected the increased openness to the management style and organizational climate in the joint venture:

> We try and put people in a non-threatening environment so that we can have good dialogue and good understanding. I think that we've also been successful in building the trust of the deputy managers, and they will let us know if there are problems and issues to be dealt with.

How did the Chinese view the Kodak environment and its relationship to motivation?

I feel deeply that the Chinese employees value their jobs very much and they work more enthusiastically here than in Fuda. They think they are treated better than before, and feel that they would have more job security than they can get in most other enterprises if they work hard here. The reason is it is relatively fair here, and people have development opportunities. Those who were recruited later, not from Fuda but from elsewhere, regard the work as just another job, and have less enthusiasm and less sense of responsibility in their work. You know the difference only after comparison, and those who did not work in Fuda do not realize how valuable the job is.

Another manager connected motivation to corporate culture:

The corporate culture in Kodak, which respects individuals and provides employees with opportunities, is the most important factor in motivating people. We have an Employee Development Planning Process. Every year, there is a review in which the employee discusses with his superior about his personal career interests and training needs. This is intended mainly to make the employees more competent for their current positions, but they can also get development opportunities that have nothing to do with their present work. It is very important to make people know that they have a future here, and that they will have chances to develop here. Kodak does not offer the highest wages, but a job at Kodak is still very attractive, because, for many people, pay is not the number one criterion for evaluating a job. In many companies, you cannot expect to get any development if you do not get along well with your boss, because the wages and promotion are all decided according to the bosses' personal wills. In Kodak, there is no such phenomenon. People feel that Kodak appreciates ability rather than relationship, and that everybody is treated fairly here.

What is apparent here is that the long-term success of technology transfer depends upon an approach to the problem which goes far beyond simple 'technical' solutions. Despite the obvious progress at Xiamen, staff were able to identify several outstanding problems.

▶ Outstanding Problems

Despite a great deal of comment being positive, Chinese managers were still able to identify room for further improvement:

The quality of managerial staff is still a problem, and Kodak should do more to improve them. On the one hand, our present system is very different from the previous Fuda system, therefore not everyone can adapt to it and work efficiently in the new organization. On the other hand, in most SOEs, many people get their managerial positions through *guanxi*, and they are not really competent. The credo for these people is 'not making mistakes is an achievement' (*wuguo bianshi gong*). When Kodak recruited people from Fuda, working experience in Fuda was valued, which was reasonable. Many Fuda employees are very skilled, but some are too old, and some find it hard to learn new things because of their educational backgrounds. Kodak needs to consider such issues well before they become apparent problems. Though the operation has been going very well, the company will need to reposition the managers and supervisors in two or three years. Therefore, performance assessment for the managers is very important. At present, the standards used to assess the supervisors are not uniform, and there are not specific requirements for managers in different positions. The management should try to improve the PA system.

More work was also needed, it was felt, at the supervisor level, 'We need to strengthen the training at the supervisor level in order to improve their way of working, management style, ability to understand policies and Kodak culture. At the manager level there are a lot of meetings and management training, and the managers have been changing fast.'

The reward system was also commented upon:

Our incentive mechanism is still far from developed. The phenomenon of 'eating from the big pot' (*daguofan*) still exists in our company. Individual performance does not yet influence one's compensation and bonuses. This has something to do with Kodak's culture, which emphasizes teams and collective performance. Personally I have not figured out very clearly whether we should stress the group or the individuals. If we stress individuals, people would possibly pull the rug from under each other's feet. If we stress collective performance, how do we give the individuals enough incentive? It is quite a subtle problem.

Despite the overwhelmingly positive tone of what was said about the Xiamen plant by both parties, at least one Chinese manager was ready to withhold judgement on the Kodak experience:

Most of us have worked in the Fuda SOE for a long time. When we come to Kodak, we should at first leave our prior experience behind, and regard ourselves as pupils, learning as much as possible how Kodak runs the operation. When we have got a clear picture of Kodak practices, we can then look back and compare. At that time, we may see some good things from the past that may be beneficial to our present operations. We do not have to reject everything that we had. And we should avoid irrational generalizations that anything Kodak is good, or anything Kodak is bad. When we understand the Kodak way thoroughly, we will be able to see our past more clearly.

Acknowledgements

Research for this case was funded and supported by the China Europe International Business School (CEIBS) in Shanghai, and was carried out with the help of CEIBS research assistant Zhang Qiang and Anna Quan.

Note

1   There are five shareholders in KCCL: Eastman Kodak (80 per cent); General Company of Shantou Gongyuan Photographic Materials Industry (about 10.3 per cent); Xiamen Fuda Photographic Materials Company (about 9.7 per cent); Guangdong International Trust and Investment Company (one share); and Fujian International Trust and Investment Company (one share).

Case Assignments

1   In terms of the level I–II typology, where is the Xiamen Branch today?
2   What were the main barriers for a move beyond level I?
3   Describe the mechanisms Kodak employed to move the Xiamen Branch beyond level I.
4   Kodak applies a 'loose' management style. How fruitful is this for knowledege transfer?
5   To what extent is 'cultural distance' a barrier for knowledge transfer?

chapter **8**

Expatriation and Repatriation

▶ Purpose

The overall purpose of this chapter is threefold. Its starting point is an overview of the various functions expatriation plays. Thereafter we examine the factors that are associated with high use of expatriates. Finally, we examine the various components of the expatriation process, including selection of personnel, training, arrival and support, repatriation and debriefing.

▶ The Functions of Expatriation

It is common to distinguish between three broad functions of expatriation: (1) position filling; (2) organization development; and (3) management development. In practice these functions are by no means mutually exclusive and frequently overlap.

Position filling

Particularly in the case of subsidiaries located in developing countries there may not be qualified host country nationals available. Expatriates are used not only to compensate for the lack of host country managers but often also to ensure the transfer of know-how to host country mangers through training and development.

Organization development

Some MNCs have a particular concern with developing a homogeneous culture. Expatriates are used to ensure the dissemination of the firm's culture. As such, the function of expatriation is one of organizational development. An additional aspect to organizational development is to ensure homogeneous practices throughout the company as well as co-ordination with headquarters corporate policies and philosophies. This second aspect to organization development is essentially a form of control by headquarters through the agency of the expatriate.

Management development

A fundamental challenge faced by MNCs is how to ensure that managers develop not only an overview of the organization in its entirety but also a 'feel' for international business. As figure 8.1 indicates an international mindset can be created and maintained in a number of ways. In figure 8.1 nine methods of internationalizing managers are indicated and ranked in terms of their importance and frequency of use in terms of a 1–5 point scale.

Four of these methods are considered by European MNCs to be of particular importance. Two of these include bringing managers from head office and the various foreign offices together for seminars and encouraging them to form networks and associations. The other two involve expatriation. One of these is to

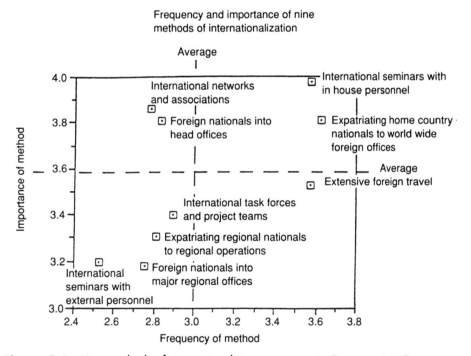

Figure 8.1 Nine methods of internationalizing managers in European MNCs: scale 1–5
Source: Oddou and Derr (1993)

Table 8.1 Average importance on a scale of 1–5 of various functions of expatriation

Function of expatriation	Mean	Standard deviation
Position-filling:		
No HCNs	3.60	1.04
Knowledge transfer	4.28	.79
Organization development:		
Transfer of culture	2.88	.93
Direct expat control	2.73	1.00
Management development	3.40	1.12

bring foreign nationals into the head offices. The other is to send home country nationals abroad. Of the two, the latter is much more frequently used. Shell, for example, despite having substantial local management resources, has over 5000 expatriates in more than 120 countries. None of these four methods are mutually exclusive, but there are undoubtedly biases within MNCs in terms of their outlook on their international operations that dictate the frequency of their use. This is particularly the case in expatriation.

In a survey of 25 headquarters of multinationals Harzing (1999) enquired about the importance they attach to the various functions of expatriation. Table 8.1 displays her main findings. The table indicates that position-filling, particularly in the sense of transferring know-how to subsidiaries, is the most important function. Management development is generally considered to be of more importance than organization development although, as the measures of standard deviation indicate, this is not necessarily always the case.

▶ Different Attitudes to International Operations

Three basic attitudes to the staffing of foreign operations can be discerned amongst MNCs (Perlmutter, 1969). Although these are radically different from one another it should be borne in mind that they may coexist within one and the same MNC in the sense that they apply to different operations.

The ethnocentric approach

It is not uncommon to find that MNCs are highly sceptical to allowing host country nationals (HCNs) manage their foreign operations. Such firms have an ethnocentric outlook on their foreign operations. They believe profoundly that the only way of maintaining control over their investments is to ensure that only individuals that are inculcated with the firm's own specific skills and values can be trusted. This does not necessarily preclude foreigners as such, but in practice that is invariably what it does.

This attitude can be justified under three conditions. First, there may well be circumstances in which a high level of technical capability is required for the foreign operation but this is objectively unavailable locally. Furthermore, a substantial proportion of this capability may consist of tacit knowledge that can only be acquired through a lengthy period of social interaction within the firm. Second, the operation may involve the use of proprietary knowledge whose dissemination to competitors would undermine the firm's competitive advantage. In such circumstances what is needed are managers who are committed to the firm regardless of the success or failure of one particular foreign operation. Third, particularly in the case of new ventures in developing countries there may be a lack of host country managerial experience.

There are, however, distinct drawbacks to maintaining an ethnocentric outlook over a longer period of time. One is that HCNs will come to perceive the firm as a dead-end in terms of career development. The lack of opportunity to progress to managerial positions is hardly conducive to long-term commitment or loyalty particularly from the most talented potential host country recruits. What is more, host country governments sooner or later tend to react negatively to MNCs that are pursuing ethnocentric staffing policies. Another drawback, and one we will discuss in more detail below, is the difficulty in maintaining a corps of expatriates who are willing to accept a string of foreign assignments.

The polycentric approach

Particularly in those MNCs we have earlier referred to as multi-domestics, the overarching approach to foreign operations is not to focus on the maintenance of close control but to appear as local as possible. As a consequence, HCNs predominate in management positions thereby giving the subsidiary a local 'face'. This polycentric approach has a number of advantages denied to MNCs with an ethnocentric outlook. Apart from speaking the local language, one advantage is that HCNs are familiar with the in and outs of local culture and have a network of local contacts. Another is that they are often more politically acceptable than foreign managers. A further advantage relates to the recruitment of well-qualified host country employees who invariably will prefer to work for MNCs without the glass-ceilings of ethnocentric MNCs. Finally, in most cases, the costs in terms of salaries involved in employing HCNs as opposed to expatriates are significantly lower.

One distinct disadvantage associated with the polycentric approach to staffing is that coordination between the parent and the subsidiary is more problematic simply because no one at headquarters has any long-term, direct experience of the subsidiary. Likewise, employees at the subsidiary will not have had any direct experience of working with anyone from the parent company. Evolving a common language and a common understanding of how the subsidiary's activities tie in with the needs of the firm as a whole is significantly more difficult than if there is a steady flow of expatriates who act as emissaries on behalf of headquarters. Moreover, the lack of foreign experience limits the opportunities for managers at headquarters to acquire a global understanding. It is therefore not uncommon that even when MNCs move away from an ethnocentric staffing approach to a more polycentric approach, they continue to send expatriates to responsible positions in their foreign operations in order to ensure that understanding.

The geocentric approach

MNCs that are aiming to achieve a global posture with strong coordination do not necessarily have to adopt an ethnocentric approach providing they can recruit third country nationals (TCNs) who can be fully integrated into the firm. MNCs that aim to make appointments solely on the basis of ability regardless of nationality have adopted a geocentric approach to staffing international operations. What is critical in making appointments for such firms is the knowledge and skills of the individual as well as the individual's commitment to the firm. In many cases the choice will therefore fall neither on PCNs nor HCNs, but on third country nationals (TCNs). For example, at Gillette only 15 per cent of the company's expatriates are US nationals, the other 85 per cent come from the other 27 countries in which the company operates. The advantage of bringing TCNs into consideration is that the firm has a greater pool for recruitment. What is more, the intake to the pool can be designed so that it includes individuals who are prepared to have expatriate careers over the long term. In other words, the aim is to acquire individuals who are multilingual, culturally flexible and equipped with a global orientation.

Some of the barriers that have to be overcome to make a geocentric approach work in practice are similar to those associated with the ethnocentric approach. First, finding individuals who are prepared to adopt a nomadic mode of existence, moving from one country to another, is hardly straightforward in an era of dual career couples. Second, host governments are no more likely to be well disposed to TCNs than they are to nationals of the parent company.

▶ Approach to Staffing International Operations

The choice of approach to staffing international operations will invariably be conditioned by the degree of authority and decision-making the firm wishes to centralize to corporate headquarters. The degree to which knowledge transfer is deemed critical and the degree to which a common corporate culture is wanted are also important considerations. The stronger the perceived need for centralization of control, the less likely it is that a polycentric approach will be viewed as viable and the more likely PCNs or possibly TCNs will be deployed at subsidiary level.

The Norwegian conglomerate Norsk Hydro has 40,000 employees spread across 60 countries of which only 16,000 are based in Norway. Firmly attached to its national roots, at any one point in time it employs some 500 expatriates and typifies the mix of reasons for having an expatriation policy:

> The priority is to satisfy a local business need for managerial, commercial, technical or other skills. However, a further aim is to improve the co-ordination of our international activities and foster the loyalty, trust and cross-divisional networking which enable Hydro to meet its business goals. This requires managers and specialists whose experience has given them the extra skills and vision which come from working outside their home country. It is through such people that we can enhance local capabilities, and thus the expatriate is often expected to develop his own local replacement.
>
> It follows that promotion to the senior appointments of the future will increasingly tend to be reserved for people with international experience. In choosing a candidate for international employment, therefore, close attention is given to this aspect of management development.
>
> International employment is a costly investment . . . which not only adds value to the individual but leads to steady and satisfying career development for those with the necessary ability, drive and readiness to meet the challenges of working abroad.
> (Norsk Hydro: International Employment Policies, §1.4)

To a large extent the need for centralized control will reflect the nature of the foreign operation. In general, short-term operations and operations involving highly valued technologies will increase the desire for the centralization of control. In turn, this will entail the deployment of expatriates as agents of control on behalf of corporate headquarters.

Two further factors affecting the use of expatriates is the technological and socio-cultural setting of the foreign location. In the case of host countries with a low level of technological development, subsidiaries will be dependent on corporate headquarters for the necessary skills and knowledge with which to run the operation. Inevitably this means that such subsidiaries will be dependent on expatriate personnel. Socio-cultural environments that are radically different to that of the parent company represent a communication challenge. Expatriates can play an important role in bridging the gulf as communication facilitators.

▶ Barriers to Expatriation

MNCs will rarely enjoy complete autonomy in regard to the deployment of expatriates. As we have mentioned, host country governments may resist the use of expatriates demanding that operational competencies and control be

Table 8.2 Factors stopping companies giving international experience to managers (Percentage of respondents who ranked a factor as among the five most important constraints in their organization)

Factors	Percentage
Disruption of children's education	77
Spouse/partner reluctant to give up own career	67
Fear of losing influence/visibility at corporate centre	54
Organisation finds difficulty in re-absorbing returning managers	52
Lack of co-ordinated approach across the company	48
Managers find reintegration difficult on return	31
Immigration/employment laws & host country restrictions	29
Financial constraints	29
Lack of perceived need	19
Elderly relatives	17
Host country subsidiaries unwilling to accept managers	8
Subsidiaries in non-parent countries unwilling to release managers	8

Source: Barham and Devine (1990).

decentralized as a condition for operating a subsidiary. A further problem faced by MNCs is that of motivating staff at corporate headquarters to actually accept foreign postings regardless of location. The lack of enthusiasm for a foreign posting rarely has anything to do with a fear of loss of earnings. Rather, as table 8.2 indicates, family concerns are the two most prevalent hindrances.

It should be noted that the 'reluctant spouse or partner' who does not want to abandon a career is nearly always a woman as expatriates have mostly been men. That this remains the case is indicated in a survey of European companies by PricewaterhouseCoopers conducted in 2000 that found that only 9 per cent of expatriates are women. However, all the indications are that the issue of the dual-career couple is not going to go away. On the contrary, it is set to become the biggest single factor in preventing staff from accepting a foreign posting (figures 8.2 and 8.3).

▶ Differences in the Deployment of Expatriates

Although there are objective factors that significantly influence MNCs in their deployment of expatriates, there are also factors of a less tangible more cultural type that influence staffing policy. This is, as Kopp's (1994) research indicates, clearly observable in cross-national comparisons. Table 8.3 shows that Japanese multinational MNCs display a strong preference for allocating top managerial positions in their subsidiaries to PCNs. Only rarely do they make use of TCNs.

The other half of the jobs equation

Many employees are unwilling to take a posting overseas because of their partner's career or family commitments, says **Alison Maitland**

Martin Frost decided to end his 10-year career as a high-flyer at Seagram, the Canadian drinks and entertainment group, when the company asked him to move to New York.

Mr Frost, head of wine and spirits in Europe and Africa, resigned rather than jeopardise the career of his wife Jane, head of brand marketing for the BBC in London, and uproot their children aged eight and six.

It was no easy decision. When Seagram decided to centralise its overseas directors in New York, "it was a catalyst for a lot of thinking about what we wanted to do", says Jane Frost. Her husband already spent 60 per cent of his time away from home and would have travelled even more from the US.

Martin Frost admits resignation was risky. "But Jane's got a good job. It just doesn't make sense for us to up sticks and move to New York," he says.

The dilemma facing the Frosts is a corporate headache too. Overseas postings are often seen as essential to groom people for senior management. But increasingly, executives with working partners and family commitments find such jobs difficult to take on.

Working spouses are now the rule rather than the exception: an estimated three-quarters of international managers have partners with careers, says Elisabeth Marx, a director of Norman Broadbent International, executive recruitment consultants. "Within a competitive job market, fewer spouses or partners are willing to take a career break and trail overseas."

Companies are sometimes failing to get their first choice for an assignment. "Or else the married person is asking to go on a single person assignment, so companies are having to consider more short-term projects and more family visits," says Ilene Dolins, senior vice-president of Windham International, a New York-based international relocation consultancy.

Windham's latest survey of 250 mainly US multinationals, to be published later this month, finds that assignments are most likely to fail because of partner dissatisfaction, family concerns or inability to adapt.

It calculates that a failed assignment costs companies three to five times the expatriate's annual income. According to the Windham survey, 70 per cent provide help to accompanying spouses, up from 59 per cent last year. But help is often minimal: only 7 per cent of companies compensate for lost income, with sums averaging just $8,500 (£5,250).

"Most companies seem to express surprise if an employee doesn't put their career first," says Peter King, director of Location Strategy Management, a UK consultancy. "They underestimate the impact of relocating on their staff."

Eastman Kodak, the US photographic group, which has about 300 expatriate staff worldwide,

·····

'You've got to be in control of your own career and not have it controlled for you'

·····

does pay compensation. Finding a job for a partner in a host country is often difficult, so Kodak pays 33 per cent of the partner's lost income, up to a maximum of $10,000 a year.

"It's a gesture," says Zoya Siddiqui, who administers assignments in Europe, Africa and the Middle East. "It's to offer encouragement to dual-career families who might be dependent on the extra income to maintain a certain lifestyle or to get their kids through school." About one in five multinational employers provides the same assistance to unmarried partners of the opposite or same sex as they do to spouses, the Windham survey shows.

Shell, with 5,000 expatriates worldwide, offers pre-assignment advice to unmarried partners regardless of the stage of the relationship. But its liberal intentions can clash with a host country's laws or culture if these do not recognise unmarried partners.

Companies also try to help by paying for career counselling, job searches or further education. Some provide seed money for partners to start a business or set up as a consultant. A few even pay for grandparents to relocate if they are the main carers of an expatriate's children.

"There's a growing number of companies that are giving spouses specific support," says Gill Mackilligin, international co-ordinator of Working Partners, a United Nations-affiliated body that matches partners' skills with the needs of host countries.

Partners may be able to help by opting for a "portable" career, says Marian Stoltz-Loike, who runs cross-cultural programmes at Windham International. Portable careers include teaching, writing, and computer analysis.

Employers cannot provide all the answers, she says. Giving up a career to follow your partner overseas is not just about losing a salary. It affects status, self-esteem and the balance of power in a relationship. "Companies are sometimes able to help with one, but not necessarily the other."

The issue is complicated because it straddles work and personal life. Even generous incentives to persuade an executive to relocate may not be enough. The Frosts explain that Edgar Bronfman Jr, chief executive of Seagram, offered to find Jane a senior post with the company in New York if Martin moved there. But neither wanted to work for the same company, nor to move at this stage.

They have both had to make tough choices before. Jane left Unilever when Martin was sent by PepsiCo to the Gulf in 1984. Fortunately she was head-hunted to set up a Middle East marketing department there for Shell. "The one thing I didn't want to be was an expat wife," she says.

Martin left PepsiCo three years later rather than take a promotion to Egypt because they did not want to be away from the UK jobs market for too long. Now he is contemplating his next move. It requires strong nerves. But he says: "I believe you've got to be in control of your own career and not have it controlled for you."

Windham International: fax 212 647 0494 or via internet: www.windhamworld.com. Working Partners, London: tel 171 823 8800 or e-mail: working.partners@virgin.net

Figure 8.2 The other half of the jobs equation

Mazda chief quits for family reasons

By Michiyo Nakamoto in Tokyo

Henry Wallace, the Scotsman who became the first foreigner to head a Japanese carmaker. has resigned as president of Mazda.

Mr Wallace, one of the most widely recognised chief executives in Japan, is leaving for family reasons and will return to the UK to take up a post at Ford. He will be succeeded by James Miller, also from Ford, who has been a vice-president since June.

The sudden resignation of Mr Wallace, who became president after Ford increased its stake in the company to 33.3 per cent last year, surprised the industry.

His tenure was very short by Japanese standards, and his admission that he was leaving for family reasons came as an eye-opener to the Japanese corporate community which considers loyalty to the company a priority for top managers.

Figure 8.3 Family reasons for departure
Source: The Financial Times (1997b)

As table 8.3 indicates, the approach of US multinationals is very different with far greater use being made of HCNs and TCNs. Kopp's research does not differentiate between the various European countries. More recent research by Harzing (1999) does and this indicates that German MNCs are similar to Japanese MNCs in that they are particularly likely to appoint PCNs as managing directors of their subsidiaries. Moreover, Japanese and German MNCs are similar in having a significant emphasis on the control function of expatriation. British and French MNCs are more similar to US MNCs in that they are less inclined to use PCNs to head their subsidiaries.

Table 8.3 Nationality of top managers in overseas operations

Headquarters country	Parent country nationals (%)	Host country nationals (%)	Third-country nationals (%)
Japan (n = 26)	74	26	0.2
Europe (n = 21)	48	44	8
USA (n = 20)	31	49	20

Source: Kopp (1994).

Table 8.4 Percentages of MNCs reporting incidence of personnel problems with host country staff

Type of problem	Japanese MNCs (n = 34) (%)	European MNCs (n = 23) (%)	US MNCs (n = 24) (%)
Difficulty in attracting high-calibre HCNs to work for the firm	44	26	21
High turnover of HCNs	32	9	4
Friction and poor communication between PCNs and HCNs	32	9	13
Complaints by HCNs that they are not able to advance in the company	21	4	8

Kopp's research indicates some of the downsides to the ethnocentric approach to staffing by Japanese multinationals. Table 8.4 indicates that not only do a substantial proportion have difficulty in attracting high-calibre HCNs to work for them but that this is coupled to a high turnover of host country employees. In addition, it indicates that there is also a significant incidence of friction and poor communication between PCNs and HCNs as well as complaints by HCNs concerning discrimination.

▶ Selection of Expatriates

Given that the function of expatriates is to represent and communicate the values of the MNC and to apply its technical and managerial competence, it is unsurprising that there has been a tendency to select expatriates first and foremost on the basis of their domestic track record and expertise. Besides they are often being sent abroad to fill a pressing business need. The consequence has been that other salient factors have often been precluded from the selection process. In particular, MNCs have frequently failed to take into account whether potential expatriates have any degree of cross-cultural awareness, the necessary openness to foreigners

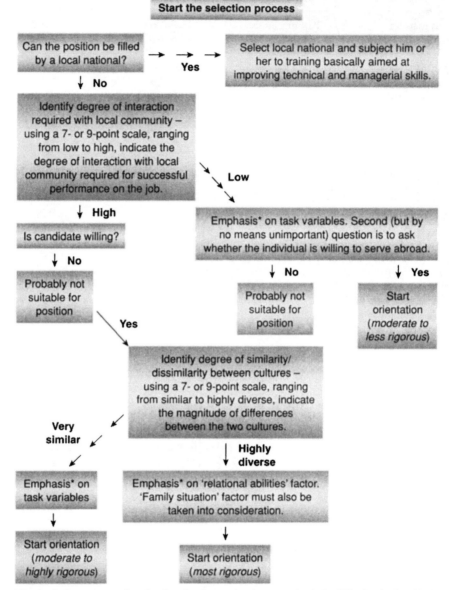

*Emphasis does not mean ignoring the other factors. It only means that it should be the dominant factor.

Figure 8.4 The selection process
Source: Tung (1981) adapted by Deresky (1997). Reprinted with permission of Elzevier Science

and new situations or whether they have the necessary interpersonal skills. Equally, the individual's family situation is often not taken directly into account when selecting for expatriation. As Tung's (1981) model in figure 8.4 indicates, the importance of taking these factors into account varies from situation to situation.

EXPATRIATION AND REPATRIATION

Table 8.5 Recall rates in American, European and Japanese Companies

Recall rate (%)	% of companies
US MNCs	
20–40	7
10–20	69
< 10	24
European MNCs	
11–15	3
6–10	38
< 5	59
Japanese MNCs	
11–19	14
6–10	10
< 5	76

Source: Tung (1982).

In some cases the appointment involves tasks of an exclusively technical nature with very little interaction with the local community. Alternatively, some assignments may be to locations that are culturally similar. In both of these cases only a relatively moderate degree of preparation for the foreign assignment will be necessary. However, in cases when these conditions are not met, considerable effort should be made in preparing the candidate and family of the candidate for the task ahead.

Expatriate failure, in the sense of early recall, is a sensitive issue for most MNCs that they generally prefer not to discuss with researchers. This largely explains the lack of broad, on-going scholarly research on recall rates and the use and misuse of anecdotal evidence and surveys that have passed their 'sell-by date'. The result has been 'the persistent myth of high expatriate failure rates' (Harzing, 1995; 2002b). Tung's (1982) findings, reproduced in table 8.5, are frequently cited but they are now 20 years old.

Tung's findings indicated that the average failure rate is around 5 per cent for Japanese and European MNCs and about 14 per cent for American MNCs. None of these rates is particularly high although the American rate is three times that of the Japanese and European rates. More recent research either substantiates the recall rate for American MNCs (Black and Gregersen, 1999) or suggests that it is not much above the European or Japanese rates (Tung, 1998).

The traditionally relatively low European recall rate has been ascribed to Europeans being more used to foreign cultures than North Americans. The low Japanese recall rate would appear to be a product of their MNCs having generally adopted a long-term attitude to preparing their candidates and their families for expatriation with the first year abroad usually devoted to acclimatization. The thoroughgoing approach of Japanese firms contrasted with that of US firms. The underlying assumption among many US MNCs was that management skills are universal and, once learned, are applicable regardless of setting. However, the apparent lowering in more recent years of the American recall rate indicates that American MNCs have learned their lessons and have a more systematic approach to expatriation. Certainly the case of Colgate-Palmolive (C-P) as described by Rosenzweig (1994) illustrates this.

Like many US companies the policy at C-P was always to set up a subsidiary wherever sales were strong. By the late 1930s C-P had subsidiaries in several European countries as well as in Argentina, Brazil, India, Mexico, South Africa and the Philippines. By 1961 it had set up nearly 40 foreign subsidiaries and continued to expand its foreign operations all of which were headed by expatriates. Indeed, the philosophy at C-P was that to become a top executive, one had to have a stint abroad. Until 1983 C-P had no formal expatriate policy. Managers were simply sent abroad with no help with housing, education or children. The assignment would last for nearly two years with only two weeks local leave at the end of the first year. Because of the difficulties in communication expatriate managers had considerable autonomy. At the most they could expect one or two visits from headquarters during their assignment.

It was only after 1983 that C-P developed an International Assignment Policy that ensured a standardized financial package, language courses for the manager and his or her spouse, tuition fees for children and extended annual home leave. Systematic selection procedures were also put in place. This policy was further strengthened in the early 1990s by offering cultural orientation programmes for the expatriates and their families. In addition, as a response to the problem of dual-career couples a spouse assistance programme was introduced that offered spouses help to gain a work permit, career advice, business start-up grants, or financial assistance for education.

Despite these developments the issue of dual-career couples remains a problem for C-P and other US and European MNCs that view international experience as a mandatory element in executive development. Although there are a variety of reasons for expatriate failure in the case of both American and European expatriates, as table 8.6 shows, the most important cause has for at least the last 20 years been related to the spouse's difficulties in adjusting to the situation. Indeed, European companies report this as the only salient factor. As table 8.6 indicates, this is not a particularly important factor for Japanese companies. This may partly reflect the status of married women in Japanese society where dual-career couples remain the exception and partly the greater investment Japanese companies make in taking the expatriate's family situation into consideration.

McKinsey has calculated that the direct cost of expatriate failure can often reach US$1 million including time and money wasted in selection, pre-assignment visits to the location, training and relocation packages (Hsieh, Lavoie and Samek, 1999). In addition there are the many indirect costs such as damage to the company's

Table 8.6 Reasons for expatriate failure in descending order of importance

American companies:
1. Inability of spouse to adjust
2. Manager's inability to adjust
3. Other family reasons
4. Manager's personal or emotional maturity
5. Inability to cope with larger overseas responsibility

Japanese companies:
1. Inability to cope with larger overseas responsibility
2. Difficulties with the new environment
3. Manager's personal or emotional problems
4. Lack of technical competence
5. Inability of spouse to adjust

European companies:
*Inability of spouse to adjust (only consistent dimension)

Source: Tung (1982).

reputation, loss of confidence among customers and suppliers, as well as the loss of self-esteem and self-confidence to the failed expatriate. Finally, expatriate failure does not enhance the attractiveness of expatriate postings within the company.

▶ Training and Development

The main function of pre-assignment training is to reduce culture shock. Culture shock is a product of lacking an interpretation system based on the new culture. Other people's behaviour is experienced as confusing and even nonsensical. Perhaps just as troubling is that one's own behaviour does not produce the desired results. Harmless jokes give offence, suggestions are regarded as unwarranted demands and demands are treated as suggestions. This deep-seated shock usually follows a predictable cycle. The first months in the new culture are often euphoric. The new culture is experienced as exciting and stimulating. However, after a few months this 'honeymoon' mood is invariably replaced by increasingly negative feelings towards the new culture. The novelty of the new environment has worn thin, the host culture is increasingly experienced as irritating and culture shock sets in. In terms of figure 8.5 the individual has reached the bottom of the U-shaped curve (Gullahorn and Gullahorn, 1963). Following the culture shock phase adaptation takes place and the curve begins to rise. However, in some cases the expatriate and the spouse are so overwhelmed by these feelings that it results in an irresolvable crisis and the abandonment of the assignment.

Pre-assignment training is designed to help the expatriate and his or her family cope with such feelings and to make an early healthy adjustment to the new

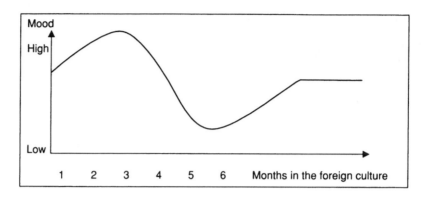

Figure 8.5 Culture shock cycle

environment. For long-term assignments it should go beyond information giving and stress reduction techniques to incorporating extensive language training, sensitivity training and cross-cultural training. The length of such a training programme will rarely be less than one month, often more than two months. As figure 8.6 indicates, shorter assignments require less rigorous and less comprehensive training programmes.

One example of a comprehensive training programme is a European Union course, known as the executive training programme (ETP). The ETP is a programme designed for European executives with no familiarity of Japan. In the space of 18 months participants are given intensive language training in Tokyo supplemented by sojourns with Japanese families and a six-month internship with one or more Japanese companies. The internships are usually located at Japanese companies that either are or are expected to be clients, joint venture partners or even competitors in the same industry. The objective is to enable participants to operate in Japan in Japanese in the sense that they have the ability to speak, read and write at a reasonable level, send e-mails and use word-processing programmes in Japanese. The effect is enhanced credibility in the eyes of Japanese companies who view the ability to work in the Japanese language as an indication of a long-term commitment to doing business in Japan. Companies such as Jaguar, Bayer, Lego and ABN Amro have all made use of ETP since it was established some 20 years ago. But they do not constitute a majority. Most companies continue to simply send expatriates to Japan in the expectation that they will pick up the language as they go along. The result is that many executives fail to get beyond reading a menu.

However, even with a thorough and well-planned pre-assignment training programme in place one must expect incidents and phases of extreme culture shock. This is not necessarily a sign of some deficiency within the expatriate. On the contrary, Raitu (1983) has observed that the most effective international managers suffer the most severe culture shock while managers evaluated as not particularly effective suffer little culture shock.

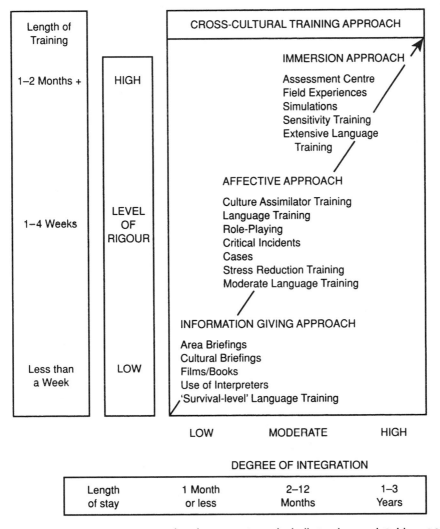

Figure 8.6 Designing cross-cultural training (Mendenhall, Dunbar and Oddou, 1987). Reprinted with permission of John Wiley & Sons Inc.

▶ Repatriation

In a survey conducted by Oddou and Mendenhall (1991) the vast majority of expatriates reported that their foreign experience had significantly increased their global perspective of their firm's business operations. Moreover, they reported on being able to communicate more effectively with people of diverse backgrounds. Many also felt that they had become more effective managers. On the other hand, reverse culture shock is also prevalent. This stems from factors such as:

- the need of the returnee to adjust to changes which have taken place in the work environment;
- the need to adjust to changes in the social environment;
- the adjustment needs of the returnee's spouse and children.

The work environment

Findings from research conducted by Black, Gregersen and Mendenhall (1992) indicate that 60 per cent of American, 80 per cent of Japanese, and 71 per cent of Finnish expatriates experienced some degree of culture shock during repatriation. There are two sources of readjustment problems. The first is job-related and involves a sense of loss of professional status. Colleagues who have not been abroad have in the meantime been promoted and there may not even be a properly defined or relevant re-entry job waiting for the returnee. This has to be negotiated on return. A survey by the US Bureau of National Affairs found that 68 per cent of managers were unsure of their re-entry position prior to returning and that 77 per cent believed that expatriation had resulted in demotion. Repatriates also report that their international experience is not always regarded as particularly important. The same survey reported that 91 per cent felt that their international experience was not valued. Finally the independence and status they enjoyed as senior figures in the subsidiary are invariably significantly reduced on their return. In general, one out of every five employees who finish an overseas assignment wants to leave the company when they return (Adler, 1991).

The social environment

The second cause of reverse culture shock is rooted in broader, social factors. One aspect is that coming home often involves taking a drop in living standard. A more important factor is that while sojourners expect to encounter changes when moving abroad, they typically do not expect to find changes when returning home. Furthermore, repatriates frequently find that their foreign experiences are unappreciated by their social circle. One experienced HRM manager with responsibility for overseeing repatriation advises returnees to 'Never talk to your friends about where you have been. Act as though you haven't been away.'

The spouse and children

On the practical side spouses have to try and resume their careers which is particularly difficult if they have not been able to work while they have been abroad. A final problem for those with teenage children is the difficulties involved in rejoining peer groups. A survey among UK repatriates revealed that nearly half had experienced some degree of difficulty in readapting to life in the UK with one in five reporting severe difficulties (Forster, 2000).

The complexity of readjustment problems depends on the number of years spent abroad, the nature of the foreign location and, not least, on whether the company has a repatriation programme in place. The most comprehensive repatriation programmes commence with expatriation. National and local newspapers are regularly mailed to the expatriate. The expatriate and family receive paid home leave in order to be able to touch base. A mentor is in place at company headquarters whose task is to ensure that the expatriate is kept abreast with developments at headquarters. At the end of the assignment it is the mentor's responsibility to reintroduce the expatriate into the company and conduct a debriefing in order for the company to garner the returnee's experience and to provide a thorough update of changes at corporate headquarters.

The prevalence of formal repatriation programmes varies. Among Scandinavian companies they are widespread (Björkman, 1990) whereas under one-third of US companies have any programme at all. This may explain the high degree of repatriate turnover for US companies that is reported as being as high as 25 per cent and the observation that overseas assignments are viewed as negative career moves.

Repatriate turnover might also be a function of restructuring that has taken place during the foreign posting. Regardless of good intentions the velocity of change is so great that it is difficult to provide any guarantees about jobs. One international assignments manager at a British IT company remarked:

> For us, this is a dark cloud on the horizon. Our assignment policy says that we will employ you in a position comparable with your overseas posting when you return to the UK – 'depending on availability'. But, there is no guarantee of this . . . The pace of change is so fast that I think a lot of them can lose touch. (Forster, 2000: 137)

 # The Cost of Expatriation

Expatriates' salaries and benefits vary significantly from company to company making it problematic to generalize. With that proviso in mind McKinsey's Shanghai office in 1997 concluded that the average annual cost of employing a senior Western manager, such as a general manager, a chief financial officer, a national sales and marketing executive or a national human-resources director, was nearly $500.000 (table 8.7).

Recent Trends

Recent research amongst mainly European big companies suggests that expatriation in the sense of long-term assignments of a year or more is some three times more widespread than short-term assignments for fixed periods of less than a year

Table 8.7 Total average package (US$)

Compensation	246,000
Additional cost to company	
Housing	84,000
Schooling	22,500
Rest-and-relaxation trips	22,500
Allowances	98,400
Other benefits	
Three-week vacation	
Medical	
Tax evaluation	
Car and driver	

Source: Hsieh, Lavoie and Samek (1999).

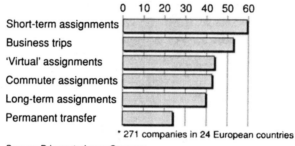

* 271 companies in 24 European countries

Source: PricewaterhouseCoopers

Figure 8.7 Percentage of large European companies experiencing an increase in each type of international assignment
Source: The Economist © The Economist Newspaper Ltd, London, 16 December, 2000

or so. While just over half had more than 50 employees on long-term assignments only about a fifth had more than 50 abroad on short-term assignments. Moreover, as figure 8.7 reveals, some 40 per cent of European companies have experienced a growth in long-term assignments. However, as figure 8.7 also indicates, short-term assignments are increasing at a significantly higher rate.

What explains this tendency to opt for short-term assignments? An increased cost consciousness amongst companies appears to be one factor. Sending an employee abroad has been estimated to cost between three and four times as much as employing a HCN. Companies appear to be less inclined to accept this expense. Another factor is that companies are increasingly conscious of the problems encountered by employees in dual-career relationships. The most important factor though in the relative growth in shorter postings is due to organizational changes in multinationals in the last decade. Whereas previously executives had regional and geographic responsibilities, they are now more likely to have global and functional responsibilities. A manager who is responsible for information technology is expected to work in all the countries in which the company has operations. This trend towards the global integration of the MNC also means that employees with specific skills, who would previously not have been sent abroad, are also increasingly liable to be sent on assignments abroad for a few weeks or months.

Although assignments of three to six months avoids the dual-career problem in the sense that spouses do not have to give up their employment, short-term assignments do put pressure on families. Harry Gram, who handles short-term assignments for IBM admits that: 'To tell individuals that they will be away from their family for six months is definitely a hardship' (*The Economist*, 2000b).

▶ Summary

Expatriation is a common feature of most MNCs, particularly those with either an ethnocentric or geocentric approach to the staffing of their subsidiaries. However, even for MNCs with a polycentric approach expatriation may be viewed as a necessity for developing managers and for the diffusion of critical competencies. The challenge for human resource departments of MNCs is not only to select the right candidates for expatriation, but also to design packages that are sufficiently motivating to overcome the barrier posed by the 'reluctant spouse or partner'. In addition, human resource departments have the responsibility of organizing appropriate pre-assignment training. The evidence is that only a minority invest substantial resources in this task. Finally, there is the issue of ensuring a smooth repatriation process. These core concerns all feature in the accompanying case, but their different weightings should give rise to discussion.

LVMH: Career Development through International Mobility[1]

Jean-Luc Cerdin

▶ Introduction

LVMH Moët Hennessy Louis Vuitton, is the leading luxury brand conglomerate in the world. Based in Paris, it employs 56,000 people, 63 per cent of whom work outside France. With more than 1,400 stores worldwide and sales of €12 billion for the year 2000 (84 per cent outside France), LVMH is a global giant.

Created in 1987, it is a portfolio of 50 prestigious luxury brands. Each one of these brands has its unique history and culture. Among them are famous names such as Château d'Yquem founded in 1593, Moët & Chandon in 1743, Hennessy in 1765, Guerlain in 1828 or Louis Vuitton in 1854. LVMH is a financial and commercial group specializing in the profitable market of luxury goods. LVMH is a young group based on timeless brands and endeavors to preserve the authenticity of all of them. Because of the strength of these brands, LVMH chose to be a decentralized organization. It is also a growing and evolving organization, constantly acquiring new businesses.

From its creation, LVMH was an international business, but its human resources were sometimes lacking in international experience. Competing in a global environment, LVMH must attract, develop and retain managers with global competence. By 2001, it had 260 expatriates and 650 other employees working abroad.

▶ History

The creation of Moët Hennessy in 1971 was a first step towards the creation of a larger group in 1987 under the name LVMH (figure H1). In 1989, the Groupe Arnault (figure H2) became a majority shareholder in LVMH. In 1997, LVMH entered the selective retailing market to better control the distribution of its goods. In 1999, it entered the Watches & Jewelry business. LVMH is organized in five business groups. In addition to *Watches and Jewelry* and *Selective Retailing*, LVMH's activities include *Wines and Spirits, Fashion and Leather Goods* and *Perfumes and Cosmetics*. The sales level of these activities is given in figure H3. The list of all of LVMH's companies can be found in figure H4.

Today the group defines its core values as 'being creative and innovative', 'aiming for product excellence', 'promoting our brands with passion', 'acting as entrepreneurs' and 'striving to be the best in all we do'.

TIMELESS BRANDS

A YOUNG GROUP

| 1593 Château d'Yquem |
| 1743 Moët & Chandon |
| 1765 Hennessy |
| 1828 Guerlain |
| 1854 Louis Vuitton |

1971 Creation of Moët Hennessy
1987 Creation of LVMH
1989 Groupe Arnault becomes a major shareholder in LVMH
1997 Entry in Selective Retailing
1999 Creation of the Watches & Jewelry Division
2001 LVMH/De Beers Jewelry Venture receives EC Clearance

Figure H1 History: a young group

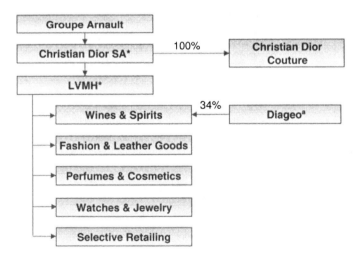

Figure H2 Group structure
Note: ᵃ Public companies

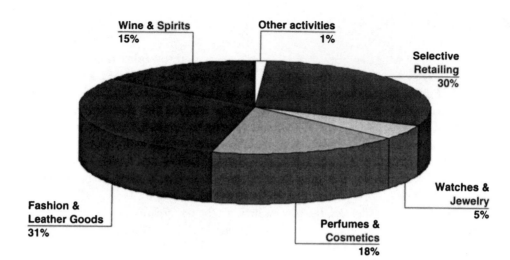

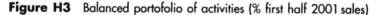

Figure H3 Balanced portofolio of activities (% first half 2001 sales)

16th

1593 Château d'Yquem

18th

1729 Ruinart
1743 Moët & Chandon
1763 Hine
1765 Hennessy
1772 Veuve Clicquot
1780 Chaumet
1796 Phillips

19th

1828 Guerlain
1836 Pommery
1843 Krug
1846 Loewe
1852 Le Bon Marché
1854 Louis Vuitton
1858 Mercier
1860 Heuer
1865 Zenith
1868 Canard Duchêne
1870 La Cote Desfossés
1870 La Samaritaine
1895 Berluti

20th

1911 Ebel
1925 Omas
1925 Fendi
1930 Acqua di Parma
1936 Dom Pérignon
1936 Fred
1945 Celine
1947 Parfums Christian Dior
1952 Givenchy
1952 Connaissance des Arts
1957 Parfums Givenchy
1958 Emilio Pucci
1960 DFS
1963 Miami Cruiseline Services
1970 Kenzo1970 Etude Tajan
1972 MountAdam
1973 Domaine Chandon
1974 Investir
1973 Sephora
1976 Cape Mentelle
1978 Newton
1979 Art & Auction
1981 Pacific Echo
1983 Radio Classique
1984 Thomas Pink
1984 Marc Jacobs
1984 Donna Karan
1985 La Tribune de l'Economie
1985 Cloudy Bay
1985 Benedom – CD Montres
1987 Christian Lacroix
1987 Parfums Kenzo
1987 Laflachère
1989 Make Up For Ever

1991 Fresh
1991 StefanoBi
1995 Hard Candy
1995 BeneFit Cosmetics
1996 Bliss1996 Urban Decay
1997 Chandon Estates
1999 Solstice
2000 eLuxury

21th

2001 LVMH/De Beers joint venture

Figure H4 History: a world-class portfolio of brands

Wines & Spirits	Fashion & Leather Goods	Perfumes & Cosmetics	Selective Retailing	Watches & Jewelry	Other Businesses
Moët & Chandon	Louis Vuitton	Parfums Christian Dior	DFS	TAG Heuer	Phillips, de Pury &
Dom Pérignon	Céline	Parfums Givenchy	Miami Cruiseline	Montres	Luxembourg
Mercier	Loewe	Guerlain Kenzo Parfums	Sephora	Christian Dior	Etude Tajan
Ruinart	Kenzo	Hard Candy	Sephora AAP	Ebel	D.I Group
Veuve Clicquot	Givenchy	Fresh	Le Bon Marché	Zenith	Investir
Ponsardin	Christian Dior[a]	Laflachère	Solstice	Omas	Radio Classique
Canard-Duchêne	Christian Lacroix	Bliss	La Samaritaine	Chaumet	La Tribune
Pommery	Marc Jacobs	Urban Decay		Fred	Jazzman
Krug	Berluti	Make Up For Ever		LVMH/De Beers	Le Monde de la
Chandon Estates	Fendi	BeneFit Cosmetics		joint venture	Musique
Cloudy Bay	StefanoBi	Acqua di Parma			System TV
Cape Mentelle	Thomas Pink				Connaissance des Arts
Newton	Emilio Pucci				Art & Auction
MountAdam	Donna Karan				Sephora.com
Hennessy					eLuxury
Hine					
Château d'Yquem					

Figure H5 Organizations in five business groups
Note: [a] Christian Dior is one of the indirect holders of LVMH

▶ Group Structure

The group's roots are French. Most headquarters of LVMH's companies are located in France. Yet, LVMH believes that its management must be multi-cultural. The group is structured around five business groups. Each business group is a collection of several strong brands, as shown in figure H5. LVMH is an aggregate, a 'confederacy' of brands, in the words of LVMH's CEO Bernard Arnault. This organization is atypical because it is a young structure that aggregates several brands, sometimes very old and independent. The strength of each brand stems from a unique culture which translates into relatively autonomous brand management.

The group is made up of 50 companies managing 450 subsidiaries. These companies are the foundation of the group. Each company has its President and its Executive Committee. Each company has its subsidiaries which report directly to it either through the President or through an International Director in charge of supervising the activities of the company's subsidiaries.

LVMH's leadership is based on its balanced presence in several key sectors of luxury goods and an even geographical split of its activities between Europe, Asia and the Americas (figure H5). It pursues an aggressive growth strategy based on a high level of innovation, control over distribution and sustained advertising and promotion.

▶ HR Structure

LVMH organizes its Human Resource Management around five main world zones, namely, France, Europe, the Americas, Pacific Asia and Japan. France and Japan are regarded as country/zones because of the size of their market (figure H6).

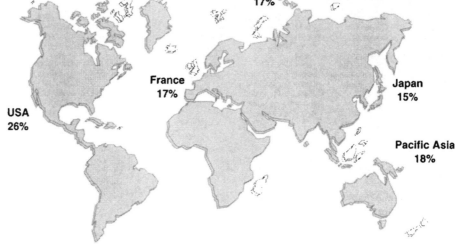

Europe w/o France
17%

France
17%

Japan
15%

USA
26%

Pacific Asia
18%

Other: 7%

Figure H6 World sales

Corporate HR policy is more than compulsory rules imposed on the business groups and on the companies. Through adaptable guidelines, it also provides management support to the companies. The role of corporate HR is to normalize certain procedures, to define strategy and to give an impetus to companies' HR teams. Regarding guidelines, corporate HR proposes but seldom imposes.

An employee deals directly with the company he or she works for, this company in turn deals with the business group which reports to corporate headquarters. Roughly 50–60 per cent of moves are handled by companies, the others being managed by the business groups or corporate.

There are four types of HR managers at LVMH. Following the group's structure, they operate on four levels: corporate, regional, business group and company level. The subsidiary HR Director, or the person acting as such, reports to the subsidiary's President. The subsidiary's HR Director gets advice and support from his company. The business group's HR Director coordinates his companies' HR Directors through monthly meetings. The purpose of these meetings is to identify vacant positions throughout the world and to study the list of the potential candidates for these positions, amongst which are the *Ready to Move*. Being a *Ready to Move* does not mean that a candidate has formally expressed a desire to move, but that the organization has identified him or her as having the potential to progress through a new assignment within the year.

The main goal of corporate HR management is to ensure information flow and to harmonize procedures, while leaving final decisions to the company, up to a point. The regional HR Director ensures that internal rules are coherently applied within his or her zone. For subsidiaries with no HR Director, recruitment is done by the Regional HR Director.

Career Development and International Mobility

LVMH was a global business from the start, however it soon realized that its human resources often lacked international skills. In 1987, too many managers were not fluent in English. Since then, LVMH has sought to create a pool of global managers, with a working knowledge of international markets. The head of LVMH's Compensation and Benefits (C&B) defines a global manager as a person with the training or the experience needed to manage a global business. He or she can perform from any place in the world thanks to a global vision and skills in managing multilingual and multicultural teams. To achieve such abilities, one must have worked in several countries so that his or her potential can be released, and noticed.

LVMH believes that the best way to develop its employees is not formal training but mobility. This includes vertical, horizontal and geographical moves within the organization. In order to facilitate mobility, employees' seniority is valued at the group level. International mobility is but one form of mobility, it accounts for one out of five moves.

Basic Principles of LVMH's Policy for International Mobility

LVMH prefers to use the term 'international mobility', rather than expatriation. Contrary to the concept of international mobility which suggests perpetual movement, the term expatriation suggests systematic repatriation. For example, a Dane leaving a Danish subsidiary of 15 people to take on an international assignment will not be expatriated. He will sign a local contract in the country of his assignment. He will be considered 'internationally mobile' because it is most unlikely that he will ever work again in Denmark for LVMH. The skills he will have acquired abroad will largely surpass the competence needed in Denmark.

The international mobility policy is part of a career development scheme which requires the training of global managers on a limited time basis. LVMH does not want to create a legion of expatriates who live out their careers outside their home base, often in the same country, maintaining their benefits. In such cases, expatriates are disconnected from their home base. Moreover, such practices are not cost effective.

LVMH strives to attract managers to international assignments through exciting career development prospects and not through economic incentives, even though its incentive programme is competitive. HR convinces a manager to become 'internationally mobile' by offering him or her a more challenging job with more freedom to perform his or her task than at home.

LVMH does not dispatch expatriates because of a lack of local talent. Most of its expatriates fit two profiles: those sent out by the corporate HQ to control its subsidiaries and protect its interests (internal auditors and financial staff) and those sent out to develop their skills. Organization development accounts for a quarter of expatriates while the rest is part of a management development scheme. Most expatriates are in charge of small subsidiaries for three years on average, very few of them stay longer. They are senior expatriates whose role is to manage the local business, train the host-country nationals and transfer corporate culture. Clearly some expatriations result from specific needs. For example, certain designers in leather goods are very hard to find and must be expatriated.

▶ International Talents

International mobility is an integral part of each high potential's career path. International mobility mainly aims at developing managers. Many expatriates are high potentials. International mobility is likely to entail a radical functional move. The head of HR development recalls the case of a French insurance specialist in the fashion business unit who was sent to Romania to head a shoe factory. LVMH recognizes the need to take risks in order to develop high potentials. It wants to put them in new situations to help them develop new skills and prove their mettle.

LVMH's career development goal is to make the mobility process smoother, particularly international moves. Indeed, HR is well aware that top management is much too ethnocentric. Half of LVMH's senior executives and 40 per cent of managerial staff are French, whereas the French account for 37 per cent of the group's global workforce. Ideally, HR wants to develop more foreign global managers so that in turn they can globalize top management. However, LVMH's mobility process works thanks to a network of HR teams mainly staffed with locals. Many heads of subsidiaries are French. Italians are also well represented at LVMH, as they are historical key players in the luxury business. The Board of Directors features French, Italian and American nationals.

Until recently, LVMH defined two types of high potentials, HP1 and HP2. An HP1 is an individual likely to achieve a top management position such as member of Board committees, Regional president or Subsidiary president. An HP2 is an employee likely to go up one or two steps in the hierarchy. For corporate HR this definition of high potential is too broad and is more relevant for flat structures. It is now considering narrowing it. It would retain the definition of HP1 and include those who are considered to be experts in their domain.

LVMH performance appraisal system is not only based on results but also on the ability to propose and implement new ideas. The group's growth and financial might allow these projects to come to life. LVMH has a career management process called Organizational and Management Review (OMR). This annual process aims at reviewing HR objectives and results. The OMR is an essential tool for LVMH's human resource planning, taking into consideration the organization's needs for the next three years. It defines succession planning and HP and *Ready to Move* lists. Employees identified on these lists are given developmental experiences which include international assignments, in order to prepare them for top management positions. The OMR particularly looks back on the previous year's objectives for HPs and those *Ready to Move* and assesses their current development. LVMH manages to staff internally two out of three executive positions.

Up until recently, the typical career path included showing one's mettle in France, moving from position to position within France in order to master the corporate culture. Once these conditions were met, the employee could be expatriated. LVMH is now willing to make expatriation happen earlier. It recognizes the risks involved in such a policy but believes that these risks are offset by the development of a young and adventurous global workforce.

▶ International Recruitment

In order to build a pool of global managers, LVMH must be able to have a worldwide recruiting process and to send its employees on global assignments. LVMH is a very attractive company for French prospects, however, it is not as successful on international labour markets. Once having achieved global recruitment, LVMH must succeed in developing its employee's global skills. Expatriation is an integral part of LVMH's HRM policy.

LVMH's natural labour market is France. LVMH is a very attractive company for early career professionals and is very active on French business campuses. An early career professional is an individual with less than five years of professional experience. Today, roughly 70 per cent of early career professionals at LVMH are recruited in France.

LVMH would like to expand its labour source to a more international level. Being a decentralized organization, their website is their main source of candidates along with on-campus job fairs. Through this website, candidates from any country can apply directly to any of LVMH's subsidiaries in a country not their own and obtain a local employment contract.

In order to support international business growth, the number of employees involved in international transfers is increasing. However, this does not mean that a rise in the number of French expatriates will drive this trend. Rather LVMH's pool of global managers will grow through third-country nationals and mostly multi-cultural profiles.

LVMH wants to recruit more individuals with international profiles. The ideal candidate is a person who has been immersed in several cultures, has travelled extensively, speaks at least three languages and has an open mind.

Today the number of expatriates at LVMH is 260 and rising, 79 per cent of them are French. Inpatriates (foreigners in France) represent 5.5 per cent and third country nationals 15.5 per cent of employees on international assignment. The average age of expatriates is 36 years, 48 per cent of them are under 35 and 5 per cent are over 50. General managers, area managers and brand managers account for 35.5 per cent of expatriates, finance and audit staff for 17.5 per cent, marketing for 12 per cent, store managers and HR staff each account for 4 per cent of expatriates, the remaining 27 per cent includes other positions. In the past years the number of expatriates as grown by approximately 30 per cent each year while the overall population of managers has grown by 20 per cent each year (figure H7).

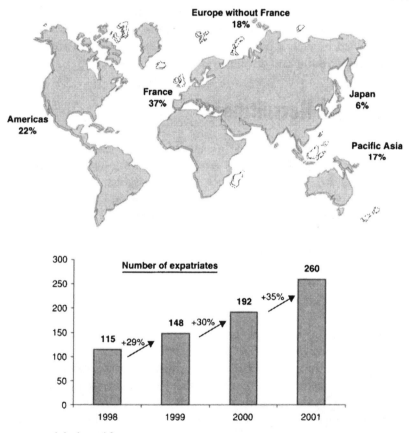

Figure H7 Global workforce
Note: This number of expatriates must be considered in light of LVMH's population of 7,300 managers (excluding DFS). Moreover, 650 other employees have a home-based salary in a country not their own, i.e. they have a local employment contract

In addition to these expatriates *per se*, 650 other employees have a home-based salary in a country not their own, they have a local employment contract. For example, an Australian recruited in France, and still working there, is not an expatriate and is not on global assignment.

▶ The International Transfer Policy

The International Transfer Department operates at the corporate level to provide support to the group's companies. It defines its role through five main functions:

- Determining expatriate packages in order to guarantee internal equity between the group's various companies.
- Helping the group's companies address specific issues regarding international transfers.
- Providing information and advice on the evolution of 'external rules' which govern international transfers, i.e. labour laws.
- Conducting, spreading and explaining LVMH's internal mobility policy.
- Monitoring of international mobility data.

Corporate HR's purpose is to define clear and simple principles that can be applied to all subsidiaries in all countries. In order to facilitate mobility within the group, LVMH is trying to harmonize its practices to allow for a more global workforce. The prime condition for achieving this goal is to make equity a priority, between both countries and employees. LVMH did not choose to set up an international corporation which would centralize HRM and would dictate the compensation policy of the entire organization. The organization would like to avoid situations where line managers are confronted with the frustrations of expatriates earning less than their colleagues in the same position. As a result the manager could feel uneasy and would not know how to cope with such discrepancies. LVMH has chosen to maintain a decentralized organization where corporate HR defines general principles.

LVMH's corporate policy of international mobility is very recent. Before 1987, each company proceeded according to its own international transfer policy. The foundation of the corporate policy was laid at the group's creation. The companies gradually adopted this policy which was eventually formalized in July 2000. Today, each company HR possesses a copy of the 'International Transfer Policy' charter which covers all main aspects of international mobility. The charter does not focus on career development but rather on the formal procedures related to international mobility. It encompasses all the aspects pertaining to an expatriate package. It is meant to be used by company HR directors. Some technical annexes are for the use of the companies' C&B staffs so as to facilitate communication with the International Transfer Department and to provide answers to potential expatriates' concerns. Indirectly, this charter helps expatriates understand their package.

The charter was first published as a paper document. It structures and formalizes past practices and tries to build a common policy. The International Transfer Department is now considering broadening its information supply to HR companies through the use of its intranet.

▶ The Expatriate Package

LVMH does not aim to attract expatriates through high compensation levels. The group is striving for cost efficiency. It is aware that a 'good' package is necessary, but that it is not the main incentive to go abroad. Research on French expatriates shows that compensation is not the main motive for accepting an international assignment (table H1).

The basic balance-sheet approach for compensation package is based on the principle that expatriates should neither lose nor gain from their move. LVMH's C&B department has retained this approach as a guide for its compensation package policy.

The home-based salary is marked up at the time of departure according to the international assignment. It will increase during the length of the assignment. It is used as a base for the calculation of social security and pension contributions. The mobility salary is compared to local labour market averages in compatible countries. LVMH delineated two types of countries, the 'compatible' countries, roughly including OECD countries, and the 'incompatible' countries.

In order to calculate an expatriate's gross salary in local currency, i.e. the mobility salary, LVMH's C&B department first considers his home-based gross salary in parent-country currency, then it calculates his net salary (by deducting theoretical home tax, social security and compulsory pension contribution.) Then is added or subtracted to this net salary in parent-country currency a cost of living allowance (COLA) and various family allowance differentials. A foreign premium

Table H1 French managers' motives for expatriation

Ranking of French managers' motives for expatriation (293 expatriates working for 12 organizations in 44 countries were asked to express their motives to go and work abroad)

Motive	Rank	%
Desire for change	1	77.7
Personal experience in another culture	2	75.3
Increased prospects of future promotion	3	49.8
Compensation	4	37.8
Immediate promotion	5	18.3
Desire to escape home country's economic and social environment	6	16.2
To distance one's self from certain personal problems	7	6.2

Source: Cerdin (2002: 65).

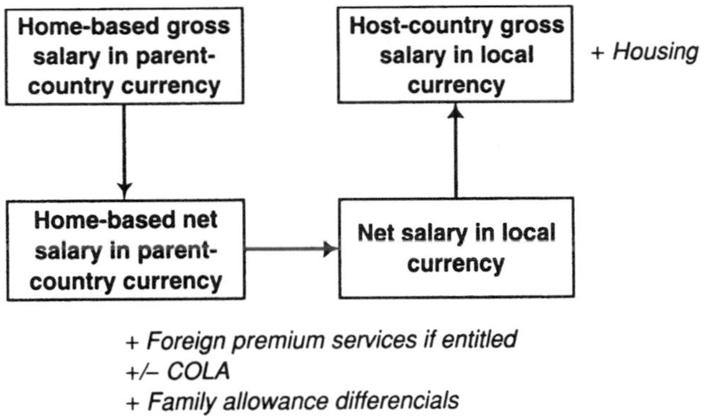

Figure H8 Basic balance sheet approach

service can also be granted. The net figure obtained is then expressed in local currency. The net salary is then 'grossed up' by adding taxes and social contribution of the host country (figure H8).

LVMH's C&B department has adapted the balance sheet approach for its housing policy. A consultancy provides them with the housing market rate for the host country. LVMH's local correspondents verify this information. Potential expatriates may also have their own knowledge of market rates. As a rule, all the parties involved are honest, but they might not always understand each other perfectly. As a company HR put it:

> Having local correspondents is one thing, understanding each other is another one. For instance, an apartment of 125 square metres in Hong Kong refers to the surface area of the apartment itself plus a proportion of the communal parts area. This is less than 125 square metres of living space. The same apartment surface might appear larger to a person used to areas where only living space is taken into account.

Once the local market rate is agreed on, LVMH will compensate the expatriate but he has to contribute 15 per cent of his home-based gross salary. For example, a French expatriate in New York will be paid an amount in US dollars equal to the average monthly market rate times twelve, minus an amount in dollars equal to 15 per cent of his yearly gross salary in France as expressed in Euros. This 15 per cent contribution is based on the assumption than a French employee's housing cost amount to roughly 15 per cent of his gross salary. LVMH believes that this estimate is below the cost effectively paid by most employees. The rationale behind this contribution is that the employee has to pay a percentage of his salary on housing at home and must also do so abroad. LVMH can directly provide housing to the expatriates or it can grant him an allowance by using the above principle. This housing allowance is also 'grossed up'. The expatriate is responsible for the cost of utilities. He is granted a relocation allowance equivalent to one month worth of gross salary upon arrival in the host country, where he must work, and after return to the home country, whence he was expatriated.

LVMH works with consulting firms specialized in overseas Cost of Living Allowances (COLA) calculation. It uses a positive index to protect its employees from losing money when they move to a country with a higher cost of living. It uses a negative index when they move to a country with a lower cost of living. Here the balance-sheet approach is strictly applied. C&B corporate relies on the internal exchange rate used by the corporate finance department, in order to avoid any complaints from financial expatriates. The calculation of the cost-of-living differential is based on the assumption that all employees, regardless of their family situation, save 30 per cent of their home-based net salary. The COLA is set at the time of departure.

C&B does not rely on outside consultancies to determine its incentive allowances. A foreign service premium is calculated by taking into account four criteria, namely, the environment (health facilities, pollution, climate), personal security, social amenities and the everyday quality of life. The granted premiums range from 0 to 30 per cent depending on the home country and the host country. For instance, for an expatriate from France, whatever his or her nationality, the premium is null when the move is within the European Zone or towards the USA. It achieves its maximum, 30 per cent, for a host country such as India.

LVMH's appeal to global managers does not rely mainly on its mobility salary but on its home-based salary, on which the mobility salary is calculated. This appeal is also greatly increased by the role of international mobility in career paths. International mobility is like an investment, the return on investment for the expatriate will be the high future incomes generated by a promotion achieved through successful international assignments.

The mobility salary also includes other aspects such as compensation of other social benefits (like family support). It also compensates for the possible loss of profit sharing benefits resulting from a move from one successful subsidiary to a less successful one. Indeed, no profit sharing schemes exists at the corporate level.

Expatriates are also entitled to additional benefits such as paid education for children, paid home-leaves, temporary housing for up to 30 days, loans for housing deposits or for purchasing a vehicle. Costs of moving are also covered. According to French labour laws, in addition to their 5-week vacation, French managers, except top executives, are entitled to have more days off. Some countries are far less advantageous in terms of vacation time. LVMH grants 4-week vacations in the USA and 5-week vacations elsewhere.

The expatriate package is prepared at the corporate level but the final decision is left up to the companies. As the companies are the ones that must pay the expatriates, they have some leeway. For instance, as expressed by a C&B manager, 'Some of them are going to give higher housing allowances, they may offer more generous home-leave allowances than those favoured by the Group, such as business-class air fare instead of less expensive economy-class ones.'

The International Transfer Department defines clear procedures, however implementing them requires some flexibility. At the company level, policies often end up being tailor-made to cope with expatriates' specific concerns. The Group's policy is to treat expatriates as locals when they are sent to compatible countries. Nevertheless, when it wishes to send an employee on an international assignment, it may have to meet his or her specific needs. A corporate manager recalls the concerns of some expatriates:

> My children have a French culture and education, and I want them to be in an international school.
> My wife has health problems, so I'd like to get this particular kind of health insurance.
> I was used to a 180 square metre apartment in Rome and for the same price, I can only afford a 35 square metre one in New York.

Negotiation with expatriates might appear time-consuming and much too focused on details for a company's HR staff. Indeed, international assignments often entail specialized, strategic and key positions, for which the company must be more flexible. This is also due to the HR structure which allows potential expatriates to negotiate, in rare instances, some non-technical aspects of the compensation package at the company level.

Harmonizing the package in the group's various companies remains a high priority. Each company is responsible for its budget. The companies can rely on the group's expertise to address certain issues, but they are the ones that implement the policies.

Expatriate compensation policies of other multinational companies may appear more advantageous than the one defined by LVMH, particularly with respect to housing allowances, car allowances and club membership allowances. The package facilitates mobility, in so far as it avoids having employees cling to a country in the hope of keeping favorable benefits. It is also a cost-effective practice and has not yet failed to attract the needed talents.

Home-based salaries may differ between individuals depending on the country and on the business group they come from. As reported by a HR manager:

> Global cash compensation for equivalent positions vary depending on the business group and on the country. Some business groups offer historically higher or lower wages than others. The purpose of LVMH's compensation policy is to reduce these differences between the various companies in the same country. Some countries offer higher wages than others because of specific labour market conditions. As a result the salary for a specific international assignment may vary according to the expatriate's previous position.

LVMH is very sensitive to international compensation market rates. It is striving to offer competitive compensation with regard to local practices. For equal qualifications, wages in the USA are much higher than in France. Relying solely on the balance sheet approach to determine the salary of a French employee sent to America would result in a low salary, not at all competitive on the American market. LVMH takes into account the local market, but does not always align its compensation with it. The reverse situation of an American sent to France is equally problematic for LVMH. The balance sheet approach implies that he or she must accept a lower gross salary according to the cost of living differential, buying power is maintained for a lower salary. Compensation first follows the balance sheet approach but then illustrates a hybrid approach in order to combine cost of living, exchange rate, housing and labour market conditions.

▶ Security Benefits

LVMH will not compromise over its expatriates' peace of mind concerning security benefits. The principle is that the chosen schemes will not penalize expatriates, i.e. they will have access to security benefits as good as those available in their home country.

Many countries have, because of their own social history, unique retirement plans. This requires the security benefits aspect of the compensation package to take into account the retirement plans expatriates have contributed to. Building compensation packages for French expatriates is particularly difficult due to the unique nature of the French retirement system.

The French retirement system is partly linked to the social security system. It is not based on capitalization like a self-funded pension scheme, but rather on a principle of wealth sharing with a contributory 'pay-as-you-go' pension scheme. Employees and employers on French territory have a legal obligation to contribute to the retirement system. In order to be eligible for full retirement benefits, a French worker must contribute to the system for 40 years. Provided that they contribute, French workers believe they are guaranteed good retirement at no risk. A French expatriate may wish to stick to the French system, particularly if he or she is to experience but one international assignment within the group. This is especially the case for older employees who have been contributing to the French system for many years. Things are different for a young graduate who is about to begin contributing to the French social security. In compatible countries, he or she can opt for another, more satisfactory, system.

Maintaining continuity between the different systems is a priority for expatriates. LVMH deems it its own responsibility. When no agreement exists between the French social security system and the host country's social security system, such as in Japan, a double contribution has to be paid. LVMH pays the French contribution to maintain the expatriates' right to retirement in France and must pay the contribution in Japan, because the Japanese system does not recognize the French one.

Most third-country nationals are dealt with differently, because many countries have implemented pension funds. LVMH analyses the employer's contribution to a retirement fund before an expatriation, it then compares it to the retirement plan of the host country. When it can find neither a solution to maintain the expatriate within the parent-country system, nor a solution in the host-country, it uses an 'off-shore' system. This 'off-shore' or international fund has no anchor in the countries involved in the move. LVMH acknowledges that there is no ideal response to the retirement issue. Generally, the parent-country scheme is maintained.

LVMH is attentive to its employees' health benefits. As a rule, the group will opt for the insurance schemes available in the host country only if they offer coverage as wide as those prevailing in the parent country. When in doubt, they provide expatriates and their families with an international insurance. Many of the group's companies have adopted this scheme. Roughly 95 per cent of the group's expatriates are covered by it. According to a C&B manager: 'Our plan is very competitive. Besides, because health is part of daily expenses and because expatriates exchange information, having various reimbursement levels would create pointless frustrations.' For life insurance and disability protection, LVMH also ensures that the level of protection is at least as good as the one before the move.

Unemployment insurance benefits reveal some intricacies. Within Europe, because of European regulation, it is not possible to maintain the system of the parent country. An employee is only entitled to receive unemployment compensation from the country he or she is working in. For a move from Europe to another country, options will depend on the host country's regulations. The group has not yet ruled on a common private scheme for all of its employees.

▶ Logistical Support

International transfer policy provides expatriates with acceptable logistical support needed to ensure smooth relocation. This amounts to support in housing search, administrative procedures, such as the lease, utilities and hook-up, etc. Relocation services also help families find schools and help them with the enrolment procedures.

International transfer experts are now working to expand their relocation services offering. Indeed, expatriates need help in finding good, experienced suppliers, such as furniture movers. It aims to provide more than financial support. These experts are writing up requirements for relocation services suppliers in order to assist companies.

▶ Support for Spouse

Very few employees turn down an international assignment. Nevertheless, LVMH acknowledges that certain employee characteristics impede their mobility. Indeed, some expatriates are hesitant to accept such a move. LVMH puts out feelers to assess employee willingness to take on international assignments. It prefers not to offer an international mobility when it anticipates reluctance or potential problems.

The issue of dual careers has become increasingly critical for any organization willing to expatriate employees. The willingness of the French to go and work abroad is rather weak compared to other nationalities in Europe. In order to cope with this issue, LVMH has agreements with other French multinational companies, which include résumé exchanges. However, they do not integrate the spouse in one of their companies to avoid any problems.

The process of identifying potential expatriates does not take into account marital and family status. Young graduates, mostly single, are keen to accept international assignments because they understand its developmental purpose. So far, most senior expatriates are males married to a non-working spouse. LVMH is well aware that this is a legacy of the past. Today, an increasing number of women are committed to their career. Today 25 per cent of expatriates are women. Besides, more and more women are appointed to high-profile positions within the group. Consequently, the number of female expatriates will rise.

▶ Intercultural Training

Intercultural training is more of a project than a reality. So far, intercultural training was not perceived as a priority because of the international profile of the expatriates. As a rule, when a candidate is sent on an international assignment, he or she has had some previous international exposure, for instance through his or her studies, or through earlier professional experience. Moreover, luxury businesses are set up in prominent locations, such as large capitals or cities like New York, Hong Kong, Singapore, or Tokyo (figure H9).

LVMH is increasingly feeling the pressure to prepare its expatriates to its international assignments in order to facilitate cross-cultural adjustment. As a result, the cross-cultural adjustment process would be accelerated. It is moving towards extending training to both the employee and his or her family. For the time being, both pre-departure and post-arrival training amounts to language courses. Moreover, an international position usually has to be filled very quickly, which leaves little time for intercultural training. Therefore very little training is provided, even for 'culturally tough' countries like Brazil or Mexico where people are expected to adjust on their own. However, they are not pressured to perform as quickly as if they had had rigorous training. Preparatory field trips are paid for and, in some cases, subsidiaries provide help to newcomers. Often, the size of the subsidiary does not allow for HR staff devoted to helping newcomers.

When intercultural training is provided, it is mainly on an ad hoc basis. It is proposed at the corporate level and some companies offer it depending on past practices or the characteristics of the host country. A Human Resource Manager stresses that: 'On international assignments, French expatriates are most likely to

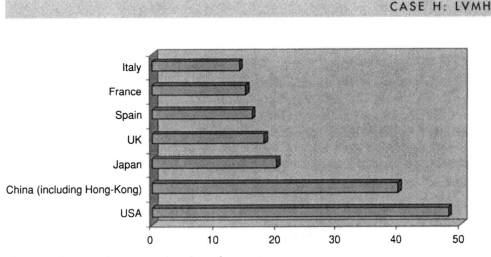

Figure H9 Key destinations/number of expatriates

find other French or European expatriates, particularly in the North America, Asia and Japan zones. To some extent, the expatriates can rely on the experience of other already adjusted expatriates.'

▶ Repatriation

Regardless of the nature of an employee's international assignment, be it an expatriation *per se* or a local contract, there is always the deliberate limitation of the length of the assignment. LVMH has always warned its companies not to create permanent expatriates. These expatriates tend to lose contact with their home country, which makes their repatriation difficult. In order to facilitate the next move or repatriation, assignments are customarily limited to a period of two to three years. When one begins a career within the LVMH group, in most cases, he or she is anchored to a home base. Throughout this career and in spite of many international moves, the home base country usually remains the same.

Even when expatriates are compensated like locals, they have a theoretical home-based salary in order to facilitate their return home. Expatriates are clearly informed that LVMH will use this theoretical home-based salary as basis for the calculation of the return compensation. The home-based anchor is upgraded each year. Upon returning home, the compensation of the international assignment is not a referent. When a promotion is granted, the home-based salary is upgraded accordingly. The theoretical home-based salary acts as a minimum guarantee referent.

The repatriation process begins at least six months to one year before the return home. It chiefly tackles career issues by addressing expatriates' concerns about return positions and career progression. Sometimes, the anticipated return is altered into another move toward a third country. Such a situation is captured by the following example: 'The Business Group Perfumes and Cosmetics recently transferred a young French expatriate from Givenchy in Sydney to manage the business group in Hong Kong. He will be on the Givenchy payroll, because the business group has no legal entity.'

Times when each company would send their employees only to their own subsidiaries are over. Thanks to the *Ready to Move* list, moves are now more frequent within a business group or between business groups. For instance, transferring employees from Veuve Clicquot France to Louis Vuitton Pacific exemplifies this inter-business group mobility. The corporate level ensures that the prevalent logic is group strategy.

▶ Looking to the Future

In spite of its young age, LVMH has already acquired an impressive expertise in international assignment policy. The International Transfer Department relies on the information flowing from LVMH's vast international networks to better determine the needs of HR decisions makers. International transfer experts can then provide a helpful framework of reference on which HR companies can rely on. Corporate HR hopes to build a global HR information system designed to provide updated and upgraded information and guidelines for HR staff around the world.

As the number of international assignments rises, the group is considering its future needs. It is looking for ways to strengthen its expertise and its ability to assist companies' HR teams. LVMH is pondering over the future of its corporate HR structure which has to cope with the group's growth and with the rising number of expatriates.

International transfer policy is an integral part of LVMH's management philosophy. It has a clear mandate to spread the group's key values which are preserving autonomy and encouraging entrepreneurship. It is also part of the process by which LVMH tries to define its future policy of career development.

The group is thinking about new ways to develop its international mobility policy so that it may better support a larger career development policy. Ultimately, the question for LVMH is to find out how such a career development strategy can better serve its strategy of international development.

Acknowledgements

This work was made possible by the cooperation of Moët-Hennessy Louis Vuitton, Paris, France. The author is very grateful for the helpful assistance of Pascal Davis-Givoiset, ESSEC MBA 2002.

Note

1   This empirical analysis constitutes a basis for discussion rather than to illustrate either effective or ineffective handling of an administrative situation.

Case Assignments

1 What are the challenges faced by LVMH regarding international mobility?
2 Why did LVMH draw up its 'International Transfer Policy' charter? Was such a policy inevitable?
3 How does LVMH tackle the issue of international adjustment? How is its international transfer policy different from those of other multinational organizations?
4 Acting as a consultant, what could be your input in order to improve LVMH's strategy of career development through international mobility?

chapter

9

Ethics and Social Responsibility in MNCs

▶ Purpose

The sheer growth in the number of MNCs, together with their increased economic and political power, has strongly accentuated the issue of their ethical responsibilities. The purpose of this chapter is to highlight core ethical challenges that MNCs and their subsidiaries must confront. The evolution in the perception of MNCs as global corporate citizens provides a general backdrop to this discussion. Thereafter various stages of ethical development are presented. Different stages in companies' development of social responsibility and ethical integrity are specified making it possible to categorize MNCs as more or less 'good global citizens'. Next, the focus is set on ethnicity and racial discrimination, corruption and bribery, child labour, and gender discrimination. This is followed by a presentation of efforts to implement and monitor corporate codes of conduct and ethics, including some specific examples of how these have been formulated in practice. Finally, we focus on whistle-blowing and loyalty, ethical absolutism versus relativism, and the relationship between profit seeking and social responsibility.

▶ The MNC as a Global Citizen

One self-evident consequence of increased globalization is that MNCs have broadened their sphere of power and influence. In Chapter 1 we indicated that some of the largest MNCs have so much economic power that in developing country settings they are capable of overshadowing the local government as the main engine of industrial development. This is one of the main reasons that ethical demands are directed at MNCs. That is not to say that ethical demands are not levelled at purely domestic firms but that they are particularly pronounced for globally visible MNCs. In particular, MNCs are experiencing a growing unwillingness among consumers in developed countries to buy goods from producers whose reputation has been tarnished either in regard to their treatment of their employees or the environment regardless of where in the world the maltreatment has occurred.

This unwillingness has undoubtedly been fuelled by the various voluntary or non-governmental organizations (NGOs) that have focused on the business conduct of MNCs worldwide. One of the most prominent of these is ATTAC but there are many other groups that are active in targeting the activities of MNCs. Traditionally, large corporations have tried to ignore such activist movements. These days few MNCs, particularly those with valuable and correspondingly vulnerable brand names, would openly persist in such an attitude. As formulated in an editorial in *Business Week*;

> [S]mart CEOs should proceed in opening a dialogue with the reformers. Many have already successfully negotiated with some of the groups. Gap Inc., Nike Inc., and others have adopted codes of conduct for their overseas plants, hiring monitors to oversee compliance. Levi Strauss Co. has ethical manufacturing standards for its overseas operations. Home Depot Inc. has adopted an eco-friendly lumber supply program with the Rainforest Action Network. Starbucks Corp. is working with Conservation International to buy coffee from farmers preserving forests. The truth is that many of the demands of the anti-globalisation groups reflect the values of middle-class consumers in the U.S. and Europe, especially the young. It may be hard, but by working with reasonable reformers of the global system, corporations can not only help others, they just might help themselves. (*Business Week*, 2001: 64)

Another feature of the past decade has been the growth of ethically oriented investment funds. Some of these have policies of avoiding investments in industrial areas such as tobacco production and the arms industry. Others have as their guiding principle not investing in firms that develop products that in any way undermine environmentally sustainable development.

MNCs are adjusting to a new set of responsibilities that go well beyond the production of goods and services in order to make profits for their shareholders. Increasingly it is expected that they display global corporate responsibility. That is they are accountable not just to their shareholders, but to a wider constituency of stakeholders which includes the local and regional communities within which they operate (Ambarao, 1993). As global 'corporate citizens' MNCs are having to accept that they will be held accountable for their impact on the economic and political development of the local communities in which they operate, as well as their employees' working conditions.

One common response from MNCs has been to create codes of conduct or 'ethical pledges' that are specific to the firm. These often feature in their annual reviews, corporate visions or strategy statements. Some have even tried to produce 'ethical audits' of their activities as part of their annual reviews that detail the ethical criteria that have influenced their investment decisions.

An example of a company that has formulated its credos and distributed it to the public is Shell through its document *People, Planet and Profits: The Shell Report 2001*. In this document the company presents its goals in this manner:

> The objectives of Royal Dutch/Shell Group of Companies are to engage efficiently, responsibly and profitably in the oil, gas, power, chemicals, renewables and other selected businesses and participate in the research and development of other sources of energy. Shell companies are committed to contribute to sustainable development. This document summarises the actions we have taken in 2001 to meet our economic, environmental and social responsibilities and describes how we are striving to create value for the future. (Shell, 2001)

Some MNCs have built their business idea and vision directly on ethical considerations. One example is the Body Shop, which has actively opposed the use of experiments and product development tests involving the use of animals. This has contributed to providing the company with a distinctly ethical image thereby making their products particularly attractive to the environmentally conscious and those concerned with animal rights.

It must be pointed out though that there is little in the way of actual legislation governing the foreign activities of developed countries' firms. One exception is the Foreign Corrupt Practices Act which the United States passed in 1977 that makes it illegal for US firms to bribe or corrupt persons in other countries. However, in countries such as Germany and France, whereas bribery within their respective national borders is a crime, its use abroad is not.

▶ Stages in Corporate Ethical Development

In table 9.1 a model containing five different stages in companies' moral development is presented, ranging from 'the amoral organization' to 'the ethical organization'. The model can be applied in two ways. First, it depicts the developmental path that a company must follow as it seeks to increase its ethical commitment and practices. Second, it can be used in a more static way, that is, as a typology or classification of different MNCs.

Stage I depicts *the amoral MNC*. Here, managers are operating according to an 'in flagrante' logic implying that as long you are not *caught* exhibiting unethical behaviour, all is well. Put differently, given that such behaviour is not uncovered there are no problems. The culture is characterized by a spirit of devil-may-care lawlessness with not even lip service paid to ethical principles or social responsibility.

Table 9.1 Stages of ethical development

Stages in Ethical Development	Management Attitude and Approach	Ethical Aspects of Corporate Culture	Corporate Ethics Artifacts
STAGE I The Amoral MNC	Get away with all you can; it's ethical as long as you're not caught; ethical violations, when caught, are a cost of doing business	Outlaw culture; live hard and fast; damn the risks; get what you can get out of it	No meaningful code of ethics or other documentation; no set of values other than greed
STAGE II The Legalistic MNC	Play within the legal rules; fight changes that affect your economic outcome; use damage control through PR when social problems occur; a reactive concern for damage to organizations from social problems	If it's legal, it's OK; work the grey areas; protect loopholes and don't give ground without a fight; economic performance dominates evaluations and rewards	The code of ethics, if it exists, is an internal document; 'don't do anything to harm the organization'
STAGE III The Responsive MNC	Management understands the value of not acting solely on a legal basis; even though they believe they could win; management still has a reactive mentality; a growing balance between profits and ethics, although a basic premise still may be cynical 'ethics pays'; management begins to test and learn from more responsive actions	There is a growing concern for corporate stakeholders other than owners; culture begins to embrace a more 'responsible citizen' attitude	Codes are more externally oriented and reflect a concern for other publics; other ethics vehicles are undeveloped
STAGE IV The Emerging Ethical MNC	First stage to exhibit an active concern for ethical outcomes; 'we want to do the right thing'; top management values become organizational values; ethical perception has focus but lacks organization and long-term planning; ethics management is characterized by successes and failures	Ethical values become part of culture; these core values provide guidance in some situations but questions exist in others; a culture that is less reactive and more proactive to social problems when they occur	Codes of ethics become action documents; code items reflect the core values of the organization; handbooks, policy statements, committees, ombudsmen are sometimes used
STAGE V The Ethical MNC	A balanced concern for ethical and economic outcomes; ethical analysis is a fully integrated partner in both the mission and strategic plan; SWOT-analysis is used to anticipate and analyse alternative outcomes	A total ethical profile, with carefully selected core values which reflect that profile, directs the culture; corporate culture is planned and managed to be ethical; hiring, training and rewards all reflect the ethical profile	Documents focus on the ethical profile and values; all phases of organizational documents reflect them

Source: Based on Reidenbach and Robin (1991).

The legalistic MNC is preoccupied with sticking to the rules and regulations, avoiding wrongdoing and violations of the laws of those countries in which it has operations. However, over and above this commitment, it is entirely reactive in relation to ethical matters. Finding legal loopholes and operating in grey areas is not considered to be amoral. In these MNCs it is evident that shareholder value is the dominant principle guiding the company. If a written code of ethics exists, this is typically an internal document and concerns the immediate interests of the organization.

Moving to stage III we find *the responsive MNC*, which takes a slightly more proactive role in its handling of ethical issues, although still being predominantly reactive. There is a notion that it may be economically profitable to go somewhat beyond the legal minimum standards that are set in each country. In that sense, there is a certain amount of 'ethical cynicism' involved. Concurrently, there is a growing concern for the multitude of stakeholders that have an interest in the conduct of the company. As a consequence there is an increasing tendency to make ethical codes and statements more externally oriented and to make them public.

The emerging ethical MNC is driven by a sincere intention to act according to ethical imperatives. To behave morally becomes a virtue and a value in itself, yet it does not penetrate the whole organization. Policies relating to ethics and codes of conduct are not fully developed and embedded in the ethical MNC's various policies and practices. However, the company may have started to produce corporate ethics artefacts, such as handbooks of acceptable conduct, internal monitoring procedures – and may have appointed ethical committees with a broad mandate.

At stage V we find *the ethical MNC* in which the ethical analysis is fully integrated in the operations, policies and organization procedures as well as in the management system. The culture is enmeshed with the moral values that the company builds on and its ethical practices are, in addition to the internal control, monitored by independent external agencies.

We shall in the next sections turn to a discussion of selected ethical issues that are of particular relevance for contemporary MNCs: ethnicity and racial discrimination, corruption and bribery, child labour and gender discrimination. This will be followed by a presentation of corporate codes of conduct, the monitoring of such codes, and whistle-blowing and loyalty. Finally, there is a discussion of the distinction between ethical absolutism and relativism.

▶ Ethnicity and Racial Discrimination

How far should an MNC go to counter racial or ethnic prejudice in the countries in which they operate? Normally, the answer would be that no kinds of such practices should be accepted within the corporation or its immediate partners. Some examples are clear-cut. There is evidence that Japanese companies have taken race into consideration when establishing factories and units in the United

States attempting to keep minority hiring to a minimum. These companies have tended to prefer geographical areas where minorities in general and blacks in particular are few. In one study it was found that Japanese companies did not establish plants within thirty miles of areas with considerable minority population concentrations: 'They ask for profiles of the community by ethnic background, by religious background, by professional makeup . . . There are demographics that they like. They like a high German content' (Cole and Deskins, 1988: 11). The result of this was the significant under-representation of Afro-Americans in Japanese car factories. As a result of this policy several Japanese MNCs in the United States have faced legal action due to complaints about discriminatory employment practices. In one case, Honda had to give almost four hundred Afro-Americans several million dollars in back pay (Hodgetts and Luthans, 1991: 446).

Yet there are other cases involving race that are more diffuse and which demand careful consideration. In contemporary times the apartheid regime in South Africa has been the most extreme case of racial discrimination in that it was based on principles of racial segregation embodied in law. Some countries chose to impose total embargoes on their companies on doing business either with or in South Africa, whereas other countries continued to do business but on the basis of particular principles. One illustration is that of the Sullivan principles that were developed in United States by the Reverend Leon H. Sullivan. He initiated meetings with US multinationals in order to develop moral principles for handling the ethical problems involved in doing business in South Africa. He succeeded in getting 12 major US MNCs to agree to abide by a code of conduct governing their operations in the country. Among the principles were non-segregation of the races in regard to all eating, comfort and work facilities, equal and fair employment for all employees, initiation of training programmes seeking to qualify non-whites for supervisory, managerial, technical and clerical jobs (Prakash Sethi and Williams, 2001). However, for many it was highly controversial that US multinationals were involved in South Africa.

Another case concerns the Norwegian, part state-owned, telecom company Telenor's operations in Malaysia. In order to be allowed to acquire majority control over the country's third largest mobile phone company, Digi, Telenor was obliged by Malaysian authorities to accept that at least 30 per cent of the shares would have to be owned by ethnic Malays. Members of the country's other ethnic groups, mainly citizens of Chinese and Indian origin, were not permitted to own more than a maximum of 9 per cent of the shares. This policy of favouring ethnic Malays, the *bumiputra*, in such contexts, was not unique to the case of Digi Telenor. Indeed the '*bumiputra* policy' is embedded in national legislation.

When asked about these conditions, one of the vice presidents of Telenor answered as follows:[1]

> This is the way Malaysian authorities do these things. We have considered the conditions and accepted them after a thorough discussion. . . . This is a part of

Malaysian reality. . . . If you go in and look at how the country is run, you will find that the authorities are very keen to secure a balance between the various ethnic groups.

This statement caused an immediate reaction from the human rights organization Amnesty International. A spokesman for Amnesty characterized Telenor's acceptance of the ethnic quota regulation as beyond belief especially because Norwegian companies have traditionally prided themselves in not having policies abroad that would be unacceptable in Norway:

Norwegian authorities have for two years been elaborating and negotiating a statement and a framework aiming at fighting ethnic discrimination and racism on all levels. Then a company with substantial government ownership accepts conditions and premises that contribute to sustaining and increasing ethnic discrimination.

The editor of the publication *Norwatch* stated that Telenor must 'be brave enough to admit that ethnicity and ownership do not belong together in a free market context'. But the debate did not stop here. Another vice president in Telenor stated that the company had no problems accepting the ownership conditions, 'since this is the way the Malaysian government tries to bring ethnic Malays into a better position compared to another economically strong ethnic group'. He furthermore drew a parallel with South Africa and Nelson Mandela's effort to create business ownership possibilities for the black population: 'This is no different from what happened when we entered South Africa. The requirement there was that the black population would have to have at least 25 per cent representation'.

A few days later, the press reported that this case could heavily damage Telenor's reputation among investors. Magne Furugard, the CEO of the Swedish investment firm, Caring Company, stated that his colleagues constantly scrutinize the degree to which specific companies their clients have invested in meet their ethical expectations. He warned that the Malaysian legislation regarding ownership quotas is in conflict with the UN's declaration of human rights that demands equal treatment of all human beings regardless of their race.

▶ Corruption and Bribery

In some countries corruption involving bribes are so widespread that it may be difficult or impossible for international companies to deal with the public authorities and local companies without becoming involved. In its most extreme form corruption is institutionalized to such an extent that public servants are dependent on such income in order to secure a standard of living above the subsistence level. Most of the countries where corruption is endemic are located in Eastern Europe, Asia and Latin America.

In the same way as the existence of corruption varies among countries, there are cross-national differences in the perception of what constitutes corruption. This was clearly indicated by a study based on a survey conducted among US, French and German managers. Considerable variations between the three groups were revealed. The managers responded to five dissimilar vignettes, including the following (Becker and Fritzsche, 1987):

> Rollfast Bicycle Company has been barred from entering the market in a large Asian country by collusive efforts of the local bicycle manufacturers. Rollfast could expect to net 5 million dollars per year from sales if it could penetrate the market. Last week a businessman from the country contacted the management of Rollfast and stated that he could smooth the way for the company to sell in his country for a price of $500,000.

Among the US managers, four out of ten considered paying this bribe to be unethical or illegal with reference to the Foreign Corrupt Practices Act. Only one out of six among the French managers viewed paying the bribe as unethical, and one out of ten German managers did. These differences may partly stem from the fact that the USA has legislation in this field that makes it a crime to bribe or corrupt officials in other countries. However, the findings also indicate that practices such as bribery and corruption are viewed dissimilarly in different countries. This is also indicated by the fact that bribes are even tax-deductible in countries such as Australia and New Zealand (Dowling, Welch and Schuler, 1999). Given these differences, some have argued that US MNCs are at a substantial comparative disadvantage since they run the risk of facing criminal prosecution if giving bribes, whereas MNCs from a number of other countries are actually given tax deductions for documented bribery expenses.

In 1993 Transparency International was founded. This is a non-governmental organization dedicated to increasing government accountability and curbing national and international corruption. It monitors and reports on global corruption and bribery and publishes its findings on an annual basis. On the basis of investigations in a large number of countries Transparency International has established a corruption index which is updated every year and is available at its website. Transparency International has also established national branches that companies can join. In a short period of time it has become a powerful force in the struggle against corruption in the world.

Since 1995, it has published the 'Corruption Perceptions Index' (CPI) which is based on several different surveys among business people, academics and risk analysts. There are 14 different surveys and at least three are required for a country to be included in the CPI. The CPI for 2001 ranked 91 countries. The top ten in respect to having little corruption were Finland, Denmark, New Zealand, Iceland, Singapore, Sweden, Canada, the Netherlands, Luxemburg and Norway (in that sequence). At the bottom of the ranking we find Bangladesh, Nigeria, Uganda, Indonesia, Kenya, Cameroon, Bolivia, Azerbaijan, Ukraine and Tanzania.

There is an obvious pattern to the ranking. The lowest levels of corruption are found in wealthy, developed nations and the highest in poor, less developed countries. High levels of corruption tend to be a feature of countries that are undergoing profound transitions, such as many of the former communist bloc states in Eastern Europe. It is worth noting that the CPI only measures corruption involving public servants or officials and that covert payments to finance political campaigns as well as money laundering and bribery involving MNCs are not included.

One of the ways Transparency International aims to reduce corruption is through its 'Islands of Integrity' concept. The basis for this is a binding agreement called an integrity pact which is signed by companies and public authorities. Company signatories commit themselves to abstaining from bribery at the same time they receive guarantees from countries' public authorities that their competitors will not be able to employ bribes to gain competitive advantage and that bidding processes will be transparent and not subject to corruption.

▶ Child Labour

It has been estimated that the exploitation of children through child labour occurs in more than two-thirds of all the countries in the world. Many of these were performing hazardous work tasks. It is important to note that the concept of child labour does not refer to children working part-time in family businesses or on farms, but to permanent employment that makes schooling either difficult or impossible. Child labour is widespread partly because children lack the resources needed to establish unions or other types of organizations that could protect them and secure their rights. It also lies in the fact that as child labour often replaces adult labour, their unemployed or under-employed parents have no choice but to force them to work.

It has to be said that many large MNCs in developed countries are no longer indifferent to the problem of child labour. What is more, their corporate codes of conduct deal with the issue in similar ways:

> Levi Strauss says child labour is not acceptable and defines a 'child' as a person under the age of fourteen or who is under the compulsory schooling age. Wal-Mart will not accept the use of child labour in the manufacture of goods that it sells. Suppliers/subcontractors must not recruit persons under the age of fifteen, or below the compulsory schooling age. If national legislation includes higher criteria, these must be applied. JC Penney will not allow the importation into the United States of merchandise manufactured by illegal child labour. The Gap states that no person under the age of fourteen may be allowed to work in a factory that produces Gap goods and that vendors must comply with local child labour laws. The FIFA [football governing body] code refers to child labour in the terms of ILO Convention 138 (i.e., children under fifteen years of age, as well as provisions for younger children in certain countries). (Golodner, 2000: 245–6)

However, as we indicated, child labour remains prevalent. In 1997 the International Labour Organization (ILO) estimated that in excess of 250 million children are child labourers (Golodner, 2000).

For advocates of cultural relativism, the degree to which this state of affairs should be condemned is not always straightforward. The following stems from an editorial in Business Week:

> Culture can be a serious problem. Child labour in factories is opposed by anti-globalization forces, but in many countries it is a major source of income, keeping families together and girls out of prostitution. Besides, it is commonly accepted on American farms today and was legal during the long period when the U.S. itself was a developing country. . . . Imposing high 21st century labour and environmental standards on developing countries runs the risk of appearing hypocritical and undermining growth. (*Business Week*, 2001: 64)

In other words, cultural relativists remind citizens of Western countries that child labour is no distant phenomenon historically in their own countries and that the idea of universal schooling is relatively recent.

▶ Gender Discrimination

Women's rights vary strongly across the world. In some cultures they are virtually non-existent in that the woman is more or less her husband's property. For instance, in Saudi Arabia women's mobility is strongly restricted. They are not permitted to drive cars or travel alone, nor can they stay in hotels or visit other people without being accompanied by a male family member. In countries, such as Pakistan and India arranged or even forced marriages are common, with 'pre-marriage' often taking place at an early age. If the woman refuses to honour the pre-marital agreement, her family is free to kill her in order to restore the 'lost honour' she has inflicted on the family members. In these cultures the position of women in regard to the labour market is very weak. In an Indian province attempts to establish a women's hospital was met with resistance and anger by local men because they wanted a veterinary hospital for their farm animals (Ramachandran, 1992). In many other Asian cultures women are generally viewed and treated as subordinate to men. Japanese and South Korean women have traditionally not continued working after getting married and not been able to reach higher-level managerial positions.

In the United States and most European countries gender equality has been established in law, yet women are significantly under-represented at managerial levels. Despite having full freedom of mobility and equal rights to education, the vast majority of women in these countries tend to earn significantly less than their male counterparts.

What are the ethical concerns of MNCs in this context and how should these be resolved? To begin with there is no doubt that MNC subsidiaries operating in fundamentalist Islamic countries or regions have virtually no degrees of freedom when it comes to treating female employees in more 'Western ways'. MNCs in Saudi Arabia cannot, for instance, insist that native female employees should be allowed to drive cars because this is the norm in Western countries. Nor could an MNC demand that in their Saudi Arabian subsidiary native women and men should work together. Likewise a subsidiary of an Arab MNC located in the United States would be obliged to adhere to the Equal Employment Opportunity (EEO) regulations that permeate US work life. In this sense there is a set of 'givens' in all contexts in the form of legal imperatives that must be abided by. However, this does not mean that MNCs should not seek out opportunities to contribute to changing discriminatory conditions, for example by providing education and training for women and by providing equal compensation for equal work regardless of gender.

▶ Codes of Conduct and Ethics

The first comprehensive international code of ethics for MNCs was elaborated in Caux in Switzerland in 1994 at a roundtable conference attended to by US, European and Japanese business people. Underlying the *Caux Principles* we can observe two fundamental ethical criteria or standards, human dignity and the Japanese principle of working together for the common good (*kyosei*):

> The Japanese concept of kyosei means living and working together for the common good – enabling cooperation and mutual prosperity to coexist with healthy and fair competition. Human dignity relates to the sacredness of value of each person as an end, not simply as the means to the fulfilment of other's purposes or even majority prescription. (Hartman, 1998)

Research has shown a marked growth in the number of MNCs adopting codes of ethics (Somers, 2001; Schwartz, 2001; Kavali *et al.*, 2001). The purpose of such codes is normally to establish an ethical climate that applies to the entire globe (Jackson, 1997; Jose and Thibodeaux, 1999).

An example of a code of conduct can be found in the Norwegian MNC Norsk Hydro, a company from which this chapter's case study is taken. It has drawn up a corporate directive called 'Community Responsibilities Attached to Industrial Development'. The directive specifies the principles and standards that give it a 'licence to operate' in local communities affected by its activities, regardless of the local level of economic development:

- Norsk Hydro supports the Universal Declaration of Human Rights and will not engage in activities that impair the enjoyment of human rights.

- Norsk Hydro will engage in open dialogue and consultation with stakeholders in local communities and elsewhere regarding impacts of company operations.
- Norsk Hydro's operations will not endanger the physical safety, security and health of members of communities affected by such operations.
- Norsk Hydro will remain neutral in respect of race, religion, gender, age, caste, cultural identity and similar factors.
- Norsk Hydro will respect the intrinsic value of diverse cultures and traditions in communities where it operates.

On a more general basis, Payne, Raiborn and Askvik (1997) recommend that ethical standards for MNCs and international operations should address six fundamental issues:

1. Organizational relations (including competitive conditions, strategic alliances and local sourcing).
2. Economic relations (including financing, taxation, transfer prices, local re-investment and equity participation).
3. Employee relations (compensation and incentives, safety and health, human rights, non-discrimination, collective bargaining, whistle-blowing, training and sexual harassment).
4. Customer relations (pricing, product and service quality, advertising).
5. Industrial relations (including technology transfer, research and development, infrastructure development and organizational stability).
6. Political relations (legal compliance, bribery, corruption, subsidies, tax incentives, environmental protection, political involvement).

Payne, Raiborn and Askvik recommend that this checklist should be applied by MNCs to analyse and systematize their ethical principles and practices each time they may enter a new country.

There are also examples of ethical codes that have been elaborated for larger groups of companies and even entire industries. A particular illustration of this is provided by the US apparel industry. In 1996 president Bill Clinton invited representatives of this industry and relevant non-governmental organizations (NGOs) to form a task force on sweatshops. The issue was how the industry could 'ensure that the products they make and sell are manufactured under decent and humane working conditions' (Golodner, 2000: 247). In addition, the industry was encouraged to provide information for consumers stating that the products are not manufactured under exploitative conditions.

On this basis the task force endeavoured to develop a common industry code partly based on existing corporate codes and partly going beyond these when necessary. This resulted in the 'White House Apparel Partnership Workplace Code of Conduct & Principles of Monitoring'. This contains elements relating to the following:

- Forced labour
- Child labour
- Harassment or abuse of employees
- Non-discrimination
- Health and safety
- Freedom of association and collective bargaining
- Wages and benefits
- Work hours and overtime compensation

Any company that chooses to adopt this Workplace Code of Conduct agrees to accept the related Principles of Monitoring, in addition to complying with the relevant laws in the country where commodities or services are produced. The same applies to a company's contractors and suppliers in that country. Thus, not only is the company itself bound by the code of conduct, but so are also the companies it does business with.

In figure 9.1 we present a code of credibility checklist containing five key questions and related issues for discussion.

In this checklist the initial focus is on who elaborates the concrete code of ethics, or more precisely, how active top management is in such efforts. Next, the question is raised as to whether standard international labour rights, human rights and environmental norms and regulations are included in the code. This is followed up by the issue of moving beyond 'the tyranny of the minimum' by adding the MNC's own internal ethical standards that supplement or exceed those stemming from international laws and regulations. A crucial point is whether and to what degree the ethical code is actively communicated to the MNC's managers and other employees. If no efforts are made to disseminate the code, no tangible results will be forthcoming. The final question relates to the monitoring of the ethical practices of the MNC and its employees. The issue of independent external insight and evaluation is critical in this context. It is to this issue we will now turn.

▶ Monitoring of Ethical Practice

One particular problem that has to be overcome if corporate and industry codes of conduct are to be effective is that of the monitoring of the actual use of such codes. There are three types of monitoring:

- internal monitoring, done by the company itself;
- hired monitoring, conducted by external consultants paid for by the company;
- independent external monitoring, often executed by NGOs and local voluntary organizations.

Question 1:
Who elaborated the code, top management or the public relations or communications function?

Issues for discussion:
It is crucial that the formulation of ethical codes is anchored in the MNC top management team. If left to the PR or communications department, it does not to the same degree become the 'property' of the top leaders. Moreover, it is symbolically important that the employees know that the ethical code or manifesto is the work of the top management.

Question 2:
Does the code include vital areas covered by key international rights, environmental standards and ILO standards?

Issues for discussion:
For most larger companies, it is vital that the standard international rights for employees' basic human rights and regulations of environmental issues are included in their ethical codes. This serves both as a signal that the organization is up to date with these international regulations and that they are taken seriously.

Question 3:
Is the code limited to the 'Tyranny of the Minimum'?

Issues for discussion:
The regulations and rights referred to above are normally interpreted as minimum standards and hence they represent the lowest level of social responsibility, that is, what we have earlier called 'social obligation'. In the short run it may seem convenient to stick to these basic regulations but at the same time that is a signal that the company does not commit itself to having an active ethical policy in these matters. Proactive companies will supplement these minimum standards with their own, more or less idiosyncratic, rules, norms and internal regulations.

Question 4:
Is the code disseminated to the individual employee and is it realized through concrete implementation steps?

Issues for discussion:
A common problem is that companies elaborate nice-sounding codes of conduct or ethics but that these remain on paper. Unless they are communicated to the individual manager and other employees they remain fairly worthless. Moreover, it is essential that the code is transformed into real action and measures – and that the way in which it is practised is closely followed by the management.

Question 5:
Is the code effectively monitored, both internally and independently by external agencies?

Issues for discussion:
An obvious minimum is that that the organization itself overlooks the practising of its ethical code, and usually this is part of the managers' jobs. Yet, the external credibility of internal evaluations is invariably fairly low. This can be compensated for by letting external agencies monitor the companies' practices on an independent basis.

Figure 9.1 Code of credibility checklist and related issues of discussion
Source: Based on Schilling (2000)

Internal monitoring carried out by employees in the MNC may to some extent be fruitful in order to ascertain that the corporate rules are followed throughout the organization. Although such monitoring may be sincerely carried out, for customers, external interest groups and the general public this is far from sufficient. Many potential customers simply will not trust internally authorized assurances that all the company's products are manufactured under ethically impeccable conditions. To some degree this also applies to the use of external consultants, most often large and renowned consulting firms. Since the work of such firms is paid for by the MNCs being monitored, the objectivity and trustworthiness are always open to being questioned.

For these reasons, there is currently an ongoing debate as to what kinds of institutions may be considered as qualified or legitimate as external monitoring agencies. Interestingly, the international consulting business has engaged itself in such activities and it appears that a new industry is under creation. A number of firms within accounting, auditing and management consulting have entered into the 'monitoring business', including PricewaterhouseCoopers, Accenture, KPMG and Ernst & Young. They have elaborated and implemented sets of social monitoring measures aimed at analysing the degree to which companies act in accordance with their own codes of conduct. Critics have contended that these firms lack the necessary experience and competencies to successfully monitor and evaluate labour conditions and violations of human rights. Monitoring these activities not only demands thoroughgoing knowledge of international labour conventions and rights but also an expertise in field-methods that these companies are unfamiliar with:

> Large accounting and consulting firms are too close to the company and too far from the local workers in plants in El Salvador, Indonesia, or China where labour violations occur. These firms are well suited to look at pages of figures, analyse data, and check for quantifiable code violations. They are ill suited for the kinds of on-the-ground detection systems needed to uncover violations of worker rights. Serious violations of freedom of association and common forms of harassment of workers often go undetected by auditors who come into an area, visit a plant for a shorter period, then leave. Independent monitors made up of local, respected nongovernmental groups – rooted in local communities and having the trust of employees – are better qualified to detect the essential, but less easily observed, elements in the workplace which relate to human respect, non-discrimination, the right to freely associate and to work in a safe environment free from fear. Local human rights and religious groups know the local social and cultural contexts, speak the local language(s), are likely to have the trust of local workers, and are ultimately accountable to their community. (Schillling, 2000: 232–233)

Essentially the same points were made in a *New York Times* editorial some years ago:

> The sneaker manufacturer Nike recently sent a civil rights leader and former United Nations representative, Andrew Young, to tour some of its factories in Asia.

Mr. Young sure had the best of intentions, but his report, which concluded that Nike had done a 'good job', revealed the problems with this kind of monitoring. His factory visits were mainly scheduled in advance and done with Nike's own translators. The better way is local, truly independent monitors who speak the language, can make unannounced visits and enjoy the trust of a largely young, female, vulnerable work force. (*New York Times*, 1997)

Indeed, empirical research indicates that non-governmental organizations (NGOs) are particularly effective at monitoring codes of conduct precisely because of their independent status (van Tulder and Kolk, 2001).

▶ Whistle-Blowing and Loyalty

In all types of organizations there is a tendency to punish or 'kill' the messenger who brings bad news. This syndrome damages companies in that the information that could create a basis for learning and therefore change is suppressed.

The multinational consulting firm KPMG has emphasized this in its internal 'Business Ethics Practice':

KPMG has established a Business Ethics practice. Its function is to help devise and evaluate management systems that, in turn, help an organization's employees *know* what's right, *do* what's right, and when they're not sure, feel confident the organization will support them if they *ask* what's right. The goal is to help clients create an environment where:

- good people aren't afraid to step forward and communicate concerns;
- where the policy and practice is not to 'shoot the messenger' but to fix the problem;
- and where bad news is sought out so that small problems can be addressed before they become big ones.

(Swenson, 2000: 4)

Transparency International emphasizes the importance of whistle-blowing and regard this as one of the most efficient means to countering corruption. Yet, there are many problems connected to whistle-blowing. One key problem is that most employees are loyal and committed to their employer, superiors and colleagues. This may cause individuals to ignore violations of ethical norms and rules by just 'looking in another direction'. The advice given by Transparency International is to initiate discussion within the organization about how existing complaints and reporting mechanisms work and to consider whether there is room for initiatives to improve these mechanisms.

However, cross-national contexts create pitfalls that domestic contexts do not. An illustration of the kind of pitfall that must be taken into consideration can be found in the differences in laws and the types of penalties between countries. These can put the issue of whistle-blowing into a rather dramatic and very uncomfortable perspective: 'Donaldson cites an example of a U.S. expatriate in China who followed her firm's policy on employee theft. On catching an employee stealing, she fired the employee and notified the relevant authorities. She was horrified to later learn that the employee had been executed' (Dowling, Welch and Schuler, 1999: 280).

▶ Ethical Absolutism or Relativism?

Fundamental to any discussion of ethics is whether there exist absolute moral imperatives. According to proponents of ethical absolutism there are certain universal values that are so fundamental that they should under no circumstances be violated, no matter what the cultural traditions in a country may be. Examples of such imperatives are that one should not torture or kill other people, that no person should be imprisoned without a fair trial and, more generally, that human rights, such as freedom of expression, should not be violated.

A key aspect to this issue is whether there exists a set of universal moral principles that is accepted by all cultures. Adherents of ethical absolutism argue that there are in fact many indications that this is the case:

> Thus ethical standards may be universal: honesty, integrity and protection of society, customer and employees. Others may remain culturally specific: reciprocity (gift-giving), whistle-blowing, profit maximization, social welfare, patent protection and price-fixing. These reflect cultural differences in importance placed on what is good for the group, rather than what is good for the individual, on achievement rather than belonging, and on social harmony rather than adherence to abstract principles. (Dowling, Welch and Schuler, 1999: 258)

Dowling, Welch and Schuler also note that while differences can be found between Western and Eastern philosophical traditions, these traditions share four fundamental core human values: good citizenship, respect for human dignity, respect for basic rights, and equity.

Furthermore, they note that a large number of comparative studies have been conducted that have uncovered only modest variations between cultures in respect to fundamental ethical beliefs: 'What differences existed between members of the various cultural groups, appeared to be more a function of differences in their reasoning and decision-making rather than core ethical values' (Dowling, Welch and Schuler, 1999: 303).

They also refer to Donaldson (1996) who has linked the Western values of individual freedom and human rights to the Japanese value of living and working together for the common good (*kyosei*) and the Muslim imperative of giving to the poor (*Zakat*).

Applications of core human values to specific duties of multinationals include the adoption of adequate workplace and environmental health and safety standards, the payment of basic living wages, equal employment opportunity, refraining from the use of child labor, providing basic employee training and education, and allowing workers to organize and form unions. Many multinationals now place considerable importance on being regarded as good global citizens and have initiated action to address public concerns about the environment and human rights. (Dowling, Welch and Schuler, 1999: 280)

However, other researchers claim that although there may be similarities in ethics across cultures, formulations of corporate and business ethics must be regarded as culturally specific. For instance, Moon and Woolliams (2000) contend that placing too great an emphasis on rational and analytic conceptions of reality may serve to hamper the development of syntheses and emotions. In addition to influencing the way business can be done across borders, this has an impact on the resolution of ethical dilemmas internationally. A consequence of this is that MNCs must put efforts into monitoring and maintaining an overview of various ethical practices in different countries of operation. On this basis it has been recommended that one should create a framework of ethical behaviour for each country 'to clarify the issues and to provide the starting point in working together to develop mutually acceptable ethical standards. This helps managers to recognize where there are differences and to understand the reasons for these differences' (Dowling, Welch and Schuler, 1999: 258).

▶ Profit Seeking and Social Responsibility

Another ongoing debate relates to whether being socially responsible and enacting ethical codes of conduct is compatible with creating wealth for the company's owners. According to neoclassical economics, or for that matter Marxist economic theory, there is no latitude for actions that conflict with profit maximization. Other theories suggest, however, that in reality companies also try to ensure their legitimacy on a broader societal level. This is especially the case for large MNCs because their size makes them particularly visible and their cross-national operations expose them to conflicting ethical principles.

It should also be noted that the norms related to profit seeking vary considerably between countries. While the United States has an individualistic profit-oriented economic ideology, there are many countries characterized by collectivistic cultures and traditions, often in the form of paternalism. As noted by Schneider and Barsoux (1997: 239):

> In Portugal, one may find a more or less explicit theory of the firm including the belief that it exists to take care of workers. This theory reflects values of paternalism (hierarchy) and collectivism which makes the idea of layoffs in economic downturn particularly difficult to accept or implement. Moreover this is reinforced by law. For

many Europeans and Asians, Americans are seen as behaving unethically when closing factories, laying off workers and neglecting their social obligations. This lack of social conscience is what is perceived as 'harsh capitalism'. It comes as a shock to many to see the huge gap between the rich and the poor in the United States, or the ratio of CEO to employee salary (Japan 17:1, Europe 21:1, US 155:1), taken as evidence of unethical exploitation.

Thus subsidiaries of MNCs have to take into account host country attitudes to profit-making as well as other values, such as the importance of taking care of employees and their families. In different countries, dissimilar stakeholders may have differing views as to what obligations the MNC and its subsidiaries should comply with. Hence, the heavy emphasis on producing maximum returns for shareholders, which is a credo in much of the business life in the United States, may be viewed as unethical in other countries.

At the corporate level, the real test of ethical principles occurs when there is direct conflict between these principles and profit making. Until a conflict arises, the principles may be no more than window dressing. Levi-Strauss is a company that has encountered such conflicts:

> Acts of corporate social responsibility may in fact be the consequence of profitability rather than the cause. It is easy to be magnanimous when things are going well. The real test is when there is a choice between acting ethically and making a profit, as in the case of the decision of US jeans company, Levi-Strauss, to pull their $40 million business out of the lucrative Chinese market in protest against human rights violations. While being a family-held business means that there is less need to worry about shareholders, Levi-Strauss has a long tradition of upholding core values (called aspirations) that have been promoted by family members over several generations. (Dowling, Welch and Schuler, 1999: 241; see also *Business Week*, 1994)

Creating a sustained and consistent ethical practice may not always be in conflict with the MNC's long-term interests. On the contrary, it may in fact generate a common goodwill and positive reputation so that ethics is good for business. Convincing companies about this is another matter. A current illustration can be found in the fruit business where well-established companies have rejected ILO employment rules and standards as well as the need to protect rain forests until other companies within the business have accepted them and used that in promoting their own produce.

▶ Summary

In this chapter, we have emphasized the need for MNCs to establish and nurture legitimacy among their various stakeholders and the groups that are affected by their operations. Today there is an increasing social commitment among consumers and new activist groups and NGOs have been established to tap into this commitment by monitoring the activities of MNCs. We have provided a typology for the different stages of ethical development in companies. Key ethical challenges facing MNCs and their subsidiaries have been discussed along with criteria for the classification of MNCs in regard to the 'good corporate citizens' concept. The importance of monitoring the implementation of ethical codes was also discussed.

Attached to this chapter is a case study featuring Norsk Hydro, a Norwegian MNC, and its venture in India, the Utkal venture. This project, which Norsk Hydro has recently withdrawn from, included the establishment of a bauxite mine and an aluminum-refining factory in the Rayagada region of Orissa in East India. It had significant social consequences and was therefore met with considerable local resistance. The case study illuminates key ethical dilemmas that MNCs regularly have to confront.

Note

1 The quotes have been translated from articles in the newspaper *Dagens Næringsliv*, August 14, 15 and 20, 2001.

Norsk Hydro's Utkal Venture in Orissa, India

Siri Ann Terjesen

▶ Introduction

This case will begin with a brief overview of the Norsk Hydro ASA's (hereinafter Hydro) Utkal Alumina International (hereinafter Utkal) project in Orissa, India, followed by cultural and ethical analyses and recommendations for next steps. Previous research suggests that corporations desire practitioner insights on this intersection of culture and ethics (e.g., Donaldson, 1989). Theory will be balanced with press releases and personal interviews with Hydro corporate offices and NGO/watch groups. The case is set in June 2001 when Hydro was still a 45 per cent shareholder. The focus will be limited to Hydro though other joint venture partners are Canadian Alcan and the Indian Aluminum Company, Indal (owned by conglomerate Indian business house Hindalco), with 35 per cent and 20 per cent ownership respectively.

Hydro was selected as this multinational corporation (MNC) has begun to engage in rigorous dialogue regarding ethical challenges and corporate social responsibility (CSR). The Utkal project site juxtaposes this ethical rhetoric with the real and continual dilemmas faced since project inception in 1993. In 2001, Indian police killed three villagers and severely injured eight others during a non-violent protest against Utkal activities.

Case overview

With an investment of US$1 billion, the Utkal project will establish a bauxite mine at the Baphlimali plateau and an alumina-refining factory in the Rayagada

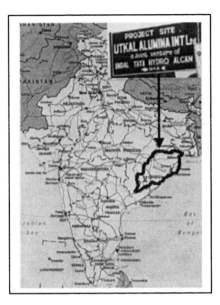

Figure II Map of India showing location of the Utkal project

district of Orissa, East India. The project is expected to supply over thirty years of alumina production for export: 1 million tons in the first phase and 2.5 million tons during the second phase. This will extract an estimated 173 million tons over a 30-year period. These alumina exports will help to meet the burgeoning international demand (4–5 per cent yearly increase) for this strong, ductile light metal. Utkal implementation is expected to begin in mid-2001, with the first production milestone set for 2005.

Meanwhile, the Utkal venture has stirred massive international controversy due to the potential human and environmental consequences. In order to acquire land, 750 people in three villages (Kucheipadar, Korala, and Komphora) will be forced to move from their homes. Approximately five hundred others will lose land and tens of villages will have reduced access to common resources such as water and agricultural and grazing lands. In total, NGOs estimate 60,000 people will be directly or indirectly negatively impacted by the Utkal venture. Most of these local inhabitants are farmers and approximately 60 per cent percent belong to native tribes in the lowest Hindu castes. Within the eastern state of Orissa (where the Utkal venture is located), 44 per cent of the population live below the poverty line, 51 per cent are illiterate, and 47 per cent do not have access to electricity, safe drinking water, and toilets. Overall, India is ranked 129th of 174 countries on the UNDP survey of human development which account for well-being components such as life expectancy, education, and gender equality. This low placement is due in part to limited government spending (just 5.1 per cent of GDP) on health and education (see table II for quality of life data.; table I2 and table I3 for macroeconomic details).

Table I1 Quality of life in India

Literacy rate %, men over 15	67
Literacy rate %, women over 15	39
Life expectancy, 1995–2000	62.6
Number of men per 100 women	106.9
Defense spending (% of GDP)	3.3
Corruption index (10 = least corrupt)	2.9
Income inequality (ratio of highest 20% to lowest 20%)	5.0

Table I2 Macroeconomic data for emerging market economies: India (1997)

1997 GDP: 1,599 in US $ Billions
1997 GDP per capita: 370 in US $
1990–7 Growth in GDP: 6.0
1990–7 Inflation: 8.8
Govt. as a percentage of 1996 GDP: 15.8
SOEs as a percentage of GDP in 1985–1990: 13.4
SOEs as a percentage of GDP in 1990–1996: 13.4
Trade as a percentage of GDP in 1987: 3.9
Trade as a percentage of GDP in 1987: 4.1
1997 tariff rate: 27.7
FDI as a percentage of 1997 GDP: 0.2

Table I3 Size of the Indian economy (1998)

Population (millions)	980
Surface Area (thousand sq. km.)	3,288
Population density (people per sq. km.)	330
GNP ($ billions)	427.4
GNP Rank	11
GNP Average annual growth rate % (87–88)	6.2
GNP per capita $	440
GNP per capita rank	161
GNP per capita average annual growth rate (87–8)	4.3
PPP GNP $ billions	2,018[a]
Per capital $	2,060[a]
Rank	151

Note: [a] These estimates are based on regression.

Environmental groups are also concerned with the effects to the land. Estimates differ. The watch group, One World, claims that the 1,750 hectares needed for facilities would result in the razing of 100 hills to the ground, and the drying up of 700 streams and numerous forests and grasslands as an area of 130,081 hectares morphs into a 'barren desert'. Meanwhile, Utkal contends that a far smaller area of land will be raised and only 10 per cent of the Bahra Nadi river (in the driest year) could be used. Utkal planted approximately 80,000 trees in the year 2000. They expect to plant a few million trees in the area. Moreover, the estimated 2 million tones of industrial sludge produced each year will silt up potable water resources and other reservoirs. Utkal contends that there will be no silting of resources, the project will utilize dry stacking with liners and collection pond and water recycling. Norwegian consultants from the Christian Michelsen Institute (CMI) initially approved the environmental assessment. However, CMI's request for more time to perform a complete analysis of social impacts was denied. Utkal's sponsors are no strangers to previous environmental catastrophes. The Indian State Pollution Control Board reports that Indal's Hirakud plant emits .5 million kg of fluorine each year – contaminating shallow ground water and soil. Hydro's S&S PVC-compound plant in Tamil Nadu, South India, was found to have 'two sets' of standards governing health, safety, and the environment. In this case, Norwatch reported the use of cadmium in the production process, the provision of asbestos gloves for workers, and the lack of an adequate waste treatment centre. All of these conditions are permissible in India, but outlawed in Norway.

Government institutions (with or without proper resource and borrowing privileges)[1] approved the project, and police and local 'authorities' have attempted to quell the non-violent village protestors. Increasingly violent measures have been used to force villagers to sign away land against their will at minimal, if any, repayment. Meanwhile, Hydro's promises to provide jobs, enable open communication, protect and enhance human welfare have generally fallen far short of expectations. Hydro contends that international NGOs have teamed with local organizations to oppose the development on political and ideological grounds.

Timeline (as of June 2001)

The following is a timeline of major events:

- 1970s: Geological survey discovers 'exceptionally rich mineral deposits' in the form of 54 meters thick of bauxite ore over a 15 square km area along India's east coast. This find accounts for 70 per cent of the country's bauxite and increased India's previous reserves estimation by a factor of six.
- 1993: Site surveys begin and the project is initially described to villagers as a malaria-prevention exercise.
- 1994: Utkal partnership is officially formed and local 'officials' began buying or seizing up land on behalf of Utkal.
- January 1998: Kucheipadar villagers set up a roadblock to prevent Utkal employees and government authorities from accessing village property. Shortly thereafter, the police destroy the roadblock and injure 17 non-violent village protestors.

- March 1998: Two Utkal employees use violence to stop further demonstrations. They were later fired.
- December 1998: Three Norsk Hydro employees are surrounded by villagers and forced to sign a protest letter renouncing the project.[2]
- October 2000: A cyclone kills 9000 across East India, though none in the Utkal region. Hydro donates one million rupees to relief efforts.
- December 15, 2000: A small number of Indian authorities, police, and journalists (writing pro-government articles) come to the Maikanch village to intimidate villagers. One of the journalists misbehaved 'with utmost contempt and vulgarity' with an 18-year-old girl. The girl and villagers are upset, and began to throw stones at the police entourage. Outnumbered, the police flee, but warn of dire consequences in the future.
- December 16, 2000: Indian police return the village with an armed force. They get out of cars and demand to see the men, 'We have got firing orders and we will put at least a few people to sleep.' The police begin to open fire on the unarmed Maikanch villagers – killing three and seriously injuring eight.
- December 18, 2000: Hydro's press release states, 'The partners in Utkal Alumina will now collectively evaluate the violent incident's impact on the development project.'
- December 18 and 19, 2000: Pro-mining and UAIL-sponsored group vandalizes most of the Agragamee (the local NGO) property.
- January 2001: A report to the President of India finds that, 'The Maikanch firing was pre-meditated, preplanned and has been done at the behest of pro-mining lobby consisting of the company, local politician apparently with support from state leadership and local police and administration officials.'
- January 29, 2001: Hydro press statement promises to reduce activities 'until acceptance from a majority of local stakeholders is manifested and a dialogue established with all organized groups that in a significant way represent these stakeholders.'
- April 2001: A Norwatch newsletter contends that Hydro is aware of who was involved in the murder. A Hydro representative is quoted as having said, 'I know who it was [behind the police action that led to the shootings] . . . I cannot tell you, because I would very much like to continue my work here in India.'[3]
- Mid-2001: Implementation is expected to begin (according to a report which pre-dates 12/2000 massacres and 1/2001 press statement)
- 2002: Final investment decision expected (according to a report which pre-dates 12/2000 massacres and 1/2001 press statement)
- 2005: First production expected (according to a report which pre-dates 12/2000 massacres and 1/2001 press statement)[4]

What has caused this downward spiral of distrust and tension that has degenerated to violence and death? This case will first examine cultural differences and

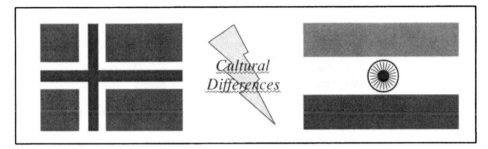

Figure 12 Cultural differences between Norway and India

ethical implications for project planning and implementation. Recommendations for immediate action are followed by a conclusion summarizing findings and suggesting implications for further research.

▶ Cultural Analysis

> Coming into India with a background in Norwegian culture and industry is hard. No question. There are no easy answers to the questions we are facing with regard to Utkal. (Hydro CEO Egil Myklebust)[5]

Culture is a learned, programmed set of common values, motivations, symbols, history, geography, philosophy, language, and preferences which gives identity and is long lasting (Falkenberg, 2001). It is important to analyse culture as this imbedded mental programming forms the process by which people solve problems (Hofstede, 1984; Trompenaars, 1993). While disparity among members of a particular culture is acknowledged; generally, divergence within one culture is considerably less than the differences present between two cultures. Furthermore, India has maintained a remarkably stable set of values and ideas over the past centuries. Hydro CEO Egil Myklebust and other Hydro executives often referred to the need for 'cultural considerations' when operating abroad, yet there is never any mention of specific cultural issues and challenges (figure 12). This section will provide a basic analysis of differences between Norwegian and Indian culture using Hofstede's four dimensions (Power Distance, Uncertainty Avoidance, Masculinity–Femininity, and Individualism–Collectivism) as a framework. This interpretation will be supplemented by other research and a general introduction to specific culture-driven issues that Hydro may face in their host country.[6]

Power distance

Power distance is the extent to which the less powerful individuals in a society accept inequality in power and consider it to be normal. India has a very high

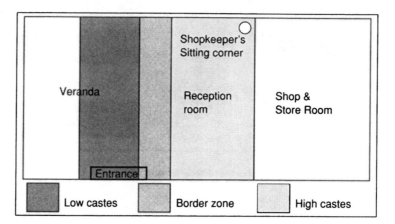

Figure 13 Untouchability: example from a shop
Source: Lunheim (1994)

power distance (77) compared to Norway (low at 27) on a scale of 11–95 (Hofstede, 1984). Thus, Indians are much more willing to accept inequalities. Psychological distance and social interactions between different groups in Indian society are contingent upon age, seniority, socio-economic class, caste affiliation, religion, and other factors (Gopalan and Stahl, 1998). There is a widespread notion of untouchability whereby low or unscheduled caste members should generally not come into contact with those of higher castes (see figures 13 and 14 for Lunheim's models of inter-caste social encounters that are context dependent). A company may face some risk when appointing a lower caste person to a supervisory position over a member of a higher caste (Terpestra and Davis, 1991). Cultural differences regarding power distance might also be linked to Indians' widespread sense of fatalism translating into a greater tolerance for poverty (Srinivas, 1971).

Norwegians, meanwhile, have been socialized in an egalitarian society characterized by the provision of capabilities and resources to achieve functioning and happiness. Scandinavians believe that investments in equality are desirable both as a means and as an end in producing a healthier, happier, and more well educated workplace which, in turn, drives efficiency (Falkenberg, 1997). Thus, Norwegians are more inclined to invest in preventative and safety net institutions to guarantee equality.[7]

On the project level, the Orissa villagers generally all belong to one of the lowest castes or unscheduled castes. As such, they are constantly subject to the will and pressure of Brahmin high caste political representatives and corporate managers. Norwegian organizations (including Hydro) operate under a flat hierarchy, which is not appreciated by Indian managers who are accustomed to a tall bureaucracy. India is the seventh most hierarchical corporate culture, Norway the fourth least, following the USA, Canada (e.g. Utkal partner Alcan), and Denmark (Trompenaars, 1993) (see figure 15 for Trompenaars' triangular hierarchy model).

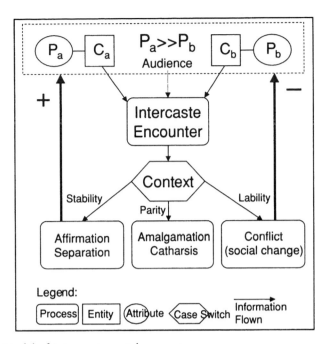

Figure 14 Model of inter-caste social encounters
Source: Lunheim (1994)
Note: This diagram illustrates that the interaction between two villagers of different and unequal castes ($Ca \neq Cb$) and different caste specific purities ($Pa \neq Pb$) depends first on caste differences, but also on the actors' attributes, the audience's presence and nature, and – most importantly – the context or interactional climate of the encounter

Masculinity–femininity

Masculinity describes the extent to which a society accepts the assertiveness, competitiveness, and the accumulation of material wealth as its most important values. Once again, India (56) and Norway (8) fall at opposite ends of the 5–95 spectrum (Hofstede, 1984). Indians operate forcefully in a male dominant environment. Meanwhile, Norway is a 'feminine' nurturing welfare state offering equal opportunities regardless of gender.

On the project site, tough Indian operatives have implemented Utkal plans. For example, police middlemen wield deadly weapons. The chief of police in one village doesn't mince words when he talks about putting an end (often violently) to protestors, 'Of course there will be resistance, and we have to tackle it when it arises.' A local authority is alleged to have said, 'If you raise your head, we know how to crush that . . . we have got firing orders and we will put at least a few people to sleep,' before killing three villagers and severely wounding eight others.

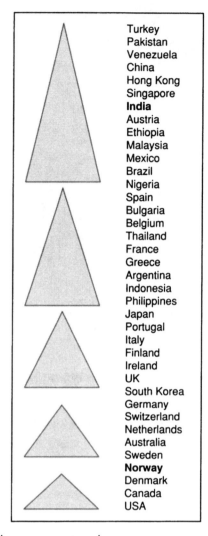

Turkey
Pakistan
Venezuela
China
Hong Kong
Singapore
India
Austria
Ethiopia
Malaysia
Mexico
Brazil
Nigeria
Spain
Bulgaria
Belgium
Thailand
France
Greece
Argentina
Indonesia
Philippines
Japan
Portugal
Italy
Finland
Ireland
UK
South Korea
Germany
Switzerland
Netherlands
Australia
Sweden
Norway
Denmark
Canada
USA

Figure 15 Hierarchical management modes
Source: Trompenaars (1993). Reprinted with permission

Norwegians are less confrontational and deliberate longer; the latest Hydro press statement stresses the need for dialogue before activities are extended. Related Scandinavian values include consensus, helpful attitude, harmony and conflict balance and cooperation and competition balance (Falkenberg, 1997).

Trompenaars (1993) has collected relevant data on perceptions of welfare provisions to displaced persons: Again, the Norwegians at Hydro may face a different perception of the need to take care of the interests of relocated villagers. Trompenaars asked respondents from India and Norway on the somewhat related idea of perceptions of the company's responsibility to provide housing for employees. Only 46 per cent of Indians believed a company held this responsibility, compared to 77 per cent of Norwegians.

Masculine cultures are often dominated by traditional gender roles such as those found in India where men rule the work place and women stay at home. This is particularly evident in rural settings. Research has highlighted the potentially serious implications from employment of women in India (Liddle and Joshi, 1986). Furthermore, multinationals might wish to exercise great care when assigning women to executive positions in Hinduism-dominated cultures (Asheghian and Ebrahimi, 1990). Orissa village women have been systematically denied access to training and means of economic self-sufficiency. Hydro managers, no doubt acting from a self-reference of empowered women in their home country, have introduced training and development programs to increase the station of women. These directives have generated both encouragement and negative reactions from villagers. Undeterred, Hydro has promoted its pro-women activities by arguing that women who can read, write, and earn additional income can provide better for their children.

Individualism–collectivism

The Individualism-Collectivism dimension describes the extent that societies focus on taking care of one's self or looking out for one another in a tight family clan. Hofstede (1984) found Norwegians to be more individualistic (69) than their Indian counterparts (48) on a scale of 12–91. *Baradari* is a Hindu word which describes this strong need for joint family or brotherhood. It can often lead to nepotism as businessmen feel obliged to favour family members when hiring (Terpstra, 1978). As particularists, Indians look for specific circumstances such as family or friend relationships which are stronger than an abstract rule of dealing equally and fairly in all cases. In the following dilemma, Norwegians responded 97 per cent, Indians 53 per cent that their friend has no right to expect a false testimony (Stouffer and Toby, 1951).

> You are riding in a car driven by a close friend. He hits a pedestrian. You know he was going at least 35 miles per hour in an area of the city where the maximum allowed speed is 20 miles per hour. There are no witnesses. His lawyer says that if you testify under oath that he was only driving 20 miles per hour it may save him from serious consequences.

Thus, Indians appear to have a stronger collective loyalty to friends and family. Similarly, they attach long-term allegiance to jobs, and do not appreciate when a job offer has been extended and then rescinded (Gopalan and Stahl, 1998). Unfortunately, Hydro is perceived to have broken many promises in this regard, further aggravating cultural tensions.

The collectivism framework may extend to interpretation of shared, traditional lands. Orissa villagers believe that land is inherited through generations as the 'womb of our motherland' and cannot be sold. As the folk song of one 16-year-old Orissa village boy pleads:

> Hey company and government!
> We are aware;
> Don't try to cheat us.
> Hear, hear, in our own village we are the government.
> In our village we will judge;
> Our land, our water cannot be traded,
> The earth is ours, the earth is ours.

The Baphimali hill has religious significance, particularly during the January festival of Pausha. The villagers have said they would not take want to mine this hill, even if they received profits for it. One villager remarked that the hill should not be ripped up because if you take the brain from a head, the person will not survive.

Village thinking could also be attributed to a cyclical time orientation. Indians view time as an infinite loop – a constant cycle of birth, death, and reincarnation. This mindset may lead to increased pride and attention to the maintenance of traditional places and beliefs for future generations (Sinha, 1990).

On the other hand, Norwegian executives have funded this project on the very premise that the land – and with it, the villagers – can be bought. Norsk Hydro describes itself as 'an industrial company based on the use of natural resources, with the aim of meeting needs for food, energy and materials. Hydro intends to create growth and development where the company can achieve good profitability through strong competitiveness.' The website highlights the motto, 'Transforming resources into the necessities of life.' This also begs the question, what about the lost necessities of life in resource-plenty, institution-deprived host countries?

Uncertainty avoidance

Uncertainty avoidance is the extent to which individuals within a culture are frustrated by unstructured, unpredictable situations. India has low uncertainty avoidance (40), indicating a willingness to accept personal risk. Norway, meanwhile, has average uncertainty avoidance (50) on a scale of 8–112 (Hofstede, 1984).

Hydro may have solicited a local partner for the venture in order to alleviate the risk of operating in an unknown environment. As Ole Lie, one of Hydro's Utkal executives, stated in my interview, 'It has been said that when a person comes to India, he knows nothing. After 6 to 12 months, he knows everything. And from then on he becomes more and more uncertain about what he knows.' Clearly, from Hydro's standpoint, truly local input was an imperative complement to Hydro and Alcan's competence as international industry leaders with proven technology, capacity for economies of scale, and other transferable resources.

India's willingness to accept increased risk may be due in part to a different control nature. According to one expert, if you're an Indian 'you can commit to a deadline – but always in the back of your mind is the thought that it'll be nice if it happens, but I can't totally control this' (Frazee, 1998). Furthermore, Hofstede (1984) finds that this low uncertainty avoidance is also expressed in less formal control systems.[8]

Cultural mindset

> Once upon a time there was a great flood, and involved in the flood were two creatures, a monkey and a fish. The monkey, being agile and experienced, was lucky enough to scramble upon a tree and escape the raging waters. As he looked down from his safe perch, he saw the poor fish struggling against the swift current. With the very best of intentions, he reached down and lifted the fish from the water. The result was inevitable. (Adams, 1969: 22–4)

Initially, Hydro took a patronizing view of their responsibilities, implementing Norwegian-culture mindset policies. The company had previous success operating with this framework: communities such as Porsgrunn, Norway, have happily relied on Hydro's fatherly-like attention and support. Several years later, CEO Myklebust speaks bluntly about the effectiveness of this strategy at Utkal, 'I can say a lot of positive things about Norwegians and their sincere desire to help people who are not well off. But I am not convinced that we always know what is best for a developing society.' Thus, Myklebust is clearly concerned with Hydro's placement on the strategic yardstick balance between local cultural attitudes and a universal set of values. What can Hydro (as the monkey) do for Utkal residents (the fish)?

Clearly, people from different cultures do not generally have the same values. Existing literature suggests that these values are linked to ethical beliefs (Hofstede, 1984; Schlegelmilch and Robertson, 1995). Thus, an understanding of a society's values should help MNCs and host countries to minimize unethical behaviour. The following section will examine how these different cultural values are linked to ethical interpretations.

▶ Ethical Analysis

> I know what I have done, and your honor knows what I have done. Somewhere between my ambition and my ideals, I have lost my ethical compass. (Jeb Stuart Magruder testifying at Watergate, June 1974)

Ethics help us to determine right from wrong, providing a standard that is relative to our culture. These frameworks focus on acts and a person's character – setting

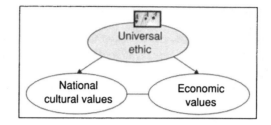

Figure 16 Universal ethics

behavioural rules that guarantee rights, justices, and happiness. As with culture, ethics can be expressed as a spectrum from cultural relativism (the equality of ethics across all cultures) to moral absolutism (one universally acceptable set of moral beliefs and values) (Donaldson, 1994). It appears as if cultural relativism is a limited perspective as Norway and India share few agreed-upon common values and principles. Furthermore, the nature of the global economy implies the need for another yardstick that is specific neither to time nor place such as the year 2001 in Orissa, India.

The universal moral compass must mitigate universal ethics with national cultural values (as examined previously) and economic motivations (figure 16); enabling universal values to trump inadequate local cultural or economic market considerations (Falkenberg, 1996).[9] For example, the universal ethic of honesty must trump local Indian practices of corruption.[10] A summary of other risks of doing business can be found in table 14. In this instance, Utkal has a 'no bribe' policy. Hydro excutive Ole Lie states that this guiding principle begins from the first solicitation, 'Never pay the first bribe.' He also believes that Utkal is 'highly respected everywhere' for not making payoffs. Norwatch and CorpWatch sources suggest otherwise – insisting that authorities are bribed through less direct channels.

Hydro and other MNCs must establish and consistently apply a universal ethical standard. This section will review and analyse the five approaches defined by Falkenberg: (1) equality; (2) just institutions; (3) rights and duties; (4) principles of integrity; and (5) responsibility.

Equality

Equality entails that individuals have equal moral worth, regardless of age, gender, race, religion, looks, language, and sexual orientation. As discussed previously, India and Norway differ greatly in their perspectives on power distance and masculinity–femininity cultural parameters. Furthermore, India has approximately 37 million 'missing women' (Sen, 1999). MNCs must act in a manner that guarantees equality of moral worth and opportunities – not equality of outcome such as equal pay or wealth for all.

Table 14 Risks of operating in developing countries

Types of Impact ⇓	Source of Risk	
	Actions of legitimate government authorities	Events caused by actors outside the control of government
Voluntary loss of control over specific assets without adequate compensation	• Total or partial expropriation • **Forced divestiture** • **Confiscation** • Cancellation or unfair calling of performance bonds • **Withdrawal of licenses or ownership of property**	• War • Revolution • **Terrorism** • Strikes • Extortion
A reduction in the value of a stream of benefits expected from the foreign controlled affiliate	• Non applicability of 'national treatment' • Restriction in access to financial, labour, or material markets • Controls on prices, outputs or activities • Currency and remittance restrictions • **Value added and export performance requirements** • Sudden cancellation or change in agreed terms of a contract • Bureaucratic blockages	• Nationalistic suppliers or buyers • Threats and disruption to operations by hostile groups • **Externally induced financial constraints** • Externally imposed limits on imports and exports • **Corruption/nepotism and 'cronyism'** • Ethical or pressure-group driven investment policies

Source: De la Torre and Neckar (1988). Reprinted with permission of Elzevier Science.
Note: **Bold** = more likely in India.

Equality trumps conflicting principles such as utilitarianism's 'greatest good for the greatest number'. Utilitarians Bentham and Mill would suggest a difficult, consequence-oriented calculation – essentially a cruel accounting exercise prescribing unethical behavior. For example, the right of the billion future recipients of lower cost, lighter weight aluminum could be determined to outweigh the homes and lives lost by a few hundred Orissa villagers, e.g.:

(# people who benefit from aluminum) ($ profit per person) + (# villagers who get jobs) ($ value each job is worth to them) > (# people who die) ($ value of person) + (# people who are injured) ($ value per person) + (# people who are forced to leave homelands) ($ value per person)

Hydro CEO Myklebust appears to utilize some degree of this human accounting. While agreeing that Utkal has both positive and negative aspects, he believes that when the 'two sides are added up and compared . . . the result for the local

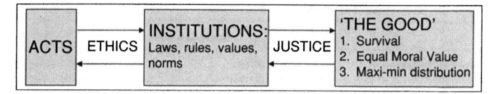

Figure 17 'The Good', Institutions and Acts

community is favorable'. One wonders what multiples Myklebust has used to account for the negative impact of lost human lives and the positive impact of sales and stockholder value.

Just institutions

As Hydro wipes the slate clean from its mid-December retreat from Utkal, the corporation has the opportunity to re-formulate its entry strategy. Rawls (1972) would suggest the 'veil of ignorance' where one determines the playing field when he/she is unaware of original (starting) position. In this scenario, a married, 30-year-old successful Hydro engineer from Oslo could easily take the station of a widowed, 70-year-old illiterate grandmother who is forced to abandon her ancestral home in Kashipur. What good principles or just institutions could be agreed upon at the original position drawing board (figure 17)? In this theory with roots from Kant's imperative and the Golden Rule, problems of cultural relativism would be avoided, and the moral compass could be extended across time and place. This could be a particularly challenging exercise for an Indian audience given their mentality that unequal stations with vastly different possibility sets (e.g. highest vs lowest caste) are inherited at birth.

'The good'

Falkenberg (2001) proposes that these individuals would agree to three basic principles which promote this good: survival (the minimum nutrition, health and education needs); ecologically sustainable level of consumption and resource utilization (to ensure survival for future generations), equality of moral value (all individuals are treated equally), and distribution of index goods according to the max–min principle (inequalities distributed so to benefit those who have the least).

Institutions

Institutional theory examines the influences of structures around organizations that help to define social and organizational behavior (Scott, 1995). These systems (including strong government and societal influences) affect the way an organization makes and implements decisions (Hoskisson *et al.*, 2000) and can ultimately be selection forces determining organizational survival (Hannan and Freeman, 1989). On the other hand, corporations can also impact institutions with strategic responses (Oliver, 1991). Due to the different nature of economic (e.g. financial institutions) and sociological orientations (e.g. provision of public services), institutional theory can be an effective tool for examining multinational companies operating in emerging market economies. Financial institutions are expected to reduce transaction and information costs by establishing stable structures that reduce uncertainty and facilitate interactions. Social institutions emphasize the role of cultural, material, and relational surroundings.

Falkenberg suggests that *just institutions* (laws, rules, values, and norms) are those which promote 'the good.' Does India have just institutions? According to Hydro's Lie:

> India has institutions which should be adequate for guaranteeing human rights. However we see very often that this is not the case. A very important reason for this is probably the high illiteracy . . . When the illiteracy is in the range of 80–85 per cent the individuals are not able to follow and understand what goes on around them. This opens up for individuals and groups to exploit the situation for their own benefit. This system goes all the way into the national politics.

Does Hydro have a just institutional framework for evaluating projects in developing countries? Hydro's five-step potential project evaluation checklist examines in descending order: (1) the strategic picture; (2) optimal ownership structure; (3) corporate social responsibility; (4) environmental issues; and (5) fundamental issues of culture. The checklist appears to promote 'the good,' beginning with what is best for the financial shareholders. The list ought better to be arranged to focus on the needs of the environment and shareholders in the host country first (see figure 18 for the current corporate strategy checklist).

Acts

Acts that are in harmony with just institutions are considered to be ethical (Falkenberg). Thus, if India's institutions and Hydro's five-step evaluation checklist were 'just', then the acts (such as establish a bauxite mine in a holy area) would be considered ethical.

Rights and duties

The human rights ethical situation (and the definition of good behavior) can be viewed in terms of Donaldson's ten rights and the corresponding expectations (X) inherent in the Utkal activities (table 15). Violations are denoted by a (✔) in

Step 1: Strategic Picture – Long term objective
  • Describe position in 10–15 years
Step 2: Optimal Ownership Structure
  • Local partner, joint venture, alone?
  • If partner:
    o Common long-term strategy?
    o Common philosophy and values?
    o Financial strength equal?
Step 3: Corporate Social Responsibility Issues
  • Define transparent information strategy
  • Active/Potential NGOs
Step 4: Environmental Issues
Step 5: Fundamentals of Culture
  • Political stability/history/values/religion/corruption
  • Industry and trading structure
  • Local expectations to project

Figure 18 Hydro Project analysis checklist

Table 15 Ten basic human rights and corresponding duties

Ten Basic Human Rights (and Corresponding Duties)	Avoid Depriving	Help Protect from Deprivation	To Aid the Deprived	Utkal Violations
Freedom of physical movement	X		O	✔
Ownership of property	X		O	✔
Freedom from torture	X		O	✔
Fair trial	X		O	✔
Non-discrimination	X	X	O	✔
Physical security	X	X	O	✔
Freedom of speech and association	X	X	O	✔
Basic education	X	X	O	✔
Political participation	X	X	O	✔
Substitutes	X	X	O	✔

the final column and examples are detailed. Hydro has attempted to establish some projects aiding the deprived (O). But, these initiatives appear to greenwash the facts and are worthless in the absence of real strategic policies guaranteeing the ten basic human rights. Examples will illustrate the human rights violations.

- *Freedom of physical movement*. Utkal has attempted to establish a wall around the future factory and mine grounds, prior to establishing the rights to these lands and to obtaining permission from local villagers. This will limit physical movement as well as critical access to water sources and agricultural land.

- *Ownership of property:* The citizens of Orissa have a right to own land. They have filed, mostly unsuccessfully, in accordance with article 226 of their Constitution and the 1894 Land Acquisition Act. These legal institutions have yet to prove themselves as guardians of justice and ethics. Watch agencies recount stories such as that of Jairam Majhi who was confronted by local authorities and told to 'abandon her family home and go elsewhere'.
- *Freedom from torture:* Young and old villagers were forced to sign away their land, by threat of gunpoint. Those shot in December were left to bleed to death on the hillside as their attackers fled the village in jeeps.
- *Fair trial:* A village man (paid by Utkal as an informant) reported three innocent young schoolchildren to the authorities for destruction of Utkal property because their parents are leaders in the struggle. The informant's claims were completely unfounded, yet police acted on them. Villager Andari Majhi describes the situation, 'Almost every other villager now has an arrest warrant against him . . . Even if you open your mouth in front of them, you could be arrested.'
- *Non-discrimination:* Again, individuals must not continue to face discrimination on the basis of caste position, family, and other variables.
- *Physical security:* Since the conflicts began nearly eight years ago, dozens of villagers have been injured, and several are dead from police attacks.
- *Freedom of speech and association:* There have been numerous attacks by police and officials (empowered indirectly or directly by Hydro) on non-violent village protestors.
- *Basic education:* By arresting innocent schoolboys, children wrongfully spend time in jail cells – not in class rooms.
- *Political Participation:* As described earlier, protestors against the local authorities do not enjoy the same capability to achieve functioning. During the process, four NGOs operating in the area have been de-registered on charges of 'backing the anti-development' efforts.
- *Substitutes:* Many villagers have not been given the right to new land because they did not hold official deeds to their current homes.[11]

Hydro, meanwhile, contends that it has 'advocated that socio-economic and cultural consequences of the project shall be a part of the management decision process . . . The ways the project will affect the local population will be given as much importance as building a plant that is both technologically and environmentally sound.' In fact, there have been many projects attempting to aid the deprived such as the 'Rehabilitation and Resettlement (R&R) Package' (to compensate individuals affected by the project) and other initiatives geared to the providing training, preventative health, improved sanitary conditions, women's grameen banking, and a weekly 'grievance day' when villagers can submit complaints to an Utkal office.

While these measures have begun to improve information flows and establish meaningful dialogues, they appear sugar-coatings to the true human rights violations of the Utkal project. A MNC cannot address projects 'to aid the deprived' without first establishing a full presence in columns A (avoid deprivation) and B (help protect from deprivation.)

Principles of integrity

In his book, *Competing with Integrity in International Business*, DeGeorge (1993) highlights seven standards for MNCs that provide a basis for evaluating and responding to the charges of unethical behavior particularly when operating in countries with inadequate background institutions:

1 *Multinationals should do no intentional harm.* It is unclear whether Hydro intended to do harm, although it is clearly a consequence.

2 *Multinationals should produce more good than harm for the host country.* Thus far, Hydro appears to have done more harm than good from the perspectives of the villagers (lost land and lives) and shareholders (no return on capital yet).

3 *Multinationals should contribute by their activity to the host country's development.* Sustainable development policies should be aimed at the interdependent three prongs: environmental sustainability, economic development and growth, and poverty alleviation (Vosti and Reardon, 1997). Hydro must champion implementation in these areas- and not contribute to the further depletion of financial, environmental, and human capital.

4 *Multinationals should respect the human rights of their employees.* Hydro has an obligation to guarantee the safety of its employees and contractors. In one case, three Hydro workers were forcibly attacked by villagers. More recently, Utkal partners have been accused of ordering contractors to attack villagers. Hydro should also not be in the position of ordering and paying (directly or indirectly) bounty hunters to commit terrible crimes.

5 *To the extent that local culture does not violate ethical norms, multinationals should respect the local culture and work with and not against it.* The Utkal partners need to assess the complete ethical and cultural environment and determine which universal ethical principles should trump national cultural values and economic incentives, e.g. caste hierarchy and bribery.

6 *Multinationals should pay their fair share of taxes.* Utkal is not currently paying taxes as it is taking advantage of an Indian government-sponsored scheme which provides a ten consecutive year tax holiday for 100 per cent export-oriented projects (Ernst & Young, 1999). Meanwhile, Utkal is heavily utilizing publicly financed and controlled resources such as water and roads.

7 *Multinationals should cooperate with the local government in developing and enforcing just background institutions.* Utkal's institutional efforts are limited

to its self-created NGO, URDS. A recent press release suggests that Hydro has adapted a hands off approach, 'A political debate is currently in progress in the State of Orissa about which areas are to be developed industrially. Utkal will not take part in this debate, but will fully support any efforts initiated by the Government of Orissa aimed at resolving the conflict in the project area. Utkal hopes that the reduction of project activities and initiative to dialogue can reduce tension in the area, which today affects the lives of many people.' How can Hydro and Utkal guarantee that the government of Orissa has been fair in resolving the conflict? Hydro and Utkal should focus on creating adequate institutions that could facilitate this important discourse.

Responsibility

The final framework examines the degree to which a company can be held responsible for the acts in its environment. In this case, the three parameters governing corporate responsibility are:

1 If I am 'response-able' or 'response-capable,' i.e. able to respond to a problem.
2 By virtue of my role: a father is responsible for his children.
3 For something that I have caused to happen: I decided to borrow the money, so I am responsible for the repayments of the loan.

In the first guideline, Hydro is both response-able and response-capable. This is particularly the case as Hydro and Norway have experience in ensuring that natural resources are used for the benefit of all. Norway is one of very few natural-resource countries with a stable socio-political environment. Following the North Sea finds in the middle of the last century, Norway created a generous welfare state guaranteeing opportunities for its citizens now and in the future (Karl, 1996). Hydro has a responsibility to share these lessons learned with developing communities in other parts of the world. In this way, Hydro can prevent the 'paradox of plenty' – where countries well endowed with natural resources are plagued by political turmoil, capital flight, and double digit inflation (Karl, 1996; Wantchekon, 1999).

In the second regard, India's political instability and lack of welfare pro-grammes help to promote paternalistic bonds between employees and organizations (Mead, 1996). Furthermore, Hydro's initial patronizing policy may have raised villagers' expectations. Hydro and the other Utkal partners are currently backing off the scale of their responsibility. As CEO Myklebust acknowledges, 'The social responsibility debate is also about more clearly defining what is, and what is not, the responsibility of business and industry, thereby clarifying the responsibilities of other parts of society.' Hydro must still accept some responsibility by virtue of its role as a multinational operating in a less-developed community.

Finally, Utkal project partners should be held responsible for events directly triggered by its venture. Utkal must accept follow up responsibility for everything from the razing of forests to the relocation of villagers. Specific examples of initiatives Hydro should be responsible for are provided in the Recommendations section.

Value chain

Ethical problems can be examined in terms of a value chain where 'networks of firms that create value for themselves and for their customers by transforming a variety of resources (human and natural) into offerings valued by end users'. These ethical challenges are particularly evident when value chain activities take place in different countries with pronounced cultural and economic differences. In the case of Utkal, light aluminum for automobiles and corporate profits for shareholders entails lost land and lives for villagers. Figure 19 (embedded picture is a collage from images of related websites)[12] illustrates this channel – where individuals at one end are smiling and enjoying the benefits of lighter, cheaper aluminium and individuals at the other end emerge dead, wounded, or with otherwise destroyed lives.

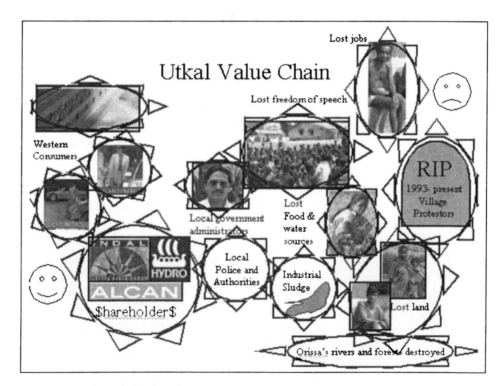

Figure 19 The Utkal value chain

▶ Recommendations

Hydro's past activities have ranged from illegal to good, honest behaviour. As a true corporate citizen, Hydro must strive to consistently act in an honest and ethical manner, following the standards so well documented and promoted in glossy corporate brochures and websites. In doing so, Hydro will promote flourishing for all by enabling people to reach their full capabilities. Additionally, other companies, particularly in the scrupulous oil industry, will be challenged by this ethical precedent and may raise social responsibility worldwide.

The author proposes action-step oriented recommendations as there is a great need to translate dialogue about ethical philosophies into strategic and implementable action steps. Hydro has two basic options: abandon the project completely (preferred) or proceed with major policy changes.

Plan A

Hydro should abandon the Utkal project. The human rights and environmental atrocities must not continue. This preference is echoed by Leer-Salvesen from Norwatch, 'Hydro should go home and find bauxite elsewhere or recycle more aluminum.' The project may also prove financially infeasible for Hydro shareholders looking for a return on investment. Already, the project is six years behind schedule, and Leer-Salvesen believes it may take another twenty to thirty years before Utkal will have full cooperation from villagers. Furthermore, if Hydro abandons the project, it is likely that Alcan will also leave and the Indian companies alone would not be able to finance the project.

Plan B

Upon re-evaluation, Hydro could choose to proceed. In this case, the following are recommended:

1   *Expand Hydro's ethical policy to include human rights regardless of the degree of the ownership structure.* According to a March press release, Hydro's current ethics policy will consider human rights only when ownership share is between 10 per cent and 50 per cent.[13] These five 'unconditional principles' are:
    - Will support the Universal Declaration of Human Rights and will not engage in activities that impair the enjoyment of human rights.
    - Will engage in open dialogue and consultation with stakeholders in local communities and elsewhere regarding impacts of company operations.

- Will not endanger the physical safety, security, or health of members of communities affected by such operations.
- Will remain neutral in respect of race, religion, gender, age, caste, cultural identity and similar factors.
- Will recognize the intrinsic value of diverse cultures and traditions in communities where it operates and will act accordingly.

This is blatantly unacceptable and begs the question-would Hydro care to stop these atrocities if it possessed a meagre 5, 8 or even 9 per cent ownership? To the same token, is it okay to sit in a room with eleven people and participate in a human rights violation, such as a rape or murder? Given Hydro's logic, none of the parties could be held accountable for his/her inaction because each possessed just 9.09 per cent (100 per cent divided by 11) of responsibility for the situation – not enough to halt or reverse the path of ethical destruction.

2 *Install more Hydro officials (with sufficient ethics and cultural training) in Orissa to initiate positive changes.* Hydro portrays itself as the victim of local officials and police who claim to have been acting on Utkal's behalf. As Union Carbide found in Bhopal, it is insufficient to blame local managers for disasters. In this regard, Hydro will be closer to the problem and therefore, hopefully also closer to a solution. For example, Hydro could directly ensure that local people, from all bases of the caste hierarchy, are involved in the decision-making.

3 *Engage future employees of Hydro in ethical dialogue.* For example, Norsk Hydro could sponsor classes at leading Norwegian institutions for research and student theses focusing on the ethical implications of strategic decision-making and management.[14] This discourse could be extended to Indian schools of business and economics. Only seven of India's 148 universities offer ethics courses.[15] (Many other leading MBA programs, particularly in the US, have a Professorship chair and champion of these activities.)

4 *Guarantee full transparency of issues.* Hydro espouses an 'openness policy' which claims to share both good and bad news on environmental and ethical fronts. Upon closer reading of fact-finding NGO newsletters, it is apparent that Hydro does not practice a full-transparency policy. For example, concerns about Utkal-paid informants in villages and destroyed forests are among those issues which have never been raised in company press releases and 'openness' documents.

5 *Invite CMI and other groups back on-site to provide status and recommendations on the current social and environmental situation.* Utkal benefits from having the most accurate and complete information, even if the picture isn't rosy. Initial projects could include a re-examination of village relocations and industrial sludge estimates and subsequent proposals for action.

6 *Agree to an ethical strategy with partners.* Hydro has said that it was not involved in the shootings, but that it cannot guarantee that its Indian partner had nothing to do these murders. Clearly, these partners need

dialogue and action. According to Norwatch's Leer-Salvesen, when ethical issues are raised, the three partners respond uniquely. Alcan will choose to 'throw money to quiet the problem.' Hydro will 'start to talk so loudly about human rights that people walk away disgusted.' And Indal 'will just shoot the villagers.'

7 *Continuously monitor the project's ethical acts and consequences.* As with all other management concerns, it is critical to continually evaluate performance (Rosenzweig & Singh, 1991). Consistent and frequent evaluation of codes of conduct can assuage the inadequate structures and economic disparities present throughout the world (Bird & Waters, 1994). As needed, Utkal partners should be prepared to enhance their corporate codes of ethics.

▶ Conclusion

If you don't know where you're going, then any road will take you there.
(Cheshire Cat to Alice in Lewis Carroll's *Alice in Wonderland*)

Hydro must choose the road it wishes to follow lest it end up on a less desirable path to the future. This Norwegian multinational should develop and actively pursue its triple bottom line: *financial, social and biophysical performance* and *responsibility*. As Hydro approaches its centenary in 2005, the company's long experience with natural resources should be expected to translate into the capability to provide flourishing for all.[16]

Efficiency (utilitarianism), equity (justice), and freedom are three equally important parameters (figure 110). Traditionally, developing countries find themselves in the lower left hand corner as centralized political and economic power

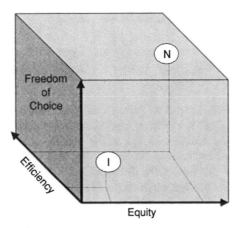

Figure 110 The equity diagram

constrain their development. When developing countries mature with just institutions and ethical acts, they will find the equitability and freedom experienced by more developed countries (Falkenberg, 2001).

In providing a brief overview of cultural and ethical issues, this paper has tried to provide a framework for cultural and ethical analysis and action for Utkal and other multinationals operating in developing countries.

Sadly, there were thousands of multinational ethical cases to choose among. Fortunately, however, corporate social responsibility is an increasingly important area of dialogue, focus, and implementation for multinational companies operating overseas. Companies recognize the short-term (valuable publicity, new customers, improved motivation and moral among workforce) and long-term (self interest and enabling flourishing for all) value of ethical practices. Multinationals are also aware of the dire social and economic penalties from unethical behaviour, such as Union Carbide's (UCC) disaster in Bhopal, India – the resulting legal precedent recognized the corporation as an ethical entity with responsibility to host society.

My corporate contacts at Hydro are currently in Orissa to 'talk and talk'. Meanwhile, Norwatch has representatives on-site to monitor the situation. Utkal's future developments will be of interest to academics, practitioners, and corporate shareholders and aluminium market analysts.

There is a need for further applied empirical and theoretical research to multinationals operating within emerging markets with different cultural and ethical frameworks. This is particularly true for private firms and international joint ventures (Childs, 1972) such as Utkal. Also, little attention has been paid to the study of organizations that run amok within their environments (Roberts, 1994). Comparatively little extant research exists for the geographical regions of India, Africa, and the Middle East; management scholars have focused primarily on the Chinese or Central and Eastern European counterparts.

Project withdrawal: December 2001

Six months after the time frame of this case, Hydro issued the following press statement on December 17, 2001, stating a withdrawal from the Utkal Project:

> Hydro Aluminium has informed its partners in Utkal Alumina International Ltd. that they wish to exit from the project. Hydro's decision is based on an assessment of the future market for alumina, as well as the positive development of the company's alumina production facilities in Brazil. The lack of progress for the Utkal alumina production is also part of the decision.
>
> Alumina, also known as aluminium oxide, is an important raw material for production of primary aluminium. Hydro has equity production of alumina in Jamaica and Brazil. The Brazilian Alunorte refinery is going through an expansion which will substantially increase Hydro's production capacity for alumina.

A balanced alumina market with a variety of suppliers is envisaged for the coming years. This will allow Hydro to pursue its strategy of alumina supply through a combination of own production, alliances and long term contracts.

The shareholders agreement of Utkal Alumina gives the remaining partners pre-emption rights. The legal process required for Hydro to leave the partnership has been initiated.

Utkal Alumina has not started any construction in the planned project area. Based on partnership policies, some socio economic development work is going on. There is also a continuous dialogue between the company, the government and the local population. The proposed host community of the project in Kashipur, Orissa is in dire need of social and economic development. Mining and industrialization, when implemented in a careful and responsible way, may contribute to a sustainable development in this area and give opportunities for thousands of below the poverty line people to better their livelihood conditions.[17]

Notes

1   Resource and borrowing privileges as defined by Thomas Pogge (2001): The international resource privilege is 'the power to confer globally valid ownership rights in the country's resources'. International borrowing privileges describe 'when a group exercises effective power within a national territory is entitled to borrow funds in the name of the whole country.'

2   During interviews, the author learned that these three employees were transferred to other Hydro divisions outside India following this incident.

3   This quote has, on several occations, been publicly denied by senior Hydro officials as totally false.

4   These events have been documented and shared mainly to Norwegian audiences by watch groups including Norwatch (daughter organization of the Future In Our Hands), the Strømme Foundation, and Norwegian Church Aid. Additionally, Indian organizations such as SODAN (South Orissa Development Alternatives Network) and international watch groups including One World have brought attention to the critical issues and tensions.

5   www.hydro.com/hits/osl02067.nsf

6   The author would have preferred to highlight the differences between high and low (or unscheduled) caste cultures in India. The best treatment of this is Rolf Lunheim's (1994) dissertation, *Desert People Caste and Community: A Rajasthani Village*. Lunheim focuses on a different geographic region of India (Rajasthan in the northwest) and his observations about high/low caste differences may not be suitable to extrapolate for the Orissa region 800 miles to the east. When applicable, insights from his thesis are included.

7   Lunheim acknowledges the difference in egalitarianism between his native Norway and host research in India. He writes that his fieldwork in the Rajasthani villages is 'intended as a journey to a place thought to be the polar opposite of egalitarian individualism, to hierarchical collectivism – caste and community.'

8   The author notes that the lack of these proper control systems may have attributed to other disasters in India such as Union Carbide in Bhopal.

9   The American Heritage dictionary describes a trump card as a 'card in the trump suit, held in reserve for winning a trick; or a key resource to be used at an opportune moment'.

10 This storm of economic liberalization beginning in the early 1990s in India exposed international companies to increased risk due to the lack of appropriate institutions. This corruption has manifested itself in artificial bid escalation, tax evasion, bank fund misappropriation, and fund diverting from productive channels (Chakraborty, 1997). The picture is perhaps best painted by a *Sunday Telegraph* editorial, 'In ancient India, kings and Emperors thought it a privilege to sit at the feet of a man of learning. In today's India, MPs and ministers think it a privilege . . . to sit at the feet of underworld dons and base businessmen to get secret donations from them and to get their blessings.' All but one of the 40 MPs in India's parliament have criminal records. In March of this year, journalists exposed several high government officials for accepting bribes in arms dealing.

11 The author elected to provide just one example (of the many documented) per human rights violation.

12 www.hydro.com, www.fivh.no/norwatch, and www.oneworld.com

13 http://osl01inet.hydro.com/HITS/OSL02008.NSF/allbyid/
1D2246679D8B42BB412568B200537E29?OpenDocument

14 The author sadly notes that Norsk Hydro representatives at the Center for Corporate Social Responsibility did not respond to repeated e-mails for their insights. She was however able to interview several other Hydro executives working closely with the Utkal project.

15 The Indian Institute of Management at Ahmedabad (set up in collaboration with Harvard Business School) does not offer ethics.

16 Ironically however, active initiatives began only in the most recent fifteen years, such as the 1988 Management Guidelines for Social Aspects of Participation in Industrial Activities and the 1993 Norsk Hydro Environmental Principles.

17 http://www.hydro.com/en/press_room/press_releases/archive/2001_12/archive.html

Case Assignments

1 Give an overview of and discuss the ethical dilemmas that Norsk Hydro faced in the Utkal Venture.

2 Discuss the statement that just institutions are those which promote 'the good'.

3 Describe Donaldson's 'ten rights' and outline Norsk Hydro's practice in relation to these.

4 In December 2001 Norsk Hydro left the Utkal Venture. Was this in your view a wise decision and, eventually, do you think the company should have done this at an earlier stage?

5 Discuss the case in regard to the corporate ethical stages outlined in Chapter 9. Websites: www.hydro.com, www.fivh.no/norwatch, www.corpwatch.com, and www.oneworld.org

Future Challenges

In this closing chapter we will outline four challenges that international managers will have to pay particular attention to during the coming decade. First, we raise the issue of whether the increased importance of competencies and networks means a shift of paradigm in the conceptualization of MNC managerial challenges. If this is the case what we will witness is the final death throes of the bureaucracy and the rise of the 'flexicracy'. The flexicracy has structural implications. Therefore, the second managerial challenge we will delineate involves the increasingly complex task of developing appropriate structures. The flexicracy also has personnel implications. It requires a new type of individual, that is individuals who not only tolerate change, but who seek it out, and who not only are prepared for learning, but who are driven by it. Hence, the third challenge we review is the challenge MNCs face in regard to attracting and retaining Generation Y employees. Finally, we are compelled to revisit the ethical dimension of MNCs. The corporate scandals of 2002 witnessed many demises but perhaps none greater than that of the multinational accountancy Arthur Andersen. Within a matter of months Arthur Andersen virtually disintegrated as its national partner firms fled the company rather than be associated with the parent company's ethical lapses. The fourth challenge that MNCs must confront is related to meaning, legitimacy and ethics. Each of these four challenges is illustrated in more detail through a series of readings.

▶ Paradigm Shift?

One of the key messages in this book is that a distinctly new, knowledge-intensive and learning-oriented phase in work life is now emerging, a phase in which the needs for competencies and transfer of knowledge are imperative. MNCs such as General Electric, have rapidly absorbed the e-based approaches pioneered by the 'new economy' enterprises. So that although the 'new economy' appears to have lost its initial gloss its approaches live on within an increasing number of MNCs.

In our view, the term 'network and competence society' epitomizes the most central contemporary trend in work life. It is no longer sufficient for MNCs to possess an impressive financial and material resource base unless this base is supplemented by excellent relations between the MNC and its customers, between its employees, and between the company and other organizations. In the network economy where cooperation both internally and externally is the key factor, much of the MNCs' vital competence resides precisely within these relations and not only in individual employees and teams.

We believe that a novel paradigm is now emerging in regard to organizational forms, managerial principles, resource utilization and cross-national coordination. The main focus is shifting from intended implementation of ideal type rational structures and working modes to how the knowledge resources of the company may best be accumulated, mobilized, shared and applied (cf. Hamel and Heene, 1994). This reflects a conceptual revolution in the sense that it is no longer financial capital, technology or other physical capital that reside at the forefront in relation to organizational success or failure. Instead companies are to a growing extent focussing on the demands for superior competencies, outstanding managerial skills and not least creativity. Concurrently, the steadily more fluid and diffuse boundaries between companies contribute to generating change and uncertainty that necessitate increased individual and organizational flexibility, which in turn will leave their imprints on managerial practices and organizational designs. In addition, there is the marked increase in the importance of operating in network modes making for a much greater emphasis on lateral relationships.

▶ The Flexicratic MNC

Because MNCs are to a growing extent focusing on nurturing superior competencies they are becoming markedly more 'organic' and equally less 'mechanistic' (cf. Burns and Stalker, 1961). The drive towards less mechanistic and more organic management practices among MNCs is not just a product of the new emphasis on intangible resources. There are other, related, factors at work. One factor is the volatility of the environment of the company that not only makes long-term strategic planning problematic (Mintzberg, 1994), but which also necessitates radically more responsive organizations.

Another factor is that relationships have become a critical resource for companies. Externally there is the need to develop relationships with customers whose needs are increasingly heterogeneous. Customers are demanding that goods and services be customized, thereby intensifying the need for innovation. In turn innovation implies a degree of creativity that necessitates the abandonment of rigid, hierarchical work structures. It is simply not possible to compel employees to be creative. Internally there is the challenge of handling relationships within fluid networks, temporary projects, centres of excellence and virtual organizations.

In sum, it is necessary to substitute the old corporate bureaucracies by organizational forms that we may, in generic terms, label 'flexicracies'. We are not postulating one single, characteristic mode of governance. It would be more accurate to say that we face a multitude of dissimilar ways of managing the activities of MNCs. What they do share is a fundamental commitment to flexibility whether this involves the outsourcing of activities, centres of excellence or strategic alliances.

In Reading A, John Storey extends this perspective in his discussion of the importance of viewing companies as networks, as global markets fragment in the wake of increasing turbulence.

▶ The Structural Challenge

In Chapter 2 we delineated four generic structures. The 'international division' structure is suitable when domestic business is still dominant and foreign subsidiaries are of little more than marginal significance. Historically, as the importance of MNCs' foreign subsidiaries grew, they adopted characteristic structures as a consequence of decisions in regard to two strategic dimensions: the importance they attached to adapting their products and services in relation to local differences in taste, and the degree to which they believed centralized global responsibility was necessary in order to achieve scale-based competitive advantage. The choice appeared to be an either–or matter. If the MNC opted for the former it adopted a 'multi-domestic' structure. If the latter, it adopted the 'global product division' structure.

During the 1980s, MNCs became less inclined to regard the issues of local sensitivity and global integration as an either–or trade matter. Some products could be developed centrally for a global market, whilst others needed to be locally adapted. Furthermore, there was an increasing recognition of the benefits in having multiple centres of technology that could draw on local capabilities. The question was how to design a structure that could take care of all three of these dimensions. The answer appeared to lie in matrix management as practised by ABB under Percy Barnevik's leadership. ABB was lauded as an example of the MNC of the future, the transnational.

However, the matrix structure proved to be so complex that it was abandoned and ABB reverted to a structure that is predominantly global product-based. In other words, of the three needs, to be able to respond to local demands, to secure a sufficient degree of global integration and that of worldwide learning, the first of these has been relegated to a more secondary status.

In Reading B, Julian Birkinshaw reviews some of the most recent ways in which MNCs are structuring their activities. These are, first and foremost, a response to the growing need to be able to serve large global customers with one-stop comprehensive, integrated offerings. In practice this means radical outsourcing and the development of new value-added services. The front-end/back-end structure he describes is, however, not without its dangers. There is for example a risk that the country dimension becomes so undermined that world-wide learning is threatened.

In addition, we have included two readings that provide brief illustrations of the ongoing challenge of developing efficient organizational structures. Reading C features the Finnish MNC, Nokia, and Reading D the Danish MNC, LEGO.

▶ The New Generation

As Readings E and F illustrate, young employees to a large degree want to work in organizations that offer substantial opportunities for personal growth, competence development and variation in work tasks. Rather than subscribing to a Protestant work ethic, they subscribe to a 'fun ethic' in the sense that their work has to be experienced as inherently challenging and interesting. If they are not challenged or if they are bored, they are inclined to look elsewhere.

What managerial challenges does this create? Traditionally, HRM has involved systematic efforts to acquire, nurture and retain the carriers of the knowledge resources that are most crucial in relation to the company's goals. This could largely be accomplished through the design and use of traditional rewards, such as salaries, fringe benefits and good working conditions. But in the case of the new generation, Generation Y, this is far from adequate. In terms of their work style and need for creative activities, these individuals often are more like artists than 'company men'. If they are managed on the basis of bureaucratic, mechanistic managerial practices they will quickly move on.

A parallel development to the emergence of Generation Y is the decline in the opportunity for vertical mobility to managerial positions due to the implementation of flatter organizational forms. For companies in general the challenge is to create meaningful lateral career opportunities and to design rewards that encourage the development of lateral careers. In this respect MNCs have a comparative advantage due to their large and geographically dispersed organizations that yield a wide range of lateral job moves for their employees. As such, MNCs can potentially offer a much greater scope for lateral career development than their domestic counterparts. On the other hand employees have to be motivated to avail themselves of these opportunities particularly if they involve periods of expatriation.

Reading E is authored by Karen Cates and Kimia D. Rahimi and Reading F by Paul Gooderham and Odd Nordhaug. Both readings deal with the characteristics of 'Generation Y', that is the coming generation of international managers.

▶ Legitimacy and Ethics as Sources of Meaning

Let us finally consider the matter of the existential basis, the very *raison d'être*, for employees of MNCs to commit themselves to their companies. A fundamental challenge is to be able to provide meaning. Ultimately this can only be accomplished through the maintenance of the MNC's reputation. To a large extent reputation has to be actively created by managers who proclaim the aim of the company through the development of images of the company both for internal and external consumption. By way of example it is worth considering the effort British Petroleum (BP) has invested in developing its 'Beyond Petroleum' image. This has paid off to such an extent that in 2001 the company was voted by a panel comprising representatives of NGOs and the media as the most respected company in the world in regard to the management of environmental resources (Skapinker, 2002).

Managers of the industrial era would perhaps have perceived the quest for creating meaning for their employees as an unnecessary luxury, but in the era of Generation Y it is an important condition for generating the type of commitment that is vital for network-based and learning-oriented MNCs. To seek meaning in what one does, to work at something one believes in, and to work with passion was the privilege of the few in the industrial age, but is now becoming a core employee demand. Without the opportunities for a sense of personal fulfilment, the facilitation of innovative and flexible business operations will be seriously undermined.

Meaning stems from legitimacy in the sense that external stakeholders and other parties view the company in a positive light. In parts of the organization theory literature it is emphasized that companies, particularly large and very visible ones, benefit from actively constructing and maintaining legitimacy (e.g., Powell and DiMaggio, 1991; Scott, 1996). One of the reasons for this is that companies are increasingly exposed to external evaluations of their actions in terms of exacting moral standards. MNCs must expect their products to be scrutinized not just for their quality but also for any possible damage they may inflict on the environment, for any use of child labour and for any maltreatment or exploitation of employees. Because of NGOs, consumer consciousness about these issues has grown markedly during the last decade. As pointed out in Chapter 9 in this book: Who wants to 'buy' child labour? Who wants to 'buy' pollution of the environment? Who wants to 'buy' brutal exploitation of employees? Who wants to 'buy' violation of basic human rights?

As a result of such external pressures and the need for employees to be engaged in meaningful activities, being able to create legitimacy and meaning is becoming a primary task for MNC managers.

In the final Reading G, Tim Dickson raises the issue of corporate social responsibility and the relationship between this and profits in companies. Written in the aftermath of the 2002 plethora of corporate scandals, he explores the concept of corporate social responsibility and discusses the attitude of companies towards this, including the possibility of 'triple-bottom-line' reporting that includes assessments of corporate economic, environmental and social performance.

reading A

When Companies Become Networks

John Storey

Even a casual observer of international business cannot help but notice that organizations seem forever in the process of reorganising. Why should this be so? Does it reflect economic reality or a superficial rearranging of the corporate furniture? Might these reforms simply be part of a cyclical fluctuation between centralization and decentralization? Do new organizational forms require different HR tasks and capabilities?

Certainly, in many cases the drama of reform disguises a more routine pattern of behaviour: changes may simply be triggered by the need to correct the deficiencies of the last restructuring. However, it would be cynical to dismiss all restructuring in this way.

One explanation is that there is no 'best way' to structure an organization so as to render it fit for all times and circumstances. Economic and industrial changes have prompted discernible patterns of organizational restructuring. For example, after the Second World War, growth in international markets based on mass production was accompanied by an expansion in the number of multinationals and led to the near-ubiquitous multi-divisional form (the 'M-Form'). This was associated with hierarchy, planned career structures and large, centralized personnel departments overseeing expatriates and home-based staff.

However, with fragmentation of markets, shorter product life cycles and greater variability of demand, the lack of responsiveness and unwieldy nature of the multinationals became apparent. Since the 1990s, other forms have been ascendant, characterized by smaller enterprises, outsourcing, joint ventures and alliances. These require new capabilities among managers, which, in turn, require different

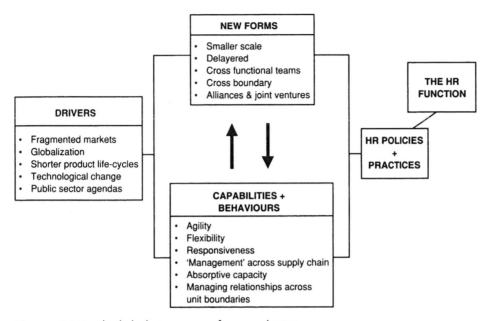

Figure RA1 The links between new forms and HRM

people management policies and practices. Figure RA1 indicates the relationship between drivers, forms, capabilities and human resource management.

As figure RA1 shows, while the drivers create 'needs' for forms and capabilities, there is also an interactive relationship between these forms and capability requirements. New forms of working and organising require new capabilities; likewise, the capabilities required by the external drivers constitute a pressure for experimenting with forms. It is worth reviewing each of the main elements in figure RA1.

▶ Drivers

As mentioned, global markets have become more fragmented and turbulent. Product life cycles are shorter and customers require more options during the life cycle of a product. Meanwhile, technological change and the number of components in a product or service mean that few single businesses can fulfil customer demands on their own.

Similar challenges face the public sector: governments in numerous countries have outsourced parts of the public services to the private sector while at the same time reforming those organizations that remain within it. These reforms are explained as attempts to make bureaucracies more responsive to the public's needs. Nonetheless, they create pressure for new organizational forms and capabilities.

▶ Forms

Over the past 15 years, when measured by numbers employed, both the size of companies and the size of workplaces have decreased. Organizations have also moved away from hierarchy and command as the prime sources of direction and control. They have responded to turbulence and fluctuations in demand by empowering employees, establishing cross-functional teams and taskforces, outsourcing non-core functions and focusing on processes rather than product lines.

In the 1980s and 1990s, the 'strategic business unit' became the focus in divisionalized corporations. This period also saw dramatic growth in new enterprises funded by venture capital. These smaller, fragmented units, while more responsive, were severely limited in their access to resources and capabilities. The trend towards vertical integration, which characterized the corporations of the early to middle part of the twentieth century, is being reversed. The value chain is becoming more clearly desegregated, as each component becomes the prime responsibility of a relatively independent unit or set of units.

In consequence, new kinds of relationship between organizations are flourishing, including joint ventures and strategic alliances; the archetypal form is now the network organization or 'N-Form'. This form is characterized by multiple inter-organizational relationships which extend beyond narrow market or contractual obligations. Firms in network relationships expect to share information, knowledge and learning. They expect to reduce risk by collaborating across the supply chain and thereby gain win-win solutions. Under these new circumstances, competition is less between individual organizations and more between entire supply chains. But managing these new forms requires new capabilities.

▶ Capabilities

Companies need to be more agile and flexible under these conditions. Standard operating procedures and long reporting lines are no longer suitable. Rapid changes in customer demand require knowledge, or access to knowledge, to be distributed around the company. In addition, since managers are increasingly working across boundaries, their ability to manage the complexities of the supply chain is at a premium. Separate units need 'absorptive capacity' – that is, the ability to make sense of, and internalize, information from partner organizations. They must be able to assimilate the knowledge they require and use it.

Where outsourcing has been established, employees must become skilled managers of contracts. Beyond formal contractual skills, they must be good at *managing relationships* across unit boundaries, which is where appropriate human resource management policies can help. Organizations may no longer need to own certain resources, but they do need to be able to access and use them effectively.

Examples of these trends can be found in many countries though it is important not to assume that large organizations have abandoned all aspects of their traditional structural characteristics. The new forms are still evolving. A recent survey of 458 firms throughout Western Europe conducted by Andrew Pettigrew and colleagues, found 74 per cent of them reporting an increase in horizontal linkages such as joint purchasing, sharing R&D across units and sharing marketing information. The survey also found extensive evidence of increased outsourcing (65 per cent of firms reporting an increase) and the formation of strategic alliances (65 per cent increase). Reinforcing these findings, an Open University Business School survey of 2,700 companies in the UK representative of all sectors and all sizes of firm (down to 100 employees each) revealed 61 per cent sharing knowledge with suppliers and 41 per cent sharing knowledge 'with other organizations in the network'. During the last five-year period, 30 per cent had increased their outsourcing of R&D. These developments were found to have implications for employment practices and HR policies.

▶ HR policies

As companies become more dependent on each other, managing relationships becomes critical. Responsiveness and flexibility are required. What are the people management implications? How, and by whom, is behaviour to be influenced? Trust becomes important, and the communication and sharing of knowledge.

Conducting relationships through the supply chain or through a network makes hierarchical control impractical. Equally, relationships are more complex than market transactions. Organizational structures are only one part of design. Other aspects include measurement, norms, expectations, culture and power – and these are often crucial in affecting behaviour.

Some organizational reforms may present HR problems. For example, the shift from a product-based mode of organizing to a process-based one can provoke anxiety and resistance. Employees may fear that re-engineering will result in job losses and extensive change. Maintaining commitment to the job and organization may be difficult during and after such reforms.

Narrow job descriptions usually have to be abandoned. For example, re-engineering consultants sometimes recommend that 'workers' become 'process performers'. If managed skilfully, this widening of responsibilities offers opportunities as well as threats; roles may be enlarged as well as changed, and employees given more autonomy, responsibility and decision-making power.

In the modern company, claims Michael Hammer, there is no organization chart, no departmental managers and virtually no hierarchy. The new psychological contract offers initiative in exchange for opportunity. No matter how well designed the organization and the processes, Hammer observes, 'it is the people who make it work'. In the long run, he maintains:

[T]he quality of an organization's coaching is a key determinant of whether it succeeds or fails. Process design alone is not enough. As more companies learn how to create the art of processes, the advantage will belong to those with an institutionalized capacity for staffing these processes with well-selected and well-trained people.

In place of hierarchy, the process-focused organization will make more use of cross-functional teams and taskforces. While some of Hammer's claims exaggerate actual practice, there is substantial evidence of extensive take-up of these latter forms.

Managers face a crucial HR challenges as a result of these developments: how should they manage those who are not direct employees, and how can they maintain and develop relationships across traditional boundaries? Should outsourced workers on the premises be included in communications, invited to meetings and expected to be involved in commitment-building initiatives?

Where activities are outsourced, a critical issue is the potential loss of expertise. Once lost, certain activities and their associated capabilities may be difficult to recover. There is danger of 'hollowing out' the organization. Innovation may be jeopardized if there is heavy reliance on strictly delineated services from external suppliers – even if service-level agreements are maintained and monitored. There is a major challenge for HR here if the organization becomes dependent on consultants and contractors.

The management writer Peter Drucker argues that companies will eventually outsource all functions that do not have a career ladder up to senior management. He contends that corporations once built 'like pyramids' will become more 'like tents' and managers will take responsibility for their own career development by exploring their competencies and making good deficiencies.

Outsourcing has other implications for HR. For staff transferred from the original employer to a service provider, different countries present different legal regulations. These typically require that prevailing terms and conditions of employment are preserved. In some cases, a task may be outsourced and the employees nominally transferred for day-to-day management purposes, while retaining their employment contract with the original employer.

Network organizations often grow out of the fact that resources and knowledge are difficult to locate within the boundaries of one organization. They are more likely to be found distributed across a network of different businesses and contractors.

If this is so, HR managers have a major task to identify, retain and develop such resources. Part of a company's know-how resides in being able to bring relevant people together and enable them to work together. In the boundaryless organization there are huge uncertainties surrounding whom, if anyone, is managing these processes. In traditional organizations there were relatively clear boundaries between insiders and outsiders. Roles and lines of accountability were relatively clear. Under the network form, 'contracts' (formal and tacit) are hybrid, that is to say, part market-based and part relational. In this environment, neither the traditional notion of win-lose competition nor hierarchical command is appropriate.

Instead of developing plans and strategies independently, planning in the network organization has to be co-ordinated and shared with other participants in the network. Information must be shared to allow managers to solve problems jointly. For example, GE Appliances collaborates with major suppliers. Together they plan for, and respond more quickly to, changes in demand and production schedules. Design, production, scheduling and sales data can be co-ordinated. Monthly sales data are shared with 25 suppliers.

Co-ordination of a value chain or network means employees need to be familiar with customer and supplier needs and preferences. One way in which this can be done is to invite suppliers and customers to meetings with employees, where outlines of goals, plans and problems can be explained and discussed. Workers can also be sent on customer and supplier field trips or seconded to these organizations. Further, companies may collaborate by giving taskforces specific aims to work across the value chain. A more ambitious step is to integrate information systems.

The difficulties associated with such innovations have led some corporate leaders to revert to traditional control systems. George Simpson, who took over as chief executive from Lord Weinstock at GEC in 1996, said he wanted to move away from 'the joint venture culture' and revert to direct investment and control by managers in targeted business sectors. The subsequent withdrawal from joint ventures (such as the one with Siemens in telecoms equipment), the choice of sell-offs, and the attempt to steer the successor company Marconi in a more focused direction turned out to be a disaster.

▶ The HR function

To what extent do the new forms represent a threat or an opportunity for HR as a specialist function? In some respects these developments offer an opportunity for HR staff to adopt a more strategic role. Many failures in strategic alliances, mergers and joint ventures have been traced to the neglect of HR issues. Consequently, this realization seems to present a strategic opportunity. In addition, many of the challenges thrown up by the new forms put a premium on strategic thinking about human resource issues.

On the other hand, it could be argued that the new forms – with their emphasis on devolved authority, flexibility and variability – are inimical to human resource management policies and procedures. In the past, personnel departments grew to a size where systems were uniformly applied across large corporations. The classic age of the personnel department was the age of the procedure manual. New contractual relationships are less conducive to investment in training and development, for example.

There is a paradoxical relationship between HRM as a relatively new movement and the transformation of organizational forms. Old-fashioned personnel management flourished in bureaucratic structures with rigid job boundaries and detailed negotiations over minor contract variations; the HRM movement sought to overturn assumptions about its role in this environment. Yet, large corporations favoured notions of 'the human resource', career planning, commitment building and other fundamental tenets of HRM. A shift to small-scale enterprises interacting through short-term market transactions does not create a favourable climate for the exercise of HRM.

▶ Conclusion

New organizational forms require new ways of influencing behaviour. The traditional reliance on consistent procedures and rules seems misplaced when corporations are increasingly fashioned around devolved, empowered and agile business units.

Companies already face this dilemma. Following a period when many aspects of HR such as selection, development and career management have been devolved, downsized HR departments are often highly uncertain about when and how to intervene in operational units. Some establish call centres to deal with routine enquiries; other routine processes are being handled via corporate intranets. When activities such as recruitment, induction, relocation and payroll have been outsourced, what role will remain for the central HR specialist? In a single organization, the question is difficult enough. When we consider a supply chain or a network, it is evident that HR specialists have a great deal yet to learn.

Acknowledgements

This article is a reprint of one published in *The Financial Times*, Monday, 19 November 2001.

Further Reading

Chandler, A. D. (1986) 'The evolution of modern global competition', in Porter, M. E. (ed.) *Competition in Global Industries*, Boston, MA: Harvard Business School Press.

Child, J. and Faulkner, D. (1998) *Strategies of Co-operation: Managing alliances, networks and joint ventures*, Oxford: Oxford University Press.

Drucker, P. (1993) *Post Capitalist Society*, New York: HarperCollins.

Hammer, M. (1996) *Beyond Re-engineering*, London: HarperCollins.

Pettigrew, A. M. and Ferlie, E. M. (2000) *The Innovating Organization*, London, Sage.

Storey, J. (ed.) (2001) *Human Resource Management: A Critical Text*, London: Thomson Learning.

Storey, J., Quintas, P., Taylor, P. and Fowle, W. (forthcoming) 'Flexible employment contracts and their implications for product and process innovation', *International Journal of Human Resource Management*, Vol. 13, No. 1.

The Customer-Focused Multinational

Julian Birkinshaw

Broad changes in today's business environment are pushing corporations away from traditional models of organization. Customers have been global in scope for decades, but they are now demanding integrated offerings from their suppliers – the right, for example, to buy the same product at the same price and service level in every country around the world. Even in industries where local regulations prohibit such integrated offerings (such as the pharmaceutical industry), the emergence of global distributors has the same effect.

Second, new kinds of enterprise have emerged that compete globally in one product area rather than attempt to provide a broad product line (Palm versus Philips, for instance). For the incumbent company, these new competitors typically expose just how slow-moving and bureaucratic they have become.

Third, competition has also intensified in traditional core businesses, leading to shrinking margins and low growth rates. Many corporations have started to look towards value-added services and solutions they can sell alongside their traditional products.

What is the best way of meeting these new demands within a traditional corporate structure? The usual approach is to put in place informal or temporary coalitions rather than create entirely new arrangements. To manage a global customer, for example, a first stage would be to appoint a global account manager whose role was to act as the internal co-ordinator of all the different businesses that sold to the customer. And if that was not sufficient, a cross-business team would be created with representatives from each business area. Such structures are usually kept informal, but they overlay all existing structures.

But while this sort of *ad hoc* solution is valid, it can quickly run out of control. It is not uncommon for a mid-level executive in a large corporation to have a 'line' job and then three or four additional responsibilities, each of which involves some form of coordination along one of these other dimensions. This approach quickly reaches the limits of internal coordination.

Is it possible to avoid these problems? Not entirely. But analysis suggests that there are certainly approaches the corporation can take to avoid the 'logjam' in coordination that is often experienced.

Espoused by such companies as IBM, HP, ABB, Citibank and EDS, a new model has emerged that attempts to satisfy two needs simultaneously: the need for integration between country or sector divisions and the need to create higher value in relationships with customers.

Its central feature is a clear split between the front end (demand side) and back end (supply side) of the corporation. The structure of the customer-oriented front end varies from case to case, but typically it is divided first into customer sectors, with specific global customers within that, and then with countries as a secondary line of reporting.

The front-end/back-end structure may be leading the effort to add value for customers, yet it also has a number of problems. Before getting into these general points, however, it is worth describing three examples of how it works in practice.

Following the success of its global services business in the early 1990s, IBM developed a form of front-end/back-end structure. The central idea was that the company would sell whatever combination of products and services the customer requested, whether that meant sourcing the products from inside IBM or selling competitors' machines.

Product development units could sell directly to customers, but they could also function as internal suppliers to the company's solution units that serve industry segments. IBM centralized the management of this front-end/back-end relationship, establishing a finance centre to manage the solutions business, internal transfer pricing, and regional leadership groups that focus on resource allocation.

In a second example, the computer group Hewlett Packard (HP) has existed for most of its 60-odd years as a highly decentralized company, with as many as 83 product units responsible for developing and manufacturing its products. Customer relationships were managed through a global sales organization, split by country first, and overlain with a global account management structure.

This structure helped to create strong managers and an impressive record in new product development. On the other hand, customers faced numerous sales and marketing staff, and the company was so focused on projects that it missed the boat on large initiatives, such as the development of a company-wide internet strategy.

When Carly Fiorina became chief executive in 2000 she quickly moved towards a customer-focused structure. The result was a structure with two back-end units developing computers and printers, and two front-end units focused on corporate sales and consumer sales. The new structure has had mixed reviews. Many HP executives enthuse about the success, and say that modifications are helping to simplify the structure and become more effective. Others are less positive, describing how the new organization created disorder and failed to win support. Some employees were also discouraged by their decreased lack of control and financial responsibility.

The third example of the front-end/back-end structure is the power and automation company ABB. It became famous for its country-business matrix in the early 1990s, but in the late 1990s it moved towards a more traditional global business unit structure, as well as developing a global account management structure on top of its sales organization. Under chief executive Jörgen Centerman, ABB has shifted further, from four industrial divisions to four customer segments (utilities, process industries, manufacturing and consumer industries, and oil, gas, and petrochemicals) and two product segments (power technology products and automation technology products).

According to a presentation by Centerman in February 2001, ABB aims 'to provide increased transparency to customers, by providing a single full-service point of entry into ABB through which we offer our full range of solutions, product and services'. The organization is expected to 'eliminate internal organizational barriers that stand in the way of satisfying customer needs'.

So what are the challenges in making front-end/back-end structures work? First, the link between the two is far from simple. Back-end businesses complain that they no longer have a direct connection to their marketplace, and that they are being asked to accept lower margins on their products which are often sold as part of a bundled offering. Front-end businesses, in turn, complain that they do not get the level of customization and attention they need from the back-end businesses, and that they spend a great deal of time haggling over transfer prices.

To make this work, the usual model is to move to market-based transfer pricing, and allow front-end businesses to source from third parties if necessary. But a strong centre is also needed to mediate disputes, such as when a front-end business wants to source a competitor's product rather than the one produced by the back-end business.

Second, as the front-end business gets closer to its customers, and starts providing complete 'solutions' to their problems, it will typically move away from relying on its traditional products. This can mean working with new partners in very different industries, as well as sourcing competitors' products.

Where does this leave the supply-side of the organization? To some extent, it can be simplified and outsourced. IBM global services, for example, could be spun off as a separate entity with little damage to the company's competitiveness.

Taken too far, though, this model can do great harm. For example, HP relies on a stream of innovative technologies for its competitive advantage, and unless the front end and back end of the company work effectively together, it will find itself in trouble. It may make sense for corporations to get out of commodity manufacturing and hence simplify large parts of their supply chain, but most have wisely recognized the importance of strong design and development capabilities – and the need to integrate them with their customer-focused operations – as central to their long-term competitiveness.

Finally, companies should disregard geography at their peril. In the global economy, the country dimension is often now regarded as less important than the customer, the segment, the product area, and function. But while deals can be done at a global level, implementation is conducted on a local-for-local basis. Most service operations, for example, rely entirely on local capabilities and relationships. So while the high-level structure of the corporation may have little space for country-level management, it has to find its way back into the organization at an operational level. And of course country management is still of great importance in the developing world, where such things as government relations are central to success. In short, the front end/back end structure offers many benefits but also opens up new management problems.

▶ A Question of Structure: Past and Present

In the past, the classic path of development for a growing business was to adopt an 'international division' structure while domestic business was still dominant, and then to move to either an 'area division' or 'global product division' structure as its business became truly international.

The area division structure, as exemplified by Philips, Shell and Nestlé in the 1970s, gave enormous power to countries and regions, but made co-ordination of product development and manufacturing across countries very difficult.

The global product division structure, as adopted by Matsushita, GE and many other corporations, had the opposite characteristics – very clear accountability for production assets worldwide, but little sensitivity to the differences in customer demands from country to country. As foreign sales increased and the range of foreign products became more diverse, companies turned to the matrix system, under which country and business unit held equal power. Matrix management was popular in the early 1980s and later in early 1990s, prompted by its highly successful use under ABB's chief executive Percy Barnevik. However, it often created such complexity as to be unworkable. New dimensions of structure – global accounts, industry sectors – were placed on top of the existing organization structure, resulting in a four- or five-dimensional matrix. Roles were blurred and managers overloaded with administrative tasks.

As a result, many corporations are experimenting with ways of simplifying their structures – they are looking for ways of reducing their portfolio of businesses, outsourcing major activities, and making use of market-like mechanisms for structuring internal relationships.

C

Nokia: An Extended Company with Local and Global Operations

Jyrki Ali-Yrkkö, Laura Paija, Petri Rouvinen and Pekka Ylä-Anttila

▶ Introduction

In 17 March 2000 lightning caused a ten-minute fire at Philips Electronics plant in New Mexico (all information regarding the incident from the *Wall Street Journal*, 29 Jan. 2001, p. A1). The news that hardly seemed noteworthy had major consequences on two Nordic mobile-phone handset manufacturers, Nokia and Ericsson, which together had acquired 40 per cent of the plant's supply of radio frequency chips (RFCs).

Three days later Nokia was informed that Philips had lost 'some wafers' but that the plant would be up in a week. Although the incident still seemed minor, at a scheduled meeting with Philips officials in Helsinki, the president of Nokia Mobile Phones Matti Alahuhta brought up the incident and stated: 'We need strong and determined action right now.' Moreover, task force members along with the chairman and chief executive office Jorma Ollila met Philips CEO Cor Boonstra in Amsterdam. The message was loud and clear: 'We can't accept the current status. It's absolutely essential we turn over every stone looking for a solution.'

Bad news travelled more slowly at Ericsson and weeks after the incident top management was unaware what they were up against with. Finally, Ericsson was millions of RFCs short whereas Nokia was able to meet its production targets despite the incident. It can be argued that Nokia's immediate and swift crisis management marked its leadership in mobile-phone handsets and Ericsson's somewhat softer response marked its declining position. Besides this incident, how did Nokia become a dominant force in mobile telecommunication industry? Why has Nokia been so successful?

In what follows, we provide some background information on the mobile telecommunication industry, consider Nokia's history and present, and shed some light on the company's internal matters. The concluding section includes some speculation on what might lie ahead.

▶ Success is Built in the Long Term

In order to understand Nokia's success one has to look back. Events and operations that Nokia faced tens of years ago explain at least part of Nokia's current success.

In 1969 a cooperative body of Danish, Finnish, Norwegian, and Swedish public telephone operators initiated a project to develop an open *Nordic Mobile Telephone* (NMT, Nordisk Mobil Telefon) standard. NMT included roaming technology, enabling a user to be served where his/her operator has not coverage, e.g., abroad. The commercial introduction of NMT in 1981 made the Nordic countries the world's largest mobile telecommunication market at the time. Local manufacturers *Ericsson* and *Nokia* came to challenge the dominant position of *Motorola* in mobile telecommunication equipment industry.

In 1988, the telecommunication authorities of the European Community published the *Digital Global System for Mobile Communication* (GSM, *Groupe Spécial Mobile*) standard. In 1991 Nokia sold its first GSM network to a small Finnish telecom operator Radiolinja which opened the first commercial GSM network in the world. This launch gave Nokia an important reference and lifted the company onto the international stage (Paija, 2001).

Later on, GSM eventually became almost universally accepted with the major exceptions of the United States, Canada and leading Latin American countries. Currently GSM is gaining ground also on these markets.

▶ Path from a Domestic to a Global Company

In the past 30 years Nokia has transformed itself from a domestically orientated conglomerate to a global mobile communication firm (Nokia's history is documented in three volumes by Häikiö, 2001). Nokia was established in 1967 as a merger of Suomen Kaapelitehdas (Finnish Cable Works), Suomen Gummitehdas (Finnish Rubber Works) and Nokia, a wood-grinding mill established in 1865, which lent its name to the new entity.

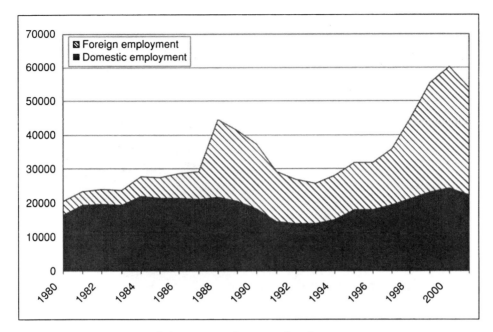

Figure RC1 Foreign and domestic employment of Nokia
Source: Ali-Yrkkö (2001)

Up till 1980, Nokia sold approximately half of its products to the domestic market and the rest was exported. In the early 1980s, however, Nokia started to strengthen its international operations (figure RC1).

A former president of Nokia (Kari Kairamo) forecast coming changes in 1984 (Nokia's annual report):

> We have attempted to change the structure of the group by directing investment and research and development activities towards high-tech products and production methods. This structural change has been supported by corporate acquisitions at home and abroad. At the same time, internationalisation has also been promoted.

Until the 1980s, Nokia's sales were mostly in Finland and the neighbouring countries. Since the early 1980s Nokia began to strengthen its global presence via acquisitions in consumer electronics (Luxor, Swedish TV manufacturer; Salora, Finnish TV manufacturer; Standard Elektrik Lorenz's, German TV and other electronics manufacturer). As a consequence, the electronics division of Nokia expanded rapidly (figure RC2). Nokia's mobile telecommunication unit, Mobira, expanded via global alliances (joint ventures in Korea and the USA with Tandy, private labelling with Radio Shack and others, etc.).

Despite the favourable developments in the mobile sector, *Nokia* was still pursuing a conglomerate strategy in the latter half of 1980s and made several

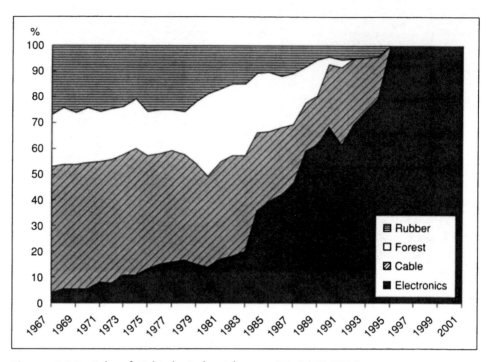

Figure RC2 Sales of Nokia by industrial group (%), 1967–2001
Source: Ali-Yrkkö, Paija, Reilly and Ylä-Anttila (2000), updated

sizable acquisitions in other sectors. As a consequence of deep financial crises related to the severe recession of the Finnish economy and internal matters, Jorma Ollila replaced Simo Vuorilehto as the chief executive officer of Nokia in 1992. Under Ollila's leadership Nokia divested activities outside the communication sector initiating an era of rapid internal growth. By and large, Nokia has not made major acquisitions in the communication sector but has rather grown internally.

Currently Nokia is a clear market leader in handsets with a global market share of over 35 per cent, and is one the dominant players in network infrastructure equipment (table RC1). In 2001, Nokia's net sales reached 31 billion euros, of which Nokia Mobile Phones accounted for 74 per cent, Nokia Networks 24 per cent and Nokia Ventures Organization 2 per cent. Ninety per cent of Nokia's stock was held abroad, 99 per cent of its net sales came abroad, it had production in ten, R&D in fifteen, and sales in over 130 countries. The most important market area is still Europe, but the most important single country is the United States. *Nokia*'s headquarters are still in Espoo, Finland. The company is lead by Jorma Ollila, and other members of the top management are also Finns. Nokia has grown to a sizable company especially with respect to its host country – in fact the company's annual sales exceed the annual budget of the state of Finland (table RC2).

Table RC1 Estimations of handset and 3G networks' market shares, 2001

Company	Mobile phones, market share (%)	Company	3G networks, market share (%)
Nokia	35	Nokia	32
Motorola	14.8	Ericsson	33
Siemens	7.4	Siemens (NEC)	15
Samsung	7.1	Nortel	8
Ericsson	6.7	Nec (Siemens)	4

Sources: Gartner Dataquest (March 2002) and UMTSWorld.com February 2002.

Table RC2 Key figures for Nokia, 1990–2001

	1990	1995	2001
Net sales, FIM	22,130	36,810	185,453
Employment	37,336	31,900	53,849
Return on capital employed, %	10	29.1	27.9
Operating profit, %	4.4	13.6	10.8
R&D, FIM	1,164	2,531	17,748
R&D, % of Net Sales	5.3	6.9	9.6

Nokia Reacts Quickly to Challenges

Although the management of Nokia has been able to build an innovation-driven culture and supporting organizational structure, flexibly exploiting both internal and external networking, Nokia has had its share of problems and challenges as well. What sets Nokia apart from many other gigantic corporations, is its ability to react quickly and improvise in a moment of crisis. As the example of fire of Philips plant showed, Nokia did not just sit and wait but started to act. A few years before this incident, Nokia made considerable losses due to a logistics glitch. Nokia has learned from its earlier mistake. Dozens of Nokia executives formed a task force addressing the problem of fire, and history was not to repeat itself.

An even better example of Nokia's reactions on problems can be found in the early 1990s. During that time Nokia was nearly bankrupt. There was even an attempt to sell the company to Ericsson, which in hindsight unwisely showed no interest. Rubber boots, car tyres, energy cables, toilet paper, etc. were divested, and a lean communication-focused company was created. The mid-1990s' logistics crisis and the mismatch of product mix and market demand shortly led to a major revision in organizational structure.

After the turn of millennium, a long-standing deep upturn of the telecommunications industry ceased. Market expectations of the stock market were revised to a more realistic level some time after the turn of the millennium. Ericsson, Lucent, Nortel, and Motorola did not react immediately but later announced layoffs in the order of tens of thousands of employees. After the first signs of weakening markets Nokia initiated a severe cost cutting programme – layoffs were in the order of hundreds and profitability remained high. In early 2002, Nokia faced rather unexpected quality problems in its handset displays. Within days of the news surfacing in the media, the company had stopped using the suspected components and switched suppliers. The organization of Nokia Mobile Phones was also revised in order to further enhance reaction speed and market responsiveness. Nokia also extended warranties of several models in case display problems were to emerge.

In their *McKinsey Quarterly* article Day *et al.* (2001) argue that Nokia's strength lies in a delicate balance between separation and integration. Various businesses have sufficient independence to develop but are simultaneously close enough to each other and to the parent company to obtain invaluable information, knowledge, and resources and to share goals, strategies, and visions. Day *et al.* note that Nokia reflects unique identity and the egalitarianism of Finnish culture and that the company relies heavily on personal networks.

▶ Make or Buy?

Rather than aim to do everything itself, Nokia is increasingly turning to outside organizations. The alliance palette includes horizontal alliances between competitors, vertical alliances between buyers and suppliers and diagonal alliances between companies in different industries (for details, see Ali-Yrkkö, 2001). Nokia's operative network includes not only companies but also universities and research institutes (figure RC3).

Since the 1980s, the scope and depth of Nokia's networking have shifted considerably. In the large scale the option of relying on outside partners was explored in the early 1990s with the manufacturing of mobile-phone handset accessories. In the late 1990s Nokia started to rely more on outside partners in other areas as well, which helped the company to respond to the challenge of shortening product life cycles and market expansion. During the past few years Nokia has also started complement in-house R&D and software development with subcontracting and partnerships (figure RC4).

By and large, Nokia's internal development activities are organized teams. In many cases a team is complemented by representatives of downstream (suppliers, subcontractors, etc.) and/or upstream (operators, end-users, etc.) partners. These extended teams work intensively to solve specific problems. As a director of a Nokia supplier notes, often these teams work so intensively together that in many cases 'it is impossible to distinguish between the two organizations'.

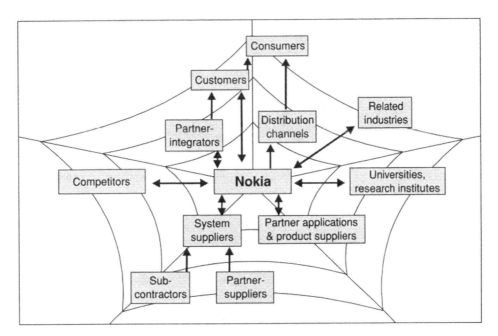

Figure RC3 Nokia's network environment
Source: Ali-Yrkkö (2001)

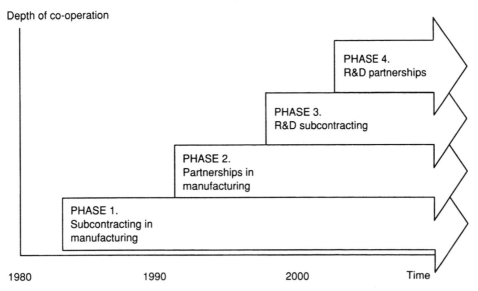

Figure RC4 The development of Nokia's co-operation with its suppliers
Source: Ali-Yrkkö (2001)

'Platform thinking' is one of the cornerstones of Nokia Mobile Phone's R&D and production strategy. The aim is to develop a manageable set of standard subsystems or platforms, a combination of which then forms a specific mobile-phone handset. A platform includes necessary design, technical, and commercial specifications. The number of specialized, as opposed to industry standard, components is kept to a minimum. As a consequence of this strategy, Nokia has been able to outsource most of component production and assembly, while focusing itself primarily on brand management, logistics, and key software components (SEC, 2001). As CEO Jorma Ollila has noted (*Talouselämä*, 18/2000): 'At Nokia key aspects of R&D as well as branding, the very soul of the company, are [always] done internally.'

▶ Listen to your Customer

Nokia's early success in the marketplace crucially depended on cooperation. For example the 1984 agreement with Tandy and the Radio Shack chain it owned gained Nokia over 7,000 consumer electronics outlets in the USA. As senior vice president Kari-Pekka Wilska notes (*Helsingin Sanomat*, 7 April 2002, p. E3), Tandy cooperation was important in other aspects as well: 'We had a Finnish engineer's mindset. As a major distributor of consumer products, Tandy's view was totally different . . . We learned that even though the product can command a high price in the market place, it does not have to be expensive to produce.'

Nokia has also built relationships with telecommunication operators, which are especially important in the USA, where most handsets are sold through them. Nokia has established an ongoing dialogue with all major operators, asking for their ideas and wishes concerning handsets and sharing ideas on market developments and long-term trends. In Wilska's words: 'One by one we went [to the operators] asking what they want. We altered our handsets to fulfil their needs.'

A few years ago Nokia reacted to its lack of direct customer interface, traditionally the domain of operators, by introducing Club Nokia in most major markets. All Nokia handset owners are invited to join; members have access to online support, services, goodies (logos, ring tones, covers, badges, etc.), games (featuring, e.g., Star Wars Episode II theme), and special promotions (e.g., advanced/specially priced concert tickets). As the head of Nokia's operations Olav Stang (*Talouselämä*, 3/1999) says: 'What is the decisive factor? To understand, what the markets want.'

▶ Successful Cooperation Requires Deep Trust

A prerequisite to fruitful partnerships is deep trust among participants, not least because partners share rather sensitive information. The concept of trust is obviously closely related to culture. Thus, a global company like Nokia needs to adapt to local variations and limitations in partnership development. For example, in Anglo-Saxon countries contracts are usually carefully drafted and enforced by law. By contrast, in Finland there is a long tradition of informal cooperation between companies, which has had an important effect on the development of, e.g., telecommunication technology. Informal agreements have been almost as, and sometimes even more, significant as formal contracts, indicating deep personal trust between partners. As the CEO of Elektrobit (one of Nokia's partners in Finland) Juha Hulkko notes, operational networks tend to create their own dynamics: 'Best-functioning firm networks are based on mutual trust. These networks cannot be [rigorously] managed – they tend to create their own set of rules. A win–win situation is a much better [incentive and disciplinary measure] than any contractual mean.'

Globalization has, however, necessitated more formal contractual habits also in domestic agreements. Aided by its strong corporate culture, Nokia nevertheless tries to maintain flexibility in these questions as well. The president of Nokia Mobile Phones Matti Alahuhta notes:

> Trust is a sum of two things. Globally uniform values [and goals] create a common frame of reference, language, and a sense of familiarity. Additionally trust has to be present each and everyone's working environment – wherever that might be. Both take considerable time to build.

▶ Suppliers Have Internationalized in the Wake of Nokia

As a global actor Nokia has contributed both directly and indirectly to the internationalization of a number of Finnish-based companies. Today, Nokia has 20 manufacturing facilities in nine countries around the world. Nokia Networks has five plants in Finland, five in China, and one in Malaysia. Nokia Mobile Phones has production units in eight countries. R&D units are located in fourteen different countries. Half of the foreign-based R&D units operate in Europe, the rest in North America and in Asia Pacific region (table RC3). We estimate, however, that more than half of Nokia's R&D is conducted in Finland. A growing share of sales comes from foreign markets: in year 2001 they accounted for 99 per cent of sales, up from 70 per cent a decade earlier.

Despite its Finnish origins, Nokia operates truly globally. As the company has grown more global, it has encouraged its Finnish subcontractors and partners to follow suit. Many supplier companies have started or increased their international operations including foreign trade, production and R&D abroad (table RC4).

Notwithstanding the fact that Nokia currently uses both local and global partners, it seems that in the future it will be more interested in suppliers capable of global operations. These suppliers operate in several continents and their plants

Table RC3 Nokia's in-house operations in different countries

R&D units	Production facilities	Listings on stock exchanges
Finland	Finland	Finland
Germany	Germany	Germany
United States	United States	United States
Hungary	Hungary	Sweden
China	China	UK
Malaysia	Malaysia	France
South Korea	South Korea	
Australia	Brazil	
UK	Mexico	
Japan		
Italy		
Canada		
Sweden		
Denmark		

Table RC4 Production plant locations of selected Finnish partner companies of Nokia in 2001

Company	Finland	Other Europe	Asia	North America	Latin America
Eimo	Yes	Yes	Yes	Yes	Yes
Elcoteq	Yes	Yes	Yes	Yes	Yes
Perlos	Yes	Yes	Yes	Yes	
Aspocomp	Yes	Yes	Yes	Yes	
Efore	Yes	Yes	Yes		
Jot-Automation	Yes	Yes		Yes	
Scanfil	Yes	Yes			

are located in logistically suitable places. The tendency toward global suppliers first occurred in electronics manufacturing services (EMS) and in component manufacturing but it will also probably take place in software development. Moving toward global partnerships places pressures on small and medium-sized Nokia's suppliers because their capability to operate globally is limited. Hence, the challenge of these companies is to grow rapidly and internationalize their operations.

Currently Nokia is outsourcing some of its business activities to further improve its flexibility and reaction speed. Outsourcing can also be seen as an additional way to manage increasing fluctuations in demand and complexity in the operating environment. Many activities are outsourced to global players as opposed to their Finnish-based counterparts. Recently Nokia Networks has sold many production units to SCI-systems. Also Nokia Mobile Phones is increasingly using global suppliers. We estimate, that in the beginning of year 2002, roughly two-thirds of network equipment and 10 to 15 per cent of mobile phone production (excl. accessories) is outsourced. Both Networks and Mobile Phones remain in control of their final assemblies, and also tightly control design, marketing, development, standards, and platforms (i.e., subsystem development) as well as manage their respective operational networks. In president Matti Alahuhta's words, 'Nokia's global network has geographical and sectoral dimensions. [Furthermore,] virtual teams cross these organizational boundaries increasing our understanding on issues affecting our future.'

▶ Nokia's Network also Includes Horizontal Alliances

As Nokia has become a dominant force in the industry, it has placed more emphasis on horizontal aspects of networking, i.e., joint ventures, alliances, and other forms of cooperation with major players in the industry and related fields as well as in the academia.

Nokia is systematically attempting to co-operate with the best universities and research units worldwide (table RC5). Besides actual research results, the

Table RC5 Nokia's most important partner universities by country, 2001

Finland		UK	
	Helsinki University of Technology		Imperial College
	Tampere University of Technology		The University of Strathclyde
	University of Oulu		University of Surrey
Denmark		United States	
	Technical University of Denmark		Massachusetts Institute of Technology
	Aalborg University		University of California, Berkeley
Germany			Texas A&M University
	University of Dortmund		Stanford University
	Aachen University	China	
Sweden			Beijing University of Posts and Telecommunications
	Linköping University		Tsinghua University
	the Royal Institute of Technology	Thailand	
Japan			Asian Institute of Technology
	University of Tokyo	Hungary	
	Tokyo Institute of Technology		Budapest University of Technology and Economics

Source: Häikiö (2001).

company is interested in being connected to leading-edge 'thinkers' of 'feelers' in order to be able to understand future developments in the market place.

Nokia has taken an active role in setting standard and even in promoting content creation for the networks and end-user terminals it provides. The company's strategy seems to be favouring open solutions and standards to proprietary ones – on more than one occasion this has positioned the company at odds with, e.g., Microsoft. Anecdotal evidence can be found at several press releases towards the end of 2001: Sony (12 Nov. 2001), with AOL TimeWarner and Nokia, announced the 'Ubiquitous Value Network', an open broadband network environment 'comprising of hardware, content and applications from diverse sectors'; Nokia (18 Dec. 2001) announced that leading IT firms, BEA Systems, Borland, HP, IBM, Oracle, and Sun, supports its 'open standards based mobile architecture that will drive the adoption of mobile software and services'; and Liberty Alliance project (Nokia, 19 Dec. 2001), 'committed to developing and deploying open standards to network identity', 'demonstrates momentum with increased membership and industry support'.

▶ Conclusion

Double-digit growth rates of the 1990s seem to be a thing of the past in the mobile telecommunication industry. Most operators in the world have overspent on network infrastructure, third generation licences, own R&D, and market share fights. Deteriorating credit ratings have added injury to insult for these heavily indebted companies. Deliveries of the third generation networks are nevertheless expected to begin in the later half of year 2002 – equipment manufacturers have been forced to carry part of the financial and commercial risk.

At the same time the general public seems to be less interested in the latest gadgets, perhaps not least because of the failed introduction of infamous WAP-based (Wireless Application Protocol) services in Europe. The issue of handset application protocols is unsettled. Japan has had early success with i-mode, which has now spreading to other markets (called m-mode in the USA). Due to the convergence of small electronic appliances, personal digital assistants, electronic organizers, laptops, palmtops, etc., mobile-phone handset manufacturers are facing (potential) competition from all directions. The eagerly waited 'killer application' for the third generation mobile networks has yet to reveal itself. Mobile corporate warriors and other heavy users aside, so far there does not seem to be a pressing need for the additional wireless bandwidth or services.

The turbulence in mobile telecommunication is likely to continue into the foreseeable future. Although the United Nations' organ International Telecommunication Union has enforced Universal Mobile Telephone Standard (UMTS) – considered a victory for the Ericsson–Nokia-led camp – standards battles are far from over. Multiple standards my not be a major problem to the manufacturers, but they certainly bring about uncertainty, deflate costs, and may even reduce the ultimate customer gain from the service, e.g., due to difficulties in roaming. Also on the network side, the convergence of information technology and telecommunication is a source of intensifying competition. Wireless local area network (WLAN) specifications may be considered wireless extensions of Internet standards. They operate on unregulated frequencies and equipment can be assembled from standard components, which makes WLANs cost effective. As far as data communication in high traffic areas such as airports is concerned, WLAN may be seen as a viable alternative to the third generation mobile networks.

As can be inferred from the discussion above, Nokia is facing an increasingly complex playing field with potential competition several directions. In the near future Nokia's fortunes are largely tied into overall market developments. It remains to be seen how the third generation mobile telecommunication will progress – both operators and equipment manufacturers desperately need a must-have killer application, that would convince customers of the need of new services and gadgets.

Nokia has taken an active role in moulding the future of its industry. The company promotes openness in both handset and network standards as well as in content and service provision. Internally outsourcing and partnerships are seen as important tools in maintaining flexibility and efficiency.

Only the future will show how Nokia responds to challenges it is facing and what role Finland will play in Nokia's operations. From Finland's point of view, it is clear that both Nokia's R&D and production will grow far faster abroad than in Finland.

Nokia's history shows that the company is able to reinvent itself – even quite radically if necessary. Thus, it seems almost impossible to forecast what kind of structure or core competencies the company will have in ten years' time.

LEGO: Moving from a Multi-Local Toy Manufacturer to a Global Brand Company

Søren Brandi and Robbert Nickolaj Stecher

▶ Background

The history of LEGO Company begins in Billund, Denmark, where in 1932 Ole Kirk Christiansen began to make wooden toys. In the years since, the Kirk Kristiansen family has transformed the little workshop into a large, successful brand company that today employs around 8,000 people. The company obtained its name 'LEGO' in 1934 when its founder combined the two Danish words 'LEg GOdt', which mean 'play well'. LEGO Company continues to be family-owned for the third generation in a row now, and today the founder's grandson, Kjeld Kirk Kristiansen, is the main shareholder, President and CEO.

The well-known LEGO brick with tubes was introduced in 1958, and in less than 50 years it has twice been named Toy of the Century. *Fortune Business Magazine* was the first in November 1999; then in January 2000 came the award from the British Association of Toy Retailers.

Today, LEGO Company is the fourth largest toy company in the world and its products are well penetrated globally – during the past 40 years, more than 300 million children have played with LEGO bricks. The company's goal is for the LEGO brand to be known as the strongest brand in the world among families with children by 2005 – a dimension on which the company already holds a position among the top 10.

LEGO play materials	• The most well-known trademarks of LEGO play materials are probably the LEGO brick and building systems with endless creative opportunities • All play material concepts are based on the LEGO core brand values emphasizing creativity, imagination, learning, fun and quality
LEGO Media	• Interactive games to support existing universes within the play materials business • IP and story development to build media based universes emphasizing child development
LEGOLAND parks	• Family Parks that offer an entertaining and developmental world primarily based on LEGO bricks
LEGO.COM	• Web-site and community inviting children to step into the LEGO universe to play and learn how to exchange information through the internet
Lego Lifestyle	• Licensed products to heighten the awareness of the LEGO brand (e.g. LEGO Wear)
LEGO Educational	• Educational products for institutions based on the LEGO play materials concepts

Figure RD1   LEGO Company's global businesses

The mission of LEGO Company is 'to nurture the child in each of us' – a mission the company will fulfil by being the world leader in providing quality products and experiences that stimulate creativity, imagination, fun and learning. This relatively broad mission statement has in recent years led to a number of natural expansions outside the core LEGO play materials business. As a result, LEGO Company today has substantial activity in its Media, LEGOLAND Park, Internet, Lifestyle licensed products and Educational businesses. An overview of LEGO Company's business activities as of 2002 can be found in figure RD1.

The LEGO brick, the LEGO building system and the LEGO values form the basis for a unique value proposition with a very universal appeal. This has been the platform from which LEGO Company successfully started international sales to Scandinavia and the German-speaking countries in the mid-1950s. At that time consolidated company sales amounted to around EUR 270 million per annum. It was really with the establishment of the international organization in 1976 and the following globalization of the company and with the new marketing model with an introduction of Play Themes (City, Castle, Pirates etc.) that sales really boomed and landed the company around EUR 1,35 billion by the turn of the century.

It has never been an ambition as such that the LEGO Company should become a transnational managed company. However, during the early 1990's the company faced declining profitability, and the time had come to accept the challenge and build a global set-up and infrastructure to continuously innovate and deliver the company value proposition and brand to the global market. Part of this included a new brand philosophy, leading to new businesses and brand

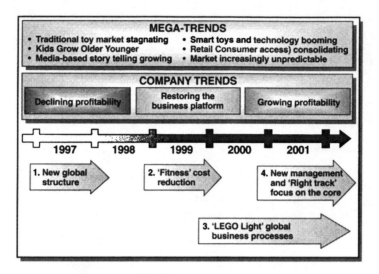

Figure RD2 LEGO Company's globalization journey

stretching and a 'soft' culture change termed Compass Management, which was introduced in 1995. The most recent events of LEGO Company's globalization journey are depicted in figure RD2.

In 1997 LEGO Company re-organized to what, by and large, is the current form and shape of the global structural set-up. Today, the Executive Office decides on the overall direction and priorities of the company, and the Global Management Team is responsible for delivering on the strategy (see figure RD3). The global organization is directed by the Global Management Team responsible for operating the global business support, global supply chain, global brand management, global market organizations and the global adjacent businesses. The responsibility for global concept and product development, brand strategy and brand communications has been placed with the Global Brand Management organization.

The second big step that was needed in LEGO Company was to dramatically adjust the cost structure, and this step was taken in 1999 with the implementation of the 'Fitness' rightsizing programme. To successfully transform the company to a healthier cost structure, the CEO and owner, Kjeld Kirk Kristiansen, hired COO Poul Plougmann to drive the change programme and subsequently turn the company into a strong global and brand-driven company. After Fitness, the third big step was to initiate implementation of global business processes to support the global structural set-up. This process was initiated in the beginning of 2000 with the change programme 'LEGO Light'.

The financial year 2000 turned out to be a disaster for the company with a total consolidated loss around EUR 135 million. It would therefore seem as if a fourth and final step was needed to really set the company on the right track.

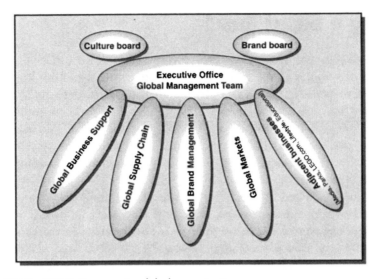

Figure RD3 LEGO Company's global organization

After several years of local initiatives and bottom-up management, the company decided to increasingly focus on its core value proposition to consumers with the project 'Right track'. The most visible results from this effort has been a stronger integration of adjacent businesses into the core play materials business and closure of business areas too far removed from the company's core.

In the following three sections, LEGO Company's change journey will be described in further detail, highlighting challenges, the rationales for the paths chosen and the difficulties in making the transformation. It is quite natural to wrap the structure around LEGO Company's three strategic priorities, i.e. a virtuous cycle of brand building, people and culture and profitable growth (see figure RD4).

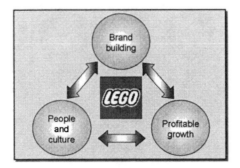

Figure RD4 LEGO Company's three strategic priorities

▶ Building a Global Brand

It has always been the *raison d'être* and driving ambition for LEGO Company to stick to its core values as the basis for its consumer promise. Both in relation to product offerings within the LEGO play materials business, but equally important for its entry into adjacent businesses. The LEGO Company consumer promise and brand position is about being a trusted provider of creative materials and experiences that empower children to create. The LEGO Company brand position emphasizes its five core values of creativity, imagination, learning, fun and quality (see figure RD5).

During the 1980s and 1990s, the company did not really deliver a truly global brand statement to the consumers. First and foremost, individual markets or regions were empowered to decide their own prioritization of marketing spendings and efforts, as well as localizing the brand expression. Second, concept and product development was given autonomy to decide on product lines with insufficient consumer focus and concept thinking. Third, the adjacent business areas were allowed too much autonomy in creating their own *raison d'être* and consequently unique interpretation of position within the overall LEGO Company value proposition.

This high degree of empowerment across the company, and with insufficient global direction setting, had a number of consequences. Most importantly, the company brand architecture was allowed to become complex and inaccessible from a consumer standpoint, and as such making it difficult for LEGO Company to achieve the intended brand position with consumers. Therefore, it was also

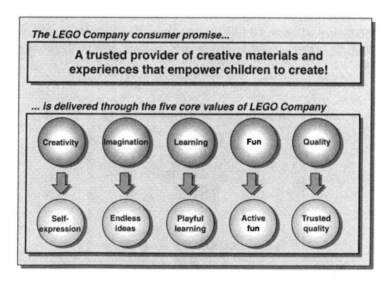

Figure RD5 The LEGO Company values

increasingly difficult to implement a universal brand position in markets across the world. As a further result, market companies increasingly reverted to focusing on meeting the current years' sales targets, and less on building a global brand position. The internal mindset can best be described as that of a 'production company' selling its products globally using the available retail structures. The key challenge to overcome was primarily to turn a decentralized and local modus operandi into a global and coordinated *modus operandi.*

As it was decided to take the necessary actions to become a truly global company around 1997, it was quite clear that the previous *modus operandi* was insufficient to deliver on the strategy. To effectively deliver on a global brand position and value proposition, LEGO Company initiated a number of key changes starting in 1997 and with some of them continuing into 2002 and onwards. The five key areas for change are listed and further elaborated on below:

1   *One global brand management organization*
    Initially, in 1997, all product development and global branding were con-solidated into three global organizations divided by age segments, i.e. pre-school, ages 4–8 and ages 8+. This set-up was chosen to ensure an improved end-consumer focus for each target group. By 2001, the foundation for improved consumer focus had been laid, and the three segment organiza-tions were again consolidated into one Global Brand Management organ-ization. This consolidation continues to ensure consumer focus, but increasingly strengthens the focus across categories and play themes, e.g. the fully integrated Racing concept for the launch year 2002 and a fully integrated Complete Discovery System for pre-schoolers in 2003.

2   *One global brand strategy with increased consumer focus*
    LEGO Company has worked intensively on improving its consumer under-standing since 1997. As a result the company will radically restructure its total value proposition around a number of more consumer-driven brand portals from 2003, i.e. consumer-driven interpretations of a logical way to access the full value proposition of LEGO Company. Specifically, an emphasis is being put on delivering the five core LEGO values in the unique LEGO way, i.e. empowering children to create emphasizing self-expression, endless ideas, playful learning, active fun and trusted quality. In short, LEGO Company intends to own the child development (learning by doing) mind-space of the consumer, as opposed to the learning-by-teaching mind-space.

3   *Combining the brand with strong story telling and external universes*
    To capture the minds of children today requires strong stories and play universes. This is evident in the current in-license portfolio, where the LEGO brand is playing on equal terms with other strong brands sharing some fundamental values regarding creativity and imagination. Good ex-amples are the Star Wars, Bob-the-Builder and Harry Potter IP franchises. They all represent unique universes and are strong stories that fit very well

with the values and the open-ended construction systems of LEGO Company. LEGO Company emphasizes strong internal story development through its LEGO Media TV business set-up. Recent examples include *Little Robots* (TV show), Jack Stone (Play theme) and Creator (basic LEGO bricks offering).

4 *Cross-functional development and global prioritization of lead propositions*
Since 1999, the notion of Big Bang teams has been introduced to reflect a fully cross-functional approach to developing and bringing to market 'lead propositions'. An example of such an effort is the Bionicle launch. Today, the GMT decides on the overall portfolio of lead propositions and there is a global prioritization process in place during which marketing funds are allocated to market regions and product lines. This process is key in ensuring a globally coordinated effort across brand management, supply chain and market regions.

5 *Improved brand control through a number of direct-to-consumer initiatives*
The LEGO Company value proposition is highly focused on the empowerment of children to create, i.e. very hands-on minds-on. This increases the importance of controlling some elements of bringing that brand position to market globally. Several initiatives have been launched and recently strengthened in regards to being integrated with the core play materials business. Most notable examples are the LEGOLAND Parks business, the LEGO catalogue and Internet sales channel, the Internet and club communities as well as a number of brand stores across the world. These channels are all key to providing the consumer with a more direct experience of the LEGO world and values.

▶ Building a Global Management Set-up

LEGO Company started the international journey by being a large Danish manufacturing company with sales companies throughout the world. A more regionalized structure replaced this set-up. In this structure regional directors controlled the Company, being responsible for all aspects of the business. The strategic direction and the brand were managed regionally, and each region controlled its own resources. At this time LEGO Company was very much a multi-domestic company operating mostly or wholly autonomous subsidiaries in multiple countries; typified by operational and functional redundancies in its various regions.

LEGO Company had been very successful, always delivering solid financial results while at the same time continuously building a strong brand in the various regions. But LEGO Company wanted to deliver a global brand position and a global value proposition. This would soon prove to be a challenge, since the management set-up and management processes applied were inadequate. At the same time turnover and profits were declining.

A number of things made it difficult to succeed in the marketplace: many new and fluctuating market conditions were making it much more difficult to predict sales and this was not a good cocktail, mixing with LEGO Company's rather inflexible cost structure.

The first big step to meet the new challenges, and thereby start on the road to globalization, was taken in 1997 where LEGO Company re-organized to what, by and large, is the current form and shape of the global structural set-up. But structure is rarely enough and proved not to be in this case either. There were also a number of problems that needed to be dealt with. Traditionally, the core competency of the company was the manufacturing moulding processes; LEGO Company was very much characterized as a Danish international manufacturing company with an old heritage and to some extent also old values and culture being used as a shield against development initiatives. Limited top-down direction and guidance also characterized the company.

To effectively change the company in this direction activities in four key areas were initiated:

1 *One Global Management Team (GMT)*
    First of all, the overall leadership structure was overly complex with five different management forums, being overlapping and to some degree without a shared sense of direction. Leadership decisions and communications were often inconsistent, unaligned and not founded in holistic portfolio management. Second, there was no clear distinction between strategic and tactical co-ordination and management processes, which seemed to cause problems in the fluctuating and complex market conditions, often demanding firm and speedy decisions on the tactical level.

    In 2000 it was concluded that there was a need for one global management team with direct representation of key business drivers, that each owns the decisions as well as the responsibility to implement those decisions in the organization. It was therefore decided to separate the strategic and tactical levels into two forums: the Executive Office consisting of CEO and owner Kjeld Kirk Kristiansen and COO Poul Plougmann; and the Global Management Team with representation of all key functional business areas, giving clear accountability and thus enabling decision competence aggregated at the right level.

2 *Global business processes*
    Across the functional global structure it soon became apparent that there was also a need for global business processes enabling delivery of the global value propositions. The lack of global business processes caused compensating and redundant work in a variety of ways combined with less structured information flow and lack of data consistency.

    Implementation of the global business processes started in 1999 with the project 'LEGO Light'. LEGO Light is a vision of a strong business foundation that will support operational excellence with a strong management

> **One global brand company.**
> An approach to sharing and applying global best practice in all areas and to organize around core global business and support processes.
>
> **Integrated.**
> An integrated way of working that ensures that skills, synergies, knowledge and business opportunities are exploited to their full potential. Clear top-down direction setting.
>
> **Simple.**
> A constant strive to simplify the way we do business in order to maintain focus on the tasks to be solved.
>
> **Change ready.**
> A leadership orientation towards continuous change and improvement. Strong action and performance drive.
>
> **Platform thinking.**
> Standardized and flexible business, product, technology, and procurement platforms leveraged across all global segments, categories and markets.

Figure RD6 Principles for LEGO Company's business foundation

support system and will foster a global mindset (see figure RD6). LEGO Light is based on an Enterprise Resource Planning (ERP) System as a vehicle for implementing the business processes. However, it has been a paramount principle that the system was implemented in order to support the business processes and not the opposite, as one so often hears.

3 *Performance culture*

The new management and the change momentum gained soon paved the way to also significantly strengthen the global performance culture. To do this, the company implemented a global Performance Management Programme (PMP). PMP supports company priorities and competence development. Individual Key Performance Indicators (KPI's) support the company priorities. All employees have KPIs in alignment with company priorities, and performance on these KPIs is reviewed on an annual basis.

The other part of PMP is the employee's development, which is addressed from two perspectives: (1) to build a common understanding of important competencies for LEGO Company, using a model focusing on five core areas: Professional skills, Consumer and brand focus, Leadership, Business drive and Living the LEGO values. Every employee has objectives for each competence area, which are evaluated on a yearly basis together with performance. (2) To support the employee in being a success during the coming year and to support an open dialogue on career perspectives, every person has an individual development plan. This plan is developed in a dialogue between leader and employee. The performance culture is now assessed in the LEGO Pulse, the yearly employee survey.

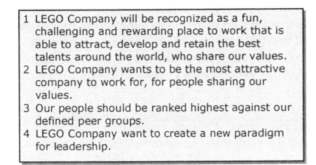

1 LEGO Company will be recognized as a fun, challenging and rewarding place to work that is able to attract, develop and retain the best talents around the world, who share our values.
2 LEGO Company wants to be the most attractive company to work for, for people sharing our values.
3 Our people should be ranked highest against our defined peer groups.
4 LEGO Company want to create a new paradigm for leadership.

Figure RD7 LEGO Company's People and Culture objectives

4 *Leadership and talent development*

LEGO Company has always prioritized building people and culture based on the LEGO values, and several programmes have been launched to develop talent and leadership (see figure RD7). A common denominator for the programmes has been a standardized common approach, which does not in all cases support the individuals' needs for development.

In 2001 LEGO Company launched a new Leadership Development Initiative for the top 90 people in the company. The process was intentionally quite simple. The people included were assessed on the competencies in scope. Based on the assessment, the individuals formulated their own strengths and development areas within the competencies in scope. This formed the background for a development plan meeting with the leader. Hereafter the focused individual development commenced.

For the majority of the leaders involved, the development plans focus on experience-based and relationship-based development strategies as opposed to traditional educational development strategies. This process with focus on company objectives and individual development needs is now cascaded throughout the organization.

▶ Building a Stronger and Flexible Operational Set-up

Quality is one of LEGO Company's core values. Hence, it has always been part of the consumer promise to deliver best-in-class products, and for that purpose the moulding and manufacturing processes were core competencies.

This mass production set-up proved itself to be inadequate at the time as markets became more fluctuating; and objectives for a new operating set-up to deliver consumer promise shifted. Focus was on building strategic agility, meaning adopt top line fluctuations, to become more responsive to changes in demand for product mix, and maybe most important, to reduce fixed costs.

In recent years, three important initiatives have been launched in order to support this more agile and effective operations set-up for LEGO Company:

1 *Fitness*
   COO Poul Plougmann initiated The Fitness programme in 1999 with the objective of rightsizing the company and taking costs out of the budget. To a large extent Fitness was the 'hard culture revolution' with emphasis on costs, structure and mindset – and as such a continuation of Compass Management introduced in 1995.

2 *Right Track*
   Fitness was a step in the right direction and it did create simplicity and a more integrated company. However, in 2000 it became evident that not all issues had been resolved. Some of the costs that were taken out in the Fitness process had been neutralized by build-up within new business areas. New business initiatives were eaten up the profitability by delivering sales with low margins. The cost structure was highly inflexible and needed to be addressed strategically in order to increase the ability to absorb fluctuations in sales.

   Right track was initiated as a task force in autumn 2000. The outcome was a strong company re-focusing by streamlining portfolio of strategic initiatives, stop for new strategic initiatives until the right growth platforms for existing businesses have been established, and right sizing of product novelty portfolio.

3 *747*
   '747' was the name of a project following Right Track aiming at restructuring the global supply chain and exploiting the potential of consolidating capacity, tying logistics operations closer to the markets and an Asian procurement set-up. All these were aiming at creating more flexibility at a lower cost level.

▶ Reflections

The whole change journey started with a vision and ambition to be a truly global and brand-driven company and the principle to use the LEGO values as a foundation for everything we do (figure RD8).

Today, we consider the LEGO Company change journey over the last decade to be a success. However, a number of key questions still remain: What was the objective of the whole change journey – and did we achieve that? Did we do the right things – and did we do them in the right order? What, if anything, should we have done differently?

> 'In my vision – my dream – the LEGO name will not only be connected to our products and to the company, and is not limited within specific intentions and strategies.
>
> The LEGO name has become a universal notion, a notion that could be described by the following words – Idea, Exuberance and values'
>
> Kjeld Kirk Kristiansen, 1988.

Figure RD8 LEGO – more than a toy

LEGO Company has always been closely connected with the Kirk Kristiansen family, and a key to understand the change journey is CEO Kjeld Kirk Kristiansen's words, when receiving the Family Business Award at IMD, Lausanne (1996):

My grandfather, Ole Kirk Christiansen's driving force was the perfection of the quality of craftsmanship. My father, Godtfred Kirk Christiansen's most important focus was the concentration on our unique product idea with all its possibilities. I see myself as the more global oriented leader who seeks to fully exploit our brand potential to further develop and expand our product portfolio and our business concept.

This remains a driving force for LEGO Company.

Algebra Lessons for Older Workers

Karen Cates and Kimia D. Rahimi

Generation Y, made up of people born between 1978 and 1994 is entering the workforce. It shares the workplace with Baby Boomers (1945 to 1961) and Generation X (1962 to 1977). Young generations emerge with their own voice, powered by affluence and characterized by a desire for change. Their arrival has sparked a good deal of debate, especially among older workers, as this new breed makes its professional needs and beliefs known.

▶ Who are They?

Generation Y has grown up in an era characterized by technology and economic prosperity. More self-obsessed than any generation before, they have a confidence and optimism that come from knowing that they are wanted. Their parents, who don't want their kids to feel the abandonment of the previous generation, shower their children with gifts, attention, and esteem-building activities. Generation X is now a stable force at work. Rebellious, resentful and realistic in the wake of their parents' experiences of redundancies, as they move into management these former latch-key children have a no-nonsense approach, sometimes shocking older workers with their cut and dried decision-making styles. Older generations scrutinized Generation X when it entered the workforce. Generation Y now enjoys the spotlight – a source of bewilderment, frustration and relief all at the same time.

The upside of working with young people originates in their early childhoods. The upside of working with late Generation X'ers and Generation Y has its origins in their early childhoods. They are used to being on the move, stimulated by activities during every waking moment. This generation does their homework in the car between school and the soccer field. Their parents filled their days with activities. According to a 1999 study conducted by the University of Michigan's Institute for Social Research, parents programme 75 per cent of their children's weekday time compared with 60 per cent in 1981 (leaving 6 hours a week of unstructured time versus 9.5 hours nearly 20 years ago). As a result, Generation Y grew up multi-tasking and knows how to make the most of every minute.

The downside of this privileged, programmed childhood emerges at work in several ways. Generation Y doesn't want to perform the menial tasks of entry-level jobs and feels comfortable voicing its dissatisfaction. They are used to getting what they want. Coddled from an early age, Generation Y seems baffled when given a project to do. Initiative was not encouraged by parents who relied on acquiescence to get through their busy days. Further, expectations of wealth and opportunity born of the boom economy of the 1990s have left Generation Y seeking ambitious salaries very early. Their confident and capable demeanour with elders and their willingness to make demands belie their inexperience and need for guidance. Impatient with over-direction, they don't always know what to do with the reins when they get them. These bright new workers demonstrate the promise and frustrations their Baby Boomer bosses experience at home with their own children. Only at work, the bratty behaviour doesn't seem so cute.

The oldest members of Generation Y are entering the workforce just as the Baby Boomer generation is poised to retire. Boomers outnumber Generation X employees by as much as 30 per cent, creating a labour shortage that employers will have to address, partly with Generation Y workers.

Not only will older workers need to manage the youthfulness of the new generations, they will also need to manage rivalry between generations X and Y: both will be vying for the Baby Boomers' vacant positions. Generation X, the resentful, achievement-oriented entrepreneurs bred by downsizing of the 1980s, will not appreciate being leap-frogged as Generation Y earns fast promotions.

Managers need to understand the opportunities and pitfalls younger workers bring. In spite of recent downturns in the economy, competition for talent continues. Companies that understand the characteristics and motivations of Generation Y, and can manage the tensions in multi-generational organizations, will have a competitive advantage when it comes to attracting and retaining these employees.

▶ Implications

Managers at all levels must understand the expectations of generations in the business and make the most of their strengths. Where Generations X and Y seek immediate recognition for their successes, Boomers embrace the notion of 'paying one's dues'. Generations X and Y may appear ungrateful for their opportunities, yet they cannot understand an organization's dedication to its 'dead wood' (overpaid executives who don't seem able to get things done). Boomers may view younger generations as slackers, always looking for more free time. Younger generations react with indignation when managers expect excessive overtime. Older generations might, for instance, regard it as reasonable to entertain clients at home over dinner. The young have no such expectations; for them, work ends at the allotted hour.

There are benefits to the views of all generations, something not always easy to acknowledge among the tensions. A company should identify how it can benefit from the expectations and values of each generation, and then sell those benefits to others. To maintain the peace, however, assumptions about the organization and how it is understood by employees need to be modified and communicated. Everything, from the organization's vision to its human resources practices, needs to be evaluated for its message to the generations. There is much of the 'old way of doing things' to be preserved but also much that can benefit from a face-lift.

Vision

Vision statements about being the biggest, best or most efficient will need more depth to motivate younger workers. Generations X and Y want to feel they are making a difference in people's lives or working for the good of society. Vision statements should incorporate a value-driven component.

For example, US carmaker Ford recently updated its vision statement, which had been: 'To become the world's leading consumer company that provides automotive products and services'. It added: 'In the process of meeting this vision, the company will focus on its customers, deliver superior shareholder returns and improve the quality of people's lives worldwide.' This emphasis of multiple bottom lines (one for the company and one for the social good) signals to younger workers that, at Ford, they are not just doing a job but also making a difference.

Strategy

The vision statement for DuPont, a global science and technology-based company, is to 'dedicate ourselves daily to the work of improving life on our planet'. To achieve this vision, DuPont has added 'corporate citizenship' to its core competencies of 'superior research and development' and 'the ability to adapt successfully to changes in the marketplace'.

Developing a competency in corporate citizenship means reviewing manufacturing policies to ensure they include protection for the environment. Recruitment would focus on people whose values match those of the organization. Performance appraisals would evaluate how well managers support environmental initiatives. Developing value-aligned strategies will demonstrate to younger workers that the organization follows through on these aspects of its vision.

Communication

Younger workers communicate directly. They expect to be involved in decisions that affect them (much like they contributed to family decisions at the kitchen table). They seek direct access to leadership. Some organizations have responded by encouraging e-mail correspondence with top managers, or scheduling on-line 'chats' with the chief executive. Opportunities for direct upward communication are valued by these workers. Top-down communication processes are scrutinized by younger workers. They do not support bureaucracy and politics, and so do not enjoy power games. More concerned with doing their work so they can focus on other aspects of their lives, young workers want clear goals, adequate resources to do their job and for managers to get out of the way so they can get their work done. For older workers used to politics and trading favours, this direct approach can appear naïve. Younger workers wonder why organizations allow older workers to waste so much time.

Culture

In general, Generation Y is attracted to team-oriented cultures. Unlike members of Generation X, who are individualistic and achievement-oriented, members of Generation Y prefer working with others and have a strong need for affiliation. Therefore, organizations should consider encouraging team-oriented behaviour if it will support their core competencies. Some solutions to encourage a culture of teamwork include: designing the workspace to accommodate the sharing of ideas (placing desks in groups); assigning projects to groups of people who are evaluated on reaching the same goal; and ensuring that appraisals assess the team as well as the individual.

Senior management

Younger workers admire honesty, integrity and ethical behaviour in their role models. They observe how leaders behave, expect them to practise what they preach and see no distinction between levels within the organization when it comes to what is considered fair.

Consider some recent instances of downsizing. Organizations that share the burden of salary cuts and redundancies across all levels are seen as more fair than those that target the lower levels. The US government's recent agreement to bail out the country's airlines prohibits the use of the money for salary increases to executives earning $300,000. Public response to this weak caveat was less than enthusiastic given the tens of thousands of employees expecting redundancy. The chairman and chief executive of American Airlines, perhaps sensing this, suspended his salary until the end of 2001.

Such gestures are not lost on young workers. Generation Y in particular is seeking a more committed employment relationship and is looking for clues that everyone in the organization is in it together – for better or worse. If they are asked to follow rules that managers ignore, they will value the employment relationship less.

▶ HR Systems

Managers should pay attention to the messages they convey when recruiting: the fairness of the appraisal system; the fairness of salaries and other rewards; and the apparent value placed on the individual when designing jobs and training systems.

Hiring strategies

Young employees evaluate every step of the recruiting process so organizations need to put their best foot forward at all times. Online advertising and targeted messages will be read by Generation X and Generation Y. Organizations may also want to send recruiting messages to their parents. A 2000 survey by the National Association of Colleges and Employers in the USA found that 45 per cent of students say their parents' opinion of a potential employer is important. For a recent student recruiting effort, KPMG used posters featuring a picture of a middle-aged couple smiling into the camera. The text read: 'Now that you've made your parents proud, join KPMG and give them something to really smile about.'

Generation Y is used to older adults who spend time on nurturing them. Make them feel sought-after by having upper-level managers meet with prospective candidates. Top managers who take time out of their busy schedules demonstrate a commitment to the candidate.

Job design

When designing jobs, treat young workers as individuals who have specific goals. Managers should find out what is important to them. Based on these interests, employees should be given information on customising their careers to give them control over their destiny and an understanding of opportunities. By giving them the tools to manage their own careers, managers will increase employees' commitment to the organization.

Baby Boomers often balk at asking what younger workers want. If open-ended questions are too threatening, give them choices. If the organization has selected them well, young workers' expectations should not be surprising or difficult to manage.

Defined goals and frequent monitoring ensure inexperienced workers have early successes. Too much handholding can foster resentment, however. Give responsibilities for manageable tasks to reduce errors and increase confidence. Focusing on outcomes rather than processes will help to challenge and develop young employees.

Training

Training should focus on specific skills needed to do the job, as well as more general skills that can be used for developmental goals. Interactive training programmes that operate online can be customized, so allowing employees to learn at their own pace. Team-based training sessions allow employees to interact with their peers, a plus for affiliation-oriented Generation Y. Finally, mentoring programmes transfer institutional knowledge as well as reducing tension between generations. Such programmes build understanding among workers.

Performance appraisals

For young workers, the process of performance appraisal is as important as the outcome. Organizations should consider using a 360-degree appraisal process in which feedback is gathered from managers, peers, subordinates, customers and the individual. These assessments tend to feel fairer because they mitigate individual biases. Emphasis should be on employee development, especially the transferable skills that are a priority for young workers. They seek constant affirmation and feedback, suggesting annual reviews be supplemented with more frequent feedback. Informal talks, at least quarterly, help keep this group on track.

Generation Y is used to being applauded by adults and feels a pressure to excel. They may feel that any criticism is a sign of failure. Therefore, negative feedback should focus on behaviour that is under the employee's control and should describe how things can be improved. Boomers may feel this as taking too much time to stroke employees. However, frequent two-way communication is an oft-cited desire of all workers.

Compensation and rewards

The carrot and not the stick drives young workers to succeed. Traditional pay packages can be fraught with inconsistencies and unclear formulas. Further, in a survey conducted by Northwestern Mutual Life/Louis Harris, only a third of Generation Y respondents said salary was most important and many would not trade free time for higher pay and gruelling hours. Motivating young employees takes creativity and an appeal to their value systems.

To accommodate their varying interests, organizations can create flexible plans that allow employees to select benefits that are most important to them. Some benefits appeal directly to young workers: paid time-off for voluntary work, days off to spend with family and friends, and tuition reimbursement. Non-monetary rewards carry weight as well. Consider memos of commendation that are copied to senior managers. Awards and gift vouchers show recognition without being costly. Young people need frequent feedback but it need not blow the departmental budget.

▶ Start Anywhere

A sixty-something graduate recently reflected: 'We wanted what they want. We just felt we couldn't ask.' Herein lies the truth: what young workers want isn't so different from what everyone else wants. However, young workers are asking for it. Granted, young workers can come to the workplace full of themselves and their ideas. And granted, they may not have the experience to manage or complete all of the ideas they bring. Having various generations working side by side can lead to stress and conflict. But it can also lead to creativity and opportunity.

The first step to making sure that generational differences work in favour of an organization is to acknowledge the differences. Then reassess the organization and the message it delivers to all of its employees through systems, policies and processes. Some of the changes that younger workers seek will be good for the organization as a whole.

Further Reading

Brooks, D. (2000) 'The organisation kid', *The Atlantic Monthly*, April, 11–12.
Howe, N. and Strauss, W. (2000) *Millennials Rising*, New York: Vintage.
O'Reilly, B. (2000) 'Today's kids', *Fortune*, July 24, 31–32.
Zamke, R., Raines, C. and Filipczak, R. (2000) *Generations at Work*, New York: Amacom.

Elite Graduate Expectations in Europe

Paul Gooderham and Odd Nordhaug

 **Introduction**

The war for business school talent in Europe is set to increase in intensity. The winners will be those firms that have the most profound understanding of what European business school graduates are seeking from employment and what they believe is required to succeed in a managerial career. In order to provide the foundations for that understanding we have carried out a comprehensive survey among students at 11 Community of European Management Schools (CEMS).

The primary goal of the survey is to gain insight into students' preferences regarding choice of job, employer and industry. Additionally we are seeking to explore national differences.

▶ The Survey

Research students travelled to each of the 11 CEMS schools involved in late autumn, 2000, and handed out questionnaires during lectures where a larger number of second and third year students were present. In this way, a high response rate was achieved. Foreign students at the individual business schools were excluded from the sample, so that it only nationals of each of the schools were included. This had a particularly marked impact on the size of the London School of Economics' sample because of its high proportion of non-British students. The sample includes 1,420 students distributed as shown in table RF1.

Table RF1   Business schools and number of respondents

Institution	Respondents
Erasmus (Holland)	187
ESADE (Spain)	122
Copenhagen Business School	113
Stockholm School of Economics	99
Helsinki School of Economics and Bus. Adm.	117
HEC (France)	80
London School of Economics and Pol.Science (England)	45
Norwegian School of Economics and Bus. Adm.	218
Università Bocconi (Italy)	181
Universität zu Köln (Germany)	144
Wirtschaftsuniversität Wien (Austria)	114

The sample comprises 42 per cent females, which approximately corresponds to the overall proportion for the schools in question. In terms of the distribution of main academic specialization, finance and strategy and organization and management were by far the largest areas represented, followed by marketing, economics, IT and accounting/auditing.

▶ Job Preferences

The students were asked about the emphasis they put on a range of factors in regard to choosing their first post-graduation job including opportunities for development, job characteristics, rewards, developmental opportunities and work environment factors. Some of the factors relate to the job itself and the nature of work tasks, while others are concerned with the personnel policy and the social environment, which are characteristics of the employer or organization itself.

Table RF2 shows a ranking of the factors we have chosen, based on an average score on a scale from 1 (low) to 5 (high). The first column gives the average for all the students in the selection, the second and third columns the results by gender.

The five highest scoring factors are interesting work, social environment at work, personal development, opportunities to develop competence, and variety in work tasks. These are followed by freedom in the job, high annual earnings/salary, a good personnel policy, the employer's reputation, pay based on individual performance, good job security and opportunities for fast promotion.

On the basis of these findings, we may conclude that the most important factors are related to four main areas:

Table RF2 The importance of factors when choosing one's first job

Factors	All students	Men	Women
1. Interesting work	4.72	4.65	4.84
2. Social environment at work	4.42	4.33	4.57
3. Personal development	4.37	4.28	4.50
4. Competence development	4.24	4.24	4.23
5. Variety in work tasks	4.20	4.13	4.30
6. Freedom in the job	3.99	3.98	4.01
7. High annual earnings/salary	3.98	4.04	3.90
8. Good personnel policy	3.92	3.76	4.17
9. The employer has a good reputation	3.74	3.71	3.79
10. Pay based on individual performance	3.68	3.74	3.60
11. Good job security	3.67	3.49	3.96
12. Opportunities for fast promotion	3.64	3.76	3.47
13. Flexible working hours	3.63	3.59	3.70
14. Opportunities to work abroad	3.57	3.54	3.62
15. Bonuses on group level	3.48	3.54	3.39
16. The position has a high status	3.33	3.43	3.18
17. Systematic career planning	3.28	3.19	3.41
18. Large amount of project work	3.17	3.09	3.29
19. Opportunity to take leaves without pay	2.99	2.93	3.07
20. Opportunities to work at home	2.80	2.68	2.98

- challenging work tasks;
- opportunities for individual development;
- social environment;
- earnings and career.

We find it particularly significant that factors related to earnings and career opportunities do not score highest. Thus the widespread perception that business school students are out-and-out careerists is not supported: 'fast career development' is ranked twelfth and 'high earnings' seventh. Although business graduates will normally obtain a high initial salary compared to many other groups of graduates money is clearly not everything. Indeed, the findings suggest that business students are, to a certain extent, willing to let pay take second place in order to secure opportunities for personal development and a good social environment at work.

It is also interesting to note that job security is not rated particularly highly – it ranks as number eleven. The greatest emphasis on job security is found among students from Italy (3.89), Austria (3.79) and Germany (3.75) with less emphasis in Sweden (3.42) and substantially less in France (2.90).

Some interesting, but not surprising, gender differences may be observed in table RF2. It is evident that female students place more emphasis on the social work environment, opportunities for personal development, personnel policy, high job security and opportunities to work from home, and less on high pay, individual performance-based compensation, fast career development and a position with a high status.

In summary, we may conclude that male students appear to be somewhat more materialistically oriented their female counterparts. The latter prioritize qualitative aspects of the work and the organization. Despite these differences, in the round there are no particularly profound differences when it comes to job preferences.

▶ Industry and Sector Preferences

The students were asked about the degree to which they are interested in working in 12 particular industries or sectors. In addition, we included a question about their inclination to start up a business on their own or in co-operation with others. The results are shown in table RF3.

Management consulting is the clear winner followed by financial services, IT/telecom and starting a company. Thereafter there are considerably weaker ratings for research and education, wholesale and retailing, tourism, hotels and restaurants, manufacturing industries, oil/energy and accounting/auditing. At the bottom we find careers in central government, voluntary organizations and local government. The Norwegian students deviate from the rest of the sample in their rating of the oil and energy sector, a reflection of the job opportunities available in oil-producing Norway. With the exception of oil/energy and manufacturing industries male and female students have a surprisingly similar ranking of their industry preferences.

Table RF3 Industry preferences (ranked; NHH, men/women)

Industry/sector	All	Men	Women
1. Management consulting	3.80	3.82	3.80
2. Financial services	3.57	3.71	3.36
3. IT/telecom	3.47	3.61	3.26
4. Start a company	3.40	3.61	3.07
5. Research/education	2.65	2.51	2.87
6. Wholesale and retail trade	2.61	2.56	2.70
7. Tourism, hotels, restaurants	2.59	2.42	2.87
8. Manufacturing industries	2.56	2.62	2.47
9. Oil and energy businesses	2.55	2.71	2.27
10. Accounting/auditing firms	2.50	2.43	2.60
11. Ministries/central government	2.29	2.22	2.40
12. Voluntary organizations	2.21	2.02	2.50
13. Local government	1.84	1.79	1.92

A Warning to the Public Sector

Table RF3 hardly makes for encouraging reading for auditing firms. They are clearly not regarded as sources of the values emphasized in table RF2 such as 'interesting work' or 'personal development'. However, table RF3 is even more discouraging for central and local government employers to the extent they need to recruit people with a background in business and administration. When asked directly if they want to work in the private sector, the public sector or within 'other sectors', 92 per cent of the sample responded that they want to work in the private sector. Only 5 per cent might be interested in a job in the public sector as their first job after graduating. Italy is the one real exception to this.

Entrepreneurialism

Throughout Europe there is a growing concern for the very large number of 'unborn businesses that must be established over the next couple of decades if employment and productivity growth are to be sustained. Table RF3 shows that establishing a business, alone or with others, is ranked highly by CEMs students: it is ranked above employment in traditional industry or retailing. There are, however, marked national differences in terms of this dimension as the following scores in table RF4 indicate.

We also asked a different, but related question: What would the students choose to do with their lives if they 'inherited or won in a lottery a large enough amount of money to be economically independent' for the rest of their lives. It emerges that as many as six out of ten would want to be self-employed, only one quarter would choose to work for an employer, and one out of six would do

Table RF4 National differences regarding entrepreneurialism

Country	Ranking
Spain	3.97
Germany	3.75
Sweden	3.67
Holland	3.56
Austria	3.39
Denmark	3.25
Italy	3.22
France	3.20
Finland	3.15
Norway	3.15
England	2.98

Table RF5 Choices if suddenly made wealthy

Country	Paid work (%)	Preferences Own business (%)	No work (%)
Denmark	37	55	8
England	23	50	27
Finland	35	52	13
France	16	36	48
Italy	12	56	32
Holland	25	64	11
Norway	41	47	12
Spain	13	81	6
Sweden	32	54	14
Germany	20	66	14
Austria	14	70	16

other things than work. There are, however, again substantial between-country differences, as shown in table RF5.

The Norwegian students stand out as the group that to the greatest extent would still prefer paid work even if they were to become economically independent, while they score relatively low on starting a business. The Spanish score highest in this category; as many as 81 per cent would prefer to run and own a business. The French, Italian and English students are those who would be most interested in doing other things than work with almost every second French student having such a preference.

Table RF5 also indicates that the Spanish students together with the Danish students are those who least of all would want to do other things than work. The question is, why these marked differences? One possible hypothesis might be that the quality of life at work varies across the countries. A second hypothesis might be that the opportunities for self-employment are different. And a third that the quality of life associated with 'doing other things' varies across the countries.

In terms of gender we found that male students would be more attracted to 'doing something else' or to running their own businesses than the female respondents who displayed a greater inclination for working for an employer.

▶ Stability

We asked the following question pertaining to stability: 'How many years do you expect to stay with your first employer after graduating before you change to another employer? Table RF6 shows how the students' expectations for the length of the first employment period are distributed, and also gives the cumulative distribution.

Table RF6 Stability expectations

	Percentage	Cumulative (%)
1 year	5	5
2 years	32	37
3 years	32	69
4 years	11	80
5 years	17	97

Table RF7 Stability distribution in years

Country	Years
Spain	2.4
Italy	2.5
France	3.0
Holland	3.1
Sweden	3.1
Norway	3.3
Austria	3.4
Finland	3.7
England	3.8
Germany	4.3
Denmark	4.4

The distribution of the students according to country is as shown in table RF7.

There are substantial differences with the Latin country students displaying much less intended loyalty to their first employer than those of Germany and Denmark.

▶ Criteria for Getting a Job

What are CEMS students' perceptions of what it is that counts in getting that first job after graduation? Do they perceive their personal qualities, their competence, their social network or the business school's reputation as critical factors? Table RF8 indicates that the students clearly believe that first and foremost it is their personality potential employers will emphasize the most. This applies regardless of nationality or gender.

The same applies to the next factor, one's own competence. However, there are some interesting differences when it comes to the reputation of the business school. In order to take a closer look at this question we have ranked the countries according to this dimension (table RF9).

Table RF8 Perceived importance of different criteria to succeed in getting one's first job

Success factors	All	Men	Women
Your personality	4.46	4.43	4.56
Your own competence	4.10	4.07	4.17
Reputation of the business school	3.47	3.47	3.47
Social networks	3.36	3.41	3.31
Your grades from business school	3.21	3.17	3.29

Table RF9 Reputation of the business school

Country	Ranking
Sweden	4.34
Norway	3.85
Spain	3.85
England	3.84
France	3.76
Finland	3.65
Germany	3.65
Austria	3.54
Holland	3.41
Denmark	2.91
Italy	2.17

The differences between these institutions are very large with students at Stockholm School of Economics attaching twice as much importance to their school's reputation as students at Bocconi in Italy.

Social network as criterion for getting a job is considered to be the second least important in our list. Finally it is evident that the students attach relatively little importance to their own grades.

All in all, our findings suggest that respondents believe that appointments will be based on their personality and real competence rather than examination grades.

▶ View on Managerial Competence

In order to gain an insight into how CEMS students view what it takes to be a successful manager, we asked them to rate the importance of a set of selected managerial competencies. The question was how important these competencies are for a person to be a good manager (table RF10).

Various types of social competence rank highest, but skills related to handling stress and uncertainty are also highly ranked, along with knowledge about the

Table RF10 Perceived importance of competences needed to be a good manager

Type of competence	All	Men	Women
Communication skills	4.52	4.49	4.58
Ability to listen to others	4.31	4.28	4.36
Co-operative skills	4.26	4.21	4.35
Stress tolerance	4.19	4.11	4.33
Knowledge about the firm's strategy	4.16	4.11	4.24
Ability to handle uncertainty	3.98	3.94	4.05
Analytical skills	3.98	3.96	4.03
Knowledge about the firm's culture	3.96	3.89	4.09
Creativity/innovativeness	3.90	3.86	3.97
Ability to command/control others	3.90	3.90	3.88
Knowledge about the industry	3.87	3.81	3.98
Personal flexibility	3.83	3.78	3.90
Political skills (power related)	3.79	3.75	3.85
Professional/technical skills	3.58	3.50	3.71
International competence	3.41	3.37	3.52
High ethical standards	3.31	3.19	3.50

firm's strategy, analytical skills and knowledge about the firm's culture. The ability to command others is not rated particularly highly except in Germany (4.56) and Austria (4.49). Indeed, German and Austrian students considered this to be the single most important competence needed to be a good manager. The scores for female students in Germany and Austria are particularly high (4.74 and 4.64, respectively). By contrast Norwegian students emphasized this skill the least of all the students (3.43) along with Finnish (3.49), Swedish (3.52) and Danish (3.61) students.

When we look at political skills, which is defined as the ability to obtain and exercise power a similar pattern emerges. The Nordic students score lowest here also, with Norwegian students (3.23) at the bottom of the list. At the top we find Spain (4.71), Germany (4.41), France (4.35) and Austria (4.24).

As for personal flexibility, this competence is ranked highest among Spanish, Dutch (4.09) and Spanish students (4.03), while German (3.36) and Austrian (3.56) students attach the least importance to this.

In last place for the student group as a whole is the importance of having high ethical standards. However, there are also significant national differences in this regard. The Spanish students (3.92) deviate from this pattern by ranking it significantly higher as do the Norwegian students (3.64). At the other end of the scale we once again find the German (2.86) and Austrian (2.91) students as well as the Italians (2.86).

Professional/technical skills are emphasized less than most of the other competencies we enquired about. Only international competence and high ethical standard score lower. The students feel, in other words, that a number of more socially and personality-related competencies, together with knowledge about the firm and the industry, are more important for good management than purely technical and professional competence. Our material indicates that the Norwegian students rank it lowest of all countries (3.15). Austrian (3.88), Italian (3.85) and German (3.82) students have the highest values for this factor. In other words we have uncovered significant differences in the perceived importance of professional and technical competence for managers.

There are also substantial variations in perceptions when it comes to international competence. The Norwegian students (3.09) are the ones who rank this lowest, together with the Danes (3.10). At the top of this list we find German (3.72), Austrian and students (3.66).

▶ What are the Lessons to be Learnt?

In the war for the talent this new cohort of Generation Y CEMS graduates represent the following challenge to companies that want to attract and recruit them:

- Firms will have to go beyond offering the traditional goods of high salaries, opportunities for fast promotion and job security. Jobs must be structured and designed in ways that offer personal growth and a good social environment. While management consulting firms appear to understand this, manufacturing industry, auditing firms and government employers clearly do not.
- Firms should attempt to harness the entrepreneurial instincts of new CEMS graduates by offering opportunities to initiate and manage small start-ups.
- Firms should accept the belief new CEMS graduates have in the importance of their personalities. These are not 'company men or women' but individualists who are nevertheless committed to working and leading through teams.

Finally, new CEMS graduates cannot be taken for granted. Firms will have to work hard at all of the above if they are to retain their services in the long term.

The Financial Case for Behaving Responsibly

Tim Dickson

Asked after a recent trade association dinner what steps were needed to turn his business into a 'sustainable' company, the finance director of a leading pharmaceuticals group thought for a moment before replying: 'Lots of lovely new drug patents!' His engagingly robust answer was not quite what the questioner had in mind – but the post-prandial exchange arguably highlights current misunderstandings and boardroom confusion over such concepts as the sustainable business, sustainable development, corporate citizenship, corporate social responsibility, business ethics and even aspects of the wider corporate governance debate.

While the semantic fog has grown thicker in the last couple of years – at times obscuring any coherent message – executives ignore the latest corporate social and environmental thinking at their peril. Acknowledging it is likely to be a minimum part of restoring their credibility and legitimacy in the wake of recent corporate scandals; embracing it, according to a growing body of opinion and even the occasional bit of empirical evidence, can offer a clear, long-term competitive advantage over rivals.

Socially responsible projects are part of a long business tradition in Europe and the USA – witness Robert Owen's early nineteenth-century New Lanark textile enterprise and the mid-to-late nineteenth-century experiments of Quaker families such as the Cadburys, Rowntrees and Hersheys. What distinguishes today's initiatives is their increasingly strategic character – by contrast with the isolated actions of philanthropic entrepreneurs – and the external forces that have pushed companies to act.

Moreover, it is clear from the examples of companies like Shell, Marks and Spencer and Diageo that activities in this area are no longer the preserve of functional specialists. Senior managers are increasingly leading these activities, and all employees need to adapt their thinking, job descriptions, performance targets and remuneration policies.

▶ Early Definitions

Perhaps the best starting point is sustainable development – a vision for society first fully articulated in the 1987 Brundtland Report (after the former Norwegian Prime Minister, Gro Harlem Brundtland) whereby economic development does not compromise the ability of future generations to enjoy the same standard of living as our own. Environmental protection was originally the paramount concern, but more recent definitions also incorporate the ambition for a just and caring society.

The reality for executives is that growing numbers of politicians, non-governmental organizations (NGOs), voters and consumers have signed up to the theory of sustainable development and increasingly use it to hold companies to account. Many analysts and advisers now promote the idea of the 'sustainable business' – one that enhances long-term shareholder value by addressing the needs of all relevant stakeholders and adding economic, environmental and social value through its core business functions.

Much depends where you stand on a divide compared by Robert Ayres, emeritus professor at Insead, to C.P. Snow's two cultures. This separates those ecologists and natural scientists who subscribe to the 'strong sustainability' school – believing human survival is tightly linked to the health of the natural world and environmental limits cannot be compromised – from those who argue that in certain circumstances environmental depletion can be offset by economic, human or social capital creation elsewhere.

▶ Corporate Social Responsibility

The business response to the challenge of sustainable development goes under various labels. But the term most widely applied is corporate social responsibility, or CSR, a catch-all to describe activities whereby companies voluntarily integrate social and environmental concerns in their business operations.

CSR initially emerged before sustainable development as a response to the social consequences of structural economic change. Just as the concept of sustainable development has been widened to include non-environmental objectives, so CSR has increasingly become the rallying cry for environmental as well as social initiatives.

Three key questions now dominate the CSR agenda. There remains a debate as to whether sustainable development should be a concern for business at all. To the extent that the consensus is 'yes', the argument rages as to whether CSR should continue to be voluntary, or whether a regulatory framework ought to establish minimum standards. Finally, disagreement remains over the business case and whether it can really be shown that CSR is good for profits.

The case for business engagement in CSR issues tends to be based on moral and ethical grounds as well as on the 'stakeholder' view of business which sees companies as societal agents with wider obligations to customers, workers and communities.

Libertarians see the arguments differently, maintaining that businesses exist only to make profits for their owners. The 'anti' argument is rarely heard from boardrooms these days – publicly at least. According to a PwC survey earlier this year, 70 per cent of global chief executives believe CSR is vital to their companies' profitability. An Environics International survey this summer, based on interviews with 1000 people in 25 countries, revealed a near global consensus that companies should go beyond financial philanthropy and apply their expertise and technology to solve social problems.

In this context should CSR be voluntary, or should governments and supranational organizations like the EU impose a mandatory set of requirements? Two developments have recently highlighted the issue – the European Commission's communication concerning CSR, published in June 2002, and the newly amended Nouvelles Regulations Economiques (NRE), a French law requiring all nationally listed corporations in France to report to shareholders and stakeholders on a range of sustainability issues from next year.

Despite submissions from trade unions and NGOs that 'voluntary initiatives are not sufficient to protect workers and citizens' rights' the Commission opposes mandatory action. But it acknowledges: 'Nevertheless, as there is evidence suggesting that CSR creates value for society by contributing to a more sustainable development, there is a role for public authorities in promoting socially and environmentally responsible practices by enterprises.' Brussels therefore aims to disseminate experience and best practice, promote CSR management skills, foster its spirit among small and medium-sized businesses, and integrate it into EU policies.

The impact of the NRE in France – which require companies to report on community activities and interactions with NGOs, on air, water and ground emissions and on the performance of their international subsidiaries with International Labour Standards – will be closely watched. French companies have not been renowned for the type of disclosure increasingly being made by other European and American corporations – in the past, indeed, the French have routinely dismissed such initiatives as an unwanted part of the Anglo-Saxon or American management model.

▶ Triple Bottom Line

'Triple-bottom-line' reporting is the measurement of a company's economic, environmental and social performance. Ten years ago a mere handful of businesses disclosed such information (most of them as monuments to their public relations department); today, according to Allen White, acting chief executive of the Global Reporting Initiative (GRI), 'more than 2,500 corporate environmental or sustainability reports have been published' by the likes of Royal Dutch/Shell, Ericsson, Ford, Canon and BASF.

Triple-bottom-line reporting is both a conscious attempt by enlightened companies to build trust and an explicit response to society's demands for 'sustainable' corporate behaviour. The GRI, launched in 1997 by the US-based Coalition for Environmentally Responsible Economies in partnership with the United Nations Environment Programme, has emerged as a *de facto* global standard-setter in this area, seeking to turn the variety of approaches into a common framework. GRI's mission, says Mr White, is to make sustainability reporting 'as routine as financial reporting', while organizations like AccountAbility (comprising large and small companies, not-for-profit businesses, accountancy organizations and academic institutions) are active in providing the 'assurance' standards that will make documents accurate and credible.

The mandatory vs voluntary debate, of course, would not be necessary if the business case for CSR were overwhelming. Even the most unrepentant corporate sinners would presumably fall into line if it could be shown unambiguously that good behaviour led to fatter profits. Numerous academic papers have concluded that improved corporate reputation, better recruitment prospects and bigger sales to environmentally conscious consumers are among the benefits. All such studies are long on description, but the vast majority are distinctly short of quantitative data.

One company that appears to have gone further than most is BT group, which earlier this year sought to respond to questions from investors. BT claims to have discovered a clear correlation between its reputation and customer satisfaction. Company analysts unravelled what contributes to that reputation and found that at least 25 per cent was broadly related to sustainable development issues. BT calculated that the cost of abandoning all its CSR activities would be a 10 per cent drop in customer satisfaction, with a consequent loss of business and profitability. 'If companies don't see the value in CSR they will do the minimum they can get away with,' says Chris Tuppen, BT's head of sustainable development and corporate accountability.

No doubt, efforts to demonstrate the link between CSR and profits will intensify – although the recent fate of a Houston-based energy company, complete with a corporate responsibility task force chaired by the chief executive and codes of conduct covering security, human rights, social investment and 'public engagement' issues in India and Brazil, is not encouraging.

That company was Enron. Which goes to show that all these activities – CSR, triple-bottom-line measurements and reports – are a waste of time without integrity, business ethics and a law-abiding culture at the top.

Acknowledgements

The Financial Times, 19 August 2002. Copyright 2002 The Financial Times Limited.

Bibliography

ABB Group (1988) *ABB Annual Report.* Zürich: ABB Corporate Communications Ltd.

ABB (1991) *Mission, Values, and Policies.* Internal document. Zürich: ABB Corporate Communications Ltd.

ABB Group (1998) *ABB Press Release.* 12. August 1998. Zürich.

ABB Group Internetpages (1998) http://www.abb.ch/abbgroup/introduction/aboutabb. html 26 November.

ABB Switzerland (1997) *ABB Switzerland Annual Report.* Baden: Author.

ABB Switzerland (1998) *Tradition und Innovation.* Baden: ABB Schweiz Kommunikation.

Adams, D. (1969) The monkey and the fish: cultural pitfalls of an educational advisor. *International Development Review,* 2, 2.

Adler, N. (1987) Pacific basin managers: a Gaijin not a woman. *Human Resource Management,* 26 (2), 162–192.

Adler, N. J. (1991) *International Dimensions of Organizational Behavior* (2nd edn). Boston, MA: PWS-Kent.

Adler, P. S. (1993) The 'learning bureaucracy': new united manufacturing, inc. *Research in Organizational Behavior,* 15, 111–194.

Albert, M. (1991) *Capitalisme contre Capitalisme.* Paris: Éditions du Seuil.

Ali-Yrkkö, J. (2001) *Nokia's Network: Gaining Competitiveness from Co-Operation.* Helsinki: Taloustieto Oy (ETLA B:174).

Ali-Yrkkö, J., Paija, L., Reilly, R. and Ylä-Anttila, P. (2000) *Nokia: A Big Company in a Small Country.* Helsinki: Taloustieto Oy (ETLA B:162).

Alkhafaji, A. F. (1995) *Competitive Global Management.* Delary Beach, FL: St.Lucie Press.

Ambarao, S. C. (1993) Multinational corporate social responsibility, ethics, interaction and third-world governments: an agenda for the 1990s. *Journal of Business Ethics,* 12 (7), 553–572.

Anderson, E. and Gatignon, H. (1986) Modes of foreign entry: a transaction cost analysis and proposition. *Journal of International Business Studies,* 17, 1–16.

Anisimova, A. (1999) Organizational culture and cross-cultural relations: the case of a Danish company in Russia. Paper presented at the CEP conference 'Cultural transformation and civil society', May, Krakow, Poland.

Ansoff, H. I. (1965) *Corporate Strategy.* New York: McGraw Hill.

Arbose, J. (1988) The new international powerhouse. *International Management*, 43 (6) 24–30.

Argyris, C. and Schön, D. A. (1978) *Organizational Learning: A Theory of Action Perspective.* Reading, MA: Addison-Wesley.

Asheghian, P. and Ebrahimi, B. (1990) *International Business: Economics, Environment and Strategies.* New York: HarperCollins.

Banner, D. K. and Gagne, T. E. (1995) *Designing Effective Organizations.* London: Sage.

Bantel, A. and Schär, M. (1998) Wir wollen allen zeigen wieviel Power wir haben, Interview with Göran Lindahl, *Cash, 33,* 14 August: 6–7.

Barham, K. and Devine, M. (1990) *The Quest for the International Manager: A Survey of Global Human Resource Strategies.* London: The Economist Intelligence Unit, Special Report no. 2098.

Barham, K. and Heimer, C. (1998) *ABB – The Dancing Giant: Creating the Globally Connected Corporation.* London: Financial Times/Pitman Publishing.

Bartlett, C. A. and Ghoshal, S. (1989) *Managing Across Borders: The Transnational Solution.* Boston: Harvard Business School Press.

Bartlett, C. and Ghoshal, S. (1990) Matrix management: not a structure, a frame of mind, *Harvard Business Review*, 68 (4), 138–145.

Bartlett, C. and Ghoshal, S. (1993) Beyond the M-Form: toward a managerial theory of the firm. *Strategic Management Journal, 14,* 23–46.

Bartlett, C. A. and Ghoshal, S. (1995) *Transnational Management: Text, Cases, and Readings in Cross-Border Management.* (2nd edn) Chicago, IL: Irwin.

BBC Group (1987) *BBC Annual Report,* Baden.

Beamish, P. W., Morrison, A. J., Rosenzweig, P. M. and Inkpen, A. C. (2000) *International Management: Text and Cases.* (4th edn). Boston: McGraw-Hill.

Beaumont, P. B. (1991) The US human resource management literature: a review. In G. Salaman (ed.) *Human Resource Strategies.* Milton Keynes: Open University Press.

Becker, G. S. (1983/1964) *Human Capital.* New York: Columbia University Press.

Becker, H. and Fritzsche, D. J. (1987) A comparison of the ethical behavior of American, French, and German managers. *Columbia Journal of World Business,* Winter, 87–95.

Beer, M., Eisenstadt, R. and Spector, B. (1990) Why change programs don't produce change. *Harvard Business Review,* November–December, 158–166.

Beer, M., Spector, B., Lawrence, P. R., Mills, D. Q. and Walton, R. E. (1984) *Managing Human Assets.* New York: Free Press.

Bennett, R. (1997) *European Business.* London: Pitman.

Berman, S. L., Wicks, A. C., Kotha, S. and Jones, T. M. (1999) Does stakeholder orientation matter? The relationship between stakeholder management models and firm financial performance. *Academy of Management Journal,* 42 (5), 488–506.

Bilanz (1998). September.

Bird, F. and Waters, J. (1994) The moral muteness of managers. *California Management Review,* 32 (1).

Birkinshaw, J. (1997) Entrepreneurship in multinational corporations: the characteristics of subsidiary initiatives. *Strategic Management Journal,* 18 (3), 207–229.

Birkinshaw, J. (2000) The structures behind global companies. Part 10 of *Mastering Management. Financial Times,* 4 December.

Björkman, I. (1990) *Expatriation and Repatriation in Finnish Companies: A Comparison With Swedish and Norwegian Practice.* Working paper. Stockholm: Stockholm School of Economics and Business Administration.

Black, J. S. and Gregersen, H. B. (1999) The right way to manage expatriates. *Harvard Business Review*. March/April, 52–63.

Black, J. S., Gregersen, H. B., and Mendenhall, M. E. (1992) *Global Assignments*. San Francisco, CA: Jossey-Bass.

Blanchard, O. (1999) European unemployment: the role of shocks and institutions. Unpublished working paper. Cambridge, MA: Massachusetts Institute of Technology.

Bleicher, K. (1991) *Das Konzept Integriertes Management*, Frankfurt: Campus.

Bolkestein, F. (1999) The Dutch model. *The Economist*, 22 May, 115–116, no. 8120.

Bond, M. H. (2002) Reclaiming the individual from Hofstede's ecological analysis: a 20-year odyssey. *Psychological Bulletin* (forthcoming).

Bowditch, J. and Buono, A. (1997) *A Primer on Organizational Behavior*. (4th edn). New York: Wiley.

Braybrooke, D. (1964) The mystery of executive success re-examined. *Administrative Science Quarterly*, 8, 533–560.

Bresman, H., Birkinshaw, J. and Nobel, R. (1999) Knowledge transfer in international acquisitions. *Journal of International Business Studies*, 30, 3, 439–462.

Brewster, C. (1994) European HRM: Reflection of, or challenge to, the American concept? In P. S. Kirkbride (ed.), *Human Resource Managment in Europe*. London: Routledge.

Brewster, C. and Lockhart, T. (1992) The EC. In C. Brewster, A. Hegewisch, L. Holden and T. Lockhart (eds) *The European Human Resource Management Guide*. London: Academic Press.

Brewster, C., Tregaskis, O., Hegewisch, A. and Mayne, L. (1996) Comparative research in human research management: a review and an example. *International Journal of Human Resource Management*, 7, 585–604.

Bronfenbrenner, U. (1970) *Two Worlds of Childhood: U.S. and USSR*. New York: Sage.

Brytting, T. (1997) Moral support structure in private industry – the Swedish case. *Journal of Business Ethics*, 16 (7), 663–697.

Buchanan, D. and Huczynski, A. (1997) *Organizational Behavior* (3rd edn). London: Prentice Hall.

Budhwar, P. S. and Sparrow, P. R. (1997) Evaluating levels of strategic integration and devolvement of human resource management in India. *International Journal of Human Resource Management*, 8 (4), 476–494.

Budhwar, P. S. and Sparrow, P. R. (1998) National factors determining Indian and British HRM practices. *Management International Review*, 38 (2), 105–121.

Burnham, J. (1941) *The Managerial Revolution*. New York: John Day.

Burns, T. and Stalker, G. M. (1961) *The Management of Innovation*. London.

Business Week (1994) Managing by values: is Levi-Strauss' approach visionary – or flaky? Author, September 12, 38–43.

Business Week (1999a) Making Microsoft, 17 May.

Business Week (1999b) 'Jack: a close-up look at how America's #1 manager runs GE', 8 June.

Business Week (2001a) The taskmaster of Nestle, 11 June.

Business Week (2001b) Confronting anti-globalism. Editorial. 6 August.

Cantwell, J. (1989) *Technological Innovation and Multinational Corporations*. Oxford: Basil Blackwell.

Cantwell, J. (1994) Introduction: transnational corporations and innovatory activities. In J. Cantwell (ed.) *Transnational Corporations and Innovatory Activities*. London: Routledge.

Cantwell, J. (1996) Transnational corporations and innovatory activities. In *Transnational Corporations and World Development*. Published by Routledge on behalf of the UNCTAD Division on Transnational Corporations and Investment. London: International Thomson Business Press.

Cantwell, J. A. and Piscitello, L. (1997) The emergence of corporate international networks for the accumulation of dispersed technological competences. In K. Macharzina, M-J. Oesterle and J. Wolf (eds) *Global Business in the Information Age*, vol. 1., 166–191. Proceedings of the 23rd Annual EIBA Conference, Stuttgart, December.

Carnevale, A. P. (1991) *America and the New Economy*. San Francisco, CA: Jossey-Bass.

Catrina, W. (1991) *BBC Glanz – Krise – Fusion 1891 – 1991 von Brown Boveri zu ABB* (2nd edn). Zürich: Orell Füssli.

Chakraborty, S. K. (1997) Business ethics in India. *Journal of Business Ethics*, 1529–1538.

Chandler, A. D. (1962) *Strategy and Structure*. Cambridge, MA: MIT Press.

Chandler, A. (1977/1980) *The Visible Hand: The Managerial Revolution in American Business*. Cambridge, MA: Harvard University Press.

Chandler, A. D. and Daems, H. (eds) (1980) *Managerial Hierarchies: Comparative Perspectives on the Rise of the Modern Industrial Enterprise*. Cambridge, MA: Harvard University Press.

Chang, S. J. and Rosenzweig, P. M. (2001) The choice of entry mode in sequential foreign direct investment. *Strategic Management Journal*, 22, 747–776.

Childs, J. (1972) Organizational structure, environment and performance: the role of strategic choice. *Sociology*, 6, 1–22.

Child, J., Faulkner, D. and Pitkethly, R. (2001) *The Management of International Acquisitions*. Oxford: Oxford University Press.

Cobb, A. T. (1986) Political diagnosis: applications in organizational development. *Academy of Management Review*, 11, 482–496.

Cohen, W. M. and Levinthal, D. (1990) Absorptive capacity: a new perspective on learning and innovation. *Administrative Science Quarterly*, 35 (1), 128–152.

Cole, R. E. and Deskins, D. R. Jr. (1988) Racial factors in site location and employment patterns of Japanese auto firms in America. *California Management Review*, Fall.

Collin, A. (1989) Managers' competence: rhetoric, reality and research. *Personnel Review*, 18 (6), 20–25.

Collins, D. E. (1997) General Johnson said . . . In O. F. Williams (ed.) *The Moral Imagination*. Notre Dame, IN: Notre Dame University Press.

Cully, M. *et al.* (1998) *The 1998 Workplace Employee Relations Survey: First Findings*. London: Department of Trade and Industry.

Cyert, R. and March, J. (1992) *A Behavioral Theory of the Firm* (2nd edn). Oxford: Blackwell.

Daft, R. L. and Weick, K. E. (1984) Toward a model of organizations as interpretation systems. *Academy of Management Review*, 9, 284–295.

Dawkins, W. (1996) Time to pull back the screen. *Financial Times*, 18 November.

Day, J. D., Mang, P. Y., Richter, A. and Roberts, J. (2001) The innovative organization: why new ventures need more than a room of their own. *The McKinsey Quarterly*, 2, 21–31.

DeGeorge, R. T. (1993). *Competing with Integrity in International Business*. New York: Oxford University Press.

De la Torre, J. and Neckar, D. H. (1988) Forecasting political risks for international operations. *International Journal of Forecasting*, 4, 221–241.

De Meyer, A. (1995) Tech talk: How managers are stimulating global R&D communication. In J. Drew (ed.) *Readings in International Enterprise*. London: Routledge.

Deresky, H. (1997) *International Management: Managing Across Borders and Cultures* (2nd edn). Reading, MA: Addison-Wesley.

Derr, C. B. and Oddou, G. (1993) Internationalizing managers: speeding up the process. *European Management Journal*, 11 (4), 435–442.

DiMaggio, P. J. and Powell, W. W. (1983) The iron cage revisited: institutional isomorphism and collective rationality in organizational fields. *American Sociological Review*, 48, 147–160.

Donaldson, T. (1989) *The Ethics of International Business*. Oxford/New York: Oxford University Press.

Donaldson, T. (1994) Global business must mind its manners. *The New York Times*, February 13: F11.

Donaldson, T. (1996) Values in tension: ethics away from home. *Harvard Business Review*, September–October, 48–62.

Dowling, P. J., Welch, D. E. and Schuler, R. S. (1999) *International Human Resource Management* (3rd edn). Cincinatti, OH: South-Western College Publishing.

Doz, Y. L. and Prahalad, C. K. (1991) Managing DMNCs: a search for a new paradigm. *Strategic Management Journal*, 12, 145–164.

Drucker, P. (1950) *The New Society: The Anatomy of the Industrial Order*. New York: Harper.

Drucker, P. (1989) *The Practice of Management*. London: Heinemann Professional Publishing (first published 1955).

Due, J., Madsen, J. S. and Jensen, C. S. (1991) The social dimension: convergence or diversification of IR in the single European market? *Industrial Relations Journal*, 22 (2), 85–102.

Dunning, J. H. (1988) The eclectic paradigm of international production: a restatement and some possible extensions. *Journal of International Business Studies*, Spring, 1–32.

Dyer, J. H. and Nobeoka, K. (2000) Creating and managing a high-performance knowledge-sharing network: the Toyota case. *Strategic Management Journal*, 21, 345–367.

Eccles, J. and Nohria, N. (1992) *Networks and Organizations: Structure, Form and Action*. Boston, MA: Harvard University School Press.

The Economist (1997) 21 June.

The Economist (1999a) A survey of pay. 8 May.

The Economist (1999b) General Electric. 18 September.

The Economist (1999c) 11 September.

The Economist (2000a) Nigeria Survey. 15 January.

The Economist (2000b) 16 December.

The Economist (2001a) Face value: Where's the beef? 3 November.

The Economist (2001b) The opacity index. 3 March.

Edwards, T. and Ferner, A. (2002) The renewed 'American Challenge': a review of employment practices in US multinationals. Forthcoming.

Eisenhardt, K. (1989) Making fast strategic decisions in high-velocity environments. *Academy of Management Journal*, 32 (3), 543–576.

Eisenhardt, K. (1990) Speed and strategic choice: how managers accelerate decision making. *California Management Review*, 32 (3), 39–54.

Ernst & Young (1999) *Doing Business in India*. Internal document.

Falkenberg, A. W. (1996) A yardstick for justice and ethical evaluations in economic organizations. *Journal of Socio Economics*.

Falkenberg, A. W. (1997) Quality of life: efficiency, equity, and freedom in the U.S. and Scandinavia. *Journal of Socio Economics*.

Falkenberg, A. W. (2001) Culture and ethics in multinational companies. Unpublished working paper. Bergen: Norwegian School of Economics and Business Administration.

Falkenberg, A. W. and Wish, J. (1980) Efficiency, equity and freedom of choice as evaluative criteria for normative marketing management. *Proceedings of the American Marketing Association's Marketing Theory Conference.*

Financial Times (1997a) 14 April.

Financial Times (1997b) 15 November.

Financial Times (1998) ABB, 13 August.

Financial Times (1999a) 2 February.

Financial Times (1999b) 4 May.

Financial Times (1999c) Varying states of start-up. 22 June.

Financial Times (2000a) 13 March.

Financial Times (2000b) Back to classic coke. 27 March.

Financial Times (2000c) 5 May.

Financial Times (2001) Corus plans to double plant investments. 16 March.

Fombrun, C. J., Tichy, N. and Devanna, M. A. (1984) *Strategic Human Resource Management.* New York: Wiley.

Fontaine, G. (1989) *Managing International Assignments: The Strategy for Success.* Englewood Cliffs, NJ: Prentice-Hall.

Forster, N. (2000) The myth of the international manager. *International Journal of Human Resource Management,* 11 (1), 126–142.

Frazee, V. (1998) Culture shock. *Global Workforce,* July.

Freeman, R. E. (1984) *Strategic Management: A Stakeholder Approach.* Englewood Cliffs, NJ: Prentice-Hall.

Garvik, O. (1997) Vinnerlaget utenfor EU. *Bergens Tidende,* 23. March.

Gatignon, E. and Anderson, E. (1988) The multinational corporation's degree of control over foreign subsidiaries. *Journal of Law, Economics and Organization,* 4, 304–336.

General Electric (1997) *Annual Report.*

Geringer, J. M., Beamish, P. W. and daCosta, R. C. (1989) Diversification strategy and internationalization: implications for MNE performance. *Strategic Management Journal,* 10 (2), 109–119.

Ghoshal, S. and Bartlett, C. A. (1990) The Multinational Corporation as an Interorganizational Network. *Academy of Management Review,* 15, 603–625.

Ghoshal, S. and Moran, P. (1996) Bad for practice: A critique of the transaction cost theory. *Academy of Management Review, 21,* 13–47.

Golodner, L. F. (2000) The apparel industry code of conduct: a consumer perspective on social responsibility. In O. F. Williams (ed.) *Global Codes of Conduct.* Notre Dame, IN: University of Notre Dame Press.

Gomez, P. (1992) Neue Trends in der Konzernorganisation. *io management,* 3, 166–172.

Goodall, K. and Warner, M. (1997) Human resources in Sino-foreign joint ventures: selected case studies in Shanghai compared with Beijing. *International Journal of Human Resource Management,* 8 (5), 569–594.

Gooderham, P. N. and Nordhaug, O. (2002) Are cultural differences in Europe on the decline? *European Business Forum,* 8, 48–53.

Gooderham, P. N., Nordhaug, O. and Ringdal, K. (1998) When in Rome, do they do as the Romans? HRM practices of US subsidiaries in Europe. *Management International Review,* 38 (2), 47–64.

Gooderham, P. N., Nordhaug, O. and Ringdal, K. (1999) Institutional and rational determinants of organizational practices: human resource management in European firms. *Administrative Science Quarterly*, 44 (3): 507–531.

Gopalan, S. and Stahl, A. (1998) Application of American management theories and practices to the Indian business environment: understanding the impact of national culture. *American Business Review*, 16 (2), 30–41.

Grønhaug, K. and Nordhaug, O. (1992) International human resource management: an environmental model. *International Journal of Human Resource Management*, 3 (1), 1–14.

Grønhaug, K. and Nordhaug, O. (1994) Strategy and competence in firms. *European Management Journal*, 10 (4), 438–444.

Guest, D. (1990) Human resource management and the American dream. *Journal of Management Studies*, 27 (4), 377–97.

Gullahorn, J. T. and Gullahorn, J. E. (1963) An extension of the U-curve hypothesis. *Journal of Social Sciences*, 19 (3), 33–47.

Gupta, A. K. and Govindarajan, V. (2000) Knowledge flows within multinational corporations. *Strategic Management Journal*, 21, 473–496.

Häikiö, M. (2001) *Nokia Oyj:n historia*. Helsinki: Edita Oyj.

Hambrick, D. C., Li, J., Xin, K. and Tsui, A. S. (2001) Compositional gaps and downward spirals in international joint venture management groups. *Strategic Management Journal*, 22, 1033–1053.

Hambrick, D. C., Nadler, D. A. and Tushman, M. L. (eds) (1998) *Navigating Change: How Ceos, Top Teams and Boards Steer Transformation*. Boston: Harvard Business School Press.

Hamel, G. and Heene, A. (eds) (1994) *Competence-Based Competition*. Chichester: Wiley.

Hannan, M. T. and Freeman, J. (1989) *Organizational Ecology*. Cambridge, MA: Harvard University Press.

Hansen, M. T., Nohria, N. and Tierney, T. (1999) What's your strategy for managing knowledge? *Harvard Business Review*, March–April, 1999.

Harbison, F. and Myers, C. A. (1959) *Management in the Industrial World: An International Analysis*. New York: McGraw-Hill.

Hartman, L. P. (1998) *Perspectives in Business Ethics*. Chicago: McGraw-Hill.

Harzing, A. W. (1995) The persistent myth of high expatriate failure rates. *International Journal of Human Resource Management*, 6 (2), 457–475.

Harzing, A. W. (1999) *Managing the Multinationals*. Cheltenham: Edward Elgar.

Harzing, A. W. (2000) An empirical test and extension of the Bartlett and Ghoshal typology of multi-national companies. *Journal of International Business Studies*, 31, 101–120.

Harzing, A. W. (2002a) Acquisitions versus greenfield investments. *Strategic Management Journal*, 32 (3), 211–227.

Harzing, A. W. (2002b) Are our referencing errors undermining our scholarship and credibility? The case of expatriate failure rates. *Journal of Organizational Behavior*, 23 (1), 127–148.

Hayes, J. and Allinson, C. W. (1988) Cultural differences in the learning styles of managers. *Management International Review*, 28 (3), 72–90.

Hedberg, B. (1981) How organizations learn and unlearn. In P. C. Nystrom and W. H. Starbuck (eds) *Handbook of Organizational Design*, 8–27. London: Oxford University Press.

Hedlund, G. (1986) The hypermodern MNC – a heterarchy? *Human Resource Management*, 25, 9–25.

Hedlund, G. (1994) A model of knowledge management and the N-form corporation. *Strategic Management Journal*, 15 (Summer), 73–90.

Hellström, T., Kemlin, P. and Malmquist, U. (2000) Knowledge and competence management at Ericsson. *Journal of Knowledge Management*, 4 (2), 99–110.

Hill, C. W. (2000) *International Business: Competing in the Global Marketplace* (3rd edn). Boston, MA: McGraw-Hill.

Hitt, M. A., Hoskisson, R. E. and Kim, H. (1997) International diversification: effects on innovation and firm performance in product–diversified firms. *Academy of Management Journal*, 40 (4): 767–798.

Hodgetts, R. M. and Luthans, F. (1991) *International Management*. (International Edition.) Singapore: McGraw-Hill.

Hodgetts, R. M. and Luthans, F. (2000) *International Management: Culture, Strategy and Behavior*. Boston: McGraw-Hill. 4th edn.

Hofstede, G. (1980a) *Culture's Consequences: International Differences in Work-Related Values*. Beverly Hills, CA: Sage.

Hofstede, G. (1980b) Motivation, leadership, and organization: do American theories apply abroad? *Organizational Dynamics*, Summer, 42–63.

Hofstede, G. (1983) National cultures in four dimensions: a research theory of cultural differences among nations. *International Studies of Management and Organization*, 13 (1), 46–64.

Hofstede, G. (1984) *Culture's Consequences: International Differences in Work-Related Values*. Newbury Park, CA: Sage.

Hofstede, G. (1991) *Cultures and Organizations: Software of the Mind*. Boston, MA: McGraw-Hill.

Hofstede, G. (1994) The business of international business is culture. *International Business Review*, 3 (1), 1–14.

Hofstede, G. (1998) Cultural constraints in personnel management. *Management International Review*, 38 (2), 7–26.

Hofstede, G. (1999) Problems remain, but theories will change. The universal and the specific in 21st-century global management. *Organizational Dynamics*, 28 (1), 34–44.

Hofstede, G. and Bond, M. H. (1988) The Confucius connection: From cultural roots to economic growth. *Organizational Dynamics*, 16 (4), 2–21.

Hollingsworth, J. R. and Boyer, R. (1997) Coordination of economic actors and social systems of production. In J. R. Hollingsworth and R. Boyer (eds) *Contemporary Capitalism*. Cambridge, MA: Harvard University Press.

Hoskisson, R., Eden, L., Laue, C. M. and Wright, M. (2000) Strategy in emerging economies. *Academy of Management Journal*, 43 (3), 249–267.

Hsieh, T-Y, Lavoie, J. and Samek, R. (1999) Are you taking your expatriate talent seriously? *The McKinsey Quarterly*, 3, 71–83.

Huber, G. P. (1991) Organizational learning: the contributing processes and the literature. *Organization Science*, 2, 88–115.

Humphrey, J. (1995) The adoption of Japanese management techniques in Brazilian industry. *Journal of Management Studies*, 32 (6), 767–788.

Hymer, S. H. (1960/1976) *The International Operations of National Firms: A Study of Direct Foreign Investment*. Cambridge, MA: MIT Press.

Ishida, H. (1986) Transferability of Japanese human resource management abroad. *Human Resource Management*, 25, 103–120.

Jackson, K. T. (1997) Globalizing corporate ethics programs: perils and prospects. *Journal of Business Ethics*, 16 (12–13), 1227–1235.

Jackson, T. (2000) Management ethics and corporate policy: A cross-cultural comparison. *Journal of Management Studies*, 37 (3), 349–369.

Johnson, G., Hendry, J. and Newton, J. (1994) *Strategic Thinking: Leadership and the Management of Change*, New York: John Wiley & Sons.

Jose, A. and Thibodeaux, M. S. (1999) Institutionalization of ethics: the perspective of managers. *Journal of Business Ethics*, 22 (1 2), 133–143.

Judy, R. W. (2002) Where on earth companies choose to do business – and why. Paper prepared for the *World Federation of Personnel Management Associations*, Mexico City, May 29.

Kanter, R. M. (1983) *The Change Masters*. New York: Simon & Schuster.

Kanter, R. M., Stein, B. A. and Jick, T. D. (1992) *The Challenge of Organizational Change. How Companies Experience It and Leaders Guide It*. New York: Free Press/Macmillan.

Karl, T. L. (1996) *Paradox of Plenty: Oil Booms and Petro-States*. Berkeley, CA: University of California Press.

Kavali, S., Tzokas, N. and Saren, M. (2001) Corporate ethics: an exploration of contemporary Greece. *Journal of Business Ethics*, 30 (1), 87–104.

Kets de Vries, M. (1994) Making a giant dance, *Across the Board*, 31, 9, Oct., pp. 27–32.

Kets de Vries, M. (1998) *The Anarchist Within: Clinical Reflections on Russian Character, Leadership Style, and Organizational Practices*. Working paper No. 96. Fontainebleau: INSEAD.

Kidger, P. J. (1991) The emergence of international human resource management. *International Human Resource Management*, 2 (2), 149–163.

Kochan, T. A., Katz, H. C. and McKersie, R. B. (1986) *The Transformation of American Industrial Relations*. New York: Basic Books.

Kochan, T. A., McKersie, R. B. and Capelli, P. (1984) Strategic choice and industrial relations theory. *Industrial Relations*, 23, 16–39.

Kogut, B. (1990) The permeability of borders and the speed of learning across countries. In J. H. Dunning, B. Kogut and M. Blomström (eds) *Globalization of Firms and the Competitiveness of Nations*, 59–90. Lund: Lund University Press.

Kogut, B. and Chang, S. J. (1991) Technological capabilities and Japanese direct investment in the United States. *Review of Economics and Statistics*, 73 (3), 401–413.

Kogut, B. and Zander, U. (1992) Knowledge of the firm, combinative capabilities, and the replication of technology. *Organization Science*, 3 (3), 383–397.

Kogut, B. and Zander, U. (1993) Knowledge of the firm and the evolutionary theory of the multinational corporation. *Journal of International Business Studies*, 24 (4), 625–646.

Kopp, R. (1994) International human resource policies and practices in Japanese, European, and United States multinationals. *Human Resource Management*, 33 (4), 581–599.

Kostova, T. and Roth, K. (2002) Adoption of an organizational practice by subsidiaries of multinational corporations: institutional and relational effects. *Academy of Management Journal*, 45 (1), 215–233.

Kotter, J. P. (1982) *The General Managers*. New York: Free Press.

Kuemmerle, W. (1997) Building effective R&D capabilities abroad. *Harvard Business Review*, March–April, 61–70.

Larson, E. and Gobeli, D. (1987) Matrix management: contradictions and insights. *California Management Review*, 29 (4), 126–138.

Lasserre, P. and Schütte, H. (1995) *Strategies for Asia Pacific*, London: Macmillan Press.

Laurent, A. (1983) The cultural diversity of Western conceptions of management. *International Studies of Management and Organization*, 13 (1–2), 75–96.

Legge, K. (1995) *Human Resource Management: Rhetorics and Realities*. London: Macmillan.

Leonard-Barton, D. (1995) *Wellsprings of Knowledge: Building and Sustaining the Sources of Innovation*. Cambridge, MA: Harvard Business School Press.

Leontiades, J. C. (1985) *Multinational Corporate Strategy*. Lexington, MA: Lexington Books.

Levitt, T. (1983) The globalisation of markets. *Harvard Business Review*, May/June, 92–102.

Liddle, J. and Joshi, R. (1986) *Daughters of Independence: Gender, Caste and Class in India*, London: Rutgers United Press/Zed Books.

Lindahl, G. (1999) Bereit für die Herausforderungen der Zukunft, *Die Volkswirtschaft – Magazin für WirtschaftsPolitik*, 3, 6–9.

Lippman, S. and Rumelt, R. (1982) Uncertain imitability: an analysis of interfirm differences in efficiencies under competition. *Bell Journal of Economics*, 13, 418–438.

Locke, R., Piore, M. and Kochan, T. (1995). Introduction. In R. Locke, T. Kochan and M. Piore (eds) *Employment Relations in a Changing World Economy*. Cambridge, Mass.: MIT Press, 7–15.

Lunheim, R. (1994) *Desert People: Caste and Community – A Rajasthani Village*. Trondheim: University of Trondheim.

Lyles, M. A. and Salk, J. E. (1996) Knowledge acquisition from foreign parents in international joint ventures: an empirical examination in the Hungarian context. *Journal of International Business Studies*, Special Issue, 877–903.

Makino, J. and Neupert, K. E. (2001) National culture, transaction costs, and the choice between joint venture and wholly owned subsidiary. *Journal of International Business Studies*, 31 (4), 705–713.

Malnight, T. W. (2001) Emerging structural patterns within multinational corporations: towards process-based structures. *Academy of Management Journal*, 44 (6), 1187–1210.

Mann, F. C. (1965) Toward an understanding of the leadership role in formal organization. In R. Dubin, G. C. Homans, F. C. Mann, and D. C. Miller (eds), *Leadership and Productivity*. San Francisco, CA: Chandler.

Markoczy, L. (1993) Managerial and organizational learning in Hungarian–Western mixed management organizations. *The International Journal of Human Resource Management*, 4 (2), 277–304.

Martin, X. and Salomon, R. (1999) Knowledge transfer capacity: implications for the theory of the multinational corporation. *Annual Academy of Management Annual Meeting*, Chicago, 6–11 August.

Maurice, M., Sellier, F. and Silvestre, J. (1986) *The Social Foundations of Industrial Power*. Cambridge, MA: The MIT Press.

Maslow, A. H. (1954) *Motivation and Personality*. New York: Harper & Row.

Mayo, E. (1945) *The Social Problems of an Industrial Civilization*. Boston: Graduate School of Business Administration, Harvard University.

McCollum, J. and Sherman, J. (1993) The matrix structure: bane or benefit to high tech organizations? *Project Management Journal*, 24 (2), June, 23–26.

McDonald, F., Tüselmann, H. and Wheeler, C. (2002) *International Business: Adjusting to New Challenges and Opportunities.* London: Palgrave.

McGregor, D. (1960) *The Human Side of the Enterprise.* New York: McGraw-Hill.

McSweeney, B. (2002) Hofstede's model of national cultural differences and their consequences: a triumph of faith – a failure of analysis. *Human Relations,* 55 (1), 5–34.

Mead, R. (1996) *International Management: Cross-Cultural Dimensions.* Cambridge, MA: Blackwell.

Mendenhall, M. E., Dunbar, E. and Oddou, G. R. (1987) Expatriate selection, training and career-pathing: a review and critique. *Human Resource Management,* 26 (3), 331–345.

Merrill Lynch (1998) *Investor Relations Report on General Electric,* Merrill Lynch & Co, Research Department, 15 Sept.

Meschi, P. X. (1997) Longevity and cultural differences of international joint ventures: toward time-based cultural management. *Human Relations,* 50 (2), 211–227.

Mezias, J. M. (2002) Labor lawsuit judgements as liabilities of foreignness. *Strategic Management Journal,* 23 (3), 229–244.

Michailova, S. and Anisimova, A. (1999) Russian voices from a Danish company. *Business Strategy Review,* 10 (4), 65–78.

Miles, R. E. and Snow, C. C. (1992) Causes of failure in network organizations. *California Management Review,* Summer: 53–72.

Mintzberg, H. (1973) *The Nature of Managerial Work.* New York: Harper & Row.

Mintzberg, H. (1994) *The Rise and Fall of Strategic Planning.* New York: Free Press.

Mintzberg, H. and Waters, J. (1982) Tracking strategy in an entrepreneurial firm. *Academy of Management Journal,* 25, 465–499.

Mitchell, D. J. B. and Zaidi, M. A. (eds) (1991) *The Economics of Human Resource Management.* Cambridge, MA: Basil Blackwell.

Mitsubishi Group (1998) *Annual Report.*

Moon, C. J. and Woolliams, P. (2000) Managing cross-cultural business ethics. *Journal of Business Ethics,* 27 (1–2), 105–115.

Moore, K. and Birkinshaw, J. (1998) Managing knowledge in global service firms: centers of excellence. *Academy of Management Executive,* 12 (4), 81–92.

Morgan, G. (1990) *Images of Organization.* London: Sage.

Morris, J. and Wilkinson, B. (1995) The transfer of Japanese management to alien institutional environments. *Journal of Management Studies,* 32 (6), 719–730.

Murakami, T. (1998) The formation of teams: a British and German comparison. *International Journal of Human Resource Management,* 9 (5), 800–817.

Murphy, P. E. (1995) Corporate ethics statements – current status and future prospects. *Journal of Business Ethics,* 14 (9), 727–740.

Nadler, D. and Tushman, M. (1988) *Strategic Organization Design: Concepts, Tools and Processes.* New York: HarperCollins.

Nelson, R. and Winter, S. (1982) *An Evolutionary Theory of Economic Change.* Cambridge, MA: Harvard University Press.

New York Times (1997) Watching the sweatshops. Editorial. 20 August.

Nicholson, N. (ed.) (1998) *The Blackwell Encyclopedic Dictionary of Organizational Behavior.* Oxford: Blackwell.

Nohria, N. and Ghoshal, S. (1997) *The Differentiated Network.* New York: Jossey-Bass.

Nokia. (18 Dec. 2001) *Leading IT infrastructure companies to support open mobile architecture initiative to drive mobile software and services market* (Press Release).

Nokia. (19 Dec. 2001) *Liberty Alliance demonstrates momentum with increased membership and industry support* (Press Release).

Nonaka, I. (1994) A dynamic theory of organizational knowledge creation. *Organization Science*, 5, 15–37.

Nonaka, I. and Takeuchi, H. (1995) *The Knowledge-creating Company: How Japanese Companies Create the Dynamics of Innovation*. New York: Oxford University Press.

Nordhaug, O. (1994) *Human Capital in Organizations: Competence, Training and Learning*. New York: Oxford University Press.

Nordhaug, O. (1998) Competence specificities: a classificatory framework. *International Studies of Management and Organization*, 28 (1), 8–29.

Nordhaug, O. and Gooderham, P. N. (1996) *Kompetanseutvikling i næringslivet*. (Competence Development in Companies). Oslo: Cappelen Akademisk Forlag.

Nordhaug, O. and Grønhaug, K. (1994) Competences as resources in firms. *International Journal of Human Resource Management*, 5, 89–106.

Norsk Hydro (1999) *International Employment Policies: Internal Corporate Procedure*. Oslo: Norsk Hydro.

Nutt, P. (1997) Better decision-making: a field study. *Business Strategy Review*, 8 (4), 45–52.

Obolonsky, A. (1995) Russian politics in the time of troubles: some basic antinomies. In A. Saikal and W. Maley (eds) *Russia in Search of its Future*. Cambridge, MA: Cambridge University Press. 12–27.

O'Connell, J. J. (ed.) (1997) *Encyclopedic Dictionary of International Management*. Oxford: Blackwell.

Oddou, G. and Mendenhall, M. (1991) Expatriate performance appraisal: problems and solutions. In M. Mendenhall and G. Oddou (eds) *Readings and Cases in International Human Resource Management*. Boston, MA: PWS-Kent.

Oddou, G. and Derr, C. B. (1993) European MNC strategies for internationalizing managers: current and future trends. In J. B. Shaw et al., *Research in Personnel and Human Resource Management*. Greenwich, Connecticut: JAI Press, 157–170.

O'Donnell, S. (2000) Managing foreign subsidiaries. *Strategic Management Journal*, 21, 525–548.

OECD (1995) *Economic Outlook*. Paris: OECD.

OECD (1998), *Economic Outlook*. Paris: OECD.

Office for National Statistics (1998) *Labour Market Trends*. London: ONS.

Oliver, C. (1991) Strategic responses to institutional processes. *Academy of Management Review*, 16, 145–179.

Osterman, P. (1994) How common is workplace transformation and how can we explain who adopts it? Results from a national survey. *Industrial and Labor Relations Review* (January), 175–188.

Paija, L. (2001) The ICT Cluster in Finland – can we explain it? In L. Paija (Ed.), *Finnish ICT Cluster in the Digital Economy*. Helsinki: Taloustieto Oy (ETLA B:176).

Pascale, R. (1990) *Managing on the Edge*. New York: Simon & Schuster.

Payne, D., Raiborn, C. and Askvik, J. (1997) A global code of business ethics. *Journal of Business Ethics*, 16, 1717–1735.

Pedder, S. (1999) A survey of France. *The Economist*, 5 June, vol. 351, no. 8122.

Perlmutter, H. V. (1969) The tortuous evolution of the multinational company. *Columbia Journal of World Business* (January–February), 9–18.

Peters, T. J. (1987) *Thriving on Chaos*. New York: Harper & Row.

Peters, T. (1993) *Liberation Management: Necessary Disorganization for the Nanosecond Nineties*. London: Pan Books.

Peters, T. and Waterman, R. (1982) *In Search of Excellence*. New York: Harper & Row.

Pettigrew, A., Ferlie, E. and McKee, L. (1992) *Shaping Strategic Change*. London: Sage.

Pfeffer, J. (1992) *Managing with Power: Politics and Influence in Organizations*. Cambridge, MA: Harvard Business School Press.

Pieper, R. (ed.) (1990) *Human Resource Management: An International Comparison*. Berlin: Walter de Gruyter.

Pinnington, A. and Edwards, T. (2000) *Introduction to Human Resource Management*. Oxford: Oxford University Press.

Pogge, T. (2001) The influence of global institutions on the prospects for genuine democracy in LDCs. *Ratio Juris* 14/3.

Polanyi, M. (1962) *Personal Knowledge: Towards a Post-Critical Philosophy*. New York: Harper Torchbooks.

Polanyi, M. (1966/1983): *The Tacit Dimension*. Gloucester, MA: Peter Smith.

Poliakov, V. (2002) Influence of cultural differences on work-related values of business school students in Norway and Russia: Comparative Study. Unpublished Master of International Business thesis. Bergen: Norwegian School of Economics and Business Administration.

Porter, M. (1980) *Competitive Strategy: Techniques for Analyzing Industries and Competitors*. New York: Free Press.

Porter, M. (1985) *Competitive Advantage: Creating and Sustaining Superior Performance*. New York: Free Press.

Powell, W. W. and DiMaggio, P. J. (1991) *The New Institutionalism in Organizational Analysis*. Chicago: University of Chicago Press.

Prakash Sethi, S. and Williams, O. F. (2001) *Economic Imperatives and Ethical Values in Global Business: The South African Experience and International Codes Today*. Notre Dame, IN: University of Notre Dame Press.

Raitu, I. (1983) Thinking internationally: a comparison of how international executives learn. *International Studies of Management and Organization*, 13, (1–2), 139–150.

Ramachandran, R. (1992) The silenced majority: sex ratio and the status of women in India. *Canadian Women Studies*, 13 (1), 60–66.

Randlesome, C., Brierly, W., Burton, K., Gordon, C. and King, P. (1990) *Business Cultures in Europe*. Oxford: Heinemann.

Rawls, J. (1972) *A Theory of Justice*. Cambridge, MA: The Bellknap Press of Harvard University Press.

Reed, R. and DeFillippi, R. J. (1990) Causal ambiguity, barriers to imitation and sustainable competitive advantage. *Academy of Management Review*, 15, 88–102.

Reger, G., 1997. Internationalisation and coordination of R&D of western European and Japanese multinational corporations. In K. Macharzina, M.-J., Oesterle, and J. Wolf (eds) *Global Business in the Information Age*, vol. 2, 573–604. *Proceedings of the 23rd Annual EIBA Conference*, Stuttgart, December.

Reidenbach, R. E. and Robin, D. P. (1991) A conceptual model of corporate moral development. *Journal of Business Ethics*, 10, 282.

Robbins, S. (1998) *Organizational Behavior: Concepts, Controversies, Applications* (8th edn)? Englewood Cliffs, NJ: Prentice-Hall.

Roberts, K. (1994) Functional and dysfunctional organizational linkages. In C. Cooper and D. M. Rousseau (eds), *Trends in Organization Behavior*. (vol. 1). Sussex: Wiley, 1–11.

Robertson, C. (1998) Developing a corporate code of ethics in MNCs. *Journal of Managerial Issues*, 10 (4), 454–468.

Roethlisberger, F. J. and Dickson, W. J. (1939) *Management and the Worker*. Cambridge, MA: Harvard University Press.

Rogers, E. M. (1962) *Diffusion of Innovations*. New York: Free Press.

Rognes, J. (2002) Organising R&D in a global environment. *European Business Forum*, 2 (10), 59–61.

Roost, A. and Meier, M. (1998) Mit Strom, Charme und neuen Chefs, Interview mit Göran Lindahl, *Bilanz*, September: 58–62.

Rosenzweig, P. M. (1994) *Colgate-Palmolive: Managing International Careers*. Harvard Business School case 394–184.

Rosenzweig, P. M. and Singh, J. (1991) Organizational environments and the multinational enterprise. *Academy of Management Review*, 116 (2), 340–361.

Rugman, A. M. (2001) The illusion of the global company. Part 13 of *Mastering Management*. *Financial Times*, 6 January.

Rugman, A. and Hodgetts, R. (1995) *International Business: A Strategic Management Approach*, New York: McGraw-Hill.

Ruigrok, W., Pettigrew, A., Peck, S. and Whittington, R. (1999) Corporate restructuring and new forms of organising: evidence from Europe. *Management International Review*, 19, special issue (July).

Sackmann, S. A. (1991) *Cultural Knowledge in Organizations: Exploring the Collective Mind*. Newbury Park, CA: Sage.

Saner, R. and Yiu, L. (1994) European and Asian resistance to the use of the American case method in management training. *International Journal of Human Resource Management*, 5 (4), 955–976.

Schneider, S. C. and Barsoux, J. L. (1997) *Managing across Cultures*. Singapore: Prentice-Hall.

SEC (2001) *FORM 20-F REPORT – Nokia Corporation*. Washington, DC: Securities and Exchange Commission.

Schilling, D. M. (2000) Making codes of conduct credible. The role of independent monitoring. In O. F. Williams (ed.), *Global Codes of Conduct*. Notre Dame, IN: University of Notre Dame Press.

Schlegelmilch, B. B. and Robertson, L. (1995) The influence of country and industry on ethical perceptions of senior executives in the U.S. and Europe. *Journal of International Business Studies*, 26 (4), 859–881.

Schneider, S. C. and Barsoux, J. L. (1997) *Managing across Cultures*. London: Prentice Hall.

Schuler, R. S. and Jackson, S. E. (1987) Linking competitive strategies with human resource management practices, *Academy of Management Executives*, 1 (3), 209–213.

Schultz, T. W. (1971) *Investment in Human Capital: The Role of Education and Research*. New York: The Free Press.

Schultz, T. W. (1981) *Investing in People: The Economics of Population Quality*. Berkeley, CA: University of California Press.

Schwartz, M. (2001) The nature of the relationship between corporate codes of ethics and behaviour. *Journal of Business Ethics*, 32 (3), 247–262.

Scott, W. R. (1995) *Institutions and Organizations*. Thousand Oaks, CA: Sage.

Sen, A. (1999) *Development as Freedom*. New York: Knopf.

Senge, P. M. (1994) *The Fifth Discipline*. New York: Doubleday.

Shell (2001) *People, Planet and Profits. The Shell Report 2001.* The Hague: Shell International B.V.

Shrader, R. G. (2001) Collaboration and performance in foreign markets: the case of young high-technology manufacturing firms. *Academy of Management Journal*, 44 (1) 45–60.

Siemens (1997) *Annual Report.*

Siemens Internetpages (1998) http://www.siemens.de/en/investor_relations/Basic_Information/index.html, 26.11.1998.

Simonin, B. L. (1999) Transfer of marketing know-how in international strategic alliances: an empirical investigation of the role and antecedents of knowledge ambiguity. *Journal of International Business Studies*, 30 (3), 463–490.

Sinha, J. M. P (1990) *Work Culture in an Indian Context.* New Delhi: Sage.

Skapinker, M. (2002) World's most respected companies. Financial Times Survey: 2002 and beyond, page 4. *Financial Times*, February 1.

Slomp, H. (1995) National variations in worker participation. In A. W. Harzing and J. van Ruysseveldt (eds) *International Human Resource Management.* London: Sage.

Smith, N. (1991) The case-study: a vital yet misunderstood research method for management. In N. Smith and P. Dainty (eds) *Management Research Handbook.* (45–158) London: Routledge.

Solenthaler, E. (1998) ABB bleibt ihrer Führungsstruktur treu, Interview mit Göran Lindahl. *Finanz und Wirtschaft*, 15 August, 62: 18–19.

Somers, M. J. (2001) Ethical codes of conduct and organizational context: A study of the relationship between codes of conduct, employee behavior and organizational values. *Journal of Business Ethics*, 30 (2), 185–195.

Sonnenberg, F. K. (1994) The age of intangibles, *Management Review*, January: 48–53.

Sony. (12 Nov. 2001) *Sony Reveals Initiatives to Create a 'Ubiquitous Value Network' – Company in Joint Efforts with AOL Time Warner and Nokia* (Press Release).

Sparrow, P. R. and Budhwar, P. S. (1997.) Competition and change: mapping the Indian HRM recipe against world wide patterns. *Journal of World Business*, 32 (3), 224–242.

Sparrow, P. and Hiltrop, M. (1994) *European Human Resource Management in Transition.* New York: Prentice Hall.

Srinivas, M. N. (1971) *Social Changes in Modern India.* Berkeley, CA: University of California Press.

Steigmeier, A. (1991) *Brown Boveri and ASEA Brown Boveri: Highlights of a Century of Company History*, Zürich: ABB.

Storey, J. (1987) *Developments in the Management of Human Resources: An Interim Report. Warwick Papers in Industrial Relations* (17) Warwick: School of Industrial and Business Studies, University of Warwick (November).

Stouffer, S. A. and Toby, J. (1951) Role conflict and personality. *American Journal of Sociology*, 56 (4), 395–406.

Swenson, W. (2000) Raising the ethics bar in a shrinking world. In O. F. Williams (ed.) *Global Codes of Conduct.* Notre Dame, IN: University of Notre Dame Press.

Szulanski, G. (1996) Exploring internal stickiness: impediments to the transfer of best practice within the firm. *Strategic Management Journal*, *17* (Winter Special Issue), 27–43.

Taggart, J. H. (1998) Strategy shifts in MNC subsidiaries. *Strategic Management Journal*, 19, 663–681.

Tamagno, S. and Aasland, T. (2000) *Invitation to a Dialogue: Corporate Social Responsibility.* Oslo: Norsk Hydro Media.

Tayeb, M. H. (1988) *Organizations and National Culture: A Comparative Analysis.* London: Sage.

Tayeb, M. (1994) Organisations and national culture: methodology considered. *Organisation Studies,* 15 (3), 429–446.

Tayeb, M. H. (1996) Hofstede. In M. Warner (ed.) *International Encyclopaedia of Business and Management.* London: Thompson Press, vol. 2, 1771–1776.

Taylor, F. (1911) *The Principles of Scientific Management.* New York: Harper & Row.

Taylor, W. (1991) The logic of global business: an interview with ABB's Percy Barnevik. *Harvard Business Review,* March/April, 91–105.

Teece, D. J. (1977) Technology transfer by multinational firms: the resource costs of transferring technological know-how. *Economic Journal,* 87, 242–61.

Teece, D. J. (1981) The market for know-how and the efficient international transfer of technology. *Annals of American Academy of Political and Social Science,* 458, 81–96.

Teece, D. J. (1992) Foreign investment and technological development in Silicon Valley. *California Management Review,* 35 (Winter), 88–106.

Templeton Global Performance Index (2000) Oxford: Templeton College, University of Oxford.

Templeton Global Performance Index (2001) Oxford: Templeton College, University of Oxford.

Terpestra, V. (1978) *The Cultural Environment of International Business.* (1st edn). Cincinnati, OH: South-Western University Press.

Terpestra, V. and Davis, K. (1991) *The Cultural Environment of International Business.* (3rd ed). Cincinnati, OH: South-Western Publishing Co.

Tewatia, D. S. and Agnivesh, S. (2001) *Police Firing on Tribals.* Report submitted to the President of India, Maikanch, Orissa.

Thill, G. and Leonard-Barton, D. (1993) *Hewlett-Packard: Singapore.* Case 694–037. Harvard Business School: Boston.

Thurley, K. and Wirdenius, H. (1991) Will management become 'European'?: Strategic choices for organizations. *European Management Journal,* 9 (2): 127–134.

Tretiak, L. D. and Holzmann, K. (1993) *Operating Joint Ventures in China.* Hong Kong: The Economist Intelligence Unit.

Trompenaars, A. (1985) Organization of meaning and the meaning of organization. a comparative study on the conception of organizational structure in different cultures. Unpublished PhD thesis. Philadelphia, PA: University of Pennsylvania (DA 8515460).

Trompenaars, A. (1993) *Riding the Waves of Culture: Understanding Cultural Diversity in Business.* London: Nicholas Brealey.

Trompenaars, F. and Hampden-Turner, C. (1997) *Riding the Waves of Culture.* (2nd edn). London: Nicholas Brealey Publishing.

Tung, R. L. (1981) Selection and training of personnel for overseas assignments. *Columbia Journal of World Business,* 16 (1), 68–78.

Tung, R. L. (1982) Selection and training procedures of U.S., European and Japanese multinationals, *California Management Review,* 25 (1), 57–71.

Tung, R. L. (1998) American expatriates abroad: from neophytes to cosmopolitans. *Journal of World Business,* 33 (2), 125–144.

UNCTAD (1999) *World Investment Report 1999.* United Nations Conference on Trade and Development. New York: United Nations.

UNCTAD (2001) *World Investment Report 2001.* United Nations Conference on Trade and Development. New York: United Nations.

Unger, B. (1999) The Economist survey of India and Pakistan: Sorry states. *The Economist*, 5 June.

van Tulder, R. and Kolk, A. (2001) Multinationality and corporate ethics: Codes of conduct in the sporting goods industry. *Journal of International Business Studies*, 32 (2), 267–283.

Vernon, R. (1966) International investment and international trade in the product cycle. *Quarterly Journal of Economics*, 80: 190–207.

Vernon, R. (1998) *In the Hurricane's Eye: The Troubled Prospects of Multinational Enterprises.* Boston, MA: Harvard University Press.

Vlachoutsicos, C. (1998) The dangers of ignoring Russian communitarianism. *Transition.* The World Bank, October, 13–14.

Von Hippel, E. (1994) 'Sticky information' and the locus of problem solving: Implications for innovation. *Management Science*, 40 (4), 429–439.

Vosti, S. and Reardon, T. (eds) (1997) *Sustainability, Growth and Poverty Alleviation: A Policy and Agroecological Perspective.* Baltimore, MD: Johns Hopkins University Press.

Walsh, J. P., Henderson, C. M. and Deighton, J. (1988) Negotiated belief structures and decision performance: an empirical investigation. *Organizational Behavior and Human Decision Processes*, 42, 194–216.

Walsh, J. P. and Ungson, G. R. (1991) Organizational memory. *Academy of Management Review*, 16, 57–91.

Wantchekon, L. (1999) Why do resource dependent countries have authoritarian governments? Personal interviews with Norwatch's Tarjei Leer-Salvesen, Hydro's Ola Lie and Jostein Flo.

Weber, M. (1946) *From Max Weber: Essays in Sociology.* Edited by H. H. Gerth and C. W. Mills. London: Routledge & Kegan Paul.

Weick, K. E. (1979) *The Social Psychology of Organizing.* Reading, MA: Addison-Wesley.

Weick, K. E. and Gilfillan, D. P. (1971) Fate of arbitrary traditions in a laboratory microculture. *Journal of Personality and Social Psychology*, 017, 179–191.

Weinstein, M. and Kochan, T. (1995) The limits of diffusion: Recent developments in industrial relations and human resource practices in the United States. In R. Locke, T. Kochan and M. Piore (eds), *Employment Relations in a Changing World Economy.* Cambridge, MA: The MIT Press.

Whitley, R. (1989) On the nature of managerial tasks and skills: their distinguishing characteristics and organization. *Journal of Management Studies*, 26, 209–224.

Whittington, R. and Mayer, M. (1997) Beyond or behind the M-form? The structures of European businesses. In H. Thomas, D. O'Neal and M. Ghertman (eds) *Strategy, Structure and Style*, Chichester: John Wiley, 241–258.

Whittington, R. *et al.* (1998) Practices and performance in the new organization: inductive and deductive explorations of complementarities. Paper presented at the *Academy of Management Annual Meeting*, San Diego August 1998.

Wilkinson, B., Morris, J. and Munday, M. (1993) Japan in Wales: a new IR. *Industrial Relations Journal*, 24 (4), 273–283.

Williams, O. F. (ed.) (2001a) *Global Codes of Conduct.* Notre Dame, IN: University of Notre Dame Press.

Williams, O. F. (ed.) (2001b) *The Moral Imagination.* Notre Dame, IN: University of Notre Dame Press.

Williamson, O. (1975) *Markets and Hierarchies: Analysis and Antitrust Implications*. New York: Free Press.

Williamson, O. (1985) *The Economic Institutions of Capitalism*. New York: Free Press.

Winter, S. G. (1987) Knowledge and competence as strategic assets. In D. J. Teece (ed.) *The Competitive Challenge*. Cambridge, MA: Ballinger.

Yin, R. (1994) *Case Study Research: Design and Methods*. Applied research metbods series. Vol. 5. (2nd edn). Thousand Oaks, CA: Sage.

Zaytseva, T. (1998) Intercultural management in Russia: a comparative analysis. *HD Forum*, 19: 4–6.

Zhu, C. J., De Cieri, H. and Dowling, P. J. (1998) The reform of employee compensation in China's industrial enterprises. *Management International Review*, 38 (2), 65–87.

Zoller, M. (1998) *Customer Focus – der gesamtunternehmerische Ansatz der ABB Schweiz*. Internal document. Baden: ABB.

Index

Lightning Source UK Ltd.
Milton Keynes UK
178582UK00008B/7/P